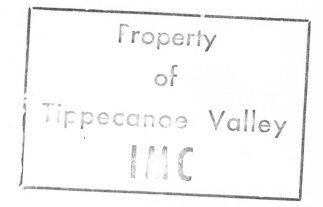

personal finance

consuming, saving and investing

W. L. Dorries

Department of Economics–Finance

East Texas State University

Arthur A. Smith

Department of Economics–Finance

East Texas State University

James R. Young

Department of Marketing–Management

East Texas State University

personal finance

consuming, saving and investing

Charles E. Merrill Publishing Company

A Bell & Howell Company

Columbus, Ohio

Published by
Charles E. Merrill Publishing Co.
A Bell & Howell Company
Columbus, Ohio 43216

Library of Congress Catalog Card Number: 73–90571
International Standard Book Number: 0–675–08839–9

Printed in the United States of America
2 3 4 5 6 7 8 9 10—78 77 76 75

preface

Ability to spend and invest money wisely is almost as important as ability to earn money. The intent of this book is to provide the materials to help make you a better money manager in your personal and family affairs. The authors planned this book to be used as a text for courses in personal finance. It presents the "fundamentals" of money management in easily understood terms for those who have no background in finance.

Part one of the book relates personal finance to generally accepted principles of business management and economics. It also discusses consumerism, a movement arising from the growing concern for consumer protection. Both businessmen and consumers will hopefully gain an insight into their responsibilities from this discussion. Included, in addition, is a section describing sales techniques, introduced for the purpose of equalizing the positions of the participants in sales situations.

Part two details characteristics of the population and discusses how income is received and spent. Family budgets are discussed as well as the use of consumer credit. Part three is unique to texts in personal finance. It includes money-saving techniques for buying food, clothing, homes, automobiles, and home appliances.

Insurance principles as well as specific recommendations on insurance purchases are presented in part four. Saving and investment programs are discussed in part five. Comparisons are made between various types of investments such as stocks, bonds, mutual funds, real estate, and real estate investment trusts, in addition to a study of savings institutions. Finally, a chapter on estate planning gives suggestions on how to conserve your estate and prepare it for distribution to heirs. Tax considerations are discussed in different chapters for their relevance to each topic.

We are indebted to the business firms and institutions who have so graciously given permission to use materials from their publications. Special thanks are given to those who read parts of the manuscript and offered valuable suggestions. Finally, we extend extra thanks to Marsha Brice, Patricia Pinkham, and Virginia Cormier for their patience and understanding while typing parts of the manuscript.

Information and institutions related to personal finance are continuously changing. We hope every reader of this book will benefit to the extent that his enjoyment is enhanced through wise use of his income.

W. L. Dorries
Arthur A. Smith
James R. Young

contents

part one

Basic Principles

1

Monetary Aspects of Personal Success

What makes a person successful? This question prompts a wide variety of answers. Ask a business man, a theologian, and an artist to explain the meaning of personal success, and they will most likely produce three quite different, but meaningful answers. Ancient and modern philosophers have imparted rules for successful living to those willing to listen. Aristotle once said, "A good man may make the best even of poverty and disease, and the other ills of life; but he can only attain happiness, under the opposite conditions. . . . This makes men fancy that external goods are the cause of happiness, yet we might as well say that a brilliant performance on the lyre was to be attributed to the instrument and not to the skill of the performer."[1]

---

[1]Ingrid H. Rima, *Readings in the History of Economic Theory* (New York: Holt, Rinehart & Winston, 1970), p. 6.

Although there are differing concepts of success, Americans and many people in other countries consider the possession of money and wealth to be an important measure of personal success. This is not to deny the significance of such often intangible factors as happiness, political power, a multitude of friends, or fame, but simply to recognize that materialism is a basis of human values. Adam Smith, often called "the father of economics," made this statement: "Every man is rich or poor according to the degree in which he can afford to enjoy the necessaries, conveniences, and amusements of human life."[2]

As a generalization, our economic well-being is a function of (1) the amount of money we have and (2) what we do with it, or how well we manage it. In economic terms, the quantities of goods and services we are able to command are limited by the amount of money we have and how wisely we spend it. This book on personal finance proceeds on the assumption that the ability to exercise good management in economic transactions will enhance family wealth and contribute to the personal satisfaction of each member of the family. Many families are not in a position to increase their income, but they can increase their purchasing power and improve their financial security by using proven practices in spending, saving, and investing the income they have.

What is Finance?

"Finance" is a general term meaning the management of monetary affairs. More specifically, we speak of public finance as the management of the monetary affairs of government; of corporate finance as the management of the monetary affairs of corporate enterprises; and of personal finance as the management of the monetary affairs of individuals and families. Occasionally, the terms "school finance," "hospital finance," "church finance," etc. may be used; but, regardless of how the term is qualified, "finance" refers to the management of monetary affairs.

Money is the medium of exchange in our society. It is used as a medium in the exchange of goods and services, as a common denominator of the value of what we own, acquire, or sell, as a store of value for future use, as a standard of deferred payments in credit transactions, and as a unit of account in the keeping of economic records. Indeed, money has many uses in our society. So important is its role that our society is often referred to as a "pecuniary" or a "monetary" society.

Importance of Money

Money is one of mankind's greatest inventions. Before money was invented, goods and services were bartered; that is, they were directly traded for other

---

[2]Adam Smith, *The Wealth of Nations* (New York: Random House, 1937), p. 30.

goods and services. Imagine how crude and cumbersome this kind of exchange must have been! Suppose you were living in a barter economy. First, you would have to find someone who had the thing you wanted, in the amount you wanted, and who, at the same time, wanted what you had to trade. If he had what you wanted and did not want what you had, you would be obliged to find some third party to trade with who had something the second party wanted and who would be willing to trade for what you had, so you then would have what the second party would accept in exchange for what you wanted.

The possibility of such elaborate complications is always present in such a primitive kind of exchange. Two complicating factors are the slowness of the process of exchange and the difficulty of reaching agreement on an equitable ratio of exchange. Moreover, some goods, such as an automobile or a cow, are not readily divisible, further creating problems in a barter economy. Finally, the difficulties of barter obviously increase as the goods to be exchanged become more numerous.

A further drawback of the barter system of exchange was that it restricted industrial development, since the barter market could not take up any considerable spatial area nor any considerable amount of time. A limited market, in turn, thwarted specialization in its fullest sense, made large-scale production impossible, and kept man's level of living relatively low and simple.

It was only after the rise of mediated exchange (the use of money) that modern industrialism could develop, thus vastly increasing production and bringing indirect methods of satisfying wants—to a large extent because the invention and use of money greatly improved the exchange process, stimulated specialization, and widened markets.

Today, producers are so specialized that they are almost completely dependent on markets. For his efforts, the worker, like all others, receives money which represents purchasing power. This enables him to buy the products that satisfy his economic wants. It is as if all producers poured their products (goods and services) into one vast reservoir and then received general claims allowing them to draw from the reservoir at will whatever goods in whatever amounts their claims allowed. Greater average shares are possible only from greater production. This highly specialized indirect process enables us to produce far more than was previously produced under the direct method of household economy when a local group produced only enough goods for internal consumption.

Think of the numerous ways in which we encounter money from day to day in one or more of its functional expressions. We buy things with money, directly or indirectly. We pay our tuition in money. Governments collect taxes from us in money. We usually borrow money and repay the loan with money. We measure our wealth (what we own) in terms of money. Businesses of all kinds compile statements of income and expenses, as well as balance sheets of assets and liabilities, always in money terms.

Money may come from one or more of numerous sources. When we are young, our parents give us money (maybe as a regular allowance or as payment for chores we do), or we work after school or during the summer at some job or jobs for which we are paid wages. Most of us, as adults, derive our incomes from wages and salaries from employment. About 70 percent of all personal income in the United States is from this source. Those who are self-employed as owners of businesses receive incomes from profits (the difference between what it costs to operate the business and what the business takes in). Others are self-employed in such professions as medicine, dentistry, or law and receive fees for their services. Real estate owners receive income in the form of rent. Owners of securities such as stocks and bonds are paid dividends as stock-holders and interest as bondholders. Indigent persons may receive welfare payments while the retired receive pensions or retirement benefits, as well as Social Security payments. There are, of course, many other sources of money income.

Differences in
Money Income

An important truth in our economic system is that all persons do not have the same amount of money income. To understand why this is the case, it is necessary to understand how our economic system works.

The economic system in the United States is frequently called a "free enter-prise system," which means that individuals and groups—such as corporations—are free to undertake, within rules and regulations, any economic activity or activities they may choose—that is, any occupation or any business enterprise for which they have the ability and the means. Broadly speaking, these are pro-ductive activities whose purpose is to produce goods and services which gratify human wants and for which people will pay.

Participants are rewarded for their contributions in the production process, not perfectly, but generally in relation to the money value of their contributions. These rewards are determined not by arbitrary, authoritative edict, but by the workings of the market system where value is largely the result of supply and demand forces.

Let us try to make this point more meaningful by an example. Why is a medical doctor's income generally more than the income of a common laborer? Each renders a valuable, useful service for which people are willing to pay, but the pay is not the same. The doctor gets more because the economic value of what he/she does is greater than the value of what the common laborer does. And why is this true? Partly because there are far more persons who can per-form common labor jobs than there are persons qualified to practice medicine. In other words, the supply of common laborers is much greater than the supply of doctors.

Why are there fewer doctors than common laborers? It is generally con-ceded that more ability is required to become a medical doctor than to become a common laborer. Furthermore, even a person with the ability might not choose the medical profession because he might be more interested in doing something else, being an engineer, for example. Or he just might not be willing to undergo the long, rigorous, and expensive training required to qualify as a physician.

Regardless of the reason or reasons for the choice, services of medical doctors are more scarce than services of common laborers. A commodity or service in short supply generally sells for more than it would if it were more plentiful. Other examples of services in limited supply might be star performers in the entertainment world, such as outstanding professional athletes and TV and cinema celebrities. These people are handsomely paid for their services. Their compensation frequently equals or exceeds that of executive managers of large business enterprises.

Many examples can be cited as evidence of how personal incomes differ. Skilled individuals generally earn more income than unskilled individuals; managers more than subordinates; professionals more than non-professionals; the educated more than the uneducated; the talented more than the untalented; and the experienced more than the inexperienced.

Ability and effort are certainly positive forces in shaping the distribution of money incomes; but if we could draw a curve of the distribution of capacity and effort and a curve of the distribution of money incomes we would see immediately that the two curves are not shaped identically. From this observation we can deduce correctly that, despite the great influence of ability and effort, there are still other causes of unequal income distribution in our economic society.

For example, the circumstance of one's birth or inheritance is often a factor. Sons and daughters of wealthy parents may inherit wealth out of proportion to their capacities or efforts. If they do not inherit wealth itself, they at least inherit an environment that affords them the very best training and other opportunities to advance economically. On the other hand, a child born to poor parents in a financially inferior environment may be endowed with exceptional ability while his environment denies him the opportunity to develop and make a contribution commensurate with his ability. Both he and society have lost.

Similarly, discrimination because of ethnic status, another circumstance of birth, has denied or restricted opportunities to many individuals and, hence, distorted the relationship between ability and income.

Society has endeavored to modify somewhat the influence of inheritance by the application of estate and inheritance taxes that reduce greatly the amount of wealth passed on to others. Also, society has sought increasingly to make quality educational training available to all, regardless of either financial condition or racial origin, and has legislated against various forms of economic discrimination. Examples are the Civil Rights Act of 1964 and the Manpower Development and Training Act of 1962.

Other factors not related to innate ability, but which affect income distribution, should be mentioned. One of these is luck or fate. It is commonplace that there are two kinds of luck: good and bad. Good luck smiled on the farmer in East Texas who was barely eking out a living on 160 acres of sandy land when oil was struck on his farm. His ability and his own efforts were in no way related to the discovery of oil; yet his income was greatly enhanced.

All of us have known of individuals plagued by misfortunes such as accidents and illness which depleted their savings and impaired their earnings, or of individuals who unwisely assumed risks that resulted in substantial losses. Nevertheless, some risks are inherent in living, and good financial management dictates that certain risks be covered by insurance, as we shall see later.

Attitudes
toward Money

There is one aspect of wealth that can never be confined to conventional measures. Varying attitudes, family backgrounds, and concepts of values shape a different meaning of "wealth" in the mind of each person. Today's counterpart of yesterday's lad who measured his wealth in agates may feel deprived if he is not allowed to own a motorbike.

Material goods may be possessed and used productively for the good of the individual and of society, or goods may literally "possess" persons to the extent that the owner of the wealth becomes dominated by it and becomes consequently less productive in helping to build a community. Occasionally we hear of someone who wants money for its own sake. The miser is a covetous, grasping individual who sometimes lives miserably in order to increase his hoard. In our study of Greek mythology we encountered Midas, the fabled king of Phrygia, who wanted gold so badly that he asked Dionysus for the power to turn everything he touched into gold. No matter how much he had, he wanted more. And who can ever forget hard, avaricious Ebenezer Scrooge? Or Uriah Heap? Or the nonfictional Hetty Green, "The Witch of Wall Street"?

At the other extreme is the spendthrift, the compulsive spender, who spends profusely or improvidently. He never seems to get ahead. He cannot manage money sensibly. He gives little thought to tomorrow, while his sense of values is dominated by the present.

Both the miser and the spendthrift have an abnormal regard for money. Fortunately, they are few in number. The great majority of people look upon money properly as a means to an end. They seek money not for money's sake, but for what money does for them—for its power to command in exchange for the things (tangible and intangible) that satisfy wants. Alfred Marshall once said: "The desire to make money does not itself necessarily proceed from motives of a low order, even when it is spent on one's self. Money is a means toward ends, and if the ends are noble, the desire for the means is not ignoble."

Having personal goals for our lives can add meaning and perspective. We must be concerned with physical, mental, and spiritual growth as well as financial objectives. Money cannot buy some of these things, but it can help us obtain better health care and provide the means to buy books or other items that improve our mental well-being. Money, indiscriminately used, can similarly buy things that contribute to unhappiness.

For most of us, economic security has considerable influence on our outlook and happiness. It may be that the current generation of young people have a more realistic attitude toward money and wealth than their parents who were reared during a period of severe economic depression. While every family needs to consider and make some provision for future security, it is possible to become overcautious and sacrifice present happiness.

Each person handles a tremendous amount of money between the time he takes his first job and the time he retires. This income could easily exceed a half million dollars. No one knows for sure what incomes will be for the next 40 years, but most economists estimate that earnings will continue to rise. The average family income in the United States was $11,583 in 1971. It is true that salaries, or wages, or profits and all other types of income can decrease, as they have done in past years.

The accompanying figures indicate what one can expect during a lifetime of work at different levels of income.

Average yearly income	*Total income over 42 years*
$ 5,000	$210,000
7,500	315,000
10,000	420,000
12,000	504,000
15,000	630,000
18,000	756,000

Of course, this is not all spendable income, since taxes must be paid; but it remains a large sum of money. How we use it is one of the most important influences on our lives.

A young family should begin financial planning early. A good program will include such things as life insurance, a regular savings plan, an emergency fund, and plans for investments. Lack of such planning brings many high-income families to retirement without adequate savings.

Quantity and Quality in Life

Although the money orientation of modern society has often been viewed as an evil that contributes to social problems, to an extent, money must be available to finance action necessary to cure these ills. It is not the authors' intention to argue this moral issue, but rather to help the reader develop a healthy respect for the important, constructive role money plays in our lives toward the end of improving the quality of life enjoyed by all.

Families can solve many of their problems if they have a reasonable level of income. They can solve even more problems by having some knowledge of financial management along with that income. People spend years learning a vocation to make money, but receive little or no training in how to spend and invest their money.

Rising incomes have given American families a high standard of living in comparison with most people in the world. We provide material goods and services for our families to an extent that few persons actually realize. For example, consider the total cost of rearing a child to adulthood. Exhibit 1–1 shows this cost in urban areas for different regions of the nation. Costs are estimated for three levels; economy, low cost, and moderate cost. According to

Exhibit 1–1   Cost of Raising a Child to Age 18 Urban Areas, 3 Cost Levels*

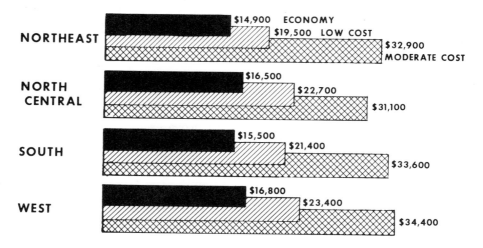

*Based on spending patterns of families with food costs at levels of 3 USDA food plans.
Derived from 1960–61 Survey of Consumer Expenditures; 1969 prices.
Source: U.S. Department of Agriculture, Agricultural Research Service

these estimates, a child may be reared for as low as $14,900 or as much as
$34,000, depending on the region and family income. Costs of rearing a child
vary less than $2,000 between regions of the country.

The Need for
Better Money Management

Decisions concerning personal income and spending are economic decisions.
It may be that the economic literacy of the American people is not keeping pace
with the increasing complexity of everyday economic affairs. Most citizens now
become involved with income taxes, property taxes, insurance programs, pension plans, and a host of other personal business matters that require at least
an elementary level of financial knowledge. This is an important aspect of life
and too many people reach adulthood without this vital knowledge.

One indication of poor family financial management is the increase in personal bankruptcies in the United States. There were over 14,000 more bankruptcy cases filed in 1970 than in 1965.[3] "Bankruptcy" means that a person
has become insolvent and has filed a legal petition in a U.S. District Court indicating that he is unable to pay his debts. Many families with relatively high
incomes file bankruptcy petitions. This seems to indicate abuse of credit
through overspending or poor financial planning. Financial counseling on the

---

[3]U. S. Department of Commerce, *Statistical Abstract of the United States, 1971*, p. 476.

use of credit is needed to help slow the growth of family money problems. This evidence also indicates that society could be better served by placing more emphasis on money management in the public school curriculums.

A significant amount of the nation's wealth is owned by widows, since women usually outlive their husbands. In 1969, 66.3 percent of ordinary life insurance death benefit payments were made to females, while only 12.2 percent were made to males.[4] This wealth is in various forms such as land, buildings, stocks, bonds, and mortgages. Too many women are shielded from or are not interested in the technicalities of the family's financial activities and holdings. Consequently, when widowed, the uninformed woman is ill-prepared to make decisions concerning property and investments for which she is suddenly responsible. It is important that women as well as men receive more training in personal financial management. This may be either formal training by taking whatever courses are available or informal training from reading current periodicals and books. If financial matters become a mutual interest between husband and wife, the learning can be helpful to both partners.

A desire for more goods and services is universal. Economists have long dwelt on the concept of the insatiability of human wants. Advertisers have done their work well in their goal to increase individuals' wants for the products of their sponsors. For many families, wants exceed ability to pay for those wants. This may be true for a high-income family as well as for one with a low income. The good life now seems to require a nice home, two cars, stylish clothes, certain recreational pursuits, travel, and a college education for the children.

With all the great variety of choices currently available for spending money, individuals must thoroughly understand themselves, and their needs, wants, and desires to make rational economic decisions. No person is a complete economic being to the extent that his money is spent in such a way as to derive the most satisfaction possible. Lack of knowledge of the multitudinous goods and services available prevents us from attaining maximum satisfaction from our incomes. But this should not prevent us from continuously striving to be better informed about finances and spending so that our economic choices will maximize our chances for personal success and happiness.

Economics teachers stress that money alone is not capable of satisfying people's wants, but it can be exchanged for products and services that do have this ability. Money then is a medium of exchange or an economic tool that we use to simplify our trading with each other. Money does produce a certain kind of happiness when we learn to use it wisely. The wise use of income is based on learning to judge value or quality when there is a choice available among items. By making a habit of careful comparative shopping, the consumer will become a demanding shopper. It is the savings from many small purchases that help to reach long-term family goals.

In most instances, whether a purchase involves buying a small consumer good or making an investment of major significance, choices must be made. Of course, all spending decisions are not of equal importance. More study must

---

[4]*Life Insurance Fact Book* (New York: Institute of Life Insurance, 1971), p. 46.

go into the purchase of a home or an automobile or a life insurance policy than into the selection of a sweater or coat. Regardless of the scale of the purchase, information is the secret to becoming a good consumer. Studying available products helps in making wise spending decisions. This is vital for large purchases and investment decisions with life-time importance. It should take much time and study to buy a life insurance or medical insurance policy, a retirement program, or a stock purchase plan. New laws are requiring producers to provide more information about their products so that all of us can be more selective consumers.

This book is written primarily for those families who have a moderate income and level of living, who will have some savings, and who wish to make a few investments. They will buy a home, a new car every few years, home furnishings, and life insurance; educate their children; and possibly purchase some stocks and bonds along with a pension plan for retirement. If the book can help this group to be better consumers and investors, its purpose will be accomplished.

Discussion Questions

1. What is finance?
2. Why is our society referred to as a "pecuniary society"?
3. What is meant by "mediated exchange"?
4. In a sense, all producers pour their products into one vast reservoir and receive general claims. Explain.
5. Why is money thought of as an economic tool?
6. What is meant by a "free enterprise system"?
7. Explain why money as a medium of exchange is better than the barter system.
8. Although the service of each is useful and valuable, why is a medical doctor's income generally more than the income of a common laborer?
9. What are some causes of unequal income distribution?
10. Explain how goods may literally "possess" persons. Give some examples.
11. Does money serve as a store of value today as well as it once did? Explain.

Economy is the science of avoiding
unnecessary expenditure, or the art of
managing our property with moderation.
[Seneca]

2

Economic Principles Related to Personal Finance

The disciplines of economics and finance are so closely related that many universities combine them into one department. Historically, economics has been classified as a social science. However, Kenneth Boulding tells us that it became known as a "behavioral science" in the 1950s to avoid any identification with socialism.[1] If we accept this new identification, we must ask the question, behavior in what areas of life? "Behavior" covers a broad range of activities. One British economist, Alfred Marshall, described economics as "a study of mankind in the ordinary business of life."[2] Combining terms, then, economics provides reasons for the behavior of man in his activities of earning and spending

[1]Kenneth Boulding, *Economics as a Science* (New York: McGraw-Hill, 1970), p. 53.
[2]Alfred Marshall, *Principles of Economics,* 8th ed. (New York: Macmillan, 1948), p. 1.

money to obtain personal satisfactions. Personal and family finance is concerned with the very same things.

Through the years, economists have developed a body of knowledge called "economic theory" which includes explanations of topics that range from methods of assigning value to commodities to the reasons for international trade. Although a detailed discussion of the extensive body of economic theory is not the purpose of this book, certain economic principles are so essential to a study of personal finance that it will be helpful to include a brief introduction to these principles in relating them to personal finance.

Consumer Satisfaction

In a free enterprise economic system where most productive resources are privately owned, individual or corporate owners earn money when those resources are utilized. The employment of our natural and human resources results in a steady output of goods and services. Only because people want these goods and services can the resource owners produce and market them at a profit. Why do people want them?

A product or service must be able to satisfy some need or desire if the consumer is to pay money for it. This makes the consumer very important in the operation of our economic system. If consumers do not want a product, it will not sell, and producers will stop making it. The use of resources will then be reoriented to produce products that consumers will buy. Since no two persons have exactly the same likes and dislikes, we have markets for thousands of different products and services. Have you silently criticized some person for spending his money on an item that seemed completely worthless to you? Most of us have. We should understand that each person's choice in spending money is conditioned by his background, living habits, friends, and general life experiences. Each person must decide what he likes best.

Producers must serve the wishes of consumers if their businesses are to make a profit. Those who are best able to anticipate and fulfill consumer demand will make the most profit. This is one criterion for good business management in a free enterprise economy.

Income and Budgeting

It may be noted that consumers can satisfy some of their wants at no direct monetary cost. Beautiful sunsets or towering mountains are natural wonders that provide a type of satisfaction to most people free of charge. However, we learn quickly that most of our wants are met only by consuming goods and services which have a monetary cost. Consequently, income becomes an all-important factor in determining the extent of our consumption of economic products.

Each person or family unit has a flow of income and possibly some savings; but, almost by definition, these are less than the consumer wants. Thus, decisions must be made as to what products to buy with the income. Spending decisions of families may be determined by the planning of a monthly or annual budget. A budget serves to allocate family income among various alternatives to obtain maximum consumer satisfaction. Chapter 8 will discuss this area of budget planning and application in greater detail.

Engel's Laws. Family spending patterns change as the level of income changes. Studies of family spending were made by Ernest Engel, a German statistician, during the 1850s. The conclusions reached in his studies became known as Engel's "Laws of Consumption."[3]

1. The percentage of a family's income spent for food tends to decrease as income increases.
2. The percentage of income spent for clothing tends to remain constant as income increases.
3. The percentage of income spent for housing, fuel, and light tends to remain constant as income increases.
4. The percentage of income spent for miscellaneous items and interests—such as education, religion, health, recreation, and luxury goods—tends to increase as income increases.

How well do American spending patterns conform to the European study? The Bureau of Labor Statistics regularly publishes data showing patterns of spending by American families. According to these studies, numbers one and four of Engel's laws have held true while two and three have not. As incomes increase, families tend to spend a smaller percentage for food while increasing the percentage for clothing, housing and household operation, and miscellaneous goods.

Spending for food does not increase as fast as income, because the amount of food a person can eat remains about the same; although it is true that low-income people improve their diets with better quality foods as income rises. After people have attained a moderate level of comfort, they being to buy for show to impress others. Economists call this *conspicuous consumption*. A big car, a cabin by the lake, or an inboard motorboat may be purchased for comfort and recreation, but the consumer may also be motivated by the status which they provide the owner. Exhibit 2–1 reveals changes in consumption patterns between 1960 and 1972.

Reconciling Income and Appetite

Goods and services to be exchanged are valued in terms of money. This value is called *price*. We receive our incomes in the form of money, and the things

---

[3]Milton H. Spencer, *Contemporary Economics* (New York: Worth, 1971), p. 145.

*Exhibit 2–1   The Composition of Personal Consumption Expenditures, 1960
and 1972*

Types of consumption	1960 Amount (bil. dol.)	1960 Percent of total	1972 Amount (bil. dol.)	1972 Percent of total
Durable goods	43.6	13.3	116.1	16.1
Automobiles and parts	18.4	5.6	52.8	7.3
Furniture and household equipment	18.4	5.6	47.6	6.6
Other	5.8	2.1	15.7	2.2
Nondurable goods	152.4	46.5	299.5	41.5
Food and beverages	80.8	24.6	144.7	20.1
Clothing and shoes	27.9	8.5	62.0	8.6
Gasoline and oil	11.7	3.6	25.2	3.5
Other	32.0	9.8	67.6	9.4
Services	131.7	40.2	305.4	42.4
Housing	42.8	13.1	107.2	14.9
Household operation	19.2	5.9	43.3	6.0
Transportation	10.5	3.1	21.7	3.0
Personal services, recreation and others	59.3	18.1	133.3	18.4
Total consumption	327.8	100.0	721.0	100.0

Source: *Survey of Current Business,* U.S. Dept. of Commerce, Feb. 1961, p. 13, and May 1973, p. 11.

we want to satisfy us are priced in terms of money. As long as our income and consumer prices change proportionally in the same direction, we do not lose purchasing power. Our income may lose or gain in purchasing power as prices or incomes change.

The relationship between family income and consumer prices determines the ability of a household to obtain goods and services.[4] Greater average shares are possible only as greater income is produced. We usually expect to find a close relationship between income and satisfaction, but many times there is no such correspondence. There are several combinations of the four factors—high and low income, high and low satisfaction.

High Income–Low Satisfaction. There are families and individuals with high incomes who get little satisfaction from their use of goods. Such people often

---

[4]Inflation is discussed in Chapter 7.

move from one house to another every two or three years. They have lived in new and old houses and large and small houses. They never find one that gives complete satisfaction. Others have the same trouble with clothes. They have closets full of clothes, but nothing satisfactory to wear. Families such as these have not made a careful study of their wants and the products necessary to satisfy these wants.

Some families are in this classification because they do not know how to spend their money. They are poor traders or bargainers. For example, they may buy items on impulse when prices are highest or they may buy poor quality merchandise from unscrupulous dealers because it looks good. These people have not learned to stretch their income; therefore, they may be getting less satisfaction from their consumption than low-income families.

Low Income–High Satisfaction. There may be just as many families as those mentioned above who have relatively low incomes but have the ability to make wise purchases and obtain a great amount of satisfaction from their consumption. These people have a reasonable understanding of which goods and services serve their needs best and they take advantage of sales prices. In many instances, they buy good quality, used merchandise. The family takes care of its possessions, and it is not unusual for one or more members of the family to be able to make repairs on many items. Someone who has a sedentary job could obtain secondary benefit by getting some physical exercise while performing simple household maintenance chores. Some manufacturers now encourage consumers who do things for themselves by including carefully written instructions with repair kits.

High Income–High Satisfaction. Another possibility is a high-income family which consumes many goods and services and receives much satisfaction. This is the normal expectation and is probably true for a majority of relatively high-income families. High-income families have the means to become good consumers, if they will make the effort.

Money Income and Real Income

Money income is the flow of money to the family from work or from the ownership of property. *Real income* is the purchasing power of money. Some economists add another classification in addition to money income called *psychic income,* the benefit or satisfaction derived from performing a job.

Unequal distribution of income not only modifies consumption by giving some the power to consume more than others, but also modifies the character of the goods chosen on each income level. Though real incomes are very unequally distributed, the differences are not so great as those indicated by the distribution of money incomes. The lower income groups do for themselves many things for which the rich pay in the market—e.g., more household production goes on in the poor household. Those in the lower income category save a smaller portion of their money income.

Measuring Satisfaction

The principal economic problem in consumption, from an individual point of view, is how to use income to obtain the most satisfaction. The great development of technique that has taken place in production during the last century and a half has not been paralleled in consumption. There are two reasons for this backwardness of consumption: (1) the very nature of the consumption problem makes it difficult to use exact measures for testing the results of individual expenditures; and (2) the household, which is the usual unit in consumption, is too small to function well economically.

The businessman tests the results of particular operations by their effect on the profits of the business. No such exact measure is as yet available for the household. The home is, of course, operated for the well-being of the family, but well-being is such a vague goal that results can be judged only in the most general way.

Households are so small that they cannot use many economical operations found in industry. Industrial purchasing has been largely specialized in the hands of expert buyers. Purchases are generally in large amounts. Household purchasing falls largely upon the housewife, who not only buys in relatively small quantities, but also has many other complex problems and duties on which to spend her time.

The Utility of Goods and Services. The extent to which a product can satisfy wants is called its *utility*. The name implies that the product is useful to the person consuming it. For example, a shirt has utility because it can satisfy a desire for protection and a good appearance.

Before goods can satisfy consumers, they must be in the right form, in the right place at the appropriate time; and the owners must be willing to sell or give possession of the goods to someone else. These are referred to as form, time, place, and possession utility. When a piece of cloth is made into a shirt, it is given form utility. When the shirt is transported to a local store and placed on a counter to be sold, it takes on time and place utility. Since the store manager is willing to transfer ownership of the shirt to anyone with adequate money or credit, he is providing possession utility. All goods in the marketplace represent varying combinations of these types of utility.

Since consumer goods have utility, they have the capability of satisfying people. However, a particular good will not provide the same satisfaction to two different people because their wants are not equal. A heavy, long-sleeve shirt may provide more satisfaction to someone in a cold climate than to another person living in mild temperatures. Some people prefer blue shirts to red shirts. Regardless of the item, however, it will have a varying utility—positive or negative—in the marketplace.

Total Utility. *Total utility* is the measure of satisfaction that is received from all of a product that is consumed in one time period. Consuming one unit of a product will provide a certain amount of utility. The second unit increases utility and a third unit will cause it to go still higher. If consumption continues with additional units of the product, a level will eventually be reached where utility will be at a maximum, a point of satiation. Additional units will cause it to start declining. We get all the satisfaction possible from one product when total utility is greatest.

We consider people's wants for all goods and services to be insatiable, but wants for a specific product can be fulfilled. To be a rational economic person, each person should have some idea of which products satisfy his wants. This means that he chooses a product because it gives more satisfaction than another product of equal cost.

Marginal Utility. Marginal utility theory was introduced by nineteenth century economists to help explain how goods and services are valued. The satisfaction received from consuming another unit of a good is the marginal utility of that unit. Our wants for a particular good at one time are satiable. If several units of a product are consumed, each unit adds less satisfaction than the previous unit. For example, a hungry person would be likely to get much satisfaction from eating a cheese sandwich. A second sandwich would add to his satisfaction, but not as much as the first. If he continued to eat them, his hunger would soon be gone and no additional utility would be provided by another cheese sandwich. In fact, he would reach a point where he would rather not have another sandwich since it would provide "disutility" if he had to consume it.

The consumption of products must be considered within a *time* framework. If we allow enough time, our consumer will be ready for more sandwiches. The principle of decreasing marginal utility may be defined as follows: when a person consumes additional units of a product during one time period, the utility added by each succeeding unit decreases. As Exhibit 2–2 shows, utility is positive, but total utility declines when negative marginal utility begins.

Exhibit 2–2   Example of Total and Marginal Utility from Consumption of Cheese Sandwiches

Number of sandwiches consumed	Total utility (units)	Marginal utility (units)
1	100	100
2	180	80
3	220	40
4	225	5
5	200	−25

Most people's wants are more than their incomes can buy. They must make a choice as to which wants to satisfy and which ones to leave unsatisfied. Not only must they choose among present goods, but they may want goods in the future which would require delaying satisfactions. We should try to distribute our spending between present and future wants in such a way that each will

have the same marginal utility. If we were assured of receiving the future benefits, we would be more willing to distribute our satisfactions evenly throughout
our lifetime, but we have no such assurance. Human nature is such that in estimating the present value of a future benefit we make a deduction from its future
value that increases as the benefit is deferred farther into the future.

The rates at which different people discount the future affect not only their
tendency to save, as the term is ordinarily understood, but also their tendency
to buy things which will be a lasting source of pleasure rather than those which
give a stronger but more transient enjoyment. The future is more important
than the present to the person who buys a new coat instead of indulging in a
drinking bout, or chooses simple furniture that will wear well, instead of showy
furniture that will soon fall to pieces.

Since income is limited, purchasing more of one product means purchasing
less of another product. As purchases of one good increase, the marginal utility
will decline, while decreasing purchases of the other good will bring about a
rising marginal utility for that product. When marginal utility becomes equal
for the last dollar spent on all goods, the total utility cannot be increased by
changing spending patterns. Utility is then as high as it can be until income,
prices, or wants change. We know that all people do not have the same wants;
nor do they get the same satisfaction from consuming the same products. For
this reason, no two people have the same total and marginal utility pattern.

Indifference Curves. Vilfredo Pareto, writing in 1906, introduced a different
view of utility which held that utility is not measurable, but has to be considered in terms of a scale of preferences without assigning numerical value to
utility functions.[5] He and Francis Edgeworth developed the *indifference curve*
theory of value. They believed that a person confronted with making a choice
between various products could rank them in order of preference but could
not determine the exact amount of satisfaction to be derived from consuming
them. For example, if a person is given a choice between a glass of milk and a
glass of cola, he can rank one over the other easier than he can place a numerical value of satisfaction on either of the products.

An indifference curve shows the preference of an individual consumer when
he chooses between goods. Assume for the moment that a person likes both
milk and cola drinks and the prices of the two are equal. His indifference curve
would show various combinations of milk and cola which would give him equal
satisfaction. Exhibit 2–3 shows various combinations of milk and cola for
which the consumer would have no preference, one over another. Each of the
three combinations represents a point on his indifference curve.

Now we can plot the combinations in Exhibit 2–3 into a graph as shown in
Exhibit 2–4. Points *A, B,* and *C* on the curve represent the various combina-
tions for which the person is indifferent. When he moves from point *A* to point
B, he is willing to trade two glasses of milk for one glass of cola. Now that he

---

[5]W. E. Kuhn, *The Evolution of Economic Thought,* 2nd ed. (Cincinnati: Southwestern, 1970), p. 174.

Exhibit 2–3   Consumer Indifference Between Milk and Cola

Combination	Milk (glasses)	Cola (glasses)
A	4	1
B	2	2
C	1	4

has only two glasses of milk, to move to point *C* and give up another glass of milk he requires two glasses of cola. This indicates that as the quantity of milk decreases, it requires an increasing amount of cola to get the consumer to part with more milk. The value placed on the last unit is high.

The indifference curve shows that the consumer is indifferent as to whether he has four glasses of cola and one of milk, two of each, or one milk and four colas; but we can logically assume that he would prefer more of both. If he could get more of both, new combinations and a new curve farther to the right on the graph would result. Certainly this would provide a greater amount of satisfaction since the consumer would be getting more of both items. If a third curve was added to the right of the second, a still higher degree of satisfaction would be provided. When several indifference curves are shown on a graph indicating different levels of satisfaction, it is called an *indifference map.*

Budget Line. Price in relation to income or budget becomes a factor that limits getting all that is wanted of the products. Let us assume that budget will allow a consumer to spend $.50 per day for milk and cola and that they cost $.10 each. He can buy any combination as long as it does not cost more than $.50 per day. By spending all the money for cola, he could get five glasses. By similarly spending $.50 for milk, he could get five glasses of milk. The budget line, or line of attainable combinations, in Exhibit 2–5 shows how much the consumer would get by spending all the money on each, as well as spending for various combinations of each that could be purchased with all the money.

Exhibit 2–4   Consumer Indifference Curve

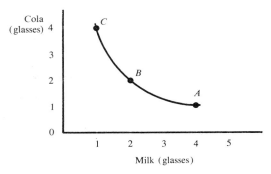

Exhibit 2–5   Budget Line or Line of Attainable Combinations

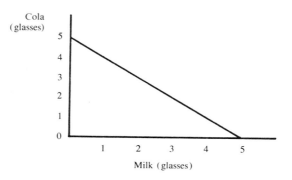

The budget line and indifference map can now be combined to see what combination the consumer should buy with the money allotted for these products
in order to get the most satisfaction possible. This is shown in Exhibit 2–6.
The best combination is where the budget line is just tangent to the highest
possible indifference curve. This is point *A* on I_2 where he would be consuming
two glasses of cola and three glasses of milk. This is the maximum level of satisfaction with the available amount of money. If the consumer decides to increase
the money for drinks or if the prices of drinks decline, he could obtain greater
satisfaction. Likewise, a smaller budget for drinks or higher prices would decrease both the quantity consumed and the satisfaction gained from consumption.

What would happen if the price of milk increased but that of cola stayed
the same? The lower end of the budget line would shift to the left. Suppose
milk increases to $.25 per glass. By spending all his money for milk, the con-
sumer could buy only two glasses. Exhibit 2–7 shows the new budget line and
new combination of products. The highest satisfaction will come from buying
one glass of milk and two and one-half glasses of cola. When the price of milk
increased, the consumer had to substitute cola for milk, but he still received
fewer total glasses of drinks and less total satisfaction than before the price in-

Exhibit 2–6   Highest Possible Consumer Satisfaction

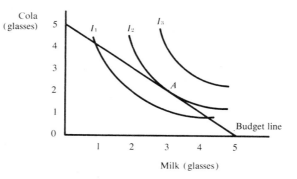

Exhibit 2–7   Highest Possible Consumer Satisfaction (milk at a higher price)

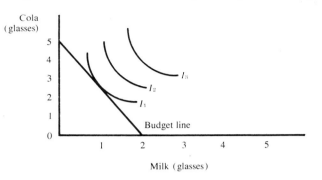

crease. A later discussion of consumer demand in this chapter will explain how the theories of utility and indifference curve analysis are used to construct a demand curve.

Balancing Income and Satisfaction. With consumer prices and family incomes continuously changing, how well do consumers obtain maximum satisfaction from their spending? Does an increase in income lead to an increase in consumption of most goods? These questions can be answered only for individual families. The degree of responsiveness of consumer expenditures to price and income changes is concerned with price and income elasticities of demand. These topics will be included later in this chapter in the discussion of demand.

Economics as a
Study of Choices

Some people may feel that their activities as individuals in the marketplace are not very important. In reality, consumers acting individually and in groups determine the success or failure of modern business firms. An example of this can be seen in the decline of the hat industry in recent years. Sales of both men's and women's hats are only a fraction of what they were in earlier years. Consumers actually influence and shape the course of business.

It is important that we as consumers learn to judge quality and values in products because, if we demand goods of high quality, this is what business will provide. When we buy poor quality merchandise, we are in effect telling producers that this is what we want. However, we should remember that producers are not completely helpless in the face of consumer power. They have many ways to influence what we purchase, such as producing a large variety of goods and conducting intensive advertising campaigns.

Without markets and consumers there would be no production. *Consumer sovereignty* is the term used by economists to refer to the power of consumers in the market. In a free market economy where resources are privately owned, producers will follow the dictates of consumers. However, our choice is not one of complete freedom without any restrictions. We have legal restrictions on the production and sale of some goods considered to be harmful to society.

Nations which provide their citizens with considerable personal and economic freedom allow people to spend time and money as they choose when they are not interfering with the freedom of other people. Such freedom has always been important to Americans. Consequently, production is constantly changing due to the wishes of the consuming public.

Scarcity of Economic Resources

The central problem of mankind in most of the world is learning how to produce enough of life's necessities. It may be that too much emphasis has been placed upon social institutions as a factor in economic progress, and too little on national resources, technological developments, and the skill of labor. Regardless of the type of economic system used, however, every nation must use the same type of resources in the production of goods and services.

Man has always had the use of natural resources such as soil, water, air, and minerals. Economists combine these into one resource and call it *land*. Many centuries ago, man learned to put his labor to work on the land to obtain useful products. Therefore, manpower, or *labor* became the second economic resource. It did not take long for man to decide that production was too slow and difficult when he had only his hands to use in working the land. He soon began to develop primitive types of tools such as wooden plows. These tools used in production, whether they be wooden plows or the most sophisticated electronic computer, are classified as *capital*. Through the years we have steadily increased and improved our capital. We include such things as buildings, machinery, equipment, and all other man-made items used in the production process.

In more recent times, we have learned how important it is to know how to combine land, labor, and capital into a profitable business. Each business requires different types and quantities of resources to be successful. The knowledge and skills used for combining resources are called *management*. As the state of technology changes, managers must make continuous changes in the types and quantities of resources used. Each day they make decisions about what and how much to produce.

The total output of goods and services in any country is determined by the quantity and quality of resources available and how well they are used. A country may have an abundance of natural resources and labor, but lack the capital and management necessary for high production. The result is a low standard of living for the people. China, for example, has a population of 800 million people with a very large land area, but possesses very little capital. However, it is possible for a country to have few natural resources and still have high production. Japan has little land but an abundance of labor, capital, and management. By using these resources and by importing raw materials, it has become highly productive.

As long as people want goods and services, economic resources will be needed. Since people's wants are increasing, the need for resources keeps growing. Unfortunately, there are not enough resources to fulfill all the wants for goods and services. For this reason, we say that economic resources are scarce. Because they are scarce, we have to pay to obtain the use of a resource. If producers have to pay for the use of resources, then they must charge for their products.

Scarcity of Economic Products—Diminishing Returns

Since economic resources are scarce, it seems reasonable to say that we should use them as efficiently as possible. Another way of saying this is to say that we should get as much output as we can from the least input of resources. Goods and services are scarce and cost money, because economic resources are scarce. Although to assume that we can double production by doubling the resources may seem intuitively correct, this is not the case. Most producers have difficulty in increasing all their resources at one time. They usually have a plant that is fixed in size with some flexibility in changing the quantity of labor and equipment. When managers begin to increase one resource while one or more is fixed, they should be aware of an economic principle called the *principle of diminishing marginal returns*.

The marginal product is the additional output (quantity of a good or service) resulting from a small increase in the use of an input (or resource) when other inputs are not changed. If this principle were not true for all experience, we could produce enough food for the entire population on a small acreage of land. In reality, when we keep adding workers on the land, we will reach a point where an additional worker will cause total output to increase by less than the amount the previous worker added. This is the beginning of diminishing returns. If more workers are added after this point, each succeeding worker adds less to total output. Continuous additions will finally cause total production to decline.

Diminishing returns can occur in any type of production, whether it is a steel mill, a farm, or an automobile assembly plant. New techniques in production can delay these results or push them back, but the principle always operates in the production process.

When a firm pushes production past the point of diminishing returns, costs of producing additional units of the product begin to increase. Competition requires businesses to keep their costs low. Each producer wants to operate with the output that will provide maximum profit. By knowing the costs of production and the demand for his product, a businessman can decide his most profitable rate of production. He may be able to substitute one resource for another to lower costs without decreasing production, but there are limits to the amount of substitution possible.

Values and Prices—Demand

In all but the most primitive societies most goods move from producer to consumer through some type of market. Markets become necessary when an economy changes from a system of barter to one using money. Some markets are highly organized while others involve only simple trades. While they vary in complexity, they are vital to a free economic system like that in the United States. In large part, we depend on the market system to keep prices at reasonable levels.

In an open market, price may be defined as the value of a good or service to the person buying it. One person may refuse to buy a particular product because he considers the price too high, while another person would willingly pay the price. Essentially, then, price is the exchange value of an item in terms of money.

Market prices serve a very important function in a free enterprise economy. The market is uninfluenced by needs or desires unless they are expressed in offers for goods in money. Each dollar, regardless of the ethical or moral situation behind its expenditure, possesses the same power in directing the productive efforts of society. Goods of society go into the hands of those who can pay for them, irrespective of the real needs of the purchasers. The consumption problem cannot be understood without a knowledge of the distribution of money incomes among the members of society; but it is important to recognize that we depend on prices not only to ration goods and services among consumers, but also to ration the limited resources among producers.

Economic goods and services must have a demand in the marketplace or production will not continue. Producers of new products do not know what their demand will be until they place some of them in the market. Consumer acceptance will determine whether production continues. The demand for a product is not an exact quantity. We define demand as *various quantities of a good or service that would be taken at various prices during a given time and at a given place.* Unless we are both willing and financially able to make a purchase, we are not part of the demand for a product. This helps to explain the difference between demand and wants. We have wants that never become part of demand because we may not have the money or credit to make a purchase.

The demand for a product depends on three things, namely: (1) number of prospective customers in the market, (2) income or money available to the prospective customers, and (3) their habits, tastes, and customs. Since people, markets, and incomes are continuously changing, we know that demands are continuously changing.

A demand curve can be explained by use of a diagram. Suppose the demand for tennis balls is as shown in Exhibit 2–8. At a price of $1.00 each, one million tennis balls will be purchased; but, if the price is lowered to $.50, three million will be taken.

We learned earlier in this chapter that consumer demand theory is built on marginal utility and indifference curve analysis. When the price is lowered, larger quantities are sold. All quantities are part of the demand. It can be seen from demand curve graphs that price and quantity can change without a change in demand, since the entire curve represents the demand. When demand changes, the curve will shift to the right or left. An increase in demand will cause the curve to shift to the right, while a decrease in demand will cause it to shift to the left (as shown in Exhibit 2–9).

Exhibit 2–8   Demand Curve for Tennis Balls

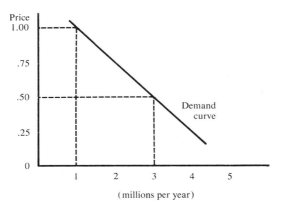

In Exhibit 2–9, the increase in demand shows that more tennis balls will be taken at every price. People are willing either to take more at the same price or take the same quantity at a higher price. This is a true indication of a higher demand. For a decrease in demand, people will take fewer at the same price or will take the same quantity at a lower price. These are new demands and they reflect the basic definition that demand reflects wants coupled with ability to pay.

Elasticity of Demand. Now look at the demand curve in Exhibit 2–8 again. Why does it have the particular shape that it has? Why is it not flatter or steeper? You can readily see that the shape of the curve will depend on the amount of change in quantity related to a change in price. A small change in price may result in either a small or a large change in quantity taken. Elasticity is defined as *the relationship of a change in quantity taken relative to the change in price.* The demand may be elastic, inelastic, or unit elastic, depending on the relationship of change. When quantity changes by a greater percentage than

Exhibit 2–9   Change in Demand for Tennis Balls

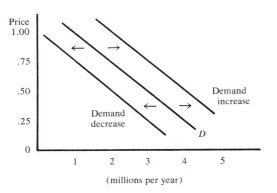

price, demand is elastic. An equal percentage change in each is unit elasticity. The following formula can be used to calculate elasticity.

$$\text{Price elasticity of demand} = \frac{\text{Percentage change in quantity}}{\text{Percentage change in price}}$$

When the price of tennis balls was lowered from $1.00 to $.75, the quantity sold increased from one to two million. Quantity sold increased 100 percent in response to a decrease of 25 percent in price. For every 1 percent decrease in price, quantity increased 4 percent. Since price changed by a smaller percentage than quantity, the demand for tennis balls was elastic.

Of what use to individuals is this concept of elasticity of demand? An elastic demand means that consumers are quite responsive to price changes. We should understand that the elasticity is not the same at all points on the demand curve. The demand for a product is more elastic at a high price than at a low price. We would likely get a greater response percentagewise from customers when the price of a tennis ball is decreased from $1.00 to $.75 than if we decreased it from $.50 to $.25. Food products, which are necessities, tend to have an inelastic demand. If you are selling a food product that already has a relatively low price, you could not expect to increase sales very much by lowering the price. Consumers could be very responsive to a decrease in price of a relatively high-priced luxury item. Exhibit 2–10 shows an inelastic demand curve and 2–11 an elastic demand curve.

Exhibit 2–10   Inelastic Demand Curve for Tennis Balls

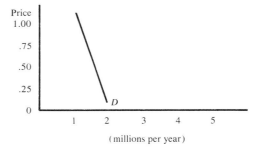

By using a method such as this, a businessman may be able to make more profit by lowering the price of a product. If he is operating in the elastic portion of his demand curve, he can lower the price and receive more revenue. His profit will rise if he can sell the additional units without increasing costs as much as revenue. When he is operating in the inelastic portion of his demand curve, his revenue can be increased only by raising prices.

Income Elasticity. Many studies have been made to determine the effects of income changes on product demand. From these studies, it has been shown that a rise in income will cause demand to increase for some products and decrease

Exhibit 2–11   Elastic Demand Curve for Tennis Balls

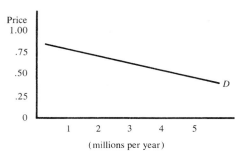

for others. For most goods and services, demand increases as a result of higher incomes. Customers buy more of the good at any price as income rises. The change in quantity related to change in income is called income elasticity and is determined by this formula.

$$\text{Income elasticity} = \frac{\text{Percent of change in quantity}}{\text{Percent of change in disposable income}}$$

Food products have very low income elasticities in highly industrial nations. This means that a very small part of any increase in income will be spent for additional food. In such a society, most people receive adequate quantities of food, so that they usually choose to spend additional income for convenience

"I'm keeping my fingers crossed, hoping the school term will end
before the class asks me to explain wage and price controls!"

Courtesy: Publishers-Hall Syndicate

items or luxuries. The low income elasticity and low price elasticity of farm
products have been largely responsible for a steady decline in number of farms.
Nevertheless, food consumption is expected to increase at about the same rate
as population.

Production and Costs—Supply

A market must have sellers as well as buyers. Thus, understanding how the
supply is obtained is an important part of understanding economic theory.
Supply is determined by producers and their willingness to offer different quantities in the market. The term "supply" may be defined as *the various quantities
that will be offered for sale at various prices at a given time and place.* In general, producers are usually willing to offer more at a high price than at lower
prices. A rising price indicates that larger quantities are needed and, given
enough time, producers will obtain resources and offer more to the market. A
rising price is usually necessary to get a larger supply offered, since costs rise
as production is increased. In the graph of this relationship, the supply curves
will slope upward to the right as shown in Exhibit 2–12.

Exhibit 2–12   Supply Curve for Tennis Balls

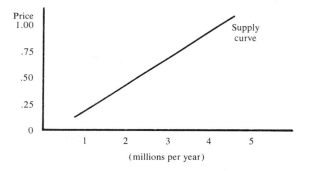

The time factor is important in assessing supply. The current supply is the
quantity that is already produced. It takes time to produce more. Sudden
changes may occur in the demand for a product, but supply changes more
slowly. If more of a product is needed, more resources may be committed to its
production. The amount of time needed will depend on the particular product.
For example, if more bicycles are needed, producers could most likely use their
resources more intensively and expand production within a few days. An increased demand for heart surgeons could be satisfied only by long periods of
training and experience.

The supply curve in Exhibit 2–12 shows that, at a price of $.25, sellers will
offer one million tennis balls; while at a price of $1.00 they will produce four
million. Price and quantity can change without a change in supply. The entire
curve represents the supply. When supply changes, the curve will shift to the

Exhibit 2–13   Change in Supply of Tennis Balls

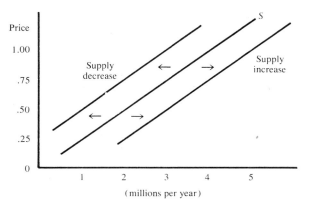

right or left. A shift to the right is an increase in supply, while a shift to the left is a decrease. Exhibit 2–13 shows these changes.

The increase in supply shows that more tennis balls will be offerred at every price. Producers are willing to offer more at the same price or offer the same quantity at a lower price. For a decrease in supply, they will offer fewer at the same price or the same quantity at a higher price. These are real changes in the supply.

Elasticity of Supply. Supply elasticity is a measure of the response of producers to price changes. It is similar to elasticity of demand, except that it is concerned with producers instead of consumers. It is defined as *the relationship of a change in quantity offered to a change in price offered.* The production of some products is more sensitive to price changes than others. Often, a producer must expect a price increase to be somewhat permanent before he will change his resources. In addition, a longer time period is required to obtain resources for higher production of some products. When, on the other hand, supply can be increased quickly, the supply is moved into and out of different types of production in response to prices of the products.

Production Possibilities. In our study of supply, it is important to understand the concept of production possibilities. Because our resources are limited, economic decisions must be made concerning what will be produced. Total production of goods and services at one time is limited by the quantity and quality of resources. Of course, we know that production can increase as these change. The individual business firm has a certain limited amount of resources to use in production at one time. If another type of good is wanted, present production must be sacrificed to produce it.

A simplified example may be used to illustrate the production possibilities principle. Suppose a farmer has fifty acres of tillable land and the necessary tools to cultivate it. Two crops are most adapted to his land—cotton and corn.

He can plant all cotton, all corn, or some combination of the two crops. He thus has to sacrifice one to get more of the other. The production possibilities curve shown in Exhibit 2–14 is the limit of production of the two crops. Any point outside the curve is not possible on this farm.

On a national basis, economists use production possibilities curves to compare large groups of goods. For example, we could compare the production of consumer goods against capital goods, or public goods against private goods. When the economy grows, the production possibilities curves shift to the right.

Opportunity Cost. Opportunity cost has a close relationship to production possibilities. It is the amount of a good that must be given up to obtain more of another good. In our previous example, we could say that the opportunity cost to the farmer for producing more cotton would be the amount of corn that he would have to give up. If the nation is using all resources and wants more capital goods, the opportunity cost will be the amount of consumer goods lost.

The opportunity cost principle can be used in a broad sense to apply to persons and to households. A family has a certain amount of income to spend. If a new automobile is purchased, the cost is the amount of other consumer goods and services given up. To some extent, individuals use the opportunity cost principle in selecting a vocation, although they may not realize it. Within the limits of his talents and ability, a person tries to obtain the highest income job. The cost of accepting a low income job is the amount he is giving up by not locating the best work possible depending on his qualifications. In another case, a factory worker may choose not to work overtime, since he values leisure time above more income. When a family takes a vacation in Mexico, it is foregoing a trip to Canada. Everything we do has an opportunity cost.

Since business managers are concerned with profits, they must consistently be considering alternatives. What is the cost of hiring another worker or installing another machine? Anytime a manager can give up less than he is getting by making a change, his profit will be enhanced.

Exhibit 2–14   Production Possibilities Curve (50 acres)

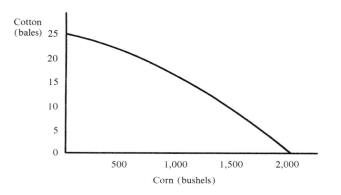

Determining Market Price

Now, by combining the demand and supply curves, it will be easy to see their relationship in determining the price of a product. The significance of these curves is not apparent until they are put together. In markets where there is competition, the interaction of demand and supply will determine the product price and the number of units sold. This can be seen by looking at the diagram in Exhibit 2–15, which combines the previous curve examples dealing with the demand and supply of tennis balls.

Exhibit 2–15   Equilibrium of Demand and Supply for Tennis Balls

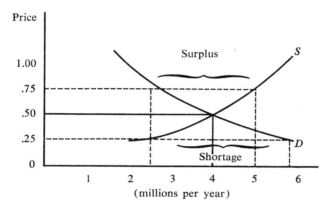

Price and quantity sold are determined at the equilibrium point of supply and demand or where the curves intersect. This is the only point where they are equal. The amount demanded just equals the amount supplied. There will be 4 million tennis balls sold at a price of $.50 each. We need to study the diagram closely to understand why price and quantity will be at the point where supply and demand are equal.

Suppose sellers try to get $.75 each for the tennis balls. At this price sellers will offer 5 million, but buyers will take only 2½ million, leaving a surplus of tennis balls. Inventories begin to build up and pressure develops to lower the price. Competition will cause some sellers to begin lowering price and then all must do so to remain in the market. This pressure on price will continue until it comes down to the equilibrium point. At this point, sellers are willing to sell 4 million tennis balls for $.50 each and buyers and willing to pay this amount for the same quantity. The pressure to lower the price is now removed; therefore, it would be folly to sell for less than is necessary.

Now let us assume that the price for tennis balls is $.25 each. At this price, sellers will offer 2½ million to the market, but buyers will take 6 million. A shortage would quickly develop, requiring producers to increase production. Buyers competing with each other for the limited supply develop pressure for the price to rise, inducing producers to offer more goods. This pressure continues until the price rises to the equilibrium point of $.50 and 4 million. With pressure removed, buyers can now get all they want at this price; therefore, it would be folly to pay more. Any producer whose costs are so high that he cannot profitably sell tennis balls for $.50 will have to become more efficient or get into another business.

How long will this market for tennis balls remain stable at a price of $.50? Will this always be the market-clearing price? No, the equillibrium price and quantity may change at a later time. In fact, we should remember that a market may not be in equilibrium very often. In free enterprise economies where markets are constantly changing, buyers and sellers are continuously searching for the equilibrium price in markets. Prices are raised and lowered as the pressure of shortages or surpluses is discovered. We can say that a competitive market discovers the true equilibrium price for a product. It takes time and many adjustments for this point to be reached. When price is above the equilibrium point and moving down, it may over-adjust and move down too far and cause a shortage of the product. How fast adjustments are made and the price moves toward equilibrium will depend on the type of market.

In some markets, price may never reach the equilibrium point of supply and demand. The pressure is always pushing price toward this point, but before it arrives, the equilibrium point may change. We learned in our earlier discussion that demand and supply are continuously changing. If either or both of these change, they will likely be equal at new price and quantity levels.

Several factors could bring about a change in demand for a product. Demand can change due to changes in the number of potential buyers, changes in incomes, tastes, and habits, and changes in the price of a close substitute. When potential buyers or their incomes increase there is a tendency for demand to increase. Conversely, a decrease in buyers or incomes brings about a decrease in demand. A decrease in the price of a close substitute can decrease demand by causing buyers to switch to the lower priced product.

Supplies of a product may change due to some technological development which lowers the cost of production. This could bring new producers into the industry to increase supply. If the price of a substitute product is lowered, some producers may have to leave the industry bringing a corresponding decrease in supply. Sometimes producers voluntarily switch to producing other goods because profit opportunities appear to be better in another industry. This change causes a decrease in supply of the former product. Although the number of firms in an industry may be decreasing, supply may increase due to the expanding output of the remaining firms.

Since demand and supply of a product change for different reasons, they are independent of each other. Demand may be falling while supply is rising. Given enough time, producers will usually respond to any change in the demand. Exhibit 2–16 shows how the equilibrium price and quantity change with changes in supply and demand.

Supply increased from S to S_1 while demand decreased from D to D_1. The equilibrium point shifted to the intersection of a new supply and demand situation. Simultaneous shifts in both demand and supply may be in the same direction or in opposite directions. Also, the change in one may be more or less than

Exhibit 2–16   Changes in Demand and Supply for Tennis Balls

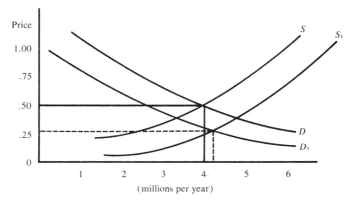

change in the other. Price may increase or decrease with little or no change in quantity demanded after the curves have shifted.

In many industries in the United States, the long-run tendency is for technology to lower production costs and for supply to increase. This allows producers to lower price and sell a larger quantity of the product. With a continuous rise in population and incomes, demand is also increasing for many products.

Our explanation of markets has been concerned with competitive markets in a free enterprise economy. This assumes that buyers and sellers are permitted to bargain freely with each other without interference from government or any other organization. In reality, there is much interference in the market place. Government frequently establishes price ceilings or price floors or regulates quality standards for products. It levies taxes on some products and not on others.

Although many restrictions are placed on markets, price is still an amazing rationing device. Shortages or surpluses usually develop when government tries to replace the market to allocate resources and consumer goods. Thus, it would seem that the interests of consumers are served by keeping most business private enterprise and maintaining a great amount of competition in the marketplace.

Discussion Questions

1. Explain conspicuous consumption and what circumstances bring it about.
2. Name and discuss the types of utility.
3. Explain the principle of decreasing marginal utility. Give an example from your own experience.
4. Explain and graphically illustrate indifference curves.
5. Explain the budget line in relation to indifference curves.
6. Explain the principle of diminishing marginal returns.
7. Define "price ceilings" and "price floors."

3

Management Principles Applied to Personal Finance

What is Management?

George R. Terry wrote: "Management deals with the establishment and the achievement of objectives. It exists to some degree in almost every human activity be it in the factory, office, school, bank, government, church, labor union, home, hotel, or hospital."[1] Writings of earliest recorded history indicate a recognition of the existence of a management process. However, the development of a body of literature which we can refer to as *management principles* has taken place principally in the twentieth century.

When we speak of these principles, we imply there are basic and fundamental truths which should be applied in the management unit involved. A logical

[1]George R. Terry, *Principles of Management,* 4th ed. (Homewood, Illinois: Richard D. Irwin, 1964), p. 3.

question follows: "What management principles should be applied in the handling of one's personal finances?"

The family unit is unique but it has characteristics and problems which are common to all organizations, be they business enterprises, governmental units, churches, civic and social organizations, or whatever. In spite of their diversity in nature and objectives, most organizations function on assumptions like the following.

Within the organization, the members recognize certain of their numbers as a manager or managers and the remainder as non-managers.

They recognize there is one person or a group which determines objectives and policies to be administered by management.

There is supposed to be *authority* in a chain of command at any one time, however tenuous or temporary it might be.

Following is a brief look at these and certain other management principles which have some relevance to personal finance.

The Decision-Making Process

Perhaps we should first review what management literature has to say about the matter of *decision making* and ask if it can be applied to any degree as an aid in the management of personal finances. Is there an orderly process for arriving at decisions? Or should we assume that each of us is endowed with varying degrees of ability to make correct decisions, and that this gift is supplemented by lessons learned from experience? Most of us, reflecting on many of our past decisions, will hope there *is* some process which would improve our performance.

Before looking for such a process, we need only examine well publicized mistakes of government, businesses, and other organizations to realize there is no infallible process which will lead us to the correct decision every time. Recognizing this fact should not diminish our desire to improve our performance in making decisions affecting our family finances.

Although writers on the subject use different terminology, essentially the decision-making process is said to consist of a sequence of five steps:

1. Recognizing and defining the problem
2. Analyzing the problem with every practical means available
3. Developing alternative solutions
4. Evaluating the alternatives
5. Deciding which alternative seems to be the best one

Although a thorough handling of a hypothetical case is outside the scope of this book, the following case study will present a brief illustration of the application of the formal decision-making process.

Indianapolis to Houston for the Frank Lewis Family

Frank Lewis has worked in the sales department of Crown Co. for ten years. He started as a salesman in St. Louis and was transferred five years later to be District Manager in Indianapolis. On April 1, he accepted a promotion as regional manager in Houston to be effective June 1. He has a wife and children ages eight and ten.

Recognize and Define the Problem. There are a number of family decisions relating to the transfer, but a very obvious one is the matter of acquiring adequate housing in Houston. The Lewises agree that they want to live in a neighborhood of families in comparable circumstances. They decide on the minimum rooms and facilities necessary. If it can be justified financially, they would much prefer to buy than rent.

Analyze the Problem. There are many facets to the problem. Their analysis includes recognition of the following:

1. *Financial limitations.* The Lewises are living in an apartment in Indianapolis and will forfeit only one month's rent if they move before June 1. Their budget permits a monthly outlay of $350 for housing, including all utilities, taxes, and maintenance. In addition, Frank has received annual bonuses from which he has been able to accumulate $10,000 in a saving and loan association. They feel they would be justified in using $7,000 of this in purchasing a home.

2. *Probable length of stay in Houston.* Lewis is happy with Crown and has every intention of making a career with them. Company officials indicate the Houston territory has as much growth potential as any other. There is a well-known but unstated company policy that a regional manager must prove himself in this position for at least ten years before being considered for the next step up—a home office executive position. The Lewises, then, can expect a lengthy stay in Houston.

3. *Transportation.* Frank has and will almost certainly continue to have a company car; therefore, locating near public transportation is no great factor for him.

4. *Schools.* Naturally the Lewises want their children to have the best education possible. If it can be determined there is a difference in the quality of schools in different parts of Houston or that some suburban school district is almost certainly superior, the Lewises want to know of this.

5. *Outlook for Houston's general economy* (particularly residential real estate values for the next decade). Lewis needs to utilize every possible source of information on this subject within reasonable limits of time available and expense involved.

6. *Anything unique about Houston about which he should be aware?*
   a. What validity is there in some of the alarming reports he has heard regarding pollution and habitability of the city in the years ahead? If this is a significant consideration with no definite answers, is there a particu-

lar suburban area which, for topographical or other reasons would be in a comparatively favorable situation should this become a problem?

b. How about Houston's uniqueness in not having any zoning laws? Frank has to keep this on his check list when evaluating each location.

Develop Alternative Solutions. Frank Lewis wisely sits down following the gathering of all information, and carefully lists each possible alternative:

1. Let Mrs. Lewis and the children remain in Indianapolis for the summer months, allowing more time to get information on which to make a decision about housing in Houston.
2. Rent an unfurnished apartment in Houston on a short-term lease to allow more time for the final decision.
3. Store the furniture in Indianapolis, and live in motel-type accommodations as long as needed to acquire a house.
4. Buy a home in Houston before June 1, and move directly from the Indianapolis apartment to the home.
5. Purchase a condominium in Houston before June 1, and move directly from the Indianapolis apartment.

Evaluate the Alternatives. So many objective and subjective factors are involved at this stage, we will not attempt to carry through on this phase. It is important for the Frank Lewises to consider *one alternative at a time,* and to be as objective as possible. A systematic approach such as the following would be helpful.

Alternative I

Mrs. Lewis and the children remain in Indianapolis for the summer.

Favorable Aspects	Unfavorable Aspects
1. More time to choose home.	1. Family separation for up to three months.
2. Mortgage loans rates expected to be reduced at any time.	2. Expense of Frank's temporary lodging.
etc.	etc.

Compiling such a listing for each of the five alternatives is almost certain to produce an orderly organization of the many factors to be considered in making a final decision. No thought should be given as to which is the best alternative until each has been fully analyzed.

Decide on the Best Alternative. The Lewises are now ready to consider the relative desirability of their alternatives. Having reduced to writing the pros and cons of each, they are less likely to rationalize and arrive at a decision which is more in keeping with what they *want* to do instead of what they can more *rationally decide.* They will likely be able to eliminate quickly some alternatives, and thus turn to consideration of the remaining two or three with more confidence. This example, admittedly oversimplified, illustrates an orderly approach to decision making. Matters involving family finances are more likely to be decided correctly if handled in this manner rather than impulsively or through trial and error.

Authority and Responsibility

Still another concept to consider is that of *authority*. What does the literature offer on this subject, and what relevance does it have to personal finance?

When we speak in terms of managing personal finances we assume that managing is *done*. An obvious question is "Which member or members of the family does the managing?" Since almost any member—even the four-year-old wanting to buy a popsicle—would volunteer for at least part of the money-managing activity, we have to assume that there is a means for someone to become a manager-in-fact.

There is certainly no absolute rule to decide the matter of who *should* have the authority in a family unit. Nevertheless, what management principles have to say about authority may aid in the assignation of that responsibility.

Sources of Authority

Let us first dispense with the obvious tenet that a manager must have *authority* to function. Reminding ourselves again that in a large family there may be several candidates for manager, let us think in terms of the *sources of authority* by which the true manager evolves.

Authority is commonly defined as power transmitted from basic social institutions to individual managers. Our laws give parents authority over minor children. This is the starting point; but, as children become adults, this legal justification for authority is no longer valid. In addition, there may be other adults within the family's scope—such as grandparents and in-laws. Thus, the matter of who is manager in certain family situations is not wholly a question resolved by law. Next, consider other potential sources of power, such as financial dependence, physical superiority, personal leadership qualities, social mores and codes of conduct. Whatever source or combination of sources of authority there may be in any one family, we can probably agree on the importance—even necessity—of resolving the question of authority in the matter of family financial management.

Nature of Authority

Two opposing theories have been propounded on the true nature of authority: *formal authority theory* and *acceptance theory of authority*. The formal theory traces specific authority in different areas within an organization from the chief executive on down through subordinates. The acceptance theory emphasizes that, even though authority is formally described and even substantiated by law and other rules, *actual* authority is on an acceptance basis—that is, there is no real authority unless a subordinate accepts it from his superior. Many parents would agree that there is some validity to the latter theory. They might agree further that authority in the day-to-day pattern of family living actually lies somewhere in between the two concepts. To the extent that the *acceptance theory* prevails in a family unit, the problem of effective management of personal finances could be even more complicated.

Responsibility

A necessary corollary of *authority* is the matter of *responsibility*. It is meaningless for a person to be chosen for and to accept the position of manager of an organization or unit if he does not accept fully the responsibility for its proper functioning. The validity of this concept seems self-evident. The *fact* of responsibility can be used as a tool in managing; and, in most instances, it is more effective and certainly more acceptable to exercise control in terms of responsibility than by authority. The further ramifications of a manager's responsibility will be pursued later in the discussion of basic management functions.

Having traveled so far afield from the subject of personal finance, we should summarize this phase of the discussion by repeating that successful handling of personal finances involves *managing* family income and expenditures and that this—by definition—makes necessary the existence of a manager with *authority* who accepts *responsibility* for family finances. This raises questions which should be considered in the formulation and enactment of a family's personal financial plan.

Four Functions
of Management

As previously stated, management is a *process* of *establishing* and *achieving* *objectives*. This process involves four basic functions: planning, organizing, directing, and controlling.

Planning

Repeating two cliches helps set the stage for our discussion of the planning function:

"From this moment on, you will spend your entire life in the future."
"Yard by yard, life is hard. Inch by inch, it's a cinch."

The future is the very essence of planning which, indeed, is defined as deciding in advance what is to be done. There is no single decision which can properly dispose of the planning function. The process of planning is best described as breaking down the elements of future aspirations into the minimum necessary components and giving detailed consideration to each of them. Writers in the field of management principles break down the planning function into an im-

Exhibit 3–1   Net Income of Leading Manufacturing Corporations for 1971 and 1972   (dollar figures in millions)

No. of cos.	Industry	Reported net income after taxes		Percent change	Net worth beginning of year 1972ᵃ	Percent return on net worth		Percent change in salesᵇ	Percent margin on salesᶜ	
		1971	1972			1971	1972		1971	1972
13	Baking	$ 88.3	$ 108.8	+23	$ 735.4	12.8	14.8	+14	2.7	2.9
12	Dairy products	321.2	345.4	+8	2,740.1	12.6	12.6	+8	3.1	3.1
38	Meatpacking	117.4	112.5	−4	1,593.9	7.7	7.1	+17	1.0	0.8
12	Sugar	75.5	66.9	−11	757.4	10.5	8.8	+4	3.7	3.1
89	Other food products	878.6	956.6	+9	7,299.8	12.3	13.1	+9	3.7	3.8
17	Soft drinks	288.0	325.2	+10	1,453.2	23.1	22.4	+10	7.1	7.3
13	Brewing	151.9	157.2	+3	1,070.0	15.8	14.7	+11	5.7	5.3
10	Distilling	194.5	217.2	+12	2,034.7	10.3	10.7	+7	4.0	4.2
12	Tobacco products	515.1	548.9	+7	3,393.9	16.6	16.2	+7	5.4	5.4
82	Textile products	264.9	331.4	+25	4,275.8	6.6	7.8	+11	2.6	2.9
108	Clothing and apparel	221.5	263.4	+19	2,381.0	10.8	11.1	+14	3.1	3.2
32	Shoes, leather, etc.	119.2	122.2	+2	1,147.3	11.0	10.6	+11	3.0	2.8
63	Rubber and allied products	468.9	587.6	+25	5,043.3	9.8	11.7	+12	3.8	4.3
29	Lumber and wood products	343.2	477.2	+39	3,442.0	11.2	13.9	+27	5.1	5.6
41	Furniture and fixtures	66.0	81.7	+24	702.5	11.9	11.6	+15	4.0	4.3
63	Paper and allied products	456.1	711.3	+56	8,147.1	5.6	8.7	+12	3.1	4.3
101	Printing and publishing	415.7	491.6	+18	3,601.1	12.6	13.7	+10	5.8	6.2
81	Chemical products	1,584.3	1,943.5	+23	17,165.1	9.7	11.3	+11	5.3	5.9
24	Paint and allied products	61.5	84.8	+38	799.7	8.1	10.6	+13	2.9	3.5
42	Drugs and medicines	1,229.4	1,428.8	+16	7,244.0	19.0	19.7	+12	9.5	9.9
36	Soap, cosmetics	539.8	626.3	+16	3,076.8	19.3	20.4	+11	6.7	7.0

Exhibit 3–1 (cont.)

No. of cos.	Industry	Reported net income after taxes			Net worth beginning of year 1972ᵃ	Percent return on net worth		Percent change in salesᵇ	Percent margin on salesᶜ	
		1971	1972	Percent change		1971	1972		1971	1972
108	Petroleum production and refining	6,400.8	6,525.0	+2	60,232.2	11.2	10.8	+9	6.9	6.5
18	Cement	95.9	118.5	+26	1,345.9	7.6	8.8	+15	5.2	5.6
14	Glass products	264.1	320.5	+21	2,560.2	11.1	12.5	+12	5.3	5.7
43	Other stone, clay products	255.8	333.7	+30	3,143.7	8.7	10.6	+13	4.6	5.3
70	Iron and steel	653.8	898.0	+37	14,510.2	4.6	6.2	+12	2.7	3.3
52	Nonferrous metals	485.7	679.8	+40	9,452.8	5.0	7.2	+13	3.1	4.0
36	Hardware and tools	157.5	212.9	+35	1,337.5	12.5	15.9	+18	5.5	6.2
52	Building, heating, plumbing equip.	159.6	221.1	+39	1,899.9	8.4	11.6	+7	2.5	3.3
66	Other metal products	251.9	303.9	+21	2,981.0	8.9	10.2	+9	3.2	3.6
49	Farm, const., material-hdlg. equip.	424.9	619.9	+46	5,111.5	8.8	12.1	+17	3.7	4.7
72	Office equipment, computers	1,310.7	1,578.3	+20	11,433.9	12.5	13.8	+14	7.3	7.7
184	Other machinery	775.9	871.7	+12	7,946.3	10.3	10.9	+11	4.3	4.3
340	Electr. equip. & electronics	2,008.5	2,616.2	+30	20,190.4	10.7	13.0	+12	3.8	4.4
17	Household appliances	267.1	358.6	+34	2,335.0	12.1	15.4	+12	4.0	4.7
12	Autos and trucks	2,692.5	3,297.9	+23	19,137.1	15.0	17.2	+14	4.9	5.2
43	Automotive parts	285.1	387.9	+36	2,967.2	10.4	13.1	+18	3.9	4.5
44	Aerospace	412.5	603.5	+46	6,838.3	6.3	8.8	0	1.7	2.5
148	Instruments, photo. goods, etc.	1,312.3	1,587.2	+21	9,421.7	15.4	16.8	+15	8.1	8.5
128	Misc. manufacturing	326.3	435.2	+33	3,467.0	9.4	12.6	+21	3.9	4.3
2,414	Total manufacturing	$26,942.3	$31,958.8	+19	$264,416.5	10.8	12.1	+12	4.7	5.0

Exhibit 3–1 (cont.)

No. of cos.	Industry	Reported net income after taxes			Net worth beginning of year 1972[a]	Percent return on net worth		Percent change in sales[b]	Percent margin on sales[c]	
		1971	1972	Percent change		1971	1972		1971	1972
23	Metal mining[d]	$ 121.9	$ 131.3	+8	$ 1,257.4	10.5	10.4	+24	11.8	11.2
15	Other mining, quarrying[d]	68.6	92.4	+35	1,062.1	6.4	8.7	+18	5.9	6.8
38	Total mining[d]	190.5	223.7	+17	2,319.5	8.5	9.6	+20	8.2	8.6
66	Food chains	432.6	301.7	−30	4,134.8	11.1	7.3	+9	1.0	1.0
126	Variety chains	493.2	558.3	+13	4,529.2	12.4	12.3	+19	2.6	2.4
86	Department and specialty	573.2	661.3	+15	5,694.2	11.2	11.6	+12	2.6	2.7
10	Mail order	628.3	707.1	+13	5,056.5	13.5	14.0	+11	4.7	4.8
248	Wholesale and misc.	539.3	623.2	+16	5,809.0	10.3	10.7	−4	1.9	2.3
536	Total trade	2,666.5	2,851.7	+7	25,223.7	11.7	11.3	+8	2.1	2.1
67	Class I railroads[e,f]	350.8	499.9	+43	16,567.6	2.0	3.0	+6	2.8	3.7
40	Common carrier trucking[e]	159.4	189.7	+19	975.7	20.0	19.4	+17	4.4	4.5
28	Air transport[e]	84.9	261.9	+209	3,973.6	2.6	6.6	+12	1.0	2.3
18	Misc. transportation[e]	116.1	137.2	+18	1,302.3	9.4	10.5	+11	2.5	2.8
153	Total transportation[e]	711.2	1,088.7	+53	22,819.1	3.1	4.8	+9	2.3	3.2
188	Electric power and gas[e]	4,540.5	5,190.6	+14	46,325.1	11.0	11.2	+12	12.1	12.4
13	Telephone and telegraph[e]	2,643.1	3,061.6	+16	31,168.5	9.2	9.8	+13	10.9	11.2
201	Total public utilities[e]	7,183.6	8,252.2	+15	77,493.6	10.3	10.6	+13	11.6	11.9

Exhibit 3–1 (cont.)

No. of cos.	Industry	Reported net income after taxes			Net worth beginning of year 1972ᵃ	Percent return on net worth		Percent change in salesᵇ	Percent margin on salesᶜ	
		1971	1972	Percent change		1971	1972		1971	1972
38	Amusements	88.6	133.5	+51	1,192.1	8.6	11.2	+19	4.3	5.5
78	Restaurants and hotels	158.1	246.6	+56	1,570.9	11.8	15.7	+18	3.6	4.8
337	Other business services	528.7	646.3	+22	4,988.2	12.2	13.0	+16	3.9	4.2
53	Construction	115.8	164.4	+42	1,451.5	8.6	11.3	–3	1.7	2.4
506	Total services	891.2	1,190.8	+34	9,202.7	11.1	12.9	+12	3.4	4.0
3,848	Total nonfinancial	38,585.2	45,565.9	+18	401,475.2	10.3	11.3	+11	4.7	5.0
64	Commercial bank holding cos.	1,987.2	2,109.5	+6	16,471.9	12.9	12.8	….	….	….
840	Property & liability ins.ᵍ	1,645.4	1,900.0	+15	15,855.0	11.6	12.0	….	….	….
245	Investment fundsʰ	1,325.4	1,250.9	–6	49,148.6	3.1	2.5	….	….	….
48	Sales finance	458.0	508.3	+11	4,953.5	9.8	10.3	….	….	….
58	Real estate	67.2	119.9	+79	935.2	9.5	12.8	….	….	….
1,255	Total financial	5,483.1	5,888.6	+7	87,364.3	7.0	6.7	….	….	….
5,103	Grand total	$44,068.3	$51,454.5	+17	$488,839.5	9.7	10.5	….	….	….

ᵃNet worth is equivalent to shareholders' equity or "book net assets" or capital and surplus. ᵇAbout 1% of nonfinancial firms with 0.7% of the income do not report sales or revenues. Data include income from investments and other sources as well as from sales. ᶜProfit margins are computed for all companies publishing sales or gross revenue figures. ᵈNet income is reported before depletion charges in some cases. ᵉDue to the large proportion of capital investment in the form of funded debt, rate of return on total property investment would be lower than that shown on net worth only. ᶠAssociation of American Railroads tabulation. ᵍEstimated by A. M. Best Co. for all stock companies on an adjusted basis. ʰIncome in most cases excludes capital gains or losses on investments.

Source: *Monthly Economic Letter,* First National City Bank, April 1973, p. 7.

43

posing list of separate factors or plans. The following selection from that list seems to provide the most appropriate analysis in managing personal finances.

Objectives
Policies
Budgets
Procedures and methods

There is at least one similarity between financial management problems of businesses and those in the family unit: no financial unit can long stay in existence unless its income equals or exceeds its expenditures. It is striking to note the very small difference between income and expenditures in industry. Exhibit 3–1 shows that among 3,848 major companies there was only a 5 percent profit margin on sales in 1972. A closer look at some of the individual industrial groups shows how precariously close this margin is. One might take exception to applying this business analogy to the family financial unit. It is true that all factors present are not the same. However, there are additional factors in the family picture—such as the presumed insatiability of human wants, pride, a desire to provide the best for the family, and the undeniable effectiveness of contemporary marketing techniques—which make it more difficult to limit expenditures to an amount less than income. Our point is that, in most institutions, regardless of their nature, the question of successful financial management is one of maintaining a very small percentage margin of income over expenditures.

Objectives. A nearly universally accepted dictum for organizations is the concept of *management by objectives.* Objectives are thought of as goals which have been carefully thought out and agreed upon. They are not meaningful until they have been described in very specific terms and understood by each level of management. In an organization there are many objectives. Since the achievement of certain ones might conflict with others, it is important to set a priority among them.

Objectives should be the first consideration in planning family finances. Let's look at two fairly typical family situations.

The Jones family, with the current month's paycheck deposited, pays the mortgage (or rent) payment, car payment, and utility bills. Afterwards, $200 remains. This is disbursed day-by-day as needs of the moment seem to justify, including a sudden decision to entertain with a steak cook-out and finally saying "yes" to son John's "heartrending" appeal to trade in his bike for a new model.

The Smiths have the same income and circumstances as the Jones. At a much earlier date they planned their personal finances, agreeing on certain objectives for the family which had monetary implications. As a result of recognizing these objectives and of their effect on previous buying decisions, $300 remains after meeting the current month's car and house payments and utility bills. The spending of this $300 is not done as a series of independent decisions, but in accordance with a monetary plan set out to achieve their objectives.

Although this is an absurdly simplistic example, it does represent two extremes in money spending patterns. The cases provide a contrast between telling the money where to go and wondering where it went.

Just as no two persons are exactly alike, no two families have the same goals. Accordingly, a listing of family objectives could be almost unlimited. The following are examples of family objectives with monetary implications:

To assure a particular type of higher education for each of the children.

To acquire certain type of home in a certain area by a certain date.

To assure financial independence of the family in the event of premature death or disability of the father or mother.

To accumulate a stated cash emergency fund in a bank or a savings and loan association.

To contribute a certain amount or percent of income to the church or other organizations.

To have a family vacation trip each year.

To foster an appreciation of money management by the children.

To foster the best possible physical and mental well-being of each member of the family (planned recreation, etc.).

This brief listing is just a starter; but it illustrates that, in a family, there is a hierarchy of objectives just as there is in other organizations. Quite obviously only a few objectives can be totally achieved, some can be partially achieved, and others cannot be achieved at all. A systematic discussion and listing of these objectives serve the multiple purposes of assessing their relative desirability and establishing a priority list for money allocations as well as providing a degree of unity within the family.

Policies. The necessity and role of *policy* in the planning function is easy to understand. Professor Flippo defines policy as a "predetermined, general course or guide established to provide direction for ensuing action."[2] Let's start with some well-known examples of policies in different organizations. The Monroe Doctrine was a *policy* followed by the United States for many decades. It was a well-defined, predetermined guide established to provide a basis for specific action the government would take in the event of a future crisis involving encroachment by a European power on the sovereignty of countries in the Western Hemisphere.

---

[2]Edwin B. Flippo, *Management: A Behavioral Approach* (Boston: Allyn and Bacon, 1966), p. 52.

What happens when a Sears-Roebuck customer, dissatisfied with a purchase, returns the article? If he cannot be made happy with the purchase, Sears' *policy* of refunding the purchase price is followed.

Pro football coach George Allen became famous for his *policy* of developing a winning team by trading draft choices to other teams for experienced players—again, an abstract statement of policy as a guide for specific future action.

Other examples of policies followed by business firms are: making promotions "only from within," not hiring salesmen who have ever worked for a competitor, or hiring as management trainees only persons with a bachelor's degree who finished in the upper half of their graduating class. The scope and list of typical business policies would be almost endless.

Now let's turn to examples of policies in managing personal finances.

To use credit (other than thirty-day charges) only for long-term capital expenditures (purchase of home, investments, and land).

To invest 10 percent of all income in excess of expenditures for necessities.

To trade cars no more frequently than every other year and then only when extra funds have been accumulated to pay cash.

To make no purchase—other than for necessities—exceeding some stated amount without observing a week-long "cooling off" period.

To avoid being ensnared by the human weakness to be *first* (buy the first model of a new item on the market, see a show at roadshow prices, etc.).

To buy food items only once a week, and to limit purchases to a shopping list.

To submit to family discussion and vote each decision concerning a choice of expenditures where there are funds available to make only one purchase at that time.

To limit certain categories of purchases by a child to the amount afforded by that child's allowance and any funds he personally earns.

And then there are unstated policies of questionable value but implied by practice:

To buy any desired consumer item which can be obtained on an installment basis.

To buy more of these wanted consumer items on an installment loan basis than monthly income permits, with the wife working part-time or the husband "moonlighting" to keep the family solvent.

To let the husband or wife make independent decisions on major purchases and argue about it later if they are not in accord.

Most people would grant there are obvious advantages to having clearly stated family objectives and policies in managing personal finances. The reader is urged to reflect on recent out-of-the-ordinary purchases to see if the existence of plausible family policies would not have helped in making a wiser buying decision.

Budgets. Management literature places budgeting under both the *planning* function and the *controlling* function. A budget is a plan of operation expressed in numerical terms. A budget is prepared in advance of the start of an accounting period and to that extent should be considered a *plan.* Once the unit—be it family, an entire business organization, or a department of that organization— moves into the accounting period, then it is not only a plan of operation but a control activity as well. We normally think of budgeting in terms of dollars of income and out-go. Budgets are also prepared in numerical terms relating to time allowed, employees used, inventory, units of production, and almost any other measurable phase of an organization's activity.

In this regard, budgeting other than in dollars may have an indirect effect on the family's finances. Most obvious is the setting of an appropriate "time to work on household chores" for younger members of the family. This could eliminate the necessity of hiring household help or purchase of certain additional household capital goods. Further, it can give the "manager" of the family unit more time and creative energy to perform family *managerial* functions— e.g., the continuing consideration of family objectives and policies for needed adjustments as time goes by; actual supervision, keeping track of and controlling family income and disbursements; making and mending of clothes; more effective control of clothing, food, and other family inventory items; more thought to and preparation of wholesome meals to promote the family's health.

Budgeting time for watching of television and setting deadlines for "lights out" have monetary as well as other advantages for the family.

Presumably there is an optimum budget in terms of all categories of family *inventory* items: food on hand; books of all kinds; accumulation of magazines and periodicals; clothing items from years back; even periodical newspaper clippings of interesting recipes which have been accumulated over a period of years. Some of us may know of families whose default on this inventory control function has resulted in a significant drain on family finances. The co-manager of the household might be one who is reluctant to throw away anything other than trash and garbage. The accumulation may have become so great through years of marriage and moving into new and larger homes that the dollar cost of providing storage space could be in the thousands. This tendency seems so widespread there is a temptation to offer a theory entitled "the insatiability of the need for household storage space."

Since budgeting is an indispensable aspect of effective personal financial management, an entire chapter (Chapter 8) is devoted to this subject.

Procedures and Methods. Where *policy* is a plan which serves as a *guide to thinking* related to achieving the organization's *objectives, procedures* are plans for *specific action.* Sears' *policy* of "satisfaction guaranteed or your money back" must be implemented by a carefully defined, step-by-step *procedure* for handling individual cases. Procedures are unquestionably necessary in a large organization such as Sears. Even though the need is not so obvious in smaller organizational units—such as the family—there is theoretically the same justification for formalized procedures.

An advantage of formalizing a *procedure* in writing is that, in so doing, the activity must be analyzed and decisions must be made about the best of alternative methods. There is a resulting efficiency, including economy of time and energy, in knowing from the start how to proceed in a particular case.

There are many examples of *procedures* necessary to implement family *policy*. Working through an example may be helpful. Assume the Green family has decided it can appreciably cut family transportation costs by following a policy of buying not new cars, but one-year old, one-owner cars with less than 25,000 mileage. Most of us would agree it would be quite an accomplishment to be absolutely sure that a car represented as such by a would-be seller actually meets these requirements. If another facet of the family *policy* in this connection is to trade every two years, we can see the financial significance of fifteen or twenty such transactions over the family's lifetime.

The Greens can be more certain of implementing their policy successfully if they follow a carefully defined *procedure*. Such a *procedure* might well involve simultaneously running an appropriate classified want-ad and carefully checking on cars listed for sale in the classified section, while calling on reliable automobile dealers. Another phase of the *procedure* would be determining steps to take, having found a car that seemed to fit the qualifications. Such a procedure might include the following steps: (1) checking the warranty card to see if the would-be seller is the original owner, (2) checking the "maintenance for warranty" record, and (3) having a reliable garage check the car's current condition including making a knowledgeable estimate as to correctness of the mileage shown. To recap, having enunciated a certain policy on buying cars, we can hardly argue against the desirability of carefully setting down a procedure to follow in implementing this policy. Otherwise, unwise decisions, triggered by emotional reactions and skillful sales efforts, might result.

Organizing

Much of our discussion attempting to relate management literature's treatment of the planning function to personal finance applies also to the *organizing, directing,* and *controlling* functions. Other chapters will deal more specifically with application of the latter three functions to our subject. This is particularly true of the treatment of budgeting in Chapter 8. Moreover, these three functions have more relevance to non-monetary aspects of the family group. For these reasons, we will confine our treatment to a definition of these management functions and a brief statement of personal financial implications.

The organizing function is a process of actually *defining* and *grouping* various activities of the unit involved and then establishing *authority relationships* among these groups.

In establishing authority relationships, the most usual concept is one of "line authority." This involves a chain of command with authority running from the top to the bottom of an organization. A simplified example for a business organization would involve a board of directors controlling a president, who is the chief executive. The president, in turn, would have under his authority several vice-presidents in charge of various activities of the business. Each of these vice-presidents would have subordinates, such as several superintendents, each of whom would have under him foremen who, in turn, would have authority over and responsibility for several workers under them.

Even though the family group must concern itself with many activities, its size limits the scope of organization. Nevertheless, effectiveness of the family as a monetary unit is somewhat dependent on the extent to which authority relationships exist.

Directing

It is one thing to do the *planning,* it is another thing to *organize* properly. It is still another thing to *initiate* and *operate* in accordance with this planning and organizing. This is the sphere of *directing,* the third management function,

To indicate the scope of management literature on the *directing* function, the following are some topics discussed in the section on directing in a leading text on principles of management:[3]

Orders
Nature of Leadership
Types of Leadership
Techniques of Positive Leadership
Leadership of Top Management
Styles of Leadership
Supervisory Management
The Training and Education
  Continuum
A Philosophy of Training
Types of Training
Training in Human Relations
Principles of Training
Company Training Programs
Evaluation of Training
Nature of Participation

Values of Participation
Prerequisite to Participation
Risks of Participation
Degrees of Participation
Participation Systems
Nature of Group Dynamics
Characteristics of the Group
Values and Danger of the Group
An Application of the Group
  Dynamics—The Conference
Nature and Significance of
  Communication
Communication Structures
Channels of Communication
The Fundamental Process of
  Communication

The topics indicate that this function is involved with interpersonal relationships and activities. Thus, as applied to the family, the directing function is only indirectly related to family finances.

---

[3]Edwin B. Flippo, *Management: A Behavioral Approach* (Boston: Allyn and Bacon, 1966), p. 52.

Controlling

Professor Haimann states: "Control is the process of checking to determine whether or not plans are being adhered to, whether or not proper progress is being made toward the objectives and goals, and acting if necessary to correct any deviations. The essence of control is action which adjusts performance to predetermined standards if deviations occur."[4]

This description of the last management function to be considered is an obvious corollary of the three previously considered functions. Thinking in terms of the family unit, the manager(s)'

> having planned the family's objectives and goals,
> having organized to carry out these plans, and then
> having initiated and put the plans into operation,

must regularly observe the results in order to make sure the plans are being achieved and to make such necessary adjustments as circumstances require. The important control device in personal finance is the budget.

The Sales Encounter[5]

Businesses must sell their products and services to survive. This involves advertising and/or personal selling. One phase of a company's operation, then, is that of *managing the sales force*. There are many aspects of this but the one which particularly relates to personal finance is the training in sales techniques given sales representatives.

Let us reflect for a moment on the situation that exists when a well-trained salesman makes a presentation to a prospect. Most consumers are not well-versed on technical aspects relating to the quality and value of the many products they purchase. However, they are more likely to make a wise buying decision if enough time transpires to permit: comparison shopping; study or research or recommendations from disinterested third-parties; and—probably most important of all—determining if their initial desire for the product is sustained to a level justifying the purchase. It is probably true that these considerations requiring time have not taken place in a signficant percent of all buying decisions. One of the reasons for this is the sales techniques employed. We are persuaded to decide *now* instead of waiting.

Thinking of a sales interview as a dialogue between the salesman and the prospect in which one of the two will prevail, we should recognize that the

---

[4]Theo Haimann, *Professional Management* (Boston: Houghton Mifflin, 1962), p. 485.

[5]As we move to this specialized aspect of management, we wish to emphasize again that this chapter is not an attempt to summarize the subject of management principles. Rather, we are merely trying to relate certain bits and pieces from the discipline which seem to have special relevance to the management of personal finances.

salesman is better prepared—has a better "game plan"—than the prospect. Is there some way the scales could be balanced a little? It is conceivable that a prospect would be less likely to be persuaded to buy prematurely if he had a *working knowledge of the salesman's basic sales techniques.* The prospect will recognize these techniques as he hears them and thus will be less likely to be affected by them. He will then be in a better position to make a rational decision based on the merits of the case. For this reason, this chapter includes a brief study of basic sales techniques.

Lest this discussion create the wrong impression of salesmen as a group, we should first emphasize the tremendous contribution and the very necessary role they play in our society. We say rather glibly that *production* consists of combining the factors of production (land, labor, capital, and enterpreneurship). As a matter of fact, no unit of these factors is committed to use unless a sale is made. The salesman, then, is the catalytic agent in the production and consumption process. He makes new products available by *creating* demand for them. In this role, he is serving to provide *product knowledge* to potential users. He helps determine the form of products by channeling back to top management what the public likes and dislikes. He keeps clients posted on new developments and gives valuable advice in fulfilling needs of customers. Also, he has the skill to help persuade clients to act *now* in circumstances where a delay would be unwise. From these credits, it is obvious we are referring to salesmen who take a professional and career approach to their work. Unfortunately, there are some who do not. Both types may use the same skills and techniques, but one puts the interests of the buyer first while the other does not.

The Emotional-
Rational Dichotomy

The starting point in selling is a recognition that *man* is a wanting being, and that his wants tend to be *insatiable.* These wants spring from *basic human needs* which are probably *innate* but some of which are magnified by his particular environment. He *reacts* to an awareness of a need, or a combination of needs, in one of two ways: *emotionally* or *logically.* Frequently, his reactions include both elements. This is the basis for the *emotional-rational dichotomy* explanation of specific behavior.[6]

Since our value system tends to frown on emotional behavior (especially in important areas such as spending money) and lauds logical behavior, we seek to give the impression to others and to ourselves that we act logically. Thus, the salesman's dilemma. He knows that a prospect buys to fulfill a need. He also knows the prospect's reaction will be emotional and/or logical. This reaction includes finally a decision to buy or not to buy. The salesman further

---

[6]For an interesting discussion of this subject read Frederich A. Russell, Frank H. Beach, and Richard D. Buskirk, *Textbook of Salesmanship,* 8th ed. (New York: McGraw-Hill, 1969).

knows that the reaction most likely to produce *action now* is an emotional one. He knows his prospect wants to think his decision is a logical one. The salesman, then, becomes a specialist in classifying basic human needs, triggering these needs to produce emotional and logical responses while convincing the prospect that he is acting on the logical ones. The salesman is, figuratively, cooking on two burners at the same time, but trying to hide the burner that is giving off more heat.

When a car salesman says "I can just see your kids' excitement if you drive this home tonight," he hopes to arouse the *parental need* to produce emotional reactions of excitement, joy, and affection. But when he says "This is the best month this year to trade," he's putting to work the need for economic security to trigger a logical reaction. When he says "This extra 1,000 pounds is just like insurance for your family's safety," he's fired two barrels to incite both emotional and logical reactions.

The Sales Process

In organizing a sales presentation, sales managers have found the most effective method is to base the presentation on a *problem recognition-problem solving* approach. In addition, it is desirable to have an opportunity to talk with the prospect on a favorable basis (Sell the Interview) and to employ special skills in persuading the prospect to *act now* (The Close). The essentials of each are described in the following sections.

Sell the Interview

There are three aspects to this: (1) the *pre-approach,* (2) the *approach,* and (3) *the company's and the salesman's prestige.* The *pre-approach* activities involve finding out everything possible about the prospect in advance (his specific needs; family information; his goals and accomplishments; his activities; his hang-ups; his philosophy on religion, politics and life in general). With this information, the salesman greatly increases the possibility of getting a favorable interview. This phase can be so well done that the prospect finds himself wanting to buy from the salesman even before essentials are discussed. The next step, *the approach,* is often referred to as the "moment of truth" in a sales interview. These first few moments are critical. Information gained from the pre-approach helps to insure the success of the approach. The *salesman's and the company's prestige* are most important in selling the interview. Some companies and some salesmen have in various ways acquired such *charisma* that many prospects will buy just to establish the personal relationship. How many pro football fans would say "No" to a telephone request from Don Meredith or Carl Ellers for an appointment to explain a unique investment opportunity? In lesser degrees, local celebrities have a similar advantage. Having *sold the interview,* the salesman proceeds to the next phase of the sales presentation.

Problem Recognition

Except in relatively rare cases, most of us will not buy something just because it is a quality product and is a bargain. We must feel we need it, whether it be to acquire a necessity or to express oneself by means of an impulsive or frivolous purchase. In this phase, the salesman concentrates on committing the prospect to specific needs and to the importance of those needs.

Problem Solving

The salesman next attempts to show how his product or service best solves the need. This involves describing the important features and relating them to the prospect's requirements. If the sales interview has proceeded *successfully* through this stage, the salesman can assume the prospect *wants to buy*.

Closing

Wanting to buy and *deciding to buy now* are two different things. There are two strong deterrents to a "buy now" decision.

1. There is an "ego" problem, stemming from our basic human need to resist domination by others. Well-trained salesmen are aware of this and look for every opportunity to let the prospect dominate the interview as long as the point involved does not leave standing an insurmountable or significant reason for not buying now.
2. It is difficult to make a final decision. Most of us, by instinct and from previous unfortunate experiences from buying hastily, would like to delay making an immediate decision, even if it is just "tomorrow" or "next month." It is comfortable enough to contemplate a purchase and even admit to yourself you plan to buy. It is still something else to do it *now*.

For these reasons, most salesmen recognize that the most difficult phase of the sales process is the *close*. At this point (with the prospect wanting to buy but instinctively resisting being pushed and being disturbed by a natural reluctance to make a final and unequivocal decision), the salesman assumes the role of *helping* the prospect decide to *act now*.[7] This involves two distinctly different phases:

1. Provide the prospect with sufficient *logical reason(s)* for acting now. The various approaches to accomplishing this may be classified as *closing strategies*.
2. Having done this, provide the easiest possible means for *finalizing* the decision. Approaches to accomplishing this may be classified as *closing techniques*.

---

[7]This is true in nearly all cases except those involving overpowering, high-pressure salesmanship directed to prospects who are by nature subject to dominance by others.

Closing Strategies

Textbooks and training manuals on salesmanship assign various labels to the closing strategies, but the most common terminology is:

> Impending Event
> Standing Room Only (SRO)
> Summary of Selling Points
> Special Offer
> Trial Offer

Impending Event. Under this strategy would fall everything that might happen in the near future which would make a delay in buying a mistake. This would include price increases and changes in warranties, credit terms, product qualities, or delivery schedules. If it can be shown that any or several of these disadvantageous happenings are imminent, the prospect has a logical reason to act immediately.

Standing Room Only. One of the impending events which is so widely used that it rates a separate classification is the likelihood that *the product or service might not be available later*. This is called the Standing Room Only (SRO) strategy. Examples we see or hear daily are: "this is the last one in stock and we can't reorder;" "don't think I'm trying to use pressure, Mr. Prospect, but I have two other families who have looked at this house several times and I really expect to hear from one or both of them any time;" "we are going to ship all that is left to our Chicago stores after we close today;" "we are allowed to place only one of these in each block;" etc.

Summary of Selling Points. Sales presentations usually involve explanation of a number of product features and advantages. When the salesman summarizes all of these, they seem to present a strong basis for acting immediately. He usually points out the extent to which he and the prospect have considered the proposition and that *now* is the best time to make a decision—that never again will they have the factors involved for making the right decision so clearly in mind. Thus, it is logical to act now, not later.

Special Offer. This strategy is also related to the impending event strategy in that it has the element of "available on this basis for a limited time only." In addition, it has the element of a concession *now* from regular terms (*price* usually, but it could involve financing, warehousing, guarantees, delivery, etc.). Some retailers base practically all their advertising on the Special Offer strategy. Retail stores of certain major tire manufacturers, for example, have full-page tire sale ads almost every week. A quick scanning of the advertising in a Thursday afternoon newspaper probably would reveal a high percent based on "special offers." In personal selling, *special offers* usually are available only "if you buy now"; thus, never again available; thus, a logical reason to buy now.

Trial Offer. This strategy is related to the special offer strategy. It is designed to make the decision to "buy now" easier and more logical by reducing the amount of money involved. It also has the logic of "Let it prove itself before spending any significant amount." It often carries a "money back if not satisfied" guarantee.

Closing Techniques

Trained salesmen recognize there always comes a time—more often "times"—in the sales interview when no more "selling" should take place. Rather, an attempt to *finalize* the sale—make it a completed transaction—should be made. Should the salesman at that point quit talking and wait for the prospect to volunteer to buy? In some cases he should, but in most instances he should make a positive attempt to bring this about. Such attempts are called *closing techniques*. They can be classified as follows:

Direct Technique. The salesman asks the prospect to buy. Thus, "Bill, authorize this contract right here with your signature and we'll get things started."

Indirect Technique. The salesman avoids a direct request, and employs an indirect technique *based on the assumption the prospect has bought.* These indirect techniques can take three forms:

1) *Assume* the prospect has bought and proceed with the mechanics of writing up the order.
2) A *choice* between two or more alternatives available, such as: "Will this be cash or charge?" or "Shall we make them all green, or would you like to mix in one-fourth yellow?" "Which of the three bonus gifts do you want?"
3) A *decision on a minor point* such as "Mr. Prospect, you do want your wife the primary beneficiary, I am sure. We should name a contingent beneficiary, however. Shall it be your son?"

In the hope that "fore-warned is fore-armed," we have attempted to brief the sales techniques you are most likely to encounter. As noted previously, when these techniques are used by a professional salesman who practices the principle that it is good business to put his client's interests above his own personal gain, these techniques can serve a useful purpose. Used as tools by an unscrupulous or disinterested salesman, they can prove costly to others. Whatever the case, your recognition of sales techniques as they are being directed to you may minimize their effect and may help you make a more rational decision.

Discussion Questions

1. Explain briefly the sequence of steps in the decision-making process.
2. Think of an important personal decision you have made in the past five years. Did you follow an orderly procedure in making the decision? If not, would

your use of the recommended steps in decision making likely have resulted in your making a better decision?

3. What is the relationship between *authority* and *responsibility?*

4. To what extent does the "acceptance theory" of authority prevail in the day-to-day activities of your family?

5. What value is there in carefully reducing to writing an individual's objectives?

6. Assume an organization is not aware of any specific objectives other than to continue pretty much as before. What affect will this have on the quality of its day-to-day decisions?

7. Explain why budgets involve both the planning and the directing function of an organization. Cite some likely examples in the handling of family finances.

8. Write down some of your personal objectives for the next twelve months. Assuming time and money won't permit attainment of all of them, assign a ranking to each so that you will have a priority of objectives on which to base decisions when they are necessary.

9. "It's a case of telling your money where to go instead of wondering where it went." What bits and pieces of management principles would help you achieve the former?

10. Define "policy" (as an element of management principles).

11. In purchases you have made recently, can you recall any "closing strategies" used by the salesmen? If so, what affect do you feel they had in your decisions to buy?

12. Which closing strategy or closing technique do each of the following statements represent?

"I can't guarantee this price beyond the next mail delivery. The company has notified us a new and higher price list is on the way."

"This is the last one we have and we cannot reorder."

"Mr. Prospect, write your authorization on this line so we can get this started."

"Is this to be cash or charge?"

"When the new models come out next week, your present car's trade-in value will decrease at least $200."

4

Consumerism— A New Era, How Much Protection?

Interest in the safety and welfare of consumers is not a new idea, but it has apparently turned into a socio-political movement in recent years. Governments and private groups have joined the march to protect the citizen from all those who want to take his money without giving fair value in return. However, the rush to help us as consumers could reach such proportions that we could conceivably need to be protected from the consumer protection laws themselves. The major question is what types of such laws are needed. In a technologically oriented world where thousands of complex products are marketed, consumers cannot be expert in chemistry, engineering, electronics, and other areas necessary to understand the workings of ordinary consumer products.

For these reasons, the consumer movement has become important enough for the President to appoint an adviser for consumer affairs. Consumers want a legitimate hearing when they have a complaint about a faulty product and it may be that businesses are neglecting this area of customer relations. It is important to businesses and to consumers that products provide a reasonable level of service. Good personal financial management dictates that we learn which companies provide good service for their products and buy from them. Because many companies are slow in improving their customer grievance procedures, federal and state governments are passing laws to give consumers more protection in the marketplace.

Our problem becomes one of deciding how much and what types of protection are necessary. Obviously we cannot pass laws to protect everyone from all risks in life. Should young couples be prevented from going deeply in debt to buy a home and furniture since they may not be able to pay for it? Should every family man be required to buy life insurance equal to five times his annual income since he may die and leave his family without any income? To what extent should the manufacturer or seller of a product be liable?

Caveat Emptor— Is It Gone?

The term *caveat emptor* means "let the buyer beware." This warning developed from early English common law and came to America as markets and trade developed. Under this doctrine it was the responsibility of a buyer to examine a product carefully before making a purchase. The seller was not obligated to reveal any information as to defects in quality since the buyer should discover these upon examination. After a purchase was made, the buyer had no legal recourse. This doctrine was considered good philosophy because it tended to sharpen the wits of buyers.

In 1870, the U. S. Supreme Court upheld this doctrine in a case where a buyer took delivery of a shipment of wool after examining four bales in the lot and finding them satisfactory. He later found damaged wool packed inside other bales. He sued the seller to collect damages, but the court ruled that *caveat emptor* relieved the seller of any obligation.[1]

Continued application of this doctrine caused suspicion and distrust to develop between buyers and sellers. As markets and products changed, it became increasingly difficult for the buyer to examine all products that he bought. Traders learned that markets operated better when buyers and sellers had mutual respect for each other. This led to more information provided by sellers about their products.

In earlier times, *caveat emptor* may have been satisfactory, but it is no longer suitable due to the complexity of many items which the average person buys. We simply have no way of knowing what to expect from using some products,

---

[1]Yearbook of Agriculture, *Marketing* (Washington, D.C.: U.S. Dept. of Agriculture, 1954), p. 266.

except what the manufacturer is willing to promise. Should a vacuum cleaner last two months or ten years? It does not matter how long it is made to provide service, as long as the buyer understands this at the time of purchase. If we are promised trouble-free service for five years, this should be provided.

Not many consumer items can be sold now on the rule of *caveat emptor.* Even foods are processed and packaged to such an extent that consumers cannot be sure of reasonable value until products are used. Clothing fibers are combined so that their identity is not recognizable except by labels. Since buyers have increasingly had to rely on the honesty or reputation of sellers, it has become necessary to pass laws concerned with negligence and fraud. The rule of "buyer beware" may not be completely dead, but it loses significance each year as new consumer protection laws come into existence. In fact, some consumers who have been harmed by faulty products have been able to collect damages from producers. Our marketing system is gradually changing from *caveat emptor,* "let the buyer beware," to *caveat venditor,* "let the seller beware."

Needed Protection— Public Health and Safety

Some types of consumer protection are much more vital than others. Regulating the contents of medicines is much more important than the interest rate paid for a loan. It is not surprising that one of the earliest aspects of consumer protection was in the sale and use of foods and drugs. Some products are useful, but dangerous when not used properly. The safe uses should be described for the consumer. It is similarly important to regulate all types of food processing plants, restaurants, and other businesses where cleanliness is essential.

While it is generally recognized that regulations for health and safety are necessary, there are disagreements as to how extensive they should be. This is a problem with any type of regulation, since there is a tendency for regulations to grow after they begin. This can readily be seen in the meat industry where numerous regulations have been added. Government-inspected meat protects the health and safety of the consumer. On the other hand, the regulations made it mandatory for the small-scale door-to-door peddling butcher to go out of business. It is easy to move on from health and safety into a degree of quality or pricing controls which may not be in the public interest.

Excessive Protection— Loss of Freedom

Congress and state legislatures pass broadly written laws and leave the interpretations and enforcement to government agencies. Such agencies establish rules or policies which must be followed by those operating under the law.

It is not unusual for these agencies to establish rules that exceed the intention of the law-making body and, quite frequently, the rules change although the law is not amended.

Again, we return to the question of what are reasonable amounts of protection for consumers. Even safety regulations can be carried to excess. It is reasonable to require manufacturers of fabrics and clothing to make their products as nonflammable as possible. But is it reasonable to require a toy manufacturer to remove a toy from the market because a lever or spring could possibly pinch a child's finger? It is not possible for the government to take each citizen by the hand and lead him through every purchase to protect his health, safety, and billfold. Any attempt to do this is a loss of freedom to both buyer and seller.

It is questionable whether government should tell us how much safety we need to purchase. Congress has decided that we need shoulder straps in our automobiles and we have no choice but to pay for them. Most studies related to the use of these straps indicate that people do not use them. We must always keep in mind that it is entirely possible to regulate a legitimate business or industry out of existence simply by adding cost upon cost in the form of protective devices until the price is out of reach of most prospective consumers.

The rapidly expanding consumer movement must be taken seriously by business management. Manufacturers are finding themselves faced with an increasing number of liability claims for injuries caused by their products. Courts often award large claims after using a very broad definition to find the product defective and at fault. What would we have to give up if consumerism brought us to the point that it is necessary to manufacture fool-proof products that cannot be used incorrectly by the most unsophisticated person?

Consumers are beginning to be heard by their government as indicated by the many consumer protection-type laws passed during the 1960s. The movement may change directions, but it will not soon decline. Recent interest is turning toward pollution and environmental protection. In the past, consumers have not had organizations to lobby for legislation in their interest as have producers. Having become more politically astute, they are learning how to register their discontent effectively.

Legal Aspects of
Business Transactions

Laws are made to regulate the relationships between individuals and to provide for an orderly society. Since laws are made by human beings, they are frequently changed and this is sometimes confusing to those who try to find absolute answers to legal questions.

Consumers cannot be expected to understand all the laws which govern their lives. Nevertheless, some laws are especially pertinent to us as consumers; so that it is wise to obtain as much understanding as we can concerning our legal rights when borrowing money, purchasing consumer goods, and performing other simple business transactions. For this reason, this chapter includes a brief examination of the legal aspects of some ordinary business activities.

Uniform Commercial Code

Businessmen and consumers encountered a need many years ago for more uniformity of state laws related to commercial transactions. A Uniform Negotiable Instruments Law was prepared by the American Bar Association as early as 1895 and submitted to many state legislatures. It was adopted by every state, although some states made changes in the law to suit particular local purposes. Other uniform laws were passed by states during later years concerning warehouse receipts, transfers of corporate securities, and selling of merchandise.

As businesses expanded to a nationwide scope, new demands were made for more legal uniformity between states. The uniform laws that were enacted applied to only certain areas of business transactions, so businessmen began to ask for a modern code of laws to include all aspects of commercial practices.

This led to the preparation of a code in 1951 jointly by the National Conference of Commissioners on Uniform State Laws and by the American Law Institute. It was adopted first by Pennsylvania in 1953 and has since become law in all states except Louisiana. It is called the Uniform Commercial Code because of its wide acceptance. The code is broad enough in scope to include most transactions in business.

The code is mostly concerned with the sale, financing, and security of personal property, both tangible and intangible. It has ten parts dealing with specific aspects of commercial transactions, such as sales, bank deposits and collection, commercial paper, letters of credit, title papers, investment securities, and bank transfers. One important part of the code is that it requires high standards of conduct for merchants by requiring them to act in "good faith." This simply means honesty and fair dealing must be part of the trade. Contracts can be prepared to suit the parties involved, but they cannot change the code obligations of good faith and reasonableness. The following discussion of laws related to business practices includes regulations set forth in the code.

Laws of Misrepresentation and Fraud

Fraud is a word with different meanings; but, in relation to contracts, it means one person willfully deceiving another to the extent that a financial loss occurs. An intent to mislead is what distinguishes an innocent misrepresentation from a fraudulent one.

Laws have been passed to prevent misrepresentation and fraud. Many business transactions are made without visual inspection of the products being purchased. For many consumers, the complexity of some products prohibits them from being able to judge values.

Any act or word by one person that creates a false impression in the mind of another person is called misrepresentation. If this is done intentionally to cause the person to give up something valuable or surrender a legal right, it becomes a fraud. Transactions can be nullified and damages claimed against the guilty person if fraud is proven. Laws such as this are necessary because honesty and fairness are essential for the proper functioning of an advanced economy.

Statute of Limitations

Placing a time limit on legal action is an old principle derived from English common law that provided for all suits to be settled in time. Later, as written laws were passed, time periods were specified for certain legal actions to be performed. For example, in some states claims against the estate of a deceased person must be filed within four months of death. Other periods of time limitation are found in state laws, but the most important in business transactions are those related to the injury or loss caused by one person to another and those dealing with contracts.

Negligence which results in injury or loss of property to another person is referred to as *tort* and state laws specify time periods for legal action to be initiated under these circumstances. Longer periods are usually allowed for filing suits for bodily injury than for loss of property.

Time limits on claims resulting from contracts apply to both oral and written contracts. Longer periods are commonly allowed for written than for oral contracts, however the statute of limitations does not apply when a party was misled into entering the contract.

Any person who thinks he has been wronged in a business transaction should request the other party to make restitution. If this is unsuccessful, a law suit can be filed in the courts until the time period expires. The Uniform Commercial Code specifies a four-year period for suits on contracts for sales of goods. Contracts not under the code depend on the particular law of the state.

Law of Contracts

When you go to the store and buy a loaf of bread, you are a party to a contract. Millions of contracts are entered into and fully performed every day without objection from either party. The oldest branch of law relating to business transactions is the law of contracts. Some type of legal enforcement of contracts is necessary for any organized society. Business depends upon contracts in a free enterprise economy.

How do contracts concern us as consumers? Every time we make a purchase, whether it is for cash or credit, we enter into a contract. We agree to buy and the seller agrees to sell an item of value for a certain price. When two competent parties (of legal age and sound mental faculty) consent to the trade of lawful objects of value, a contract has been made. In many cases, then, it is not necessary for a contract to be in writing. In fact, most contracts are oral; however some must be written, as we will discuss later.

Parties to a contract can set their own terms as long as the contract complies with rules of law. For example, two persons cannot contract to deal in products that are forbidden by laws (such as narcotics). Contracts must follow rules of law because the courts are expected to settle disputes of contract violation.

When one party to a contract does not meet his obligation, he is liable for damages where the other party has suffered a loss. The amount of damage is usually a sum of money necessary to place the injured party in the same position he would have been had the contract been fulfilled. If the court decides that it is a legal and enforceable contract, the court will require the offending party to comply with the contract or it will set appropriate damages.

Law of Sales

Most business transactions involve the transfer of an item of property from one person to another. Since there are so many transactions involved in the marketing of goods and services, laws have been provided which apply primarily to selling practices. Prior to adoption of the Uniform Commercial Code, sales were judged according to the Uniform Sales Act and the law of contracts. The code, however, provides special rules for contracts involving the sale of goods of a tangible, physical nature, although it does not apply to the sale of services. This limitation excludes real estate and financial securities, such as stocks and bonds.

Consumers are becoming more concerned about the apparent disinterest of some sellers in standing behind products. What consumers are most interested in concerning the law of sales is their rights to return merchandise and obtain reasonable warranties that will be honored.

A normal practice in selling goods is for the buyer and seller to discuss the merits of a product before completion of sale. Statements made by the seller are important unless they are generalities, such as "this is a fine product," or other simple statements of opinion. Two types of warranties relating to product quality are recognized by law. When the seller makes representations or certain claims for his product, this is an *express warranty*. If he intentionally misrepresents the product, he is liable for fraud. Any promises made—whether they are oral statements by the retailer or advertising claims by the manufacturer—are considered to be express warranties.

Implied warranties are another type. Law requires that sellers assume a certain level of responsibility for their products although no claims may be made. All goods sold must be of a "merchantable," or average quality. For example, when we go to a restaurant to eat we assume that the food will be fit for human consumption. If we find evidence that it is not, the seller is liable. The law requires a minimum level of serviceability for products, which is an implied warranty. The warranty may be modified or excluded by agreement of the parties to the sale.

Laws are not always clear relating to product liability. Too, each case seems to have unusual circumstances that are not clearly defined by laws. This is why one person may be awarded damages for an injury in a court suit while another may get nothing in what appears to be a very similar claim.

The general rule has been that a seller is liable for damages only to the immediate purchaser. This required consumers to make their claims to retailers rather than going directly to manufacturers. The code took no position on whether an injured purchaser could bring suit directly against the manufacturer. Today, court cases have weakened the seller's position to such an extent that he has difficulty disclaiming product liability. Manufacturers are being held liable to consumers for faulty products and this becomes more important when physical safety is involved. Court decisions are definitely causing a reduction in the marketing of unsafe products.

Bailment

Instances where one person loans, rents, or temporarily surrenders an item of personal property to another are referred to as bailment. It is a transfer of possession for a particular purpose. It may be a repair transaction, such as when you leave your watch at the jewelers for repairs. A bailment exists when a person legally has possession of an item which he does not own and there is a duty for it to be returned to the owner. A bailment exists if you lend your paint brush to a neighbor.

Bailment is important to us as consumers since we leave items of personal property in repair or service shops. Examples are household appliance repair shops, automobile repair shops, laundries, dry cleaning firms and shoe repair shops. What are your rights if your property is lost or damaged while in temporary possession of another person? Does the shop owner have a right to use your property while it is in his care?

Most bailments are of a commercial nature, that is, both parties expect a benefit. When you take your car to the mechanic, you get your car repaired and he gets paid. This is a mutual benefit. For commercial bailments, the holder of the product must exercise reasonable care to prevent damage to your goods, but he is not held liable unless negligence is proven.

A bailment that benefits only the owner of property is another type. You may agree to keep the neighbors' dog while they are out of town and no pay is received. In this instance, you are liable only if you do nothing to prevent injury or loss when you could easily do so without substantial cost or sacrifice. Your responsibility for loss is slight, in a legal sense.

Still another type of bailment is one where the temporary holder of the propery receives all the benefit. If you borrow a hoe from the neighbor and break the handle, are you liable? Here you must exercise great care in using the item because you are getting the benefit. You would be liable for replacing the hoe handle.

Some business firms buy liability insurance to protect themselves when holding property of others. Also, contracts between two parties may be made to increase or decrease liability of either party. Usually a person cannot relieve himself of liability due to his own negligence since this is against public policy.

Negotiable Instruments

Items such as bank checks, promissory notes, certificates of deposit and drafts are examples of commercial paper used in business transactions. Commercial paper is a legal contract which serves as credit or represents money. To be negotiable, it must be transferrable from one person to another.

Some types of commercial paper have been used for centuries. With the development of trade and commerce on a national basis, uniformity of these instruments became necessary to protect the rights of all parties in business transactions. This came with the Uniform Commercial Code which has a section relating to the use of commercial paper.

Instruments such as corporation stocks and bonds and negotiable warehouse receipts are examples of negotiable instruments, but they are not classified as commercial paper since they do not contain a promise to pay a certain sum of money. They do contain the element of transferability.

A person may transfer his rights in an instrument by *assignment* or by *negotiation*. When a contract is assigned to another person, the person assigning property can assign what he owns or controls and the person receiving the contract can receive only what is contained in the contract. Where contracts involve performance by personal skill and judgment, they are not assignable. Contracts to sell land and different kinds of merchandise are assignable.

An instrument may be transferred in two ways by negotiation. A paper that is payable to bearer (anyone holding the paper) may be negotiated by delivery alone. However, if it is payable to the order of a person, then it must be endorsed by this person or someone legally approved by him.

Great care should be exercised in the use of business papers, since the protection of ordinary contracts does not exist for the holder of some types of commercial paper, and some instruments must be freely negotiable to serve business needs of speed and convenience.

Consumer
Legislation

It is appropriate to review the most significant consumer protection laws. Although some laws benefit consumers only in an indirect way; in some respects, all laws are consumer protection laws since they are passed for the benefit of the people and all people are consumers. However, since we cannot discuss all legislation here, this chapter includes only selected specific consumer protection laws. The laws are classified under three headings: (1) consumer information to protect from deception and fraud, (2) consumer personal health and safety, and (3) economic protection. These federal laws are listed in the appendix at the end of this chapter.

Since federal laws to protect consumers apply only to businesses operating in interstate trade, you may ask about regulations on those doing all their business within one state. If their selling practices are regulated, it must be done by the state or local government.

We can safely say that state legislatures have shown little interest in consumer protection. This attitude may be changing. Some states have recently passed such laws. The Federal Trade Commission made a survey in 1967 and found that only nineteen states have satisfactory laws prohibiting deceptive selling practices.[2] States with the least consumer protection legislation are Alabama, Arkansas, Indiana, Mississippi, New Hampshire, North Carolina, Ohio, Oklahoma, South Carolina, South Dakota, Tennessee, Texas, Virginia, West Virginia, and Wyoming.

Until states provide better legal protection for consumers, we must learn to recognize deceptive practices. Seldom is it necessary to buy products from strange salesmen traveling through the area, especially when the buyer is required to sign a written contract. Even where state laws are effective, more satisfaction will usually be obtained by trading with local dealers who have a reputation to maintain. The outlook for state-initiated consumer protection legislation may be improving, however. Congress responded to growing consumer pressures with many laws during the 1960s. Is it possible that these pressures could be turned toward the state legislatures in the 1970s?

Overseers for
the Consumer

Public Agencies

To enforce such an array of consumer protection laws, federal agencies and commissions have been established. The Federal Trade Commission, established by the *Federal Trade Commission Act of 1914,* was responsible for investigating and controlling unfair trade practices which reduce competition. It has since been given the responsibility for enforcing other laws—namely, the Wool Products Labeling Act, the Fur Products Labeling Act, the Wheeler-Lea Act, the Textile Fiber Products Identification Act, the Flammable Fabrics Act, the Fair Packaging and Labeling Act, and others. This commission has, to a large extent, become a consumer protection agency.

The Food and Drug Administration is an agency with broad powers. It is responsible for preparing standards and product tolerances for safety in the sale of foods, drugs, and chemical consumer products. This agency was established by the Pure Food and Drug Act of 1906. Its responsibility has grown as

---

[2]David A. Aaker and George S. Day, *Consumerism* (New York: Free Press, 1971), p. 207.

other laws were added such as the Food, Drug, and Cosmetic Act, the Food Additives Amendment, the Color Additive Amendment, the Pesticide Amendment, the Drug Industry Act, the Drug Abuse Control Act, and others. The Meat Inspection Act and Poultry Products Inspection Act are supervised by the U. S. Department of Agriculture.

Other agencies responsibile for consumer protection laws are the Federal Deposit Insurance Corporation which guarantees bank accounts, the Securities and Exchange Commission which regulates trading in securities, and the many state insurance commissions which enforce state insurance laws. In some instances, responsibilities of regulatory groups overlap. This requires cooperation in their work.

Private Organizations and Consumer Groups

It is not surprising that consumers are becoming more vocal in their discontent with shoddy products and misleading advertising. They are looking for ways to get more information about the quality and reliability of various products. Publications issued by such consumer organizations as Consumers Research, Inc., and Consumers Union are used by many people to get this type of information. Local Better Business Bureaus, while organized to serve business interests, have helped to rid communities of unscrupulous dealers.

Some individuals outside of government have become outspoken leaders for consumer interests. Much has been written in recent years about the work of Ralph Nader and his so-called "Nader's Raiders." He has received credit for developing enough public interest in automobile safety to lead to federal legislation in the 1960s.

A Consumer Movement

The decade of the 1960s witnessed the beginning of a consumer movement that could bring vast changes in our producing and marketing system. All kinds of producers are feeling the pressure to make changes, whether it is for a safer product or a better-written warranty. In addition, the credibility of many business practices is being questioned by aroused consumers.

Why have consumers become discontented with products and markets? Do businessmen still believe in the old marketing concept of learning what consumers want and producing it at a competitive price? Have businesses come to rely too much on advertising which tries to shape consumer demand to what is being produced?

The years since World War II have been a time of rising incomes, production, and sales. When business is good, the manufacturer may give too much attention to meeting production quotas and tend to neglect quality and the changing needs of the consumer. If this continues, he may eventually find that he is producing for a non-existent market. At the same time, the consumer may be expecting too much from his purchases, but he has been told by advertisers that products are getting better all the time. If he finds products that do not meet his high expectations, he will demand changes. All the while he sees and hears publicity given to findings and opinions of consumer protagonists such as Ralph Nader and others. When enough people become dissatisfied, the result is a consumer movement, and legislators respond to the demands of large concerned groups by passing new laws.

We do not need much imagination to see how a consumer movement can lead to over-regulation or over-protection. Excessive and unnecessary standardization of products can reduce competition and hinder the development of new products. Businesses and consumers should look upon each other as being essential parts of a complex marketing system. They need each other to survive and prosper.

Poor regulations and inefficient enforcement may be as bad as no regulation at all. In recent years, new laws have come so rapidly that the regulatory agencies have not been able to expand fast enough to assume properly the added responsibility. Businesses are faced with new regulations, but they do not know how to meet them. As a consequence, there is the danger of seriously harming businesses without providing benefits to consumers.

Businessmen must assume some responsibility for the sudden upsurge in consumer protection laws. Some have neglected quality and service. It is very frustrating to the customer for a new machine to break down and then to have to listen to reasons why the warranty does not cover the repair. Sears Roebuck Company became the nation's largest retailer by guaranteeing satisfaction or refunding the customer's money. If all businesses had operated in this manner, there would not have been as many regulatory laws passed. By improving quality and service now, there will be fewer regulatory laws in the future.

Future Directions

Business executives are beginning to realize the significance of rising expectations of millions of consumers for higher quality and reliability in what they buy. Most publicity has been related to what the federal government is trying to do, but many state and local governments are passing consumer legislation. Also, there appears to be no end to the possible areas for regulation of business practices. States are beginning to create agencies to deal with consumer problems. For example, New York has a State Consumer Protection Board and California has established a Division of Consumer Services.

Problems recently receiving attention are the costs of automobile repairs, no-fault auto insurance, health services for rural areas, and the dating of packages for perishable foods. We should remember that laws without effective enforcement provisions do little good. When new laws are passed, an agency must be given responsibility and the necessary funds for enforcement.

The consumer movement is growing rapidly, but it has little coordination. Different groups spring up quickly to get on the bandwagon and their efforts sometimes duplicate the work of others. The President has established an

Office of Consumer Affairs to give consumers greater access to government, to promote consumer education, to encourage voluntary efforts by business, to work with state and local governments, and to help the federal government improve its consumer-related activities.[3] There is no doubt that the consumer movement is growing and increasing in scope of interests. What is needed now to increase its effectiveness is better organization and coordination.

Discussion Questions

1. Briefly define *caveat emptor* and relate this term to the consumer movement that has taken place in recent years.
2. Discuss the needed government protection in the public health and safety area.
3. In your opinion, is there too much (or too little) government protection for consumers? Why?
4. Give a brief history of the reasons for adopting a Uniform Commercial Code.
5. Why was the Interstate Commerce Act of 1887 passed? What powers are presently held by the Interstate Commerce Commission?
6. Comment on the Federal Trade Commission and its position as a consumer protection agency.
7. There has been recent talk of a consumer revolution on the horizon. In your opinion as a consumer, is there justification for a consumer revolt?

---

appendix

Examples of Consumer Protection Legislation

Consumer Information Legislation

Wool Products Labeling Act of 1939

This act requires the manufacturers of woolen products to list the percentages of each fabric and information on whether the wool is new or reused. It was the intention of Congress that this act would stop the practice of selling reused wool as

---

[3]"President's Message to Congress on the State of the Union," *U.S. News and World Report,* Jan. 31, 1972, p. 75.

new and the selling of blended fabrics as all wool. Rugs, carpets, and upholstery
materials are exempt from the requirements.

Fur Products Labeling Act of 1951

The purpose of this act was to protect consumers as well as the industry from
deception and false advertising in the sale of furs. Blends of furs were being falsely
labeled. This act requires manufacturers to label fur products by name of the animals, with information on fur color (whether the fur is bleached or dyed), and by
the part of the animal from which it came.

Fair Packaging and Labeling Act of 1966

The primary intent of this act was to prevent the use of deceptive and unfair
methods of packaging and labeling consumer products. It applied to most consumer
products not already covered in other legislation, such as meat and tobacco products, prescription drugs, alcoholic beverages, seeds, and insecticides. Congress expected this legislation to help consumers obtain accurate information as to the contents of packages so they could make value comparisons of products. Packages must
show the name of the product, a list of ingredients, name and address of the manufacturer, and weight or volume of the contents.

Consumer Personal Health
and Safety Legislation

Pure Food and Drug Act of 1906

After considerable publicity about unsanitary conditions in meat packing plants,
this act was passed to prohibit the misbranding and adulteration of foods and drugs.
The act was amended in 1938 to include cosmetics and therapeutic devices. Other
amendments, in 1958 and 1960, were related to coloring and other types of food
additives. Any food additive intended for public consumption must be either generally recognized as safe or it must conform with a regulation indicating safe conditions for use of the additive. The Food and Drug Administration establishes standards for food additives before they can be used.

Drug Amendments Act of 1962

An amendment entitled the Drug Amendments Act of 1962 increased restrictions
on the manufacture and sale of drugs. This resulted from publicity concerning the
fetus-deforming drug thalidomide being taken by pregnant women in Europe. This
far-reaching law requires manufacturers to prove safety and effectiveness of drugs
before they can be sold. The Food and Drug Administration has established testing
procedures for drug firms to follow before receiving approval of products. Labels
and advertising must be accurate and must include warnings of possible side effects.

Drug Abuse Control Act of 1965

With increasing use of narcotic-type drugs, the Drug Abuse Control Act of 1965 was passed to provide better controls over the manufacture and sale of stimulants and depressants. Legal handlers of dangerous drugs must keep records of all sales. Additional control over drugs came with passage of the Drug Abuse Act of 1970. This act required strict regulation of production and distribution of most commonly prescribed depressants, stimulants, and tranquilizers. Penalties were lessened for drug possession, but increased for illegal narcotics sellers. Funds were provided to increase preventive drug education and rehabilitation by the National Institute of Mental Health.

The Pesticide Amendment of 1954

This amendment was concerned with the sales and use of poisons for crop, livestock, and household insects. This law and later amendments require manufacturers to label these products with directions for their use and to provide warnings as to their hazards. Instances of harm to wildlife and fish have been found and residues are sometimes left on plants that make them harmful for use as food. All pesticides and herbicides must be registered with the Secretary of Agriculture before they can be marketed.

Hazardous Substances Labeling Act of 1960

Many children have been injured and killed by hazardous household products such as cleaning agents, paint removers, laundry supplies, and sprays. The Hazardous Substances Labeling Act of 1960 requires manufacturers of toxic and flammable products to place warnings about their use on the labels. In 1966, it was amended as the Child Protection Act and gave the FDA authority to ban or seize items too hazardous for common use.

Further to prevent personal injury from radiation emissions from improperly constructed color television sets and x-ray machines, Congress passed the Hazardous Radiation Act in 1968. This act empowered the Secretary of Health, Education and Welfare to establish standards to be used in the production of these items.

Federal Cigarette Labeling and Advertising Act

After many studies were made indicating that cigarette smoking increases a person's chances for lung cancer and heart disease, the Federal Cigarette Labeling and Advertising Act was passed in 1965. It required manufacturers to place warning labels regarding the possible hazards to health on each package. Later legislation stopped all cigarette advertising on television after 1970.

Food processing regulations have been aimed at wholesomeness and edibility more than at grades of products. Official or standard grades are not required for many foods. Some food processors establish their own grading system by using a different brand name for each grade. They hope to develop more customer loyalty by establishing brand names on the housewife's mind rather than to reveal actual grading judgments. When official grading is required, it is usually by state laws.

Meat Inspection Act of 1906

One of the first federal laws concerned with food wholesomeness was the Meat Inspection Act of 1906. This act required inspectors in packing plants who deal in interstate trade to inspect animals before slaughter for disease and the meat after slaughter for its desirability as human food. Until recent years, a large percentage of meat sold was slaughtered within the state, which made the law inapplicable. Congress extended the requirements to intrastate shipments in 1967. Poultry meat was not included under this legislation since it had little importance at the time.

Poultry Products Inspection Act of 1957

Poultry became an important meat with development of the broiler industry during the 1930s and 1940s. This created the need for inspection, which resulted in the Poultry Products Inspection Act of 1957. At this time, inspection began at all slaughter plants selling in interstate trade. In 1968, this system was extended to intrastate shipments. Sea food inspection came with the Sea Food Act of 1934.

Flammable Fabrics Act of 1953

Personal safety was the intent of Congress in the passage of The Flammable Fabrics Act of 1953. Some types of clothing were being manufactured using highly flammable fabrics which resulted in serious injury and death. The manufacture and sale of articles of clothing from highly flammable materials are prohibited by this act.

National Traffic and Motor Vehicle Safety Act of 1966

One of the most far-reaching pieces of legislation to be concerned with safety was the National Traffic and Motor Vehicle Safety Act of 1966. As the number of injuries and deaths on highways increased each year, Congress intended to determine reasons for this and to establish safety requirements for automobile manufacturers. A National Highway Safety Agency was established to conduct research into the causes of accidents and establish requirements to be met by the manufacturers. The first safety standards were required on 1968 models. Some of these were headrests on front seats, seat belts, and red and amber lights on the sides of the car. Each year the agency has required additional safety items as standard equipment. Manufacturers are required to recall cars and repair them when safety-related defects are discovered.

As safety items are added to automobiles, prices increase to cover their cost. No sensible person can object to paying for something that will save his life; however, the agency must be sure that it is not forcing some items on the public that have little safety value. A high percentage of accidents are found to have drinking drivers involved. Safety features do little to prevent these accidents. This raises the philosophical question of the relative importance of mechanical auto safety legislation and the enforcement of appropriate driving while intoxicated legislation in the ultimate protection of automobile purchasers.

1969 Child Protection and Toy Safety Act

The 1969 Child Protection and Toy Safety Act was passed to keep potentially harmful toys off the market. Toys that contain parts that can inflict puncture wounds or that present mechanical or electrical hazards are banned. The Food and

Drug Administration has responsibility for enforcement of this law working with toy manufacturers to get changes made in hazardous toys.

Economic Protection
Legislation

It is in the area of economic protection that the tendency for over-protection becomes great. Many economic-type regulations are serving the consumer well, but some laws in recent years appear to be replacing (reducing) competition in the marketplace. Others may increase a seller's costs with much or all of these costs being passed on to consumers. These higher prices may offset the benefits received from the regulation.

Federal Deposit Insurance Corporation

Most laws that we have classified as providing economic protection came with the depression of the 1930s and later. The Federal Deposit Insurance Corporation was established in 1933 to protect bank depositors from loss of their funds. During this time, banks were failing daily and many people were losing their life savings. Most banks now have this insurance to protect their customers' accounts. The same protection was extended to savings accounts in savings banks and savings and loan associations in 1934. The latter are insured by the Federal Savings and Loan Insurance Corporation.

Security Exchange Acts

Investors in stocks had such large losses in the depression that Congress enacted the Securities Act of 1933 and the Securities Exchange Act of 1934. These laws placed restrictions on the issuance and sale of securities. They do not prevent losses in stock trading, but require companies and securities dealers to provide accurate information so that buyers will have a better basis for making decisions. The Securities and Exchange Commission was established to regulate securities dealers and stock exchanges.

The Investment Companies and Investment Advisers Act of 1940

This act brought various types of investment trusts and investment advisers under regulation of the SEC. Any person selling advice about securities must be registered by SEC. His charges are regulated, and he is required to follow ethical business practices in advising his clients.

Securities Acts Amendment

In 1964, the Securities Acts Amendment resulted from an extensive study made of securities markets. This act placed additional restrictions on brokers and dealers, such as licensing, financial responsibility, and character requirements. Entry into the securities business was made more difficult.

McCarran Act of 1945

This act was concerned with the insurance industry. This is a highly specialized and technical area where consumers need protection, since they may have little understanding of the soundness of a company or the relative value of its policies.

When we pay annual premiums for many years to obtain insurance, we want some assurance that the company can pay the insurance when it becomes due. Safety and soundness of insurance companies are left to state regulations. The McCarran Act was concerned with competition and the anti-trust laws. Until 1944, insurance companies were considered to be intrastate and not subject to federal regulation. The McCarran Act, following a Supreme Court decision which declared insurance interstate commerce, exempted insurance companies from federal legislation as long as the Congress felt state regulation was appropriately protecting the public. There remains the possibility that Congress may decide to assume this regulatory function.

State insurance laws of some states do a reasonably good job of maintaining the financial safety of insurance companies by requiring adequate reserves and placing certain restrictions on their investments.

Automobile Information Disclosure Act of 1958

Another law that was intended to provide economic protection to consumers was the Automobile Information Disclosure Act of 1958. This act requires manufacturers to place suggested retail prices on all new automobiles and to include the price of each item of optional equipment. The intention of this law was to give the customer accurate information about the trade-in value of his car as related to selling price of the new car. Few apparent benefits have resulted from the law, since the suggested prices are usually much higher than prices dealers are willing to accept. There is little price competition in the automobile industry and this law did little to increase it.

Growth of consumer credit during recent years increased concern for regulations dealing with interest rates. Complaints were made about the numerous methods used to calculate interest costs of consumer credit. Many times, the actual rate paid was much higher than the contract or advertised rate. Some installment loans and revolving charge accounts were made in such ways that the customer could not determine the actual rate of interest paid.

Consumer Credit Protection Act

To provide more information for consumers, Congress passed the Consumer Credit Protection Act in 1968. This act requires that borrowers be informed in writing of the exact cost of credit both in dollars and in annual interest rates. This law applies to all types of loans including home mortgages, charge accounts at stores, installment loans, and personal loans. The law does not regulate the amount of interest that can be charged, but only requires that the borrower know exactly how much he is paying. Presumably, if the interest rate seems high, the borrower will decline the credit. There is little evidence that this act has had an effect on the use of consumer credit.

Wheeler-Lea Act of 1938

A discussion of consumer protection would not be complete without mentioning the Wheeler-Lea Act of 1938. This act was passed to prevent false advertising on foods, drugs, cosmetics, and therapeutic devices. Any advertising that is deceptive or misleading is illegal under this statute. The intent of the law was good, but it has been very difficult to enforce.

Money makes money, and the money
money makes, makes more money.
[Benjamin Franklin]

5

Mathematics of Personal Finance

The purpose of this chapter is to teach a few basic mathematical fundamentals that are needed in making decisions related to earning, consuming, and investing. It will present problems and situations having a functional bearing on family finance. Since the subject of mathematics is related to almost all chapters of this book, some problems discussed here will be similar to those found under the special topics. Hopefully, the repetition in this mathematical context will help to increase understanding of these aspects of personal finance.

Costs of Borrowing Money

To borrow money or buy merchandise on credit is to use another person's money; and, in most cases, it is necessary to pay for that privilege. Payment for the use of money is called interest and is usually stated as an annual rate or percent. Whether you borrow money and pay cash for the goods or buy on credit, you are getting the use of a product for which you have not paid. The usual sources of short-term borrowing are commercial banks and finance companies, while long-term loans for purchasing real estate are secured from savings and loan associations, life insurance companies, savings banks, or government agencies. When you buy merchandise on credit, the dealer or store sometimes carries the loan, but usually the note is sold to a bank or finance company.

Calculating Interest

Not many people go through life without either borrowing or lending. The following formulas are useful for determining the amount of interest in dollars, the rate in percent, and the amount of principal in dollars.

1. Principal (amount loaned or borrowed) × rate (in decimals) × time (fraction of year) = interest (dollars). In symbols: $prt = i$, where $p =$ principal, $r =$ rate of interest, $t =$ time, $i =$ interest.

   Example: What is the interest on a principal of $850 at a rate of 7% over a period of ten months ($\frac{5}{6}$ year)?

   $850 × .07 × \frac{5}{6}$ = $49.58 interest

2. Interest (in dollar and cents) ÷ principal (amount loaned or borrowed) × time money used = rate of interest (in decimals). Symbolically $prt = i$ or $r = (i ÷ pt) × 100$.

   Example: What is the rate of interest on a $925 debt when the interest paid is $72 for 9 months?

   $72 ÷ ($925 × $\frac{3}{4}$) × 100 = 10.4% (rate)

3. Interest (dollars and cents) ÷ rate × time = principal. Symbolically: $prt = i$ or $p = i ÷ rt$.

   Example: How much money was borrowed for a loan with an interest rate of 9% when the interest paid was $325 for 15 months?

   $325 ÷ (9 × $\frac{5}{4}$) = $2,889 (principal)

Methods of Charging Interest

Methods of applying stated interest charges in themselves are confusing, to say nothing of the additional confusion contributed by various other charges. For example, an advertised 6 percent charge for a loan standing by itself is meaningless unless it is clear how the 6 percent is applied. It could be applied in one of several methods.

Discount Method. This method is frequently applied to home repair and modernization loans and to personal loans. The loan is made for one year, but interest is taken out in advance. A loan of $1,000 for one year at 8 percent interest would cost $80. The lender takes the $80 out in advance, and the borrower receives only $920. When the loan is due in one year, he repays $1,000. He is paying $80 for the use of $920, which is actually 8.7 percent. The following formula can be used.

$$\text{Actual rate charged} = \frac{2 \times b \times I}{P(n + 1)} = \frac{2 \times 1 \times 80}{920 \times 2} = 8.7\%$$

b = number of payments in a year
I = credit cost in dollars
P = amount of money actually used
n = number of total payments

Minimum Charge Instead of Annual Rate. The loan is made for a period of less than a year but interest is charged for the full year. A loan of $1,000 for six months at 8 percent would cost $80 if charged for a full year, but would be only $40 at an annual rate. The minimum charge method would be an actual rate of 16 percent.

Service Fee Charge. The lender may charge a service fee for making a credit investigation. This adds to total loan costs and may be considered the same as interest costs. A loan of $1,000 at 8 percent for one year with a $20 service fee will cost $100. This raises the actual rate paid to 10 percent instead of 8 percent.

$$r = \frac{i}{p\,r} = \frac{\$100}{\$1,000 \times 1} \times 100 = 10\%$$

Annual Interest on Unpaid Balance. When interest is calculated on the unpaid balance, the borrower is paying on the money actually used. The contract rate and actual rate are then the same.

Example: A $1,200 loan is to be repaid in 12 equal monthly payments at 6% interest. Interest will be $6.00 the first month and will decline $.50 each month for a total of $39.00 interest paid.

$$\text{actual rate} = \frac{2 \times b \times I}{p\,(n + 1)} = \frac{2 \times 12 \times 39}{1,200\,(13)} \times 100 = 6\%$$

Installment Credit Charges. Installment credit is a method of repaying a debt by making regular payments at specified intervals, rather than repaying the total in one lump-sum payment. These loans are usually repaid on a monthly basis. Interest may be figured on the outstanding balance of the principal or on the full amount for the full time. If the charge is a certain percentage of the unpaid balance per month, the borrower should multiply this rate by 12 to get the annual rate as shown in the table on the top of page 78.

If the monthly rate is	The true annual rate is
¾ of 1%	9%
1%	12%
1½ %	18%
2%	24%
2½ %	30%

The monthly payments may be calculated by taking a percentage of the total principal over the full period, adding the product to the principal, and dividing the resulting sum by the number of months.

$$m.p. = \frac{prt + p}{n}$$

$m.p.$ = monthly payment
n = number of months

Example: You trade your car for a new one and owe a difference of $2,450. This is to be paid in 36 monthly installments at 7% interest.

Interest for one year $2,450 × 7% = $171.50
Interest for three years $171.50 × 3 = $514.50
Amount to be paid $2,450 + $514.50 = $2,964.50
Monthly payment $2,964.50 ÷ 36 = $82.35

The stated rate of interest is 7%. What is the actual rate paid? Using the previously listed formula, we can determine the rate.

$$\frac{2 \times 12 \times 514.50}{2,450 \times 37} \times 100 = 13.6\% \text{ actual rate paid}$$

The "Add On" Charge Method. A lender may quote his charge as a certain number of dollars per 100 dollars borrowed per year. He may specify a charge of $5 per $100. The borrower receives $100 and pays back $105 in contrast to the "discount method" where he would receive $95 and pay back $100. This would appear to be a 5 percent loan, but it is actually more because the borrower does not use the full amount for an entire year. This method is com-

Exhibit 5–1   True Annual Rates on Loans Repaid in 12 Monthly Installments

If the credit charge per year is	The quoted rate per year is	The true rate per year is	
		For "add on"	For "discount"
$4 per $100	4%	7.4%	7.7%
$6 per $100	6%	11.1%	11.8%
$8 per $100	8%	14.8%	16.1%
$10 per $100	10%	18.5%	20.5%
$12 per $100	12%	22.2%	25.2%

Source: *Consumers All,* U.S. Department of Agriculture Yearbook (Washington, 1965), p. 159.

monly used in installment sales of automobiles and other consumer durables. Exhibit 5–1 compares annual rates of interest for the "add on" and "discount" methods. The discount rate is consistently more expensive.

The rates in Exhibit 5–1 can be calculated by using the formula given under the discount method. An example follows.

$$R = \frac{2 \times 12 \times 4}{100 \, (12 + 1)} = .074; \, .074 \times 100 = 7.4\% \text{ (add on)}$$

$$R = \frac{2 \times 12 \times 4}{96 \, (12 + 1)} = .077; \, .077 \times 100 = 7.7\% \text{ (discount)}$$

It may have more meaning to look at the actual dollar costs of credit. Costs rise rapidly as the installment period is extended. Exhibit 5–2 shows credit costs for the "add on" and "percent of unpaid balance" methods for different installment periods.

Exhibit 5–2 Dollar Cost of Credit Charges on a $1,000 Loan at Different Rates, Repaid in Different Numbers of Installments

Method of charging interest	Dollar cost of credit charges when number of monthly installments is—					
	12	*18*	*24*	*30*	*36*	*42*
"Add-on" Rate:						
$4 per $100 per year	$ 40	$ 60	$ 80	$100	$120	$140
$6 per $100 per year	60	90	120	150	180	210
$8 per $100 per year	80	120	160	200	240	280
$10 per $100 per year	100	150	200	250	300	350
$12 per $100 per year	120	180	240	300	360	420
Percent of unpaid balance:						
¾ of 1% per month	49	73	96	120	145	169
1% per month	66	98	130	162	196	230
1½% per month	100	149	198	249	301	355
2% per month	135	201	269	340	412	488
2½% per month	170	254	342	433	528	627

Source: *Consumers All,* U.S. Department of Agriculture Yearbook (Washington, 1965), p. 160.

In some instances a borrower may need to calculate interest for a certain number of days. The following rules can be used for this purpose.

At 3%, multiply the principal by the number of days and divide by 120.
At 4%, multiply the principal by the number of days and divide by 90.
At 5%, multiply the principal by the number of days and divide by 72.
At 6%, multiply the principal by the number of days and divide by 60.
At 7%, multiply the principal by the number of days and divide by 52.

At 8%, multiply the principal by the number of days and divide by 45.
At 9%, multiply the principal by the number of days and divide by 40.
At 10%, multiply the principal by the number of days and divide by 36.

Example: Jim Jones paid his charge account at the store. The store charges 8% interest and the debt was owed for 48 days. How much interest should he pay on a debt of $90?

$90 \times 48 \div 45 = \$.96$ interest

Other Charges. A lender may quote a low rate of interest but add other incidental charges to the loan cost. A carrying charge or fee for life insurance may be added. All extra charges should be combined with interest costs for determination of rates.

Another factor which can make credit cost comparisons difficult is the price of an article bought on credit. Here is an example:

Let us assume a consumer is considering the purchase of a color TV set. He finds what he wants at Store A priced at $650. The clerk tells him that the down payment is $50 and that the balance of $600 is payable in twelve monthly payments of $50 each with no charge for credit. At Store B he is offered an identical TV set for $610 cash, or he may buy it on a twelve-month installment plan which involves a $50 down payment and a 6 percent credit charge on the balance of $560. If he buys using Store B's credit offer, his total obligation will be $560 plus $33.60 *add on,* or $593.60; and the monthly payments will be $593.60 ÷ 12, or $49.47.

Note that although Store A advertised no credit cost, the buyer would pay more there than at Store B where he used credit.

Amortized Loans

Some loans are made to be repaid over many years. When purchasing a home, a family will be likely to assume a large debt requiring monthly payments over a period of twenty or twenty-five years. Amortization is a method of financing through which the purchaser pays a debt in small installments rather than in a lump sum at the end of the loan period. The payments, which include both principal and interest, may be equal or unequal depending on the method of amortization.

To determine the size of payments for amortizing a debt, the following formula can be used:

$$R = An \left(\frac{1}{a \, \overline{n} \, i} \right)$$

Example: Bill and Sara Jones purchased a $30,000 house and made a $6,000 down payment. They agreed to pay the balance in equal monthly payments for 20 years. The interest rate is 7% compounded monthly. What is the amount of their monthly payments?

$An = \$24{,}000$

$i = 7\%/12 = \frac{7}{12}\%$ (per month)

$n = 20 \times 12 = 240$ monthly payments

By using Exhibit 5–6 (Exhibits 5–3 through 5–6 are at the end of the chapter), we can substitute a value for the formula as follows:

$$R = \$24{,}000 \times \text{value from Exhibit 5–6}$$

Look under the column for $\frac{7}{12}\%$ with an n period of 240. The value is 0.00775299.

$$R = \$24{,}000 \times 0.00775299 = \$186.07$$

Thus, the monthly payment is $186.07.

Truth in Lending Act

The "add on" and "discount" methods of charging interest may have lost some significance since passage of the Consumer Credit Protection Act of 1968 (see Chapter 9). Also, the practice of quoting interest rates by the month (e.g., 1 percent per month) may be used less frequently. This act, sometimes called the "Truth in Lending Act," required that customers who borrow money and buy merchandise on credit, be notified in writing as to the amount of money and interest rate they are paying annually. The law was passed not to specify maximum rates that can be charged, but rather to help consumers understand and be better prepared to compare credit costs. This law may help consumers with loans and credit purchases, but it does not negate the need for understanding how to calculate interest charges.

Interest on Savings Accounts

The formulas given in the first part of this chapter under the heading "calculating interest" can be used to determine interest received on savings accounts just as it was used to calculate interest paid for loans. If the interest is paid annually, the method of determining interest is the same whether you are paying or receiving it. A common practice of some financial institutions is to compound the interest either semiannually or quarterly. When interest is compounded, the actual rate is higher than the contractual annual rate. The principal becomes larger by the amount of interest added to the account at the end of the period. Then interest is calculated on the larger principal during the next period. The following computations show how interest is compounded quarterly on a $500 deposit at a rate of 5 percent.

1st three months interest $= \$500 \times \frac{3}{12} \times .05 = \$6.25$

2nd three months interest $= \$506.25 \times \frac{3}{12} \times .05 = \$6.33$

3rd three months interest $= \$512.58 \times \frac{3}{12} \times .05 = \$6.41$
4th three months interest $= \$518.99 \times \frac{3}{12} \times .05 = \$6.49$

Total interest received for the year equals $25.48

The actual rate of interest received is determined by the following:

$$\text{Rate} = \$25.48 \div \$500 = .051 \times 100 = 5.1\%$$

The annual rate is 5 percent, while the compounded rate is 5.1 percent. Exhibit 5–4 shows how much $1 will grow at compound interest for various rates in twenty-five periods. The periods are not necessarily in years. Figures in the table are compounded annually, but the table can be used to show compounding on a quarterly or semiannual basis. If the interest is to be compounded semiannually, use one-half of the given rate and twice as many periods as the number of years.

> *Example:* Find the amount of $80 invested for 5 years at 4% compounded semiannually. In Exhibit 5–4 find the amount of $1 at 2% for 10 periods and multiply by $80.
>
> $1.218994 \times \$80 = \$97.52$

For quarterly compounding, use one-fourth of the given rate and four times as many periods as the number of years.

> *Example:* Find the amount of $80 invested for 5 years at 4% compounded quarterly. In Exhibit 5–4 find the amount of $1 at 1% for 20 periods and multiply by $80.
>
> $1.220190 \times \$80 = \$97.62$

Banks and savings and loan associations have their own rules for calculating interest on savings accounts. Customers make deposits and withdrawals according to their needs and may not consider the effects on interest earnings. If a patron makes a withdrawal a week before interest is to be deposited to his account, he may lose the interest on that amount for the full three or six-month period. Learn the procedures used where the family's savings account is kept.

Some institutions calculate interest by using the lowest passbook balance during the period. Others pay by calculating the number of days each balance was maintained. Still others may figure the interest for each whole month a balance was kept. Examples will help to understand these methods. Compare the amount of interest paid at different institutions compounding interest quarterly on a savings account. Mr. John Doe has a savings passbook as follows:

Date	Interest	Withdrawals	Deposits	Balance
10–2			150.	150.00
10–22			85.	235.00
11–1		30.		205.00
11–17			60.	265.00
12–17		75.		190.00

If interest for the quarter is figured by paying 4 percent on the lowest balance, the calculation would be

$$\$150 \times .04 \times \tfrac{1}{4} = \$1.50$$

On January 1, $1.50 interest would be added to his account giving a balance of $191.50.

When interest is calculated on the number of days each balance is maintained, the following method would be used.

$$\$150 \times 20/365 \times .04 = 0.33$$
$$235 \times 10/365 \times .04 = 0.26$$
$$205 \times 16/365 \times .04 = 0.36$$
$$365 \times 30/365 \times .04 = 0.87$$
$$190 \times 14/365 \times .04 = 0.29$$
$$\overline{\$2.11}$$

This method would pay $2.11 to give a balance of $192.11 on January 1.

Another method would be to calculate interest on the lowest balance for each month.

$$\text{October } \$150 \times \tfrac{1}{12} \times .04 = 0.50$$
$$\text{November } \$205 \times \tfrac{1}{12} \times .04 = 0.68$$
$$\text{December } \$190 \times \tfrac{1}{12} \times .04 = 0.63$$
$$\text{Total} \quad \$1.81$$

This method would pay $1.81 to give a balance of $191.81 on January 1.

By timing withdrawals to the beginning of interest-paying periods, money may be saved. If an emergency arises where more money must be obtained, it may pay to borrow the money instead of withdrawing it from a savings account. This would be true at the end of an interest-paying period when a withdrawal would cause a loss of interest for the entire period. Interest paid on a loan for a few days would be less than the loss from making the withdrawal.

To attract the savings of more persons, some institutions are beginning to compound savings accounts on a monthly, weekly, or daily basis. Compare the yields by frequency of compounding an account by studying Exhibit 5–3.

Savings accounts do not pay interest rates as high as those rates charged for borrowing money. Loan rates are usually about double the rates on savings accounts. For this reason, a family will normally not find it profitable to borrow money just to maintain a savings account. When money is needed, it will usually cost less to take it out of savings than to borrow it.

Balancing the Checkbook and Bank Statement

It is exasperating when the bank statement at the end of the month does not balance with the checkbook record. After trying for two or three months to reconcile these two balances, it is tempting to quit trying. The difficulty is that checks written during the last few days will not have been cleared through the bank. In addition, the bank may have a service charge subtracted from the account which has not yet been entered in the checkbook. The following bank statement for March details the activity for the month in John Doe's checking account.

Checks		Deposits	Date	No. of checks paid	Balance
Balance brought forward			Mar. 8		873.31
2.25	.50				
9.49	3.00		Mar. 11	4	858.07
107.55			Mar. 15	5	750.52
5.00	75.00				
10.99			Mar. 22	8	659.53
19.71	350.25		Mar. 25	10	289.57
18.78		59.00	Mar. 28	11	329.79
		899.59	Apr. 1		1,229.38
80.00			Apr. 3	12	1,149.38
175.50	12.05				
107.55			Apr. 4	15	854.28
5.10			Apr. 5	16	849.18
45.00	45.00				
20.00			Apr. 6	19	739.18
4.00	13.25		Apr. 7	21	721.93

Although the bank statement balance may be larger or smaller than that in the checkbook, it usually is larger since all the checks written usually have not been cashed. Occasionally, even checks written five or six weeks prior to the statement have not reached the bank. With the possibility of such complications, it is easier to account for all checks if they are numbered. When John Doe received his bank statement, it showed a balance of $721.93. His checkbook showed that on April 8 he wrote two checks, one for $12.80 and another for $61.39, leaving a balance of $647.74. By using the accompanying form, he can reconcile the statement and checkbook. (Often a similar form is printed on the back of the bank statement.)

Since the bank did not make a service charge in March, the checkbook balance was correct. The two outstanding checks put the two accounts in balance when they were subtracted from the bank statement balance. If the accounts had still been out of balance, John Doe would have had to look for an error in the checkbook by refiguring the check entries for the entire month. If no error was then found, he would proceed to check all figures on the bank statement. This can be done by adding all deposits to the beginning balance and subtracting the total of all checks written. The result should be the ending balance. It is also a good practice to examine each canceled check to be sure that it was written by you and has not been altered by someone else.

Balancing checkbook with bank statement

		Date April 10	
Bank statement balance	$721.93	Checkbook balance	$647.74
Subtract:		Subtract:	
Checks not cashed		Service charges	
No. 67	12.80		
68	61.39		
Total checks	74.19		
Adjusted balance	$647.74	Adjusted balance	$ 647.74

Using Index Numbers

Index numbers are used to make comparisons or show changes from one time period to another. Economists frequently use them to show changes in production, sales, and prices. Price indexes are used to show changes in the purchasing power of money. The Consumer Price Index calculated by the U.S. Department of Labor may be the most popular index number in use. It is used to show changes in the cost of living. The formula for calculating an index number is as follows:

$$\frac{\text{current period}}{\text{base period}} \times 100 = \text{index number in percent}$$

Example: If the price of a gallon of gasoline increased from 32 cents to 36 cents between 1970 and 1973, what is the price index?

$$\frac{36}{32} \times 100 = 112.5\%, \text{ or } 112.5$$

The price of gasoline in 1973 was 112.5 percent of the price in 1970, or it was 12.5 percent higher in 1973 than 1970.

The time period does not need to be a year. Index numbers can be used to show changes between any periods.

Example: Acme Merchandising Company sold 46 refrigerators during the month of April but only 38 in May. Show the change as an index number.

$$\frac{38}{46} \times 100 = 82.6\%, \text{ or } 82.6$$

Sales in May were only 82.6 percent of April, or they decreased by 17.4 percent.

Index numbers could be used to determine the extent to which a family is gaining or losing purchasing power. The Consumer Price Index is calculated using 1967 costs as the base. The CPI was 125.3 in 1972 which was an increase of 25.3 percent over 1967. Family income should have increased this amount to prevent the loss of purchasing power.

Example: The Wilson family income was $6,785 after income taxes were paid in 1967. The after-tax income for 1972 was $7,130. Did the family purchasing power increase or decrease?

$7,130
  6,785 $345 ÷ $6,785 × 100 = 5.1%
$ 345

Income increased only 5.1 percent while consumer prices were increasing 25.3 percent. The family lost purchasing power during this period. Additional information concerning the Consumer Price Index can be found in Chapter 7.

Return on Investments

Investors want to get the greatest return for their money. It is a common procedure to calculate returns from investments into percentages for comparative purposes. This is referred to as the rate of return and can be determined whether the investment is in stocks, bonds, mutual funds, real estate, or other types of investments. The return may be called interest, rent, dividends, or profits. The formula for determining the rate of return (the net dollar return per $100 invested) is as follows:

$$\text{Rate of return} = \frac{\text{yearly net return}}{\text{amount invested}} \times 100$$

Example: What is the rate of return on a share of stock that will cost $86 and pays annual dividends of $4.50 per share?

$$\frac{\$4.50}{\$86.00} \times 100 = 5.2\% \text{ return}$$

Securities

The return on a preferred share of corporation stock can be determined since the company promises to pay a fixed rate of the par value of the stock.

Example: What is the rate of return on a preferred stock that pays 5% on a par value of $30? The stock can be purchased for $27.50 per share.

$$\frac{\$1.50}{\$27.50} \times 100 = 5.4\% \text{ return}$$

Investments may be made in government or corporation bonds. A fixed rate of interest is paid on the par value or face value at the time the bond was issued. The current selling price may be higher or lower than the par value. A bond may be quoted as follows:

U.S. Treasury 7% Bond 1981   106.12

This is a $1,000 par value bond that pays $70.00 per year and will cost the buyer $1,061.25. The current rate of return is as follows:

$$\frac{\$70.00}{\$1,061.25} \times 100 = 6.6\% \text{ return}$$

Like government bonds, corporate bonds are quoted as a percentage of par value. Bonds are rated as to investment quality. High-rated bonds yield a low rate of interest in relation to lower-rated bonds. Market prices on bonds fluctuate to provide the investor with a yield which reflects changing market conditions.

Example: A General Electric Co. 6¼%, 1979 bond sells for 99. What is the rate of return?

$$\frac{\$62.50}{\$990.00} \times 100 = 6.31\%$$

Real Estate

Investors in real estate must obtain net income figures by making reasonable estimates of ownership expenses to subtract from gross income. If the property has not been income-producing property, it may be necessary to estimate gross income before expenses are determined. For example, an investor may want to consider the purchase of a home for use as a rental house. Since the property has not been rented before, he must determine how much rental income it will produce. The income must produce a fair return or one that compares well with other investment possibilities. The following example shows how this can be estimated.

Description of property
   3 bedroom, 2 bath, brick veneer house that is 5 years old and in good condition
   Price is $26,000 (includes closing costs)
   Down payment required: $5,000
   Loan of $21,000 for 25 years at 7% interest

Annual gross income
   $300 monthly rental × 12 months $3,600
   Less expected vacancy—3%   108
   Effective gross income $3,492

Annual ownership expenses
   Property taxes $ 525

Insurance	135
Repairs and advertising	350
	$1,010
Net operating income	$2,482
Less interest on mortgage (7% on $21,000)	1,470
Gross income on owner's equity	$1,012
Less depreciation (30 years on building value of $20,000, straight line method)	667
Return for your investment and management	$ 345
Percent return on your equity ($5,000)	6.9%

Estimating Savings Needed
for Specified Objectives

A good savings program will include funds necessary to obtain long-term family objectives. Families who have no retirement program other than the federal Social Security program may need to start a savings account to provide funds for retirement. The amount of savings required each month or year will be determined by how soon before retirement the program is started and how much income will be needed during retirement. Often, families begin setting aside a small amount each month while the children are small in order to have money available for a college education. It is possible to calculate the amount of savings needed to meet these future objectives.

Setting aside regular amounts of money over a specified period of time is called establishing an *annuity*. Annuity contracts are usually made with life insurance companies to which the individual agrees to make regular payments in return for a lump sum amount at some period in the future or in return for a series of small regular payments. Annuities can be bought to provide an education fund for the children or a retirement fund for the parents. The same purpose can be accomplished by establishing a savings account if the investor calculates the amount to be deposited regularly to obtain his specified objective. Since saving accounts accumulate interest, the fund will grow and more money will be available for use than was deposited. How fast it grows will depend on the rate of interest paid for the savings and how often it is compounded.

Annuity tables have been compiled giving the values for $1 invested for different rates of interest and different periods of time. Exhibit 5–5 on page 95 is a table of annuity values. The following formula may be used for calculating annuities.

R = amount of each regular payment
i = interest rate per conversion period
n = number of payments during term of annuity or number of conversion periods
S = amount of annuity

$$S = R \times \frac{(1 + i)^n - 1}{i}$$

Values in Exhibit 5–5 are obtained from the preceding formula; therefore, values from the table can be substituted for the formula in the following manner.

$$S = R \times \text{value from Exhibit 5–5}$$

Example: John Jones deposits $50 per month in a savings account paying 6% interest compounded monthly. How much is in the account at the end of 5 years?

50×69.7700 (annuity table – $\frac{1}{2}\%$, 60 periods) = $3,488.50

Example: Bill Smith deposits $100 each quarter in a savings account paying 5% interest compounded quarterly. How much is in the account after 10 years?

100×51.4896 (annuity table – $1\frac{1}{4}\%$, 40 periods) = $5,148.96

Present Value of an Annuity

The present value of an annuity is the amount of money needed to provide payments of a certain amount for a given number of periods at a specified interest rate. If you want to establish a savings account to be used as an education fund, how much must be set aside to provide the desired amount? The following formula can be used to calculate the size of each periodic payment.

$$R = Sn \left(\frac{1}{a\,\overline{n}|\,i} - i \right)$$

Sn = amount needed
i = interest rate per conversion period
n = number of payments
R = periodic payment

Values in Exhibit 5–6 are obtained from the above formula; therefore, values from the table can be substituted for the formula according to the following:

$$R = S \times \text{value from Exhibit 5–6}$$

Example: Bill Smith is 50 years of age. He has decided that when he retires at age 65, his Social Security pension will not pay enough for an adequate income. He wants to establish a savings account now that will provide additional income for 10 years beginning at age 65. He wants the fund to be $18,000 when he begins retirement. How much must be saved each month to obtain this amount? His savings account pays 6% compounded monthly.

$Sn = \$18,000$
$i = 6\%/12 = \frac{1}{2}\%$ (per month)
$n = 15 \times 12 = 180$ (month)
$R = \$18,000 \times 0.00843857 - .005) = 61.89$ per month

Now we can reverse this problem.

> *Example:* Mr. Smith has now reached retirement age and has his $18,000
> fund saved. He has it invested at 6% compounded monthly. How
> much can he withdraw each month if the fund is to last 10 years?
> $i = \frac{1}{2}\%$ per month
> $n = 10 \times 12 = 120$ months
> $R = \$18,000 \times 0.01110205$ (Exhibit 5–6) $= \$199.84$

He will have an income of $199.84 per month to supplement his Social Security
pension.

Finding the Annuity Term

When saving for a specific objective, most families need to save small amounts
on a regular basis. For example, if we know how much we can save each month
and how much will be needed for the future objective, we can determine how
long it will take to save this amount.

> *Example:* Sam Jones wants to establish an educational fund for his 6-year-
> old son. He estimates that it will take $8,000, and that he can
> save and invest $50 per month at 6% interest compounded
> monthly. How long will it take to build this fund?
> $S = \$8,000$
> $R = \$50$
> $i = 6\%/12 = \frac{1}{2}\%$ (month)
> $n =$ number of months required
> $$\frac{8,000}{50} = 160$$

Turn to Exhibit 5–5 on page 95 to the $\frac{1}{2}\%$ column. The 117th period is
158.4752 while the 118th is 160.2676. It would take 118 months or 9 years
and 10 months to accumulate this fund; however, it would be slightly above
$8,000 at this time. Mr. Jones would need to begin the savings account when
his son is eight years old.

> *Example:* Bill and Sara Jones want to buy a home freezer, but they plan to
> save the money before purchasing it. They can put $50 each
> quarter into a savings account that pays 5% compounded quar-
> terly. The freezer costs $225. How long will it take to save this
> amount?
> $S = \$225$
> $R = \$50$
> $i = 5\%/4 = 1\frac{1}{4}\%$ (quarter)
> $$\frac{225}{50} = 4.5 \text{ quarters}$$

Turn to Exhibit 5–5 (to the 1¼% column). The fourth period is 4.0756 and the fifth period is 5.1265. It will take about 4½ quarters or one year and one month to save enough for the freezer.

Computing
Depreciation

Reduction in the value of property due to age, wear, and obsolescence is called "depreciation." As a general rule, used items usually sell for less than when they are new. By determining the depreciation on a piece of property, its book value can be calculated at any time during its life. The three most popular methods of calculating depreciation are (1) straight-line, (2) declining balance or fixed rate, and (3) sum-of-years or declining rate.

The *straight-line* method uses the following formula:

$$\frac{\text{cost} - \text{estimated salvage value at end of useful life}}{\text{estimated years of useful life}}$$

Example: A new car costs $4,250 and is expected to have a trade-in value of $800 after 5 years of use.

$$\frac{\$4,250 - \$800}{5} = \$690 \text{ annual depreciation}$$

The car would decline in value $690 each year or an annual rate of 16.2%.

The *declining balance* or *fixed rate* method uses a set percentage of the preceding year's value. Depreciation will not be the same amount each year as with the straight-line method. The rate stays the same, but the actual dollar amount declines each year. Usually this method is double the rate for the straight-line method, but this is not a requirement.

Example: A car purchased for $4,250 is expected to be used for 5 years before trading. What is the depreciation using the declining balance method?

First, determine the fixed rate by dividing the estimated years of use into 100. Then take this percentage of the remaining value each year to find depreciation for that year.

$$\frac{100}{5} = 20\% = \text{fixed rate}$$

1st year—$4,250 × 20% = $850 depreciation
2nd year—$3,400 × 20% = $680 depreciation
3rd year—$2,720 × 20% = $544 depreciation
4th year—$2,176 × 20% = $435 depreciation
5th year—$1,741 × 20% = $348 depreciation
Trade-in value after 5 years = $1,393

The *sum-of-years* or *declining rate* method uses a decreasing percentage each year of the original cost of the item after an estimate of the salvage or trade-in value has been subtracted. The percentage used will be determined by the number of years the item is to last. For example, an item that will last five years will have 33⅓% depreciation the first year. This percentage is arrived at by adding together the estimated years of life to create a denominator for calculating rates $(1 + 2 + 3 + 4 + 5 = 15)$. Then, in reverse order, each year of life becomes the numerator. Depreciation the first year is $\frac{5}{15}$, the second year $\frac{4}{15}$, the third year $\frac{3}{15}$, the fourth year $\frac{2}{15}$, and the fifth year $\frac{1}{15}$, for a total of $\frac{15}{15}$ or 100%.

> *Example:* A new car costs $4,250 and is expected to have a trade-in value of $800 after 5 years of use. How much will it depreciate each year using the sum-of-years method?
>
> $4,250 − $800 salvage value = $3,450 to be depreciated
> $1 + 2 + 3 + 4 + 5 = 15$ which becomes the denominator
> 1st year depreciation = $\frac{5}{15} = 33.3\% = \$1,150$
> 2nd year depreciation = $\frac{4}{15} = 26.7\% = \$921$
> 3rd year depreciation = $\frac{3}{15} = 20\% = \$690$
> 4th year depreciation = $\frac{2}{15} = 13.3\% = \$458$
> 5th year depreciation = $\frac{1}{15} = 6.7\% = \$231$

Good business management requires the owner of property to calculate depreciation on items that last longer than a year. The federal government allows owners of income property to deduct depreciation as an expense for tax purposes. Theoretically, the owner should be setting aside this amount of money each year to replace the property when it is no longer useful. By keeping a record of depreciation, the owner will know the current value of an item any time during its period of usefulness.

Problems

1. What is the interest on $945 at a rate of 6% for 8 months?
2. Find the rate of interest on $850 when the interest paid is $29.75 for 6 months.
3. Given: rate = 8%, time = 2 years, interest = $240
   Find: principal
4. You trade your old console television for a new one. The difference to be paid in 12 monthly installments at a rate of 6% is $450. What is the actual rate paid?
5. Bob and Jill Smith purchased a $30,000 house and made a down payment of $8,000. They agreed to pay the balance in equal monthly payments for 15 years. The interest rate is 7% compounded monthly. What is the amount of their monthly payments?
6. Find the amount resulting from $90 invested for 6 years at 4%, compounded quarterly.
7. Find the amount resulting from $70 invested for 4 years at 7%, compounded semiannually.

8. If the price of a dozen eggs was 47¢ in 1970 and 52¢ in 1972, what is the price index?

9.

Date	Interest	Withdrawals	Deposits	Balance
10–11			200.	200.
10–18		50.		150.
11–13			75.	225.
11–22		140.		85.
12–06			40.	125.

Compute interest at a rate of 5% in the following ways:
   (a) for the quarter, paying interest on the lowest balance
   (b) on the number of days each balance is maintained
   (c) on the lowest balance for each month

10. Poster Row sold 75 posters during the first week of September, but only 40 during the last week in this month. Show the change as an index number.

11. The Colby family's income for 1967, after income taxes were paid, was $6,450. Their after-tax income for 1972 was $7,675. Did the family's purchasing power increase or decrease?

12. What is the rate of return on a share of stock that costs $78 and pays dividends of $3.50 per share?

appendix

Tables

Exhibit 5–3   How Frequency of Compounding Affects Yield on $1,000 in One Year

Stated rate	When compounded				
	Semiannually	Quarterly	Monthly	Weekly	Daily
3.00%	$30.23	$30.34	$30.42	$30.44	$30.45
3.50	35.31	35.46	35.57	35.61	35.62
4.00	40.40	40.60	40.74	40.79	40.81
4.50	45.51	45.76	45.94	46.00	46.02
5.00	50.63	50.95	51.16	51.25	51.27
5.50	55.76	56.14	56.41	56.51	56.54
6.00	60.90	61.36	61.68	61.80	61.83
6.50	66.06	66.60	66.97	67.12	67.15
7.00	71.23	71.86	72.29	72.46	72.50
7.50	76.41	77.14	77.63	77.83	77.88
8.00	81.60	82.43	83.00	83.22	83.28

Exhibit 5-4   A Compound Interest Table—Total Amount of $1 Invested at Specified Rate for Specified Number of Periods

Periods	½%	1%	1½%	2%	2½%	3%	3½%	4%	4½%	5%	5½%	6%
1	1.005000	1.010000	1.015000	1.020000	1.025000	1.030000	1.035000	1.040000	1.045000	1.050000	1.055000	1.060000
2	1.010025	1.020100	1.030225	1.040400	1.050625	1.060900	1.071225	1.081600	1.092025	1.102500	1.113025	1.123600
3	1.015075	1.030301	1.045678	1.061208	1.076891	1.092727	1.108718	1.124864	1.141166	1.157625	1.174241	1.191016
4	1.020151	1.040604	1.061364	1.082432	1.103813	1.125509	1.147523	1.169859	1.192519	1.215506	1.238825	1.262477
5	1.025251	1.051010	1.077284	1.104081	1.131408	1.159274	1.187686	1.216653	1.246182	1.276282	1.306960	1.338226
6	1.030378	1.061520	1.093443	1.126162	1.159693	1.194052	1.229255	1.265319	1.302260	1.340096	1.378843	1.418519
7	1.035529	1.072135	1.109845	1.148686	1.188686	1.229874	1.272279	1.315932	1.360862	1.407100	1.454679	1.503630
8	1.040707	1.082857	1.126493	1.171659	1.218403	1.266770	1.316809	1.368569	1.422101	1.477455	1.534687	1.593848
9	1.045911	1.093685	1.143390	1.195093	1.248863	1.304773	1.362897	1.423312	1.486095	1.551328	1.619094	1.689479
10	1.051140	1.104622	1.160541	1.218994	1.280085	1.343916	1.410599	1.480244	1.552969	1.628895	1.708144	1.790848
11	1.056396	1.115668	1.177949	1.243374	1.312087	1.384234	1.459970	1.539454	1.622853	1.710339	1.802092	1.898299
12	1.061678	1.126825	1.195618	1.268242	1.344889	1.425761	1.511069	1.601032	1.695881	1.795856	1.901207	2.012196
13	1.066986	1.138093	1.213552	1.293607	1.378511	1.468534	1.563956	1.665074	1.772196	1.885649	2.005774	2.132928
14	1.072321	1.149474	1.231756	1.319479	1.412974	1.512590	1.618695	1.731676	1.851945	1.979932	2.116091	2.260904
15	1.077683	1.160969	1.250232	1.345868	1.448298	1.557967	1.675349	1.800944	1.935282	2.078928	2.232476	2.396558
16	1.083071	1.172579	1.268986	1.372786	1.484506	1.604706	1.733986	1.872981	2.022370	2.182875	2.355263	2.540352
17	1.088487	1.184304	1.288020	1.400241	1.521618	1.652848	1.794676	1.947901	2.113377	2.292018	2.484802	2.692773
18	1.093929	1.196147	1.307341	1.428246	1.559659	1.702433	1.857489	2.025817	2.208479	2.406619	2.621466	2.854339
19	1.099399	1.208109	1.326951	1.456811	1.598650	1.753506	1.922501	2.106849	2.307860	2.526950	2.765647	3.025600
20	1.104896	1.220190	1.346855	1.485947	1.638616	1.806111	1.989789	2.191123	2.411714	2.653298	2.917757	3.207135
21	1.110420	1.232392	1.367058	1.515666	1.679582	1.860295	2.059431	2.278768	2.520241	2.785963	3.078234	3.399564
22	1.115972	1.244716	1.387564	1.545980	1.721571	1.916103	2.131512	2.369919	2.633652	2.925261	3.247537	3.603537
23	1.121552	1.257163	1.408377	1.576899	1.764611	1.973587	2.206114	2.464716	2.752166	3.071524	3.426152	3.819750
24	1.127160	1.269735	1.429503	1.608437	1.808726	2.032794	2.283328	2.563304	2.876014	3.225100	3.614590	4.048935
25	1.132796	1.282432	1.450945	1.640606	1.853944	2.093778	2.363245	2.665836	3.005434	3.386355	3.813392	4.291871

Source: Page 132 from *Business and Consumer Arithmetic* by Milton C. Olson and A. E. McNelly © 1969 by Prentice-Hall, Inc., Englewood Cliffs, N.J. Reprinted by permission.

Exhibit 5–5   Amount of Annuity (when periodic payment is 1)

$$S_{\overline{n}|i} = \frac{(1+i)^n - 1}{i}$$

n	1/2%	13/24%	7/12%	5/8%	2/3%	n
1	1.0000 0000	1.0000 0000	1.0000 0000	1.0000 0000	1.0000 0000	1
2	2.0050 0000	2.0054 1667	2.0058 3333	2.0062 5000	2.0066 6667	2
3	3.0150 2500	3.0162 7934	3.0175 3403	3.0187 8906	3.0200 4444	3
4	4.0301 0012	4.0326 1752	4.0351 3631	4.0376 5649	4.0401 7807	4
5	5.0502 5063	5.0544 6086	5.0586 7460	5.0628 9185	5.0671 1259	5
6	6.0755 0188	6.0818 3919	6.0881 8354	6.0945 3492	6.1008 9335	6
7	7.1058 7939	7.1147 8249	7.1236 9794	7.1326 2576	7.1415 6597	7
8	8.1414 0879	8.1533 2090	8.1652 5285	8.1772 0468	8.1891 7641	8
9	9.1821 1583	9.1974 8472	9.2128 8349	9.2283 1220	9.2437 7092	9
10	10.2280 2641	10.2473 0443	10.2666 2531	10.2859 8916	10.3053 9606	10
11	11.2791 6654	11.3028 1066	11.3265 1396	11.3502 7659	11.3740 9870	11
12	12.3355 6237	12.3640 3422	12.3925 8529	12.4212 1582	12.4499 2602	12
13	13.3972 4018	13.4310 0607	13.4648 7537	13.4988 4842	13.5329 2553	13
14	14.4642 2639	14.5037 5735	14.5434 2048	14.5832 1622	14.6231 4503	14
15	15.5365 4752	15.5823 1937	15.6282 5710	15.6743 6132	15.7206 3267	15
16	16.6142 3026	16.6667 2360	16.7194 2193	16.7723 2608	16.8254 3688	16
17	17.6973 0141	17.7570 0169	17.8169 5189	17.8771 5312	17.9376 0646	17
18	18.7857 8791	18.8531 8544	18.9208 8411	18.9888 8532	19.0571 9051	18
19	19.8797 1685	19.9553 0687	20.0312 5593	20.1075 6586	20.1842 3844	19
20	20.9791 1544	21.0633 9811	21.1481 0493	21.2332 3814	21.3188 0003	20
21	22.0840 1101	22.1774 9152	22.2714 6887	22.3659 4588	22.4609 2537	21
22	23.1944 3107	23.2976 1960	23.4013 8577	23.5057 3304	23.6106 6487	22
23	24.3104 0322	24.4238 1504	24.5378 9386	24.6526 4387	24.7680 6930	23
24	25.4319 5524	25.5561 1070	25.6810 3157	25.8067 2290	25.9331 8976	24
25	26.5591 1502	26.6945 3963	26.8308 3759	26.9680 1492	27.1060 7769	25
26	27.6919 1059	27.8391 3506	27.9873 5081	28.1365 6501	28.2867 8488	26
27	28.8303 7015	28.9899 3037	29.1506 1035	29.3124 1854	29.4753 6344	27
28	29.9745 2200	30.1469 5916	30.3203 5558	30.4956 2116	30.6718 6587	28
29	31.1243 9461	31.3102 5519	31.4975 2607	31.6862 1879	31.8763 4497	29
30	32.2800 1658	32.4798 5241	32.6812 6164	32.8842 5766	33.0888 5394	30
31	33.4414 1666	33.6557 8494	33.8719 0233	34.0897 8427	34.3094 4630	31
32	34.6086 2375	34.8380 8711	35.0694 8843	35.3028 4542	35.5381 7594	32
33	35.7816 6686	36.0267 9341	36.2740 6045	36.5234 8820	36.7750 9711	33
34	36.9605 7520	37.2219 3854	37.4856 5913	37.7517 6000	38.0202 6443	34
35	38.1453 7807	38.4235 5738	38.7043 2548	38.9877 0850	39.2737 3286	35
36	39.3361 0496	39.6316 8498	39.9301 0071	40.2313 8168	40.5355 5774	36
37	40.5327 8549	40.8463 5661	41.1630 2630	41.4828 2782	41.8057 9479	37
38	41.7354 4942	42.0676 0771	42.4031 4395	42.7420 9549	43.0845 0009	38
39	42.9441 2666	43.2954 7391	43.6504 9562	44.0092 3359	44.3717 3009	39
40	44.1588 4730	44.5299 9106	44.9051 2352	45.2842 9130	45.6675 4163	40
41	45.3796 4153	45.7711 9518	46.1670 7007	46.5673 1812	46.9719 9191	41
42	46.6065 3974	47.0191 2249	47.4363 7798	47.8583 6386	48.2851 3852	42
43	47.8395 7244	48.2738 0940	48.7130 9018	49.1574 7863	49.6070 3944	43
44	49.0787 7030	49.5352 9254	49.9972 4988	50.4647 1287	50.9377 5304	44
45	50.3241 6415	50.8036 0871	51.2889 0050	51.7801 1733	52.2773 3806	45
46	51.5757 8497	52.0787 9492	52.5880 8575	53.1037 4306	53.6258 5365	46
47	52.8336 6390	53.3608 8839	53.8948 4959	54.4356 4146	54.9833 5934	47
48	54.0978 3222	54.6499 2654	55.2092 3621	55.7758 6421	56.3499 1507	48
49	55.3683 2138	55.9459 4697	56.5312 9009	57.1244 6337	57.7255 8117	49
50	56.6451 6299	57.2489 8752	57.8610 5595	58.4814 9126	59.1104 1837	50

Exhibit 5–5 (*cont.*)

$$S_{\overline{n}|i} = \frac{(1 + i)^n - 1}{i}$$

n	1/2%	13/24%	7/12%	5/8%	2/3%	n
51	57.9283 8880	58.5590 8620	59.1985 7877	59.8470 0058	60.5044 8783	51
52	59.2180 3075	59.8762 8125	60.5439 0381	61.2210 4434	61.9078 5108	52
53	60.5141 2090	61.2006 1111	61.8970 7659	62.6036 7586	63.3205 7009	53
54	61.8166 9150	62.5321 1442	63.2581 4287	63.9949 4884	64.7427 0722	54
55	63.1257 7496	63.8708 3004	64.6271 4870	65.3949 1727	66.1743 2527	55
56	64.4414 0384	65.2167 9703	66.0041 4040	66.8036 3550	67.6154 8744	56
57	65.7636 1086	66.5700 5469	67.3891 6455	68.2211 5822	69.0662 5736	57
58	67.0924 2891	67.9306 4248	68.7822 6801	69.6475 4046	70.5266 9907	58
59	68.4278 9105	69.2986 0013	70.1834 9791	71.0828 3759	71.9968 7706	59
60	69.7700 3051	70.6739 6755	71.5929 0165	72.5271 0532	73.4768 5625	60
61	71.1188 8066	72.0567 8487	73.0105 2691	73.9803 9973	74.9667 0195	61
62	72.4744 7507	73.4470 9245	74.4364 2165	75.4427 7723	76.4664 7997	62
63	73.8368 4744	74.8449 3087	75.8706 3411	76.9142 9459	77.9762 5650	63
64	75.2060 3168	76.2503 4091	77.3132 1281	78.3950 0893	79.4960 9821	64
65	76.5820 6184	77.6633 6359	78.7642 0655	79.8849 7774	81.0260 7220	65
66	77.9649 7215	79.0840 4015	80.2236 6442	81.3842 5885	82.5662 4601	66
67	79.3547 9701	80.5124 1203	81.6916 3580	82.8929 1046	84.1166 8765	67
68	80.7515 7099	81.9485 2093	83.1681 7034	84.4109 9115	85.6774 6557	68
69	82.1553 2885	83.3924 0875	84.6533 1800	85.9385 5985	87.2486 4867	69
70	83.5661 0549	84.8441 1763	86.1471 2902	87.4756 7585	88.8303 0633	70
71	84.9839 3602	86.3036 8994	87.6496 5394	89.0223 9882	90.4224 0857	71
72	86.4088 5570	87.7711 6826	89.1609 4359	90.5787 8882	92.0253 2510	72
73	87.8408 9998	89.2465 9542	90.6810 4909	92.1449 0625	93.6388 2726	73
74	89.2801 0448	90.7300 1448	92.2100 2188	93.7208 1191	95.2630 8611	74
75	90.7265 0500	92.2214 6872	93.7479 1367	95.3065 6698	96.8981 7335	75
76	92.1801 3752	93.7210 0168	95.2947 7650	96.9022 3303	98.5441 6118	76
77	93.6410 3821	95.2286 5710	96.8506 6270	98.5078 7198	100.2011 2225	77
78	95.1092 4340	96.7444 7900	98.4156 2490	100.1235 4618	101.8691 2973	78
79	96.5847 8962	98.2685 1159	99.9897 1604	101.7493 1835	103.5482 5726	79
80	98.0677 1357	99.8007 9936	101.5729 8939	103.3852 5159	105.2385 7898	80
81	99.5580 5214	101.3413 8702	103.1654 9849	105.0314 0941	106.9401 6950	81
82	101.0558 4240	102.8903 1954	104.7672 9723	106.6878 5572	108.6531 0397	82
83	102.5611 2161	104.4476 4210	106.3784 3980	108.3546 5482	110.3774 5799	83
84	104.0739 2722	106.0134 0016	107.9989 8070	110.0318 7141	112.1133 0771	84
85	105.5942 9685	107.5876 3941	109.6289 7475	111.7195 7061	113.8607 2977	85
86	107.1222 6834	109.1704 0579	111.2684 7710	113.4178 1792	115.6198 0130	86
87	108.6578 7968	110.7617 4549	112.9175 4322	115.1266 7928	117.3905 9997	87
88	110.2011 6908	112.3617 0495	114.5762 2889	116.8362 2103	119.1732 0397	88
89	111.7521 7492	113.9703 3085	116.2445 9022	118.5765 0991	120.9676 9200	89
90	113.3109 3580	115.5876 7014	117.9226 8367	120.3176 1310	122.7741 4328	90
91	114.8774 9048	117.2137 7002	119.6105 6599	122.0695 9818	124.5926 3757	91
92	116.4518 7793	118.8486 7794	121.3082 9429	123.8325 3317	126.4232 5515	92
93	118.0341 3732	120.4924 4161	123.0159 2601	125.6064 8650	128.2660 7685	93
94	119.6243 0800	122.1451 0901	124.7335 1891	127.3915 2704	130.1211 8403	94
95	121.2224 2954	123.8067 2835	126.4611 3110	129.1877 2408	131.9886 5859	95
96	122.8285 4169	125.4773 4812	128.1988 2103	130.9951 4736	133.8685 8298	96
97	124.4426 8440	127.1570 1709	129.9466 4749	132.8138 6703	135.7610 4020	97
98	126.0648 9782	128.8457 8427	131.7046 6960	134.6439 5370	137.6661 1380	98
99	127.6952 2231	130.5436 9893	133.4729 4684	136.4854 7841	139.5838 8790	99
100	129.3336 9842	132.2508 1064	135.2515 3903	138.3385 1265	141.5144 4715	100

Exhibit 5–5 (cont.)

$$S_{\overline{n}|i} = \frac{(1+i)^n - 1}{i}$$

n	1/2%	13/24%	7/12%	5/8%	2/3%	n
101	130.9803 6692	133.9671 6919	137.0405 0634	140.2031 2836	143.4578 7680	101
102	132.6352 6875	135.6928 2469	138.8399 0929	142.0793 9791	145.4142 6264	102
103	134.2984 4509	137.4278 2750	140.6498 0877	143.9673 9414	147.3836 9106	103
104	135.9699 3732	139.1722 2823	142.4702 6598	145.8671 9036	149.3662 4900	104
105	137.6497 8701	140.9260 7780	144.3013 4253	147.7788 6030	151.3620 2399	105
106	139.3380 3594	142.6894 2738	146.1431 0037	149.7024 7817	153.3711 0415	106
107	141.0347 2612	144.4623 2845	147.9956 0178	151.6381 1866	155.3935 7818	107
108	142.7398 9975	146.2448 3273	149.8589 0946	153.5858 5690	157.4295 3537	108
109	144.4535 9925	148.0369 9224	151.7330 8643	155.5457 6851	159.4790 6560	109
110	146.1758 6725	149.8388 5928	153.6181 9610	157.5179 2956	161.5422 5937	110
111	147.9067 4658	151.6504 8644	155.5143 0225	159.5024 1662	163.6192 0777	111
112	149.6462 8032	153.4719 2657	157.4214 6901	161.4993 0673	165.7100 0249	112
113	151.3945 1172	155.3032 3284	159.3397 6091	163.5086 7739	167.8147 3584	113
114	153.1514 8428	157.1444 5868	161.2692 4285	165.5306 0663	169.9335 0074	114
115	154.9172 4170	158.9956 5783	163.2099 8010	167.5651 7292	172.0663 9075	115
116	156.6918 2791	160.8568 8431	165.1620 3832	169.6124 5525	174.2135 0002	116
117	158.4752 8704	162.7281 9244	167.1254 8354	171.6725 3310	176.3749 2335	117
118	160.2676 6348	164.6096 3681	169.1003 8220	173.7454 8643	178.5507 5618	118
119	162.0690 0180	166.5012 7235	171.0868 0109	175.8313 9572	180.7410 9455	119
120	163.8793 4681	168.4031 5424	173.0848 0743	177.9303 4194	182.9460 3518	120

n	1 1/4%	1 3/8%	1 1/2%	1 5/8%	n
1	1.0000 0000	1.0000 0000	1.0000 0000	1.0000 0000	1
2	2.0125 0000	2.0137 5000	2.0150 0000	2.0162 5000	2
3	3.0376 5625	3.0414 3906	3.0452 2500	3.0490 1406	3
4	4.0756 2695	4.0832 5885	4.0909 0338	4.0985 6054	4
5	5.1265 7229	5.1394 0366	5.1522 6693	5.1651 6215	5
6	6.1906 5444	6.2100 7046	6.2295 5093	6.2490 9603	6
7	7.2680 3762	7.2954 5893	7.3229 9419	7.3506 4385	7
8	8.3588 8809	8.3957 7149	8.4328 3911	8.4700 9181	8
9	9.4633 7420	9.5112 1335	9.5593 3169	9.6077 3080	9
10	10.5816 6637	10.6419 9253	10.7027 2167	10.7638 5643	10
11	11.7139 3720	11.7883 1993	11.8632 6249	11.9387 6909	11
12	12.8603 6142	12.9504 0933	13.0412 1143	13.1327 7409	12
13	14.0211 1594	14.1284 7745	14.2368 2960	14.3461 8167	13
14	15.1963 7988	15.3227 4402	15.4503 8205	15.5793 0712	14
15	16.3863 3463	16.5334 3175	16.6821 3778	16.8324 7086	15
16	17.5911 6382	17.7607 6644	17.9323 6984	18.1059 9851	16
17	18.8110 5336	19.0049 7697	19.2013 5539	19.4002 2099	17
18	20.0461 9153	20.2662 9541	20.4893 7572	20.7154 7458	18
19	21.2967 6893	21.5449 5697	21.7967 1636	22.0521 0104	19
20	22.5629 7854	22.8412 0013	23.1236 6710	23.4104 4768	20
21	23.8450 1577	24.1552 6663	24.4705 2211	24.7908 6746	21
22	25.1430 7847	25.4874 0155	25.8375 7994	26.1937 1905	22
23	26.4573 6695	26.8378 5332	27.2251 4364	27.6193 6699	23
24	27.7880 8403	28.2068 7380	28.6335 2080	29.0681 8170	24
25	29.1354 3508	29.5947 1832	30.0630 2361	30.5405 3966	25

Exhibit 5–5 (*cont.*)

$$S_{\overline{n}|i} = \frac{(1 + i)^n - 1}{i}$$

n	1 1/4%	1 3/8%	1 1/2%	1 5/8%	n
26	30.4996 2802	31.0016 4569	31.5139 6896	32.0368 2343	26
27	31.8808 7337	32.4279 1832	32.9866 7850	33.5574 2181	27
28	33.2793 8429	33.8738 0220	34.4814 7867	35.1027 2991	28
29	34.6953 7659	35.3395 6698	35.9987 0085	36.6731 4927	29
30	36.1290 6880	36.8254 8602	37.5386 8137	38.2690 8795	30
31	37.5806 8216	38.3318 3646	39.1017 6159	39.8909 6063	31
32	39.0504 4069	39.8588 9921	40.6882 8801	41.5391 8874	32
33	40.5385 7120	41.4069 5907	42.2986 1233	43.2142 0055	33
34	42.0453 0334	42.9763 0476	43.9330 9152	44.9164 3131	34
35	43.5708 6963	44.5672 2895	45.5920 8789	46.6463 2332	35
36	45.1155 0550	46.1800 2835	47.2759 6921	48.4043 2608	36
37	46.6794 4932	47.8150 0374	48.9851 0874	50.1908 9637	37
38	48.2629 4243	49.4724 6004	50.7198 8538	52.0064 9844	38
39	49.8662 2921	51.1527 0636	52.4806 8366	53.8516 0404	39
40	51.4895 5708	52.8560 5608	54.2678 9391	55.7266 9261	40
41	53.1331 7654	54.5828 2685	56.0819 1232	57.6322 5136	41
42	54.7973 4125	56.3333 4072	57.9231 4100	59.5687 7544	42
43	56.4823 0801	58.1079 2415	59.7919 8812	61.5367 6805	43
44	58.1883 3686	59.9069 0811	61.6888 6794	63.5367 4053	44
45	59.9156 9108	61.7306 2810	63.6142 0096	65.5692 1256	45
46	61.6646 3721	63.5794 2423	65.5684 1398	67.6347 1226	46
47	63.4354 4518	65.4536 4131	67.5519 4018	69.7337 7634	47
48	65.2283 8824	67.3536 2888	69.5652 1929	71.8669 5020	48
49	67.0437 4310	69.2797 4128	71.6086 9758	74.0347 8814	49
50	68.8817 8989	71.2323 3772	73.6828 2804	76.2378 5345	50

Source: Charles H. Gushee, *Financial Compound Interest and Annuity Tables* (Boston: Financial Publishing Co., 1970). Reprinted by permission.

Exhibit 5–6   *Periodic Payment* (*when present value of annuity is 1*)

$$\frac{1}{a_{\overline{n}|i}} = \frac{i}{1 - (1 + i)^{-n}} \quad \text{Note:} \quad \frac{1}{S_{\overline{n}|i}} = \frac{1}{a_{\overline{n}|i}} - i$$

n	1/2%	13/24%	7/12%	5/8%	2/3%	n
1	1.0050 0000	1.0054 1667	1.0058 3333	1.0062 5000	1.0066 6667	1
2	0.5037 5312	0.5040 6616	0.5043 7924	0.5046 9237	0.5050 0554	2
3	0.3366 7221	0.3369 5095	0.3372 2976	0.3375 0865	0.3377 8762	3
4	0.2531 3279	0.2533 9457	0.2536 5644	0.2539 1842	0.2541 8051	4
5	0.2030 0997	0.2032 6170	0.2035 1357	0.2037 6558	0.2040 1772	5
6	0.1695 9546	0.1698 4061	0.1700 8594	0.1703 3143	0.1705 7709	6
7	0.1457 2843	0.1459 6910	0.1462 0986	0.1464 5082	0.1466 9198	7
8	0.1278 2886	0.1280 6608	0.1283 0351	0.1285 4118	0.1287 7907	8
9	0.1139 0736	0.1141 4204	0.1143 7698	0.1146 1218	0.1148 4763	9
10	0.1027 7057	0.1030 0331	0.1032 3632	0.1034 6963	0.1037 0321	10
11	0.0936 5903	0.0938 9024	0.0941 2175	0.0943 5358	0.0945 8572	11
12	0.0860 6643	0.0862 9642	0.0865 2675	0.0867 5742	0.0869 8843	12
13	0.0796 4224	0.0798 7125	0.0801 0064	0.0803 3039	0.0805 6052	13
14	0.0741 3609	0.0743 6432	0.0745 9295	0.0748 2198	0.0750 5141	14
15	0.0693 6436	0.0695 9197	0.0693 1999	0.0700 4845	0.0702 7734	15

Exhibit 5–6 (*cont.*)

$$\frac{1}{a_{\overline{n}|i}} = \frac{i}{1-(1+i)^{-n}} \quad \text{Note: } \frac{1}{S_{\overline{n}|i}} = \frac{1}{a_{\overline{n}|i}} - i$$

n	1/2%	13/24%	7/12%	5/8%	2/3%	n
16	0.0651 8937	0.0654 1646	0.0656 4401	0.0658 7202	0.0661 0049	16
17	0.0615 0579	0.0617 3248	0.0619 5966	0.0621 8732	0.0624 1546	17
18	0.0582 3173	0.0584 5810	0.0586 8499	0.0589 1239	0.0591 4030	18
19	0.0553 0253	0.0555 2865	0.0557 5532	0.0559 8252	0.0562 1027	19
20	0.0526 6645	0.0528 9239	0.0531 1889	0.0533 4597	0.0535 7362	20
21	0.0502 8163	0.0505 0743	0.0507 3383	0.0509 6083	0.0511 8843	21
22	0.0481 1380	0.0483 3951	0.0485 6585	0.0487 9281	0.0490 2041	22
23	0.0461 3465	0.0463 6031	0.0465 8663	0.0468 1360	0.0470 4123	23
24	0.0443 2061	0.0445 4625	0.0447 7258	0.0449 9959	0.0452 2729	24
25	0.0426 5186	0.0428 7751	0.0431 0388	0.0433 3096	0.0435 5876	25
26	0.0411 1163	0.0413 3732	0.0415 6376	0.0417 9094	0.0420 1886	26
27	0.0396 8565	0.0399 1140	0.0401 3793	0.0403 6523	0.0405 9331	27
28	0.0383 6167	0.0385 8751	0.0388 1415	0.0390 4159	0.0392 6983	28
29	0.0371 2914	0.0373 5508	0.0375 8186	0.0378 0946	0.0380 3789	29
30	0.0359 7892	0.0362 0498	0.0364 3191	0.0366 5969	0.0368 8832	30
31	0.0349 0304	0.0351 2924	0.0353 5633	0.0355 8430	0.0358 1316	31
32	0.0338 9453	0.0341 2088	0.0343 4815	0.0345 7633	0.0348 0542	32
33	0.0329 4727	0.0331 7379	0.0334 0124	0.0336 2964	0.0338 5898	33
34	0.0320 5586	0.0322 8254	0.0325 1020	0.0327 3883	0.0329 6843	34
35	0.0312 1550	0.0314 4237	0.0316 7024	0.0318 9911	0.0321 2898	35
36	0.0304 2194	0.0306 4900	0.0308 7710	0.0311 0622	0.0313 3637	36
37	0.0296 7139	0.0298 9865	0.0301 2698	0.0303 5636	0.0305 8680	37
38	0.0298 6045	0.0291 8793	0.0294 1649	0.0296 4614	0.0298 7687	38
39	0.0282 8607	0.0285 1377	0.0287 4258	0.0289 7250	0.0292 0354	39
40	0.0276 4552	0.0278 7344	0.0281 0251	0.0283 3271	0.0285 6406	40
41	0.0270 3631	0.0272 6447	0.0274 9379	0.0277 2429	0.0279 5595	41
42	0.0264 5622	0.0266 8461	0.0269 1420	0.0271 4499	0.0273 7697	42
43	0.0259 0320	0.0261 3183	0.0263 6170	0.0265 9278	0.0268 2510	43
44	0.0253 7541	0.0256 0429	0.0258 3443	0.0260 6583	0.0262 9847	44
45	0.0248 7117	0.0251 0031	0.0253 3073	0.0255 6243	0.0257 9541	45
46	0.0243 8894	0.0246 1834	0.0248 4905	0.0250 8106	0.0253 1439	46
47	0.0239 2733	0.0241 5698	0.0243 8798	0.0246 2032	0.0248 5399	47
48	0.0234 8503	0.0237 1495	0.0239 4624	0.0241 7890	0.0244 1292	48
49	0.0230 6087	0.0232 9106	0.0235 2265	0.0237 5563	0.0239 9001	49
50	0.0226 5376	0.0228 8422	0.0231 1612	0.0233 4943	0.0235 8416	50
51	0.0222 6269	0.0224 9344	0.0227 2563	0.0229 5928	0.0231 9437	51
52	0.0218 8675	0.0221 1777	0.0223 5027	0.0225 8425	0.0228 1971	52
53	0.0215 2507	0.0217 5637	0.0219 8919	0.0222 2350	0.0224 5932	53
54	0.0211 7686	0.0214 0845	0.0216 4157	0.0218 7623	0.0221 1242	54
55	0.0208 4139	0.0210 7327	0.0213 0671	0.0215 4171	0.0217 7827	55
56	0.0205 1797	0.0207 5014	0.0209 8390	0.0212 1925	0.0214 5618	56
57	0.0202 0598	0.0204 3844	0.0206 7251	0.0209 0821	0.0211 4552	57
58	0.0199 0481	0.0201 3756	0.0203 7196	0.0206 0801	0.0208 4569	58
59	0.0196 1392	0.0198 4697	0.0200 8170	0.0203 1809	0.0205 5616	59
60	0.0193 3280	0.0195 6615	0.0198 0120	0.0200 3795	0.0202 7639	60
61	0.0190 6096	0.0192 9461	0.0195 2999	0.0197 6709	0.0200 0592	61
62	0.0187 9796	0.0190 3191	0.0192 6762	0.0195 0508	0.0197 4429	62
63	0.0185 4337	0.0187 7762	0.0190 1366	0.0192 5148	0.0194 9108	63
64	0.0182 9681	0.0185 3136	0.0187 6773	0.0190 0591	0.0192 4590	64
65	0.0180 5789	0.0182 9275	0.0185 2946	0.0187 6800	0.0190 0837	65

Exhibit 5–6 (cont.)

$$\frac{1}{a_{\overline{n}|i}} = \frac{i}{1 - (1 + i)^{-n}} \quad \text{Note: } \frac{1}{s_{\overline{n}|i}} = \frac{1}{a_{\overline{n}|i}} - i$$

n	1/2%	13/24%	7/12%	5/8%	2/3%	n
66	0.0178 2627	0.0180 6144	0.0182 9848	0.0185 3739	0.0187 7815	66
67	0.0176 0163	0.0178 3711	0.0180 7449	0.0183 1376	0.0185 5491	67
68	0.0173 8366	0.0176 1945	0.0178 5716	0.0180 9680	0.0183 3835	68
69	0.0171 7206	0.0174 0817	0.0176 4622	0.0178 8622	0.0181 2816	69
70	0.0169 6657	0.0172 0299	0.0174 4138	0.0176 8175	0.0179 2409	70
71	0.0167 6693	0.0170 0366	0.0172 4239	0.0174 8313	0.0177 2586	71
72	0.0165 7289	0.0168 0993	0.0170 4901	0.0172 9011	0.0175 3324	72
73	0.0163 8422	0.0166 2158	0.0168 6100	0.0171 0247	0.0173 4600	73
74	0.0162 0070	0.0164 3838	0.0166 7814	0.0169 1999	0.0171 6391	74
75	0.0160 2214	0.0162 6013	0.0165 0024	0.0167 4246	0.0169 8678	75
76	0.0158 4832	0.0160 8663	0.0163 2709	0.0165 6968	0.0168 1440	76
77	0.0156 7908	0.0159 1771	0.0161 5851	0.0164 0147	0.0166 4659	77
78	0.0155 1423	0.0157 5317	0.0159 9432	0.0162 3766	0.0164 8318	78
79	0.0153 5360	0.0155 9287	0.0158 3436	0.0160 7808	0.0163 2400	79
80	0.0151 9704	0.0154 3663	0.0156 7847	0.0159 2256	0.0161 6889	80
81	0.0150 4439	0.0152 8430	0.0155 2650	0.0157 7096	0.0160 1769	81
82	0.0148 9552	0.0151 3575	0.0153 7830	0.0156 2314	0.0158 7027	82
83	0.0147 5028	0.0149 9084	0.0152 3373	0.0154 7895	0.0157 2649	83
84	0.0146 0855	0.0148 4944	0.0150 9268	0.0153 3828	0.0155 8621	84
85	0.0144 7021	0.0147 1141	0.0149 5501	0.0152 0098	0.0154 4933	85
86	0.0143 3513	0.0145 7666	0.0148 2060	0.0150 6696	0.0153 1570	86
87	0.0142 0320	0.0144 4505	0.0146 8935	0.0149 3608	0.0151 8524	87
88	0.0140 7431	0.0143 1650	0.0145 6115	0.0148 0826	0.0150 5781	88
89	0.0139 4837	0.0141 9088	0.0144 3588	0.0146 8337	0.0149 3334	89
90	0.0138 2527	0.0140 6811	0.0143 1347	0.0145 6134	0.0148 1170	90
91	0.0137 0493	0.0139 4809	0.0141 9380	0.0144 4205	0.0146 9282	91
92	0.0135 8724	0.0138 3073	0.0140 7679	0.0143 2542	0.0145 7660	92
93	0.0134 7213	0.0137 1594	0.0139 6236	0.0142 1137	0.0144 6296	93
94	0.0135 5950	0.0136 0365	0.0138 5042	0.0140 9982	0.0143 5181	94
95	0.0132 4930	0.0134 9377	0.0137 4090	0.0139 9067	0.0142 4308	95
96	0.0131 4143	0.0133 8623	0.0136 3372	0.0138 8387	0.0141 3668	96
97	0.0130 3583	0.0132 8096	0.0135 2880	0.0137 7933	0.0140 3255	97
98	0.0129 3242	0.0131 7788	0.0134 2608	0.0136 7700	0.0139 3062	98
99	0.0128 3115	0.0130 7694	0.0133 2549	0.0135 7679	0.0138 3082	99
100	0.0127 3194	0.0129 7806	0.0132 2696	0.0134 7864	0.0137 3308	100
101	0.0126 3473	0.0128 8118	0.0131 3045	0.0133 8251	0.0136 3735	101
102	0.0125 3947	0.0127 8625	0.0130 3587	0.0132 8832	0.0135 4357	102
103	0.0124 4610	0.0126 9321	0.0129 4319	0.0131 9602	0.0134 5168	103
104	0.0123 5457	0.0126 0201	0.0128 5234	0.0131 0555	0.0133 6162	104
105	0.0122 6481	0.0125 1259	0.0127 6328	0.0130 1687	0.0132 7334	105
106	0.0121 7679	0.0124 2489	0.0126 7594	0.0129 2992	0.0131 8680	106
107	0.0120 9045	0.0123 3889	0.0125 9029	0.0128 4465	0.0131 0194	107
108	0.0120 0575	0.0122 5452	0.0125 0628	0.0127 6102	0.0130 1871	108
109	0.0119 2264	0.0121 7174	0.0124 2385	0.0126 7898	0.0129 3708	109
110	0.0118 4107	0.0120 9050	0.0123 4298	0.0125 9848	0.0128 5700	110
111	0.0117 6102	0.0120 1078	0.0122 6361	0.0125 1950	0.0127 7842	111
112	0.0116 8242	0.0119 3252	0.0121 8571	0.0124 4198	0.0127 0131	112
113	0.0116 0526	0.0118 5568	0.0121 0923	0.0123 6588	0.0126 2562	113
114	0.0115 2948	0.0117 8024	0.0120 3414	0.0122 9118	0.0125 5132	114
115	0.0114 5506	0.0117 0615	0.0119 6041	0.0122 1783	0.0124 7838	115

Exhibit 5–6 (cont.)

$$\frac{1}{a_{\overline{n}|i}} = \frac{i}{1 - (1 + i)^{-n}} \quad \text{Note: } \frac{1}{S_{\overline{n}|i}} = \frac{1}{a_{\overline{n}|i}} - i$$

n	1/2%	13/24%	7/12%	5/8%	2/3%	n
116	0.0113 8195	0.0116 3337	0.0118 8799	0.0121 4579	0.0124 0675	116
117	0.0113 1013	0.0115 6188	0.0118 1686	0.0120 7504	0.0123 3641	117
118	0.0112 3956	0.0114 9165	0.0117 4698	0.0120 0555	0.0122 6732	118
119	0.0111 7021	0.0114 2263	0.0116 7832	0.0119 3727	0.0121 9944	119
120	0.0111 0205	0.0113 5480	0.0116 1085	0.0118 7018	0.0121 3276	120
121	0.0110 3505	0.0112 8813	0.0115 4454	0.0118 0425	0.0120 6724	121
122	0.0109 6918	0.0112 2259	0.0114 7936	0.0117 3945	0.0120 0284	122
123	0.0109 0441	0.0111 5816	0.0114 1528	0.0116 7575	0.0119 3955	123
124	0.0108 4072	0.0110 9480	0.0113 5228	0.0116 1313	0.0118 7734	124
125	0.0107 7808	0.0110 3249	0.0112 9033	0.0115 5157	0.0118 1618	125
126	0.0107 1647	0.0109 7121	0.0112 2941	0.0114 9102	0.0117 5604	126
127	0.0106 5586	0.0109 1093	0.0111 6948	0.0114 3148	0.0116 9690	127
128	0.0105 9623	0.0108 5163	0.0111 1054	0.0113 7292	0.0116 3875	128
129	0.0105 3755	0.0107 9329	0.0110 5255	0.0113 1531	0.0115 8154	129
130	0.0104 7981	0.0107 3588	0.0109 9550	0.0112 5864	0.0115 2527	130
131	0.0104 2298	0.0106 7938	0.0109 3935	0.0112 0288	0.0114 6992	131
132	0.0103 6703	0.0106 2377	0.0108 8410	0.0111 4800	0.0114 1545	132
133	0.0103 1197	0.0105 6903	0.0108 2972	0.0110 9400	0.0113 6185	133
134	0.0102 5775	0.0105 1514	0.0107 7619	0.0110 4086	0.0113 0910	134
135	0.0102 0436	0.0104 6209	0.0107 2349	0.0109 8854	0.0112 5719	135
136	0.0101 5179	0.0104 0985	0.0106 7161	0.0109 3703	0.0112 0609	136
137	0.0101 0002	0.0103 5841	0.0106 2052	0.0108 8633	0.0111 5578	137
138	0.0100 4902	0.0103 0774	0.0105 7021	0.0108 3640	0.0111 0625	138
139	0.0099 9879	0.0102 5784	0.0105 2067	0.0107 8723	0.0110 5749	139
140	0.0099 4930	0.0102 0869	0.0104 7187	0.0107 3881	0.0110 0947	140
141	0.0099 0055	0.0101 6026	0.0104 2380	0.0106 9111	0.0109 6218	141
142	0.0098 5250	0.0101 1255	0.0103 7644	0.0106 4414	0.0109 1560	142
143	0.0098 0516	0.0100 6554	0.0103 2978	0.0105 9786	0.0108 6972	143
144	0.0097 5850	0.0100 1921	0.0102 8381	0.0105 5226	0.0108 2453	144
145	0.0097 1252	0.0099 7355	0.0102 3851	0.0105 0734	0.0107 8000	145
146	0.0096 6718	0.0099 2855	0.0101 9386	0.0104 6307	0.0107 3613	146
147	0.0096 2250	0.0098 8420	0.0101 4986	0.0104 1944	0.0106 9291	147
148	0.0095 7844	0.0098 4047	0.0101 0649	0.0103 7645	0.0106 5031	148
149	0.0095 3500	0.0097 9736	0.0100 6374	0.0103 3407	0.0106 0833	149
150	0.0094 9217	0.0097 5486	0.0100 2159	0.0102 9230	0.0105 6695	150
151	0.0094 4993	0.0097 1295	0.0099 8003	0.0102 5112	0.0105 2617	151
152	0.0094 0827	0.0096 7162	0.0099 3905	0.0102 1052	0.0104 8597	152
153	0.0093 6719	0.0096 3087	0.0098 9865	0.0101 7049	0.0104 4633	153
154	0.0093 2666	0.0095 9067	0.0098 5880	0.0101 3102	0.0104 0726	154
155	0.0092 8668	0.0095 5102	0.0098 1950	0.0100 9209	0.0103 6873	155
156	0.0092 4723	0.0095 1190	0.0097 8074	0.0100 5370	0.0103 3074	156
157	0.0092 0832	0.0094 7332	0.0097 4251	0.0100 1584	0.0102 9327	157
158	0.0091 6992	0.0094 3525	0.0097 0479	0.0099 7850	0.0102 5632	158
159	0.0091 3203	0.0093 9768	0.0096 6758	0.0099 4166	0.0102 1988	159
160	0.0090 9464	0.0093 6062	0.0096 3087	0.0099 0532	0.0101 8394	160
161	0.0090 5773	0.0093 2404	0.0095 9464	0.0098 6947	0.0101 5858	161
162	0.0090 2131	0.0092 8795	0.0095 5890	0.0098 3410	0.0101 1350	162
163	0.0089 8536	0.0092 5232	0.0095 2362	0.0097 9919	0.0100 7899	163
164	0.0089 4987	0.0092 1716	0.0094 8881	0.0097 6475	0.0100 4494	164
165	0.0089 1483	0.0091 8245	0.0094 5445	0.0097 3076	0.0100 1134	165

Exhibit 5–6 (*cont.*)

$$\frac{1}{a_{\overline{n}|i}} = \frac{i}{1 - (1 + i)^{-n}} \quad \text{Note:} \frac{1}{S_{\overline{n}|i}} = \frac{1}{a_{\overline{n}|i}} - i$$

n	1/2%	13/24%	7/12%	5/8%	2/3%	n
166	0.0088 8024	0.0091 4819	0.0094 2053	0.0096 9722	0.0099 7819	166
167	0.0088 4608	0.0091 1436	0.0093 8705	0.0096 6411	0.0099 4547	167
168	0.0088 1236	0.0090 8096	0.0093 5401	0.0096 3143	0.0099 1318	168
169	0.0087 7906	0.0090 4798	0.0093 2138	0.0095 9918	0.0098 8131	169
170	0.0087 4617	0.0090 1542	0.0092 8917	0.0095 6733	0.0098 4986	170
171	0.0087 1369	0.0089 8327	0.0092 5736	0.0095 3589	0.0098 1881	171
172	0.0086 8161	0.0089 5151	0.0092 2595	0.0095 0486	0.0097 8816	172
173	0.0086 4992	0.0089 2015	0.0091 9494	0.0094 7421	0.0097 5791	173
174	0.0086 1862	0.0088 8918	0.0091 6431	0.0094 4395	0.0097 2803	174
175	0.0085 8770	0.0088 5858	0.0091 3406	0.0094 1407	0.0096 9854	175
176	0.0085 5715	0.0088 2836	0.0091 0418	0.0093 8456	0.0096 6942	176
177	0.0085 2697	0.0087 9850	0.0090 7468	0.0093 5542	0.0096 4066	177
178	0.0084 9715	0.0087 6901	0.0090 4553	0.0093 2664	0.0096 1226	178
179	0.0084 6768	0.0087 3987	0.0090 1673	0.0092 9821	0.0095 8422	179
180	0.0084 3857	0.0087 1107	0.0089 8828	0.0092 7012	0.0095 5652	180
181	0.0084 0979	0.0086 8262	0.0089 6018	0.0092 4238	0.0095 2917	181
182	0.0083 8136	0.0086 5451	0.0089 3241	0.0092 1498	0.0095 0215	182
183	0.0083 5352	0.0086 2673	0.0089 0497	0.0091 8791	0.0094 7546	183
184	0.0083 2547	0.0085 9927	0.0088 7786	0.0091 6116	0.0094 4909	184
185	0.0082 9802	0.0085 7214	0.0088 5107	0.0091 3473	0.0094 2305	185
186	0.0082 7038	0.0085 4532	0.0088 2459	0.0091 0862	0.0093 9732	186
187	0.0082 4404	0.0085 1881	0.0087 9843	0.0090 8282	0.0093 7189	187
188	0.0082 1752	0.0084 9261	0.0087 7257	0.0090 5732	0.0093 4678	188
189	0.0081 9129	0.0084 6670	0.0087 4701	0.0090 3212	0.0093 2196	189
190	0.0081 6537	0.0084 4110	0.0087 2174	0.0090 0722	0.0092 9743	190
191	0.0081 3973	0.0084 1578	0.0086 9677	0.0089 8260	0.0092 7320	191
192	0.0081 1438	0.0083 9075	0.0086 7208	0.0089 5828	0.0092 4925	192
193	0.0080 8931	0.0083 6601	0.0086 4767	0.0089 3423	0.0092 2558	193
194	0.0080 6452	0.0083 4154	0.0086 2355	0.0089 1046	0.0092 0219	194
195	0.0080 4000	0.0083 1734	0.0085 9969	0.0088 8696	0.0091 7907	195
196	0.0080 1576	0.0082 9341	0.0085 7610	0.0088 6374	0.0091 5622	196
197	0.0079 9178	0.0082 6975	0.0085 5278	0.0088 4077	0.0091 3363	197
198	0.0079 6806	0.0082 4635	0.0085 2972	0.0088 1807	0.0091 1130	198
199	0.0079 4459	0.0082 2321	0.0085 0691	0.0087 9562	0.0090 8923	199
200	0.0079 2138	0.0082 0032	0.0084 8436	0.0087 7343	0.0090 6741	200
201	0.0078 9843	0.0081 7768	0.0084 6206	0.0087 5148	0.0090 4584	201
202	0.0078 7571	0.0081 5528	0.0084 4000	0.0087 2978	0.0090 2451	202
203	0.0078 5324	0.0081 3313	0.0084 1818	0.0087 0832	0.0090 0342	203
204	0.0078 3101	0.0081 1121	0.0083 9661	0.0086 8709	0.0089 8257	204
205	0.0078 0901	0.0080 8953	0.0083 7526	0.0086 6610	0.0089 6195	205
206	0.0077 8724	0.0080 6808	0.0083 5415	0.0086 4535	0.0089 4156	206
207	0.0077 6571	0.0080 4686	0.0083 3327	0.0086 2482	0.0089 2140	207
208	0.0077 4440	0.0080 2587	0.0083 1261	0.0086 0451	0.0089 0146	208
209	0.0077 2330	0.0080 0509	0.0082 9217	0.0085 8442	0.0088 8175	209
210	0.0077 0243	0.0079 8454	0.0082 7194	0.0085 6455	0.0088 6225	210
211	0.0076 8178	0.0079 6419	0.0082 5194	0.0085 4490	0.0088 4296	211
212	0.0076 6133	0.0079 4407	0.0082 3214	0.0085 2545	0.0088 2388	212
213	0.0076 4110	0.0079 2415	0.0082 1256	0.0085 0622	0.0088 0512	213
214	0.0076 2107	0.0079 0443	0.0081 9318	0.0084 8719	0.0087 8635	214
215	0.0076 0125	0.0078 8492	0.0081 7400	0.0084 6836	0.0087 6789	215

Exhibit 5–6 (cont.)

$$\frac{1}{a_{\overline{n}|i}} = \frac{i}{1 - (1 + i)^{-n}} \quad \text{Note:} \frac{1}{s_{\overline{n}|i}} = \frac{1}{a_{\overline{n}|i}} - i$$

n	1/2%	13/24%	7/12%	5/8%	2/3%	n
216	0.0075 8162	0.0078 6561	0.0081 5502	0.0084 4973	0.0087 4963	216
217	0.0075 6220	0.0078 4650	0.0081 3624	0.0084 3130	0.0087 3156	217
218	0.0075 4297	0.0078 2758	0.0081 1766	0.0084 1306	0.0087 1369	218
219	0.0075 2393	0.0078 0886	0.0080 9926	0.0083 9502	0.0086 9600	219
220	0.0075 0508	0.0077 9032	0.0080 8106	0.0083 7716	0.0086 7851	220
221	0.0074 8642	0.0077 7197	0.0080 6304	0.0083 5949	0.0086 6120	221
222	0.0074 6794	0.0077 5381	0.0080 4520	0.0083 4200	0.0086 4407	222
223	0.0074 4965	0.0077 3583	0.0080 2755	0.0083 2469	0.0086 2713	223
224	0.0074 3154	0.0077 1802	0.0080 1008	0.0083 0757	0.0086 1036	224
225	0.0074 1360	0.0077 0040	0.0079 9278	0.0082 9061	0.0085 9376	225
226	0.0073 9584	0.0076 8295	0.0079 7566	0.0082 7383	0.0085 7734	226
227	0.0073 7825	0.0076 6567	0.0079 5871	0.0082 5723	0.0085 6109	227
228	0.0073 6083	0.0076 4856	0.0079 4192	0.0082 4079	0.0085 4501	228
229	0.0073 4358	0.0076 3162	0.0079 2531	0.0082 2452	0.0085 2910	229
230	0.0073 2649	0.0076 1484	0.0079 0886	0.0082 0841	0.0085 1335	230
231	0.0073 0957	0.0075 9823	0.0078 9257	0.0081 9247	0.0084 9776	231
232	0.0072 9281	0.0075 8178	0.0078 7645	0.0081 7668	0.0084 8233	232
223	0.0072 7621	0.0075 6549	0.0078 6048	0.0081 6105	0.0084 6706	233
234	0.0072 5977	0.0075 4935	0.0078 4467	0.0081 4558	0.0084 5194	234
235	0.0072 4348	0.0075 3337	0.0078 2902	0.0081 3027	0.0084 3698	235
236	0.0072 2735	0.0075 1755	0.0078 1351	0.0081 1511	0.0084 2217	236
237	0.0072 1137	0.0075 0187	0.0077 9816	0.0081 0009	0.0084 0751	237
238	0.0071 9554	0.0074 8634	0.0077 8296	0.0080 8523	0.0083 9299	238
239	0.0071 7985	0.0074 7097	0.0077 6790	0.0080 7051	0.0083 7863	239
240	0.0071 6431	0.0074 5573	0.0077 5299	0.0080 5593	0.0083 6440	240

References

Aaker, David A., and George S. Day, *Consumerism,* New York, Free Press, 1971.

Boulding, Kenneth E., *Economics as a Science,* New York, McGraw-Hill, 1970.

Britton, Virginia, *Personal Finance,* New York, American Book Company, 1968.

Corley, Robert N., and William J. Robert, *Principles of Business Law,* 9th ed., Englewood Cliffs, N. J., Prentice Hall, 1971.

Dale, Ernest, *Management: Theory and Practice,* 2nd ed., New York, McGraw-Hill, 1969.

Dolphin, Robert Jr., *Self-Correcting Problems in Personal Finance,* Boston, Allyn and Bacon, 1970.

Donaldson, Elvin F., and John K. Pfahl, *Personal Finance,* New York, Ronald Press, 1966.

Dooley, Peter C., *Elementary Price Theory,* New York, Appleton, 1967.

Gordon, Sanford D., and George G. Dawson, *Introductory Economics,* Lexington, Mass., D. C. Heath, 1972.

Huffman, Harry, Ruth M. Twiss, and Leslie J. Whale, *Mathematics for Business Occupations,* New York, McGraw-Hill, 1968.

Killough, Hugh B., and Barrington Associates, *The Economics of Marketing,* New York, Harper and Bros., 1933.

Klein, Jacob, and Woolf Colvin, *Economic Problems of Today,* Chicago, Lyons and Carnahan, 1953.

Locke, Flora M., *College Mathematics for Business,* New York, John Wiley & Sons, 1969.

Lusk, Harold F., et al., *Business Law Principles and Cases,* Homewood, Ill., Richard D. Irwin, 1970.

McGregor, Douglas, *The Human Side of Enterprise,* New York, McGraw-Hill, 1960.

McMurry, Robert N., "The Case For Benevolent Autocracy," *Harvard Business Review,* Vol. 36, No. 1, January–February, 1958.

McNelly, A. E., L. J. Adams, and Milton C. Olson, *Business and Consumer Arithmetic,* Englewood Cliffs, New Jersey, Prentice-Hall, 1964.

Morell, Robert W., *Managerial Decision-Making,* Milwaukee, Bruce Publishing, 1960.

Mund, Vernon A., *Government and Business,* 4th ed., New York, Harper and Row, 1965.

Paust, Jordan L. and Robert D. Upp, *Business Law for Two Year Colleges,* St. Paul, Minn., West Publishing Co., 1969.

Peterson, Willis L., *Principles of Economics: Micro,* Homewood, Ill., Richard D. Irwin, 1971.

Phillips, E. Bryant, and Sylvia Lane, *Personal Finance,* New York, John Wiley & Sons, Inc., 1969.

Rosenberg, R. Robert, and Harry Lewis, *Business Mathematics,* New York, McGraw-Hill, 1963.

Sanborn, Henry N., *What, How, For Whom: The Decisions of Economic Organization,* Baltimore, Cotter-Barnard, 1972.

Shao, Stephen P., *Mathematics for Management and Finance,* Cincinnati, South-Western Publishing, 1969.

Shields, H. G., and W. Harmon Wilson, *Consumer Economic Problems,* Cincinnati, South-Western Publishing, 1940.

Sisk, Henry L., *Principles of Management,* Cincinnati, South-Western Publishing, 1969.

Strohm, John, *The Ford Almanac,* New York, Golden Press, 1966.

Tannenbaum, Robert, "Managerial Decision Making," *Journal of Business,* Vol. XXIII, January, 1950.

Watson, Donald S., *Economic Policy, Business and Government,* Boston, Houghton Mifflin, 1960.

Wilcox, Clair, *Public Policies Toward Business,* 4th ed., Homewood, Ill., Richard D. Irwin, 1971.

Willett, Edward R., *Personal Finance,* Columbus, Ohio, Charles E. Merrill, 1964.

part two

Income and Family Financial Planning

*The public is the only critic whose
opinion is worth anything at all.*
[*Mark Twain*]

6

Population as Household Units and Workers

America has historically been a vital nation, its rapid industrial growth creating a continuous need for more workers. Consequently, this country was open to all who wanted to come and begin a new life. Needs were great for both skilled and unskilled workers to help build industry and settle the new land, and people came from all parts of the world. Few restrictions were placed on immigration before the first world war. The seventy-five years between the Civil War and World War I recorded 25 million immigrants to our land.

Although many new workers were needed to take jobs in new industries that were developing, at times the labor supply increased faster than job openings. This had a tendency to depress wages for short periods of time. The western frontier served as a relief valve for those who could not find work in the industrial cities. The westward migratory movement of people from cities to farms continued until about 1890. By this time, most of the good land in the west was settled and the migration reversed and began to flow from farms to cities. It has continued in this direction.

America had an agrarian economy before the twentieth century when most workers were on farms. Many nations still have this type of economy, while America has long since industrialized. Nations that are still basically agricultural in their output are sometimes called "underdeveloped countries."

Population Characteristics

Population increased from 5 million to 75 million between 1800 and 1900. It took only seventy more years for it to exceed 205 million. The Census Bureau has projected a population of 224 million by 1980 and 246 million by 1990.[1] However, the percentage of increase shown each decade is declining. Population growth was 18.5 percent during the 1950s, but only 13.4 percent for the 1960s. This is the lowest rate for any decade except for the 1930s. During the late 1960s, the rate of growth was only 1 percent per year. The Census Bureau has projected a growth rate of 9.4 percent for the 1970s and 10.0 percent for the 1980s.

Household Units

In analyzing statistics, it is useful to understand how the population is organized. The Census Bureau defines a "household" as all persons who occupy a housing unit, be it a house, apartment, or single room. A "family" is considered to be

Exhibit 6–1   Household Units by Type, U.S. 1960–1970 (numbers in thousands)

	March 1970		March 1965	March 1960
Type of unit	*Number*	*Percent*		
Families	51,110	81.3	47,720	44,905
Husband-wife	44,408	70.6	41,588	39,254
Other male head	1,209	1.9	1,168	1,228
Female head	5,493	8.7	4,964	4,422
Individuals	11,765	18.7	9,531	7,895
Male	3,971	6.3	3,271	2,716
Female	7,794	12.4	6,260	5,179
Total households	62,874	100.0	57,251	52,799

Source: U.S. Dept. of Commerce, Bureau of Census, Population Characteristics, Series P–20, No. 218, March 23, 1971.

[1] *Manpower Report of the President* (Washington, D.C., U.S. Government Printing Office, March, 1973), p. 219.

two or more persons related by blood, marriage, or adoption who are residing together. Thus, our households are composed of family units and individuals living alone. Economists look at them as consumer units. Exhibit 6–1 shows that, in 1970, 81 percent of households were families while almost 19 percent were individuals. Households composed of individuals increased 49 percent during the 1960s while family units were increasing only 13.8 percent. Households are increasing by more than one million each year, and should increase to 76 million by 1980, since marriageable age groups in the population are increasing. The percentage of families with a female head increased slightly during the 1960s, while it is even more noticeable that over 21 percent of all households are female or have a female head of the family.

Households as Resource Suppliers and Income Receivers

Economists consider these households to be the most important force in the economy. They not only furnish many resources for production but also provide about 65 percent of all spending in the economy. Members of households are paid in the form of wages, rent, interest, and profits for their resources used for production. Since households are consumers, they usually spend about 92 percent of income and save the remainder. This saving serves an important economic function, since a great part of it is loaned to business firms and governments to be used for producing more goods and services.

Producers of consumer goods and services study changes in population and household composition to get an indication of future demand for their products. Some items have a higher demand by certain age groups. According to Exhibit 6–5 (on page 117), large increases are expected during the 1970s for ages 20 to 35. These are ages when most marriages occur and families are started. This decade should witness a rising demand for homes, apartments, furniture, and all the things that young families purchase.

Population as
a Work Force

The quantity of goods and services available in the marketplace is largely dependent on the number of people engaged in productive work. Quantity and quality of workers are both necessary to achieve high production. No country in the world has been able to achieve our degree of production and level of living. The number of people in the labor force does change; but, over the history of this nation, the number working has steadily increased. Most people work to support a family; although, in some families, the housewife takes a paid job to obtain additional income. Those who have a choice of working or not working give flexibility to the labor force, but also make it difficult to estimate future growth of employment.

The labor force, briefly described, includes all persons 16 years of age and above who are working for pay, plus those seeking work. It includes both full-time and part-time workers. This figure for 1970 was 85 million people and is expected to be 100 million by 1980. (Exhibit 6–2). The labor force grew at a faster rate than total population during the 1960s and is expected to do the same during the 1970s. This raises the important question: can enough new jobs be created to give these people employment? The answer to this question is made even more significant in view of the expected technological replacement of labor as wages tend to increase beyond their productivity.

The number of jobs had a significant increase during the 1960s. Civilian employment increased 20 percent as compared to a 17 percent increase in the noninstitutional population. Naturally, persons in institutions such as prisons and mental institutions are not counted in the labor force. Unemployment rates are usually given such emphasis that we sometimes overlook the increase in jobs. The total labor force includes our armed forces while they are omitted in counting the civilian labor force. Unemployment normally ranges between 4 and 6 percent of the labor force. Economists consider that it will not get below 4 percent due to voluntary changes in jobs, etc. Full employment thus exists when unemployment is not above 4 percent of the labor force.

Exhibit 6–2   Employment Status of the Noninstitutional Population 16 Years and Over by Sex for Selected Years (in thousands) (1980 est.)

| | | Total labor force | | Civilian labor force | | |
| | Non-institutional | | Percent of | | Unemployed percent of | Not in labor |
Year	population	Number	population	Employed	labor force	force
Male						
1950	52,352	45,446	86.8	41,580	5.1	6,906
1960	58,144	48,870	84.0	43,904	5.4	9,274
1970	67,409	54,343	80.6	48,960	4.4	13,066
1980	80,332	63,612	79.2	—	—	—
Female						
1950	54,293	18,412	33.9	17,340	5.7	35,881
1960	61,615	23,272	37.8	21,874	5.9	38,343
1970	72,774	31,560	43.4	29,667	5.9	41,214
1980	84,394	37,115	43.9	—	—	—
Total						
1950	106,645	63,858	59.9	58,920	5.3	42,787
1960	119,759	72,142	60.2	65,778	5.5	47,617
1970	140,182	85,903	61.3	78,627	4.9	54,280
1980	164,726	100,727	61.2	—	—	—

Source: Bureau of Labor Statistics, Washington, D.C., U.S. Dept. of Labor, Employment and Earnings, Vol. 18, No. 2, August, 1971.

Women in the Labor Force

A very significant factor to note is the decreasing number of males in the labor force as a percent of the population in contrast to an increasing rate for females. Women now make up more than one-third of the total labor force. It is expected that the labor force will continue at about 60 percent of the population over 16 years of age, but the proportion will decrease for men and increase for women. Since men are staying in school longer and retiring earlier, their proportion in the total labor force is decreasing, while the growing number of women taking jobs outside the home adds to the proportion of women in the labor force.

Since a higher proportion of women are receiving some college education, as shown in Exhibit 6–8 on page 120, many are entering the professions. The professions employing most women are teaching, nursing, social and welfare work, libary science, and dietetics. Teaching and nursing employ two out of every three women professional workers.[2] There is a growing need for the acceptance of women in professions where they are not usually employed.

About the same proportion of women in the labor force have college degrees as do men. However, college degrees do not completely eliminate employer resistance when women seek employment outside their traditional fields. Equal employment opportunities for women are not yet a reality, although federal legislation does forbid discrimination on the basis of sex.

There are indications that women are slowly moving into management positions in private industry, taking such jobs as systems analysts, marketing direc-

Exhibit 6–3   Wives in the Labor Force (by income of husband and age of children), 1971

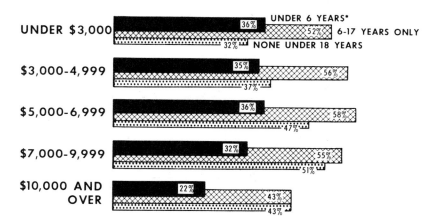

Source: U.S. Department of Agriculture, Agricultural Research Service.

---

[2]*Manpower Report of the President* (Washington, D.C.: U.S. Government Printing Office, March, 1970), pp. 188–189.

Exhibit 6–4 Employment Status of Women by Marital Status, 1950–1972 (numbers in thousands)

Period	Single			Married, spouse present			Widowed, divorced, separated		
	Female population	Number in labor force	Percent of population	Female population	Number in labor force	Percent of population	Female population	Number in labor force	Percent of population
March, 1950	11,126	5,621	50.5	35,925	8,550	23.8	9,584	3,624	37.8
April, 1955	10,962	5,087	46.4	37,570	10,423	27.7	11,718	4,643	39.6
March, 1960	12,252	5,401	44.1	40,205	12,253	30.5	12,150	4,861	40.0
March, 1965	14,607	5,912	40.5	42,367	14,708	34.7	13,717	5,332	38.9
March, 1970	13,141	6,965	53.0	45,055	18,377	40.8	15,065	5,891	39.1
March, 1972	13,610	7,477	54.9	46,400	19,249	41.5	15,496	6,213	40.1

Source: *Manpower Report of the President*, Washington, D.C., U.S. Govt. Printing Office, March, 1973, p. 165.

tors, and management trainees. The U.S. Labor Department has stated that it will be necessary to employ more women in management jobs during the next decade if the services of all those seeking employment are to be utilized.

Married women account for the major share of increase in women workers. By 1980, the number of women at work is projected to double the 1950 figure, reflecting a major change in American life style. This increase from 18 million in 1950 to 37 million in 1980 will make the labor force almost 40 percent female. Of the 30 million women currently in the labor force, 18 million are married.

Exhibit 6–4 shows the number and percentage of women in the labor force according to their marital status. Almost two-thirds of the women working outside the home are married and living with their husbands. This group is also responsible for most of the increase in working women. In 1950, 23.8 percent of married women were in the labor force, while, in 1972, this percentage had increased to 41.5. For females who are single or have been widowed, separated, or divorced, approximately the same percentage were in the labor force in 1972 as in 1950.

There are many reasons for this steady movement of housewives into the labor force. A second income for the family can sometimes provide those extra things that make for better living. Some women seek employment after their children leave home, because they no longer feel needed at home. Modern household appliances make it possible for women to spend more time outside the home. This trend is likely to continue. In families where the husband has a low-paying job, it may be necessary for the wife to supplement their income by working, even if she would prefer to remain at home caring for the children.

Day-Care Centers. Since working women have not yet obtained equality with men in pay scales, some jobs fail to increase family income when it is necessary to hire someone to care for small children during working hours. Community day schools and nurseries are available in some areas where the low wages of the husband make another income a necessity. For a nominal fee, or perhaps in proportion to ability to pay, children are cared for during the mother's working hours. This assistance is lacking in most communities, and young children are sometimes left at home with no supervision at all or in the care of an older child who should be in school.

Facilities for keeping children of working mothers are sponsored by such organizations as churches, local women's liberation groups, labor unions, and governmental organizations. Federal funds are being used to provide day care for children of migrant workers and for welfare mothers participating in the Work Incentive Program.[3] Where facilities are licensed by the state and provide adequate care, charges for keeping a pre-school child may amount to $2,000 per year. This would be excessive for low-income mothers providing the only income for the family. Some day-care centers are operated by individuals as profit-making businesses. These may be more expensive than centers oper-

---

[3]U.S. Congress, House Committee on Ways and Means, *Hearings on Social Security and Welfare Proposals,* 91st Congress (Washington, 1969), Part 1, pp. 288–294.

ated by nonprofit organizations, since the latter may be subsidized or may have volunteer workers. The greatest need for more centers appears to be in areas with a concentration of low-income families. These families have a high proportion of working mothers. Increasing numbers of employers who hire a significant number of women are providing day care on the premises either as a part of fringe benefits or at a nominal charge. Parents are encouraged to come to the nursery at intervals during the day to check on the child or perhaps to give necessary medicine or special care.

Specially trained career women in fields with a higher wage scale often feel they can contribute more to society as well as to the family income by continuing in their jobs or professions, employing housekeepers and child-care personnel. Some less highly trained women receive greater satisfaction from a job outside the home, even though the salary they make may leave little profit after deducting expenses.

The Women's Liberation Movement. The advent of children into the family keeps most women out of the labor force, at least until the children are in school —some because of necessity and many by their own choice. Proponents of women's liberation challenge the traditions and system that make motherhood a hindrance to a woman's career. These advocates see no reason why a valuable worker becomes less valuable simply because of pregnancy and motherhood. They question the necessity (and economy) of lengthy mandatory pregnancy leaves. They feel such leave should be determined by a woman's health and her doctor's judgment, in the same way that an ulcer patient is given leave as the individual case requires and not as a specified amount of time determined by the employer. They agree that cooperation of the worker is vital here. Of course, women cannot expect to have special demands met if they demand equal or impartial treatment. One suggestion which has grown out of the women's liberation movement is the advocacy of "paternal" leave, a benefit that would allow a new father to share in the care of the baby and thus reduce the length of time the mother must be off the job, at the same time allowing the father to become comfortable in his parenthood role and increasing his familiarity and closeness to the children.

The women's liberation movement is responsible for many of the demands from working women for fair consideration in job choices and in pay and benefits. Those who choose to join the labor or professional force as an alternative to the housewife's job ask for more than legalistic equal pay for equal work; they hope for removal of prejudices and preconceived ideas that prescribe what women should or should not do. They resent being pigeonholed as secretaries and maids. An oft-cited example of the special ("sexist") treatment afforded women professionals describes the case of a man and woman of equal training applying for a teaching position in a university. Both applicants were told that nothing was available, but the woman was told that, if she could type, she could apply for a secretarial vacancy. It never occurred to anyone to offer the highly educated male a secretarial job.

One of the ideas of women's liberation that may seem impractical, but might be beneficial to both sexes, is the division of responsibility at home and at the job. Claiming that most fathers rarely see their children, the liberationists advocate a split day or week or month on the job, with the husband assuming child care and household chores on his days off, while his wife takes her turn on the job. One aim of this proposal, to decrease job pressure on the male, may be well-founded, considering that population figures show that women outlive men and many would point to job tension as a cause of this phenomenon. Nevertheless, adapting such a schedule to the business world as a whole may well be another story, although it has been done successfully in small private businesses and offices.

It appears, then, that the women's liberation movement has provided a direction and a set of goals to allow the labor force to accommodate the rising number of women who wish to enter the job market, at the same time recognizing the need for changes in the business world and family structure and making proposals to accomplish those changes.

Population Age Groups

Exhibit 6–5 shows the change in population by age groups for the 1960s and estimates for the 1970s. The 16–24 age groups had large increases during the 1960s. For the 1970s, the dramatic increase will be among young adults—ages 25–34—those entering their prime working years. These figures indicate that there will be a need to create many new jobs because of this large movement of young people into the labor force.

Productivity and Education of Workers

Worker productivity tends to drop as the nation approaches full employment, since the least productive workers are presumably the last to be hired, and also because work incentives are lessened due to apparent job security. The rate of productivity growth decreased in the late 1960s, averaging only 2.1 percent

Exhibit 6–5   U.S. Population Changes by Age Groups, 1960–1970, estimated for 1970–80 (in millions)

Age group	1960	1970	1980	1960–70 percent change	1970–80 percent change
Under 5 yrs.	20	18	23	−13	31
5–15 yrs.	39	45	42	18	−7
16–19 yrs.	11	15	17	41	12
20–24 yrs.	11	17	21	55	22
25–34 yrs.	23	25	37	11	45
35–44 yrs.	24	23	26	−5	11
45–54 yrs.	21	23	22	14	−4
55–64 yrs.	16	19	21	18	14
65 & over	17	20	23	19	18

Source: U.S. Bureau of Census, Washington, D.C., Current Population Reports, Series P–25, No. 311, 314, 448.

annually from 1965 to 1970. In 1970, the rate of growth was only 1.0 percent, while 1971 showed a 3.6 percent increase and 1972, 4.2 percent. Although this is a low rate of growth, American workers are still the most productive in the world due to the high level of education of the work force and the large amounts of capital used in production processes. When productivity is rising less than wage rates, total labor costs increase and contribute to price inflation. Unit labor costs, or costs of producing one unit of a product, increased most years during the 1960s and were rising 6 percent per year in 1970. They declined to 1.9 percent in 1972. Worker productivity is a measure of the output per hour of work. Many economists suggest and it has often been stated as a national policy goal that a minimum of 4 or 5 percent annual increase in productivity is necessary for workers to get higher wages or to work fewer hours for the same pay without seriously affecting consumer prices.

Exhibit 6–6   Indexes of Output per Man-Hour and Unit Labor Costs for the Private Economy 1955–1972, (1967 = 100)

| Year | Total private | | Farm | Manufacturing | | Non-manufacturing | |
	Output per man-hour	Unit labor costs	Output per man-hour	Output per man-hour	Unit labor costs	Output per man-hour	Unit labor costs
1955	69.9	80.1	49.5	73.7	81.4	73.4	78.4
1960	78.2	91.8	64.9	79.9	95.9	80.6	90.0
1965	94.2	93.8	86.9	98.3	92.8	93.5	94.7
1970	104.3	119.4	119.6	108.1	112.9	101.7	122.7
1972	112.7	125.7	112.5	119.1	116.4	109.4	130.1

Source: *Manpower Report of the President,* Washington, D.C., U.S. Government Printing Office, March, 1973, pp. 240–242.

Exhibit 6–6 compares productivity of workers in the farm, manufacturing, and non-manufacturing sectors of the economy. Output per man-hour increased more in the farm sector than in the others between 1955 and 1972. The non-manufacturing sector had the least increase in output. This is to be expected since this sector includes the service industries, that area least susceptible to automation. Productivity increases faster in those industries which are able to substitute capital for labor.

Industries with a relatively large growth in productivity during the 1960s were air transportation, electric and gas utilities, petroleum refining, major household appliances, and coal mining. Some with low rates of growth during the same period were footwear, steel, glass containers, and the canning and preserving industry. Since increasing productivity of workers is largely a matter of improving efficiency, more and better machines, which eliminate some jobs, make it possible for workers who remain to be more productive.

Productivity rates are projected to 1980 in Exhibit 6–7. Rates are expected to increase in mining and manufacturing but decrease in farming, communications and public utilities, transportation, and trade. The average annual rate of 3 percent, which we achieved for all industries between 1950 and 1970, will remain about the same until 1980.

Since there is an increase in the number of people employed each year, the total output of goods and services rises. This has helped provide the rising level of living that Americans now take for granted. An important national problem for the 1970s will be to make certain that jobs are available for the growing labor force and to provide enough education and capital to assure that worker productivity equals or exceeds increases in wages.

The strong emphasis that is placed on a college education may be partly responsible for a reduction in the flow of workers into the skilled crafts. Secondary school counselors must find better ways to help students learn about vocational opportunities and requirements. Unfortunately, the vocational training available in many schools prepares students for jobs that no longer exist. Our economy has the capability to provide jobs for everyone, but we will need to improve our system of counseling, training, and job-matching to accomplish our goal of steady full employment. It is not necessary to force people into certain types of work, just because they are needed, but it is reasonable to inform them of alternatives so that they can choose a vocation that gives optimal personal satisfaction. Parents and educators may be guilty of encouraging students to enter college who have neither the ability nor the desire to attend.

Exhibit 6–7   Productivity Trends, Total Private Economy and Selected Sectors, 1950–70 and 1965–80

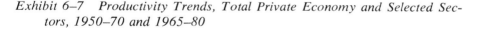

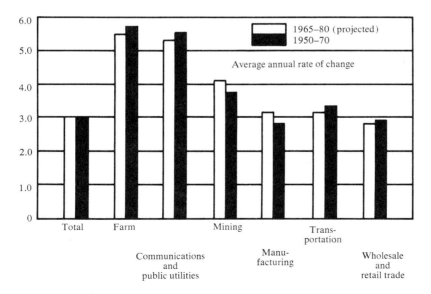

Source: U.S. Department of Labor, Bureau of Labor Statistics.

Federal legislation during the 1960s established new types of vocational and technical education programs. Since industry demand for unskilled labor is expected to continue downward, workers who do not obtain adequate preparation will find it difficult to secure satisfactory jobs. Exhibit 6–8 shows that young people are staying in school longer. The percent of young men and women who had gone on to college after completing their high school education was higher in 1970 than in 1960. In 1970, 52 percent of the men twenty to twenty-four years old who were high school graduates had also completed some college work, as compared to 42 percent in 1960. The comparable figures for women were 42 percent in 1970, as compared with 33 percent in 1960. Additional information relating to income by levels of education can be found in Chapter 7.

Exhibit 6–8   High School Graduates 20 to 24 Years Old Who Have Completed One Year of College or More: 1960–1970 (numbers in thousands)

		Completed one year of college or more	
Year	*Total, high school graduates*	*Number*	*Percent*
Male			
1970	5,774	3,028	52.4
1969	5,267	2,741	52.0
1968	5,090	2,688	52.8
1965	4,413	2,017	45.7
1960	3,269	1,379	42.2
Female			
1970	6,777	2,824	41.7
1969	6,310	2,542	40.3
1968	5,990	2,497	41.7
1965	4,933	1,655	33.5
1960	3,598	1,179	32.8

Source: Census Bureau, U.S. Department of Commerce, Characteristics of American Youth, 1970, Series P–23, No. 34, Feb. 1, 1971.

Importance of Part-Time Workers

A significant part of the production of goods and services comes from those who work part-time. The proportion of workers preferring part-time employment increased rapidly during the 1960s and, if the same trend continues during the 1970s, one out of every seven persons will be a part-time worker by 1980. Most part-time opportunities are provided by the service-oriented industries.

Those most interested in part-time employment are found in three groups: namely, the sixteen to twenty-four-year-olds who are usually still in high school and college but want some work, married women who do not want to leave their homes long enough to work full-time, and older workers who have retired from their full-time professions but are still physically able to perform some work. Since these three groups are increasing in size, and since they tend to work for lower pay, we expect part-time work opportunities to expand during the 1970s. Estimates made by the Labor Department show the service-oriented industries to have the greatest growth of all industries during this decade. This will also provide an increasing demand for part-time workers.

Occupational Changes

Great changes are occurring in the kinds of occupations open to workers. Technology creates new vocations while it destroys others. It becomes more difficult for young people to choose a lifework, since many occupations require a college education, yet there is no assurance that that type of work will not become obsolete. While income is not the only consideration in choosing a vocation, it is an important one. Distribution of employment by industries is shown in Exhibit 6–9.

Exhibit 6–9 Employment by Industry Division, 1970, and Estimates for 1980 (in millions)

Industry	Employment 1970	Expected employment 1980	Increase or decrease
Manufacturing	19.4	21.9	2.5
Wholesale & retail trade	14.9	17.6	2.7
Services	11.6	16.1	4.5
State & local government	9.8	13.8	4.0
Finance, insurance & real estate	3.7	4.3	0.6
Construction	3.3	4.6	1.3
Federal government	2.7	3.0	0.3
Transportation	2.7	2.9	0.2
Communications, utilities	1.8	1.8	—
Agriculture	3.5	3.0	−0.5
Mining	0.6	0.5	−0.1

Source: *Manpower Report of the President,* Washington, D.C., U.S. Government Printing Office, March, 1973, p. 225.

Projections of employment opportunities indicate that, by 1980, most growth will be occurring in services, government, and trade. The greatest declines will be in agriculture and mining. Exhibit 6–9 does not include self-employed people. The self-employed group includes many professional and technical workers; and Labor Department estimates indicate that demand for professional and technical workers will also continue to increase.

In this world of technology and changing occupational requirements, educators and others are raising questions about the effectiveness of our educational system.[4] Public attitudes that only careers requiring a college education are good may need to change. Since 45 percent of high school graduates do not enter college and only 10 to 12 percent of high school students prepare for careers in vocational-technical programs, educators should consider changes in the school system.

The U.S. Office of Education has suggested a refocusing of education to give young people a more realistic preparation for the job market, whether they leave high school without graduating or go on to college.[5] A new career education approach is in the developmental stage by the Office of Education. Career education would provide information on job alternatives beginning with the first grade and will continue with this task throughout high school. Career opportunities and requirements would be built around basic subjects with only general information provided in the elementary grades.

As students enter junior high school, they would begin to explore certain clusters of occupations through classroom instruction and field trips. At the senior high school level, they would select one of three options: intensive job preparation for entry into the labor market immediately upon leaving high school, preparation for a special type of occupational education after high school, or preparation for college.

Every student would leave the system with at least entry-level job skills and with a background in basic academic subjects to permit further education. His combination of occupational and academic training would vary, depending on the option selected. The occupational clusters explored in junior high school would be broad—for example, allied health fields, construction trades, and business occupations.

The Office of Education also has experimental programs for school drop-outs between the ages of 13 and 20 and for adults who want to improve their skills. The program for young people is in cooperation with employers who provide certain work experiences and training. The program for adults is home-based, relying on television programs and training clinics.

More workers are beginning to accept continuing education as a necessity in a rapidly changing world of work. Cooperation of business, labor unions, and government will be necessary if we are to keep the labor force employed. More research and data collection are needed concerning national occupational requirements. In addition, these needs will have to be more effectively communicated to the teachers and counselors in educational institutions.

Discussion Questions

1. Distinguish between a "household" and a "family."
2. Trace the development of the American economy and show how the changing characteristics of the population have influenced this development.

---

[4]"New Ideas for Better Schools," *U.S. News & World Report,* November 1, 1971.

[5]Sidney P. Marland, Jr., address to the Convention of the National Association of Secondary School Principals, *Career Education Now,* Houston, Texas, Jan. 23, 1971.

3. Give some reasons why women are increasingly joining the nation's work force. Do you think this trend will continue? Why?

4. Comment on the authenticity of the statement that "for workers to receive an increase in wages, the productivity of these workers must increase."

5. What are some of the changes that can result in higher worker productivity? What are some of the benefits of higher productivity?

6. Do you think more emphasis should be placed on vocational education (use statistics to support your answer)?

7. An important national problem facing this country today is making certain that jobs are available for the growing labor force. What are some of the changes that our school system will have to make to help solve this problem?

7

Household
Income

The growth in family income of Americans has been phenomenal in recent years. Yet, we find that people's demands for goods and services tend to keep pace with their incomes. Family income is rising at a much faster rate than the number of people in the labor force, indicating that married women are entering the labor force to secure a second income for the family, or that more men are taking second jobs.

No other country in the world has developed its productive ability and provided comparably high individual incomes so that its citizens could have such an array of consumer goods and services. Not only are U.S. living standards high in relation to other countries, but they continue to rise at a faster rate, widening the gap between this country and most others.

Most people agree that it is difficult to measure a family's *level of living.* Is there a better measure than amount of income? Some writers point out that 95 percent of all families have at least one television set, or that three families in four have washing machines. These are simply indications that U.S. consumers do have increasing incomes and purchasing power, and that they choose to make life more comfortable by purchasing homes, cars, and home appliances.

The Economy's Production

A brief description of terms used in measuring national economic performance should provide some insight for a better understanding of household and family incomes. Since our economy produces a variety of goods and services and we cannot add unlike units such as cars and refrigerators, it is necessary to use a common denominator. By adding prices of all final goods and services produced in a year, we have a measure of total economic performance. This is called *Gross National Product* (GNP).

All economic resources—land, labor, capital, and management—are combined in various proportions to bring about production. Capital, which includes machinery and equipment, was produced during previous years and is now used for current production. This process of integrating capital into the production system is called "depreciation of capital" or "capital consumption." To obtain an accurate figure for the year's net national production, we subtract capital consumption from GNP. The result is called *Net National Product.*

Governments are not considered to be resources of production, but they do consume some of the nation's total production through collection of taxes and borrowing. By subtracting various types of taxes and adding transfer payments, measures for *National Income* and *Personal Income* are obtained. (See Exhibit 7–1). Personal Income is the income received by all households before income taxes are deducted.

Earnings and Income

There are instances when the distinction between earnings and income should be made. Earnings are the return to someone who is gainfully employed in a business of his own or by someone else. They are also called "wages" or "salary" if the worker is employed by another person and "profits" if he is self-employed. Those who have only their time and energy to sell will receive all their income in these forms.

Some families have sources of income other than their labor. Returns from land and capital are called "rent" and "interest" or "dividends." A person may be unemployed and still have a high income because he has many resources for which others are willing to pay. The purchasing power and standard of living

Exhibit 7–1   Calculation of Personal Income, Disposable Income, and Personal Saving, 1972

	Billions of dollars
National income (income earned)	$935.6
Social security contributions	−74.0
Corporate income taxes	−41.3
Undistributed corporate profits	−26.6
Transfer payments[1]	+142.2
Personal income	$935.9
Personal income	$935.9
Personal taxes	−140.8
Disposable income (after tax income)	795.1
Disposable income	795.1
Personal consumption	−721.0
Interest paid by consumers	−18.2
Personal saving	$ 55.9

[1]Transfer payments—income from government for which no current services are provided. Social security income, welfare payments, etc.

For a more complete method of calculating measures of income, see Campbell R. McConnell, *Economics*, 5th ed., New York, McGraw-Hill, 1972, pp. 168–171.

Source: Adapted from Federal Reserve Bulletin, June, 1973.

then will be determined by the income from all sources, after allowing for payment of income taxes.

"Personal income" is the actual income received by individuals from all sources. From this amount we subtract personal income taxes to obtain dispos-

Exhibit 7–2   Sources of Disposable Income—1967–72 (billions of dollars)

	1967	1968	1969	1970	1971	1972
Wages & salaries	423.1	489.2	509.6	541.4	573.5	626.5
Other labor income	22.3	25.4	28.2	30.8	36.5	40.3
Proprietor's income	62.1	63.8	67.1	66.9	70.0	75.2
Income from rent, interest, & dividends	90.6	98.4	105.8	113.0	119.5	124.9
Income from transfer payments	52.0	59.2	65.9	79.6	93.6	104.4
Less income taxes & personal Social Security contributions	103.5	120.5	142.5	143.9	148.2	176.2
Disposable income	546.3	590.0	634.1	687.8	744.9	795.1

Source: Federal Reserve Bulletin, June, 1973.

able income, the money remaining to be spent as the person desires. As we observed from Exhibit 7–1, most of disposable income is spent, but a small part is saved. The sixty-three million households in America have steadily increased their consumption of goods and services as disposable income grew, but the increase in total expenditure as a percent of earnings has not increased.

Changes in Earnings and Income

Wages and salaries have risen faster than other sources of income in recent years. More than two-thirds of total personal income is from wages and salaries (see Exhibit 7–2).

There is such a variation in family incomes that figures have little meaning unless they are analyzed very closely. For example, family income usually increases for those in some occupations until near retirement age. In other occupations, earnings tend to peak much earlier (e.g., the professional athlete as opposed to the professional businessman). Also, incomes tend to be higher as the level of formal education increases. In some families, the housewife has a paying job to provide additional income, while in others there is only one paycheck.

Some of the lowest income households have no wage earners, so they must obtain their income through some type of welfare program. Their inability to obtain work may be due to a lack of education, health problems, environmental handicaps, or a lack of ambition. These families have a greater need than any for good financial management, yet they are usually the least educated in financial matters.

Exhibit 7–3 reveals that both families and individual households are changing into higher income groups, although 7.2 percent of families and 43.9 percent of individual households still had less than $3,000 annual income in 1972. Most would agree this is below a subsistence level in the absence of welfare assistance. Progress in raising income levels seems slow for those in individual households, but we should remember that many of these people are not in the labor force due to age or disability. Their income is from pensions, investments, or welfare programs. It is encouraging to see that more than half of all families had incomes above $10,000 in 1972.

Income by Family Characteristics

The highest income families have more persons in the family and more wage earners. As Exhibit 7–4 indicates, the lowest income families have less than one full-time earner. Families with one or more earners had incomes above $4,000 in 1971. The average family size was 3.53 persons with 1.66 of the members being wage earners. Families with the oldest heads and fewest years of schooling were in the low income groups. The highest income families had 3.62 members with 1.94 earners. Also, in these families, the head was about 52 years of age with more than 16 years of school completed.

Exhibit 7–3   Distribution of Income of Families and Individual Households by Percentages for 1960, 1965, and 1972

Income groups	1960 Families	1960 Individual households	1965 Families	1965 Individual households	1972 Families	1972 Individual households
Number—(thousands)	45,456	11,081	48,279	12,132	54,373	16,811
Percent	100	100	100	100	100	100
Under $3,000	15.6	58.2	11.8	54.4	7.2	43.9
3,000–4,999	14.1	16.8	12.3	15.8	9.4	18.5
5,000–6,999	16.7	13.2	13.7	12.6	10.2	12.0
7,000–9,999	24.7	8.3	23.2	10.8	16.8	13.2
10,000–14,999	19.3 }	3.2	24.3 }	6.5	26.1	8.5
15,000 & over	9.5 }		14.6 }		30.3	3.8
Median income	7,376	2,256	8,559	2,650	11,116	3,521

Source: Bureau of Census, Current Population Reports, *Consumer Income*, Series P–60, No. 85, Dec. 1972, p. 37 and No. 87, June 1973, p. 4.

Exhibit 7–4   Family Characteristics by Money Income, 1971

Income	Average family income (dollars)	Per capita family income (dollars)	Average no. of Persons per family	Average no. of Earners per family	Median age of head of family	Median* school years completed
Total	$11,583	$ 3,279	3.53	1.66	45.6	12.3
Under $1,000	−161	−52	3.11	0.83	44.0	10.5
1,000–1,499	1,261	433	2.91	0.71	50.5	8.5
1,500–1,999	1,750	634	2.76	0.68	58.8	8.4
2,000–2,499	2,238	780	2.87	0.67	55.4	8.8
2,500–2,999	2,737	973	2.81	0.73	58.7	8.7
3,000–3,499	3,223	1,066	3.02	0.88	53.7	8.8
3,500–3,999	3,734	1,246	3.00	0.95	55.7	9.1
4,000–4,999	4,502	1,470	3.06	1.07	52.3	9.3
5,000–5,999	5,466	1,668	3.28	1.27	47.4	10.3
6,000–6,999	6,456	1,928	3.35	1.37	44.8	11.2
7,000–7,999	7,461	2,149	3.47	1.46	42.0	11.9
8,000–8,999	8,446	2,383	3.54	1.57	43.4	12.1
9,000–9,999	9,448	2,613	3.62	1.63	39.9	12.2
10,000–11,999	10,887	2,979	3.65	1.74	42.4	12.3
12,000–14,999	13,325	3,565	3.74	1.94	43.2	12.5
15,000–24,999	18,514	4,841	3.82	2.24	46.5	12.8
25,000–49,999	31,179	7,723	4.04	2.40	49.2	15.6
50,000 & over	66,988	18,505	3.62	1.94	51.6	16.3

*Restricted to families with head 25 years old and over.

Source: Bureau of Census, Current Population Reports, *Consumer Income,* Series P–60, No. 85, December, 1972, p. 23.

Additional analysis of family and individual household incomes can be made by studying Exhibit 7–5. Families consistently moved from low to higher income groups between 1959 and 1971. Only 6.7 percent of all families had incomes of $15,000 or more in 1959, while 19.5 percent earned this amount in 1971. It is interesting to note how family income changed with the number of earners. In 1971, there were more families with two earners than with one. One-earner families decreased between 1959 and 1971, while increases were noted in all other groups. The number of families with three or more earners almost doubled during this period. Families with no earners increased.

Most individual household persons are earners. But these earners have relatively low incomes, and the non-earner persons have even lower incomes. Over 25 percent of the earners and 77 percent of the non-earners had incomes below $3,000 in 1971. There were more than eleven million households with no earners in 1971.

Income by Occupation and Education

The income of many occupational groups fluctuates with national economic conditions. Wage rates and incomes vary even within occupations because of such things as geographic location, level of education, type of industry, and

Exhibit 7–5 Number and Percent of Earners—Families and Individual Households by Income, 1959 & 1971

	Total		None		One		Two		Three or more		Individual households Total	Earners	Non-earners
	1959	1971	1959	1971	1959	1971	1959	1971	1959	1971	1971	1971	1971
No.—thousands	45,004	53,296	3,555	5,100	21,653	20,104	15,745	20,602	4,051	7,490	16,311	9,826	6,485
Percent	100	100	100	100	100	100	100	100	100	100	100	100	100
Under $3,000	16.4	8.3	73.8	39.1	16.0	8.5	7.2	2.8	5.1	1.1	46.4	25.9	77.3
3,000–6,999	33.0	21.4	21.4	47.4	41.2	27.2	28.8	14.8	16.7	6.3	30.6	38.7	18.2
7,000–8,999	17.3	12.2	1.7	5.9	18.1	16.1	20.6	12.2	14.5	5.8	9.3	14.3	1.8
9,000–14,999	24.5	33.2	2.2	5.5	17.6	32.5	34.8	41.1	40.3	30.8	10.6	16.5	1.7
15,000–24,999	6.7	19.5	0.8	1.6	4.8	11.7	7.0	24.2	20.2	41.2	2.4	3.6	0.5
25,000 & over	2.2	5.3	0.5	0.5	2.5	3.9	1.9	5.0	3.2	14.8	0.7	1.0	0.3
Average income (dollars)	8,212	11,583	2,585	4,409	7,664	10,119	9,283	12,844	11,918	17,481	4,774	6,280	2,491

Note: The "None", "One", "Two", and "Three or more" columns fall under the heading *Families having specified number of earners*, within the broader *Families* section. The last three columns fall under *Individual households*, with "Non-earners" as the final column.

Source: U.S. Bureau of the Census, Social and Economic Characteristics of the Population, P-23, No. 37, June 24, 1971, and Current Population Reports, P-60, No. 85, Dec., 1972, p. 79.

local supply and demand for workers. Workers in some occupations are paid on an hourly basis. The majority of these hourly workers are now members of labor unions.

In other types of work, pay is based on a weekly, monthly, or annual basis. The payment period does not necessarily determine who will receive the highest income. Some workers who are paid by the hour receive higher annual incomes than some who are paid a yearly salary. Income from jobs requiring the most education is usually paid by the month or year.

Most high school and college students have become aware of the influence of education on future income. Perhaps this is partly responsible for the rising level of education of the population and labor force. Many young people still do not complete high school; however, some take a specialized course of study that prepares them for a job after dropping out of high school.

A survey was made by the U.S. Department of Labor in October, 1968, to determine what had happened to those who had graduated or dropped out of school during 1968. Results of this survey are shown in Exhibit 7–6. Of 2.6 million high school graduates, slightly more than one-half entered college. Five percent entered other types of schools for more education while 30 percent took jobs. Of 610,000 school dropouts, 50 percent found jobs while only 3 percent entered other types of schools for additional training.

Exhibit 7–6 shows further that only 4 percent of high school graduates were unemployed in 1968, while well over 13 percent of high school dropouts were not employed. The quality and productivity of individual lives cannot be judged from the exhibit's objective figures and inexplicit terms, such as "to other pursuits," but it appears that a valid question at this point is: are we providing high school students who do not plan to enter college with suitable preparation to become productive workers?

Exhibit 7–6   Pursuits of 1968 High School Graduates and School Dropouts in October, 1968

High school graduates—2.6 Million		*School dropouts—610,000*[1]	
To college	1.4 mil.	To special training	20,000
To more training	134,000	To jobs	305,000
To jobs	782,000	To unemployment	85,000
To unemployment	122,000	To other pursuits	200,000
To other pursuits	124,000		

[1]People 16–24 years old who dropped out before finishing high school.
Source: Occupational Outlook Quarterly, Fall, 1969, U.S. Department of Labor, Washington, D.C., pp. 30, 31.

Exhibit 7–7 shows how income varies with the level of formal education. These figures are similar to most studies which indicate that incomes rise with the years of school completed. This is easy to understand by contrasting the low and high income groups. Family heads who have only an elementary school education or less had incomes averaging $7,976 in 1971. High school gradu-

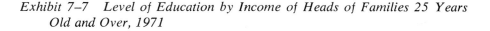

Exhibit 7–7   Level of Education by Income of Heads of Families 25 Years
            Old and Over, 1971

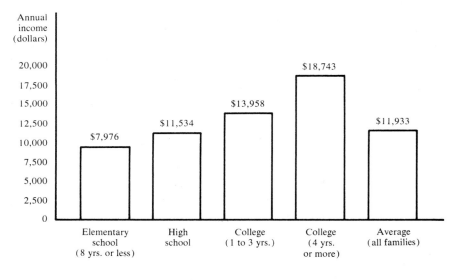

Level of education

ates were earning $11,534 at the same time and college graduates $18,743. The average income for all families in 1971 was $11,933.

A rapid growth in the demand for professional and technical workers during the early 1960s coincided with a relatively small supply of new college graduates. Enrollments in colleges increased to such an extent that, in 1970, over a million degrees were granted—more than double the number for 1960. By the early 1970s, the scarcity of manpower had changed to a scarcity of jobs in many professions. As more students prepared for professional occupations, a noticeable shortage of workers began to develop in semi-skilled and skilled trades. Fortunately, emphasis on career education appears to be shifting more to vocational training in secondary schools and community colleges.

It is helpful to study income changes in various industries and occupations to learn how occupational needs and the demand for workers is changing. In addition, incomes can be compared by industry and by occupation groups. As Exhibit 7–8 shows, incomes increased in all industries and occupations for both males and females between 1939 and 1971. A distinction that is still very clear is the difference in income between male and female workers in all industries and occupations.

The highest incomes by industry for males in 1971 were in finance, insurance, and real estate and, for females, in public administration. Lowest incomes for males were in agriculture, forestry, and fisheries and, for females, in personal services. Among occupational groups, males had the highest income as managers, officials, and proprietors, and the lowest income as farm laborers

Exhibit 7–8   Median Wage or Salary Income of Workers 14 Years Old and Over by Sex, Industry and Occupation, 1939 and 1971

Industry and occupation groups	Full-time workers			
	Male		Female	
	1971	*1939**	*1971*	*1939**
Major industry group				
Agr., forestry, and fisheries	$ 4,458	$ 381	$ —	$ 266
Mining	10,318	1,550	—	1,331
Construction	9,483	1,276	6,199	1,042
Manufacturing	9,544	1,416	5,488	869
Transportation, communications & public utilities	10,130	1,649	6,238	1,158
Wholesale trade	9,890	1,527	5,606	1,029
Retail trade	8,071	1,196	4,402	761
Finance, insurance & real estate	11,036	1,636	5,606	1,064
Business and repair services	8,663	1,232	5,321	1,016
Personal services	6,973	940	3,070	390
Entertainment & recreation services	9,082	1,291	—	840
Professional & related services	10,081	1,349	6,497	998
Public administration	10,943	1,843	7,055	1,339
Total	9,399	1,361	5,593	788
Major occupation group				
Professional, technical & kindred workers	$12,842	$2,100	$8,515	$1,277
Farmers & farm managers	4,915	430	—	403
Managers, officials & proprietors (except farm)	13,087	2,254	6,960	1,218
Clerical & kindred workers	9,512	1,564	5,820	1,072
Sales workers	11,122	1,451	4,681	745
Craftsmen, foremen & kindred workers	9,779	1,562	5,493	995
Operative & kindred workers	8,069	1,268	4,884	742
Private household workers	—	549	2,328	339
Service workers (except private households)	7,484	1,019	4,375	607
Farm laborers & foremen	3,806	365	—	245
Laborers, except in farms & mines	7,063	991	4,486	738
Total	9,685	1,356	5,746	788

*Excludes public emergency workers but includes members of armed forces.

Source: Bureau of Census, Current Population Reports, *Consumer Income*, Series P–60, No. 85, December, 1972, p. 120.

and foremen. For females, the highest income was for professional and technical workers, while the lowest was received by private household workers. These figures again reflect the importance of education to income. The highest income occupations for both male and female are those requiring the most formal education.

Exhibit 7-9 Age—Persons 14 Years Old and Over by Total Money Income in 1972, by Sex
(persons 14 years old and over as of March, 1973)

Total money income	Total	Male Age (years)						
		14 to 19	20 to 24	25 to 34	35 to 44	45 to 54	55 to 64	65 and over
Number of persons (thousands)	73 572	11 997	8 507	13 638	10 920	11 246	8 923	8 340
Number of persons with income (thousands)	67 474	6 891	8 007	13 462	10 854	11 157	8 836	8 267
Percent	100.0	100.0	100.0	100.0	100.0	100.0	100.0	100.0
$1 to $499 or less	5.3	37.9	4.5	1.2	1.0	1.3	1.8	0.6
$500 to $999	3.6	19.0	5.5	1.1	0.7	1.0	1.3	2.7
$1,000 to $1,499	3.6	11.6	6.7	1.4	0.9	1.1	2.6	5.8
$1,500 to $1,999	3.5	7.6	5.3	1.2	0.9	1.5	2.9	8.8
$2,000 to $2,499	3.7	5.7	5.9	1.5	1.1	1.2	3.3	11.0
$2,500 to $2,999	3.1	3.9	4.9	1.8	0.9	1.3	2.3	8.7
$3,000 to $3,999	6.4	5.3	11.0	4.2	2.8	3.1	5.1	16.5
$4,000 to $4,999	5.9	3.6	10.2	5.0	3.6	3.8	5.3	11.8
$5,000 to $5,999	6.0	2.3	10.6	6.0	4.8	5.0	5.5	8.1
$6,000 to $6,999	6.1	1.3	8.5	7.6	5.6	5.3	6.6	6.1
$7,000 to $7,999	6.2	0.6	8.5	8.2	6.0	6.7	7.1	4.3
$8,000 to $9,999	12.0	0.7	10.6	17.8	15.2	13.9	13.7	5.2
$10,000 to $14,999	20.9	0.3	6.9	30.4	30.9	30.5	25.3	5.7
$15,000 to $24,999	10.2	0.1	0.8	11.0	19.4	17.4	12.0	2.9
$25,000 and over	3.4	0.1	0.3	1.7	6.1	6.8	5.2	1.9

134

Exhibit 7–9 (cont.)

| | | Male | | | | | | |
| | | Age (years) | | | | | | |
Total money income	Total	14 to 19	20 to 24	25 to 34	35 to 44	45 to 54	55 to 64	65 and over
Median income (dollars)	7 450	817	4 614	9 218	11 035	10 771	8 902	3 746
Mean income (dollars)	8 635	1 426	5 058	9 628	12 172	12 092	10 320	5 384
Year-round full-time workers								
Percent of civilian income								
Recipients	57.4	7.4	42.9	75.3	82.4	80.1	66.2	12.6
Median income (dollars)	10 538	4 225	7 019	10 329	11 986	11 840	10 763	7 757
Mean income (dollars)	11 797	4 151	7 237	10 846	13 234	13 339	12 365	10 547

		Female						
Number of persons (thousands)	80 896	11 983	9 114	14 155	11 541	12 203	10 123	11 777
Number of persons with income (thousands)	54 487	5 919	7 116	9 043	7 425	7 869	7 014	10 101
Percent	100.0	100.0	100.0	100.0	100.0	100.0	100.0	100.0
$1 to $499 or less	13.0	48.8	12.1	10.9	10.6	8.7	8.9	2.8
$500 to $999	9.9	16.1	9.8	7.2	6.8	6.2	9.4	13.9
$1,000 to $1,499	10.1	11.1	8.6	6.7	6.2	6.3	10.0	19.3
$1,500 to $1,999	8.4	6.5	7.0	5.8	5.6	5.4	7.9	17.4
$2,000 to $2,499	7.5	5.9	7.8	5.8	5.8	6.0	6.4	13.1
$2,500 to $2,999	5.5	3.1	6.0	4.9	5.0	4.8	5.1	8.5
$3,000 to $3,999	10.1	3.5	12.4	10.9	11.5	11.7	10.7	8.9
$4,000 to $4,999	8.4	2.2	11.1	9.9	10.3	10.8	9.6	4.5

135

Exhibit 7–9 (cont.)

		Female						
				Age (years)				
Total money income	Total	14 to 19	20 to 24	25 to 34	35 to 44	45 to 54	55 to 64	65 and over
$5,000 to $5,999	7.1	1.1	10.3	8.7	9.4	9.2	7.6	3.3
$6,000 to $6,999	5.5	0.8	6.8	7.7	7.6	7.8	5.8	1.9
$7,000 to $7,999	4.6	0.4	3.9	7.6	6.3	6.7	5.1	1.5
$8,000 to $9,999	5.0	0.3	3.3	8.0	6.8	8.0	5.8	2.0
$10,000 to $14,999	4.0	0.1	0.7	5.4	6.6	6.5	6.1	1.8
$15,000 to $24,999	0.8	–	0.1	0.5	1.2	1.5	1.4	0.6
$25,000 and over	0.2	(z)	(z)	0.1	0.3	0.4	0.3	0.3
Median income (dollars)	2 599	537	2 884	3 805	3 862	4 067	3 209	1 899
Mean income (dollars)	3 577	1 055	3 225	4 278	4 482	4 715	4 125	2 743
Year-round full-time workers								
Percent of civilian income								
Recipients	30.7	6.3	34.2	40.5	42.7	50.1	38.5	4.2
Median income (dollars)	6 053	3 745	5 361	6 706	6 266	6 193	6 080	5 731
Mean income (dollars)	6 526	3 825	5 339	6 843	6 801	6 846	6 717	6 738

Source: Bureau of Census, Current Population Reports, *Consumer Income*, Series P–60, No. 87, June 1973, p. 5.

Income by Age and Residence

Another interesting element in the study of income is the variation of income by age for both men and women. A significant pattern can be seen for both groups. The preceding chart, Exhibit 7–9, indicates that income for males is low during early working years but gradually rises to a peak at about 45 or 55 years of age when it starts declining. The highest income years usually occur from age 35 to 55 or 60. Low income is obtained during the early work years and again after 65.

The same pattern of income by age exists for women as for men—that is, higher incomes at older ages until about retirement age. The great difference in the two groups is that incomes of women are lower than men for all age groups. Over 40 percent of women have incomes under $2,000, while only 16 percent of men have income at that level. Over 10 percent of men have incomes above $15,000, while 1 percent of women attain that level. The average income in 1972 for men of all ages was $8,635 ($3,577 for women).

Income differences between men and women for similar work are receiving more attention as women's organizations push for laws and regulations to obtain equality in pay, as well as in other areas. There is no valid economic reason for women to receive less pay than men when they are equally qualified. Custom and attitudes change slowly, but women are being accepted in more types of jobs than previously. Equal treatment in pay may be a reality in the future.

Another significant income comparison is for residents of different regions of the country (see Exhibit 7–10). The highest incomes are received by persons living in the Western states with the average being $8,379 for males in 1971. Almost as high were incomes of workers in the Northeastern states. The lowest income region was the South with an average of $7,131 for males. Regional differences in income were not the same for women. Highest incomes were in the Northeast and lowest in the South. In all regions, the average income for women was less than half of the amount received by men.

When we compare incomes of persons living in large cities with those in the suburbs and in rural areas, we can get a better understanding of why people continue to migrate from rural areas. Exhibit 7–11 shows that incomes of suburban residents are higher than those within the cities for both large and small cities. Lowest incomes are found in rural areas with farm incomes being lower than non-farm rural residents. Average income of persons in rural areas is much below that received by those living in cities and their suburbs. More than 42 percent of farm residents had incomes below $2,000 in 1971. The number of persons 14 years of age and over who live in metropolitan areas is more than double the number living in rural areas. People will continue to migrate from rural to urban areas as long as such disparity in incomes exists.

Too many people are still trying to earn their living by farming. The lowest income farmers often have inadequate facilities to keep them fully employed. They need a larger farming operation or a part-time job off the farm. Some

Exhibit 7–10 Percentage of Persons 14 Years Old and Over by Income Groups, Region, and Sex, 1971*

Income groups	Male					Female				
	Total	North-east	North central	South	West	Total	North-east	North central	South	West
Total	100.0	24.0	27.5	30.8	17.7	100.0	24.2	27.4	31.2	17.2
Percent	100.0	100.0	100.0	100.0	100.0	100.0	100.0	100.0	100.0	100.0
Under $2,000	17.5	14.8	17.1	20.1	16.4	44.2	39.5	44.3	48.6	42.4
2,000–3,999	13.9	12.3	12.9	16.0	13.8	22.6	23.6	21.9	22.2	22.8
4,000–5,999	12.9	12.8	11.3	15.2	11.1	15.9	17.4	15.9	15.4	14.7
6,000–7,999	13.7	14.6	13.4	14.2	11.9	9.3	10.6	9.4	7.7	9.8
8,000–9,999	12.5	13.6	13.2	11.2	12.4	4.4	4.3	4.9	3.4	5.2
10,000–14,999	19.0	20.4	21.7	14.6	20.6	3.0	3.6	3.0	2.1	3.9
15,000–24,999	8.1	9.0	8.0	6.4	9.8	0.6	0.7	0.5	0.4	0.8
25,000 & over	2.5	2.6	2.4	2.4	2.9	0.2	0.1	0.1	0.2	0.3
Average income	$7,892	$8,275	$8,093	$7,131	$8,379	$3,333	$3,587	$3,331	$3,022	$3,543

*Northeast: Conn., Maine, Mass., N.H., N.J., Penn., R.I., Vermont. North Central: Ill., Ind., Iowa, Kansas, Mich., Minn., Mo., N.D., S.D., Ohio, Wis. South: Ala., Ark., Del., D.C., Fla., Ga., Ky., La., Miss., Maryland, N.C., Okla., S.C., Tenn., Tex., Va., West Va. West: Ariz., Col., Calif., Idaho, Mont., Nev., N. Mex., Oregon, Utah, Wash., Wyo., Alaska, Hawaii.

Source: U.S. Bureau of the Census, Current Population Reports, Consumer Income, Series P–60, No. 85, Dec., 1972, p. 110.

Exhibit 7-11   Percentage of Persons in Income Groups—14 Years Old and Over by Type of Residence, 1971

		In metropolitan areas							Outside metropolitan areas		
	United States		*1,000,000 or more*			*Under 1,000,000*					
Income groups	*Total*	*Total*	*Total*	*In central cities*	*Outside central cities*	*Total*	*In central cities*	*Outside central cities*	*Total*	*Non-farm*	*Farm*
No.—in thousands	152,034	104,820	59,101	25,608	33,493	45,718	21,888	23,831	47,214	41,176	6,038
Percent	100.0	100.0	100.0	100.0	100.0	100.0	100.0	100.0	100.0	100.0	100.0
Under $2,000	29.2	26.7	25.1	24.4	25.9	28.5	28.6	28.6	35.1	34.0	42.3
2,000–2,999	9.5	9.2	9.1	10.7	8.0	9.2	10.2	8.1	10.1	10.1	10.8
3,000–3,999	8.2	7.9	7.5	8.5	6.7	8.4	9.2	7.7	9.1	9.2	8.4
4,000–4,999	7.5	7.2	6.8	8.1	5.9	7.6	8.2	7.1	8.1	8.1	7.2
5,000–5,999	6.7	6.7	6.6	7.5	6.0	6.8	7.1	6.5	6.8	6.8	6.1
6,000–6,999	5.9	6.1	6.0	6.8	5.5	6.1	6.1	6.1	5.7	5.7	5.3
7,000–7,999	5.8	6.0	6.0	6.5	5.7	5.9	5.7	6.2	5.3	5.4	4.1
8,000–9,999	8.9	9.5	9.5	9.3	9.6	9.5	9.0	9.9	7.7	8.0	5.4
10,000–14,999	12.0	13.5	14.5	12.3	16.1	12.3	10.8	13.7	8.5	8.8	6.8
15,000–24,999	4.8	5.6	6.5	4.5	8.1	4.4	3.8	4.9	2.4	3.0	2.5
25,000 & over	1.5	1.8	2.2	1.5	2.6	1.3	1.3	1.3	0.8	0.9	1.0
Average income	$5,878	$6,341	$6,730	$6,125	$7,206	$5,841	$5,616	$6,056	$4,848	$4,948	$4,121

Source: U.S. Bureau of the Census, Current Population Reports, *Consumer Income*, P-60, No. 85, Dec., 1972, p. 99.

attention has been given to encouraging corporations to build new plants in small cities. Government payments to farmers have slowed the migration of people out of farming and tended to bring about a misallocation of resources. Many influential organizations, including some in agriculture, have recommended that government regulation of production and pricing be withdrawn. Current government policy appears to be moving in that direction. With fewer farms and the increasing demand for food and fibers, farm incomes should become more comparable to those of non-farm workers.

Wives' Contribution
to Family Income

A question being asked by an increasing number of housewives is, "Should I look for a job to supplement the family income?" In some instances, it is only a part-time job under consideration, but many women are accepting employment to provide more spending power for the family. Public attitudes concerning working housewives have changed so that it is now quite acceptable for women to take a job and leave their children at a nursery, at a playschool, or with a private sitter. Women who have trained for a career which they enjoy are more likely to be entering the labor force. Also, those who worked before marriage are more willing to re-enter the labor market than women who did not work before marriage. Of course, women who do not marry or who become widowed before retirement age usually work due to economic necessity. Before a housewife accepts work outside the home, the family should consider several important items concerned with job-related expenses and expected income.

Exhibit 7–12   Median Income of Families by Age and Sex of Head, 1969

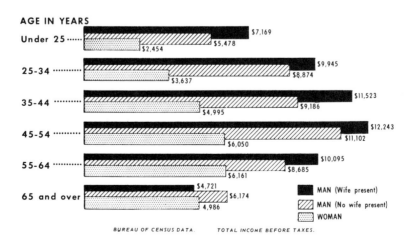

Source: U.S. Department of Agriculture, Agricultural Research Data

It is best to study job possibilities, prospective salaries, and extra costs involved before the wife accepts employment. First, she should find out how much will be withheld for taxes and estimate how much will be needed for transportation costs, lunches, additional clothing, and hired household help. Job-related expenses will depend on the type of work. It is better to over-estimate the expenses involved with working than to under-estimate. The result of such consideration will indicate the net gain in income for the family.

It is possible, given women's salaries at the present time, that the prospective net income from a job is not a reasonable gain considering the options a wife must forego. The net income could possibly put the family in a higher tax bracket when added to the husband's salary. However, just a small addition to the income may be enough to provide some of the extra things that add so much to family enjoyment. All family members should take part in the decision, because the husband and children will, in many cases, be expected to accept new responsibilities in the home. Data showing the number of women in the labor force was given in Chapter 6.

Prices and Costs of Living

Perhaps no topic has received more attention by the news media in recent years than the cost of living and prices of consumer goods and services. These economic indicators are important because they reveal how well the family's income will provide both necessities and luxuries. When prices are rising, purchasing power of a static income falls. The relationship of price changes to income changes will determine what happens to purchasing power.

For the past thirty years, prices of consumer items have risen almost continuously. Of course, prices of all products do not rise or fall at the same time or at the same rate. Some are rising while others are falling. To provide a useful measure, the average level of prices is calculated. The U.S. Department of Labor calculates a Consumer Price Index (CPI) by using prices of about 400 items found in most family budgets. Regular surveys are made in about 18,000 retail establishments to collect price information on these items. If prices rise on some items more than they fall on others, the average will rise to denote inflation or a higher cost of living.

Although this index does provide an indication of changes in living costs, all families will not be affected the same since they do not buy equal quantities of items used in making the price index. The index is a percentage figure with a base year denoted as 100. If the index increased from 100 to 116 in four years, the cost of living would be rising by an annual average of 4 percent. Living costs were 36 percent higher in 1972 than in 1960 (Exhibit 7–13).

Families whose income tends to increase at the same rate as prices will maintain their purchasing power. Some labor unions have included automatic wage changes in their contracts to vary with the CPI. Those who are most adversely affected by rising prices are retired people and others whose income tends to be fixed. In recent years, inflation has accelerated to the extent that the problem is acute for many families.

How well have workers fared in the race to keep their income rising faster than consumer prices? Consider, for example, the average weekly earnings of production workers in private employment. Their earnings increased from $95.06 in 1965 to $135.78 in 1972, an increase of 43 percent.[1] During this same period, consumer prices increased 30.8 percent. Since state and local tax rates have been rising, this apparent gain of 12 percent almost disappears. Real income increased very little during this period for the average worker.

Exhibit 7–13   Consumer Price Index, 1960–72 (1967 = 100)

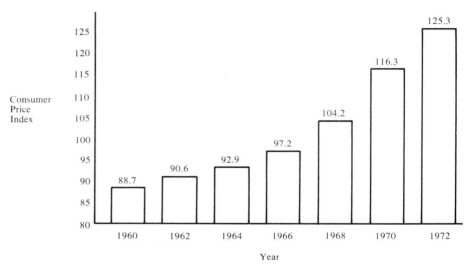

However, median annual family income increased faster than weekly earnings during this same period. Family income changed from $6,957 in 1965 to $10,285 in 1971, an increase of 48 percent. The difference here reflects more than one working family member, or some additional source of income for the family.

The continued rapid rise in consumer prices resulted in a 90-day freeze on wages and prices in late 1971. At the end of this period, the President established a Pay Board and a Price Commission to hold wage and salary increases to 5.5 percent or less and price increases to not more than 2.5 percent a year. These guidelines were set to allow for a 3 percent average increase in productivity of workers. But, controls of this type are very difficult to use with any degree of success in a democratic country, except in periods of national emergency.

---

[1]*Manpower Report of the President* (Washington, D.C.: U.S. Government Printing Office, March, 1973), p. 191.

In early 1973, controls on wages and prices were eased. The Pay Board and Price Commission were dissolved with the job of monitoring price and wage changes going to the Cost of Living Council. It has been found that more flexibility was needed in the program. Prices were rising fastest in the health, construction, and food industries. Special committees were established to work with leaders in these industries to help moderate price changes. Prices continued to increase to such an extent that the President ordered a new 60-day price freeze in June, 1973.

Inflation not only reduces a family's current purchasing power, but it also reduces the value of some kinds of savings. Those who have saved by accumulating a bank account, buying life insurance, or investing in government bonds will see the value of these savings gradually decline. This subject will be considered more extensively in Chapter 19.

Continuous price increases tend to make workers and business firms less efficient. As long as higher costs can be passed on to the consumer without much resistance, business management will not feel the necessity for efficiency. The ability of business managers is given its greatest test during periods of declining prices.

Prices of services have been rising faster than those for products. Consumers are increasing their demands for services which involve mostly labor costs. While prices of all items in the consumer price index rose 36 percent between 1960 and 1972, prices of services rose 41 percent. Professional services such as those of doctors, dentists, lawyers, and accountants are also being used more. Also, taxes are rising at a rapid rate. State and local tax rates are increasing faster than federal taxes. If we continue to ask for more highways, schools, playgrounds, additional taxes will be necessary.

Inflation would be easier to control if the blame could be placed upon one group in our society. Some individuals try to blame labor unions, government, or big business; but all of these plus other groups must share the responsibility. When Congress fails to balance the federal budget, or when labor unions acquire wage increases in excess of labor productivity increases, and when business executives raise prices of products to increase profits, inflation is being fed. In the rush for a higher standard of living, each group wants a larger share than it is reasonable to obtain. Sometimes economists make a game of trying to decide what group is causing prices to rise. Usually, however, they must identify more than one such group, and it is difficult to determine who is influencing prices most.

Wages have increased faster than production during recent years (Exhibit 6–6). This raises the cost of production for each unit of product. When unit labor costs are rising, the producer must take less profit or raise the price to the consumer. Unit labor costs rose 31.9 percent while consumer prices increased 30.8 percent between 1965 and 1972, indicating that all increases in cost were not passed on to consumers.

While some groups are able to keep their incomes rising as fast as prices increase, others are not. This results in hardships and distortions in purchasing power between various groups. If for no other reason than this, it is imperative that the rate of inflation be reduced. Economists do not agree on a permissible rate for prices to increase, but 2 to 3 percent per year appears to be a reasonable range that would prevent excessive hardships on any group. Of course, a stable price level is a desirable objective, but this does not appear to be possible in the near future.

When inflation is allowed to continue and increase, it becomes more difficult to control. People learn to make adjustments in expectation of higher prices. Wage contracts include *escalation clauses* which give automatic wage increases as prices rise. Business managers learn to make adjustments to keep the higher wages from reducing profits. As inflation feeds on itself in a vicious circle, it becomes more difficult to stop, while stopping it becomes more and more essential.

Discussion Questions

1. Explain why family income is rising at a much faster rate than growth in the number of people in the labor force.
2. Distinguish between earnings and income.
3. How may a person be unemployed and still have a high income?
4. Define "disposable income."
5. For what reasons do people migrate from rural to urban areas?
6. What important items should a family consider before the wife accepts employment?
7. Explain why rising purchasing power as a result of falling prices produces a decline in purchasing if income does not change.
8. What does a rise in the average level of prices indicate?
9. What led the President to establish a Pay Board and a Price Commission in 1971? What was the purpose of these organizations?
10. Name some of the means by which inflation continues to be fed.
11. What is the purpose of the escalation clauses that are found in wage contracts?

He who reigns within himself and rules his
passions, desires and fears is more than a king.
[Milton.]

8

Budgeting
the Income

Getting the most from the family income requires planning and budgeting. Too many families spend their income haphazardly—buying by impulse, using too much credit, being surprised that so many bills come at the end of the month, and wondering why their bank accounts always seem overdrawn. Such a financial bind can be overcome, simply by preparing plans for using the family income. The money will actually go farther in satisfying the family's needs. The time needed for preparing a family budget will be well spent, and may help avoid end of the year recriminations such as "where has our money gone?"

A budget is simply a plan for spending and saving. It need not be so rigid that it becomes a heavy burden, but it should serve a need if it is to be kept. The purpose of a budget is to show where the money goes and, with the study and planning necessary in keeping it, to help get more goods and services from that income. At the same time, it may serve an educational purpose in teaching the children to be good money managers.

Most of us have limited incomes so that it is necessary to keep expenditures balanced with income and, if possible, to set aside some savings. Any family budget needs to be somewhat flexible if it is to serve its purpose. Since budgets are plans for the future, unexpected events frequently necessitate changes or adjustments while the budget is being used.

It is often said that families must learn to live within their incomes. If a budget serves its purpose, a family can live even better within its income. Managers of businesses would not consider trying to operate without preparing a budget. If it helps a business to be more successful, it seems reasonable to believe that a family can benefit by making financial plans. Why not consider family income and spending as a business? Some families manage their income reasonably well without a written budget, but these instances are probably rare.

Who Needs to Budget his Income?

Have you ever thought that if your income were just a little larger you would not need to be such a penny-pincher? Most of us have probably believed that at one time or another. Statistics show that this is not usually the case, however. As family income rises, so does spending. Thus, the need for better money management exists in high-income families as much as in others. Our desire for more goods and services always seems to grow just a little faster than income. This is why we use credit.

Instances of family dissension over "too little money" or "too much spending" are not uncommon. A husband may have the attitude that he should give his wife a small allowance for family spending each week without considering needs or desires. He may have a hobby such as golf or hunting and fishing on which he spends excessive amounts, while family needs are sacrificed. An equally distorted budget might be at the mercy of a wife who cannot resist antique sales when the money is needed for clothing. Attitudes about money may need changing and individual desires may need to be compromised with family needs to form "family desires."

Why is it that more families do not prepare budgets for income and spending? There are probably many reasons. One reason is that some people do not know what kind of records to keep and how to prepare them. Some are afraid that they would not know how to analyze and use them after they are completed. Others do not want to recognize the reality of their particular financial constraints in order to make necessary adjustments in the family's life style. So, for these and other reasons, no records are kept. The motive for budgeting is not strong enough until all family members understand the need for it and what can be accomplished by using it.

By learning to prepare budgets and plan spending during the early years of marriage while the income is usually low, a good base is prepared for later use of higher incomes. Budgeting and keeping records will become a habit. After a few years, this record-keeping will become indispensable. Some items of family expenses, such as medical costs, can be used to lower income taxes paid, but records must be kept so that the spending can be proven. A budget, then, can be useful to any size family at all levels of income.

The Budgeting Process

Preparing a system for spending is not difficult, but some plans and records do have to be prepared. The first step is to determine how much income is available for family spending. This is the income from all sources that will go into the budget. The next step is to recognize both short and long-term goals. The goals will include plans for regular family needs as well as relatively expensive items that are purchased irregularly. Spending goals will also include some amount for savings.

After goals are prepared, the next job is to allocate the expected income to the goals. The short-term goals will be covered first with remaining income allocated to long-term goals. When this step is completed, it is time to begin using the budget. After it is put into use, some changes and adjustments will need to be made. Then, at the end of the year, it will help to restudy the budget to find places where it did not operate as expected. Corrections and improvements can be made for the next year's budget.

Setting Goals

The planning of any type of project requires a reason. This means that there must be an objective or goal—a purpose for preparing and using a family budget. If we will accept the general purpose of budgeting to be obtaining more goods and services from our income, then we can be more specific by classifying our goals according to long and short-term time periods. It will help just to write down all the things the family wants to buy during the next few years. Each item can be given a priority and placed in the long-term goals category. The family may want to plan for a washing machine in two years, a dryer two years after that, and a replacement for the refrigerator in six years.

Consumer spending is usually classified by products and services with products being further divided on the basis of how long they will last. The Department of Commerce classifies consumer spending as (1) expenditures on nondurables, (2) expenditures on durables, and (3) expenditures on services.[1] Durable goods have an expected life of one year or more, while nondurables last less than a year. Furniture, home appliances, and automobiles are examples of durable goods. Nondurables include food and clothing, while services are the work of people such as plumbers, barbers, beauticians, doctors, and mechanics.

---

[1]Campbell R. McConnell, *Economics,* 5th ed. (New York: McGraw-Hill, 1972), p. 114.

Exhibit 8–1 indicates how consumers divided their spending in 1972 among goods and services. Consumers decide what to buy in accordance with their desires, incomes, and prices. The price system guides resources into industries producing those items most wanted by consumers. If consumers are not willing to pay prices that will allow a producer to make a profit, the firm will have to stop production. Prices not only ration goods and services among consumers, but they also ration resources among producers.

Exhibit 8–1   Consumer Spending—Goods and Services, 1968–72 (billions of dollars)

Item	1968	1969	1970	1971	1972
Personal consumption spending	536.2	579.5	616.8	664.9	721.0
Durable goods	84.0	90.8	90.5	103.5	116.1
Nondurable goods	230.8	245.9	264.4	278.1	299.5
Services	221.3	242.7	261.8	283.3	305.4

Source: Federal Reserve Bulletin, May, 1973.

There are many similarities in the way families spend their money, yet there are also significant differences. For example, most families have a car and some furniture, and all families buy food, clothing, and medical services. However, the quantities of these items purchased will vary greatly among families, and certain items will be desired by some but not by others. It is good for each member of the family to help plan the budget so that the desires of each member will be included.

When a family has not kept any records of family spending before and has no idea of how much is spent on various items, it may be better to keep a record of expenses for a year before planning a budget. A small notebook is suitable for this purpose. Expenses can be kept according to the following headings—food and drinks, clothing, automobile and public transportation, furniture and appliances, home operation and utilities, medical care and drugs, personal care, education and recreation, and gifts. A more suitable grouping of expenses may be used if it fits the family situation better. If a year seems to long to wait to begin the budget, all available records—such as checkbook stubs, store receipts, and other records can be useful in preparing a budget from the previous year.

Family spending in some categories develops into a pattern according to individual needs and desires and will change very little except for changes in the size of family or for emergencies such as major medical expenses. After keeping spending records for a few months, it is easy to see certain patterns forming which will help the family in estimating the amounts needed for these items in the budget.

Long-Term Goals. High-cost items that are purchased infrequently should be planned for over a period of years and placed in the budget by setting aside a certain amount each month to save for the item or to repay the loan, if the item has already been purchased. This includes such items as a home, a car, large home appliances and pieces of furniture, education for the children, and a savings account for emergencies. A record should be made of the expected date of purchase. For example, if the budget specifies paying cash for a clothes dryer in two years, the purchase price should be divided by twenty-four, with the resulting amount to be set aside each month in a savings account for this purpose. If this amount is too much to be taken from the income, a longer time period must be allowed.

In buying a home and possibly in purchasing a car, it is not very practical to try to save the full purchase price in advance. A down payment can be saved before purchase with the balance being paid later by including the actual payments required in the budget. For less expensive items than these, it seems practical to place them in the budget and save for them before they are purchased. This may not be common practice because most buyers of large home appliances use credit, but it is these purchases that require high interest rates and consequently reduce the family's consuming power excessively. Planning ahead for these items can lower their cost and provide savings to be used for other purposes. Also, when the money is saved in advance, it can be drawing interest in a savings account which will lower the total amount that needs to be saved.

Short-Term Goals. Planning for short-term goals in a budget includes mostly items that are purchased regularly. Such planning should not last longer than one year. The budget may be made to include items of infrequent purchase such as small home appliances that are relatively inexpensive. An item of this nature may be purchased from one month's income or spread over three or four months, depending on its cost. If saving is to take more than one month, the cost should be apportioned and saved over the number of months selected. Some items of expense occur only one or two times a year, such as insurance premiums and property taxes. An amount should be set aside each month during the year so the money will be available when it is due.

After some experience with keeping expense records, the family will be able to make reasonable estimates for regular purchases such as food, clothing, utility bills, and car expenses. These should be estimated on a monthly basis and placed in the budget. It is also a good idea to give each person a personal allowance, even if it is small. An example of a monthly budget plan is shown in Exhibit 8–2.

Determining Income that Will Be Available

An important part of budget planning is determining how much money will be available for spending. Expected income from all sources should be included. Only the income after taxes, or what is actually available for spending, should

Exhibit 8–2   A Short-Term Budget Form

Monthly Budget Plan

Regular monthly expenses:
  Rent or house payment $_____
  Utilities
  Debt payments
  Personal allowances
  Other
  Total

Savings:
  Future goals and emergencies
  Seasonal and irregular expense
  Total

Regular day-to-day expenses:
  Food and drinks
  Clothing
  Automobile and public transportation
  Home operation
  Medical care and drugs
  Personal care and miscellaneous
  Education and recreation
  Gifts
  Total
      Total monthly spending plan $_____
      Total monthly income after taxes $_____

Source: Adapted from *Consumers All,* U.S. Dept. of Agriculture Yearbook, Washington, D.C., 1965, p. 164.

be counted from salaries. If income is expected from other sources, but the amount is uncertain, a conservative estimate should be included.

The form on the next page can be used as a guide for estimating family income. All funds to be received during the planning period should be recorded.

Sometimes it is difficult to determine future income because the family workers receive commissions or because the income is based on profits from a business. Previous income records and estimates should be used in these instances. The children may have income from a paper route or another part-time job. A decision must be made concerning the inclusion of all or part of this income in the budget. Such involvement is good training and gives the children a greater interest in the budget if they are required to include a part of their income.

Teaching children the basics of money management is an important part of their education. During early years, their spending should be supervised and they can learn how to save money from their allowance or earnings to get things they want. By the time they reach high school age, it is time for them to

Estimated income for _____ (period) _____

Item	Amount
Wage or salary of—	
Husband	$_____
Wife	_____
Net profit from business, farm, or profession	_____
Interest, dividends	_____
Other	_____
Total	$_____

Source: A Guide to Budgeting for the Family, Home and Garden Bulletin No. 108, U.S. Dept. of Agriculture, Washington, D.C., 1968, p. 3.

keep their money in bank accounts and learn how to write checks and keep their accounts balanced.

Allocating Money to Attain Goals

The next and most difficult task is to allocate the expected income according to the long- and short-term family goals. Previous obligations made should be considered first, such as house payments, insurance premiums, property taxes, and other debts. The remaining income can then be allocated according to family desires. Estimates for food, clothing, car expenses, and other regular expenses should be listed next. Any remaining income can be used for saving to buy items classified as long-term goals.

Occasionally the income may not be sufficient to allow for regular expenses. In that case, some adjustments will need to be made. The important thing is not to be discouraged and scrap the budget if the first try is unsuccessful. It will become easier with work and practice. Look over all expenses again and reduce items that appear least desirable to the family. If a large part of the income is necessary to pay previous debt obligations, a savings fund may have to be postponed until these debts are reduced. Reducing debts may thus be viewed as making progress toward goals. Just having plans, seeing expected income and spending written down, will allow a better perspective on the family financial situation.

Another alternative, if the budget does not balance, is to consider prospects of increasing the family income. The husband may be able to get more over-time work, or his wife may find it desirable to accept a part-time job. Seasonal work may be available when expenses are greatest, such as at Christmas. Another possibility is for children who are old enough to earn part of the money for items they want in the budget. This will not only help them to get things they want, but will give them a sense of responsibility. Every possibility for increasing income should be explored. Each family will know its own situation well enough to know what can be tried. If it is not possible to have a savings item in the budget during the first year, it should be added as soon as possible. Remember, the savings item in the budget is the setting aside of money for future purchases. If your budget will not allow for this item now, it does not mean that the family has no saving. Other items in the budget, such as house payments and life insurance premiums, are actually family savings.

"You take advantage of me, Roscoe . . . a budget should only include things I buy with money, not with things I charge!"

Courtesy: Publishers-Hall Syndicate

Trying the Plan

After the budget is balanced, it is ready to be used. It is not necessary to keep a record of every penny spent to use a budget. Enough records should be kept to make sure that the family is not overspending in some areas of expense. If the husband and wife use a joint checking account at the bank, all income can be deposited and checks written for expenses. Receipts and cancelled checks provide a good record of where the money is going. Also, minor adjustments may need to be made in the budget as it is used because of items overlooked and errors in making estimates.

If spending in a certain area continuously exceeds the budget, it may be necessary to keep a detailed record of expenses in that area for a few weeks to learn why the plan is not working. After gaining experience by using a family budget, the family should have better control of spending and should gain more satisfaction from its income. Two or three years of practice may be required before the full benefits of budgeting are realized, but money problems can bring much unhappiness to a family; and, although money cannot guarantee happiness, a reasonable amount of financial independence can sometimes reduce other family problems. Many families can improve their economic security by planning and using a budget.

The Single Person and Budgeting

A single person who works and has no family to support may think that plans for spending are unnecessary. In most cases, a single person, whether a man or woman, tends to do more impulse buying than someone buying for a family. It is difficult to prepare food for one person without some waste. Unless a single person becomes adept at cooking and meal planning, his food expense may be as large as a family with two or three persons. Single persons dine out more often than married couples and purchase more prepared or ready-to-cook foods than families do—another factor in increased food costs.

Single persons are often easy victims of impulse buying for decorating living quarters. This may be a greater problem for women than for men; because, although single women spend less than single men for food, they spend more for home furnishings and decorations. Large and heavy furnishings should be avoided by single persons whose career advancement or way of life demand mobility. If marriage is included in long-range plans, expensive items should be adaptable to family living. The portion of income spent on clothing will vary according to individual personalities and life styles. The single person who has no dependents can indulge more freely in special desires for clothes, home furnishings, or automobiles than persons with families to consider.

In preparing a budget, it is important to know how much to allow for special wants. The budget is not meant to frustrate these wants, but rather to plan how much to allow for them. After studying the budget, items which give little satisfaction may be reduced in the budget in order to have more items of special significance. The budget for a single person should include all the basic necessities found in a family budget, but in smaller amounts. It is for this reason that single people need budgets.

Major differences in budgets for families and single persons are in the long-range goals. Each should have a savings item. The family may be saving for a new washing machine or dryer, while the single person may be saving for a trip to Europe. The family may be saving for the children's education, while the single person is saving to buy an antique clock. So, goals and budgets can be just as useful in helping to satisfy more wants for single persons as they can be for families.

Family Spending
Patterns

No two families are exactly alike in their desires for different kinds of products, nor would they spend exactly alike even if their income and family size were the same. Such diversity in demands has given us a wide variety of goods in the marketplace. Knowing how other families spend may help us to allocate money for various items in our budget.

Income has an important influence on the type and kinds of goods purchased by families. All families must give first attention to the necessities of food, clothing, and shelter in making spending decisions. For the lowest income families, these items may take up all the income and still not provide what is considered to be a satisfactory level of living. Decisions will still be necessary to allocate the inadequate income among necessities. As income rises above the level needed for basic necessities, a wider spending choice becomes available. Chapter 7 showed that family incomes are rising faster than consumer prices, so that most families are enjoying a growing purchasing power. The average family annual income is over $11,000 while 22 percent have incomes above $15,000.[2] Household income distribution can be seen in Exhibit 7–2.

Material possessions of Americans have increased phenomenally. The number of two-car families increases each year, as does the number of families with color television sets, home freezers, automatic dishwashers, and stereophonic record players. The list is endless. These purchases would not be possible without rising purchasing power.

While families do spend their income for a variety of things, we have learned by studying spending records that certain patterns exist in amounts spent for basic necessities according to a family's size and income. We know that equal-size families will spend about the same percentage of income for food when incomes are similar. The same is true for other major expenditure groups.

Exhibit 8–3 shows estimates of spending by families with two to five members at various levels of income. These figures are averages and are not expected to fit each family's spending exactly. They can be used as a guide to compare a family's spending patterns with those of other families. Each family has certain desires and needs unlike those of any other family and is willing to spend less on other items to satisfy these extra demands. For example, some families prefer to spend less than average for furniture or clothing so that they will be able to own a second automobile. Consumer choice in spending helps to satisfy the demands of each family.

Take-home pay is the amount left for a family to spend after such items as income taxes and Social Security contributions have been withheld. These cannot be part of the budget. If medical or life insurance payments are withheld, they should be included as part of the income since these are expense items in

---

[2]Bureau of Census, Current Population Reports, *Consumer Income,* Series P–60, No. 80, Oct. 4, 1971, pp. 17–23.

Exhibit 8-3   Estimates of Average Family Spending by Size of Family and Income

Monthly take-home pay & no. in family	Food[1]	House operation[2]	Clothing[3]	Shelter[4]	Transportation[5]	Pers. Advancement[6]	Total family exp.	Saving, ins. & contrib.[7]	Take-home pay
$250—2	69.75	35.25	19.75	50.00	26.75	31.50	233.00	17.00	250.00
3	72.25	35.25	22.25	50.00	26.75	31.50	238.00	12.00	250.00
4	74.75	35.25	24.75	50.00	26.75	31.50	243.00	7.00	250.00
5	77.25	35.25	27.25	52.50	26.75	29.00	248.00	2.00	250.00
$300—2	83.70	42.30	23.70	54.00	32.10	43.80	279.60	20.40	300.00
3	86.70	42.30	26.70	56.00	32.10	41.80	285.60	14.40	300.00
4	89.70	42.30	29.70	58.00	32.10	39.80	291.60	8.40	300.00
5	92.70	42.30	32.70	60.00	32.10	37.80	297.60	2.40	300.00
$350—2	92.40	50.05	26.95	55.00	49.00	44.75	318.15	31.85	350.00
3	95.90	50.05	30.45	57.00	49.00	42.75	325.15	24.85	350.00
4	99.40	50.05	33.95	59.00	49.00	40.75	332.15	17.85	350.00
5	102.90	50.05	37.45	61.00	49.00	38.75	339.15	10.85	350.00
$400—2	105.60	57.20	30.80	62.00	56.00	52.00	363.60	36.40	400.00
3	109.60	57.20	34.80	64.00	56.00	50.00	371.60	28.40	400.00
4	113.60	57.20	38.80	64.00	56.00	50.00	379.60	20.40	400.00
5	117.60	57.20	42.80	68.00	56.00	46.00	387.60	12.40	400.00

Family spending & saving

Exhibit 8–3 (cont.)

Monthly take-home pay & no. in family	Food[1]	House operation[2]	Clothing[3]	Shelter[4]	Trans-portation[5]	Pers. advance-ment[6]	Total family exp.	Saving, ins. & contrib.[7]	Take-home pay
$450—2	113.40	61.65	33.30	66.60	57.60	59.85	392.40	57.60	450.00
3	117.90	61.65	37.80	69.00	57.60	57.45	401.40	48.60	450.00
4	122.40	61.65	42.30	69.00	57.60	57.45	410.40	39.60	450.00
5	126.90	61.65	46.80	72.00	57.60	54.45	419.40	30.60	450.00
$500—2	126.00	68.50	37.00	74.00	64.00	66.50	436.00	64.00	500.00
3	131.00	68.50	42.00	75.00	64.00	65.50	446.00	54.00	500.00
4	136.00	68.50	47.00	75.00	64.00	65.50	456.00	44.00	500.00
5	141.00	68.50	52.00	78.00	64.00	62.50	466.00	34.00	500.00
$600—2	141.00	85.20	42.60	80.40	77.40	90.00	516.60	83.40	600.00
3	147.00	85.20	48.60	83.00	77.40	87.40	528.60	71.40	600.00
4	153.00	85.20	54.60	85.00	77.40	85.40	540.60	59.40	600.00
5	159.00	85.20	60.60	87.00	77.40	83.40	552.60	47.40	600.00
$700—2	150.50	91.00	55.30	84.70	98.70	96.60	576.80	123.20	700.00
3	157.50	91.00	62.30	86.00	98.70	95.30	590.80	109.20	700.00
4	164.50	91.00	69.30	90.00	98.70	91.30	604.80	95.20	700.00
5	171.50	91.00	76.30	91.00	98.70	90.30	618.80	81.20	700.00
$800—2	172.00	104.00	63.20	96.80	112.80	110.40	659.20	140.80	800.00
3	180.00	104.00	71.20	98.00	112.80	109.20	675.20	124.80	800.00
4	188.00	104.00	79.20	101.00	112.80	106.20	691.20	108.80	800.00
5	196.00	104.00	87.20	101.00	112.80	106.20	707.20	92.80	800.00

Family spending & saving

	1	2	3	4	5	6			
$900—2	173.70	108.90	74.70	98.00	126.00	132.40	713.70	186.30	900.00
3	182.70	108.90	83.70	99.00	126.00	131.40	731.70	168.30	900.00
4	191.70	108.90	92.70	101.00	126.00	129.40	749.70	150.30	900.00
5	200.70	108.90	101.70	101.00	126.00	129.40	767.70	132.30	900.00
$1000—2	193.00	121.00	83.00	107.00	140.00	149.00	793.00	207.00	1000.00
3	203.00	121.00	93.00	112.00	140.00	144.00	813.00	187.00	1000.00
4	213.00	121.00	103.00	112.00	140.00	144.00	833.00	167.00	1000.00
5	223.00	121.00	113.00	122.00	140.00	134.00	853.00	147.00	1000.00
$1100—2	212.30	133.10	91.30	117.70	154.00	163.90	872.30	227.70	1100.00
3	223.30	133.10	102.30	120.00	154.00	161.60	894.30	205.70	1100.00
4	234.30	133.10	113.30	120.00	154.00	161.60	916.30	183.70	1100.00
5	245.30	133.10	124.30	131.00	154.00	150.60	938.30	161.70	1100.00

[1]Groceries: meat, milk, vegetables, eggs, fruit, tobacco, beverages; cost of meals eaten out, etc.
[2]Fuel, light, gas, telephone, water, household help, gardener, household supplies, cash or credit payment for furniture & home appliances, draperies, linen, etc.
[3]Clothing for all family members, dry cleaning, laundry, pressing, etc.
[4]Rent or payment for interest on home mortgage property improvement, real and personal property taxes (except car), fire insurance, etc.
[5]Carfare, automobile payments, auto insurance, repairs, tires, gas, oil, upkeep on car, etc.
[6]Health, health insurance, education, recreation, vacation expense, newspapers, magazines, books, hobbies, dues, state income taxes, membership fees, allowances, baby sitter, entertainment, etc.
[7]Savings accounts, retirement programs, life insurance, stocks, bonds, payment on home mortgage principal. Contributions to churches, charities, gifts, etc.
Source: Adapted from National Consumer Finance Association, Washington, D.C.

157

the budget. The lowest income families have very little left for saving and insurance programs. As income rises, the item for saving, insurance, and contributions increases faster than each item of spending. For example, a family of
four will almost double its spending when income increases from $400 to $800
per month, while the item for saving, insurance, and contributions increases
over five times.

The average family spending by categories in different income groups is
revealing when grouped as a percentage of income:

Food	19 to 31%
Clothing	8 to 11%
Shelter	11 to 21%
Household operation	12 to 14%
Transportation	14 to 10%
Personal advancement	15 to 12%
Savings	21 to 1%

The first number in the table is the proportion spent by highest-income families,
while the second figure is for the lowest-income families. High-income families
use lower percentages for the necessities—food, clothing, shelter, and household operation. These same families use higher percentages for the luxuries—
transportation, personal advancement, and savings.

Of course, spending habits are not static; they change over time. Technology
brings new products to market to compete for our income, and desires for
particular items change. As the nation continues to urbanize, a greater amount
of processing of food becomes necessary. This adds to food costs, yet the proportion of family income spent for food continues to decline. Slight declines
are also occurring in clothing and household operating expenditures. Increases
are occurring in the other classifications, with the largest being in transportation
and medical care.

There are no absolute answers to questions concerning the proper amounts
families should spend for different categories of goods and services. Exhibit
8–4 shows examples of annual budgets for a family of four with three levels of
income.

Need Psychology
and the Budget

While we have difficulty trying to measure individual needs and wants, they do
exist and vary greatly between family members. Most likely, the only persons
who would possibly be satisfied with the basic necessities—food, clothing, and
shelter—would be the very young or the very old. Most people have desires
for many things beyond these necessities and these needs can present a considerable monetary difference. Certainly, our needs and wants change at almost
every age level, and it is an unusual family money manager who understands

Exhibit 8–4   Annual Budgets for Three Living Standards; Urban U.S. Autumn 1971; Family of Four—Husband, Wife, Boy (13), and Girl (8).

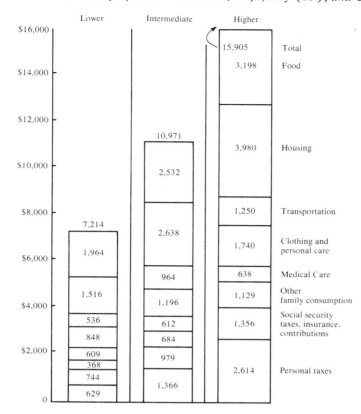

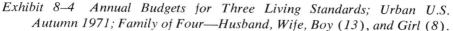

Source: Finance Facts, National Consumer Finance Association, Washington, June, 1972.

these changes and can use the income to satisfy these desires while maintaining some savings.

Economists frequently talk about the importance of consumer spending to a healthy economy. But how much do we know about what makes people buy? When incomes are rising, do we decide to save rather than spend more? According to Keynesian economic theory, consumers should spend more when incomes are rising.

Some examples indicate that consumer spending patterns are becoming more difficult to predict. Consider this example: Jim Smith is a 26-year-old mathematics teacher. His wife Gloria is a secretary in a real estate office. They have been married two years and live in a one-bedroom apartment. They had saved $2,000 for a down payment on a house, but this year they decided to use it for a trip to Europe. This example may not be typical of modern consumers, but it is happening more often as young people become more educated and have steadily rising incomes.

Many companies conduct customer interviews and surveys to aid in understanding more about consumers. This is a good policy from the consumer's point of view because it promotes competition to estimate consumer demand and keeps industry changing to provide better products and services.

Problems

1. You are having problems making your income meet all your needs; however, you have never really taken time to see where your money is going. Prepare a detailed estimate of all your expenses on a monthly basis.

2. You have a salary of $600/month, you own a car that is paid for, and you would like to start buying a house. You are also married, although your spouse does not work, and you have decided you should be able to save a small amount each month. Prepare a realistic budget showing a list of expected monthly expenditures. (Figure your income taxes to be 15 percent of your salary.)

3. Your son Timmy, age 12, has a paper route that you encouraged him to take to learn something about managing money. He has 100 customers on his route and receives $.50/month from the newspaper company for each customer. He wants a new bicycle that costs $75, and needs to start a fund to pay for his college education. For school activities and spending money he has been on an allowance of $5/week. Help him prepare a monthly budget.

4. You estimate that you will need a new car in about two years. The car you want is expected to cost $3,000. Also, the family will need to purchase a new automatic washer and dryer in about a year. You expect this will cost $500. The insurance premium on your car is expected to be $100 semiannually. How much should you budget on a monthly basis to these three items?

Discussion Questions

1. Why is a personal family budget desirable? What are some of the characteristics of a good budget?

2. Give your opinion about the statement "For a budget to be effective it is necessary that detailed records be kept and that special record forms be used."

3. Distinguish between budgeting for long-term goals and budgeting for short-term goals. Which is more important? (Give reasons)

4. Since a person must know how much he will receive in order to plan a budget, what problems does this create for the proprietor of a small business? What is your advice to the proprietor concerning budgeting?

5. What three broad categories mentioned by the text can expenditures be classified into? Which of these are most critical to the success of the budget? Explain.

6. How do prior debts fit into any budget plans?

7. Describe how a checking account at a bank can be used as a budget tool.

8. Discuss how the budget of a single person differs from that of a family. Point

out some of the problems facing the single person. Do the long-range goals of these two groups differ? How?

9. What do we mean when we say that a person's purchasing power is growing? Give some tangible evidence that this is happening in this country.

10. Comment on the statement "In the past several years, consumer expenditures have become relatively unpredictable." Speculate on the reasons for this development.

Everything that exceeds the bounds of
moderation has an unstable foundation.
[Anonymous]

9

Consumer Credit

Effective management of personal finance in these times is possible only if the individual and the family are knowledgeable about credit. A basic truth in our economic lives is that money income too frequently does not coincide or synchronize with our needs and wants. Without credit we would have to save enough to acquire more costly items after a time; whereas, with the use of credit, goods can be bought now to be enjoyed while credit is being repaid. In this way, we obtain present satisfactions in anticipation of future income.

No other country approaches the United States in volume of credit extended to consumers. Foreigners call Americans "the world's most ardent debtors," because the use of consumer credit here is an established, widespread practice. Furthermore, credit has contributed greatly to the growth of our economy. Making credit available to consumers has brought about mass buying, and this in turn has supported mass production which has created more jobs, distributed more income, and made possible the enjoyment of a higher level of living.

It is no coincidence that the country most advanced in the use of credit and the country with the world's highest standard of living are one and the same. If the consumer had to pay cash for everything he bought, economies of mass production could not be realized and prices of automobiles, refrigerators, televisions sets, etc., would be too high for most families to pay. But, credit puts these things in easy reach of millions of families at lower prices and in better quality because of volume production. On the whole, the value of these advantages far exceeds the cost of credit itself.

The purpose of this chapter is to provide information that will help in understanding credit—its kinds, its sources, its administration, its costs, and its use.

The Meaning and Classification of Credit

Credit has several meanings, but for our purposes it is the ability or capacity to obtain money, goods, property, or services in exchange for a promise to pay at some future time. A credit contract involves two parties: (1) the *creditor,* the one who gives up the thing borrowed, and (2) the *debtor,* the one who promises to pay later an agreed value, usually in money, in consideration for the thing borrowed.

Credit may be classified in different ways. One significant classification is on the basis of use for which credit is issued.

Production Credit

Production credit or *producer credit* is used for business purposes by merchants, manufacturers, farmers, and other entrepreneurs. Since this kind of credit is expected to increase output and, hence, create the means of its own repayment, we often refer to it as "self-liquidating."

Consumption Credit

Consumption or *consumer credit,* sometimes called personal credit, is used by individuals to obtain goods and services to satisfy personal wants. Generally, this kind of credit is not self-liquidating, but is instead a lien upon future income. In other words, the borrower commits future income in exchange for present value. It is sometimes argued that some uses of consumer credit might enhance the borrower's earning power and, therefore, increase his capacity to repay. Likewise, there are many instances where consumer credit is used to buy something which renders a service that the individual would have to buy otherwise. (Example: The purchase of a mechanical refrigerator saves having to buy ice.)

Occasionally, the borrower will encounter the terms *sales credit* and *loan credit.* The distinction is in the proceeds obtained from the credit transaction.

Credit used in a transaction from which the consumer-borrower obtains directly a good or service is referred to as *sales credit*. An example would be credit extended by a retailer to sell a TV set. Credit used in a transaction from which the borrower receives cash is referred to as *loan credit*. Money borrowed from a commercial bank is an example of loan credit regardless of how the cash is ultimately spent.

Speculative Credit

The definition of *speculative credit* overlaps to some extent with that of production credit, depending upon strictness of definition. Here we shall distinguish speculative credit by confining it to those instances where the borrower uses it solely to buy or sell something in expectation of favorable changes in prices. For example, where someone borrows to buy land or securities expecting to sell at a higher price or prices, he is using speculative credit.

Our concern in the field of personal finance is most obviously with consumer credit. Broadly speaking, this includes credit applying to purchases of homes, although homeowner credit will be treated separately here.

Another classification of credit is based upon the period of time covered by the credit agreement. When the credit period is a year or less, it is regarded as *short-term*. More than a year but less than five years is called *intermediate* credit. If the credit period is five years or more, it is referred to as *long-term*.

The method of repaying a credit obligation constitutes still another classification. When a debt is paid in a series of periodic payments, it is called *installment* credit. A debt which is to be paid entirely in one payment is referred to as *single payment* or *noninstallment credit*.

Finally, credit can also be classified as either *secured* or *unsecured*. When something of value (tangible, such as real property, furniture, automobiles, jewelry, etc., or intangible, such as stocks, bonds, patent rights, or royalties) is pledged to assure payment of a loan, we refer to the credit as being secured. Credit is called unsecured if the promise to repay rests solely upon the financial ability of the debtor. Nothing specific is pledged. Nevertheless, if the borrower owns vast amounts of assets, the loan is perfectly safe. In truth, unsecured loans are often as safe as secured ones.

Why Borrowers Borrow

The creation of credit is a function of the borrower's desire to use credit and the creditor's willingness to grant credit. From this self-evident truth, we can analyze, in a general way, what happens before a credit agreement is made.

Individuals desire credit for a variety of reasons:

(1) To meet emergencies such as illness, accident, death, unemployment, or property loss. Not all families have enough cash to meet sudden and unexpected needs. Although some families may have insurance protection, even insurance settlements take time and the need for cash is immediate in emer-

gency situations. Except in charity cases, use of credit is the customary solution.

(2) To buy something "on time." Typical "big ticket" items most often bought with credit are automobiles, boats, television sets, furniture, air conditioners, refrigerators, and other household appliances. Many a young man has bought an engagement ring "on time." Now it is a common practice to use credit for vacations and air travel, as well as for education.

An option open to an individual is to save until he has accumulated enough to pay cash for what he wants. However, this requires self-discipline and patience which not everyone has. Furthermore, the buyer simply might want the commodity now, even though he has the will to save in advance for it. Of course, making regular payments on credit obligations also requires self-discipline.

(3) To exercise a convenience option usually in the form of charge accounts with merchants. Purchases are made in person, by mail, or by telephone during the month, and the customer pays in one sum at the end of the period. This avoids writing a check or paying cash each time something is bought. It also has the advantage of providing a record of expenditures for families that keep a budget. Others believe that an unsatisfactory article which has been bought on a charge account is more easily returned than one bought for cash.

Why Lenders Lend

Some factors which affect a creditor's willingness to provide consumer credit to those who want it are:

(1) It is profitable to do so. The extensive desire (demand) for credit has created a distinct business out of making credit available. Users of credit are expected to pay for it just as they pay for a commodity or any other service which they buy. Institutions supplying credit operate to make a profit by charging more for credit than the costs and expenses incurred in rendering the service. Remember that these institutions seek and welcome qualified borrowers as much as any business seeks and welcomes customers.

(2) Credit may serve as a selling adjunct. Retail merchants supply consumer credit to aid or stimulate sales. This is particularly true of retailers who sell "big ticket" items and those who extend credit as a convenience.

(3) The borrower is qualified for credit. As you might expect, a creditor's primary concern is in being repaid for the loan extended. A creditor's willingness to provide credit depends upon whether he thinks he will get his money back plus financing charges. This is a judgment matter which we shall examine.

How to Qualify for Credit

What does a creditor want to know about us before he makes a judgment as to whether to grant our request for credit? It is highly unlikely that he cares whether we have light or dark hair, blue or brown eyes, or whether we are tall or short, fat or thin. None of these characteristics has any proven relation to credit worthiness.

In the field of credit, however, a number of factors do have a significant bearing upon a person's ability and willingness to pay debt obligations. A trained credit administrator looks for them when he investigates an applicant. Basically, these factors can be classified under (a) character, (b) capacity, and (c) capital. These are the ageless three "C's" of credit. *Character,* for this purpose, is determined by the applicant's willingness to pay his bills, as indicated by his credit record. A person of good character generally regards obligations seriously and tends to be careful not to incur a debt when he cannot see beforehand a way to pay. This type of person also will make an extra effort to pay even though misfortunes may have overtaken him.

Creditors know from experience that an individual's personal habits, his style of living, including his wife's ambitions even, and his reputation for honest dealing are all important indicators of how faithful he will be to his credit obligations. At the other extreme are persons described as "deadbeats" who deliberately seek to use credit without paying. Somewhere in the middle lie those who are notoriously slow in fulfilling their credit obligations, even though they may have the means.

Capacity refers to one's ability to pay his debts out of current or future income. No matter how willing a person is to honor his credit agreements, he must have the means of doing so. What is the applicant's occupation? How long has he worked in his present job? Is he regarded as a competent employee? How well is he educated or technically trained? What is his monthly income? How many dependents does he have? How much does he already owe? Does he own his home or does he rent? These and other questions provide clues as to the credit applicant's capacity.

Capital is a term referring to the amount of property or assets owned by the credit applicant. When a debtor cannot meet a debt obligation out of current or future income, he may be able to do so by selling assets. In case a debtor proves unwilling to pay, a lien may be obtained against his property, which legally can be sold to satisfy his debts.[1] Creditors do not like to take such legal action against a debtor and, as a consequence, they rely more upon character and capacity than upon capital in rating a borrower. The amount of capital one owns, however, may reveal something about his character and his capacity. Also, if the creditor is reluctant to make a loan without security, he can require the applicant to put up some capital as collateral.

From this discussion it seems fair to say that credit is based upon confidence on the part of lenders that borrowers will pay their debts. Actually the word "credit" is derived from the Latin "credere," meaning to have confidence in or to trust.

---

[1]Some assets cannot be attached and sold to satisfy debts—such as a homestead property or items needed to carry on one's occupation (e.g.—carpenter's tools owned by the carpenter or professional books used by a teacher).

In small communities where everyone seems to know everyone else, it is not difficult for a merchant or a lender to make a credit judgment about someone. In larger cities, where it is virtually impossible to know everyone personally, credit analysts must depend upon an investigation for information about customers. The investigation usually begins with a credit application form which the customer is required to fill out. A specimen of such a form is shown in Exhibit 9–1.

Exhibit 9–1   A Credit Application Form

Promenade National Bank, Richardson, Texas
Installment Finance Department

First Time-Pay
Loan Application

I wish to apply for $_____ which I can repay in _____ monthly payments.

This loan is to be used for _____

My Full Name _____ (PRINT)   Wife's First Name _____   Home Phone _____

Home Address _____ (NUMBER AND STREET) (CITY) (STATE)   How Long _____ Years _____ Months

Previous Address _____ (NUMBER AND STREET) (CITY) (STATE)   How Long _____ Years _____ Months

Age _____ Single ☐ Married ☐   Number of Dependents Including self _____   I Prefer My Payments on the   1st ☐ 11th ☐ 21st ☐   6th ☐ 16th ☐ 26th ☐

INCOME STATISTICS (Employment or Business)

Employed by _____

Address _____

Phone No. _____ How Long There _____ Years _____ Months

Position _____ Department _____

Kind of Business _____

Monthly Salary $_____ Other Income $_____

Source of Other Income _____

Previous Employer _____

Address _____ How Long There _____

Wife Employed by _____

Phone No. _____ How Long There _____ Years _____ Months

Position _____ Monthly Salary $_____

TWO CLOSE RELATIVES (Not Living With You)

Name _____

Address _____ (RELATIONSHIP)

Name _____

Address _____ (RELATIONSHIP)

BANK REFERENCES

Bank Account With _____ (NAME OF BANK)   ☐ Checking   ☐ Savings

Name of Account _____

Credit Union _____ (NAME OF COMPANY)   Value of Shares $_____

RENT PAID OR REAL ESTATE OWNED

Location _____ My Cost $_____

Title in Name of _____

1st Mortgage $_____ 2nd Mortgage $_____

Mortgage Held by _____

Mortgage Payment or—If You Rent—Rent per Month $_____

Other Real Estate Owned _____

Automobile Owned _____ (YEAR) (MAKE) (MODEL)

Financed by _____

Amount Owing $_____ Monthly Payments $_____

Stocks and Bonds Owned — Value $_____

Description _____

LIFE INSURANCE

Amount $_____ Loans $_____

LOANS, DEBTS AND ACCOUNTS OWING -- OTHER THAN ABOVE (Include Any With Credit Unions)

NAME OF BANK, COMPANY OR INDIVIDUAL	UNPAID BALANCE	MONTHLY PAYMENT	NAME OF BANK, COMPANY OR INDIVIDUAL	UNPAID BALANCE	MONTHLY PAYMENT
1.	$	$	6.	$	$
2.	$	$	7.	$	$
3.	$	$	8.	$	$
4.	$	$	9.	$	$
5.	$	$	10.	$	$

Any other information or paid loan reference that you care to submit _____

The information above is true and complete and is given to induce you to grant credit to the undersigned.

Date _____   Signed _____

The credit department of a store or lending institution where a credit application is made verifies employment and contacts places where the applicant has charge accounts or where he has done financial business. In addition, they may contact references listed in the application.

Most merchants and lenders, however, subscribe to services of a retail credit bureau, a specialized clearinghouse of information about consumers. Credit bureaus accumulate a vast amount of knowledge about individuals from cooperating merchants, banks and other financial institutions, employers, neighbors, and public records.

With correct and meaningful information at hand, a well-trained and experienced credit man can determine with great accuracy whether a potential client is a good risk.

Credit Responsibility

As a general rule, it is not difficult to obtain credit within the limits of an applicant's ability to handle that credit. However, both the applicant and the credit grantor have a responsibility to see that the credit is properly granted and properly used.

It is a sound credit practice to be sure that those who administer credit are confident that the borrower is able and willing to repay. Mistakes are sometimes made, of course, either as a result of inadequate or incorrect information or due to an error in the grantor's interpretation of what facts he has.

It is occasionally alleged that credit induces people to live beyond their means. Undoubtedly there are some instances where this is true. Frequently this situation is due to liberal extension of credit by eager sellers of goods whose profit margins are large—so large that above-average credit losses are easily absorbed. But the consumer must assume some responsibility. Proper use of credit by a borrower means that he will buy with credit only what he would have bought had he had money of his own all along. In other words, availability of credit should not induce him to spend differently than if he had his own cash.

The proper use of credit also means that the borrower fully expects to pay and is willing to pay out of current and future income or from the liquidation of assets. Furthermore, that he will avoid using more credit than he can carry.

True, some people abuse credit or use it unwisely, just as they use money itself unwisely sometimes. Moreover, there are a few borrowers who slip through the credit grantor's screen who are not entitled to credit and who will not pay for whatever reason.

However, judging from evidence that shows losses amounting to a relatively small part of total credit extended, consumer credit on the whole can be said to be efficiently administered and properly used. However, this does not mean that all creditors and all debtors are free of credit troubles. Nor does it mean that the granting of credit and its use are simple matters.

Your Credit Rating

Properly administered credit is beneficial to both lender and borrower. A credit manager is pleased when an applicant qualifies for credit. He is in business to extend credit. Moreover, if a client meets the lender's criteria, he will have no problem obtaining credit. The lender's decision is based upon information about the client himself; so, in the final analysis, he—more than anyone else—is responsible for his own credit standing. Since this credit rating is very important, it should be sustained on a high level. A few simple rules will help.

(1) Know definitely what the credit agreement entails and comply with it. Know how much is supposed to be paid, when and where it is to be paid. Then faithfully keep the payment schedule. Remember, prompt payments strengthen a credit record; delinquent payments weaken it.

(2) Do not overextend the ability to pay; that is, do not take on so much debt that it cannot be handled without reducing current living standards. One effective way to avoid this plight is to live by a budget through which the use of resources can be planned. If there is a temptation to incur a debt that will require, for example, $100 a month to meet, first determine whether this additional outlay can fit comfortably into the budget. If it necessitates reducing expenditures elsewhere, then a choice must be made. To take on an additional debt service burden without means of carrying it can only result in defaults and serious damage to your credit rating.

(3) Go to your creditors at once when you are in financial trouble. If, for any reason, debt payments cannot be met, report this to the creditors before the bill becomes delinquent. Explain honestly why the payments cannot be met. In all probability, a revised payment plan can be worked out which will remove some of the payment pressure, and will do so without injuring your credit rating. As a rule, the sooner the inability to pay is recognized and reported the easier something can be arranged. Creditors do not want another collection problem and they will help as much as they can.

(4) If there is a change in address, all creditors should be notified. This not only makes a good impression, but it is the borrower's responsibility to do so. If such notice is not given, creditors must initiate "skip tracing" (a hunt for the borrower).

(5) Watch for possible errors that might harm your credit rating. Since credit men depend upon information collected from many sources, possibilities of error are great, especially when the borrower has a common name such as Jones, Smith, Johnson, Williams, Brown, etc.

The Fair Credit Reporting Act. Until 1970, credit reports were veiled in secrecy. The borrower could not see what was reported about his credit rating and reputation. But now, under the Fair Credit Reporting Act,[2] anyone can demand to know what is in his file. Incorrect or unverified information must be removed from the file and a correction notice sent to all who have received a report containing false information.

Credit reports, because of the extensive information they contain, are commonly used for other purposes than to determine eligibility for credit. Insurance companies use them for underwriting purposes. Employers use them to evalu-

---

[2]Public Law 91–508, enacted October 26, 1970.

ate a job applicant. Thus, it is vitally important to make sure the information in the files is accurate and up-to-date.

Under the law, a credit reporting agency must advise a person that he is currently being investigated and that he is entitled to know what is in the report. If it is requested, the agency must reveal who has received the report during the past two years, if the request was for employment purposes, and during the past six months, if for credit or other purposes.

The Fair Credit Reporting Act makes it unlawful for an agency to report any of the following information:

1. A bankruptcy that occurred more than fourteen years ago.
2. An arrest, indictment, or conviction for a crime after seven years from date of disposition, release, or parole.
3. A suit or judgment that occurred more than seven years ago.
4. A past due account, a tax lien, or any other kind of unfavorable information after seven years.

If a client has sought credit directly and has been turned down by a store or financial institution because of information contained in a report from a credit bureau, the law requires the store or financial institution to advise him of the credit bureau's name and address. A simple disclosure notice like the one shown in Exhibit 9–2, or one very similar, is what he should receive.

If the rejection is due to information received from someone other than a credit bureau, the store or financial institution must clearly and accurately disclose the fact at the time of rejection and advise the customer that he has sixty days in which to request in writing reasons for the turndown.

In this instance, he might receive a notice very similar to the following:

N O T I C E

Date of Credit Request_____

We have denied your request for credit because of information obtained by us. Upon your written request, received by us within sixty days of your receipt of this notice, we will disclose the nature of such information to you.

Dated:_____   _____

(Name of Institution)

If credit has been denied based upon information that the client himself has supplied, then he would receive a notice worded along the following lines.

N O T I C E

Date of Credit Request_____

We have denied your request for credit. Upon your written request, received by us within sixty days of your receipt of this notice, we will tell you the reason(s) for such denial.

Dated:_____   _____

(Name of Institution)

Exhibit 9–2   A Simple Disclosure Notice

```
                        N O T I C E
                Date of Credit Request_____
    We have denied your request for credit because of information contained
    in a credit report from:

    _____
                    (Name of Credit Bureau)

    _____
                    (Address of Credit Bureau)

    Dated:_____    _____
                                         (Name of Institution)
```

Types of
Consumer Credit

Sales Credit

Charge Accounts. Charge accounts are instruments of sales credit. They are used in the sale of goods and services by retail merchants, oil companies, airlines, doctors, dentists, utility companies, and many others who sell to consumers.

Basically there are two kinds of consumer charge accounts: (a) simple charge accounts—sometimes called 30-day charge accounts—and (b) installment charge accounts.

The simple charge account is used mostly for convenience. As a rule, no written promise to pay is required of the customer. The obligation is understood. The creditor expects the account to be paid at regular intervals, usually monthly. The seller generally extends and carries the credit himself showing amounts due him as "accounts receivable" on his books.

The simple charge account is an old form of credit once used extensively by most local merchants, including grocers, druggists, dry goods, clothing, and hardware merchants. However, emergence of food supermarkets and discount houses aggressively engaged in price competition and selling for cash only has reduced greatly the amount of convenience goods sold on simple charge accounts. On the other hand, the amount of charge account business done by department stores and by specialty stores has grown substantially in recent years.

Charge account customers who desire longer credit terms may qualify for some type of installment charge account which permits them to pay the amount owed in installments over a period of several months, normally up to as many as twelve. Some plans allow the option of paying a bill in full without any credit cost or paying in installments with a credit charge added, commonly 1.5 percent of the unpaid balance each month, or 18 percent a year.

Installment charge accounts are prearranged between the retail store and the customer, the latter applying for credit and agreeing to pay a certain portion of his bill each month with a minimum dollar amount specified. The store's credit department, after investigation, will set a credit limit for the customer which will allow him to continue to make purchases on account until the sum owed reaches this limit. An arrangement of this kind is called a *revolving credit account*.

For example, let's say that a customer applies for the privilege of buying merchandise on an installment charge account from Store Z. The store's credit department makes a careful investigation of his credit history and economic circumstances and concludes that he can pay as much as $50 a month debt service without straining his budget. If the store's policy is to limit a customer's outstanding credit to ten times the amount the customer can pay monthly, then his maximum line of credit will be $500.

Installment Sales Contracts. Because charge accounts generally are a form of unsecured credit and to some extent are granted for convenience, their dollar limits tend to be relatively modest. Therefore, sales of "big ticket" durable items involving credit are normally not made on charge account but under a written installment credit contract calling for equal payments at stated regular intervals. Each installment sale is ordinarily made under a separate contract; whereas, with an installment charge account, a customer can buy any kind of goods from time to time without making a new contract with each purchase, so long as his credit limit is not exceeded.

Monthly payments on installment sales contracts generally extend over a longer period of time than is the case with installment charge accounts. Another difference is in the security required for an installment sale contract. The seller (lender) will ask the buyer (borrower) to sign a contract of sale under which the buyer gives the seller a promissory note secured by what is called a security agreement.[3] The latter instrument is evidence of the creditor's security interest in the personal property (the goods bought), identified as collateral, and must be signed by the debtor.

Installment sales credit, unlike installment charge account credit, is frequently sold or assigned by retailers to financial institutions, more especially commercial banks and sales finance companies.[4] This enables the retailer to get his money at once and not have his capital tied up in credit. Debtors under this arrangement make installment payments directly to the new owners of the credit paper which may be assigned either with recourse or without recourse. *Without recourse* means the retailer is free of liability if the debtor fails

---

[3]The instrument known as a security agreement has come into common use under the Uniform Commercial Code, largely replacing the chattel mortgage and the conditional sales contract.

[4]Retailers at times do pledge their accounts receivable (charge accounts and installment charge accounts) as security for loans from financial institutions.

to pay. *With recourse* means the retailer will have to pay the bank or sales finance company if the debtor defaults.

As Exhibit 9–3 shows, purchases of automobiles involve the use of more credit than any other consumer item. Buying an automobile is the second largest single expenditure most families will ever make, exceeded only by the cost of a home. For this reason, only about one of every three automobiles is bought with cash.

Exhibit 9–3   Consumer Credit Outstanding (year end, in billions)

	1950	1960	1965	1970	1972
Total	$21.5	$56.1	$90.3	$126.8	$157.6
Installment	14.7	43.0	71.3	101.2	127.3
Automobile paper	6.1	17.7	28.6	35.5	44.1
Other consumer goods paper	4.8	11.5	18.6	29.9	40.1
Repair and modernization loans	1.0	3.1	3.7	4.1	6.2
Personal loans	2.8	10.6	20.4	31.6	36.9
Non-installment	6.8	13.2	19.0	25.6	30.2
Single payment loans	1.8	4.5	7.7	9.5	12.3
Charge accounts	3.4	5.3	6.4	8.8	9.0
Service credit	1.6	3.4	4.9	7.3	8.9

Note: Data may not sum exactly due to rounding.
Source: Federal Reserve Bulletins

However, not many car dealers extend credit themselves. This is most often true of dealers in large cities. They have tie-ins with commercial banks or sales finance companies that actually provide the credit. (See Exhibit 9–4). In fact, a car dealer may have direct wire communication with a bank where a facsimile of the buyer's application is received by a terminal machine and immediately reviewed and approved or denied by a bank loan officer, with the decision sometimes coming back to the dealer before the buyer is through admiring the

Exhibit 9–4   Holders of Automobile Credit Paper

	1960	1965	1968	1970	1972
Finance companies	43.6%	32.8%	30.1%	28.0%	23.1%
Commercial banks	46.1	55.5	56.6	56.4	61.3
Other financial lenders*	8.3	10.6	12.4	14.7	14.9
Automobile dealers	2.0	1.1	0.9	0.9	0.7
	100.0%	100.0%	100.0%	100.0%	100.0%

*Credit unions, savings and loan associations, and mutual savings banks.
Source: Federal Reserve Bulletins

car he proposes to buy. Although most credit decisions are not made this quickly, banks try to process every application in not more than one day.

When an automobile installment note is in default and the bank incurs a loss, there is what might be called indirect recourse on the dealer. Here is how it works: banks handling automobile paper for dealers commonly require each dealer to set up a loss reserve which must equal a certain percentage of his total loans outstanding (usually a 3 percent reserve). Losses are charged to this reserve.

Loan Credit

Thus far we have discussed forms of sales credit. We now turn to forms of loan credit by which a borrower obtains money to be used as he sees fit. From one point of view, it may be said that sales credit simply amounts to borrowing money from a retailer and in turn using it to buy goods from him; but, in reality, the distinction between sales credit and loan credit lies in what a borrower actually obtains directly from the credit transaction itself. In one case it is merchandise and in the other it is cash.

There are many reasons for consumers to borrow cash. Studies show that the leading reason is to consolidate overdue accounts. Some consumers incur a number of debts with different creditors and, as a result, find themselves burdened with payment commitments that put them in a financial bind.

Under such circumstances it is easy to fall behind in payments. Often the best course to follow is to borrow enough cash to pay off all other creditors and thereby consolidate many debts. Payments on the new loan may be extended over a longer period of time, thus reducing the drain on monthly income, since payments will be smaller when maturity is lengthened.

A second important reason for a consumer to borrow cash is to buy automobiles, home furnishings, appliances, and other items ordinarily bought with sales credit. Some consumers prefer to borrow and pay cash for such goods because they often find it is more economical to do so. With cash they can take advantage of lower prices and frequently can obtain a better bargain when buying automobiles. Also, consumers with good credit ratings often find that the cost of a cash loan at a commercial bank is less than the cost of retail sales credit.

Borrowing cash to meet unemployment, medical, dental, hospital, and funeral emergencies has been declining in frequency largely due to increased coverage by social and private insurance. On the other hand, borrowing cash to pay for travel, vacation, and education expenses has been increasing significantly.

Individuals used to borrow considerably more to pay taxes, especially federal incomes taxes, than they do now. Withholding of taxes at the source of income has been responsible for the decline.

Loan credit may be extended on a secured or unsecured basis and be payable in installments or by a single payment at maturity. Consumers with good credit standing often borrow money without security and with an option of installment or single payment liquidation. However, many loans are secured with the borrower pledging such financial assets as a life insurance policy with cash surrender value, savings accounts, or marketable securities—such as stocks and bonds. With easily marketable assets pledged, a borrower can usually obtain funds on a single payment basis and at a lower interest cost.

If a consumer is unable or unwilling to pledge assets, he still may qualify for a loan; but the lender is likely to restrict the total amount of the loan, require weekly or monthly installment payments, and limit the payout (maturity) period of the credit contract.

Credit Cards

Non-Bank Credit Cards. A variation of charge accounts involves credit cards whose initial use dates back to the early 1920s. A few hotels, retail stores, and oil companies pioneered in the use of credit cards. Earliest credit cards were issued as evidence of the holder's right to credit in buying from a specific card issuer. In other words, they were two-party instruments, meaning that the holder could buy on credit only from the firm which issued the card.

In later years, there emerged what might be called multi-party credit cards —some of the first being American Express, Diner's Club, and Carte Blanche —which were valid in all restaurants, hotels, motels, and retail establishments cooperating with the central issuing agency.

Multi-party cards are issued upon application. Approved applicants pay an annual fee of $15 or so to the issuer. Participating sellers of goods and services are relieved of cost of credit investigation and of credit risk, but in return must pay the central agency a percentage of the amount sold on credit, called a "discount fee," which in some instances ranges as high as 7 percent.

Suppose a customer has been approved for an American Express membership. He is issued a credit card which enables him to buy on credit at any place of business which honors the American Express card. Let's say he and his family are on vacation and stop at a motel where he tenders his credit card to pay for food and lodging amounting to $80. When he "checks out," he will be asked to sign a statement which shows the total of itemized amounts. At the same time, his credit card number will be recorded on the statement. He then goes on his way, without having to pay until he is billed by American Express, such billing being monthly and including all charges he has made during the period.

If he is slow about paying and is in arrears by, say, two months, he will be charged a penalty, perhaps 1½ percent per month. More likely, however, he will be denied further credit.

How does the motel come out? It is paid $80 less the discount fee by American Express, regardless of whether the latter ever collects from the customer.

Inter-Bank Credit Cards. The most advanced use of credit cards has come within recent years in the form of interbank credit cards. With the development of electronic accounting (computers), commercial banks saw almost unlimited possibilities of extending credit service and doing so more efficiently.

Today, several interbank credit card services are in operation. The two most widely used are BankAmericard and Master Charge. Most commercial banks offer one of these services. At these banks, a person may apply for a card which will be honored by all businesses that have contracted to participate.

First, he will be required to fill out a credit application. (See Master Charge Application, Exhibit 9–5.) The bank will then check his qualifications for credit. If he is accepted, he will be extended a revolving line of credit in an

Exhibit 9–5 An Application for a Credit Card

MASTER CHARGE® APPLICATION

FIRST NATIONAL BANK IN DALLAS
Dallas, Texas

MR ☐ MRS ☐ MISS ☐ FIRST NAME	MIDDLE	LAST	BIRTHDATE	SOCIAL SECURITY NUMBER	
STREET ADDRESS	CITY	STATE	ZIP CODE	HOW LONG?	HOME PHONE	SINGLE ☐ MARRIED ☐ WIDOWED ☐ DIVORCED ☐

Please indicate the following accounts you have at the bank listed in the heading above:

Checking Account Number (list one account number only) __________

Savings Account Number (list one account number only) __________

If you have a Master Charge card from another bank, please indicate your Account Number __________

OWN HOME ☐ RENT ☐	MORTGAGE HOLDER OR LANDLORD	PREVIOUS ADDRESS	CITY	STATE	HOW LONG?
EMPLOYER	HOW LONG?	OCCUPATION	NO. OF CHILDREN		
EMPLOYER'S ADDRESS	CITY	STATE	BUSINESS PHONE	MONTHLY INCOME	
YOUR PREVIOUS EMPLOYER	ADDRESS	CITY	STATE		
HOW LONG?	OCCUPATION	MONTHLY INCOME			
SPOUSE'S FIRST NAME	SPOUSE'S EMPLOYER & ADDRESS	CITY	STATE		
HOW LONG?	OCCUPATION	MONTHLY INCOME	BUSINESS PHONE	SOURCE OF OTHER INCOME	OTHER INCOME
NEAREST RELATIVE NOT LIVING WITH YOU	ADDRESS	CITY	STATE	RELATIONSHIP	
YOUR BANK	CITY	STATE			
CAR MAKE, MODEL & YEAR	WHERE FINANCED?	MONTHLY AUTO LOAN PAYMENT			

LOANS, DEBTS AND ACCOUNTS OWED

Name of Bank, Company or Retail Department Store	Unpaid Balance	Monthly Payment	Name of Bank, Company or Retail Department Store	Unpaid Balance	Monthly Payment
1.	$	$	5.	$	$
2.	$	$	6.	$	$
3.	$	$	7.	$	$
4.	$	$	8.	$	$

AMOUNT OF CREDIT DESIRED

$400 ☐ $500 ☐ $600 ☐ $700 ☐ $800 ☐ $900 ☐ OTHER __$______ NO. OF CREDIT CARDS NEEDED ______ amount the bank thinks his circumstances justify, but usually not more than $2,500.

A billfold-size card will be issued to him showing the issuing bank's name and number, the customer's name, the card's expiration month and year, his account number, and his line of credit. On the reverse side will be space for an authorized signature.

The card holder may obtain duplicate cards for other members of his family, but he is the person who will be held responsible, since the cards were issued upon his application and he signed the agreement.

Bank credit card holders pay no membership fee. However, merchants and others from whom purchases are made using the card have to pay the bank a discount fee on the amount charged to each account. The latter fee is a service charge the bank makes for handling details of the credit such as billing and collecting, and for assuming the credit risk, since there is no recourse upon the seller in case of a credit loss.

Purchases on a credit card are accumulated and a statement is issued each month. If the new balance is paid on or before the date indicated on the statement (which is at least twenty-five days after statement closing date), no finance charge is made. However, if the card holder prefers to pay in installments, a finance charge is attached. This charge will be made monthly at a rate of 1.5 percent, or 18 percent a year on the average daily unpaid balance up to $1,500. Then, at a periodic rate of 1 percent or 12 percent a year, charges are made on the next $1,000 of average daily balance.

Most bank officials think that the interbank credit card is only the beginning of an amazing development in the consumer credit field. Retail merchants are expected ultimately to discontinue credit service, leaving credit functions largely to banks. Qualified consumers will be extended lines of credit which will be merged with checking accounts. A single universal credit card will be in use. This card will carry the customer's name, address, account number at his bank, and the name and number of his bank. It will be coded to indicate the customer's line of credit. Every merchant and every business will be similarly identified. The cardholder's signature will appear on the face of the card and will be identical to the signature on records of the issuing bank. A thumbprint or photograph might also be used.

Something like this will happen: a customer will make a purchase (say of a shirt) at a store—price, $8.75. He neither charges the purchase nor pays cash. Instead, he hands the clerk his bank card which she puts in a small terminal machine connected directly by wire with an electronics accounting machine in the bank, and also connected with the store's own accounting machine. At the same time, a sales slip in duplicate is inserted or perhaps is already in the machine. The machine will have a small keyboard on which the clerk will record stock number and price of the item. She then presses an activating bar and the machine sends an impulse to the store's bank which causes the store's account to be credited. If the customer has his account at the same bank, the machine will debit his account there. If he has his account with some other bank, the machine in the store's bank will clear instantaneously through some central point like a Federal Reserve Bank or a clearinghouse or directly with the second bank whose machine will debit the customer's account on its books and credit the store's bank.

The terminal machine at the clerk's counter will also send simultaneously an impulse to the store's electronics accounting machine where the sale is recorded showing the stock item, the number of the clerk making the sale, and an increase in the store's bank account by $8.75. The store's accounting machine will not only keep an up-to-the-minute inventory of all items in the store, but will know costs, prices, and gross margins. If clerks are on commission, the machine will calculate and record this information to each clerk's credit. At any moment, the store manager will be able to get a printout showing a current inventory breakdown, sales by items, and sales by clerks; and he also can confirm the store's bank balance.

One other thing will happen when the clerk presses the activating bar on the store's terminal machine. The machine will impress on a sales slip, in duplicate, information from the customer's card plus the number of the item bought and the price, as well as the time of purchase. The clerk then will require the customer's signature on the sales slip, checking to see that that signature matches the one on the customer's bank card. A copy of the sales ticket will be handed to the customer for his records or for possible use should he return the merchandise. In the latter case, the whole banking process will be reversed.

An interesting sidelight of the above procedure is that if the customer has no balance in his bank at time of purchase, having used up his line of credit as well as all he has deposited, the bank's machine will reject the store's draw on it, and there will be no sale.

It might appear that the enormous cost of such an arrangement will eliminate small banks. Not so, because large banks will handle a major part of processing for many smaller institutions, or a group of the latter might process through a cooperative center. Such a system, however, is several years from realization, since it necessitates the standardization of credit cards and the installation of a tremendous amount of equipment.

Sources of Consumer Credit

Financial Institutions

All financial institutions that supply credit to consumers are not alike in the services they provide, in the charges they make, or in the risks they are willing to assume. It is important to be able to distinguish these institutions and to know how they differ.

The principal ones are *commercial banks, credit unions, industrial banks, consumer finance companies,* and *installment sales finance companies.* The first three are referred to as intermediaries, because they obtain most of their funds from depositors. The others obtain the money they lend from capital furnished by owners and funds borrowed from the public and/or other financial institutions. The easiest way to distinguish intermediaries and nonintermediaries is to remember that the former are savings institutions in whole or in part, whereas the latter are not.

Commercial Banks. Commercial banks are the most common of the intermediaries. They are widely distributed geographically and range in size from relatively small units in towns and villages to multi-billion dollar institutions in large cities. There are about 14,000 commercial banks in the United States, virtually all of which engage in some form of consumer credit activity. They not only make direct personal loans to consumers, but also buy automobile and other installment paper from retailers. As we have seen, commercial banks are also active in promoting use of interbank credit card services. Some banks offer what are called check-loan or check-credit plans to individuals. Such plans actually extend a personal line of credit to a customer usually in the form of specially designed checks which he can use as he wishes and for any purpose he chooses, repaying the loan in monthly installments.

Commercial banks generally charge lower rates on consumer loans than do other institutions, but they are also somewhat stricter in granting credit. If you have a deposit account with a bank and your record is good, you most likely will be able to borrow there with little or no delay. At first the bank probably will require collateral as security for a loan, but as you establish your credit worthiness, you will be able to borrow without collateral. In fact, most banks try to grant credit on an unsecured basis and do so when earning power and net worth justify it. Unsecured loans tend to build goodwill for the bank.

Credit Unions. A credit union is essentially a cooperative made up of members "who agree to save their money together and make loans to each other at low interest." A credit union is organized by people who have some common bond such as working for the same employer, or having membership in the same fraternal order, church, or labor union, or living in some closely knit community.

Loanable funds of credit unions come not only from savings of members who receive shares in return, but also from money borrowed by the union from commercial banks.

Loans are made to members only and at an interest rate customarily 1 percent a month on the unpaid balance. Credit losses generally are at a minimum because of intimate personal acquaintanceship among members and a strong compulsion to repay what is borrowed from one's fellows. Also, employers tend to work closely with credit union officials in making collections. It is claimed that losses average less than ⅕ of 1 percent.

Laws are favorable to credit unions, the chief advantage being exemption from income taxes. Credit unions are also able to keep operational costs down, since their operations tend to be simple; and they have a captive market, even if small. Frequently the employer whose employees operate a credit union will furnish free office space, utilities, and sometimes even secretarial and clerical help. It is not necessary for credit unions to impress the public, and, therefore, be obliged to advertise expensively or to furnish their offices elaborately.

As in the case of commercial banks and other financial institutions, credit unions are supervised and examined by the respective governments from which their charters are obtained. Historically, the record of credit unions has been quite good. An opportunity for membership in a credit union should be seriously considered.

Exhibit 9–6   Holders of Consumer Installment Credit, Year End (in billions)

	1950	1960	1965	1970	1972
Total	$14.7	$43.0	$71.3	$101.2	$127.3
Commercial banks	5.8	16.7	29.0	41.9	59.8
Finance companies	5.0	15.3	24.3	31.1	32.1
Credit unions	.6	3.9	7.3	12.5	16.9
Retail outlets	2.9	6.3	9.8	14.1	15.9
Miscellaneous lenders	.4	.8	1.0	1.5	2.6

Note: Data may not sum exactly due to rounding.
Source: Federal Reserve Bulletins

Industrial Banks. Industrial banks (some are known as Morris Plan banks) were originally created to make loans to consumers, mostly industrial wage earners—hence the word industrial. These institutions lend to consumers under an agreement whereby a borrower obligates himself to make savings deposits of a definite amount at regular intervals, usually monthly, until enough is accumulated to pay the loan plus a finance charge.

Operational details of industrial banks differ considerably as a result of variations in legal status from state to state. In some states, they are not allowed to use the word "bank" in their titles. Instead they are known as industrial loan companies and, as such, are not allowed to extend checking account privileges. On the other hand, industrial banks which still adhere to Morris Plan principles are deposit institutions, obtaining funds from savings and checking accounts of customers who, in many instances, are also borrowers.

Industrial banks and industrial loan companies now make all kinds of consumer loans at rates generally higher than those of commercial banks, but less than small loan company rates.

Consumer Finance Companies. Consumer finance companies, also called *small loan companies* and *personal loan companies,* specialize in making small cash loans to individuals. Repayment is mostly on an installment basis, commonly up to a thirty-six-month period.

These companies are strictly licensed and operate under the Uniform Small Loan Law in effect in almost all states.

In order to obtain a license to operate a consumer finance company, an applicant must establish that he is of good character and be able to post a surety bond. The business is subject to supervision and to examination by state authorities annually, or more frequently if deemed necessary.

Limits are set by statute on both the amount that may be loaned to one borrower and the interest rate that may be charged. In the beginning of licensed small loan companies, the maximum loan that could be made was $300. The law has since been amended in most states to permit higher maximum loans, ranging from $500 to $5,000. Similarly, interest rates now vary among the states from 2 percent to as high as 4 percent a month; but, in most instances, the maximum rate applies only to the first specified amount of a loan, say the first $300, with lower rates on the next specified amount or amounts above the first.

Consumer finance companies make smaller loans generally involving greater risk than commercial banks make and, therefore, charge higher rates. Both secured and unsecured loans are made. Small amounts are often loaned solely on the borrower's character and ability to pay, but security—such as a chattel mortgage on furniture or on an automobile—is required for relatively large loans. Borrowers of larger sums might also be required to buy credit life insurance to pay the loan in case of death. In states that permit it, the lender might ask the borrower to sign a wage or salary assignment enabling the lender to collect from the borrower's employer if the borrower fails to pay.

There are numerous consumer finance companies, the great majority of which are small; but there are a few quite large ones with many branch offices scattered across the country. Familiar by name to most of us are two big ones: Household Finance Corporation and Beneficial Finance Company.

Installment Sales Finance Companies. These are roundabout sources of consumer credit because they, as such, do not make loans directly to individuals. In a technical sense, they do not lend money but buy (discount) installment paper from dealers and merchants who have made credit sales. However, these companies do exert considerable influence upon the retailer's credit policies, and even furnish contract forms, rate charts, etc., to the retailer.

Installment credit paper arising from automobile sales constitutes the largest part of the business of sales finance companies. In fact, the earliest of these companies were formed for the specific purpose of acquiring automobile paper. Some, like General Motors Acceptance Corporation (GMAC) and Ford Motor Credit Company, are subsidiaries of automobile manufacturers.

Security

Most consumer credit is used to buy durable goods under an installment sale contract. The lender almost always takes as security a lien upon the goods bought. It is in the lender's interest to see that the loan period is less than the

"We adhere strictly to the principle of truth-in-lending, Figby! . . .
No need to tell a customer that the interest is going to be fantastic!"

Reprinted by permission: Publishers-Hall Syndicate

useful life of the pledged asset, because at all times the lender wants the value of collateral to exceed the balance of the debt. Borrowers are less likely to default when pledged assets are worth more than amount owed.

Some durable items like automobiles depreciate in value quickly in early months of use. Sound credit policy requires the borrower to make a down payment at time of purchase, thus beginning with an equity in the asset.

When a borrower puts up intangible assets as collateral, such as stocks and bonds, which are subject to market price fluctuations, the lender as a rule will ask for collateral value well in excess of the amount of the loan. In fact, financial institutions are restricted in the amount they can lend on securities listed for trading on organized exchanges. The restriction is usually expressed as a percentage of market value of the collateral. When market value drops, the borrower must either put up more security or reduce the loan. If he is unable to do either, the lender can sell the securities under what is called "stock power" which the borrower signed when the loan was granted. (See Exhibit 9–7.)

A lender will sometimes require a borrower to have an accommodation endorser to co-sign before a loan is made. If the debtor does not pay the note when due, the co-signer is legally obligated to do so, because the effect of co-signing is to guarantee the loan.

Less than 3 percent of all loans extended are endorsed or co-signed, and most of these involve personal relationships such as a father co-signing a son's note at a bank. Students who borrow to go to college usually have not established a credit record, and the lender will ask for a co-signer.

As a rule, co-signing someone's promise to pay a debt is not a wise thing to do. Certainly you should not do so without very carefully considering the possibilities of embarrassment later. Would you lend the borrower the money yourself? If so, it probably would be better to make the loan than to guarantee his

Exhibit 9–7 A Stock Power Form

RAUSCHER PIERCE SECURITIES CORPORATION

IRREVOCABLE STOCK OR BOND POWER

FOR VALUE RECEIVED, the undersigned does (do) hereby sell, assign and transfer to

_____

(Social Security or Taxpayer Identifying No.)

IF STOCK,
COMPLETE
THIS
PORTION

_____ shares of the _____ stock of _____ represented by Certificate(s) No(s). _____ inclusive, standing in the name of the undersigned on the books of said Company.

IF BONDS,
COMPLETE
THIS
PORTION

_____ bonds of _____ in the principal amount of $_____. No(s). _____ inclusive, standing in the name of undersigned on the books of said Company.

The undersigned does (do) hereby irrevocably constitute and appoint _____ _____ attorney to transfer the said stock or bond(s), as the case may be, on the books of said Company, with full power of substitution in the premises.

Dated _____

In Presence of _____

IMPORTANT – READ CAREFULLY

The signature(s) to this Power must correspond with the name(s) as written upon the face of the certificate(s) or bond(s) in every particular without alteration or enlargement or any change whatever. Signature guarantee should be made by a member or member organization of the New York Stock Exchange, members of other Exchanges having signatures on file with transfer agent or by a commercial bank or trust company having its principal office or correspondent in the City of New York.

Signature _____

Name Printed _____

Account Number _____

note. Remember that the credit rating of the party you are accommodating is not good enough to obtain a loan without a co-signer.

When a Borrower
Cannot Pay

No matter how careful a creditor might be in investigating loan applicants or how honest borrowers might be in their determination to pay whatever debts they incur, there are always some loans that go sour. Fortunately, the number of defaults is quite small in relation to total number of consumers who use credit, and the dollar amount of losses from bad debts is similarly small in relation to the immense total of consumer credit outstanding.

A person who is unable to pay his debts is said to be "insolvent." Certain things can and likely will happen. Secured creditors will take the assets pledged as security. Unsecured creditors may enter court and bring suit to obtain a judgment against the insolvent person. If the court grants the judgment, the debtor's property may be seized and sold to satisfy the judgment (be applied to the debt).

The debtor, however, may not have any personal property or real estate that can be taken. In that case, in most states, his wages can be attached, if he is a worker. In other words, his employer can be ordered by the court to pay out of the worker's wages up to the amount he owes. This process is called *garnishment,* and the employer is known as the *garnishee.*

Laws applying to garnishment vary considerably among the fifty states, ranging from (1) no garnishment of wages at all in Texas, to (2) at the discretion of the court in Florida, to (3) different amounts or percentages of wages that can be attached in other states.

Title III of the Truth in Lending Act of 1968 establishes a new federal garnishment restriction. Under it, the maximum amount of a person's earnings subject to garnishment is the lesser of (a) 25 percent of his disposable weekly earnings or (b) the amount by which his weekly disposable earnings for any one week exceed thirty times the federal minimum hourly wage. The act also prohibits an employer from discharging any employee on the grounds that the employee's earnings have been subject to garnishment for debt.

Suppose a debtor's weekly gross wages are $120 and, after income tax withholding and other allowable deductions, his weekly disposable (take-home) earnings are $100. Suppose also the federal minimum hourly wage is $2 at the time. Then only $25 of his wages (25 percent of $100) is subject to garnishment under the federal law, because $25 is less than $100 minus thirty times the federal minimum hourly wage.

When a debtor owes a number of creditors and is unable to pay, his situation becomes quite complicated. The laws of some states allow an insolvent person to make an assignment for the benefit of his creditors. The assignment process is relatively simple. The debtor turns all of his property over to an assignee who publishes a notice of assignment so that creditors may file claims. After a certain period of time, the assignee sells the property and pays the creditors on a pro rata basis.

A disadvantage of this arrangement is that if proceeds from the debtor's property are insufficient to pay the indebtedness fully, the balance remains outstanding. This disadvantage can be avoided by what is known as "a composition with creditors" which means that the assignee persuades the creditors to settle for the amount of the proceeds.

Similar to a composition is a procedure known as "voluntary arrangement" which is processed under the jurisdiction of the Federal courts. Essentially it is an insolvent debtor's plan for settling his unsecured debts and is initiated only by the debtor in accordance with Chapter XI of the bankruptcy law.

The debtor's petition for an arrangement is referred by the court to a referee who calls a creditors' meeting. The creditors file proof of their respective claims and pass upon the debtor's plan of settlement. If a majority of creditors having more than half of the total dollar amount of claims approve the arrangement, the proposal is then reviewed by the court. If the court approves, the debtor is discharged from all debts covered by the arrangement.

When the arrangement is neither accepted by creditors nor approved by the court, the debtor is declared a bankrupt, and the matter proceeds as any ordinary bankruptcy case.

The principal advantage of a voluntary arrangement is that it may be filed before a bankruptcy proceeding is begun, thus affording a chance of avoiding the stigma of bankruptcy.

When an insolvent individual is unable to work out a satisfactory settlement with his creditors by assignment or by arrangement or to get them to agree to stretch out the period of time for him to pay what he owes, he may have himself declared a bankrupt under the National Bankruptcy Act. This latter step is called *voluntary bankruptcy.*

If he does not take the initiative himself, his creditors may force him into bankruptcy by filing against him, this procedure is known as *involuntary bankruptcy.*

In a bankruptcy case, the court-appointed referee selects a trustee to take over all assets of the insolvent debtor and to receive creditors' claims. With permission of the referee, the trustee will then sell the assets and distribute the money to the creditors as far as it will go.

Secured creditors and certain prior claims such as those for taxes, rent, workers wages, and administrative expenses of the bankruptcy are paid first. General creditors receive what is left on a pro rata basis.

After the trustee has made the distribution, the court, upon recommendation of the referee, will issue an order discharging the debtor from bankruptcy and freeing him from all debts covered in the proceedings.

The philosophy underlying the National Bankruptcy Act is that it will help liberate a deeply involved debtor and enable him to get a new financial start.

The Cost of
Consumer Credit

Credit, like other commercial services, costs money. In fact, consumer credit is relatively expensive. Much of the advantage in prices that stores selling for cash only have over retailers who extend credit service is in the cost to the latter of providing credit.

Consider expenses of investigating applicants, then add bookkeeping, billing, and collection costs, as well as losses from accounts that turn bad and the value of money (interest) the seller ties up in credit sales, and it is readily understandable how stores selling for cash can usually do so at lower prices. Stores extending credit must recover these costs some way—either by charging merchandise prices high enough to absorb them, or by passing credit costs directly to the consumer. Similarly, consumer financing agencies must charge enough to cover their costs and leave a reasonable profit.

Most of the elements that constitute total costs of credit are of a fixed nature; that is, they are the same or nearly so whether the amount of credit or the size of the loan is large or small. For example, it costs about as much to investigate a borrower of $50 as a borrower of $500. The same is true of bookkeeping, billing, and collection costs. Only two credit costs are strictly variable in character—interest on money used and losses from bad debts.

Consumers, therefore, should understand that the economics of credit tends to work heavily against the small borrower, costing him much more per dollar of credit than it costs the larger user of credit. This mostly explains why consumer finance companies (small loan companies) legally can charge an annual percentage rate of as much as 48 percent in some states.

Whether use of credit is worth what it costs a borrower is a subjective matter. Only the buyer himself can decide. But one thing is certain: he cannot make a sensible decision if he does not know how much the credit costs; nor can he shop for better credit terms.

On May 29, 1968, Congress passed the Consumer Protection Act, more popularly known as the Truth-in-Lending Act. The essence of the law is that it requires all lenders who extend credit to people for personal, family, household, or agricultural purposes to show how much is being charged in dollars and cents for the credit and what this cost amounts to in relative annual percentage terms. Full disclosure of credit charges is presumed to help the consumer to decide for himself the reasonableness of credit charges and to give him the means of shopping for credit at least cost. The law does not regulate amount of interest and other credit costs, nor does it regulate terms and conditions under which credit may be extended.

An abundance of evidence was presented at both the House and the Senate committee hearings showing that consumers were generally unaware of the actual financing rates that they were paying. Surveys revealed that there was such widespread use of misleading and deceptive methods of stating the price of credit that ordinary citizens found it difficult to make meaningful comparisons and therefore intelligent choices of various credit terms offered to them. Lenders were quoting finance charges on an add-on basis or some other basis difficult for borrowers to understand. Furthermore, a variety of fees, penalties, and other charges were being piled on. Only a well-trained mathematician could convert these charges to a percentage of unpaid balance. Little wonder it was beyond the ability of most consumers to do so. In many instances, borrowers did not even know the dollars-and-cents amount of a finance charge.

The Truth-In-Lending Law

Open-end Credit. Now let's examine in some detail what the Truth-in-Lending Law requires. For purposes of the law, consumer credit is classified into open-end credit, which we have previously referred to as revolving credit, and non-open-end credit which is a single credit transaction.

The law requires a merchant or lender before opening an account under an open-end consumer credit plan to disclose to the customer the following information.

1. The conditions under which a finance charge may be imposed, including the time period within which any credit extended may be repaid without incurring a finance charge.
2. The method of determining the balance upon which a finance charge will be imposed.
3. The method of determining the amount of finance charge including any minimum or fixed amount imposed as a finance charge.
4. Where one or more periodic rates may be used to compute the finance charge, each such rate, the range of balances to which it is applicable and the corresponding nominal annual percentage rate, determined by multiplying the periodic rate by the number of periods in a year.
5. The conditions under which any other charges may be imposed and methods by which they will be determined.
6. The conditions under which the creditor may retain or acquire any security interest in any property to secure payment of any credit extended under the plan, and a description of the interest or interests which may be so retained or acquired.

The intention of the law here is for the customer to have full knowledge in advance of how his account will be handled. If he does not agree, he can shop elsewhere for better terms or forego use of such a credit plan.

If a customer agrees to the plan and uses it, he is entitled under the law to receive in his statement each billing period the following information.

1. Outstanding balance in the account at the beginning of the statement period.
2. Amount and date of each extension of credit during the period and, if a purchase was involved, a brief identification of the goods or services purchased.
3. Total amount credited to the account during the period.
4. Amount of any finance charge added to the account during the period, itemized to show how much is due to the application of percentage rates and how much is imposed as a minimum or fixed charge.
5. Where one or more periodic rates may be used to compute the finance charge, each such rate, the range of balances to which it is applicable, and the corresponding nominal annual percentage rate determined by multiplying the periodic rate by the number of periods in a year.
6. The balance on which the finance charge was computed and a statement of how the balance was determined. If the balance is determined without first deducting all credits during the period, that fact and the amount of such payment shall also be disclosed.
7. The outstanding balance in the account at the end of the period.
8. The date by which, or the period within which, payment must be made to avoid additional finance charges.

In the case of an open-end credit account, the periodic rate is convertible into an annual rate simply by multiplying the periodic rate by the number of billing cycles in a year. For example, if the billing is monthly and the periodic rate is 1.5 percent, then the annual percentage rate is 12 × 1.5 percent or 18 percent. If the finance charge is the result of the application of more than one periodic rate, the annual percentage rate is determined by dividing the total finance charge for the billing cycle by the sum of the balances to which the periodic rates were applied and multiplying the quotient in percentage terms by the number of billing cycles in a year.

For example, suppose the department store where you have an open-end credit account shows on your monthly statement that the balance you owe is $500 of which the first $200 carries a periodic rate of 1.5 percent, or a finance charge of $3; and the remaining $300 carries a periodic rate of 1 percent, or a finance charge of $3. The annual percentage rate would be figured by adding the two finance charges, or a total of $6, and dividing by $500, making 1.2 percent the weighted average periodic rate, then multiplying by twelve to get an annual rate of 14.4 percent.

Non-Open-End Credit. As we have noted, many "big ticket" items such as automobiles are sold under non-open-end credit plans, each transaction being a separate credit contract. In connection with such consumer credit sales, the seller or creditor in each instance is required to disclose:

1. The cash price of the item purchased.
2. The sum of any amounts credited as down payment, including any trade-ins.
3. The unpaid balance of the cash price.
4. All other charges, individually itemized, which are included in the amount of credit extended but which are not part of the finance charge.
5. The total amount to be financed.
6. The amount of the finance charge.
7. The finance charge expressed as an annual percentage rate.
8. The number, amount, and due dates or periods of payments scheduled to repay the indebtedness.
9. The charges payable in the event of default or due to late payments.
10. A description of any security interest held or to be retained or acquired by the creditor in connection with the extension of credit, and a clear identification of the property to which the security interest relates.

All the above information must be disclosed before the credit is extended. The disclosures must be made in writing to the customer and must be clear, conspicuous, and in meaningful sequence. The terms "finance charge" and "annual percentage rate" must be used whenever they are required and must be printed more conspicuously than other terminology required by the regulations. At the time disclosures are made, the creditor must furnish the customer with a duplicate of the instrument, or a statement in which required disclosures are made. The creditor must be identified by name on this instrument.

It is important to point out that the term "finance charge," as used in the Truth-in-Lending Law, is not synonymous with the word "interest" as the latter is commonly understood in finance. The law says that the amount of the finance charge is the sum of all charges imposed by the creditor as an incident to the extension of credit, including any and all the following types of charges.

1. Interest, time-price differential, and any amount payable under a point, discount, or other system of additional charges.
2. Service or carrying charge.
3. Loan fee, finder's fee, or similar charge.
4. Fee for an investigation or a credit report.
5. Premium or other charge for any guarantee or insurance protecting the creditor against the customer's default or other credit loss.

Once the finance charge is determined in dollars and cents, the annual percentage rate is to be calculated within an accuracy of at least ¼ percent.

The Truth-in-Lending Law applies only to the extension of credit to natural persons. It does not apply to extensions of credit to governments, business, or other organizations. Clearly, Congress was concerned about protecting the average consumer, particularly the consumer of limited means, because if the total amount financed in a credit arrangement exceeds $25,000, the transaction is exempt from the law, except in case of real estate credit. Any credit involving a security interest in real estate extended for a personal, family, household, or agricultural purpose is covered, regardless of the amount financed.

Since there have been so many instances of credit abuses relating to home modernization and repairs, Congress sought to protect homeowners from hastily signed contracts by giving them the right to rescind a transaction until midnight of the third business day following consummation of the transaction or delivery of the disclosures required. The law states that the *right of rescission* applies to any credit transaction in which a security interest is or may be retained or acquired in any real property that is used or is expected to be used as the residence of the person to whom the credit is extended.

Full Disclosure in Advertising. The Truth-in-Lending Act also applies to advertising of credit and affects all types of advertising to aid or promote any extension of consumer credit. Anyone who regularly extends credit to consumers, whether in the form of sales credit or cash loans, is subject to the act and its regulations. Generally, no individual or business is permitted to advertise any specific credit terms unless all other credit terms are clearly stated and can be plainly seen.

Full disclosure in an advertisement concerning open-end credit is substantially the same in detail as that which must be furnished a customer before he opens an account. In advertising credit other than open-end, the advertiser, if he mentions any specific credit detail, must state all of the following.

(1) The cash price.
(2) The amount of the down payment required, or that no down payment is required.
(3) The number, amount, and due-dates or period of payments scheduled to repay the indebtedness if the credit is extended.

(4) The deferred payment price or the sum of the payments.

(5) The rate of the finance charge expressed as an annual percentage rate.

A merchant advertising a revolving credit (open-end) service would meet the letter of the law if he used the following wording, or something similar.

> NO FINANCE CHARGE when payment is received within thirty days from the closing date shown on your monthly billing statement. If any purchase remains unpaid for thirty days from the closing date shown on the monthly billing statement, a FINANCE CHARGE at the periodic rate of 1.5 percent per month on the previous balance without adding purchases or deducting payments and credits during the current billing period shall be imposed. This is an ANNUAL PERCENTAGE RATE of 18 percent. The minimum monthly payment is $10.

The following advertisement by an automobile dealer presumably satisfies legal requirements relating to non-open-end credit.

> '72 FORD CUSTOM RANCH WAGON. Six passenger with Selectaire air conditioner, 400 CID V-8 engine power steering, automatic transmission, power disc brakes, luggage rack, tinted glass complete, H78 × 15 whitewalls, wheel covers, etc.
> Cash Price $3,940 • Down payment $350
> 36 Monthly Payments at $122 • Deferred payment price $4,742
> ANNUAL PERCENTAGE RATE 13.50%

Prior to the Truth-In-Lending Act, credit advertising commonly stated only dollar cost of the loan, making no reference to annual percentage rate. For example, a consumer finance company advertised a "GET ACQUAINTED OFFER. Fifty dollars for 30 days on your name only, total cost $1.75. No extras." Calculated on a 360-day year basis, what appears to be a very modest charge amounts to an annual interest rate of 42 percent.

Another practice was to advertise sales credit stating only the amount of each monthly payment with no indication of the price of the article or how many months the buyer would have to pay before he owned the article bought. A typical advertisement would read something like this: "NO MONEY DOWN. 17″ General Electric Television. Now only $5.49 per month." Both these practices are now illegal.

Administration of the Law. The Board of Governors of the Federal Reserve System is responsible for the issuance of regulations under the Truth-In-Lending Law. The Board has issued Regulation Z which sets forth disclosure requirements applying to consumer credit transactions under the law.

Enforcement of Regulation Z is distributed among nine federal agencies, each with a specified jurisdiction as follows: (1) the Comptroller of the Currency over national banks; (2) the Board of Governors of the Federal Reserve System over state member banks of the Federal Reserve System; (3) the Federal Deposit Insurance Corporation over state non-member insured commercial banks; (4) the Federal Home Loan Bank Board over savings and loan associations; (5) the Civil Aeronautics Board over air carriers; (6) the Interstate Commerce Commission over common carriers, such as railroads, bus lines, and truck lines; (7) the Bureau of Federal Credit Unions over federal credit unions; (8) the Secretary of Agriculture over creditors subject to the Packers and Stockyards Act; (9) the Federal Trade Commission over retailers, consumer finance companies, sales finance companies, and all other creditors.

Discussion Questions

1. Distinguish between secured and unsecured credit.
2. Explain three reasons an individual might desire credit.
3. Lenders lend for various reasons. Name three.
4. What are the three C's a trained credit administrator looks for when he investigates an applicant?
5. What information does the Fair Credit Reporting Act make unlawful for an agency to report about a consumer?
6. Explain the types of consumer credit.
7. Distinguish between simple charge accounts and installment charge accounts.
8. Name the five principal financial institutions that supply credit to consumers.
9. Suppose your weekly gross wages are $200 and after income tax withholding and other allowable deductions, your weekly disposable earnings are $150. Suppose also the federal minimum hourly wage is $2.25 at the time. How much of your wages is subject to garnishment under the federal law?
10. What information does the Truth-in-Lending Law require the lender to disclose to the customer before opening an account under an open-end consumer credit plan?

References

Arnold, Pauline and Percival White, *Money—Make it, Spend it, Save it,* New York, Holiday House, 1962.

"Bank Credit-Card and Check-Credit Plans," Washington, D.C., Federal Reserve Board, July, 1968.

Britton, Virginia, *Personal Finance,* New York, American Book Company, 1968.

Chapman, John M., "The Consumer Finance Industry: Its Costs and Regulation," New York, Columbia University Press, 1967.

Cohen, Jerome B. and Arthur W. Hanson, *Personal Finance,* Homewood, Illinois, Richard D. Irwin, 1972.

"Consumer Credit Labeling Bill," Hearings before a subcommittee of the Committee on Banking and Currency, United States Senate, 86th Congress Second Session on S. 2755, Washington, D.C., United States Government Printing Office, 1960.

"Credit Union Yearbook, The," The Credit Union National Association, Washington, D.C. (published annually).

Delehanty, John A., *Manpower Problems and Policies,* Scranton, Pa., International Book, 1969.

Donaldson, Elvin F. and Pfahl, John K., "Personal Finance," 4th ed., New York, Ronald Press, 1964, chs. 3 and 4.

Farwell, Loring C., "Financial Institutions," 4th ed., Homewood, Illinois, Richard D. Irwin, 1966, ch. 22.

"Finance Facts Yearbook," National Consumer Finance Association, Washington, D.C. (published annually).

Hawyer, Carl F., "Family Money and Credit Management," Washington, D.C., National Consumer Finance Association, 1962.

Juster, Francis T., "Consumer Sensitivity to Finance Rates," New York, National Bureau of Economic Research, 1964.

Lasser, J. K. and Sylvia Porter, *Managing Your Money,* New York, Henry Holt, 1953.

Lindberg, P., "Ten Most Misunderstood Points About Borrowing Money," *Better Homes and Gardens,* August, 1969.

Moore, Geoffrey H., "The Quality of Consumer Installment Credit," New York, Columbia University Press, 1967.

Mors, Wallace P., "Small Loan Laws," rev. ed., Cleveland, Bureau of Business Research, Western Reserve University, 1961.

Neifeld, Morris R., "Manual on Consumer Credit," Easton, Pa., Mack Publishing, 1961.

Unger, Maurice A., and Wolf, Harold S., "Personal Finance," 3rd ed., Boston, Mass., Allyn and Bacon, 1972, chs. 6 and 7.

U.S. Department of Commerce, Bureau of the Census, *Population Estimates and Projections,* Series P–25, No. 448, August 6, 1970.

U.S. Department of Labor, *1973 Manpower Report of the President,* Washington, D.C.

U.S. Department of Labor, *U.S. Manpower in the 1970s, Opportunity and Challenge,* Washington, D.C.

"What You Ought to Know About Truth in Lending: Consumer Credit Cost Disclosure," Washington, D.C., Board of Governors of the Federal Reserve System, 1969.

Willett, Edward R., *Personal Finance,* Columbus, Ohio, Charles E. Merrill, 1964.

Yearbook of Agriculture, *Consumers All,* U.S. Department of Agriculture, Washington, D.C., 1965.

part three

Spending for the Family's Needs

A wise man will make more
opportunities than he finds.

[*Francis Bacon*]

10

Securing a Home

So many questions must be asked and decisions made when the time comes to look for a place to live that it is difficult to know where to begin. Things to be considered are size of the family, distance of the house from work, types of transportation available, family income, possibility of being transferred to another town, and a host of other items related to the family situation. There is usually a wide range of choices—such as living in the country or in a suburb and commuting to work or living at a downtown location. In any one of these general locations, a house, an apartment, or a condominium are possible choices.

A few years ago, it was not uncommon to find families who had spent almost a lifetime living in one house. This is no longer the case, since Americans have become a mobile people with 20 to 25 percent of all families changing their place of residence each year. Nevertheless, although the selection of a place to live may be for only a short time, some thought should be given to its selection.

Choosing
a Location

People move to a house in the country to escape crowds in the city, to reduce the cost of living by growing a garden, to have a better place to rear their children, or just to satisfy a romantic ideal. At least, these are some of the reasons they offer. It is easy to make a costly mistake in choosing a location to build or buy a home. What are the choices in selecting a location? You may consider these possibilities—namely, (1) to build or buy a house in the country, (2) to rent a house or apartment in the country, (3) to rent or buy a house in the suburbs of a city, (4) to rent an apartment in the suburbs, (5) to rent or buy a house in the downtown area of a city, (6) to rent an apartment in the downtown area, (7) to buy a condominium, or (8) to buy or rent a house, apartment, or mobile home in a small town.

Living in the Country

Working in the city and living in the country is a practice that is appealing to a growing number of people. It is not uncommon to find workers who commute forty or fifty miles to their job each day. In considering this choice, compare the costs of commuting in money, time, and fatigue with the advantages of privacy and space for the family. Also, remember that there may be fewer public services such as fire and police protection, and that any children in the family may have to commute several miles to school. In addition, medical and health facilities may be unsatisfactory. The lack of public water facilities, a former disadvantage of rural living, has been reduced with the construction of public water systems. These are being extended to homes many miles from town. Taxes on country property are usually lower than on city property, but fire insurance is more expensive because protection is inadequate. There are many rewards to country living, but before making a decision, it is important to make sure the entire family has considered the advantages and disadvantages.

Once the decision has been made to live in the country, it may be necessary to buy some land in a desirable area and build a house. Very few country homes are available for rent, although some apartment houses are being built near lakes for city people who want to live near a recreation area and commute to their jobs. When buying land, consider the possibility that the city may grow out into the area. An industrial or commercial development near-by may leave the location undesirable for a home.

The quality of rural housing has improved markedly in recent years; however it is still inferior to that in urban areas. A 1968 census survey showed 17.1 percent substandard housing in rural areas, 5.7 percent in central cities, and 4.0 percent in the suburbs.[1] In the country, an increasing number of families are living in mobile homes. City housing regulations usually limit mobile homes to special areas set aside for them, but most rural areas have no restrictions on the location and use of mobile homes.

Living in the Suburbs

Suburban housing developments have spread around cities of almost every size during the past thirty years. People have spilled out of the central cities to get more room for growing families. Developers filled these needs by mass production of homes outside the city limits. Here they could get land at reasonable prices with less strict building codes and zoning restrictions. As home buyers moved into these developments, the pattern of commuting several miles to the city for work became established. The suburbs continue to move farther out into rural areas as new housing developments are built. Of course, these new living patterns necessitate the construction of shopping centers and, thus, further development in the suburbs.

Suburban dwellers are sometimes called "exurbanites." They accept the disadvantage of commuting to work so they can have less crowded living conditions, a more leisurely pace, and a more informal neighborhood. In some cases, workers move to the suburbs to find something to offset the monotonous conditions of their job. Despite their expressed goals, exurbanites sometimes find that they have little time for family life. The father may spend two hours each day getting to the job and back while the mother takes care of the children and develops her own interests in the neighborhood. At the same time, the children get involved in interests of their own age groups.

Property taxes can become an increasing burden for the exurbanite. City governments in growing suburbs usually have difficulty providing public services demanded by new residents. There is a never-ending need for more streets, water, schools, police and fire protection. If the area has no industrial plants, the full costs of these services must be met by homeowners and local merchants.

Apparently, most families think the advantages of suburban living outweigh the disadvantages, since the suburbs continue to grow. Often, young families move to the suburbs and they have the desire and enthusiasm to overcome the problems associated with this type of living pattern.

Living in the Central City

Living in the downtown areas of cities has usually meant residing in a large apartment building. Nearness to all services and facilities is considered to be the greatest advantage of this type of residence. Accessibility of cultural and entertainment opportunities is an inviting prospect, along with the convenience of being near a job. Many people living in the central cities find that they can

---

[1]*Rural Housing: Trends and Prospects* (Washington, D.C.), U.S. Dept. of Agriculture, Report no. 193, Sept. 1970, p. 8.

reduce their expenses by not owning an automobile, since public transportation is available when they need to travel in the city.

Families without children may find apartment living suitable, but those with children prefer to live where more play space is available. It is possible to own a home or a condominium in the central city, but space is still limited. Children may still have to rely on public parks or school grounds for play space.

Condominiums are gaining in popularity in the cities, since they combine some of the advantages of home ownership with those of apartment living. A condominium is somewhat like a large apartment house, although the resident buys his apartment rather than renting it. He pays a monthly fee for his share of services provided to all apartments—such as garbage collection, swimming pool and lawn maintenance. A well-managed condominium in a good location may be less expensive than renting a similar apartment or buying a house. A distinction should be made here between condominiums and cooperative apartments. Tenants in a cooperative own a share of the entire building, while a condominium owner has equity only in his apartment. However, the condominium owner has more freedom to sell and mortgage his apartment than the owner of a cooperative apartment.

Regardless of the type of housing, living in the city has lost favor with young families. Unless commuting becomes an overwhelming burden, central cities are not likely to become popular residential areas again for those who have the financial ability to live elsewhere, since noise and air pollution certainly lessen the desirability of city living.

Living in a Small Town

City workers who are considering living in a small town should consider family needs in relation to the life style in such a community. Families whose entire life is wrapped up in the theatre, big-time sports, or the symphony might find commuting to work by day and to their chosen activities by night and weekends wearying and expensive. The make-up of small town populations may be changing to a more cosmopolitan nature as city workers migrate to them, or as industry in the form of a manufacturing plant moving from the city comes to town or to a rural site nearby. But it is true that each small town has its own degree of openness or provincialism, of progressive spirit or community lethargy.

These factors being favorable, it is a good idea to do further analysis of the town. Good schools are a necessity for the family with children. Adequate medical care for treatment of ailments not requiring a specialist is also a reasonable requirement. Financially, it is wise to investigate tax rates and to look for those that are reasonable. Excessively low rates may mean poor schools and sub-standard streets, parks and other city facilities.

Many small towns have no city zoning codes. In such a case, although a homesite may be carefully chosen, its property value may drop when a business moves nearby. On the other hand, this "unplanned" quality which may be a hazard also has its advantages. You may find the neighborhood grocery down the street convenient; certainly such a convenience may be lacking in the rigidly zoned residential areas of most suburbs.

The cost of a homesite in a small town should be less than a comparable place in the city or in the suburbs, and the cost of labor for construction may be a little less; but materials should cost about the same as in larger cities. As in any area, care should be given to selection of the site taking into consideration personal preferences for such things as quiet and privacy.

Transportation can be a problem in the small town for the one-car family. Often bus service to school is restricted to students living a certain distance from school or, simply, to rural students—even though the in-town child's home is too far from school to walk. Car pools to take dad to work or junior to school may be the answer, but there may be no city bus to take mother downtown, while taxi service may be poor or nonexistent.

To Buy
or to Rent

Many factors have a bearing on whether a family should rent or buy a home. Each family should weigh these factors in its own way to make a final decision. Many young couples just beginning married life prefer renting a small apartment. Many reasons dictate this choice: they have little furniture, they want to live in the city near their work and may have only one car, they are not settled on a permanent job, or may still be going to college, or they may be in a type of work that requires frequent transfers. Under these circumstances, it would be folly to consider buying a home since considerable time and expense are required in such a purchase. Nevertheless, some young couples are willing to buy in expectation of possible property appreciation.

Home ownership is most often related to stages in the life cycle. The typical pattern is to upgrade the living quarters as age and financial assets increase. The cycle may begin by renting a small, furnished apartment. A family's first move could be to a larger unfurnished apartment or to a mobile home. When the first child arrives, a new or used small house may be acquired. Often this occurs around the ages twenty-five to thirty. By the time a couple has reached thirty-five, a second child may necessitate buying a larger house. Another house may be needed by age forty-five to fifty when the children need still more space and family income is nearing a peak. This house may be in a suburb or in the country where animals can be kept. It may be the last house until retirement age when the children are gone and smaller quarters are more appropriate. Of course, such a pattern does not apply to families who have to move frequently in their jobs. Certainly, the individual situation dictates the pattern of living quarters as much as convention.

Buying a home should be considered as the family size begins to increase and as the job holders in the family achieve some degree of stability in job location. Families move more now than in past years, so it is not necessary to plan a lifetime in one location before a home is purchased. However, unless there are plans to be in one place at least five years, there would probably not be any advantage in buying; since the first few years of mortgage payments on a house are mostly for interest, with little equity in the home being acquired.

Advantages of Renting

Since circumstances vary for each family, the decision to rent or buy a home should be made only after weighing the advantages and disadvantages of each alternative in relation to the family situation. There are many advantages to renting. The type of person who has neither the desire nor talent to perform house repairs and maintenance chores should, most often, choose to rent. Even if a person does have such an inclination, his job may leave little time for these chores. And, even if there is the time available, he may prefer to use it for recreation rather than for working around the house.

Another consideration is the amount of money needed for the down payment on a house. A large amount may be needed for the type of house being considered. Renting may help accumulate the down payment for a house, since repair and maintenance costs are included in the monthly rental. Renting is also better for those who may have to move to another town on short notice. Job promotions sometimes require changing locations and young persons just beginning their careers need such freedom of mobility.

Advantages of Owning

An additional choice of home ownership has been extended with the growing popularity of mobile homes and condominiums. There are intangibles to ownership that are impossible to measure. How do you place a value on prestige of ownership or family privacy?

A great advantage to owning a home is the freedom to redecorate and make structural changes. If a person enjoys working around the house—making simple repairs, gardening and landscaping—then he will get many satisfactions from home ownership. More space for storage and for children to play may also come with ownership.

It is important to remember the income tax advantages of home ownership. Owners get deductions for property taxes and interest paid on mortgages which help to reduce the costs of owning a home. Usually homeowners have better credit ratings because they are considered to be more stable members of the community.

Buying a house is an investment. For those who find it difficult to save money, making regular monthly payments on a home can be a type of forced saving. Each payment increases equity in the house. For many families, their house is a major part of their accumulated estate.

Houses depreciate, which means they decline in value due to age, wear, and obsolescence. During times of inflation when prices of goods and services are rising, a house that is well-maintained may actually increase in value more than it depreciates. Renting is usually considered to be less expensive than owning a home, but inflation may make ownership more economical.

Economic considerations of renting and owning are important, but other considerations should have first priority. The economic gain in ownership is long-term. After years of saving and making payments, a home is a tangible asset that is valuable. The renter does not gain this asset. However, if, after considering the many factors related to ownership, renting is the choice, the money saved from renting can be invested toward building an estate that may be as valuable as a home would be.

It is impossible to make exact cost comparisons between owning and renting. We usually demand more when buying. Examples of comparisons may not show all actual costs or returns. But this should not stop us from making some comparisons since they can help us to understand more about what is involved in owning a home. The example shown in Exhibit 10–1 is one method of figuring the costs and benefits of home ownership.

These figures show a considerable variation when depreciation and price inflation are taken into account. Property values rise with inflation and housing values may rise faster than the average level of prices. This will be true if construction costs rise faster than costs in other industries. It is certainly not unusual to find homes in good neighborhoods that maintain their value or even increase in value. The estimates show the cost of ownership with depreciation and price inflation offsetting each other at 3 percent per year. The cost of $169.41 per month is for no inflation and a 3 percent annual depreciation rate on the house. When inflation is 6 percent and depreciation is 3 percent, the house is increasing in value at a 3 percent annual rate. This lowers the actual monthly cost of ownership to $69.41.

A landlord using the house for rental would not have the same ownership costs as an owner living in it. Rental property becomes a business operation and landlords can include all costs, including depreciation, when they calculate profit for income tax records. The monthly cost of ownership would be less for a landlord; however, he would need to include enough profit in the monthly rent to provide him with a reasonable return on his investment.

After learning how to calculate the cost of owning a home, you may want to make actual comparisons of the cost of owning and renting. The worksheet shown in Exhibit 10–2 can be used to make such comparisons.

How Much to Pay for a House. Once the decision has been made to buy a house, the next consideration is how much to spend for it. This information is necessary before beginning to shop around, since the price range will determine the type and size of house to consider. Reviewing the family budget or income and expense records, it can be determined how much has been spent for housing. The next step is to make an estimate of changes that may occur in the family income and expenses by considering size of family and stability of employment. Be sure to allow for savings for the children's education and for retirement.

Numerous ratios have been suggested between a family's net income (after income taxes) and the price it can prudently pay for a home. The U.S. Depart-

Exhibit 10–1   The Costs and Benefits of Home Ownership

	Cost of house	$20,000
	Down payment	5,000
	Mortgage	15,000
	Interest rate	6% per year
	Mortgage term	20 years
	Income tax rate	20%

	Monthly cost of ownership	*Monthly benefits from ownership*
Mortgage cost		
Principal and interest payment	$107.55	
Amount of payment for principal		53.78
Estimated amount of income tax reduction due to interest paid if tax rate is 20% (20% × $53.77)		10.75
Estimated interest that money used for down payment could have earned in another investment ($5,000 × 5% interest ÷ 12 months)	20.83	
Property taxes	33.08	
Amount of income tax deduction for property taxes (20% × $33.08)		6.62
Insurance	9.10	
Repairs and maintenance	20.00	
Cost of ownership	190.56	71.15
Less benefits received	71.15	
Monthly cost of home ownership (assumes inflation will offset depreciation—house will maintain its value)	119.41	
Monthly cost with 3% annual depreciation allowance	169.41	
Monthly cost with 3% annual depreciation and 6% inflation rate (house increases in value)	69.41	

Exhibit 10–2   Estimated Costs of Buying or Renting a Home

	Monthly cost	
	Renting	Buying
Monthly payment (loan payment for owner, rental payment for tenant)	$_____	$_____
Fire insurance for owner	_____	_____
Property taxes for owner	_____	_____
Repairs and maintenance for owner (allow 1% of cost for a new house and 2% for an older house)	_____	_____
Depreciation (allow 3% of cost of house for annual amount of depreciation)	_____	_____
Utilities (this item should be omitted if rental payment does not include utilities)	_____	_____
Total cost per month	$_____	$_____

ment of Housing and Urban Development has recommended that the price of a home should not exceed two to two-and-one-half times the annual family income and that a homeowner should not pay more than 25 percent of income for monthly housing expenses (payment on the mortgage loan plus average cost of heat, utilities, repair, and maintenance).[2] A young couple should stay on the low side of this estimate. According to this rule, an after-tax annual income of $8,000 will allow the purchase of a $20,000 house, while a $10,000 income will pay for a $25,000 house.

Another method of calculating the housing allowance is to look at monthly expense records or estimate the family expenses and subtract these from the monthly after-tax income. These expenses should exclude the current spending for housing but should include an allowance for savings. The balance is what could be spent for housing. Consider the case of a family with $300 per month to buy a house on a thirty-year mortgage after paying a 10 percent down payment. A reasonable estimate of monthly housing expense is 1 percent of the home's total cost.

Now we can use these figures to determine how much house to buy.

$300 = 1% of house price
$300 ÷ .01 = $30,000
$30,000 = 90% of house price
$30,000 ÷ .90 = $33,333.

[2] *Wise Home Buying*, U.S. Department of Housing and Urban Development, Bulletin No. 267–F, March, 1972.

This is approximately the price the family can afford to pay. If the loan is for less than thirty years, the price would be somewhat less. This $300 per month estimate would include the mortgage payment, taxes, insurance, maintenance, and utilities. Because standard rules are not always a suitable guide, each family should decide on the basis of its personal situation and the relative value it places on home ownership in comparison with other desires.

Building construction costs have been rising rapidly. When looking at new homes or drawing plans to build one, it is tempting to want a house that the family cannot afford. Despite this desire, it is a good practice to leave a margin for safety when becoming obligated to a long-term debt. Exhibit 10–3 shows estimates of the size of mortgage that are reasonable to carry in relation to a corresponding amount of income.

It may be difficult to determine an annual income for making these housing estimates. Should a wife's income be included? What about small amounts of income from sources not related to jobs. These are personal situations that each family will have to decide. Any income used in the housing calculations should be stable or the family could get into a financial bind. In any case, mortgage lenders at banks and savings and loan associations can help decide what types of income should be used in determining the ability to carry a debt.

How Much Down Payment? The down payment on a home purchase will depend on the purchase price and policies of the lender. Also, the interest rate charged and the number of years for repayment can have some influence on down payment. It appears that society's attitude toward credit is changing to the extent that people are willing to assume more debt. At the same time, lenders are lowering the required down payment on home-mortgage loans, leaving a larger balance to be repaid. Young people may have a different attitude toward credit than their parents who lived through an economic depression. Although they have little for a down payment on a house, they may still believe that they have the potential for large monthly payments.

Attitudes also appear to be changing in relation to approving more home mortgages for women and for older people. Formerly, it was considered a poor business practice to make a long-term loan to someone who is too old to live that long. Now the loans are being approved with the expectation that the property will maintain its value to the extent that no loss would occur to the lender. As women become a larger part of the labor force and their pay becomes comparable with men's, long-term credit should become easier to obtain.

New plans are being tried in the financing of homes. Since interest rates have fluctuated more in recent years, the chairman of the Federal Home Loan Bank Board has announced that his agency expects to propose a *variable-rate mortgage* plan for savings and loan associations. Under a variable-rate plan, which until now has been tried only on an experimental basis by a relatively few mortgage lenders, the interest rate on a home loan would move up and down in line with long-term rates in the open market. This is in contrast to a fixed rate for the entire life of the loan. An example of what payments would be on a variable-rate mortgage is shown in Exhibit 10–4 with interest rates rising one-

Exhibit 10–3   Repayment Capacity of Mortgage Loans by Amount of Income

Amount of loan which income for housing will finance

Income available for housing		At 6 percent			At 6½ percent			At 7 percent			At 7½ percent			At 8 percent		
Monthly	Annual	10 yrs.	15 yrs.	20 yrs.	10 yrs.	15 yrs.	20 yrs.	10 yrs.	15 yrs.	20 yrs.	10 yrs.	15 yrs.	20 yrs.	10 yrs.	15 yrs.	20 yrs.
$ 50	$ 600	$ 4,500	$ 5,920	$ 6,970	$ 4,400	$ 5,730	$ 6,700	$ 4,300	$ 5,560	$ 6,440	$ 4,200	$ 5,380	$ 6,200	$ 4,110	$ 5,230	$ 5,970
60	720	5,400	7,100	8,360	5,280	6,880	8,040	5,160	6,670	7,730	5,050	6,460	7,440	4,940	6,270	7,160
80	960	7,200	9,470	11,150	7,040	9,170	10,720	6,880	8,890	10,300	6,730	8,620	9,920	6,580	8,360	9,550
100	1,200	9,000	11,840	13,940	8,800	11,460	13,400	8,600	11,120	12,880	8,410	10,770	12,400	8,230	10,460	11,940
125	1,500	11,250	14,810	17,430	11,000	14,330	16,750	10,750	13,900	16,100	10,520	13,460	15,500	10,290	13,070	14,930
150	1,800	13,500	17,770	20,920	13,200	17,200	20,100	12,900	16,680	19,320	12,620	16,160	18,610	12,350	15,690	17,920
175	2,100	15,750	20,730	24,400	15,400	20,060	23,450	15,060	19,460	22,550	14,730	18,850	21,710	14,410	18,300	20,900
200	2,400	18,000	23,690	27,890	17,600	22,930	26,800	17,210	22,240	25,770	16,830	21,550	24,810	16,470	20,920	23,890
225	2,700	20,250	26,650	31,380	19,800	25,800	30,160	19,360	25,020	28,990	18,930	24,240	27,910	18,530	23,530	26,880
250	3,000	22,500	29,620	34,860	22,000	28,660	33,510	21,510	27,800	32,210	21,040	26,930	31,010	20,590	26,150	29,860
275	3,300	24,750	32,580	38,350	24,200	31,530	36,860	23,660	30,580	35,430	23,140	29,630	34,110	22,650	28,760	32,850
300	3,600	27,000	35,540	41,840	26,400	34,400	40,210	25,810	33,370	38,650	25,250	32,320	37,220	24,710	31,380	35,840
325	3,900	29,250	38,500	45,320	28,600	37,270	43,560	27,960	36,150	41,880	27,350	35,020	40,320	26,770	33,990	38,820
350	4,200	31,500	41,460	48,810	30,800	40,130	46,910	30,120	38,930	45,100	29,460	37,710	43,420	28,830	36,610	41,810
375	4,500	33,750	44,430	52,300	33,010	43,000	50,260	32,270	41,710	48,320	31,560	40,400	46,520	30,880	39,220	44,800
400	4,800	36,000	47,390	55,780	35,210	45,870	53,610	34,420	44,490	51,540	33,670	43,100	49,620	32,940	41,840	47,780

Source: U.S. Savings and Loan League.

half percent every five years and falling one-half percent every five years. Rates would change only if market rates had changed during the specified period.

Exhibit 10–4   Monthly Payments for a Variable-Rate Home Loan Mortgage

Example: a 30-year home loan of $25,000 starting at 7 percent interest			
	Monthly payments on standard mortgage with 7% interest rate fixed for life of loan	*Monthly payments on variable-rate plan—*	
		If interest rates rise (figures assume rates go up one-half percent every 5 years)	*If interest rates decline (figures assume rates drop one half percent every 5 years)*
1st 5 years	$166.33	$166.33	$166.33
2nd 5 years	$166.33	$173.85	$159.03
3rd 5 years	$166.33	$180.54	$152.83
4th 5 years	$166.33	$185.89	$148.00
5th 5 years	$166.33	$189.83	$144.53
Last 5 years	$166.33	$191.98	$142.69
Home-Owner's Payments Over a 30-Year Period			
On principal	$25,000	$25,000	$25,000
On interest	$34,879	$40,305	$29,805
Total payments	$59,879	$65,305	$54,805

Note: One form of "variable-rate mortgage," which might become popular, would keep the monthly payment unchanged and lengthen or shorten the maturity of the loan as interest rates rise or fall.
Basic data: Federal Home Loan Bank Board

Reprinted from *U.S. News and World Report*, Aug. 21, 1972. Copyright 1972, U.S. News & World Report, Inc.

Another unusual practice being tried for home loans is the use of *variable-payment mortgages*. This is a system of establishing the monthly payments to increase over the years, since the income of the borrower is expected to increase as he gets older and acquires more seniority on his job. For example, the monthly payment may be $135 for the first five years of the mortgage, $140 for the second five years, $145 for the third five years with continuous increases every five years until the loan is completely repaid. In some instances, a small balance may remain to be paid as the final term payment.

Another plan that may be used is a *partial-payment mortgage*. With this plan, the monthly payments remain the same; but, at the end of the mortgage term, a small balance remains to be paid either in a lump sum or under new loan agreement. This plan assumes that the borrower would be at his peak earning power by the end of the mortgage term and would be financially able to make a lump sum payment of five or six thousand dollars. These two plans are compared with the standard mortgage payment plan in Exhibit 10–5.

Exhibit 10–5   Old-style vs. New-style Mortgages

	Standard mortgage	Partial-payment mortgage	Variable-payment mortgage
			1st 5 years: $135
			2nd 5 years: $140
Monthly payment	$147.80 for 25 years	$141.10 for 25 years	3rd 5 years: $145
			4th 5 years: $150
			5th 5 years: $155
Payments over 25 years			
On principal	$20,000	$14,124	$13,520
On interest	$24,340	$28,206	$29,980
Total payments	$44,340	$42,330	$43,500
Amount owed after 25 years	0	$ 5,876	$ 6,480

Example: a 25-year home loan of $20,000 at 7½ percent

Note: People who buy homes with proposed new mortgages can pay off final amounts owed in a single lump sum, or refinance the amount due—if they have not already sold their homes or refinanced their loans.

Reprinted from *U.S. News and World Report,* Dec. 27, 1971. Copyright 1971, U.S. News & World Report, Inc.

Another consideration in deciding on the amount of down payment for a home loan is how much interest will be paid during the life of the loan. A small down payment means a larger loan and higher interest costs. If a buyer borrows $20,000 at 9 percent interest with payments over a period of twenty-five years, he will pay $30,220 interest for the use of that money.[3]

Loan Maturity. Should a home mortgage loan be repaid as quickly as possible? Home loans usually vary from fifteen to thirty years depending on the source of credit and amount of down payment. Long-term loans allow for small monthly payments, but total interest cost will be large. Exhibit 10–6 shows how much smaller monthly payments can be as the loan term increases by various interest rates. It is good management to repay the loan in as short a period as possible

[3]U.S. Department of Agriculture, *Selecting and Financing a Home,* Home and Garden Bulletin No. 182 (Washington, Dec., 1971).

to save interest costs. Payments should be small enough, however, to provide a margin of safety in the event of a temporary loss of income. Exhibit 10–7 shows the monthly payment required to retire a loan by various interest rates and maturities.

Exhibit 10–6 *Effect of Longer Maturity on Amount of Monthly Payment on a $20,000 Loan (amount payment decreases)*

Loan term increases from:	Rates of interest					
	5%	*5.5%*	*6%*	*6.5%*	*7%*	*7.5%*
15 to 20 years	−26.16	−25.84	−25.49	−25.11	−24.71	−24.29
20 to 25 years	−15.08	−14.76	−14.42	−14.07	−13.70	−13.32
25 to 30 years	− 9.50	− 9.26	− 8.95	− 8.63	− 8.29	− 7.95
30 to 35 years	− 6.40	− 6.15	− 5.88	− 5.58	− 5.29	− 5.00

There are other considerations. Is inflation likely to continue? If so, it may be better to make a small down payment. Your income a few years later will be worth less than present income. If your income rises, you may want to increase payments. However, this may be unwise if you are borrowing money on short-term loans and paying a higher interest rate than for the home loan. Usually home loans have lower interest rates than loans obtained for other purposes.

Exhibit 10–7 *Monthly Payments on a $20,000 Loan by Different Rates and Different Maturities*

Interest rates	Maturities					
	15 years	*20 years*	*25 years*	*30 years*	*35 years*	*40 years*
5.0%	$158.14	$131.98	$116.90	$107.40	$101.00	$ 96.60
5.5%	163.42	137.58	122.82	113.56	107.41	103.16
6.0%	168.78	143.29	128.87	119.92	114.04	110.05
6.5%	174.23	149.12	135.05	126.42	120.84	117.10
7.0%	179.77	155.06	141.36	133.07	127.78	124.29
7.5%	185.41	161.12	147.80	139.85	134.85	131.62

Interest payments can be deducted as an expense on income tax records, but this is hardly a reason by itself for making a low down payment on a home. Families who move frequently will find that the house is easier to sell when their equity is small. Lenders usually recommend that you make as large a down payment as you can. This leaves a smaller debt on which interest must be paid and will allow for smaller monthly payments. Remember that you will have some unexpected costs involved in buying a home and moving. If you allow enough for these expenses, then it is well to use any available surplus funds for adding to the required down payment.

Loan and Property Transfer Costs. After you have agreed on the purchase price of a home and arranged for financing, it is time for the closing transactions. It is important to follow proper legal procedures since this is a transfer of property that involves a large sum of money. It will take several days or possibly weeks to complete the closing transactions. Legal instruments that you will be likely to use are a *warranty deed, deed of trust* or *mortgage, abstract* or *title insurance,* and a *mortgage note.*

Instruments used in the transfer of real estate vary to some extent due to differences in the laws of each state. A *warranty deed* is provided by the seller which warrants that he owns the property and that it is clear of debt unless otherwise stated. A *deed of trust* or *mortgage* pledges the real estate as security for a loan and is held by the lender. The *abstract of title* is a history of all recorded documents related to the land. Any claims on the property from previous owners, their heirs or creditors can be determined from an abstract, which should be provided by the seller. It is a common practice now for buyers to accept title insurance in place of an abstract. Such insurance gives the buyer protection against ownership disputes as long as he owns the property. A mortgage may be used in place of a deed of trust. It is a conditional transfer of title to real estate as security for a loan. The mortgage note is a promissory note that is secured by a mortgage.

Closing costs for purchasing a home will depend on purchase price and the number of legal instruments involved. There may be a mortgage service fee charged by the lender for preparation of the mortgage and loan papers. It could also include an appraisal fee for appraisal of the property and a charge for a credit report on the borrower. Property taxes will be prorated between seller and buyer according to the number of months the property was owned by each for the year of sale. Usually the seller pays to the buyer his portion of the year's taxes and then the buyer pays all taxes for the year. The lender will require the buyer to provide property insurance at the time of closing.

The first document signed after selecting the house is usually a sales contract. Although it may contain special provisions, it basically obligates the buyer and seller to complete the transaction and will require a cash deposit as evidence of good faith. Sales contracts specify the terms and conditions of sale and the obligations of each person. It is good business for the buyer to understand exactly what he is expected to do before signing the contract. Failure to fulfill the contract can result in loss of the deposit.

After all documents have been prepared and signed for completing the property transfer, the buyer will have a deed, mortgage, survey of the property, and abstract of title or title insurance policy. If he is receiving an abstract, it should be examined by an attorney for assurance that it is a good and merchantable title. The abstract will include a tax statement indicating any unpaid property taxes. The following closing costs are an example of transferring a $30,000 house with a $25,000 mortgage. Costs may vary considerably in different areas with different requirements. All of these costs, except those for title insurance, are paid by the buyer.

Survey	$ 75.00
Appraisal fee & credit report	75.00
Title insurance	110.00
Recording fees	8.00
State tax stamps	27.50
Attorney's fee for preparation and examination of documents	150.00
Mortgage service fee	100.00
	$545.50

In addition to the above closing costs, a specified amount may be required for taxes and property insurance. The deed and mortgage must be recorded in the county clerk's office for protection of both the lender and home buyer. When the loan is repaid, a release is given by the lender which will be recorded to show that the property has been cleared of debt.

The appraisal and credit report will be needed by the lender. An appraiser is a real estate specialist who inspects the property and determines its value. The credit report is a record of the buyer's debts, income, and ability to repay a home loan. The survey is made by an engineer or public official to locate property boundaries and compare them with descriptions in the documents. Some lenders will require the buyer to purchase a mortgage cancellation life insurance policy. This is a policy on the family income earner equal to the amount of the loan. Policy value declines as the mortgage debt declines. If the borrower dies before the debt is paid, the insurance company will pay the balance of the debt. Premium costs are relatively low due to the declining value of the policy. The policy expires when the loan is completely repaid.

It should be evident by now that it takes considerable time and money to transfer real estate from one person to another. It is not unusual for closing costs to be more than originally expected. The buyer will always be expected to pay these costs at the time of closing along with the down payment.

Comparing New and Old Houses

Several options are available when a family decides to buy a home. A family may consider buying a used house that is many years old or one that is relatively new. Other choices are a house that is currently under construction or one that has recently been completed and is still unsold. A final possibility is buying a lot and having a new house built according to personal specifications. In any case, the decision should be made only after a careful study of available houses, financing and down payments required, construction costs, and the needs and desires of the family.

Buying a Used House

Styles of old and recently built houses are usually quite different. Some families like old houses that need some remodeling so they can use their skills and artistic ability to create something unique. These houses will usually have more space and can be purchased for a lower price than houses that are relatively new. One very important point to consider, however, is the location. An old house in a declining neighborhood can lose value rapidly regardless of how well it is kept repaired. The buyer should be sure the neighborhood is one where the family will enjoy living. This will include a consideration of schools, churches, shopping facilities, and distance from work. The location of a house is also important to its resale value. After the family is satisfied that the location is suitable, then the condition of the house must be examined.

Structural Condition. All houses depreciate in value as they get older, but the depreciation is less if they are well maintained. While inspecting a used house, the buyer should look for such things as cracks in the floors or foundation, cracks in the walls around doors and windows, floorboards that are out of alignment and uneven roof lines. A house that will soon need repainting or a new roof may require $1,000 for repairs as soon as the family moves in. Closet and built-in cabinet space should also be examined since many old houses do not have adequate closet space. Another consideration is that costly repairs tend to increase with the age of a house. Finally, a termite inspection is advisable (particularly in the West and South) as a further indication of an older house's structural condition.

Electrical and Plumbing Fixtures. Probably the greatest drawback to buying an old house is the lack of electrical wiring and outlets. Families use electric appliances to such an extent today that houses built fifteen or twenty years ago do not have adequate wiring. In addition, plumbing pipes and fixtures may be ready for replacement in houses of this age. Replacing the wiring and plumbing is a major repair that could cost hundreds of dollars. An out-dated or inadequate heating system is another frequent fault with older houses.

Buyers should also be wary of buying an old house that may be beautiful simply because of furnishings that the present residents will take with them. Ask to be allowed to examine areas under rugs or behind furniture. In one instance, after a cursory examination of a house, a young woman felt it was the only one for her, and her husband was easily talked into buying it. Moving day came and the buyers moved into a bleak house with many flaws in the interior. All had been cleverly disguised by quaint curtains, lovely antique furnishings, and innumerable throw rugs. Unexpected and unbudgeted expense was necessary to make the place livable. Many towns have families that supplement their income substantially by buying old homes, cleverly decorating with their movable furnishings, and selling at a profit to someone intrigued with the interior decorating and ignorant of what the place is like underneath the superficial polish.

Unless there is some overriding consideration, most families should not consider purchasing a house that is more than five to ten years old. Older houses have too much upkeep and their type of architecture makes them less marketable if they must be sold. A house that is relatively new will have a modern style and fixtures, less upkeep, and a better resale value. Also, it will be easier to finance and may require less down payment. Closing costs could be less if the buyer assumes an existing mortgage. In addition, any repairs needed will be more likely to be minor than in the case of an old house.

Buying a New House

If the family plans to live in a new house, it may choose between having a house built according to personally designed plans and specifications or buying one that is already built or under construction. There are many things to consider before making this choice. First, a custom-built house will cost more than a ready-made house per square foot of floor space and will most likely require a larger down payment. It will also require a considerable amount of supervisory time during construction to select various types of materials. On the other hand, it is relatively easy to obtain a loan and buy a ready-built house.

Many people are willing to put forth the extra effort and expense to get the house of their dreams. If a family plans to live in one place for many years, the satisfactions from personally planning a home can outweigh the extra trouble. Anyone who has some knowledge of construction and home decorating will enjoy the many details of selecting colors and choosing materials that are a part of custom building. Let us assume that you have decided to have a house built for your family. What are the steps to be followed?

Obtain Building Plans. The first step is to find a suitable building lot. The same care should be used in selecting a lot that was described earlier in this chapter for finding a place to live. This is where you will be living and where your money will be invested, so be sure to select a good neighborhood with building codes and zoning laws if you choose a city or suburban area. After securing the lot, you are ready to prepare building plans. Should you try to draw your own plans or hire an architect? Unless you have had experience with architectural design or have special knowledge of construction, it will probably be necessary to consult an architect.

An architect will draw a complete set of building plans. He will be able to make suggestions on types of materials and methods of reducing costs. After completing the plans, he will help you to distribute the plans to several contractors to get bids on construction costs. He will also be acquainted with the most reputable builders in the area. After a contractor has been selected and actual construction is started, the architect can inspect the work to see that the plans are followed and that the specified materials are used. This work should continue until the house is complete and you are ready to move in. What do you pay for services of an architect? Costs vary with the price of the house. His fee is usually a percentage which may vary from ten to fifteen percent of the total house cost.

It is certainly possible to have your own home constructed without the services of an architect, although you may have to be more flexible in the personal specifications you have in mind. Contractors, lumber dealers, and others types of suppliers have an assortment of house plans of many sizes and arrangements. If you find a suitable plan from among these, the blueprint can be purchased at a very modest cost. These plans can then be taken to contractors to obtain bids on building costs. The disadvantage of these plans is that they may not include all the arrangements you wanted and contractors will allow few or no changes to be made in the plans. In addition, without an architect, you will need to make periodic inspections during construction to see that plans are being followed.

Secure Financing. The next step after preparing plans and specifications and receiving bids on costs from contractors is to obtain financing. Now that costs are known, you can go to various real estate lenders to obtain financing. They will want to see copies of the house plan and bids for construction before determining arrangements for a loan. Sources of housing loans are discussed in a later section of this chapter. It is wise to go to more than one of these lenders to be sure that you are getting the lowest cost credit available.

Select a Contractor. After arranging the loan, you are ready to select a contractor and begin construction. Be prepared to wait from six months to a year for the house to be completed after choosing the contractor. It is important that you investigate the builder's reputation thoroughly before giving him the contract to build your house. He should be honest and financially reliable. You may want to talk to people whose homes he has built and look at the quality of his work. A builder with satisfied customers usually can be relied upon. It is better to pay a higher price if necessary to get a reputable contractor. There are too many ways to skimp on costs by using poor quality materials to rely on an unknown contractor.

A good builder will employ and be responsible for paying subcontractors such as electricians, plumbers, and bricklayers. He will carry insurance on the building while it is under construction and will follow local construction codes. Some builders require payment in three stages. A certain amount is due when the foundation is completed, with the second payment after the framework and roof are built and the third after the house is completed and ready for occupancy.

Although a contractor is responsible for overseeing the construction work, you should visit the site regularly to answer any questions that may arise and to see how the work is progressing. Being the owner, you will have many decisions to make—such as the type of hardware to use, the kind of electric fixtures, type and color of brick, the choice of carpets, and many other selections. Remember that basic changes in the plan cannot be made without adding to the cost. Most builders will allow some minor changes after construction has begun, but these should be kept to a minimum. When the house is completed, make a thorough inspection to see that all work is done according to plans before you make final payment to the builder.

Buying a Ready-Built House

Most home buyers choose a ready-built house. Not many families have the desire to go through the long and tedious process of building a custom home. Probably the major reason that most families select a ready-built home is the lower cost per square foot of space. Builders keep costs down by constructing several houses in an area at one time. These are sometimes referred to as tract or development houses. To construct such a development, a builder will buy several acres of land and building materials in volume to get low prices. He will have a few basic house plans and these will be varied in the development so that all houses will not look alike.

One disadvantage of purchasing a development home is that you will not likely be able to find a plan that fits your family situation exactly. Plan to make some compromises on the number of rooms, their sizes, or the overall floor plan. Another disadvantage is that you will not know in advance how high property taxes will be on the house. In a new development, taxes may be high to pay for new schools and other necessary improvements.

Since builders of development homes use several floor plans and room arrangements, you can choose a plan that best fits your family's size and desires. Many single persons are finding that they prefer buying a house to living in an apartment. In their own home, they get more privacy and find that the income tax laws have special provisions for home owners, making a home a good investment.

A well-planned house should have defined areas for different uses. The bedrooms should be an area away from noisy work areas. The kitchen and living area should be convenient and planned for play and other activities. Be sure to look for a floor plan that has plenty of closets and storage space. Each bedroom and bathroom should have closet space and it is desirable to have a closet in or near the living room or in the entrance corridor. Similarly, the kitchen should have plenty of cabinet space. The functional layout of the house is more important than decorations or extras that may be added to get your attention. A self-cleaning oven is not as important as the number of bathrooms or the size of the bedrooms.

It is wise to take plenty of time to look at homes being built by different builders. In most cities there will be housing developments under construction in several locations. If more than one location is suitable, you may have a wider choice of house plans by looking in more than one development. By taking your time and looking at all that is available, you may find a plan that is almost what you want while obtaining savings that would not be possible in a custom-built house.

Sources of
Housing Loans

Financing of homes requires large quantities of capital. In 1890, about one-half of all families in the United States owned their own homes, while in 1970, almost two-thirds had achieved this goal.[4] Rising incomes have made home ownership possible for many people, but the development of long-term mortgage credit has been the most significant factor to such growth. Home ownership varies with family income and age of the household head, and it increases with age and income. Most home owners are over thirty-five years of age. The

Exhibit 10–8   Mortgage Debt Outstanding on Nonfarm 1- to 4-family Properties (in billions of dollars)

| End of period | Total | Government-underwritten | | | Conventional |
		Total	FHA-insured	VA-guaran-teed[1]	
1945	18.6	4.3	4.1	.2	14.3
1963	182.2	65.9	35.0	30.9	116.3
1964	197.6	69.2	38.3	30.9	128.3
1965	212.9	73.1	42.0	31.1	139.8
1966	223.6	76.1	44.8	31.3	147.6
1967	236.1	79.9	47.4	32.5	156.1
1968	251.2	84.4	50.6	33.8	166.8
1969	266.8	90.2	54.5	35.7	176.6
1970	280.2	97.2	59.9	37.3	182.9
1970—IV	280.2	97.2	59.9	37.3	182.9
1971—I[p]	283.6	98.3	61.0	37.3	185.3
II[p]	290.9	100.4	62.8	37.6	190.5
III[p]	299.7	102.9	64.4	38.5	196.8
IV[p]	307.8	105.2	65.7	39.5	202.6
1972—I[p]	314.1	107.5	66.8	40.7	206.6
II[p]	324.6	109.6	67.6	42.0	215.0
III[p]	335.8	111.5	68.4	43.1	224.3

[1]Includes outstanding amount of VA vendee accounts held by private investors under repurchase agreement.

Note: For total debt outstanding, figures are FHLBB and F.R. estimates. For conventional, figures are derived. Based on data from FHLBB, Federal Housing Admin., and Veterans Admin.

Source: Federal Reserve Bulletin, May, 1973.

---

[4]United States Savings and Loan League, *Savings and Loan Fact Book, 1973* (Chicago, 1971), p. 43.

same holds true for families with vacation or second homes. A high percentage of these owners are retired people.

Most home buyers must obtain credit to make their purchase. Exhibit 10–8 shows the growth in residential mortgage debt.

A mortgage loan is a special loan for purchasing real estate. The person receiving the loan is called a mortgagor and he signs a legal document which requires him to make regular payments for a certain number of years to the lender or mortgagee. The property is pledged as security for the loan and the borrower promises to keep the house insured and to pay the property taxes. If payments are not made on the loan, the lender can foreclose and take the property.

It is a good practice to compare types of loans made by leading home mortgage lenders. They are not alike in interest rates, terms for repayment privileges and penalties for advance payments. Lenders may be divided into two groups, public and private. Private lenders are commercial banks, insurance companies, savings banks, savings and loan associations, and individuals. Public lenders are those related to government, such as Federal Housing Administration, Veterans' Administration, and—in rural areas—the Farmers Home Administration and Federal Land Banks. Many loans are made by one of the private lenders and guaranteed by a public lender. Loans made by private lenders without the benefit of government insurance or guarantees are referred to as conventional loans. Interest rates and terms on these loans vary with local practices and policies. Exhibit 10–9 shows the total mortgage loans in 1972 by type of property and type of lender. Savings associations accounted for 35 percent of all mortgage loans, more than any other type of lender. When we consider only loans for one- to four-family homes, savings associations made over 46 percent of the loans.

It is interesting to see how the rankings of mortgage lenders have changed since 1950 (see Exhibit 10–10). Life insurance companies, commercial banks

Exhibit 10–9   Total Mortgage Loans Outstanding, Year-End 1972

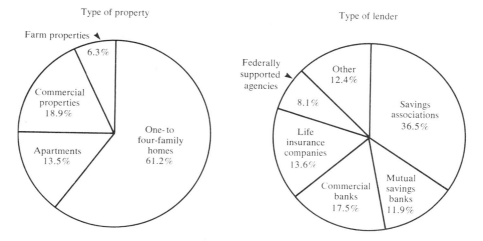

Source: U.S. Savings and Loan League, *Savings and Loan Fact Book, 1972*. p. 36.

Exhibit 10–10   Mortgage Loans Outstanding on One- to Four-Family Non-farm Homes, by Type of Lender, Year-End 1950 and 1972

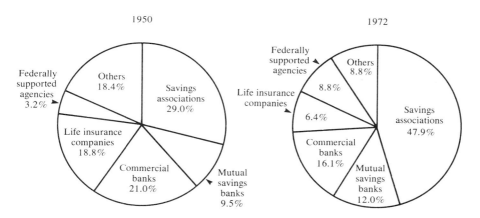

Source: U.S. Savings and Loan League, *Savings and Loan Fact Book,* 1972, p. 37.

and individuals have decreased in their percentage of the total loans for one- to four-family homes, while mutual savings banks, savings associations, and government agencies have increased their percentages.

Commercial Banks

Commercial banks are not very active in making real estate mortgage loans because they are not in a good position to make long-term loans. Money placed in checking accounts in banks fluctuates very much because the owners of these accounts can withdraw their money at any time. Banks must always remain in a position to pay this money to owners when they demand it. The nature of commercial banking makes these institutions more adapted to participating in short-term loans. Banks do not make many loans for terms of longer than five years, and such terms are not suitable for housing loans. This limited amount of time would probably require that the loan be renegotiated, since few borrowers would be able to repay this type of loan in such a short time period. Banks are better suited for home remodeling loans, since such loans can be repaid in a shorter period than home-purchase loans. These smaller loans may be used to add a room, a garage, a swimming pool, or any other type of major improvement to the property. Bank loans can also be insured by the Federal Housing Administration. Interest rates and closing costs for bank loans compare favorably with those from other private lenders.

Mutual Savings Banks and Savings and Loan Associations

Almost 60 percent of home mortgage loans are made by mutual savings banks and savings and loan associations. These are private organizations operating under state and federal laws. Their funds are almost wholly used for real estate loans, although savings and loan associations have recently obtained permission to make loans for other purposes. They accept the savings of millions of people and pay interest on these accounts. In turn, the funds are loaned to others who want to purchase real estate. Their operating expense and profit comes from charging a higher rate of interest for loans than that interest paid on the savings accounts.

Since savings banks and savings and loan associations are private businesses, their loan requirements and operating procedures will vary in different regions. On conventional loans, their interest rates may be slightly higher than other lenders, but their required down payment will usually be lower.

Some savings and loan associations are chartered and operate under state laws, while others have federal charters and regulations. Federal associations are supervised by the Federal Home Loan Bank Board. Savings and loan associations, like commercial banks, are found in both large and small cities. Doing business with a local institution is more convenient for the borrower.

Life Insurance Companies

Life insurance companies make home mortgage loans, but they account for only 8 percent of these loans. Their loans compare favorably with those from other lenders, but the life insurance company must depend on an agent or banker in the smaller towns to originate the loans. Since these companies do not have offices or company agents in many towns, potential borrowers may not know how to apply for a mortgage loan with an insurance company.

In recent years, life insurance companies have not been aggressive in the home mortgage market. They prefer large loans that involve such construction projects as office buildings and apartment houses. Consequently, their share of home mortgages has declined. Nevertheless, in seeking a home loan, it could be worthwhile to try an insurance company. They will likely require a higher down payment than other lenders, but they may allow a longer repayment term. The local banker or a life insurance salesman can supply information on how to apply for one of these loans. The owner of a life insurance policy can write to his own company to inquire about their home loans.

Federal Housing Administration

The Federal Housing Administration was created by the National Housing Act of 1934 and is now in the Department of Housing and Urban Development. It does not make loans, but it does insure those made by private lenders, such as commercial banks and savings and loan associations. Lenders making FHA-insured loans must abide by the limits on interest rate, down payment, and other terms established by FHA regulations. These loans usually have smaller down payments and lower interest rates than conventional loans. Lenders can afford to do this, since they have less risk on these government-guaranteed loans. A loan may be made for up to 97 percent of the first $15,000 of appraised value, 90 percent of the next $10,000, and 80 percent of the value over $25,000. On a $30,000 home, the loan could be $27,550, or 91.8 percent of the appraised value, and terms could allow thirty years for repayment.[5]

On FHA-insured loans, borrowers pay a monthly insurance premium of .5 percent on the principal outstanding. Interest rate ceilings are set at that level required to meet market conditions. They have varied from 4¼ percent in 1950 to 8½ percent in 1970. The rate dropped to 7 percent in 1971. The .5 percent insurance premium is added to these rates.

The FHA loan program was liberalized in 1959, when an interest subsidy program was authorized. Borrowers whose income is below a specified level have part of their interest paid by the government. Laws passed in 1968 and 1969 provided additional assistance for low-income families in the purchase or rental of homes. Mobile homes may also be purchased with government assistance. Those families with poor credit histories can become eligible for loans.

Sometimes lenders add "points" to government-insured loans, since the interest rate they are allowed to charge may be below the rate on conventional loans. A point is 1 percent of the mortgage and it is charged only one time. For example, with a $25,000 mortgage, one point would be $250. The seller of the house may be required to pay the points, but the cost will be passed on to the buyer in the price of the house.

Houses must be constructed to meet FHA specifications in order to receive an insured loan. Builders and real estate agents can provide information about housing loans and application for an FHA-insured loan. About 25 percent of the residential mortgages outstanding are loans insured by FHA or guaranteed by the Veterans' Administration. Almost all of these loans are in urban and suburban areas. Housing loans are more difficult to get in rural areas, since these areas do not necessarily have community loan services and rural homes are less marketable than those near cities. The shortage of housing credit in rural areas has been partly alleviated by expansion of Farmers Home Administration, an agency of the U.S. Department of Agriculture.

Farmers Home Administration

The Farmers Home Administration makes loans to repair, remodel, and build homes in rural areas and in communities of up to 10,000 population. These are direct government loans and this organization has offices in many county-seat towns. These low-interest loans have repayment periods of up to thirty-three years. Requirements specify that loans can be made only to families who do not qualify for loans at private credit agencies. This credit can be used to construct new homes, while Federal Housing Administration loans are made only on completed structures. The Farmers Home Administration program has expanded rapidly in recent years.

---

[5]U.S. Savings and Loan League, *Savings and Loan Fact Book, 1972* (Chicago, 1971), p. 127.

Veterans' Administration

Veterans of military service are eligible for government-guaranteed home loans made by private lending institutions. In rural areas and small towns where credit is not available, the Veterans' Administration can make direct loans. When loans are guaranteed to private lenders, the VA enters into an agreement with the lender to guarantee only part of the loan, but to do this in such a way that the lender has little chance of loss. The down payment is smaller than for conventional loans and the repayment period may be as long as thirty years. These mortgages allow the borrower to make payment ahead of schedule without penalty, while many conventional mortgages make a charge for advance payments. Interest rate ceilings are the same as those for FHA loans, except that the borrower pays no insurance premium.

Other Loan Alternatives

Assuming a Loan. In the purchase of an existing house, chances are good that it has a current loan and mortgage. Should the buyer assume the present owner's loan or find a new credit source and repay the existing loan? It would certainly be an advantage to assume the old loan, if the interest rate is lower than rates for new loans. Sometimes, mortgages cannot be assumed by new borrowers except at current (higher) interest rates. Another advantage to assuming an existing loan is the possibility of lower closing costs. Moreover, a property survey will not be needed and less legal work is required. One difficulty in assuming a loan is that more money may be needed for a down payment. The present owner may have made payments long enough to have a large equity in the house. If this large payment is necessary, the buyer should be able to borrow enough for the larger down payment from another lender and give him a second mortgage.

Loans insured by FHA or guaranteed by VA cannot be assumed by a new borrower unless the agency gives permission. A conventional loan could be assumed without the lenders' permission; however, the original borrower would be taking extra risk. He would still be liable for the debt if the person assuming the loan stopped making payments.

Another method of transferring a home loan obligation to someone else is called *novation*. A person entitled to receive payment on a loan may agree to release the person obligated when a third person agrees to take his place. Actually, the new party is not assuming the loan, but a new contract is made. Since the old contract is nullified, the first payer is released from all obligation.

Second Mortgages. Some houses are sold by the use of a second mortgage. A second mortgage is a debt instrument given to a lender using security that already has a lien on it. The second mortgage holder has a lower claim on the property than the first mortgage holder. Sometimes a seller will take a second mortgage for his equity in a house when the buyer does not have a down payment. In considering the purchase of a house that will require payments to two lenders at the same time, it is important to be sure that the budget provides for this expense without undue hardship on the family, since housing costs could take too large a share of income. Since there is more risk involved in accepting second mortgages, these loans usually require higher interest rates than first mortgages. Unless the housing market is weak or the house is in a poor location, the seller should not need to take a second mortgage, if he is asking a reasonable price for his property.

Using a Real Estate Agent

A prospective home buyer or seller often considers going to a real estate agent. These agents or brokers are professional people in the business of buying, selling, renting, and managing real estate. They perform valuable services just as do other professional people. There are instances when a real estate agent is not needed, but in most places their service is worth the fee. For example, after having lived in a town for a long time and having become familiar with housing developments and neighborhoods, a buyer may learn of a house that is for sale that he likes. He could investigate prices of other houses in the area to see if he would be paying a fair price for the house. However, in most cases, it takes time and some knowledge of real estate transactions to buy or sell a home without using the services of professional agents. They do perform valuable services which the buyer must be prepared to undertake if he chooses not to consult an agent.

Why are real estate agents needed? These people have more general information about the town and new developments than the average person does. They know the locations of schools, churches, and stores. Above all, they can help a buyer obtain financing and save time by showing him only the houses in his price range. On the first visit to an agent's office, a prospective buyer should tell him about what size and type of house he wants, the approximate price he can afford to pay, and the general area he wants to live in. The agent wants a satisfied buyer and seller, so this information is important. Ultimately, the agent's fee is paid by the seller and it will vary from 5 to 10 percent of the selling price.

If time is not a vital factor when a person decides to sell his house, there is no reason he cannot try to sell it without an agent's help, providing he knows what is a reasonable asking price. A sign can be placed in the front yard and an advertisement listed in the newspaper. He must be prepared to show prospective buyers through the house at all hours. When an agent is involved, this can be done by appointment. After a period of trying to sell without satisfaction, a seller can always consult an agent.

It is a good business practice to have an independent appraisal before buying a house. The agent represents the seller so he will usually try to raise the price as much as he can. A buyer can apply for FHA-insured financing and receive an appraisal as a part of that process, even though he may plan to use a conventional loan. This is good protection from paying an excessively high price.

Although real estate dealers are licensed and supposedly trustworthy, a buyer should demand more than vague verbal descriptions of boundary lines when he makes his choice. One example of the results of such a vague description concerns a young couple new to a small town who were shown an attractive house that seemed just the right size for their family and their pocket book. One of the features that attracted them to the house was a breezeway and garage unit that had been added. The real estate dealer pointed out the usefulness of the large back yard and, when asked about property lines, pointed in the general direction of what appeared to be the back corner of the lot. The deal was closed and the family lived comfortably in the new home for several months until, they were pleased to learn, street improvements were to be made. Since the owner was to pay a certain amount per foot for curbing, the young owner compared the footage given on his deed with actual measurements he had made and found that the two did not compare. To his consternation, he found that the garage was actually sitting on the adjoining vacant lot. He was fortunate enough to be able to purchase the lot and later to sell the unneeded portion of it, but the situation could easily have been past remedy.

Despite the grim picture of real estate agents that such a story presents, a good real estate agent will learn what the buyer wants and try to find the right property to satisfy his needs. After the buyer has selected the house, the agent will proceed with completing the transaction. If any obstacle arises during closing, he will try to remove it. If there is trouble with financing or in getting a survey completed, he will make arrangements to get the job completed. Thus, it is important to use reasonable care in selecting the agent. In return, he will save the buyer time and money and make the selling or buying of a home a more pleasant task. Since real estate agents are licensed by the state, local chambers of commerce or better business bureaus should be able to supply the names of reputable agents.

Discussion Questions

1. Discuss some of the advantages and disadvantages of being an exurbanite.
2. What are condominiums? Discuss the difference between a cooperative apartment and a condominium.
3. What are the income tax advantages of home ownership?
4. Explain the variable-rate mortgage plan for savings and loan associations.
5. Explain what is meant by variable-payment mortgages and give an example of how they work.
6. What is the *Abstract of Title?* What is included in it?
7. What are tract or development houses? What are some disadvantages of purchasing this type of house?
8. Discuss the two groups of home mortgage lenders.
9. Identify FHA and give its purpose. Discuss the program FHA offers.
10. Why are real estate agents needed?

He that lives upon hope will die fasting.
[Benjamin Franklin]

11

Buying
Food

The Need for
Consumer Education

Advertisers have deluged us with so much information about their products that some practical guidance is needed. Television commercials and features, magazine advertisements and articles, books on nutrition and dieting supply harmful and helpful—but always enticing—information. The besieged consumer must evaluate and choose what is best for the family's health and budget. Food and nutrition education is essential for consumers and is most important for those trying to manage with low incomes. A study of low-income families who are participating in a nutrition education program of the U.S. Department of Agriculture revealed that only 9 percent of homemakers entering the program were serving their families foods recommended for an adequate diet.[1]

---

[1]U.S. Department of Agriculture, *Marketing and Transportation Situation* (November, 1970), p. 23.

However, poor diets and unwise spending are not confined to low-income families.

One consumer in nineteen spends $50 a year on unnecessary or falsely represented vitamin products and so-called health foods.[2] Nationally, this amounts to over $500 million a year. Weight-consciousness with its fads and facts has added to the confusion. Promoters have found weight-reducing products to be a lucrative field.

To aid consumers in evaluating prospective purchases, federal and state governments have passed laws to require that foods be truthfully labeled, as well as safe for consumption. Although there is much discussion about the use of insecticides and pesticides in the production of our food supply, few informed persons will deny that we have the safest and most wholesome foods in the world. One amusing and reassuring result of our food safety and labeling laws was the case of the sudden reduction in the amount of "Vermont Maple Syrup" on the market. At one time, the quantity reported sold amounted to ten times the production capacity of Vermont. Consumer protection laws for food are discussed in Chapter 4.

Protection insured by laws and the honesty of producers is not enough to make sure all people have balanced nutrition. The shopper who wants to get the best food at the most reasonable cost must learn to evaluate the information available. The family's or individual's needs must be taken into account along with the limitations and possibilities of the food dollar. Experience and careful planning and shopping combined with common sense and a mind open to new ideas should guarantee good nutrition without damaging the budget.

While adequate income and education do not assure good family diets, apparently they help. Two studies were made in 1955 and 1965 which permitted comparisons of family diets for their adequacy of meeting recommended nutrition requirements.[3] The studies revealed that dietary adequacy was related to family income and the level of education of the homemaker. The higher level of education did not necessarily include courses in foods, but it presumably helped the homemaker to use educational materials from other sources.

There is evidence to indicate that dietary levels of American families are not increasing as fast as incomes. The 1955 and 1965 studies mentioned earlier showed a 10 percent decrease in the proportion of family diets meeting the 1963 Recommended Dietary Allowances of the Food and Nutrition Board of the National Research Council.[4] One reason given for the decrease was unwise consumer choice of goods—such as a higher consumption of soft drinks and lower consumption of milk.

If educational programs do not improve family dietary levels, then other methods must be used. The food processing and marketing system can be im-

---

[2]*Consumers All, Yearbook of Agriculture* (Washington, D.C.: U.S. Dept. of Agriculture, 1965), p. 402.

[3]Address by Trienah Meyers, Economic Research Service, U.S. Department of Agriculture, at Third International Congress, Food Science and Technology (Washington, D.C., August 9, 1970).

[4]Address by Joan C. Courtless, Agriculture Research Service, at the 1971 National Agriculture Outlook Conference (Washington, D.C., February 24, 1971).

proved by fortifying more foods with vitamins and minerals and by better handling and storage practices. Families receiving foods on welfare programs can be provided with those items that assure minimum nutrition requirements. We can make nutritious foods available, but freedom of choice prevails in the marketplace, still allowing consumers to buy less nutritious foods.

Changes in Food
Consumption Patterns

Food stores display between 8,000 and 18,000 different items on their shelves. Fifty-five percent of these did not exist ten years ago. Only one-third of the new items accepted by grocers will survive more than a year.

Food consumption patterns have changed in the United States as population shifted and new technology appeared. On the early self-contained farm, most food items were raised at home, supplemented by a few items—such as tea and coffee—which had to be purchased. Out-of-season fruits, because of inadequate transportation and storage facilities, were a rare luxury indeed. As people began to specialize in their vocations, they came to depend on those who specialized in food production to provide food of all kinds.

Of course, as living patterns changed, packaging and merchandising had to change. When most people lived on farms, they did not go to town often, so they had to purchase foods in quantity. Their large houses usually provided ample storage space. As people moved to the cities, they lived in small houses and apartments with little space for storage. This necessitated small and frequent purchases. To meet this need, food processors began reducing the size of packages. Refrigeration and better transportation have added a new dimension to the food industry by making more foods available in all seasons.

It is encouraging that research shows diseases due to improper food have declined sharply—an improvement over the 1930s, when President Franklin D. Roosevelt stated that one-third of our population was ill-fed. Studies by the Department of Agriculture and other surveys had disclosed that deficiency diseases were widespread at that time.

Today, sanitation, cleanliness, and safety in foods is taken for granted. There is a vast difference between good quality, graded eggs produced on a modern poultry farm, taken directly to the wholesaler, and then to the retailer and his customer at controlled temperatures, and eggs found in stores in the "good old days," when customers in the grocery store found eggs of doubtful heritage and age. In those days, eggs may have been relayed at a leisurely pace from the farmer to the small town merchant to traveling egg and chicken buyers and at last to the city retailer and the customer. The latter could only hope the product still edible.

Quality testing and pasteurization of milk are expected by the customer, who also takes for granted that meats are government inspected. Cleanliness and careful handling are taken for granted, while produce is expected to be fresh and top quality. Extra costs are naturally incurred when so many services must be performed.

Besides benefiting from better quality foods, the grocery shopper finds convenience foods one of the pleasant changes in foods. A family where both husband and wife work or a higher income family will find these foods better bargains than a person or a family with a lower food budget. As a later discussion in this chapter will show, certain convenience foods may actually be cheaper than those in raw forms.

Changing life styles have brought changes in the types of foods needed. Since many people today exert minimal physical effort in their jobs, they need a smaller quantity of food and fewer calories. Not everyone has adapted to this change automatically—hence the necessity of another noticeable change in recent years, the increase in dieting and weight-watching. (See *Planning for Balanced Diets* later in this chapter.)

Changing prices bring changes in food consumption also. In times of rising prices, shoppers tend to be more alert to specials, to try different, less-expensive cuts of meat, and to take more time selecting needed items. In 1972, according to the United States Department of Agriculture, food expenditures were $124 billion, a 6 percent increase from 1971. The 5 percent rise in food prices accounts for a large part of that increase. Food consumption per person in 1972 averaged only .5 percent higher than in 1971. Inflation does not affect the family's needs, but it does have an effect on the ultimate selection of food available within the bounds of a given food allowance.

The size of our supermarket bill depends on

Our incomes	*Our families'* *wants and needs*	*Non-food* *purchases*
As our incomes go up, we buy . . .	Number in the family	Toothpaste
	Ages of family	Lightbulbs
More steaks and roasts	members	Cigarettes
More fruits and vege-	Amount of entertaining	Paper towels and tissues
tables out of season	done at home	Soaps and detergents
More convenience foods		Pet food
More delicacies		Hair sprays and shampoos
We spend . . .		Socks and shirts
		Medical Products
More total dollars, but . . .		
A smaller percentage of		These things are not food,
our incomes for food		but they can add up to 23¢
		out of each dollar we
		spend at the supermarket.

Food Costs

Food is now the second largest recurring expense in most family budgets. Housing costs have exceeded food costs. More than a hundred years ago, Ernest Engel concluded, after a study of the expenditure of Belgian workingmen's families at all income levels, "The poorer a family, the greater propor-

---

[5]Economic Research Service Leaflet 308 (Washington, D.C.: U.S. Department of Agriculture, Jan., 1971).

tion of total outgo that must be used for food."[6] Later investigations have confirmed Engel's conclusion. While the proportion is declining, spending for food including meals at home or away from home takes nearly 25 percent of the total consumer income in the United States (see Exhibit 11–1).

Exhibit 11–1   Intermediate Family Budget, United States: Where the Dollar Goes, Autumn 1971

Four-person family budget, intermediate level[1]

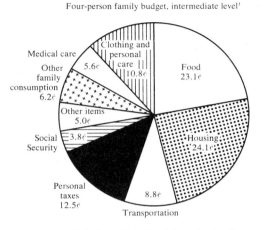

Retired couple's budget, intermediate level[2]

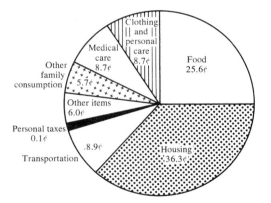

[1]Intermediate level income is $10,971 (4 persons).
[2]Intermediate level income is $4,776 (retired couple).
Source: U.S. Dept. of Labor, Family Budget Levels in the Southwest, Regional Report No. 5, Nov., 1972, p. 3.

The current trend of inflation is one reason that the proportion of income spent for food does not drop sharply with a rise in income. Inflation brings rising food prices along with income increases, so the proportion spent remains relatively large. However, food prices have not risen as fast as wages. Few people who look back at 59¢ sirloin steaks, milk at 10¢ a quart and 5¢ loaves

[6]*Food, The Yearbook of Agriculture* (Washington, D.C.: U.S. Department of Agriculture, 1959), p. 559.

of bread would want to go back to the wages that accompanied those prices. A factory worker's hourly wage would bring home less than a pound of bacon in 1914, 2 pounds in 1939, and 3½ pounds today.

Buying foods partly for style keeps the higher income consumer's food costs up—throwing parties with exotic food to impress guests, dining out at expensive restaurants, endeavoring to keep up with (or ahead of) the Joneses. Economist Thornstein Veblen called this "conspicuous consumption." This phenomenon is not limited to high-income groups, however. What family does not take pride in offering special delicacies to guests?

Inflation has also made grocery shopping a nightmare for extremely low-income people. A look around almost any supermarket will usually reveal at least one or two persons with items in their baskets reminiscent of depression days—flour, beans, salt pork, lard—with only a few fresh or canned fruits or vegetables or high protein foods. The old-age pension or day-labor dollar stretches very thin at today's prices. The hopelessness of low-income old age is balanced at the other end of the life cycle by the hopefulness of another low-income group—young married students. Again, a picture in the supermarket is easy to evoke: a boy and girl huddle together comparing the costs of the items in their shopping basket against the few dollars in their pockets. If the student couple can hang on a few more months or years until they become full-time wage earners, their food consumption pattern will change. Unfortunately, the pensioner or fixed-low-income buyer has little hope for improvement.

To understand part of the system which produces these extremes, economists refer to certain indicators. The Consumer Price Index (discussed more thoroughly in Chapter 7) is calculated by the U.S. Bureau of Labor Statistics to show relative monthly and yearly changes in costs of certain consumer items. Food is a significant part of this index. Of 398 items included in the index, 105 are foods. Prices are noted at intervals ranging from once every month to once every three months, and these samples are taken in various size cities in all parts of the country. While this price index is not a perfect measure of change in the cost of living for any particular family, it does indicate general price changes. It is more accurate for those living in the largest cities of the midwest and northeastern regions, since samples are taken more frequently in these areas.

Food Needs According to Family Size and Ages

Each family is unique. Aside from known basic daily nutritional requirements established for individuals according to age, sex, and activity, any one family's food requirements cannot be copied from a plan set out by someone else. Most could exist on these minimum requirements, but the quality of life rather than mere maintenance of life is dear to Americans. One family may save as much as possible on food, while splurging on other budget items. To others, food without frills would be a near-calamity. For a poor family, a near-Spartan diet may be a necessity.

Exhibit 11–2   The Changing Family Food Bill

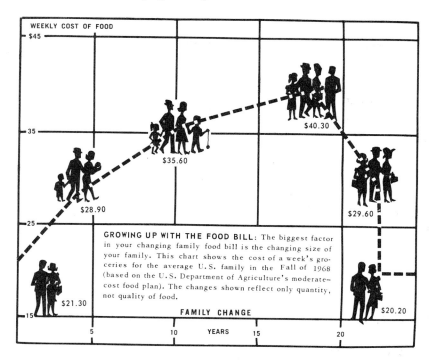

GROWING UP WITH THE FOOD BILL: The biggest factor in your changing family food bill is the changing size of your family. This chart shows the cost of a week's groceries for the average U.S. family in the Fall of 1968 (based on the U.S. Department of Agriculture's moderate-cost food plan). The changes shown reflect only quantity, not quality of food.

Source: U.S. Department of Agriculture

Thus, no one can arbitrarily set a budget item for food to satisfy "a family of four." It is all-important who the "four" are—husband, wife, and two small children (requiring special baby foods); husband, wife and two ravenous teen-agers; with a husband whose job is sedentary or a husband whose work is hard physical labor; a family all in normal health or one with family members ill or elderly and requiring special diets. Each person responsible must know the needs of the family and must acquire a knowledge of the best use of the money available for food.

That segment of the population which is composed of single adults—particularly elderly people—often voices displeasure at certain popular practices of food stores, such as carrying items in packs of four or more servings and eggs by the dozen. These people are often limited to a small weekly grocery allowance and more often than not have little refrigerator or freezer space. Thus, large packages are a problem from several standpoints. One might well use a whole chicken before it spoiled, but the prospect of chicken three or four days in a row is not desirable psychologically or nutritionally. Some stores do provide small packages of chicken and meats; but, if they do not, what can a single person do? First, he can try asking the store to break sizes. If they refuse and patronizing another store would be inconvenient, friends might make joint purchases and later divide the larger packages among themselves. Mrs. Smith splits a package of cutlets with Mrs. Green, who in turn divides a fryer with her. They share the cost equally and both have variety in their diets. Some gregarious and variety-minded single persons even take turns preparing complete meals for two or more friends, providing more incentive for variety and enjoyment.

Unfortunately, due to lack of energy and incentive, elderly people tend to take the easy route and consume too many bland, easy-to-eat foods that are often low in nutritive value. They should be encouraged to get plenty of protein and a balanced diet.

Young people often tend to ignore the need for a balanced diet and require special family guidance.

Whatever its size, the family's ability to plan, shop wisely, prepare food well, avoid waste, and guide each member in being reasonable in his requirements has much influence on the family's food budget—and on its well-being and happiness. If the children learn to exercise good judgment in choice of foods, the parents will have succeeded in teaching as well as feeding the family.

Planning for
Balanced Diets

Modern families have little excuse for unbalanced diets or malnutrition, but both conditions do exist—even in high-income families. Elementary schools teach children the necessity for careful choice of foods; almost every magazine, newspaper, and complete cookbook gives a guide to proper diet. The United States Department of Agriculture and other government and commercial services offer booklets for a few cents—sometimes free. It seems repetitious to enumerate these guidelines here. However, food fads, careless food choice habits, inflation woes, and misinformation make it mandatory that we occasionally review a fitness guide and the Basic Seven Food Groups. These groups consist of the following:

1. Milk, cheese, and ice cream
2. Meat, poultry, fish, eggs, dried peas, and beans
3. Leafy, green and yellow vegetables
4. Citrus fruit, tomatoes, and raw cabbage
5. Potatoes and other vegetables and fruits
6. Bread, flour, and cereals
7. Butter and margarine

Although no two families' food needs are the same, for purposes of listing basic food requirements we shall use the term "typical family." Money-wise in the typical family, one-half of the food money goes for milk, meat, eggs, one-fifth for fruits and vegetables, and the remainder is about equally divided as follows: grain products; fats, oils, sugars, and sweets; miscellaneous items—such as coffee, tea and other beverages, leavening agents, spices, and vinegar.

The basic seven food groups allow wide latitudes in budgets, tastes, and seasonal abundance in their requirements. Not all beef need be choice cuts. "Regardless of cost, you get about the same food value from equal-size servings of cooked lean from different types and cuts of meats. Exceptions are frankfurters, sausages, bacon, and some meats with breaded coatings. Amounts of these meats usually served may cost less than servings of average size of other meats but do not give as much in food value."[7]

It is important to note that the above quotation refers to equal-size servings of lean meat. In choosing meat, the consumer must learn to identify packages containing a good amount of lean meat with a minimum of gristle, fat, and bone. A higher priced roast containing only enough fat to make it tender and little or no gristle and bone may be a better buy than a much lower priced cut made up largely of waste. A practiced eye can decide which is the bargain.

Think in terms of portions:

Amount of meat needed per person	*Type of meat*
¼ lb.	meat with little fat and no bone
⅓ lb.	meat with some fat and a small amount of bone
½ to ¾ lb.	substantial amount of fat and bone
1 lb.	great deal of fat and bone

Amount of fish needed per person
1 lb. of whole fish
½ lb. of dressed fish
⅓ lb. of frozen fish

Acceptable occasional substitutes for meat, fish, and poultry are eggs, dry beans, and peanut butter.

The food groups or a daily guide is only a framework around which to plan the daily diet. After the essential amounts from each group are included, the individual adds other foods from the groups plus butter or margarine, salad dressings, and various sweets, depending on the number of calories needed daily.

Calorie content is important in planning balanced diets. With calorie charts available in nearly every cookbook and on every newsstand as well as from the family doctor, it is superfluous to try to reproduce calorie charts here. Of course, the dieter must learn to obtain basic daily requirements from lower calorie foods. Since we can get calcium requirements in skim milk or cottage cheese, the calorie budget will not permit indulgence in the amount of richer ice cream required to supply an equal amount of calcium. The budget-minded dieter should also note that expensive "diet" foods are often more expensive and less suitable than carefully chosen and properly prepared meats, vegetables, fruits, and dairy products.

---

[7]*Consumers All*, p. 417.

Careful shopping for food to find the best quality nutritive food for the money available is important. But, no matter how wisely the shopper chooses, he must remember to enlist his family's cooperation and to cater to (or "train") their tastes. "The family's approval is important. No food is a bargain or a body builder if it is not eaten. Keeping waste to a minimum is a big step toward keeping food costs down."[8]

Buying in Quantity and on "Specials"

The grocer's vegetable bin features choice crisp lettuce at a "special" price. Two heads are usually the family's limit on one shopping trip. Nevertheless, the low price and the quality of the product convince our average consumer that purchasing four heads is economical. Putting away the groceries at home, the shopper can find room in the refrigerator for only two heads (the usual limit). Consequently, two heads are left in the bag on the cabinet, waiting for refrigerator space. After several hours, the room-stored lettuce has deteriorated in taste and nutritive value. Even refrigerated lettuce, kept for several days, retains only 75 percent of its A and C vitamins. If kept only twenty-four hours, 90 percent of these are retained. This kind of venture into quantity buying of specials can leave the consumer with a supply of unappetizing, deteriorated food. This is an example of unplanned, impractical quantity buying.

Quantity buying can be a money-saver to the food buyer if these points are considered:

1. Is there a substantial saving over purchasing in smaller amounts?
2. Is the quality good?
3. Will the family receive added benefit in enjoyment and nutrition from having this food in additional amounts?
4. Is space available for storing this food under conditions that will retain its nutritive value and prevent spoilage and waste?

A twenty-pound bag of potatoes at a bargain price is a bargain only if storage space at the proper temperature and humidity is available. A twenty-pound bag of potatoes spoiled before they can be used is no bargain at any price.

The object of quantity buying is usually to save money. Another consideration is that quantity buying may enable the homemaker to purchase higher quality food at lower prices by buying in large amounts.

If the primary object is economy, the shopper must be careful not to spend the usual amount for groceries in weeks following a quantity purchase. For instance, if a shopper has purchased a dozen cans of green beans at a reduced price and has a side of beef in the freezer, his grocery bill should not be as much as if he were still buying beans and beef each week.

---

[8]*Consumers All*, p. 416.

Of course, a strict weekly allowance is a disadvantage for buying in quantity. If the budget is rigid, some juggling may be necessary, such as postponing the purchase of certain items for a week in order to take advantage of a current sale. For the purchase of meat in quantity on a set budget, saving and economizing in advance may be the answer. Fortunate is the buyer who has a reserve of cash, even a small amount, if it makes saving possible by buying when items are on "special."

Family packs of meats and other items frequently offer a saving, but the shopper should be alert to quality and the real value in content.

Specials and Sales

Grocery stores offer specials or sales for various reasons. Year-end inventory time is the season for sales on frozen and canned goods and odd and slow-selling items. Other reasons may be seasonal harvest or over-supply. One of the most frequent uses of specials is as a "come-on" to bring the customer to the store. In the case of the latter type of special, the consumer must compare prices on other items. Some staples or other "steady sellers" may be marked up to compensate for planned losses on "loss leaders." The change in price may not be marked on each item in special sales, so the shopper should watch as the salesperson checks the groceries. He may unintentionally overcharge for unmarked items. One way to avoid this overcharge is to take a copy of the ad to the store or list prices on advertised specials. Then, with careful observation, the consumer can make sure of getting the advertised price. He should also be careful in buying specials to group like items together for quicker and more efficient checking, with only advertised items in such a group. If cut green beans are selling at four for $1.00, the shopper loses the advantage of the sale if he carelessly picks up three cans of cut green beans and one of long or French-cut beans. Clerks usually point out such apparent mistakes, but exchanging for the proper item is an unnecessary waste of time.

If adequate freezer space is available, meat specials can save money and help to feed the family better. If buying a large portion of beef is not desirable, special sales offer an opportunity to get good values on a supply of the consumer's choice of particular cuts. Frying chickens are often found as specials and as much as $.10 per pound can often be saved. The extra amount could be frozen for future use or, if the family plans to entertain guests, a chicken dish could be substituted for some other choice on the menu.

Many stores offer "rain checks" if advertised specials run out of stock. The shopper should ask for one if the items he needs are out-of-stock. The store offers this service in good faith in order to encourage the shopper to become or remain a regular customer.

The price of foods is influenced by seasonal supply. Improved transportation and storage have made seasonal changes less marked than a few years ago, but the price of fresh and frozen fruits and vegetables still fluctuates with the crop year. Exhibit 11–3 shows this seasonal price change for some products. Newspaper food sections feature recipes and advertisements for fruits, produce, and

Exhibit 11–3   Retail Price Seasonality

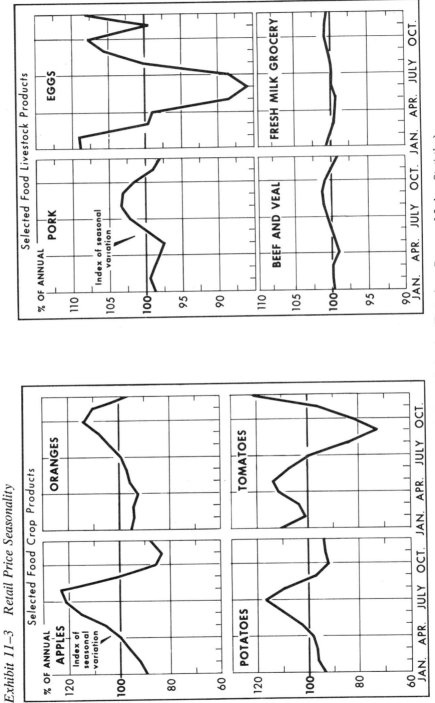

Source: U.S. Department of Agriculture, Economic Research Service (Data from Bureau of Labor Statistics)

even meats that are in season. Radio stations offer consumer reports. Thus, there is ample information for the wise shopper to judge which meals, using in-season ingredients, should be planned. Unless a special occasion calls for serving expensive, out-of-season fresh strawberries, it is a good idea to use the frozen ones at a more reasonable cost.

Sometimes in seasons when fresh produce is in plentiful supply, frozen fruits and vegetables are also more likely to be reduced in price. This is the time to add to the freezer supply.

Convenience Foods

There are several misconceptions concerning convenience foods.

(1) One of the most widely accepted assumptions is that *convenience foods are always more expensive than foods prepared entirely from raw products*. This is not always true. A study by the U.S. Department of Agriculture of 158 foods showed that 42 of them were less expensive as convenience foods than if they had been prepared at home. Frozen whole kernel corn costs less per serving than fresh corn. Orange juice squeezed at home costs much more than that made from frozen juice concentrate. Some cakes made from mixes are less expensive than those baked from home ingredients, but frozen prepared baked goods are usually higher than the homemade. Carrots and potatoes cost less if prepared from fresh vegetables because they are more economically stored than more perishable produce. Canned and frozen peas are cheaper because they have a longer shelf life and are more compact to ship and store.

(2) *Individually packaged foods are usually a luxury*. Whether or not this is true depends on the use intended for the items. Individually packaged servings of sugar, sugar substitutes, and salt do cost more, but under certain circumstances they may be needed—such as at picnics where food is not easily served in bulk form. Chips are more expensive in individual packages than in a large bag, but if they are more readily kept fresh and are more easily served in small bags they may well be worth the extra cost.

(3) There are a few "die-hards" who maintain that *only lazy or rich housewives should use convenience foods*. Happy is the wife who twenty years ago cringed as her mother-in-law, sampling a pudding, queried ruefully, "Did you make this from a mix?" and now observes mother-in-law matter-of-factly serving "store-bought" frozen pies and cakes made from a mix. For some individuals or families, using convenience foods may be the only means of obtaining household help. For those employed outside the home, convenience foods are almost like having a maid. The use of convenience foods by the non-working homemaker may give her more time with the family, time for sewing, for interior decorating, or for community activities. Any extra costs should be bal-

anced against extra satisfactions for the entire family. Entire cookbooks have been written on using convenience foods as a basis for interesting new dishes.

If the time permits and the prospect is desirable, a homemaker should, by all means, prepare as much food from raw products as is feasible. It is sometimes necessary to do so with items that cost more in prepared form. But, if the resulting dishes are consistently less appetizing to the family, the resulting waste from homemade throw-a-ways may make them more expensive than the mixes.

Each person must be guided in the decision as to how many prepared foods to use by the amount of time, money, and degree of cooking skill available.

One problem with convenience foods that should be considered is that of additives. To improve color and conserve freshness, various chemicals are added. From time to time, public concern is aroused as to the safety of some of these chemicals. The best advice on this topic is that all consumers should remain alert but not alarmed and keep up with consumer reports on this subject.

Ways to Guard
Your Pocketbook

Although it may sound like an admonition to a child, this heading might well be taken literally, since it is often a careless habit of many adults to leave valuables in the grocery basket while wandering about searching for an item.

But there are other "figurative" ways to guard the pocketbook. If food bills are too high, consider these steps:

1. Entertain less often or less expensively. "An ounce of ingenuity is often worth a pound of money."

2. Avoid restaurant meals when you can dine at home. Family members working or attending school might take lunches.

3. Check for expense leaks in your buying habits, storage facilities, cooking.

4. Avail yourself of every opportunity to adopt ideas on worthwhile money-saving methods of meal planning, cooking, and food selection.

5. Halt impulse buying.

6. See if you are paying for services you can't afford. Milk delivered to your door costs more than in the store. (Warning: If you cannot resist impulse buying you *might* spend more at the store on unnecessary items when you go to the store to pick up milk.) Can you afford baked goods and some of the admittedly more expensive convenience foods?

7. Make a shopping list (and stick with it, unless you find less expensive substitutes) from menus that you have planned that take into account the food on hand. "It can help you avoid the pitfall of impulse buying

—the out-of-season fruit and the costly ready-prepared items or snacks that add little to the diet and much to the grocery bill."[9]

8. Compare prices by the ounce, when possible. Your grocers may have (or you may buy) a plastic or cardboard wheel-type computing device that makes it easy to compare prices.

9. If your children accompany you to the store, don't let them load your cart with eye-catching extras.

10. Take advantage of specials and quantity buying, but make sure you are not continuing to spend as much for groceries in the weeks following special purchases as you did before these items were in your pantry.

11. If you shop with a friend, decide if you may be buying extras because he or she does.

12. Check your purchases to determine if you are adding an excessive amount of non-grocery items. At the same time, check your budget to see if you have allowed enough money for needed non-grocery items. The deficit could be a matter of wrong judgment rather than over-spending.

Trading Stamps and Credit

Two important considerations for the shopper who is serious about saving money are whether to shop at stores which offer trading stamps and premiums or provide extra services, such as "free" delivery or extending credit to customers.

As for trading stamps, the customer must learn to judge by prices whether the stamps are costing extra money. Compare prices at stores that give stamps with those at stores that do not offer such "bonuses" and shop accordingly. A few stores offer a cash discount equal to the value of the stamps. Each shopper must decide which means more to him—the cash or collecting stamps to trade for some wanted article. Many grocery stores claim that offering stamps helps them to maintain such a large volume of sales that they are able to offer stamps at no extra cost to their patrons. Even when stamps do add a slight cost to groceries, it is still a matter of personal decision. The items obtained from redeemed stamps are often things that add to the enjoyment of the home but might never be purchased if it were necessary to pay cash for them—a disguised or fairy-tale type of saving toward a goal.

Stores that offer credit usually must charge everyone a little more to balance bad debts. Again, the customer must compare prices at other stores. Buying on credit also adds a disadvantage for the credit shopper himself. The credit shopper must accept what is available at the store where he has established credit and cannot shop around for bargains.

Comparison of prices is the answer in deciding whether to shop at stores that offer delivery service. People who are confined to their homes or who have no

[9]*Consumers All*, p. 416.

means of transportation may, of necessity, have to shop at these stores by telephone, even if prices are higher. The irony of the credit and delivery situations is that so often those who can least afford the extra charges are the ones who are forced by their life situations to pay them.

Brand Names and Labels

Brand-name buying is an important shopping consideration. There is an element of snobbery with some people who consistently purchase brand-name products. Purchasing "brand x" may be a threat to the stability of such a person's self-image.

There are legitimate reasons for purchasing brand-name merchandise, however. Young people are likely to purchase brand-name products because they are not yet experienced enough to judge between different brands. One distinct advantage of brand names is that the product may be expected to be consistent all over the country. It takes experience and trial and error to learn which lesser-known brands measure up in quality. Grocery chains usually have their own brands. To find if these brands are good, the consumer must often try them. Usually they are good. The A & P chain, for example, has three different brand names for many of its products, rated according to quality and price. The chains and independent grocery co-ops often have a contract with one of the "name brand" companies to make goods under the chain or co-op's label. They are less expensive than under the original name. Companies, such as Del Monte, may market their first quality products under the brand name and a good, but not so fancy, product under other names. The consumer should learn to recognize the name of the packing company on the label.

A shopper can also guard the family's pocketbook by learning to read labels and figure prices by the ounce. The label must show the contents of the package and their source, the name of the product, and the name and address of the packer, manufacturer, or distributor. It must also detail, in descending order of importance, the ingredients of the product. In the lower third of the panel, in readable type, the net weight must be shown. For easier comparison, packages over one pound but under four pounds must give the weight in both pounds and ounces or quarts and ounces and in ounces alone. The number and description of size of servings must be given if the word is mentioned. A necessary amount of empty space for certain products is permitted, but packages deceiving in size are illegal. A dieter should always check the calorie count on a label before he pays extra for a so-called low-calorie food.

The Bargain Hunter—The Hunter or the Hunted?

A bargain is a bargain only when it is something a consumer needs, will use, and can afford.

Stores naturally employ customer psychology in their displays. This is not dishonest, but it is to the consumer's benefit to learn some of their wiles in order to curb some of his own habits that cost money.

(1) Stores use the principle of juxtaposition to sell items that do not sell well. The ten items most sought by customers are coffee, cookies and crackers, canned vegetables, baking needs, paper products, canned soups, laundry supplies, cereals, sugar, and salad dressings and oil. These items are strategically placed around the store among poorer sellers. When a shopper starts down an aisle to buy what he came for, he must learn to ignore other attractive but unnecessary items. Related products are often placed side by side to entice the shopper to buy both when only one is needed. For example, candy is placed alongside the cookies and crackers (usually easily within a child's reach).

(2) Mid-aisle and color displays may cause a shopper to lose his head and his money.

(3) A shopper should never rush or allow himself to be rushed. Shopping comparatively should be the aim.

(4) Another counter-strategy is to avoid being lured into adding unneeded items just to get the coffee or sugar special available with a $5.00 purchase.

(5) A good comparative shopper should learn to evaluate specials to determine if they are really "good buys."

Discussion Questions

1. What have the federal and state governments done to help the consumer buy better food? Do you think their efforts have been effective?

2. Why does a higher level of education ostensibly make for improved food purchasing?

3. Trace how food consumption patterns in the U.S. have varied in the past several years. How has the cost of food in relation to incomes varied during this period? How has food quality varied?

4. How does inflation of food prices affect the consumer? Does it hurt any particular group?

5. Would you agree with the statement "For a family of four, food purchases are essentially standard from one family to the next"? Why?

6. List the seven basic food groups necessary for good nutrition.

7. Give some of the situations where it may be possible to save money by buying food in relatively large quantities.

8. How can a stringent weekly allowance be a disadvantage to buying in quantity?

9. Discuss the rationale behind a grocery store's use of a so-called "loss leader."

10. It is a misconception that all convenience foods cost more than unprepared foods. Why do some convenience foods cost less than their unprepared counterparts?

11. What are some other misconceptions concerning convenience foods?

12. What are three common practices of grocery stores that may add to the cost that one pays for food? Which of these is practiced most widely today?

The best things carried to excess are wrong.
[Churchill]

12

Purchasing Clothing and Major Household Appliances

Although the major portion of a family's income is spent on nondurable goods, durable goods—such as household appliances—do require large expenditures. Clothing also accounts for a large portion of the average family's budget. An approach different from the considerations given to food purchases is needed when planning these expenditures, because we purchase these items less frequently, invest more in each of them, and expect them to last much longer. Careful planning and wise shopping methods must be employed to keep expenses for clothing and appliances at a reasonable level.

Clothing

Knowing Fabrics

Fabrics and clothing have become more versatile since the development of synthetic fibers and the production of a variety of new blends using natural fibers.

In order to benefit from these new products, the consumer must learn more about them. The multiplicity of fabrics makes the task of selecting, purchasing, and caring for the family's clothing more difficult, but the advantages of improved materials outweigh the initial disadvantage of extra thought and effort. A few years ago the choice of fabrics was chiefly between cotton, wool, linen, and silk. It was relatively simple to learn how to clean and care for clothing made from these natural fibers, although there was usually more work involved in care of the old type of fibers than that required for the new. Now the number of blends of natural and synthetic fibers is almost unlimited. Exhibits 12–1 and 12–2 show the major manmade fibers, a few important blends, and their uses.

Planning a Wardrobe

Clothing needs vary with climate, occupation, activities, age, and personal priorities. The proportionate amount of income spent on clothing has not increased with the rise in incomes as much as other family budget items. Although all clothing has become more expensive because of increased production costs, the trend to more casual dress has paralleled a decline in selection of clothing for prestige. Long considered the third necessity of life (after food and shelter), clothing is now in fourth place in amount spent on it, having been superseded by transportation.

Clothing that is comfortable, attractive, and suited to a person's activities greatly improves his self-image and affects the impression he makes on other people. Acquisition and upkeep of clothing and accessories consume an average of 9 percent of disposable income.

The amount a family should spend for clothing may be determined by assessing the amount of income and the family situation. The needs of each family member will dictate the way a clothing allowance is spent. Some family members will need more money for clothes than others. The occupations of family members employed outside the home and the standards of dress they must maintain at work determine certain needs. Home, school, community and social life, and recreation dictate other needs for all persons. Young people in the home pose a special clothing problem. Not only are they still growing and hard to fit, but peer pressures to conform and their style-consciousness shorten the wear-life of most garments. It is necessary to see that the family clothing allowance is not too far slanted in their favor, at the same time remembering that late teen and early adult years are one of the periods of most clothing expenditure. Children need clothing that is comfortable, durable, and easily cleaned. Since children grow so rapidly, it is best to plan on frequent laundering and cleaning so that a smaller wardrobe is needed. It is more economical to wash the playclothes twice a week or more often than try to buy enough soon-to-be-outgrown clothes to last a whole week.

A family must plan purchases, based on knowledge of past records of expenditures and on projected needs. Planning includes taking an inventory of usable clothing on hand and allotting available money for clothing. The inventory should be taken twice a year. It requires time and family cooperation. Each

Exhibit 12–1 *Major Manmade Fibers*

Generic name	Manufacturer's trade name	Manufacturer	Fiber type	Major end uses
Acetate	Celanese Estron* Avisco* Acele*	Celanese Fibers Co. Eastman Chemical Products, Inc. American Viscose Div. (FMC) E. I. du Pont de Nemours & Co.	Secondary cellulose acetate, filament and staple	Lingerie, dress goods, drapery, sports and casual wear. Fiberfil.
Triacetate	Arnel*	Celanese Fibers Co.	Cellulose triacetate, filament and staple	Tricot lingerie and outerwear dress goods, sports and casual wear.
Acrylic	Orlon* Acrilan* Creslan*	E. I. du Pont de Nemours & Co. Chemstrand Co. American Cyanamid Co.	Polyacrylonitrile (primarily staple)	Sweaters, knit goods, men's and women's slacks, carpets, blankets.
Nylon 66	Du Pont* Chemstrand* Celanese Beaunit	E. I. du Pont de Nemours & Co. Chemstrand Co. Celanese Fibers Co. Beaunit Fibers	Polyamide (primarily continuous filament)	Hosiery and socks, lingerie, dress goods, blouses, upholstery, carpets, knit sports goods, uniforms and work clothing, and industrial yarns.
Nylon 6	Caprolan* Enka* Beaunit Firestone*	Allied Chemical Corp. American Enka Corp. Beaunit Fibers Firestone Synthetic Fibers Co.	Same as for Nylon 66	Same as for Nylon 66.

244

Generic name	Manufacturer's trade name	Manufacturer	Fiber type	Major end uses
Polyester	Dacron* Fortrel* Kodel* Vycron*	E. I. du Pont de Nemours & Co. Fiber Industries, Inc. Eastman Chemical Products, Inc. Beaunit Fibers	Polyester (primarily staple), filament for special applications	Blends with cotton for shirting, sports clothing, dress goods, slacks. Blends with wool for suitings. Knit goods for shirting and sports wear. Fiberfil.
Rayon	Avril* Zantrel* Cuprammonium Fibro*	American Viscose Div. (FMC) American Enka Corp. Beaunit Fibers Courtaulds North America, Inc.	Regenerated cellulose filament and staple	Men's and women's slacks and suitings. Women's wear. Linings and drapery. Blankets, carpets, industrial yards.
Glass	Fiberglas* Beta Fiberglas PPG* Garon* Vitron*	Owens-Corning Fiberglas Corp. Owens-Corning Fiberglas Corp. Pittsburgh Plate Glass Co. Johns-Manville Fiber Glass, Inc. Johns-Manville Fiber Glass, Inc.	Silicon dioxide (sand) plus fluxes to lower melting point	Nonflammable drapes, curtains, bedspreads, industrial fabrics.

*Registered trademark.
Source: *Consumers All*, U.S. Department of Agriculture Yearbook, 1965, p. 366.

Exhibit 12–2 A Few of the Important Blends and Their Applications

End use	Fiber blends	Fabric construction	Important properties
Dress shirts	65/35 polyester/cotton	Batiste Broadcloth Oxford	Ease of care, fast drying, wrinkle resistant, durability.
Blouse	65/35 polyester/cotton	Broadcloth Crepe Combinations Taffetas Failles	Ease of care, lightweight, appearance retention, fast drying, durability.
Dress goods Printed and plain Dyed	65/35 polyester/cotton 50/50 polyester/cotton 50/50 polyester/rayon 50/50 triacetate/cotton	Broadcloth Challis Checks Crepes Twills Linens	Washability, ease of care, color styling, shape retention.

End use	Fiber blends	Fabric construction	Important properties
Sportswear Shirting Circular knit goods Slacks	65/35 polyester/cotton 50/50 polyester/cotton 55/45 acrylic/wool 50/50 acrylic/rayon	Sharkskin Serge Twills Linens Poplins Sateens Oxfords Flannels	Ease of care, durability, appearance retention, color styling, pleatability.
Slacks Casual Dress	65/35 polyester/cotton 50/50 polyester/cotton 55/45 polyester/wool 55/45 acrylic/wool 70/30 polyester/acrylic 50/50 triacetate/rayon 50/50 acetate/rayon	Gabardine Twills Tropicals Denims Sharkskin	Appearance retention, washable or drycleanable (wool), ease of care.
Lightweight	55/45 polyester/wool 50/50 acrylic/wool	Gabardine Tropical worsted Twills Flannels Serge	Durability, shape retention, ease of care.

Source: *Consumers All*, U.S. Department of Agriculture Yearbook, 1965, p. 367.

family member should look at the clothing on hand and decide what is wearable. Slight alterations and mending may save the purchase of a new garment. Garments should be tried on to make sure they still fit and look well. If one family member has forgotten the still attractive blue woolen dress put away in moth balls, the inventory will refresh her memory so that she will not return from a fall shopping trip with a new dress almost the same color.

Allotting money for clothing should consist of dividing the money both by seasons and by individual needs. If an overcoat is to be handed down from one child to another, the amount needed for the child receiving the coat can be reduced. However, if this happens very often, some special items—perhaps accessories he particularly likes—should be added to the younger child's wardrobe, so he will not feel that he always comes out second best.

In allotting the money for garments, it is wise to set a price limit for each item. This saves both time and money. However, if possible, the limit should be flexible. If a much more handsome, better quality coat can be purchased for a few dollars more than an unsatisfactory garment that fits into the arbitrary price range, it is a good idea to try economizing on another item to allow for its purchase.

Choosing a Store

Types of stores patronized by the shopper vary with the locality and the life situation of the buyer. Two people living within thirty miles of a large city may shop entirely differently. Mrs. Affluent may patronize prestigious department stores in the city, seldom shopping in her small home town. Mrs. Retiree, no longer able to drive a car and limited in means, may do most of her shopping at home from a mail-order catalog, supplemented by items from local stores. Both will have a variety of garments to choose from.

The new shopping centers, even in small towns, have lured many customers away from the downtown area. Shopping centers usually make shopping easier for young families who must take along the children. Types of stores, not all found in all areas, include department stores, chain and catalog stores, home "dry goods" stores, boutiques, specialty shops, and factory outlets.

Department Stores. These stores offer an advantage if a family member is hard to fit because they may have various specialty shops under one roof. Charge accounts are available from such stores, and it is usually possible to shop by mail or phone. Adequate sales help is almost always available. In some cases, the stores will deliver purchases (there may or may not be a charge for this service). A wide choice of merchandise is offered. This may not always be true of suburban branches, although some of them will get a wanted item for a customer from a downtown store. The decor of some large department stores makes shopping more pleasant. The prestige attached by some people to being able to engage in "name-dropping" of the prestigious store their clothes came from may be an additional factor in choice of stores.

Chain and Catalog Stores. Chain stores have an advantage because of quantity buying and inventory controls for keeping merchandise up-to-date. Not all chain stores with the same company name are alike. Although the basic goods available are the same, management does make a difference in individual stores. Failure to be impressed by goods and services of a chain store in one city should not convince you that all stores of that chain are mediocre. Mail-order houses offer services by mail or from catalog stores. Catalog stores receive orders in person or by phone and the article may be picked up on arrival or delivered by mail. Leading chain and catalog stores are no longer lagging behind in fashion. Most of them carry up-to-the-minute fashion garments, some quite expensive, as well as the moderately priced and inexpensive clothing which made them famous. Some of the larger chains have their own labels, with most of these goods produced by well-known manufacturers who market them at a lower price without the "prestige" label in the garment or on the material.

Home "Dry Goods" and Independent Stores. These stores may range from small-scale department stores to stores with limited or specialized stock. Often faced with strong competition from large chains, they may survive by providing personalized service, competitive pricing, or local leadership within the community that is not part of the "conscience" of the out-of-town merchandiser.

The Boutique. Originally a small shop within a specialty store, the boutique has evolved into a type of retail store. It is sometimes owned by a designer and may carry only a few items in each style. Garments may also be made to order. High-fashion accessories are usually offered. The boutique can be expected to be expensive; thus, it is only a "special occasion" shop for budget-minded people.

Specialty Shops. These stores provide quality merchandise of special types. Many of them stress classic good taste, workmanship, and fit instead of high style, and may be the place to look for a really good suit or coat that is to be worn a long time. Some specialize in one item, such as lingerie or shoes, and their personnel may become experts in their line of goods. The one-item shop, while offering the very best, may also carry bargains in seconds and irregulars. Irregular items of clothing are those not perfectly sized, while "seconds" refers to items with a flaw in material or construction. Specialty shops offer many of the services available at department stores.

Factory Outlets and Discount Stores, and Stores Specializing in Irregulars. These stores are all very economical if the shopper is a judge of the quality of material and workmanship. Discount stores may not have the familiar name brands and customers will not usually find many of the services offered in other types of stores, but the lack of these "extras" is one of the reasons these stores are able to offer lower prices. In factory outlet stores and stores that sell irregulars, bargains can be found by the knowledgable shopper.

Wise Shopping

The key to wise shopping is being a comparative shopper. The customer should familiarize himself with shops and stores and compare brands, quality, and price of merchandise. He must also learn to know textiles and fiber content and to interpret tags and labels.

Wise shopping includes learning to detect these signs of good workmanship:

1. Seams wide enough to allow for letting out and to withstand strain and finished enough to prevent fraying.
2. Garment cut with the grain of the goods.
3. Close and uniform stitching.
4. Hems and facings adequately attached but not showing on the outside of garment. Two-inch hems on skirts and dresses.
5. Reinforced weak points and properly sewn zippers and other fasteners.
6. Firmly and evenly stitched buttonholes, if they are machine-made.
7. Stripes, checks, and plaids matched at seams and openings.
8. Materials with nap, such as corduroy and velvet, cut so that the surface looks alike when viewed from the same angle. If one panel of the skirt looks light and the other dark, it is incorrectly cut. A quick test is to run the fingers over different panels in the same direction to detect differences in smoothness.

Some of the above points, if not in a garment, are unalterable. Nevertheless, a person who sews can plan to make a few changes on an inexpensive item to give it some of the long-wear characteristics of an expensive garment. For example, with the zig-zag attachment, a seam can be finished to prevent fraying, if the seam is wide enough. Uneven stitching may be remedied or a hem repaired so that the stitches do not show from the outside. Skill in sewing will also help determine which weak points can be reinforced at home, and whether poorly made buttonholes can be strengthened, but the basic cut and design of a garment cannot be changed. Most permanent press fashions may be taken in, but it is inadvisable to try to let them out because stitching and creases usually show permanently.

Who to take on a shopping trip can be an important consideration. Husbands and wives sometimes like to shop together for major purchases. Some shoppers like to take along a friend for the advantage of another opinion. However, sometimes having a friend along encourages shoppers to overspend or to waste time. Should the children come along? Yes, if the shopping is for their clothing. Garments may need to be fitted, and as the children grow older they enjoy making or choosing their own clothes, and the experience is good training for them. However, if a parent is shopping for himself, the children may disrupt and interfere with his good judgment. Another precaution suggested is that in shopping with teens, some homework is helpful before making the shopping trip. Nowhere is the generation gap more evident than when a budding beauty is trying on clothing and mother is (not very tactfully) trying to hold onto the purse strings and the last vestiges of decency in attire. Some salespersons, eager to make a sale, effusively assure the teenager that the skimpy, expensive, high-fashion or fad garment is "oh-so-becoming" and just meant for her. Mother fumes, saleslady effuses, and teenager argues. A child old enough to be so demanding is old enough to be told these basic facts in the privacy of home before the shopping trip:

1. A certain amount of money is allotted to be spent on certain items of clothing.
2. Salespersons are sometimes sincere in compliments, but their comments may occasionally be intended only to insure a sale.
3. Since there is a limit on the amount of money available to each member of the family, too many fad items are not practical; and, even if an item is in good taste and practical, we cannot always afford the most expensive garments.

Thus, if the youngster's heart is set on a certain expensive item, he must understand that he will have less money to spend on other wardrobe items.

When shopping, it is a good idea either to wear or take along shoes and important items that will be worn with the garment to be bought. If a woman wears an old, limp girdle and loafers to try on a dinner dress, only fond imagination can tell how it will really look when she wears it.

The purchase of accessories must also be planned, since this is one of the sources of overspending in many family budgets. Moreover, accessories should be coordinated so that one is not tempted to overbuy.

If a family member likes to sew, this may be an additional source of saving and perhaps a way to ensure better quality garments.

If, despite all these precautions, on reaching home the merchandise is found to be faulty, it should be returned. Labels should not be removed or sales tickets destroyed until one is absolutely sure the garment or material is without flaws.

Finally, families should discourage impulse buying. Who needs a pair of purple slacks if there is nothing suitable to wear with them?

Beginning Clothing Care at the Store

Care in laundering and cleaning begins in the planning and shopping stage. Tags should be examined and filed for later reference use. Understanding clothing care terminology is important. "Wash 'n Wear," "Drip Dry," and "Little or No Ironing" usually mean a little ironing for best appearance. The easy care principle is based on chemical treatment and resins. "Perma Prest," "Permanent Press," and "Durable Press" are among the terms that mean no ironing if tumbled dry. These fabrics are usually a blend of polyester and cotton or avril rayon. Automatic washers with at least two cycles are needed for "no press" clothing. The very hard spin used for towels may leave permanent creases in permanent press clothes. Also, if the dryer is not equipped with a special cycle for these garments, the dial should be hand operable so that it can be set to start at the last twenty (cooler) minutes of the drying cycle and, thus, will not subject the garments to extreme wrinkle-setting heat.

Clothing labels should contain information as to size, fiber content, special finish, and fabric construction. Good labeling instructs as to the care required. Special finishes on both ready-made clothing and uncut material include treatment for resistance to wrinkles, flame, soil, insects, or rain. Even so, many seamstresses prefer to launder washable material before making a garment to be sure there will be no further shrinkage. If this is done, zippers and trim should also be prewashed for possible shrinkage.

A permanent care labeling rule by the Federal Trade Commission which became effective July 3, 1972, required that articles of clothing manufactured after that date contain permanent labels giving laundering or dry cleaning instructions as well as warnings against what not to do when caring for the garment. Articles to be retailed for $3 or less which are completely washable under normal circumstances and articles which would be impaired in utility or appearance if a label were attached were excluded. Home sewing fabrics are included. They must be labeled on the bolt and on separate labels to be given the individual purchaser.

This law, which requires so much of manufacturers, is quite useless if customers are careless or do not understand directions. For this reason, families should be sure that they do understand what kind of care each article of clothing needs—either by reading the label thoroughly, or (if that is not adequate) by consulting a chart or pamphlet on clothing care.

The type of yarn and weave or construction affects the quality of the fabric and the type of care needed. Some woolens are now machine washable, while others must be dry cleaned. Good material should be resilient when crushed or, as the professionals say, should have a good "hand." To a certain extent each consumer can learn to judge materials, but accurate labels are a better guide.

Evaluating Sales

Sales are useful only if a shopper buys only what he really needs and intends to buy anyway. Good sale strategy is to go early, inspect carefully, and know what is needed and how much the budget allows for certain types of clothing.

Marketing practices have made special sales an important marketing device in the clothing industry. There are "good" sales, which the consumer cannot afford to miss, and there are "poor" sales, which he cannot afford to attend.

In order to sell merchandise that is to be replaced with new, good stores hold sales at regular intervals and stand behind the quality of their products. Less reputable stores regularly stage "going-out-of-business" or "moving to new location" sales, yet never move or go out of business, or perhaps, move just around the corner. Surprising quantities of shoddy goods brought in for these sales are sold to gullible people. Even at legitimate sales the customer must judge critically. Terms to watch for in ads and on tags, especially at promotional sales, are "marked down from" and "special purchase." If accurately tagged, the former should be regular stock marked down for the sale, while the latter may be brought in especially for the sale and may not be the store's regular brand of merchandise. The "special purchase" items may mean a savings for you, but may require more care in choice than those marked down from regular stock. Beware of sales of quantities of obviously shoddy clothing brought in for a special promotion. A knowledge of fabrics and construction, and the ability to judge size is required for finding bargains at these sales. Good buys often appear at clearance sales at chain stores when merchandise is being moved from one store location to another.

Saving substantial amounts of money on major clothing items can be just as much an investment as putting the same amount of money in a savings account —in some cases more. If a $100 suit is purchased on sale for $80, a 20 percent saving has been made.

The consumer who prefers to buy clothing at will, with little planning by use of a budget or little concern for the timing of purchases, may derive less overall benefit from sales than the person who plans ahead. Likewise, the wearer of high-style and fad clothing will find sales of little value. If such garments were purchased at sale prices late in the season, much of their value will be gone because of the time element involved in the wearability of high-style clothing. The style or fad garment may be preempted all too soon by another extreme trend. Better to pay the full, early season price and get a full season's wear from the garment.

Children's clothing is not very well adapted to seasonal sale buying. Because of a child's unpredictable growth, buying at the end of the season expecting to guess the size needed for the same season next year is risky. It is best simply to replace children's clothing when the old wears out or is outgrown. Back-to-school sales and promotions often have special values for growing children.

Most sale items are not returnable, so they should be examined carefully and, if possible, tried on. If they cannot be tried on and it is not possible to estimate the actual size (marked sizes on different brands vary), it is better to pass up the bargain. Sales merchandise should be returned for adjustment if it is defective, unless it was purchased at the bargain counter.

The best way to take advantage of sales and get the necessary clothes for less money, or better clothes for the same amount of money, is to plan ahead a season at a time. Certain articles of clothing may be wisely bought at sales, while others may be most economically bought from regular stock at the beginning of the season. Aside from the usual end-of-the-month sales and other regular promotional sales, it is a good idea to learn the time of year special types of garments are placed on sale.

Men's suits and coats for winter go on sale in December and January, while summer clothing is on sale in June. Prices are marked down and there is still a reasonable choice of styles and sizes. If a customer is easy to fit and easy to please, he may profit by waiting for more drastic mark-downs at inventory time, but he cannot expect much choice at that time. The best time for buying men's dress shirts is November. Whether it is wise to buy quantities of shirts on sales depends on how conservatively an individual dresses.

Sale times on fabrics vary, although usually January or February offers the best winter values and summer materials go on sale in June. Woolens may go on sale in late September or October. Factory Outlet and Discount Fabric Shops offer year-round savings. At these stores, ask the clerk to roll out the yardage required so that you may examine it for flaws. Reputable stores are glad to allow you to do this. They often unroll bolts of new material looking for obvious faulty areas.

Women's clothing sales have several seasons, except for lingerie, which is usually placed on sale in late December and early January. Hosiery, put on sale periodically, is a good sale purchase. Sales of hosiery are usually based on purchase of several pairs for a certain amount and hosiery lasts longer if several pairs of one color are purchased so that when one is damaged the mate may still be used with remaining hose of the lot. This applies also to men's and children's socks. If a winter coat is needed, start looking for mark-downs in October and November. The most drastic discounts come in December, especially after Christmas, and the first few days in January; but the stock may be almost depleted by this time. Dresses are marked down at the end of each retail season, with special markdowns on cocktail and dressy dresses after Christmas.

Sportswear is most likely to go on sale in October and November, May and June, and July and August. Some stores stay so far ahead in stocking their seasonal garments that it is difficult to find summer clothing in August. The customer who dashes to the store to add a lightweight garment to his wardrobe for a late vacation trip may be greeted with store displays of woolens and back-to-school wear.

Swimsuits are put on sale as late as possible. Stores sometimes watch each other and sales may start the same day in rival stores. If last year's suit can be worn until July (often after July 4th), a substantial saving can usually be made.

In buying strategy, it helps to learn the customary times when sales will be advertised in the papers. Often, if a customer is in a store the day before a sale begins while the store personnel are marking down items, he might be allowed to purchase the marked-down items at the new price before they have been picked over. Not all stores allow this practice, however. Certainly, it could not be done during big inventory sales, when many stores close their doors for a day while taking inventory and marking down prices.

Bargain counters sometimes actually yield bargains. Occasionally, a good shopper can find perfectly good garments that are only shop-worn, one-of-a-kind, soiled, ripped, or missing a button. He must balance the chances of being able to clean or repair the garment successfully against the possibility that the stain is permanent or the garment irreparable before deciding whether or not to make the purchase.

The best clothing sales seem to come when we have spent our money. Large expenses for Christmas leave us unprepared for the January sales and the same thing happens after the family vacation in July. This is why these months have become the best months for sales. Since they are normally slow months for merchandising, the sales are planned to get people in the stores at times when they would not otherwise be there.

One of the advantages of having a family budget is that a wise shopper can plan for these sales. Not only does this rule apply to clothing purchases but also to furniture and home furnishings. January is known for its "white goods" sales. By learning the best "sales" months for many items that are regularly needed and planning the budget around these periods, we can easily stretch our budget by 15 to 20 percent.

Always remember that most sales indicate that the merchants are attempting to get rid of an item which has not sold, regardless of the reason. Caution is the responsibility of sales merchandise buyers.

Major Home Appliances

All types of household appliances are important purchases, but we will distinguish between large and small appliances. Our discussion will be concerned with the former, since they are more expensive and extra planning is needed for their purchase. We consider major appliances to be such items as kitchen ranges, refrigerators, freezers, clothes washers and dryers, dishwashers, and television sets. These may be distinguished from furniture in that they contain mechanical, electrical, or moving parts that cause them to need replacement more often than most pieces of furniture. Otherwise, the same considerations may be given to purchases of furniture as are given to major appliances.

Deciding What Appliances to Buy

A kitchen range and a refrigerator are essential appliances for the family, while a freezer, washer, and dryer provide important services but are purchased partly for their convenience. Since frozen foods can be bought each week and kept in the freezer compartment of the refrigerator, a separate freezer may not be economical. The same may be true for a washer and dryer now that almost every shopping center has self-service coin-operated laundry facilities. A dishwasher is certainly a labor-saving appliance, but is it worth more to the family than some other item? Many things must be considered before these decisions can be made.

The two most important considerations in deciding about purchasing the less-essential appliances are family income and whether the housewife is employed outside the home. Another factor almost as important is the size of family. Of course, the space needed for these appliances and plumbing or electrical wiring costs may also be part of the decision to buy such appliances.

Completely objective answers cannot be given concerning the purchase of appliances since each family situation is different. The subjective factors of convenience, enjoyment, likes, and dislikes will have to be weighed against other possible uses for the money before purchases are made. However, the costs of purchase and use can be estimated for each appliance and should weigh heavily in decision-making concerning the spending of family income.

Costs of Large Appliances

Home Freezers. How many consumers have the impression that they could reduce food costs considerably if only they could buy a half or quarter of beef at one time? They may also think about the savings from buying several loaves of day-old bread and freezing it. It is true that a freezer can save on food costs when used at full capacity. Thus, with this restriction, a small family should buy a small freezer or one that they can use to capacity. Freezers are now available from 3.2 to 30.1 cubic feet in size.

A seventeen cubic-foot freezer (a medium-size freezer) can be purchased for about $235 and will store about 590 pounds of food. A rough guide to determine optimal freezer size is to allot four cubic feet per person. Prices are higher for frost-free freezers and they cost more to operate since the added frost-free feature draws considerably more electricity. Prices of upright freezers are slightly higher than the low, chest types, but they take less space and less time to defrost. The following estimate can be used as a guide for annual ownership costs of a seventeen cubic foot freezer that is purchased for $235 and lasts for fifteen years. A charge of 6 percent on one-half the original price is made for the use of money. If the freezer is bought on credit, this amount or more will be paid for interest. For a cash purchase, it is added in as a charge for use of the money which could be put to another use. One-half the original price is its average value during the entire life of the appliance and thus is a convenient figure to use as its yearly value. Since this method of calculating costs makes a reasonable charge for interest, it makes no difference whether the item is purchased for cash or credit.

Annual ownership costs of freezer (filled once per year)

Depreciation	$15.67
Interest	7.05
Repairs	5.00
Electricity & packaging	30.00
Total	$57.72

Cost per pound of food = 9.8 cents

Annual ownership costs of freezer (filled three times per year)

Depreciation	$15.67
Interest	7.05
Repairs	5.00
Electricity & packaging	50.00
Total	$77.72

Cost per pound of food = 4.4 cents

An important consideration which can not be shown in these cost figures is the enjoyment of the added convenience of a freezer—including the trips to the store saved and the savings in annual food spoilage. Buying food in quantity may not be a saving if it costs almost $.10 per pound to freeze and store it. However, by filling the freezer two or three times per year the cost per pound is reduced so that buying foods on sale and in quantity can be a real saving.

If buying a freezer does work out to be an economical purchase, certain practices should be followed when making the purchase. The most important consideration is to select a brand manufactured by a reliable company and retailed by a dealer who will service the freezer as provided in the warranty. A few dollars saved on the purchase price can be very uneconomical if good service is not available. Any bargaining on purchase price should be with dealers of equally good brands and service.

Clothes Washers and Dryers. Washers and dryers are the greatest time-saving appliances available. Few people enjoy going to a public laundry for two or more hours each week. Automatic washers and dryers have removed much of the work from a formerly arduous chore. Prices for these appliances vary according to the automatic controls available. Washers have settings for different types of fabric—including spin speeds, several cycles, different water temperatures and levels, and automatic bleach and detergent dispensers. Dryers are available with controls for different levels of heat, several cycles for different fabrics, and sensing devices to stop the machine when the right amount of moisture is removed from the clothing.

Some automatic controls are more important than others. In shopping for a first washer and dryer, the shopper should be prepared to take plenty of time and look at different brands and models. He must get all the information he can about what the machines will do. If he is not sure about which automatic controls are most valuable, talking to friends or neighbors who have washers and dryers may be helpful. Ultimately, a rule of thumb that has proven true on most appliances is that repair bills and service calls usually increase with the number of controls available.

It may be that personal finances will necessitate buying only one appliance at a time. For most families, the washer should be first purchase. A clothesline for outside drying can be installed with little expense, and weather conditions make this a feasible drying method for several months during the year. At other times, automatic dryers at the public laundries can be used. Automatic washers cost more than dryers, because they have more parts and are more complicated machines. Automatic washers range in price from about $170.00 for a portable, one-speed, one-cycle machine to $335.00 for one with three speeds, ten cycles, and other features. Dryers range in price from about $105.00 for a one-cycle, one-heat temperature setting to $285.00 for one with automatic temperature control, automatic or timed cycle, and an electronic sensor for measuring dryness.

Are washers and dryers economical for all families? Without considering convenience and the user's time, we can make good estimates for comparing ownership costs with costs of using coin-operated machines at public laundries. A family of two people will have three or four washer loads per week, while a family of four with the children above infancy may have six to eight washer loads each week. A medium-priced washer will cost $200.00 and should last ten years. Interest should be charged at 6 percent on one-half the price to allow for a credit or cash purchase. The following are ownership cost estimates for an automatic washer.

Annual ownership costs of automatic washers (7 loads per week)

Depreciation	$20.00
Interest	6.00
Repairs	7.50
Electricity and water	30.00
Total	$ 63.50

Cost per load = $.18

This estimated cost of $.18 per load compares favorably with the $.25 needed in coin-operated machines. Thus, a family of four can save money by owning a washing machine. Convenience and time saved is in addition to these costs. A family of two persons washing only four loads per week would have about the same costs for owning a machine as the public laundries charge. Families of this size, then, should also buy a washer for convenience and time-saving reasons.

A medium-priced dryer will cost $170.00 and should last fourteen years. The following are ownership cost estimates for an automatic electric dryer.

Annual ownership costs of electric dryer (7 loads per week)

Depreciation	$11.43
Interest	4.80
Repairs	6.00
Electricity	18.00
Total	$40.23

Cost per load = $.11

Since coin-operated dryers are usually $.25, a greater saving is made by owning a dryer than a washing machine. Ownership costs rise with less use, but a family drying only three or four loads per week can save by owning the appliance. An additional saving not included here is the savings in electricity and labor from a reduction in necessary ironing if clothes are properly dried. This is particularly true of permanent press garments.

Kitchen Ranges and Refrigerators. A range and refrigerator are essential for housekeeping, so the problem is to determine what types and sizes will satisfy the family's needs and fit the budget. These appliances are available in small apartment sizes at a relatively low price or they can be purchased in large sizes with many accessories.

Cooking ranges are available as freestanding, self-contained units or the oven and burner units can be purchased separately and built into a cabinet. Both electric and gas ranges have four surface burners with a selection of heat-level settings. A small apartment-type range can be purchased new for about $135.00, but prices range up to $700.00 for those with self-cleaning or electronic ovens. Each brand and model is somewhat different; some features are found on one model but not on another. Electronic ovens, a recent invention, cook food with microwaves without heating the air inside the oven. Much less time is required for cooking with this type of oven. Ovens on most medium to higher-priced ranges have a clock that can be set to automatically time the cooking period.

Refrigerators are also made in many brands, models, and sizes. Small portable refrigerators are available, but they are not suitable for home use unless space is inadequate for a larger model. Small refrigerators can be purchased with a single door and a small freezer compartment inside. The most popular unit appears to be a combination refrigerator and freezer with separate outside doors. Some units have the freezer compartment below the refrigerator and some above. In recent years, a model called the side-by-side has also been produced in which the two compartments are beside each other. New models are available with both refrigerator and freezer compartments that are frost-free and have separate drawers for meats and vegetables. More expensive models have automatic ice makers and cold water dispensers. Prices range from about $175.00 for a small, single-door refrigerator to $750.00 for a large side-by-side combination refrigerator-freezer with automatic ice maker and cold water dispenser.

The family's choice in selecting a refrigerator-freezer will depend on whether they already own a separate freezer or plan to get one. It will not be necessary to have a large freezer compartment with the refrigerator if a separate freezer is available. Small families or those that do not purchase foods in quantity will find it most economical to buy a medium to large combination refrigerator-freezer. A very large family that purchases food carefully may be able to own both and save on the food budget. Each family will need to make a careful study of its needs and compare alternatives after learning prices of different makes and models.

In some circumstances, the most economical alternative in selecting a range or refrigerator may be a used appliance. Furniture and appliance stores may have a good selection of used appliances, some of which can give many years of service. Families with low incomes should investigate this alternative as a way of saving money for other important needs. Those who have jobs that require them to move frequently may prefer to study the possibility of purchasing used appliances. Expensive appliances are easily damaged with frequent moving. Refrigerators and ranges should provide good service for fifteen years when they receive good care. Excessive moving will shorten this period and require additional service costs.

Dishwashers and Air Conditioners. If any large appliances can be considered luxuries, possibly dishwashers and air conditioners would have to be in the group. A dishwasher could be economical for a homemaker who works outside the home and employs a maid to help with housework. The dishwasher might, in that case, possibly reduce the amount of work hired enough to pay for its cost. For most families, however, these appliances are purchased for convenience and comfort.

Portable and built-in dishwashers are available in several brands and in models that range in price from about $165.00 to $300.00. The higher priced models have more wash cycles and automatic controls. For a rented house or apartment, it would be wise to buy a portable model, although storage space is needed when it is not in use. These machines are usually rolled near the sink and connected to the water faucets for use. They are less convenient than built-in models, but they can be moved when the family moves to another house.

Dishwashers should provide good service for ten years and can be used by any size family. For more economical operation, a small family should accumulate dishes until the machine is filled before they wash them. Whether to buy a dishwasher or not will depend on the family desires and financial condition. It may be an item that is saved for as a long-range goal. Since hand washing of dishes is a substitute, most families place a higher priority on other appliances to obtain services for which no substitute is available. When finances permit the purchase of non-essential appliances, each family will have to determine its own priorities for the kinds and times of purchase.

Air conditioner units are gaining in popularity and have almost become a necessity in regions where the summers are hot and long. In moderate climates, air conditioners (including air humidifiers and purifiers) are now being used because of the "smog" situation. When the whole house is to be air conditioned, it is most economical to install a central unit with ducts carrying the air to each room. Houses need better insulation to ensure economical cooling than they do for heating purposes. Most medium and higher priced homes built in the southern United States have central air conditioning installed during construction. It is difficult to estimate the cost of a central unit because the size of the unit will be determined by the size of the house. Since extra insulation is necessary, the cost of central air conditioning in a moderately priced six-room house could easily amount to $1,500 to $2,000. It could be even more expensive to have a unit installed in an older house. These figures include only installation costs. Electricity for operation costs from $1.00 to $1.50 per day for a moderately insulated house of about 2,000 square feet of floor space during the hot summer months. Also, central air conditioning units require considerable servicing. In parts of the South where air conditioning is needed for about five months of the year, a reasonable estimate for total costs of owning and operating a central unit in an average home would be about $300 per year. Costs would be slightly lower in other regions.

If only a part of the house is to be air conditioned, units of various sizes are available to be installed in a window. A small unit to cool one room may be used or a unit large enough to cool several rooms can be obtained. The air does not circulate well between rooms when too large an area is cooled with one unit. Window air conditioners range in price from about $150 for a one-room unit to $475 for one large enough to cool four or five rooms. Installation of these units is simple if the house has proper electrical wiring. Better circulation of the air results if two or three units are spaced around the house than that achieved by trying to cool the entire house with one unit, although the cost would be somewhat higher.

Window air conditioners will use as much electricity as a central unit if they are of equal size. However, a window unit will last longer and require less servicing. There is little difference in total costs for the type of unit used to get the same area cooled. To cool only a part of the house, it is more economical to use a window unit. For an entire house of five or more rooms, it is probably just as economical to install a central unit.

Safety in Home Appliances

Safety is an important consideration in the purchase of home appliances, since they are built to use electricity or gas. Two organizations, the Underwriters Laboratories and American Gas Association, are concerned with testing and approval of appliances for safety. When these organizations approve a manufacturer's brand of appliance, they attach a seal indicating such approval. It is a good practice to look for this seal because appliances with improper connections can cause a fire or electrical shock. The Association of Home Appliance Manufacturers is a trade group that is interested in quality and sales practices in the home appliance industry. It is not a safety testing organization, but it is concerned with all practices related to the manufacture and sale of home appliances.

Discussion Questions

1. Why is it considered wise to plan before you shop?
2. In what way(s) can taking an inventory of usable clothing on hand prove rewarding to a family?
3. What are some of the signs of good workmanship that a shopper should look for in buying clothes?
4. What basic facts should a child who has reached the age of reason be told before he is taken on a shopping trip?
5. List some of the advantages of shopping in department stores?
6. What information should clothing labels contain?
7. Although "marked down from" and "special purchase" are both sale terms, the former offers an advantage when accurately tagged. What is it?
8. Why are men's suits and coats for winter usually put on sale in December?
9. Of the major appliances usually purchased by families which would you consider most essential, and why?
10. What is the Association of Home Appliance Manufacturers?

Fidelity bought with money
is overcome by money.

[*Seneca*]

13

Purchase and Operation Costs of an Automobile

If we figured the actual cost of owning and operating an automobile, many of us would most likely be shocked. People who use their cars for business purposes keep records for tax or reimbursement allowances; but others who use their cars only for family service and pleasure have a tendency to overlook the costs. One reason for this may be that it requires considerable time and effort to keep a complete record of automobile expenses. Unless there is a real need for doing so, we usually do not put forth the effort.

But poor planning in the use of an automobile is one of the best means of disrupting a family budget. Large auto expense items have a habit of coming when they are least expected or when the budget has no provision for them. It is important to remember that expenses of keeping an automobile rank near the top along with food and housing costs. When allowances are made for this expense in the budget, many problems will be alleviated.

As we learned in Chapter 8, families spend from 10 to 14 percent of their income for transportation. Higher income families spend a slightly larger proportion of income for this purpose since they tend to buy more expensive automobiles and often drive more miles. While auto costs are large, if family members understand this and want to spend their income for this purpose, the expenditure should be made. This chapter is designed to help the consumer obtain satisfactory transportation as economically as possible. There are many things to consider in accomplishing this goal.

The Importance of Automobiles

An automobile has become a necessity for most American families. Living patterns have changed to such an extent that many families may even need two automobiles. Families living in the suburbs and in rural areas need transportation to jobs, schools, and shopping areas. Public transportation is oftentimes either not available or not a satisfactory method for meeting all of these needs. So, for most families, the choice is not whether to own an automobile, but how to keep automobile ownership costs to a suitable level in the budget.

Eighty percent of American households have one or more cars. Some of the remaining families need a car but, because of age or health reasons, cannot drive safely. Others have suitable public transportation to meet their needs and do not care to bear the expense of car ownership. Exhibit 13–1 shows that car ownership varies with income. Most households without cars have low incomes and those with higher incomes have more than one car.

The age of the household head is also related to car ownership. Over 45 percent of those age sixty-five and over had no car in 1971, but 81 percent of those under sixty-five had at least one car. Households with two or more cars reach a peak about middle-age and then decline. Ages forty-five to fifty-four is the period when a family has the most cars and this is also when family income is approaching its peak, as well as the usual time that teenagers learn to drive.

The region of highest car ownership is in the West while the Northeast is lowest. This is a reflection of population concentration. In large metropolitan areas and especially in the central cities, cars are less of a necessity. Highest ownership of cars by residence is in suburban areas outside the central cities.

According to the Interstate Commerce Commission, 87 percent of all intercity traveling in 1971 was by car.[1] Since more than half of all trips made are less than five miles, the car has become an item of convenience for local travel. Even where considerable effort has been made to get workers to ride public transportation to their jobs to relieve congestion in cities, 85 percent still use cars. Cars were driven 1.2 trillion miles in 1971 and that mileage is increasing by almost 50 billion miles each year.

---

[1]*Automobile Facts and Figures, 1972,* Motor Vehicle Manufacturers Association, Inc., (Detroit, Michigan, 1973), p. 37.

Exhibit 13–1   Automobile Ownership by Income, Age, Region and Residence, 1971

	Percent of households owning				
	No car	At least one car	One car	Two cars	Three or more cars
Household income					
Under $3,000	56.4%	43.6%	38.0%	5.1%	0.5%
$ 3,000–$ 4,999	29.8	70.2	58.9	10.8	0.5
$ 5,000–$ 7,499	14.8	85.2	62.8	20.3	2.1
$ 7,500–$ 9,999	8.7	91.3	58.4	28.1	4.8
$10,000–$14,999	5.1	94.9	48.6	38.7	7.6
$15,000 and over	3.4	96.6	33.9	47.9	14.8
Age of household head					
Under 25	16.9%	83.1%	62.8%	18.7%	1.6%
25–29	12.4	87.6	61.0	25.2	1.4
30–34	12.5	87.5	55.8	29.7	2.0
35–44	11.9	88.1	45.9	35.0	7.2
45–54	12.1	87.9	44.7	32.6	10.6
55–64	18.6	81.4	52.8	23.8	4.8
65 and over	45.4	54.6	45.2	8.3	1.1
Region					
Northeast	26.9%	73.1%	47.3%	21.3%	4.5%
New England	19.6	80.4	51.0	23.3	6.1
Middle Atlantic	28.8	71.2	46.3	20.8	4.1
North Central	16.4	83.6	51.6	26.3	5.7
East North Central	16.6	83.4	50.7	26.7	6.0
West North Central	15.7	84.3	54.1	25.4	4.8
South	20.8	79.2	50.2	24.9	4.1
South Atlantic	22.0	78.0	49.1	24.5	4.4
East South Central	21.4	78.6	47.0	27.5	**4.1**
West South Central	18.4	81.6	54.1	24.0	3.5
West	14.1	85.9	52.6	28.1	5.2
Mountain	12.3	87.7	53.6	28.0	6.1
Pacific	14.7	85.3	52.2	28.1	5.0
Residence					
Metropolitan areas	21.7%	78.3%	47.6%	25.5%	5.2%
Central cities	32.3	67.7	46.9	17.8	3.0
3 million or more	46.6	53.4	42.2	9.6	1.6
1 million to 2,999,999	38.4	61.6	44.5	15.6	1.5
250,000 to 999,999	23.8	76.2	50.3	21.8	4.1
Less than 250,000	19.8	80.2	50.3	25.5	4.4
Suburban rings	12.1	87.9	48.4	32.4	7.1
Outside metropolitan areas	16.8	83.2	55.1	23.9	4.2
All households	20.0%	80.0%	50.2%	25.0%	4.8%

Source: *Automobile Facts and Figures, 1972,* Motor Vehicle Manufacturers Association of the U.S., Inc., Detroit, p. 38.

The automobile has become so important to Americans that millions of workers now depend on the automobile industry for their jobs. American families spent about $37 billion in 1971 for pleasure and vacation travel by car. Twenty-four percent of all retail trade is related to the automotive industry. Not only is the automobile significant to business, but governments (federal, state and local) received over $18 billion in taxes and fees from the use of motor vehicles in 1971. States received 19 percent of their total revenue from this source. Most families buy several cars, either new or used, in the course of a lifetime. When all of these costs are added together, some families find that they have spent more for automobiles than for a home.

For this reason, we should take great care and use every means available to get the most economical trade when we enter the market for a car. Certain steps can be taken to help a buyer obtain the type of transportation needed for the best possible price.

Purchasing an Automobile

Frequency of purchasing an automobile varies considerably by families. Some like to trade every year, but it appears that most families like to keep their cars about five or six years. The Automobile Manufacturing Association estimated the average age of all passenger cars to be 5.7 years in 1971. Of course, the amount of traveling a family does will influence its trading practices. If a family buys used cars, it may be necessary to trade more often. If a buyer is trying to decide between the purchase of a new or used car, the ownership costs of each should be estimated. Buying a good used car that is two or three years old eliminates initial high depreciation costs. However, this advantage might be offset by maintenance expenses, if the car is not in good condition.

Before comparing costs, a buyer should decide whether he needs a small, medium, or large car. The size of the family and the amount of traveling will influence this decision. Exhibit 13–2 lists advantages and disadvantages of various sizes and models of cars. Depending on the family's needs, it might want to purchase a new, small car for about the same price of a used, medium-size car. If the decision is to try a new car, plenty of time should be allowed for shopping before making a final decision.

Shopping for a New Car

Unless a buyer has firmly decided on the kind of car he wants and what optional equipment to include, the first shopping trip may be used to see what is available. There are so many types and body styles in cars that one trip is not enough time to see all of them. Even if it were possible to see them all, it would likely be confusing and would thus make a decision even more difficult. After a shopping trip, then, is time to decide exactly what make and body style are desirable including the optional equipment. After making this decision, a

Exhibit 13–2   Advantages and Disadvantages of Cars by Size and Models

Size	Advantages	Disadvantages
Subcompact	Lowest-cost available in U.S. Extremely easy to handle, park, garage. Excellent fuel mileage. Low operating, maintenance costs. Uncomplicated engines, usually 4-cylinder. Good second, or son-and-daughter car.	Slightly stiffer ride usually because of short wheelbase and light weight. Limited space for passengers, cargo. Fewer choices and options in colors, equipment, etc.
Compact	Low initial cost. Low operating, maintenance cost. Good fuel mileage. Easy to handle, park, garage. Fair cross-country car. Excellent for commuting. Good size for family of two adults, two small children.	Less smooth ride than next sizes up. Less comfortable than larger cars for frequent long trips. Passenger and cargo space somewhat limited. Instruments, option choices somewhat limited.
Intermediate	Good room and comfort at low cost. Not as bulky as full-size cars. Easy to handle in traffic, to park, to garage. Relatively low-cost operation and maintenance. Well balanced for long-trip road car; gives good ride. Adequate passenger and cargo space. Good choice of engines, options, etc. Fairly good on fuel mileage.	Not as spacious for big families or those with lots of luggage. Not as well suited for heavy loads or heavy-duty trailer towing. May need V-8 engine for hill country operation.
Full size	Most stability and riding comfort. Widest choice of options and equipment. Best long-trip car. Hauls heavy loads. Tows trailers easiest. Excellent for bigger families. Provides most space for passengers, cargo.	Costs more to buy, operate, maintain. Lower fuel mileage. A bigger size to handle, park, garage. More complicated and heavier.

Exhibit 13–2 (Cont.)

Size	Advantages	Disadvantages
Sedan, 2-door	Lowest-cost in a given line. Good family car for those with small children (no doors in rear). Sturdy, least subject to body squeaks as it ages. Rigid body-and-pillar design.	Awkward getting in and out of, or loading rear seat. Wider doors make it somewhat more difficult to get in and out of car in tight parking places.
Sedan, 4-door	Good family car; 4 doors make easy entrance and exit to both front and rear, especially for older people. Sturdy because it has between-side-windows pillars. Narrower doors make it somewhat easier for you to get in and out of car in tight parking places.	More doors may subject car to more squeaks, drafts, as it ages. More doors and windows to lock for secure parking. Children in rear have access to rear-door locks and handles.
Hardtops, 2- and 4-door	Judged to be smarter in appearance. Side views unobstructed by body pillars, with all side windows down. Hold resale value better than sedans.	Least rigid structure of all the metal-roof cars. Cost more. In 4-door models, children in rear have access to rear-door locks and handles.
Convertible	Unique design, compared to metal-roof cars—"different." Provides full open-air-and-sunshine driving. Usually has heavier, lower-center-of-gravity construction to compensate for lack of metal-roof rigidity and bracing.	Least rigid roof structure of all cars. Upkeep of fabric roof and raise-lower mechanism required. More subject to theft and vandalism by slashing roof. Depending on design, rearward visibility limited with top up. Most squeaks and rattles, as car ages.
Station wagon	Highly useful all-purpose vehicle. Most states recognize as car and avoid "commercial vehicle" taxing on private family car use.	Slightly noisier than sedans. Larger interior with big window area takes longer to heat in cold weather, or cool in hot weather. Subject to more rattles and

Exhibit 13–2 (Cont.)

Size	Advantages	Disadvantages
	Carries most passengers and cargo of all car-line vehicles. Versatile, rugged, adaptable. Has good resale value.	squeaks than sedans, as it ages. Higher-priced than sedans.
Small specialty/ sports car	Good eye appeal. Options offered in wide range. Usually has more horsepower per pound of vehicle to give greater performance.	Higher-priced, compared to more conventional models. Higher-cost insurance probable if it has a high-powered engine. Limited number of passengers, up to four, with crowded rear seat. More subject to theft.
Vans/buses	Most space enclosed in least amount of body. Versatile, all-purpose passenger and cargo carriers. Easy handling. Low-cost operation, maintenance. Good forward visibility.	Noisier. More subject to wind forces. Subject to rattles, squeaks and drafts, as they age. Not the best road performers. Require care to guard from overloading.
Light trucks	Versatile, multiple-purpose design. Good rural-area type of transportation. Good stability and performance with loads. Good "second car" for rural-area family. Good commercial vehicle for contractors, others who work from job-site to job-site.	Limited to three passengers, in cab. Commercial or farm licensing normally required. Open-box type exposes uncovered cargo to all weather. No cargo security when parked and left unattended.

Source: *Car Buying Made Easier,* Ford Motor Company, Dearborn, 1972.

buyer is ready to begin talking business with a salesman. Accessories can easily add $800.00 to the base price of a car. In addition, the smallest car that will serve the family's needs will be the most economical to operate.

Money can be saved if the many extras which only add to appearance are eliminated. For example, additional costs come with whitewall tires, large wheel covers, more chrome, vinyl-covered roof, and these items add nothing to safety or service of the car. If the aim is to get transportation at the least cost, a buyer must be prepared to resist when all cars in the showroom appear to have some extras and the salesman explains how long it will take to get one without extra specifications. Basic transportation can still be obtained at a reasonable cost. It is the many added accessories which are causing automobile costs to rise so rapidly.

It is a good policy to write down on paper the exact specifications and let the salesman list a price for each item. This list should include any federal and state tax, and registration and title papers. By summing this list, the selling price for the kind of car the buyer has chosen can be determined. This price will probably be several hundred dollars less than the sticker price on the car window. If the old car is to be traded in, the trade allowance can then be subtracted from the new car price to obtain the difference to be paid. This procedure should be repeated with at least three dealers before agreeing on the purchase. By comparing the same type of car and the same optional equipment, a buyer can make a good price comparison. If the purchaser has saved the money to pay cash, this will be his cost; but with credit there will be interest to pay.

"So that's your 'manufacturer's suggested retail price'? . . . Now would you like to hear my 'buyer's suggested retail price'?"

Courtesy: Publishers-Hall Syndicate

A buyer may want to price two different makes of cars before making a decision. If this is the case, he should get prices from at least three dealers for each make he is considering. It is impossible to make reasonable price comparisons on different makes of cars. Buyers should also remember that it is an expensive practice to accept unwanted equipment on a car just because the dealer does not have what he wants in stock. The dealer can order such a car or the buyer can find it at another dealer.

Credit for Automobile Purchases

It does make a great deal of difference where a buyer finances the purchase of a new car. He has a choice of several sources of credit and selecting the right source is just as important as shopping for the car. There can be a considerable difference in the cost of borrowing money. The car dealer will probably offer to finance it, but this is usually high-cost credit. In fact, a dealer may insist that his customer buy on credit, but it is not required. The automobile manufacturers have finance companies for this purpose. From them, interest and carrying charges are 15 to 18 percent per year and a buyer may be required to buy high-cost insurance from them rather than being able to choose a local agent. Two-thirds of all new car buyers in 1969 used some credit in making their purchases.

Exhibit 13–3   Calculator for Purchasing and Financing a New Car

2-step financing calculator

Step 1: The price of the new car

A. Write in the price of the car   _____

B. Write in the prices of options:

Engine	_____
Transmission	_____
Other:	
_____	_____
_____	_____

C. Write in totals of A. and B.   _____

D. Write in the trade-in value of your present car   _____

Note: This will have to be your best estimate of value, from local used-car newspaper advertising, from knowledgeable friends, or perhaps from an actual dealer appraisal. If you plan to pay cash for a down payment, enter that figure here, instead.

E. Subtract D. from C. above   _____

    This is the amount to be financed on your new car.

Step 2: Monthly payment calculation

To work out monthly payments for the new-car balance, you begin with the amount to be financed on the new car shown in E. of Step 1. Next, you select the time-period plan you want to use—24, 30, or

Exhibit 13–3 (cont'd)

36 months*—and multiply it by the figure shown for that payment time plan.

Example: If the Amount Financed in E. of Step 1 is $2,000 and you want to spread the payments over 36

___

*Most people who finance their new cars use 24, 30 or 36 month payment plans: however, 12 and 18 month plans are also available.

months, then you multiply the $2,000 by the factor of .03278 (*annual percentage rate—11.08%*). This shows that each payment for the 36 months will be $65.56.

This calculator will not give an exact figure because there are variations in local finance rates, taxes, insurance and other charges, but it's a useful approximation for many areas.

24-month plan ⎰	Amount (E., Step 1, from preceding page) to be financed on new car	$ _____
	Multiply by	× .04667[a]
	24 monthly payments of:	$ _____
	[a]Annual percentage rate—11.13%	
30-month plan ⎰	Amount (E., Step 1, from preceding page) to be financed on new car	$ _____
	Multiply by	× .03833[b]
	30 monthly payments of:	$ _____
	[b]Annual percentage rate—11.12%	
36-month plan ⎰	Amount (E., Step 1, from preceding page) to be financed on new car	$ _____
	Multiply by	× .03278[c]
	36 monthly payments of:	$ _____
	[c]Annual percentage rate—11.08%	

Should you pay cash for your car?

Your own personal financial situation will be a factor in deciding whether to pay cash or finance your new car.

These are some of the bases on which you must decide whether or not to pay cash for your car:

Do you have the necessary amount of cash available?

By using your cash for the car, will you seriously jeopardize other important purchase or travel plans?

Will you still have a cash reserve for emergencies?

Because most people cannot satisfy all of the above conditions, it is estimated that 2 out of 3 buyers finance their new cars.

Source: *Car Buying Made Easier,* Ford Motor Company, Dearborn, 1973.

Personal loan companies also make credit available for car purchases, but again it is high-cost credit. These agencies specialize in short-term loans, many of which are high-risk loans. Interest costs could easily be greater than those offered by the car dealer.

Bank loans are usually available at the lowest interest cost. Being a local institution, a bank will try to arrange payments to fit personal income situations. A bank loan officer will calculate the monthly interest payment on the outstanding balance and he will take a mortgage on the new car and permit the buyer to choose the insurance agent. If the buyer has a good credit rating, the bank may give him an annual loan on a personal note without taking a mortgage on the car. Since no monthly payments would be made under this system, the buyer could establish a savings account in the bank and deposit a monthly sum in the account to be used for a large payment on the note when it becomes due. If the total amount is not available when the note has matured, the balance can be renewed for another year.

The best idea is to shop for the best credit arrangement just as is done in searching out the best car price. If a buyer belongs to a credit union, interest costs should compare favorably with bank credit. Once loan arrangements have been made, the buyer is ready to close the transaction for the car and pay cash.

Shopping for a Used Car

Buying a used car at a reasonable price can be a difficult task for someone who has little mechanical knowledge. The best-looking used car may give the poorest service. A buyer must expect to have more repair costs on a used car than on a new car, since these costs increase with age and service. However, with careful selection, a used car should be less expensive than a new car, when all costs are considered.

Shopping for a used car is quite different than looking around for a new car because no two used cars are alike. Each must be judged according to its condition and price. This does not reduce the necessity for visiting several dealers, however. Another choice the buyer must make is that of either buying the used car from a new car dealer who has a service department or buying one from a used car dealer with no service department. Although a dealer may not have a service department, he may still provide warranties and service through independent garages or he may pay for servicing at the shop of a new car dealer.

It is usually not economical to buy a used car that is more than three years old unless the previous owner can be contacted. Mileage shown on the odometer is frequently not accurate because some dealers change the reading to show low mileage. This should be less of a problem in the future since Federal law now forbids changing mileage on the odometer before selling a car.

A small car that is two years old is often available for a price as low or lower than that of a larger car that is four years old. The small car would certainly be more economical if it is suitable for your needs.

Some seasonal difference does exist in the prices of used cars. Prices may drop as much as 5 percent during the winter months. Business is slow during this period, so dealers are more anxious to bargain for a sale. It may be necessary to do more shopping for a used car than for a new car since the buyer ought to learn what current prices are for somewhat similar cars. Newspaper advertisements can help in comparing prices, but it is necessary to see the car to make the best comparison.

Once a used car has been found that appears suitable, it can be worth the cost to let a trusted mechanic inspect the car before the transaction is concluded. Needless to say, he should be independent of the seller so that he will give an unbiased opinion of the car's mechanical condition.

Probably the most important point to remember in buying a used car is to check the reputation of the dealer. A warranty or guarantee is only as good as the seller's reputation. It is more economical to pay a few additional dollars if necessary to know that the dealer will fulfill his promises. The average person cannot be an expert automobile mechanic, so he must rely on the dealer to some extent. Cars are too complex and expensive to rely solely on such limited judgment when purchasing a used one.

Ownership and Operating Costs

Costs of owning and operating an automobile vary widely from family to family. Because of this, the figures given here will probably not fit any family exactly; but, if approximate costs are known, they can be used in any budget. Two major factors affect both annual cost and cost per mile of owning a car. These are the original purchase price and the number of miles driven. This explains in part why large automobiles sold at a high price are more expensive to own.

As soon as a car is purchased, some costs of ownership begin, and these *fixed* costs continue as long as the car is owned. Fixed costs are not the same each year, but they are present regardless of how much the car is used. Other costs are called *variable* costs, since they depend on the amount of use the car is put to. The more it is driven, the higher variable costs are. If the car is not used, there are no variable costs, only fixed costs. When these two types of costs are combined we have the total cost of owning and operating an automobile. The following items are classified according to fixed and variable costs.

Fixed costs	*Variable costs*
Depreciation	Gasoline and oil
Interest on loan	Repairs (parts and labor)
License	Servicing costs
Insurance	Parking costs
Property taxes	Traffic tickets
Inspection fees	
Shelter	

A person may not have all of the above listed costs. For example, if a person pays cash for his car, there will be no interest expense. Not all states require an annual inspection, nor is it necessary to provide shelter. Depreciation is the decline in value from year to year due to wear, age, and obsolescence. This cost is incurred on all cars and the amount each year will depend on the purchase price, the length of time one owns the car, and—to some extent—how much the car is driven. Both fixed and variable costs may change considerably from year to year.

Exhibit 13–4 shows estimates of ownership costs of an automobile purchased for $4,000 and used for six years. Interest cost is charged during the first three years because these are the years when it is actually paid. It could have been divided equally over the entire six years to lower the costs during the first three years and raise them during the last three.

The estimate of $.21 per mile for the first year may appear high. Over one-half of this cost, however, is due to the large amount of depreciation. It is a suitable method to use an equal amount of depreciation each year over the life of the car, but this is not as accurate as the declining balance method, since a car actually loses more value during the early years.

In our example, the cost per mile decreases each year until the sixth year when it shows a slight increase. This increase is due to the cost of new tires and a battery during that year. These costs would have been averaged over a three-year period since they were replaced every three years, but the outlay of cash actually occurred in the third and sixth years. It is important to notice that fixed costs far exceed variable costs in the early years, but eventually the variable costs overtake and exceed fixed costs. This is mostly due to a decline in depreciation and a rise in repair costs as the car gets older. Ownership and operating costs during the entire six years amount to $10,278, or $.143 per mile.

It should be understood that automobile costs per mile will decrease as the number of miles driven increases, since the high fixed costs are spread over more miles. In our example, we used 12,000 miles per year, an average mileage for American families. If a car exceeds this amount, the cost per mile should be lower. Also, if a family decides to keep the car for seven or eight years, the cost will continue to decline. These figures help to explain why a person who buys a new car every two or three years has higher automobile costs than one who trades every six years. If he drives his car from 12,000 to 15,000 miles per year and wants to get the most for his money, there is no reason why a new car should not give satisfactory service for six or seven years. To trade more often will require allotting a considerable amount for transportation in the family budget.

As shown in Exhibit 13–5, variable costs begin to exceed fixed costs after the fifth year. Repair costs will most likely rise rapidly after this point. This is an economical time to trade—before repair and upkeep costs exceed total value of the car.

A study made by the U.S. Department of Transportation reveals operating costs for cars driven 100,000 miles over a ten-year period.[2] A standard-size car is shown to cost $.1604 per mile the first year, and declines each year to a cost of $.1043 cents during the tenth year. Average cost for the full ten years is $.1355 per mile. A compact-size car is estimated at $.1118 per mile the

[2]Federal Highway Administration, Department of Transportation, *Cost of Operating an Automobile* (Washington, D.C.), 1972, p. 2.

Exhibit 13–4 Estimated Annual and Per Mile Cost of Automobile Ownership and Operation—Purchase Price of $4000 on a Car Driven 12,000 Miles Per Year

Costs	1st year	2nd year	3rd year	4th year	5th year	6th year	Total. 6 years
Fixed costs:							
Depreciation[1]	$ 1320	$ 800	$ 480	$ 320	$ 240	$ 160	$ 3320
Interest[2]	240	240	240	—	—	—	720
License	20	20	20	20	20	20	120
Insurance	250	235	220	205	190	175	1275
Property taxes	75	65	55	45	35	25	300
Inspection	3	3	3	3	3	3	18
Shelter	180	180	180	180	180	180	1080
Total fixed costs	$ 2088	$ 1543	$ 1198	$ 773	$ 668	$ 563	$ 6833
Variable costs:							
Gasoline and oil	$ 295	$ 295	$ 295	$ 295	$ 295	$ 295	$ 1770
Repairs[3]	50	75	300	125	150	375	1075
Servicing	25	25	25	25	25	25	150
Parking and other costs	75	75	75	75	75	75	450
Total variable costs	$ 445	$ 470	$ 695	$ 520	$ 545	$ 770	$ 3445
Total costs	$ 2533	$ 2013	$ 1893	$ 1293	$ 1213	$ 1333	$10,278
Costs per mile	0.211	0.168	0.158	0.108	0.101	0.111	0.143

[1]Depreciation estimated at 33% first year, 20% second year, 12% third year, 8% fourth year, 6% fifth year, 4% sixth year with 17% remaining as trade-in value.
[2]Assumes $3,000 borrowed for 3 years at 8% interest.
[3]Assumes replacement of tires and battery every 3 years.

Exhibit 13–5   Comparison of Fixed and Variable Costs of Automobile Ownership Using Figures in Exhibit 13–4

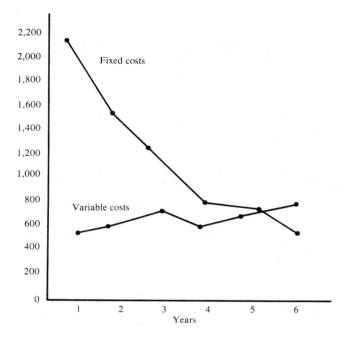

first year and decreases to $.0967 during the tenth year. Average for the compact car is $.1081 over the entire period. Costs of owning a subcompact car were also estimated but for less than a ten-year period, since these cars are relatively new. The study showed costs for this size car to be $.0944 cents per mile.

Most people do not keep a car for ten years. The Motor Vehicle Manufacturers Association reports that in 1971, only 41 percent of cars in use were six to seven years old or older.[3]

Lowering
Ownership Costs

A car can provide better service at a lower operating cost if it is given proper maintenance attention. Automobiles are somewhat like people in this respect —that is, they will have a longer and healthier life if preventive measures are used. Small and regular maintenance costs can prevent major repairs. A car that is well maintained is safer to drive and will command a higher price at

---

[3]Motor Vehicle Manufacturers Assoc., *1972 Automobile Facts and Figures* (Detroit, 1973), p. 31.

trade-in time. Of course, the mechanical parts—such as the engine and brakes —are most important, but a car maintains its value and appearance better when the paint and upholstery also receive good care. Appearance is a major factor in selling a car.

Modern cars are powerful and complex machines. They have many parts that can stop working at any time. Regular inspections and servicing should be made by qualified mechanics. Car owners can learn to perform minor servicing to make the car last longer and save on maintenance costs. New car buyers can follow service recommendations in the owner's manual that comes with the car. The same maintenance practices should be used on cars of any age. The following are recommended practices to get better and lower cost performance from a car.

1. Check air pressure in the tires often and rotate wheels every 5,000 miles for longer tire life. Wheel alignment and balance should be checked once each year.

2. An engine tune-up once a year is necessary for best operation. If the family drives an average of about 10,000 miles per year, the tune-up should include new spark plugs, distributor points, condenser, and carburetor adjustment. Also, the air, gasoline, and crankcase ventilation systems will need new filters.

   The oil filter is usually changed more than once a year. Oil changes and proper lubrication will be needed two or three times a year under normal driving habits. Brakes should be checked once a year and new linings installed when needed.

3. At each gasoline purchase it is a good practice to check the engine oil level, and water levels in the battery and radiator. Of course, a good grade of anti-freeze should be kept in the radiator at all times.

4. As for appearance, keeping both inside and outside of the car clean is all that is necessary. An occasional waxing of the exterior paint can help to keep it clean.

Insuring the Family Automobile

The frequency and high cost of automobile accidents make it imperative that every car owner have liability insurance. High repair costs have forced insurance companies to raise policy rates. Adequate liability insurance coverage can protect the owner from losing his lifetime savings in the event of an accident.

The most expensive part of automobile insurance is for collision, that feature of the policy which pays to repair the car. Whether this coverage is included is a personal decision. A moderate-income family should have this insurance while the car is new; but, after three or four years, they may want to accept the risk of loss from a collision, since the car has already lost much of its value. For more details on purchasing automobile insurance, read Chapter 18.

Leasing
a Car

The automobile leasing business has grown rapidly in recent years. It is now possible to lease a car for an hour, a day, or a year. Some families can save money by leasing rather than owning a car. Families living in large cities where public transportation is good may have little need to own an automobile. If there is only an occasional need for private transportation, it may be more economical to lease. Most automobile leasing is done for business purposes, because leasing is more expensive than owning for the average family. Business firms like leasing arrangements because they do not have their capital invested and leased cars are less trouble to the operator.

Exhibit 13–6 compares costs of ownership with those for leasing a car on a one-year or a two-year lease agreement. When all costs are considered, there is very little difference in owning or leasing during the first year. If the car is driven more than average mileage, ownership costs decrease in comparison to leasing costs. The big saving in ownership comes after the second year. Leasing costs will equal the value of the car in two years, but the car is still not owned. Those who buy a new car every year could possibly save money by leasing, if the mileage driven is average or below.

Exhibit 13–6   Comparison of Ownership and Leasing Costs of Medium Size Automobiles Driven 12,000 Miles

	Ownership Costs	Leasing[1] Costs
Annual Cost (1st year)	$2,533	$2,335
Cost per mile	0.211	0.195
Annual Cost (2nd year)	2,013	2,275
Cost per mile	0.168	0.190

[1]Cost of one year is figured at $170 per month, not including gas and oil; $165 per month for the second year on a 2-year lease.

If the family needs private transportation only a few times during the year —possibly for a vacation or a few week-end trips—it is less expensive to rent than to own a car. Medium-size cars can be rented for $15 per day, or $75 per week, plus $.15 per mile driven (this includes gas and oil). For most families, owning a car is necessary because it is needed frequently.

Discussion Questions

1. What are some reasons why the use of a car today is considered a necessity?

2. You are trying to decide whether to purchase a new car or a used car. Make a list of the advantages of each of these alternatives.

3. Before buying any car outline and discuss the steps a buyer should go through up to purchase.

4. Elaborate on why more than one dealer should be seen before a car is bought.

5. What are some of the sources of credit for the purchase of a car? How do these sources differ?

6. Give some of the reasons why a person should be careful in buying a car that is over three years old. Is there anything he can do to reduce these risks?

7. Distinguish between *variable* and *fixed* automobile costs. Give some examples of each.

8. Why does the cost per mile of driving an automobile become less the older the car becomes?

9. Even though variable costs may exceed fixed costs by the time a car reaches five years of age, why may it be desirable to keep the car another two years or longer?

10. What are some situations when the leasing of a car may be more economical than outright ownership? Explain why.

11. Why is preventive maintenance on a car desirable?

References

Arnold, Pauline and White, Percival, *Money; Make It, Spend It, Save It,* New York, Holiday House, 1962.

Beloisen, Arletta M., "Seasonal Variations in U.S. Diets," U.S. Department of Agriculture, Agricultural Research Service, Consumer and Food Economics Research Division, 1971.

Britton, Virginia, *Personal Finance,* New York, American Book Company, 1968.

Cohen, Jerome B. and Arthur W. Hanson, *Personal Finance,* 4th ed., Homewood, Ill., Richard D. Irwin, 1972.

DeBenedictis, Daniel J., *The Complete Real Estate Adviser,* New York, Trident Press, 1969.

Economic Research Service, U.S. Department of Agriculture, *What Makes Food Prices?* Rensid, October, 1970.

Hastings, Paul and Norbert Nietus, *Personal Finance,* New York, McGraw-Hill, 1972.

Lasser, J. K. and Porter, Sylvia F., *Managing Your Money,* New York, Henry Holt, 1953.

Nielsen, Jens and Jackie, *How to Save or Make Thousands When You Buy or Sell Your House,* Garden City, New York, Doubleday, 1971.

Reader's Digest, *How to Live on Your Income,* Pleasantville, N.Y., Reader's Digest Association, 1970.

Smith, Carlton and Richard Pratt, *The Time-Life Book of Family Finance,* New York, Time Inc., 1970.

U.S. Department of Agriculture, *Consumers All, The Yearbook of Agriculture,* 1965.

U.S. Department of Agriculture, *Food, The Yearbook of Agriculture, 1959,* Washington, D.C., The United States Department of Agriculture, 1959.

U.S. Department of Agriculture Leaflet No. 424 "Food for Fitness—A Daily Food Guide."

U.S. Department of Housing and Urban Development, *Wise Home Buying,* Bulletin 267–F, March, 1972.

U.S. News & World Report, *How to Buy Real Estate,* Washington, 1970.

U.S. Savings and Loan League, *Savings and Loan Fact Book, 1973,* Chicago, 1973.

Willett, Edward R., *Personal Finance,* Columbus, Ohio, Charles E. Merrill, 1964.

Wodecka, Virgil O., Ph.D., "Food Safety," Bureau of Foods, Food and Drug Administration, U.S. Department of Agriculture, February 23, 1971.

part four

Reducing Losses Through Insurance

There is none so blind as
they that won't see.

[Jonathan Swift]

14

Making Basic Insurance Decisions

Insurance—a Method
of Reducing Losses

We as individuals and as family units are beset on every hand by the possibility of *direct* and *consequential* financial losses. The scope of these possible losses is great. In the realm of exposure to *direct* losses, we recognize such possibilities as theft; destruction of property from various perils; loss of earnings through unemployment, disability, and premature death; losses resulting from medical and rehabilitation expenses. *Consequential* losses vary widely among situations such as the following:

Additional living expenses incurred during the rebuilding of a home destroyed by fire or other perils.

Profit and overhead losses sustained while a business is shut down following destruction of the premises.

Reduced earning potential caused by failure to attain educational or training objectives.

Future income lost as a result of divorce or from the premature death of a breadwinner.

Many of these losses can be reduced or eliminated through our own personal efforts. Others—such as premature death, medical expenses, and destruction of property through the carelessness or intent of others—may be beyond our control. It is in the area of losses *beyond our control* that the institution of insurance can be of help.

For reasons which we shall note, we cannot be protected by insurance from all of this category of losses.

Insurance—a
Pooling Operation

Insurance is essentially a "pooling" operation whereby a large number of people who are subject to the same risk contribute to a pool, from which those who actually sustain a loss from the peril insured against are reimbursed. The insurance theory is basically that simple, and *there is no other approach to the insurance mechanism*. For the risk to be subject to "pooling" and to be fair to all, certain requirements must be met:

1. The individuals contributing to the pool should have similar characteristics relating to their chances of loss during the period of time in which the pool is operating.
2. It must be possible to determine that a loss has actually occurred and what the amount of the loss is.
3. No member of the group should have any control over the occurrence of a loss. In other words, the loss must be accidental or fortuitous.
4. Last, but as important as any of the other requirements, it must be possible to predict in advance with a relatively high degree of accuracy the amount of losses for the entire group.

From these requirements we can see that many risks facing the individual and the family cannot be handled through the insurance device. Some examples of uninsurable risks are:

Failure to earn a college degree—the individual has some control over this.

Decline in stock market values—it is impossible to predict the occurrence, duration, or severity of each market decline.

Wearing out of a car or household appliance—this is not accidental; also, the owner has a degree of control over this.

Possibility of injury or death from a space flight—at this date, at least, there is not a large enough group subject to this loss to organize a pool.

Financial consequences of divorce—again, this is not an accidental or fortuitous event. It would be interesting to contemplate how many additional divorces there would be in the next twelve months if each wife had a *$100,000 Divorce Policy* on which she could collect by divorcing her husband. Yet, even scholars sometimes seriously propose using insurance as a means of reducing personal losses from perils for which the insurance mechanism is totally unworkable. Note the following June 13, 1970 news item:

INSURANCE SUGGESTED
FOR FAMILY BREAKUPS

(Dispatch of *The Times,* London)

LONDON   To protect wives whose marriages break up, compulsory insurance, much on the lines of automobile coverage, was suggested as a possible answer to the difficulty of supporting two homes and often two families.

Colin Gibson, Principal research officer in the legal research unit at Bedford College, London, said that when a marriage broke up and the breadwinner remarried or set up a home with another woman, there usually was not enough money, and the Supplementary Benefits Commission had to come to the rescue of the former wife.

The *pooling* aspect of insurance should be understood and recognized by a person contemplating the purchase of insurance. It is the very nature of a pool for the individual to contribute, along with many more, a small certain amount for the unlikely possibility of receiving a relatively large amount from the pool in the event of a loss. From this reasoning, we can define insurance as *the substitution of a relatively small certain loss* (the premium) *for the possibility of a relatively large uncertain loss.* For example, it is possible to purchase a $10,000 one-year term life insurance policy at age 21 for $30.00 which would guarantee payment of $10,000 in the event of death within the next twelve months. The $30 premium is the substitution of a relatively small certain loss for the unlikely receipt of a relatively large $10,000 amount as partial reimbursement for the loss of future earnings through premature death. The prospective insurance buyer should therefore be forearmed with the knowledge that:

1. The purchase of insurance involves a small *loss*.
2. There is no such thing as free insurance.
3. There *should* be no possibility of profiting from insurance.

The Large
Loss Principle

A closely related concept of insurance buying is the large loss principle.[1] This principle simply means that it is not sensible or economical to insure against small losses. To use our previous terminology, it is not wise to substitute a *small certain loss* for a *small relatively certain loss*. Stated in such a way, the proposition becomes a truism and a paradox. In the purchase of insurance, because of the administrative and sales costs of insurance, it is nearly certain that a person will lose in the long run with such an insurance-buying philosophy.

We frequently hear the virtue of $50 deductible on collision insurance for our car as opposed to $100 or $250 deductible. The differences in the annual premium charge between these deductibles vary from state to state and from period to period; but, in one specific case, the $50 deductible cost $21 more than $100 deductible, $60 more than $250 deductible. Thus, for twelve months: $50 more collision insurance ($50 deductible instead of $100) costs $21, and $200 more collision insurance ($50 deductible instead of $250) costs $60. Most would agree this is a very high cost to pay, and the example well illustrates the expense, even folly, of insuring against small losses.

With the same automobile insurance policy, the buyer should probably purchase liability insurance which would protect him against claims of legal liability to others arising out of negligence in connection with the use of his automobile. In too many cases, the amount of coverage buyers choose is $20,000 per occurrence. This is a pitifully small amount of protection in terms of the possible liability judgment the insured might incur. Given the present inflationary incomes and costs, it is easy to see that if the negligence involved the death, permanent disability, or even major medical expenses of another party, the actual amount of damages inflicted could well be as much as $100,000 or several times that.

Thus, the automobile insurance buyer should consider the desirability of transferring some of the premium money spent to insure the small—but admittedly more frequent—losses from collision to buying insurance protection for the much less likely but still very possibly catastrophic losses resulting from negligence liability. Again, the premiums vary with the state and also with the rating groups; but the same $21 previously mentioned would typically raise the liability protection from $20,000 per occurrence to $300,000 per occurrence.

This example illustrates the large loss principle, which suggests the wisdom of spending a limited insurance budget dollar to purchase protection against the large catastrophic loss, regardless of how unlikely it is to occur, as opposed to spending the same dollar to purchase protection against small frequent

---

[1]For an excellent and lively discussion of the large loss principle, read Mehr and Cammach, *Principles of Insurance,* 4th ed. (Homewood, Illinois: Richard D. Irwin), pp. 603–606.

losses. To the insurance practitioner, it is truly astounding that so many otherwise sophisticated buyers violate this large loss principle in their insurance-buying decisions.

How Much Insurance?

Indemnification and the Ability to Pay Premiums

A first consideration in the question of how much insurance one should buy is to acquire an understanding of the principle of *indemnification*. A typical dictionary definition of the word *indemnify* is "to compensate for damage or loss sustained." *Compensate* does not mean to reward or make a profit from loss sustained. Nor is that what the principle of idemnification in insurance means. Insurance should not be owned with the purpose or possibility of making a profit from a claim. We can readily see why this would tend to increase the number and amount of losses, thus resulting in needless destruction of the wealth of our country.

Insurance regulatory laws generally back up this principle by making void or even illegal any insurance contract from which a person can profit. Such policies are categorized as gambling contracts harmful to public welfare. The only basic difference between insurance and gambling (which is also a pool) is this matter of *indemnification against loss*. A hoaried story related to the principle of indemnification has to do with the farmer whose $10,000 barn burned. He asked his insurance agent to just give him a check for $10,000, to which the agent demurred, "Sorry, my company doesn't pay in cash; we simply replace with another just like it." To which the farmer countered, "Well, if that's the way you operate, you can just cancel that policy on my wife."

The answer to the question of "How much insurance?" centers around two questions: "How much do I need?" "How much can I afford?" The answers to these two questions in terms of kinds of coverage and amounts of coverage are almost never the same. Loss exposures for which insurance protection can be bought are so many in number and so great in amount that the typical person has to forego some protection, choosing the kinds and amounts which his limited budget permits. Insurance *protection* would be self-defeating if a family's total premiums were so great that not enough money was left to provide the necessities of life.

The best guides in making this compromise are the *large loss principle* and the *principle of indemnification. It is most important to the insurance buyer to have his own understanding of these concepts in his dealing with insurance agents.* As will be explained in a later chapter, insurance agents vary from one extreme to another in terms of their own knowledge of insurance and in their professional approach to service. It is easy to understand the temptation to an agent—even the most professional—to violate these principles in his recommendations. This is especially so with certain types of prospects. In the previous example on automobile insurance, the agent realized from previous sad experience—sad in terms of the policyholder's unhappiness and also in terms of losing his business—the results of convincing his client to buy $250 deductible on collision and $1,000,000 liability protection, as opposed to a policy at the same cost with $50 deductible collision and only $20,000 liability protection. It is difficult for many insureds to keep their objectivity at the prospect of accepting a collision claim check for $250 less than the costs of repairs and

Exhibit 14–1   An Illustration of Insuring a Family's Three Greatest Financial Assets

I. Automobiles
$6,000 Asset

II. The Family Home
$30,000 Asset

III. Future Earning Power
of Family Provider
$113,797 Asset[1]

Two Family Cars
Insured for $5,900
(98.3% of value)

Insured for $25,000
(Lot worth $5,000)
(100% of value)

$10,000	16th year Child age 18
$10,000	15th year Child age 17
$10,000	14th year Child age 16
$10,000	13th year Child age 15
$10,000	12th year Child age 14
$10,000	11th year Child age 13
$10,000	10th year Child age 12
$10,000	9th year Child age 11
$10,000	8th year Child age 10
$10,000	7th year Child age 9
$10,000	6th year Child age 8
$10,000	5th year Child age 7
$10,000	4th year Child age 6

[1]Present value of $10,000 per year for number of years indicated, discounted at 5%.

Exhibit 14–1 (Cont.)

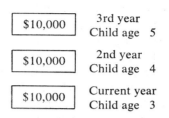

| $10,000 | 3rd year Child age 5 |

| $10,000 | 2nd year Child age 4 |

| $10,000 | Current year Child age 3 |

Breadwinner's Net Pay
Checks Until Youngest
Child is Grown
Insured for $15,000[2]
(13.2% of value)

[2]This total does not include Social Security Survivorship benefits which are in the nature of compulsory decreasing term life insurance. The present value of these benefits would be substantial. However, part of this might have to be forfeited. In any event, counting the survivorshop benefit as life insurance, we can say the family's biggest "asset" is insured for substantially less than its present value for middle and higher income wage earners.

still feel good that, even though it possibly will never happen, he does have $1,000,000 protection against an automobile negligence liability claim.

A guide in answering the question of "How much insurance?" is to ask "How much could I lose in the event of the worst possible loss from the exposure involved?" The answer is relatively simple in insuring property, such as the home and the automobile. It is basically a matter of how much it costs to replace the property. The question of "how much" becomes more difficult in the areas of negligence liability; health insurance; and loss of earning power through disability, death, or old age.

Since loss through negligence liability involves an order from the court allowing the injured party to take the negligent party's property up to a stated amount, we might be tempted to answer in terms of not only how much property we now have but also how much we might acquire in the future. Depending on the particular state and the nature of the action, judgments are enforceable typically from five to ten years and may be renewed. When the college student recognizes that he will spend probably a third and almost certainly the most productive part of his working life in the twenty-first century and when he considers the likely technological and productivity miracles of the next four or five decades, it is easy to recognize the potential magnitude of his future earnings and property accumulations. The bright side of this negligence liability protection picture is that the cost of increasing the amount of protection to substantial figures is minimal.

In considering the matter of health insurance, the buyer should recognize that medical costs have risen so greatly in the past decade and are continuing to do so at a rapid rate. Thus the insurance buyer is cautioned to review this aspect of his insurance program at relatively short intervals. Where a combined hospital and health insurance policy with a $5,000 maximum benefit was fairly typical in 1950, the subsequent progression to a $10,000 maximum is now being discarded for maximums of $30,000, $50,000, and even $75,000.

The question of "how much insurance on the individual's life?" involves two separate exposures to the deceased's survivors: (1) the estimated cost of death expenses and (2) the amount of financial dependency of survivors on the deceased. The significance of the answer to each of these questions will be developed in Chapter 17. It is pertinent to observe at this point, in the matter of concepts, the rather unbelievable practice that persists in many family insurance programs. Exhibit 14–1 illustrates this point.

At this point, the buyer of life insurance should take note of the "human life value" concept developed by Professor Solomon S. Huebner.[2] The following example may be helpful in introducing the subject. Let us assume the law allowed a person to make a contract selling for cash all his future earnings to another party.[3] Then let us ask "For what cash amount *today* would he sell all his future earnings?" If given only a few minutes to decide, he would make a quick assumption as to his probable average yearly earnings for the remainder of his working life and then estimate the present value of these total savings. It is quickly apparent that even the most modest assumption of average annual earning for forty years or more would have a very substantial present value.

Suppose we estimate a value of $300,000 for these future earnings. If it happened that this person owned a warehouse with the same future earning power—thus possessing the same present value—would he hesitate to insure the warehouse for much less than the $300,000? Almost certainly not, and the matter would probably be one of such urgency that he likely would not let a moment pass before getting this protection in force.

Dr. Huebner's reasoning was that it is just as illogical to delay insuring the present value of an individual's future earning power. It is difficult to argue with his premise. One might point out there is one difference: destruction of future earning power by death will mean nothing to the individual who dies. But the same point would apply to the value of the building in the event of the insured's death.

In the same book, Dr. Huebner discussed the matter of *economic* death, relating to the situation where a person is alive but has physically lost his earning power. This arises from two conditions—disability and old age. Theoretically, there is the same need to insure in proper amounts for these two contingencies.

---

[2] S. S. Huebner, *The Economics of Life Insurance* (New York: Appleton, 1959), pp. 18–71.

[3] This idea is not as "far out" as it might seem. In past eras of human slavery, we can assume the market price of each slave tended to approach the present value of his future productivity. Current examples of athletes signing contracts for long-time services for $1,000,000 and more further illustrate the point.

The Fallacy of
"Limited" Insurance

A *limited* insurance policy is generally described as one where the insurance company's promise to pay is limited to those losses resulting from certain specified causes (perils), with those causes representing a relatively small percentage of all causes. This definition has legal origins (Uniform Individual Policy Provisions of 1950) and institutional origins (as a term used frequently in insurance literature). "Limited policies" most often refers to:

1. Life insurance contracts which pay only when death is caused by *accidents* (e.g., double indemnity) or by *certain types* of accidents (e.g., flight insurance), or by accidents occurring only under *special conditions* (e.g., vacation trip insurance).
2. Health insurance contracts which pay only under accidental circumstances enumerated above, or only for certain specified illnesses (e.g., "cancer" insurance, "dreaded disease" insurance, etc.).

This analogy seems justified: why build a fence for security where the height varies at random places from six to twenty feet and where certain sections of it are only one foot high or nonexistent? Let us say six feet is considered an adequate height for guarding a thousand feet of property line against possible harmful intrusions of all categories: thiefs, rioters, vandals, animals, windblown trash, etc. If the fence was built a section at a time over a period of years as the property owner had the money and the inclination, the fence would look like the sketch in Exhibit 14–2.

Such a fence is ridiculous, of course. How much more logical is a "fence" giving financial protection against the intrusion of death that has a similar profile? For example, let us consider the safety height (amount of cash needed at death for surviving dependents) to be $25,000. The insured has a $20,000 ordinary life policy that will pay this amount regardless of the cause of death.

Exhibit 14–2

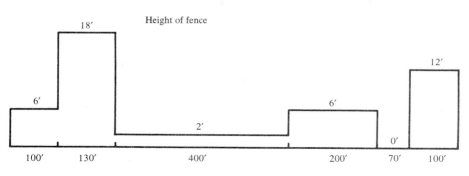

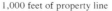

1,000 feet of property line

In addition, other policies were acquired through the years—all limited to death by accident—that produce a profile of his "life insurance" fence like that shown in Exhibit 14–3.

Exhibit 14–3

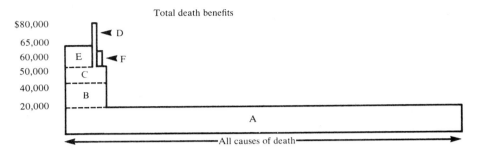

A. $20,000 Whole life
B. $20,000 Accidental death (Double Indemnity) rider to A
C. $10,000 Accidental death policy (purchased through a credit card and paid with other monthly billings)
D. $30,000 Flight insurance (pays if killed as commercial air passenger; purchased through world-wide credit card and paid with other monthly billings)
E. $15,000 Auto accident (pays if killed in car accident; purchased through college alumnae organization)
F. $10,000 Bicycle accident insurance (pays if killed while riding bicycle; purchased as part of maintenance contract from manufacturer)

The "life insurance" fence is $5,000 too low for 93.4 percent of the distance, since all policies except the $20,000 whole life pay off only in the event of accidental death.[4] It is likely that if the premiums spent on the five accident policies were applied to the purchase of more whole life—or even term life for the remainder of the family dependency period—the height of the protection fence could be built up well beyond the $25,000 adequacy level.

Just as an actual fence should normally be the same height at every point, so should a wall of life insurance protection. The same is true of property insurance, medical expense insurance, and disability income insurance.[5] The following generalization seems valid: *the amount of insurance in force should be the same for all causes of loss.*

When we recognize that most individual and family insurance budgets do not permit purchasing all the protection needed, it is axiomatic that buying *duplicating* insurance protection is unwise. Limited policies (of the type de-

---

[4]Institute of Life Insurance, *Life Insurance Fact Book* (New York, 1971), p. 92. In a table giving the percentage distribution by cause of death among ordinary policyholders in all United States life insurance companies, accidents were shown as the cause of 6.6 percent of the deaths.

[5]This is not to say that in some insuring situations the amount needed does not change frequently.

fined here) *are* duplicating coverages. It is difficult to make a case for spending money on such policies.[6]

Selection Against
the Insurance Company

The insurance buyer should understand that one of the great problems of insurance companies lies in the concept of "selection against the insurer." This means simply that insurance rates are based on aggregate losses for the total number in the insured group and that members of this "pool" must be a relatively homogeneous group (in relation to the exposure involved). The insurer recognizes there is always a possibility that certain individuals applying for insurance have special reason to suspect or expect a loss in the near future. If the carrier does not keep this "adverse selection" factor to a minimum, it will experience greater losses than expected.

When an insurance company, in its consideration of an application for a policy, decides the applicant is not an average or typical risk for the group, it either (1) rejects the applicant, (2) offers him the applied-for insurance at a higher premium, or (3) offers him a more restricted contract. The insured is not always aware that he has been put in this category, and it may be that the abnormal risk decision was based on incorrect information or erroneous judgment on the part of an insurance company underwriter.

Rate
Classifications

In addition to the *adverse selection factor,* the insurance company has an additional problem, that of deciding in which particular rate group a certain applicant should be placed. The insurance pricing system justifiably is based on dividing applicants into different homogeneous groups in order to be as fair as possible to the individual. Awareness on the part of the insurance buyer of the existence of these rating groups and an expressed interest in the categories will increase the likelihood of his being placed in the most advantageous price classification. Following is an actual example illustrating the point.

Quotation from *Consumer Reports,* July, 1970, page 427:

> While almost all insurance companies will put you through the same sort of rating mill, they will not by any means grind out identical prices.

---

[6]There remain only two reasons for buying such limited policies: (1) they seem to be a bargain (and in Chapter 17 we will note the opposite is usually the case); (2) a perhaps subconscious feeling that having an excessive amount of insurance in force on a particularly dreaded peril (i.e. cancer, death from a plane crash) reduces the likelihood of the actual event: buying peace of mind.

Premiums for roughly the same basic liability and medical-payments policy for the same hypothetical motorist in Jacksonville, Fla., early this year ranged from $78 to $264, a spread of 339 percent, depending on the company. That included only the top 20 companies (otherwise unidentified) in an industry-sponsored survey. Eliminating the three highest prices (which were probably from high-risk companies), the range was still from $78 to $125.20, a spread of 60 percent.

Another survey, this one published by the Georgia Insurance Department, showed rates of 169 companies as of December 31, 1968, for 10/20/10 liability coverage on a 45-year-old man in the company's lowest premium classification. In Atlanta, the price ranged from $35 at the Pennsylvania General Insurance Co. to $83 at the Aetna Casualty & Surety Co. That was a spread of 237 percent.

All Insurance is
Term Insurance

John Citizen pays $200 a year for his automobile insurance for fifty years. At the end of fifty years and after having paid $10,000 for fifty "one-year term" automobile insurance policies, he is not the least bit concerned that the insurance company owes him no money of any kind—that the insurance policy has no "cash value." The same John Citizen pays another $200 a year for each of fifty years on a life insurance policy and at the end of the time would likely be outraged if the insurance company did not owe him some money or—to put it more accurately—if the insurance policy did not have a cash value roughly equal to the total premiums paid. Why is this? Is there something basically different between automobile (and other property insurance) and life insurance? There *is* a difference in the *contract* with the insurance company, but there is *no* difference in the insurance part of these contracts.

All insurance is *term* insurance—i.e., protection for a stated period of time. For calculation purposes and for other logical reasons the most typical *term* is one year. Life insurance is no different from all other insurance in that the basic calculation is one-year term.[7] Homogeneity of each group insured is established by age and "normal" health for that particular age. We can insure only against the possibility of death during a particular year of life (i.e., one-year term for each year of life). The problem is that ultimate death is a certainty. It follows that as we approach the age of certain death (age 100 arbitrarily chosen by actuaries), the one-year term rates become prohibitive. Exhibit 14–4 reflects this.

A question logically follows: if there is only one kind of life insurance—*term*—how do we reconcile the fact that there are many policies with different

---

[7]Actuaries would question this in terms of their complex calculation on most policies, but not in terms of the theoretical basic ingredient. For those interested in a more detailed treatment of this concept the following references are recommended: Robert I. Mehr, *Life Insurance Theory and Practice* (Austin: Business Publications Inc., 1970), pp. 6–23. Huebner and Black, *Life Insurance* (New York: Appleton, 1969), pp. 9–11.

names such as "ordinary life," "twenty-pay life," and "endowment at sixty-five"? In answering, a distinction must be made between the terms *life insurance* and *life insurance policies*. The typical life insurance company rate book contains prices and other details for many distinctly different policies (contracts). Some of these policies involve only insurance; others involve insurance and a systematic savings account not too different from savings accounts at banks and savings and loan associations. In such policies, the annual premium contains a charge for the life insurance as well as the savings deposit. Hence, the frequently heard statement: "There are many kinds of life insurance *policies,* but only one kind of *life insurance.*"

Exhibit 14–4   Mortality Cost of $1,000 One-year Term Life Insurance*

Age	Cost	Age	Cost	Age	Cost
25	$1.91	41	$ 3.79	57	$ 15.35
26	1.94	42	4.12	58	16.79
27	1.97	43	4.47	59	18.36
28	2.01	44	4.86	60	20.09
29	2.05	45	5.28	61	21.97
30	2.10	46	5.76	62	24.01
31	2.16	47	6.28	63	26.24
32	2.22	48	6.86	64	28.68
33	2.29	49	7.51	65	31.36
34	2.37	50	8.22	70	49.18
35	2.48	51	9.00	75	72.47
36	2.61	52	9.84	80	108.63
37	2.77	53	10.76	85	159.16
38	2.97	54	11.75	90	225.34
39	3.21	55	12.84	95	346.93
40	3.49	56	14.04	99	987.73

*Commissioners Standard Ordinary Mortality Table (1958), 2½% interest. No expense costs included.

The Life Insurance Policy as a Simple Two-Piece Jigsaw Puzzle

In examining that category of life insurance policies which include a savings element, we might gain an understanding of how they work by thinking of them in terms of a simple two-piece jigsaw puzzle. Forgetting for a moment any previous concept we may have had concerning life insurance, let's take an example.

Bill Savor wants to accumulate $1,000 in ten years by making equal annual deposits in a savings account at the bank or savings and loan. He is told that, at the current 4.65 percent compound interest rate, he can achieve this by depositing $77.22 now and making similar deposits for nine consecutive years. Bill decides to do this and asks the bank to show him what his savings account balance will be at the end of each of the ten years. He is furnished the information in the form shown in Exhibit 14–5.

Exhibit 14–5

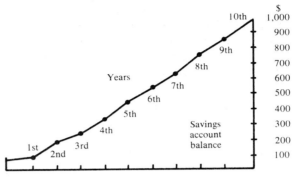

Amount at end of year

Bill, who is rather sharp in logic and mathematics, reasons to himself "it will be nice having that $1,000 cash ten years from now but what if I die during that period? My estate would surely need that full $1,000 to pay off bills." He quickly recognizes that if he bought term life insurance each year with a death benefit equal to $1,000 less the savings account balance, his estate would have that $1,000 upon his death.

Bill Savor, age fifty-five, knowing that the rate for term life insurance is different for each year of age, quickly makes the following notation of how much one-year term he will need each of these years and what his age will be at that time.

Year	1st	2nd	3rd	4th	5th	6th	7th	8th	9th	10th
Age	55	56	57	58	59	60	61	62	63	64
Amount of Term Life Needed	$923	835	746	654	557	545	349	238	122	40

He takes this notation to Ajax Life Insurance Company and asks them if they will sell him a ten-year term policy with the death benefit decreasing each year to the amount shown and if they would quote him a premium which would be the same each year. The Ajax representative gladly offers to do this, assuming Bill is insurable, and quotes him an annual rate of $19.00.[8]

---

[8]Ajax would very likely agree to a term contract (policy) such as this, but would probably require a six or seven year premium paying period rather than ten years. The amount of insurance is so little during the last years that Bill might be tempted to drop the policy and save the premium. In other words, the insurance company would need to get the total premiums for the ten different years of coverage before the amount in force became so little that the premium would seem "high" in the last years.

When Bill gets home with the policy he draws a graph (see Exhibit 14–6) showing the amount of one-year term insurance to be in force each of the ten years.

Exhibit 14–6

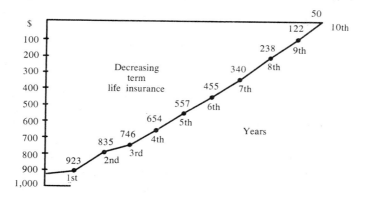

If Bill joins these two graphs together (as in Exhibit 14–7), they fit like a two-piece jigsaw puzzle. For any one of the ten years, adding the amount of the savings account balance and the amount of term insurance in force equals the $1,000 that Bill wanted to have in the event of his death or at the end of ten years.

Exhibit 14–7

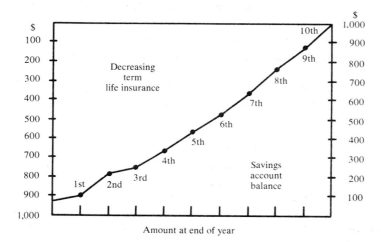

These two combined figures would also graphically reflect the workings of a ten-year endowment policy. From Bill Savor's standpoint, he could accomplish his original purposes by applying to Ajax Life Insurance for a ten-year endowment. He would be quoted an annual premium of approximately $99, such

premium to be paid at the first of each year for 10 years with the policy providing for $1,000 cash at the end of ten years or $1,000 cash, should Bill die
prior to the end of ten years. This same analogy could be used to explain the
workings of a twenty-year endowment, an endowment at sixty-five, an ordinary life (endowment at 100), and any other policy. The only difference would
be the duration. Thus, at an insured's age thirty-five, an endowment at age
sixty-five would constitute a thirty-year savings account with the complemen-
tary thirty-year decreasing term life insurance. An ordinary life policy provides
for payment of the face amount at age 100 and thus at age thirty-five would
involve a sixty-five-year accumulation period on the savings account with the
corresponding sixty-five years of decreasing term.

   Not mentioned in this analogy is a third factor which goes into the "making"
of a life insurance policy: the *loading*. This is a calculation of the life insurance
company's other costs which are added to the money requirements for the savings account and the decreasing term life to produce the level annual premium
quoted to the buyer. These other costs in issuing a policy include such things as
sales costs, underwriting costs (medical examinations, inspection reports, etc.),
as well as the usual overhead of such a business. Since many of these costs are
fixed costs regardless of the size of the policy and some are "one-time, first-
year" items, some insurance companies charge a policy fee in addition to the
annual premium. They are also allowed to charge a "surrender charge" against
the savings balance if the policy is discontinued in the early years.

   We must emphasize that this analogy was used as a means to bring about
an understanding of what a life insurance policy is, and *not* as an advocacy
of buying only term life insurance and putting *all* savings in other savings institutions. The opposite is true. Everyone needs a permanent life insurance program (one that does not pay until death) and it is not possible to buy term insurance for advanced ages. Even if it were, it is not likely one would maintain
the savings account and the term policy through a thirty, forty, or fifty year
period. There are also tax and legal advantages to life insurance over other
types of savings. For most families, a balanced financial program includes both
term and "cash value" life insurance, as well as other types of savings and
investments. The latter will be explored in Chapter 17 and in Part V.

"Life" Insurance
for Property

Since most property is also faced with ultimate "death" (from wear and tear,
obsolescence, etc.), there could be similar "life" insurance contracts for property insurance. As an example, assume a new $1,000 vending machine would
have only junk value at the end of five years. It would be possible for a property insurance company to sell a "life" insurance policy which would provide
$1,000 cash at the end of five years and would also pay $1,000 any time during
the five-year period if it was destroyed by fire or any other peril, or lost through
theft. This would be a "five-year endowment" vending machine policy. As it

happens, of course, owners of vending machines and other property handle the "certain death" problem by setting up a depreciation reserve, and handle the destruction part by purchasing "one year term" each year for the depreciated value of the property (i.e., theoretically the difference between the $1,000 cost, and the amount of the depreciation reserve that year).[9] Where inflation or economic conditions have *appreciated* the property's value, insurance is increased instead of decreased.

Understanding the one-year term aspect of *all* life insurance policies forearms the life insurance buyer for the misrepresentations and inaccurate presentations of certain insurance agents. Any agent's statement that a certain policy "provides free insurance to age 65 plus a certain amount of profit on all premiums paid" would be more accurately explained with the statement "the compound interest earnings on the savings (cash value) by age 65 exceed the cost of the yearly insurance protection and other costs by 'x' amount of dollars."

The same understanding of the essential "one-year term" aspect of all insurance contracts also protects the buyer from sales presentations based on a "revolutionary *new* type policy." Sophisticated insurance buyers know there just is no such a thing.

Discussion Questions

1. Insurance is a "pooling" operation. Discuss.
2. What is meant by the "large loss principle"? Give an example.
3. Discuss the principle of indemnification in insurance.
4. What is meant by economic death?
5. What is the reasoning behind the phrase "the fallacy of limited insurance"?
6. What are three alternatives an insurance company has when, after considering the application, it decides the applicant is not an average or typical risk for the group?
7. A third factor which goes into the making of a life insurance policy is the "loading." Discuss.
8. Why have *permanent* property *life* insurance policies not been developed?
9. Using the "two-piece jigsaw puzzle" analysis of life insurance, explain the difference in the shape of the two pieces of a ten-year endowment as compared to a whole life policy. Assume age at issue is twenty-five for each policy.
10. Explain the meaning of the statement: "All insurance is term insurance."

---

[9]There was an enterprising group at the end of World War II which toyed with the idea of forming a "car life insurance company." It happened that most cars in 1945—contrary to any subsequent period—were owned free and clear of debt. The idea was to offer a four, five, or six year "car endowment" policy involving monthly savings deposits plus a monthly charge for the yearly insurance premium. The policy would pay for damage to or destruction of the car during the period and would also give the insured a check for the "face amount" (value of the car) with which to pay cash for his new car at the end of the period.

Hope for the best, but
prepare for the worst.

[*English Proverb*]

15

Buying
Insurance

Insurance Available
(Overview)

Having acquired an understanding of basic insurance concepts and principles from the preceding chapter, we—as insurance buyers—would do well to survey the insurance environment in which we find ourselves. An overview of all the insurance coverages available should impress us with the scope and magnitude of the insurance mechanism. Further examination of the many different types of insurers can offer some understanding of the characteristics, advantages, and disadvantages of each of these types. Because of their great significance in terms of premiums involved and protection afforded, Chapter 16 will also deal with *benefits available* and *important policy provisions*. This treatment applies to social security programs for old age, survivor's, disability, and health insurance protection, as well as to similar protection offered by private insurers. Lastly, the important benefits and provisions of policies insuring us against loss resulting from damage to our property will be considered.

Following is an outline of insurance coverages currently available to an individual. The outline is presented to afford an overview and to act as a point of reference. The outline is organized on the basis of the degree to which the "purchase" is voluntary or compulsory.

A. Compulsory insurance with the insured required to pay at least part of insurance premiums
   1. Federal Social Security Program
      a. Retirement benefits
      b. Survivorship benefits (monthly income to insured's dependent survivors)
      c. Disability income
      d. Health insurance (Medicare)
   2. FHA Mortgage Insurance (required when purchasing a home financed under FHA program)
   3. Automobile personal and property damage liability (protection to others harmed by the insured's legal negligence in connection with ownership or driving an automobile; compulsory in varying degrees among the fifty states in connection with state financial responsibility laws; also, in connection with automobile *no fault* legislation, compulsory health and disability insurance—a fast changing picture varying greatly among states with such legislation)

B. Compulsory, with the insured not paying a premium *per se*
   1. Employee benefit plans paid for wholely by employer
   2. Unemployment Insurance
   3. Workman's Compensation Insurance
   4. Federal Deposit Insurance (insurance of deposits in banks)
   5. Federal Savings and Loan Insurance (insurance of deposits in savings and loan associations)

C. Semi-compulsory insurance with varying degrees of compulsion to buy and from whom to buy; insured pays premiums (these same coverages are also voluntary purchases in different circumstances)
   1. Employee benefit plan where employee pays part or all of premium
   2. Title insurance (in connection with real estate mortgages, protecting against loss from title defects)
   3. Credit life and disability insurance (in connection with installment purchases paying off balance of loan if insured dies, or paying current installments if insured is disabled)
   4. Life insurance (other than credit life) involving large individual or business loans where the lender is made beneficiary during the period of the loan
   5. Fire insurance and other peril insurance protecting mortgage companies and property owner from direct loss (always required where improved property is pledged to secure a loan)

6. Automobile collision and other direct loss perils (always required in connection with automobile finance loans)

D. Voluntary, insured pays premium, free to make own decision whether to buy,
how much to buy, and from which insurer to make the purchase

1. All forms of life insurance
2. All forms of health insurance (hospitalization, other medical expenses,
disability)
3. All forms of property insurance and liability insurance
4. The medical insurance part of Social Security health insurance (pays doctors and other non-hospital expenses; not free to choose insurer since
available only through Social Security Agency)

The total premiums involved in these insurance operations are tremendous as
we can see from the following premium income figures for 1971.

Premium income 1971 (in billions) [1]

Property insurance companies	$ 38.2
Life insurance companies	$ 42.4
Blue Cross-Blue Shield type associations	$ 9.8
Social Security old age, survivors, disability, and Health Insurance contributions	$ 47.1
	$137.5

This shows an amount exceeding 10 percent of the gross national product is
involved in gigantic *pooling* operations which provide Americans a greater
degree of security by allowing them to share financial uncertainties with each
other.

Types of Insurers:
Considerations in Choosing an Insurer

It is important to an individual, not only in his personal insurance-buying
decisions but also in the exercise of his influence (voting, contact with public
officials, etc.), to have some knowledge regarding the various types of insurers.
In considering a particular insurer, questions as to its ownership and organizational structure are pertinent.

The following is a classification of insurers on the basis of their nature as
private or government institutions.

---

[1]Amounts are approximate. Property insurer data from *Insurance Facts, 1972* (New
York: Insurance Information Institute), p. 9; Blue-Cross data from *Argus Chart, 1972*
(Cincinnati: The National Underwriter Co.), p. 112; life insurer data from *Best's Insurance Reports, Life and Health, 1972* (New Jersey: Alfred M. Best), p. vii; OASDHI
data from *Social Security Bulletin*, U.S. Department of Health, Education, and Welfare,
Social Security Administration, Jan., 1973, pp. 40, 43, 45. This total does not include
various federal, state, and local civil service, unemployment and other programs, nor self-
insured programs of private industry.

A. Private insurers
   1. Proprietary (ostensibly operated for the profit of the owners)
      a. Incorporated insurers (property insurance companies usually referred to as capital stock companies; life insurance companies referred to as old-line, legal reserve capital stock companies)

      Examples: Travelers, Aetna, Insurance Company of North America, Franklin Life, Connecticut General

      b. Unincorporated proprietary insurers

      Example: Lloyd's of London

   2. Non-proprietary
      a. Unincorporated insurers (reciprocal insurance exchanges)

      Examples: Farmer's Insurance Exchange, United Services Automobile Association

      b. Incorporated insurers
         (1) Consumer cooperatives (owned and theoretically controlled by policy holders)
             (a) Assessment mutuals
             (b) Advanced premium mutuals

             Life insurance company examples: Metropolitan Life, Prudential, John Hancock
             Property insurance company example: Liberty Mutual

         (2) Non-profit by charter, but ownership and control by other than policy holders

             Examples: Blue Cross-Blue Shield, United Mine Workers of America Welfare and Retirement Fund, various community plans, and private group clinics

B. Government insurers (agencies of government and quasi-public insurers backed by government)

   1. Federal government insurers
      a. Social Security Board of the Department of Health, Education and Welfare (old age, death, disability, medical care insurance)
      b. Railroad Retirement Board (administering railroad retirement system insurance benefits)
      c. Veteran's Administration (service men's life and disability insurance and mortgage loan insurance for veterans)
      d. Federal Housing Administration (mortgage and property improvement loan insurance)
      e. Federal Deposit Insurance Corporation (insuring bank deposits against bank failure)
      f. Federal Savings and Loan Insurance Corporation (insurance of savings and loan deposits against failure of the Savings and Loan Association)
      g. Federal Crop Insurance Corporation (insuring against crop failure caused by perils of nature)
      h. National Insurance Development Fund (reinsures private insurers against risk of excessive losses from civil disorders)

    i. National Flood Insurance Fund (reinsures private insurers to make it possible for them to offer flood insurance)

    j. Securities Investment Protection Development Fund (insures investors for losses caused by brokerage house insolvencies)

2. State insurers (varies greatly among states)

    a. Unemployment Insurance (All states offer this under a grant-in-aid program under federal social security act.)

    b. Workmen's compensation (Six states have a monopoly, twelve states have state funds competing with private insurers.)

    c. Very few states offer hail insurance, disability income insurance, title insurance. Only Wisconsin offers life insurance.

From this overview, we must be impressed with the pervasiveness and complexity of insurance in our personal and family affairs. We are relieved of much of the decision making in personal insurance matters because of the compulsory "purchase" aspect of so much of the protection. The decision-making area lies in those voluntary purchases which we make from private insurers. In Chapter 17 and 18, we will consider which coverages it is best to have. This chapter will deal with the characteristics of the various types of private insurers while suggesting some objectives to pursue in finally deciding on a particular insurer.

Types of Private Insurers

When we buy from a private insurer, we pick from among several types whether by chance or by choice. All of the different types can be assumed to be offering worthy insurance service or they could not survive in competition with others. There are, however, significant differences to be considered when purchasing a particular insurance policy, especially in (1) the *type* of insurer chosen and (2) the *particular insurer* selected from that category.[2]

The basic types of insurers are (1) stock companies, (2) mutuals, (3) reciprocal exchanges, and (4) Lloyd's Associations. In addition, in the field of health insurance, there have developed various forms of health insurance associations. Before examining these types of insurers, an overview of their relative importance in the three different lines of insurance may be useful.

Property insurance. In terms of premium income, the capital stock property insurance companies dominate, as Exhibit 15–1 indicates.

Life insurance and annuities. In 1971, life insurance companies collected over $29.5 billion of life insurance and annuity premiums.[3] With 1,818 legal reserve life insurance companies doing business, 1,664 were capital stock companies and 154 were mutual companies.[4] The mutuals, representing less than 10 percent of the total number, had about two-thirds of the assets of all U.S.

---

[2]For an extensive treatment of this subject, see Mehr and Cammack, *Principles of Insurance,* 4th ed. (Homewood, Illinois: Richard D. Irwin, 1966), Chapters 23, 24, 25.

[3]*Best's Insurance Reports, Life and Health, 1972* (New Jersey: Alfred M. Best, 1973), p. vii.

[4]*Life Insurance Fact Book, 1972* (New York: Institute of Life Insurance, 1972), p. 89.

Exhibit 15–1   Premiums Written by Private Property Insurers, 1971*

		Amount (in billions)	% of total
839	capital stock companies	$24.96	70.65
418	mutual companies	8.65	24.48
69	reciprocals and Lloyd's	1.72	4.87
		$35.33	100.00

*Data compiled from *Argus Chart FCS*, 1972 (Cincinnati: National Underwriter Co.), p. 202. Premiums written total less than the $38.2 billion previously shown because approximately $2 million of health insurance premiums are excluded, $800 million written by four factory mutuals are excluded, and some of the smaller companies are excluded.

companies and over one-half of the life insurance in force.[5] The reason for this seeming disparity is principally that the mutuals include among their numbers some of the oldest and largest companies, as Exhibit 15–2 indicates.

Exhibit 15–2   Fifty Largest Life Insurance Companies (December 31, 1971)*

Company	Total assets		Ins. in force	
	Rank	(Mil. $)	Rank	(Mil. $)
†Prudential	1	31,160	2	168,253
†Metropolitan Life	2	29,163	1	177,014
†Equitable Society	3	15,395	3	82,777
†New York Life	4	11,268	7	54,058
†John Hancock	5	10,604	4	64,827
Aetna Life	6	7,804	5	62,907
†Northwestern Mutual	7	6,453	11	21,216
Connecticut General	8	5,669	8	36,497
Travelers	9	5,044	6	59,651
†Massachusetts Mutual	10	4,566	12	20,907
†Mutual of New York	11	3,947	15	16,988
Sun Life, Canada	12	3,874	13	19,968
†New England Life	13	3,752	16	16,285
†Connecticut Mutual	14	2,922	24	11,338
†Mutual Benefit	15	2,698	18	14,195
Teachers Ins. & Ann.	16	2,597	100	2,577
†Penn Mutual	17	2,512	33	9,607
Lincoln National	18	2,364	10	22,768
†The Bankers Life	19	2,251	26	11,265
†Manufacturers Life, Canada	20	2,193	30	10,066
†Western & Southern	21	1,980	29	10,164
National Life & Acc. (NLT Corp.)	22	1,890	23	11,553

[5]*Life Insurance Fact Book*, p. 87.

Exhibit 15–2 (Cont.)

Company	Total assets		Ins. in force	
	Rank	(Mil. $)	Rank	(Mil. $)
Occidental Life (Transamerica)	23	1,796	9	26,710
Continental Assurance (CNA)	24	1,770	17	15,333
London Life, Canada	25	1,734	19	12,424
Great-West, Canada	26	1,634	22	11,591
†National Life, Vermont	27	1,522	48	5,888
American National	28	1,487	28	10,469
†Phoenix Mutual	29	1,447	35	8,409
†Canada Life	30	1,407	32	9,753
Franklin Life	31	1,311	39	8,182
†State Mutual	32	1,305	40	8,025
†Mutual Life, Canada	33	1,288	41	7,987
†Provident Mutual	34	1,191	49	5,823
Southwestern Life	35	1,122	55	5,565
Jefferson Standard (Jeff.-Pilot)	36	1,056	66	3,963
†Guardian Life	37	993	47	6,076
†Pacific Mutual	38	992	53	5,667
Equitable Life, Iowa	39	958	88	2,857
†Confederation Life, Canada	40	934	38	8,234
†Union Central	41	919	63	4,195
State Farm Life	42	902	25	11,274
Life of Virginia (Richmond Corp.)	43	895	45	6,478
†Home Life, New York	44	885	44	6,578
Liberty National	45	865	57	5,500
†Crown Life, Canada	46	810	34	9,405
United Benefit	47	770	37	8,322
No. Amer. Life, Canada	48	749	46	6,159
Provident Life & Acc.	49	718	21	11,682
†Minnesota Mutual	50	695	20	12,211

*Includes Canadian cos.
†Denotes mutual cos.
Note: Company in parentheses indicates parent organization.
Source: A. M. Best Co. Standard and Poor's "Industry Surveys," January 18, 1973, p. I 14.

Health insurance. Health insurance is the one line that is sold by both property insurance companies and life insurance companies. In addition, a group of associations have developed which specialize in providing health services on an insurance pool basis. The most prominent of this type by far are the Blue Cross-Blue Shield associations. In 1971, nearly $24 billion in premiums were collected for health insurance. This was divided among the insurer types as follows:[6]

---

[6]*Argus Chart, Health Insurance, 1972* (Cincinnati: National Underwriter Co., 1972), p. 112. Totals for a few, smaller insurers not included.

Life insurance companies $11.88 billion (50.2 percent of total)
Property insurance companies $ 1.97 billion (8.3 percent of total)
Blue Cross-Blue Shield type
    organizations $ 9.82 billion (41.5 percent of total)

Reciprocals and Lloyds associations write only negligible amounts of health insurance.

Stock Companies. The *stock company* is a corporation owned by the stockholders and operated for profit. It is also called a *capital stock* company. Stock companies selling life insurance are often referred to as *old line legal reserve* stock companies. The term "old line" has no legal or other significance. It probably grew out of competition during the nineteenth century with other insurers, principally fraternals and assessment mutuals, which were operating on various assessment pooling bases.

The term *legal reserve* does have legal as well as practical significance. A life insurer cannot represent itself to be a "legal reserve" company unless its corporate charter requires the company to maintain (1) minimum *legal reserves* on policyholders' premium payments, (2) minimum stated capital and surplus funds, and (3) other operating safeguards. The term "legal reserve" applies to both capital stock and mutual companies which qualify as such.

Mutual Companies. Mutual companies operate under a charter but have no stockholders; ownership is vested in the policyholders. There are two basic types of mutuals: *assessment mutuals* and *advanced premium mutuals*.

Assessment mutuals are so named because they choose to assess their insureds when it is necessary to accumulate funds in the pool from which claims are paid—this, instead of the more usual practice of charging adequate *premiums* in advance. The frequency and amount of these assessments vary greatly among the different mutuals. Most use a hybrid pricing system by charging advance premiums but reserving the right to assess sporadically when the funds in the pool are not adequate.

There are many mutual assessment property insurers, but their operations typically are local in nature, consisting primarily of insuring rural properties—hence their most typical designation: "county mutuals." In this activity, they serve a market a part of which other type insurers do not normally pursue energetically. An unpainted barn or isolated farmhouse are properties that many stock companies would be willing to allow—even strongly prefer—someone else to insure. These are specialty risks where the chance of loss varies greatly because of local conditions. Well-managed county mutuals serve an important function in such cases.

Assessment mutual property insurers in many states are subjected to somewhat less rigid regulations, including lenient licensing requirements for their agents. For this reason, they are sometimes used by large stock companies for special or unusual situations—such companies reinsuring the assessment mutuals to assure financial stability. We find an example in the insuring of mobile homes by using an auto insurance policy form instead of a residential policy, creating more flexibility in the rate structure, and permitting mobile home dealers to sell the insurance where they are not licensed to sell other lines of property insurance.

In the field of insuring human lives on a permanent basis, the assessment approach has proved unworkable. Such an insurance pool might seem to be operating successfully for a period of years; but, sooner or later, as the *average age* of the insureds increases, the younger persons drop out or refuse to join, preferring the guaranteed lower cost protection of legal reserve companies. The assessment mutual life insurance companies which exist today have switched over to varying degrees of actuarially sound *advanced premium* methods involving accumulation of reserves. Some of these are referred to as "stipulated premium" or "legal reserve assessment" companies.

The most significant group of insurers in this category are known as *fraternals*. Fraternals, even though usually considered a separate *type* of insurer, are mutuals in the sense that they operate under a government charter, have no stockholders, and have members who are jointly liable to the insurance pool. A difference lies in the "open" nature of the insurance contract, which makes the insurance agreement subject to the fraternal charter and by-laws in addition to the terms of the policy itself. Even though fraternals have played a significant role in the development of this country's life insurance industry, they account for less than 2 percent of the insurance now in force.[7] Many of the fraternals have changed to full legal reserve basis.

Assessment mutuals play a very small role in the health insurance field. In some states, there are assessment mutuals operating as health insurers selling individual policies. Many of their policyholders are not aware of the legal nature of their contracts.

In considering a mutual assessment insurer, we should recognize that such companies may rate from "A" to "Z" on financial condition and performance. We should make appropriate investigation before buying from them. Other things being equal and assuming the buyer has a choice, a more dominant insurer type should normally be chosen. A factor of special significance is that former members of a defunct and insolvent assessment mutual may in some circumstances be further assessed by state officials to pay claims outstanding against the company.

Advance premium mutuals have three significant characteristics:

1. They operate on an *advance premium* basis as do stock companies.
2. They may qualify with the state regulatory bodies to issue a policy which is non-assessable and to have a charter or other provision guaranteeing that the insured has no contingent liability as an "owner-member" of the

---

[7]*Life Insurance Fact Book,* pp. 28, 100.

mutual. One important requirement to qualify for this is the establishment of specified surplus and reserve funds.

3. They are subjected to the same relatively strict regulation as the stock insurers.

From the standpoint of his financial responsibility as a policyholder, an individual owning a policy with such a mutual is in the same position as with a capital stock insurer.

There are many such advance premium mutuals in the property, life, and health insurance fields. Their importance in each of these fields has been previously noted.

Reciprocal Exchanges. A reciprocal exchange is legally and theoretically an entirely different approach to pooling risks. An exchange is not an insurer, but a facility (personnel and physical accommodations for the activities necessary) through which each member reciprocally insures all other members individually (not jointly as in a mutual). In a "reciprocal exchange of insurance agreements" among, for example, 1,000 individuals wishing the same amount and kind of insurance, each individual insures every other for $\frac{1}{1000}$ of the amount of protection. This theoretically complicated procedure is simplified through the wording of a single policy issued to the insured.

An attorney-in-fact is empowered by each insured to act for him. The attorney-in-fact performs all the necessary activities of an insurance pooling operation, such as getting new members, rejecting would-be members who are not acceptable risks, determining premiums, paying claims and making investments. The attorney-in-fact is compensated for his services usually in terms of a stated percentage of the premiums. Where the premiums collected are not adequate, each member can be assessed for the deficiency. Some reciprocals have accumulated such large surpluses that the possibility of assessments is very unlikely. In fact, some states permit issuance of a non-assessable reciprocal insuring contract where surpluses and other aspects of the "Exchange" meet specified requirements. Where this is the case, the reciprocal is practically the same as an advanced premium mutual from the standpoint of the insurance buyer's position. Reciprocal exchanges operate primarily in the property insurance field and handle a very small percent of the total premiums paid to insurance companies. There are fewer than fifty reciprocals in operation.

A prospective member of a reciprocal should make a careful investigation with special attention given to the financial history, scope of operation, surplus funds and management (attorney-in-fact), and any contingent liability there might be from membership.

Lloyd's Associations. We probably should first point out that the only significant Lloyd's operating in our country is Lloyd's of London. There are currently only thirteen Lloyd's associations in the United States, and all but two of those are in Texas.

The role of Lloyd's of London in the United States is basically the reinsuring of certain policies placed by other insurers where the amount of risk is beyond the limit of the individual insurer and the insuring of unique and unusual risks which conventional companies would not undertake. If Joey Heatherton, Raquel Welch, Joe Namath, or Paul Newman—recognizing their earning potential for the next ten years is related to their physical allure—wanted to buy $5 million insurance against the risk of physical disfigurement, the insurance almost certainly would have to be placed with Lloyd's of London. Such a policy probably fails the tests for an insurable risk (see Chapter 14). Where such is the case, the insurer is gambling with the unknown. Lloyd's of London's history started with this "liberal" view; hence their willingness (coupled with the financial strength, "know how," and very substantial premium charges for such risks) to insure risks other insurers will not consider.

A Lloyd's Association theoretically is not an insurer in itself, but it provides certain services such as (1) underwriting information, (2) writing and issuing policies, (3) loss adjustments, and (4) office space for member *underwriters*. These underwriters join together in insuring individual risks, each underwriter agreeing to insure a specified amount of the total protection stated in the policy. Indeed, Lloyd's of London was formed in 1769 for just such a group of underwriters who wanted to organize and formalize their previous practice of "betting," along with several others, on the successful completion of the voyage of a cargo ship to the new world or other areas. Shipowners were willing to undertake such activities when they could substitute a small certain loss (payment of premiums to underwriters at Lloyd's) for the relatively large uncertain loss (total loss of ship and cargo). There are currently about 6,000 underwriter members of Lloyd's of London.

Lest the unusual operations of Lloyd's sidetrack us from the basic assumption that insurance is simply a pooling arrangement whereby a large number of people contribute to a pool from which the relatively few who suffer losses are indemnified, we should point out that Lloyd's cooperating underwriters perform this pooling function.

American Lloyd's. Even though the circumstances of a particular American Lloyd's association might well be very substantial and able to perform a worthwhile insuring function, a would-be insurance buyer should keep in mind that their financial resources are often relatively meager. The number of underwriters is very small and they are usually represented by an attorney-in-fact speaking for all the underwriters.

Health Associations. Mid-twentieth century saw the concern and fear of Americans over medical expenses reflected in the emergence of many types of private arrangements for sharing these expenses. An example was a group of school teachers in Dallas who, in 1929, joined together in a contract with Baylor Hospital for prepaid hospital services. This was the origin of the Blue Cross concept.[8] By 1971, it had expanded to over 150 Blue Cross, Blue Shield,

---

[8]*Source Book of Health Insurance Data* (New York: Health Insurance Institute, 1970), p. 6.

and similar organizations with approximately 40 percent of the over $20 billion private health insurance industry. The existing private insurance industry accounted for the balance (approximately 50 percent for life insurance companies and 10 percent for property insurance companies).[9]

A Blue Cross Association is a non-profit insurance corporation approved by the American Hospital Association and controlled by the hospital members making up the Association. The specific provisions for control vary among the different Blue Cross groups. They generally do not compete with each other; each serves its own territory. Usually the controlling board of directors includes hospital directors, physicians, and representatives of the general public.

The Blue Shield Associations are technically separate insurers, but in practice they work in conjunction with Blue Cross. Originally organized and controlled by cooperating doctors, each Blue Shield Association is usually like its corresponding Blue Cross Association. With Blue Cross primarily offering insurance to pay for hospital expenses and Blue Shield providing insurance to pay for physician fees, these plans have had to work out administrative and competition problems with the emergence of major medical coverages. Since major medical pays for all health expenses (including hospital, medicines, treatment, as well as physician fees) in excess of the basic hospital and surgical fee plan, it became impractical for the two groups to confine their coverages to their original areas. The resulting trend has been for Blue Cross and Blue Shield associations to have closer identity with one another, although in some instances they are competing in the sale of major medical insurance.

Other cooperative type health associations center around industry and union employee groups, consumer groups, medical associations, hospitals, and medical clinics. These are essentially mutual insurance associations with control and financial responsibility resting with the consumers in some groups, with the organizers or operators in other groups.

Further Considerations in Choosing an Insurer

A Priority of Objectives

If, with the preceding brief orientation on the types of insurance companies as a starter, a family were buying an insurance policy today, how should it go about choosing an insurer? Where is reliable information available about insurance companies? How much faith can be placed in insurance agents' recommendations? Are there any special pitfalls to avoid? Is one particular company or one particular type of company likely to give a better price or a better policy, or both?

Recognizing that, in this country, there are presently over 2,700 property insurance companies, over 1,800 life insurance companies, plus many health associations, we know at least that we can be selective.

---

[9]*Argus Chart,* p. 112.

Choosing the insurer from which to buy is a last step in a larger decision. When we arrive at this point we have already surveyed our current and future financial uncertainties, decided which ones could best be handled through insurance, have probably found that our insurance budget does not permit full coverage of all these particular risks, and have accordingly decided which insurance purchases would give us the greatest total security. Only *then* are we ready to do business with an insurance company.[10]

Even though we are not likely to be making the decision on the same basis, the matter of choosing an insurer is not too unlike the problem of choosing a spouse: there are many choices; we have long sought the perfect one and found there is none; many are acceptable on all counts with varying degrees of excellence in various desirable attributes; and, in some instances, it might well be a lifetime association. This analogy suggests the need to describe these desired attributes and then to decide on their relative importance. In the case of the insurer decision, we accordingly should describe any significant objectives (attributes of the insurer) and then establish a relative priority among the objectives.

Suggested important objectives in choosing an insurer are, in order of priority: (1) the strength and stability of the company, (2) a quality product (favorable policy benefits and provisions), (3) good service, and (4) the lowest price commensurate with the other objectives.

Strength and stability. Rights and obligations under a contract are one thing. The ability of the parties to perform their obligations is something else. We might have contract rights that are exceedingly favorable, but they are of little value if the other party cannot perform. Since we buy insurance to *eliminate* financial risks, we probably should make present and future financial strength the first and most important consideration in choosing an insurer. One need only look at the several-page listing of "Retired Insurers" in Best's annual reports to find examples of insurance company failures, including companies of all types (stock, mutual, etc.) and all lines (property, life and health).

The Alfred M. Best Company reports on insurance companies and the insurance industry. It annually publishes *Best's Insurance Reports, Life and Health,* and *Best's Insurance Reports, Property and Casualty* in which it (1) assigns ratings to property insurers and (2) gives either varying degrees of recommendation to life insurers or chooses not to recommend them. Best's is generally acknowledged as an authoritative and reliable insurance reporting service. These annual reports are available in most of the larger libraries. Dunne's International Insurance Reports of Louisville, Kentucky also publishes reports in which insurers are rated. It is a matter of record that Dunne's gives very favorable ratings to hundreds of companies which Best's chooses not to recommend.

Lest the preceding discussion leave the impression that private insurance has a questionable record on company failures, the contrary should be emphasized.

---

[10]The text handling of this sequence is found in Chapters 17 and 18.

Probably no other industry, including other fiduciary institutions—such as banks and savings and loan associations—has performed as well through the years. The "retiring" of most insurance companies from business involves mergers with other insurers and changes in corporate structures. Even so, there have been failures with losses to policyholders, and there will likely be more. It behooves the family insurance decision-maker to be aware of this.

Product (*Policy Benefits and Provisions*). Like most everything else we buy, insurance policies vary in quality—in terms of benefits and provisions in the contract. There are significant exceptions. The family automobile policy has been standardized to the point of being almost completely uniform in all fifty states. This situation has been brought about through joint action of the insurance companies and the insurance regulating authorities of all the states.[11] There is also a high degree of uniformity in inland marine (property "on the move") and comprehensive personal liability coverages. The basic fire insurance policy is uniform in each state and, to high degree, among all states. Many states also require uniformity on additional protection issued along with the fire policies. The most notable examples are *extended coverage* (windstorm, hail, explosion, riot and civil commotion, damage by aircraft or vehicle, and smoke damage) and the *homeowner's* policy. Since the above described coverages represent most of the property insurance a family or individual buys, we can say there is a fairly high degree of uniform quality of the products offered by the competing property insurers. There are exceptions, which might be more liberal or less liberal. The individual buyer of property insurance should think in these terms: "Am I getting the standard policy? If not, how does it differ from the standard?"

In the life insurance field, there is no such thing as a uniform policy offered by all insurers. However, there are uniform basic provisions which the states require in *all* policies. These uniform provisions cover the most important aspects of the life policy and—even though the marketing efforts of the competing companies make much of the infinite differences in the non-uniform provisions—the buyer is fairly well protected on the quality aspect of the basic life *policy form*. The all-important provisions are those relating to payment of the death, endowment, and cash-or-loan provisions. The state-imposed uniform provisions adequately insure the quality of all legal reserve life policies on these points.

Other provisions such as (1) reinstatement, (2) change of plan, and (3) settlement options—even though significant in special instances—are relatively unimportant. It is in these areas that the life policies vary greatly in "quality" among the offerings of the different insurers. The same is true of various *riders* to the basic life policy, such as premium waiver, accidental death, and guaranteed insurability. A rider to an insurance policy amends the basic contract. In the case of life insurance, most riders are actually additional insurance cover-

---

[11]Even this uniformity can be undone in some instances in this and other uniform policies through endorsements which alter the terms of the basic policy.

age. Here there are almost infinite "quality" differences among the offerings of the over 1,800 life insurance companies. The extent of these differences will be illustrated in Chapter 16.

It is in the health insurance field that quality of product in terms of the policy benefits and provisions varies the greatest. There is a higher degree of uniformity in the group health insurance coverages than in individual policies; but even here there are significant differences. Among the various types of insurers there are tendencies toward quality differences, but no definitive studies are available to justify enunciating these. In addition, health insurance is such a volatile field that what may be true now may not be so later. We are justified in pointing out that there are a number of examples of health insurers among the stock and mutuals whose policies, in the aggregate, pay out an unconscionably low percent of the premium dollar in benefits. Specific information relative to this is available in the annual report of the insurers to the state insurance departments. A more convenient source is the annual edition of the *Argus Chart,* which compiles this information from the state insurance department reports and from information supplied by the insurance companies. The *Argus Chart* is available in many libraries or can be ordered directly from the publisher at a nominal price.[12]

Service (Facilities, Performance Record and Reputation, Agency Representation.) An individual purchasing an insurance policy starts a business relationship with the insurer that may continue for years—even for a lifetime. From the standpoint of the service he will receive, consideration should be given to the company's physical and personnel facilities for providing service, to its performance record and reputation on service, and to the quality of its agency representation.

In many matters, it is difficult to communicate effectively and expeditiously on insurance by correspondence alone. Where personal service seems important, an individual should find out as best he can what facilities the company has locally. Questions pertinent to the insurer representative may include: "Do you have local service offices?" "How long have you maintained such a local office?" "Is it strictly a sales office, or are there adequate claim and other service facilities?"

The best assurance for satisfactory service in the future is a history of favorable performance in the past. Finding such information is not easy, nor is it always possible; but a buyer should recognize its importance and find what he can. The questions raised in the previous paragraph might yield such information, as may contacts with references, other policyholders, and firms with previous and continuing dealings with the insurer.

The matter of the quality of a company's agency representation is probably the most significant aspect of an insurer's service. There are over 450,000 people engaged in sales work for private insurers—an average of approxi-

---

[12]*Argus Chart,* National Underwriter Co., 420 East Fourth Street, Cincinnati, Ohio, 45202 (single copy—$4).

mately one per 500 in the population. Since most agents specialize in either personal insurance or property insurance, the ratio is, in actuality, more like one per 1,000 of population for each type of insurance. Their employment status varies from salaried and commissioned agency employees to independent agents and brokers. The latter two are not company employees and are engaged solely in negotiating insurance contracts between the insurer and the insured. There are many pros and cons in determining which is the preferable status from the buyer's point-of-view. There is no basis for making general conclusions on this, but the insurance buyer should be aware of the particular employment status of the salesman.

Probably the most important aspects of an agent's service are his recommendations on which coverages to purchase and his role in persuading a buyer to act *now* on needed protection. The qualitative aspect of these recommendations is *compatibility with the needs of the insured.* Since individual and family needs change through the years, the agent should keep informed and make appropriate recommendations for changes. If the agent is to perform this service well, he should possess a number of qualifications. Among the more significant of these are:

1. A professional approach based on putting the insured's welfare before his own material gain

2. A broad educational background *and* specialized, continuing education and training in insurance

3. A commitment to sell for a company or companies which he considers to be the best or as good as the best

4. Experience and intellect to make sound judgements and recommendations

These qualifications may seem too stringent to be realistic, but as insurance buyers we should ask ourselves: "Would we like to deal with an agent who is seriously lacking in any of these?"

There is no sure way of determining whether an agent is so qualified, but it is not as impossible as it may seem. The agent's approach to offering his services tells much. Talking first of the customer's *needs* and *interests* is desirable—this as opposed to a "package sale" approach, trying to sell a special policy, often represented as "revolutionary in nature" with added special features such as "paying quadruple benefits if killed while a passenger on a common carrier wrecked by a tornado."

Attainment of the professional designation, C.L.U. (Chartered Life Underwriter) and C.P.C.U. (Chartered Property and Casualty Underwriter) by the agent is further assurance of competence, even though there are thousands of dedicated and able insurance agents who do not have either designation. There are other indicators, such as his reputation in the business and in the community; a recommendation by attorneys, bankers, and accountants; and his length of time in the business. The latter qualification is prejudicial to the new agent and it is true that all good agents were new at one time. This is, of course, a common dilemma in all areas of society.

The insurance industry practice of compensating agents on a commission basis is generally compatible with the insured's best interest, but there is one related problem area in the life insurance business. The basis of most life insurance companies' arrangements with their agents is a "graded scale" commission. Depending on the company and the limitations imposed on it by the states in which it operates, the maximum commission on the first year's premium varies among companies from 55 percent to rare cases of 100 percent.[13]

Let's take an example. Mr. Smith is thirty years old and has a wife and four young children wholly dependent on his earnings. He has now only $5,000 life insurance in force. The Smiths have determined the absolute maximum life insurance expenditure they can put into their present budget is $200 annually. If agent Jones is on a "top 55 percent" commission contract, he will make $110 first year commission if he recommends whole life; he would probably make less than $50 if he recommended buying all twenty year family income protection.[14] In such a case, the agent may be forced to choose between his own greater profit and the client's greater benefit.

It is a matter of record that there is higher turnover of agents selling individual life and health insurance than is found among those selling property insurance. Since there is definitely a service aspect related to such a turnover, the insurance buyer should be especially selective in choosing the agent with whom he will deal on life and health insurance matters.

Price. Recognizing that most family budgets do not permit buying enough insurance protection to guard against all contingencies, we can accept the desirability of making *price* one of the objectives in the buying decision. It follows that the lower the price of each insurance unit, the more insurance units can be purchased.

What potential is there for an astute insurance buyer to affect lower unit costs? Unhappily, no simple or completely accurate answer is possible. There *are* price differences on some coverages but—in a specific buying instance—the individual must seek these out. Only general comments on the pricing situation in the various lines of insurance can be made. Before doing so, we should emphasize that price comparisons are difficult where the products (policy benefits and provisions) are not uniform. Our earlier comments on the degree of uniformity among the various lines should be kept in mind. Where there are not great differences in the product, examples of the extremes in price

---

[13]Some states set a maximum which any company operating in that state and other states may pay. A company operating in New York cannot pay more than 55 percent of the first year premiums to any of its agents, no matter where they work. The word *maximum* is used because the first year commission as a percent of the premium is graded down to as low as 10 percent, depending on the life insurance policy sold. The highest commission is paid on whole life, the lowest on one-year renewable term.

[14]It should be pointed out that the matter of which policy or combination of policies to buy may be a more philosophical than ethical question. Who is to say how much of the $200 should be spent for protection on the one in eight chance that Smith will not live until the youngest child is grown; and what part of the $200, if any, should represent an increasing savings account in a whole life policy, thus assuring more permanent insurance beyond the family period?

variation among competing companies range from no variation (in some states where policy form and price are set by the state) to a difference of 200 percent and even 300 percent (example: $1,000 accidental death benefit priced from $.55 to $1.75 per year). Recall also the examples in Chapter 14.

Rate classifications. The matter of the *rate classification* assigned us is often very significant. As noted in Chapter 14, the insurance industry has developed a system of charging different prices for the same policy through a system of grouping insureds in different rate classes. Classes are based on differences in the probability of loss. Assigning rate classifications to individual risks is not automatic and is often based on the judgment of the agent and home office underwriters. This is true in all lines. Herein lies a significant area of price savings for the family insurance buyer: to secure the most favorable possible rate classification, even if it requires applying to more than one company.

Dividends. Policy dividends are often thought of solely as a return of a mutual insurance company's profits to its owners, the policyholders. This is only partially true. A more accurate picture requires considering dividends in the property insurance field separately from dividends in life insurance.

Property insurance dividends. In property insurance, policy dividends do originate as mutual insurance company profits distributed to its owner-policyholders rather than to a group of stockholders. If these dividends were solely funds that would otherwise be paid to stockholders, the amount would often be relatively small.[15]

In order to get more substantial dividends, the mutual property insurers have tended to seek out "better" risks; they have also increased their dividend fund through lower marketing costs (lower commissions to agents or—in some companies—use of salaried agents). In response to this competition, many capital stock property insurers have followed these practices, typically using an affiliated stock company which pays dividends. How does the individual get his insurance in such a stock company? It is not necessarily automatic. Some agents and some companies are inconsistent, issuing the dividend policy only when the buyer expects or requests it. Here again is a possible source of saving to the buyer.

Life insurance dividends. An area of confusion of life insurance policy dividends arises from two contrasting philosophies on the proper approach to pricing life insurance. The "par" philosophy is associated with mutual legal reserve companies; "non-par" with capital stock legal reserve companies, even though some of the latter type companies offer both "par" and "non-par" prices.

Proponents of the participating ("par") plan point out that when an insurance company issues a life insurance contract it may be required to perform

---

[15]Capital stock proponents counter with the traditional argument that the efficiencies resulting from the profit motive produce the lowest price possible. The mutuals retort that (1) they are competing in the same market and therefore must be just as efficient to survive and (2) their top decision makers (Board of Directors) are of the same nature as their capital stock counterparts: ownership so splintered geographically and percentagewise that control tends to be vested in a self-perpetuating group.

under it for many years into the future. For example: A whole life policy is issued to a child at birth who lives to be age 100 and who then leaves the proceeds to a beneficiary age fifty under a life income option who lives also to age 100. The insurer would have contractual obligations under this policy for 150 years. During each of these years it would experience mortality, interest, and administrative costs. This example would be most unusual, but it is very typical for life insurance companies to be obligated under a substantial proportion of their policies for periods of several decades. Exhibit 15–3 indicates the range of the duration of life policies which become death claims. The proceeds of many of these are left with the insurer and paid out to beneficiaries over an additional period of years.

Exhibit 15–3   Duration of an Ordinary Life Insurance Policy when it became a Death Claim, May, 1969*

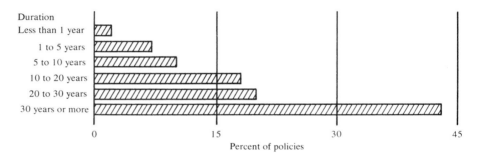

*"Ordinary" in this context refers to all legal reserve life insurance other than group and industrial.

Source: *Life Insurance Fact Book, 1971* (New York: Institute of Life Insurance), p. 47.

Because of this time factor, the "Par" proponents reason it is impossible to look into the future and determine mortality, interest returns and administrative costs (including taxes) precisely enough to set a level annual premium and other policy provisions cheap enough to the insured and safe enough to the company. The obvious alternative, it is reasoned, is to calculate the cost based on reasonable current assumptions and then add an admitted overcharge as a safety factor. With this is a contractual obligation to refund (usually annually) as much of this overcharge as possible on the basis of actual experience. A mutual company further agrees to include with this overcharge each year any distributable profits from the company's operations. Hence, the unfortunate term "dividend" was applied to this periodic (in nearly all cases annual) refund of an admitted overcharge.[16] More logically the payment would be divided into two parts: (1) annual refund (2) annual company profit dividend.

The mutual companies embraced this pricing policy from the beginning. They were no doubt influenced during the nineteenth century not only by a recognition of a relatively meager surplus but also by the uncertainties of future

---

[16]The Internal Revenue Department recognizes these "dividends" are substantially a refund of premiums and accordingly does not require reporting them as dividends.

cost factors in the then young and developing country. This may partially account for what to some might seem to be a large overcharge of typically 15 to 30 percent. The amount of this overcharge has tended to persist to the present, but the past decade has seen a trend of reducing "par" premiums. Very possibly strong competition in price and in numbers by capital stock companies has influenced this trend.

The case for the non-participating ("non-par") pricing philosophy involves a rebuttal of some of the theory of the par proponents as well as additional arguments. An insurance policy on a non-par basis provides for a fixed price for each of the years the policy is in force without any refunds or dividends of any nature. The reasoning would include the following. Mortality costs are the most precise and most predictable of all insurable risks. Interest rates do vary but not greatly—even in the short run, for the type of investments made by life insurance companies—and tend to average out in the long run (especially with the interest rate "managing" characteristic of our present day political economy). Administrative costs are a relatively small part of the policy costs and do not vary greatly over a period of time. A cost *advantage* of the non-par system lies in the absence of dividends and the costs attendant to 1) determining how much in total dividends should be paid, 2) calculating how much of the profits is attributal to each policy contract plus 3) the administrative cost of handling the dividend on each policy. Par advocates would minimize these factors in this computer age. A lower selling cost advantage is also claimed for non-par policies, attributed to the system in which an agent's commissions are based on percentage of the premium (resulting in a lower dollar commission). Some "par" companies rebut this by claiming that their commission scale is lower resulting in a lower dollar amount of commission.

The bromide, "the proof of the pudding is in the eating," would appear to apply here, since we have a performance history of well over a century. And, indeed, a few generalizations may be made concerning *participating* policies sold by mutual companies and *non-participating* policies sold by stock companies.

1. By definition, the "par" plan gives an additional financial safety factor to the insurer.

2. In the early policy years, the non-par premium is usually less than the par premium minus the dividend. In later years the reverse is usually true.

3. Most people don't die prematurely and—based on actual dividend histories—a young person in most instances has paid less net premiums under participating policies of mutual companies than under non-participating policies of stock companies.[17]

---

[17]This has been generally true, but there are exceptions among companies. Illustrations of actual dividend histories for all of the larger life companies can be found in annual editions of *Flitcraft Compend,* Flitcraft, Inc., Morristown, New Jersey, and in *Life Rates and Data* (formerly *Little Gem*), National Underwriter Co., Cincinnati. Many libraries have copies, as do most life insurance sales offices.

There still remains the question of the advisability of purchasing a "par" policy from a capital stock company. For this question, the individual is left to decide on the basis of all the factual information he can gather and to ponder philosophical considerations.

Discussion Questions

1. Explain the difference in terms of ownership between the following types of insurance companies: capital stock, mutual, reciprocal exchange, Lloyds, and Blue Cross-Blue Shield.

2. Why is it that over 90 percent of all life insurance companies are capital stock, yet they account for less than half the amount of life insurance in force?

3. What is the one line of insurance sold by both property insurers and life insurers? Which is the more active in this line?

4. What do we mean by the term "advance premium" mutuals?

5. What problems did the emergence of major medical coverage present to Blue Cross and Blue Shield organizations?

6. "In the life insurance field, there is no such thing as a uniform policy offered by all insurers." What have the states done to afford some protection to the public in regard to important provisions of life insurance policies?

7. What are the two most important aspects of an insurance agent's service?

8. What is meant by the initials C.L.U. and C.P.C.U.?

9. Explain the rationales behind the "par" and "non-par" life insurance pricing philosophies.

10. Roughly what percent of life insurance death claims involve policies which have been in force ten years or more?

11. How does the Internal Revenue Department treat dividends on life insurance policies?

We may take fancy for a companion, but
must follow reason as our guide.
[*Samuel Johnson*]

16

Policy Benefits and Provisions

The rationale for this chapter in relation to the preceding and following chapters can be viewed as a "who," "what," "where" approach.

"Who?" In the preceding chapter, after taking a brief overview of the scope of the insurance environment, we explored the matter of *who* the different insurer groups are (government and private, and the different classes of private insurers).

"What?" In this chapter, we will consider *what* specific insurance *benefits* are available and *what* provisions are stated in connection with qualifying for the benefits offered. This will be organized under four groupings: social security, life insurance, health insurance, and property insurance.

"Where?" The following two chapters will sort out our various personal exposures to losses and attempt to show *where* the many insurance benefits available might be used in connection with other means of dealing with these uncertainties. Another aspect of the *where* inquiry will be *whether* to use all, part, or none of the insurance benefits (protection) in preparing for various possible losses.

Social Security

Since our federal social security program is compulsory and woven permanently into our social fabric, it might seem academic to ask "why do we have it?" Even so, as we incorporate its benefits in our personal financial planning, we might gain some satisfaction in knowing of its origin and history.

The industrial revolution, with the resulting urbanization, specialization, and interdependence of labor, made inevitable the development of social insurance. The impact of a wide range of financial uncertainties facing the individual is much more acute in urban society than in the rural. In the rural economy, an individual could produce much of what he needed and could further count on the custom of reciprocal assistance from his neighbor. Both of these security factors largely disappeared for his urban counterpart.

Western civilization in the past century has gradually accepted the concept of having to choose between total welfare for large segments of society or a social *insurance* program to augment private *insurance,* plus a welfare program for the indigent sector. Germany pioneered modern social insurance in the late nineteenth century. Other nations followed during the early twentieth century. The United States was a latecomer in the field when it adopted a comprehensive program in 1935. Since then amendments liberalizing and extending its benefits were passed in 1939, 1946, 1950, 1952, 1954, 1956, 1958, 1960, 1961, 1965, 1967, 1969, 1971, and 1972.[1]

An individual dependent on his earnings for a livelihood is faced with the uncertainties of *unemployment, disability,* and *old age.* Others dependent on his earnings are further threatened with the possibility of his *premature death.* Recognition of these uncertainties is reflected in the various benefits of social security.

The Social Security Act provides for three separate programs: the Federal Old-Age, Survivors, Disability, and Health Insurance (OASDHI) program, more popularly known as "social security"; Public Assistance programs for people in need; and Unemployment Insurance for unemployed workers. The remainder of this section on "social security" will be concerned with the OASDHI program which provides four kinds of protection:

---

[1]Facts related here are based on the act as amended in 1972. The Social Security Administration issues a revised booklet, *Your Social Security,* each time the program is changed. Even more detailed information on changes is given in its monthly *Social Security Bulletin.* Any branch Social Security office will supply the current booklet and arrange a subscription to the monthly bulletin. Most libraries subscribe to the latter publication.

1. *Retirement Benefits*—To the retired worker at sixty-two or later and to his wife (or dependent husband) and dependent children.
2. *Disability Benefits*—To the worker under sixty-five (and to his dependents) who becomes severely disabled for a year or more and cannot work.
3. *Survivor Benefits*—To the widow (or dependent widower), children, and certain other dependents of a worker who was insured under social security.
4. *Medicare Health Insurance*—A hospital and medical insurance plan available to most people at sixty-five to help pay hospital, doctor, and other medical bills. Disabled people who have been getting benefit checks at least two years also have Medicare.

In addition to the above, a lump-sum death payment—generally $255—is payable upon the death of an insured worker.

These federal benefits are administered by the Social Security Administration (SSA), through its approximately 1,000 field offices and with help from state agencies in administering the disability program and aid from private insurance and other organizations in administering Medicare. Starting January 1974, SSA was also responsible for administering a new federalized supplemental security income program which provides a floor of income for the needy, aged, blind, and disabled. Before 1974, these programs were administered by individual states.

Wise family financial planning requires a fairly precise knowledge of what the benefits are and what their approximate amount will be in a specific family situation. Beyond this, it is practicable to have only an understanding of the scope and complexity of the administrative aspects of the social security program. With such a background, we will know how to get expert information (at the nearest social security office) when it appears we might be eligible for a benefit; we will also be aware of the need to know specifically what is required to *retain* eligibility once payments start. The following treatment of social security benefits and provisions is organized accordingly.

An exception to the rationale for the organization of Part IV, Reducing Losses through Insurance, will be made regarding social security unemployment insurance and medicare health insurance. Because of the uniqueness of these two coverages in the overall social security program, details regarding benefits and provisions will be related in the appropriate "where to use insurance" discussions in Chapters 17 and 18.

Cost

The cost of social security is shared equally by the employer and the employee. A self-employed person is given a concession on this cost; previously he paid three-fourths of the employer and employee's total; he now pays less than seven-tenths of the total. The employer must deduct from the employee's paycheck the percent of earnings applicable at the time. This amount and its matching contribution of the employer are continued during the calendar year until the stated *taxable earnings* amount has been reached during that year. In 1974, the rate was 5.85% *each* on earnings up to $12,000. The amount of these deductions is shown on most payroll statements under "FICA" (Federal Insurance Contributions Act).

Comment on the "costs" of these Social Security benefits is not necessary; the figures speak for themselves. An employee earning at the maximum rate in 1974 had nearly $60.00 a month deducted from his pay and—to the extent that the employer's contribution might be passed on to the employee in lower ultimate wages—his contribution is even more.

Over 90 percent of all wage earners are now covered under social security on a compulsory basis. Those not covered include: (1) most Federal Government employees, covered by Civil Service or certain other plans; (2) career railroad employees who are covered under a federally administered Railroad Retirement Act; and (3) state and local government and non-profit organization employees whose employers have not chosen to make the special arrangements required to have the coverage.

Professional men, clergymen, and members of religious orders who have not taken the vow of poverty are covered (those who *have* taken the vow can be covered under certain conditions). Active duty in the military service is covered; and noncontributory wage credits of $300 a quarter are granted for each quarter of active duty pay after 1957.

Eligibility

For a worker and/or his family to get monthly cash payments when he becomes disabled or retires or dies, he must first have credit for a certain amount of work under social security. This credit may have been earned at any time after 1936.

Most non-farm employees get credit for one-fourth year of work (called a "quarter of coverage") if they are paid $50 or more in a three-month calendar quarter. Also, a person may receive a full year of credit if his self-employment net income is $400 or more in the year. A person who has covered farm wages receives one-fourth year of credit for each $100 in wages he has (up to $400) in a year. In addition, any employee who earns the maximum wages creditable for social security for a year (i.e., $10,800 in 1973 and $12,000 in 1974) receives a full year of credit even if he works only part of the year.

If a person stops working under social security before he becomes insured, credits for the earnings reported for him will remain on his social security record. He can add to them if he later returns to covered work. No benefits based on his earnings can be paid to him or his family, however, until he has credit for enough earnings to become insured.

Certain types of benefits are payable if a person is currently insured, fully insured, or meets the special requirements for disability insurance protection.[2]

---

[2]A fourth insured status, "transitional," applies to certain persons who became 72 before 1972. Under specified conditions, such persons may receive a monthly life income of $58 a month ($87 for a couple).

Currently Insured. Even if a worker is not fully insured, benefits may be paid to his widow and their children if he is "currently insured" when he dies. He is currently insured if he has credit for at least 1½ years of work within three years before his death.

Fully Insured. If you are fully insured when you reach retirement age, you and certain members of your family can get monthly benefits. If you are fully insured at death, benefits can be paid to certain members of your family.

No one can be fully insured with credit for less than 1½ years of work, and a person who has credit for ten years of work can be sure that he will be fully insured for life. Having credit for sufficient work, however, means only that certain *kinds* of benefits may be payable—it does not determine the amount. The amount will depend on your average earnings over a period of years.

This chart shows how much work is needed to be fully insured for retirement or survivor benefits:

Worker who reaches 62 or dies in	Will need credit for no more than this much work
1974–75	6 years*
1976	6¼
1977	6½
1978	6¾
1979	7
1983	8
1987	9
1991 & later	10

*A woman needed less work for 1973 (5½ years) and 1974 (5¾ yr).
Note: Workers born after 1929 who die before age sixty-two would need even less work than that shown above.

Work Credits for Disability. If you become disabled before you are twenty-four, you need credit for 1½ years of work in the three years before you become disabled.

If you are between twenty-four and thirty-one, you must have credit for half the time between your twenty-first birthday and the time you become disabled.

If you become disabled at thirty-one or later, you need the same credit that you would need if you reached retirement age in the year you are disabled (see retirement chart), and five years of work must be in the ten-year period just before you become disabled.

Work Credits for Medicare. If you are eligible for a social security or railroad retirement check—as a worker, dependent, or survivor—you automatically have hospital insurance protection at sixty-five. If you are not eligible for a check, you need credit for some work under social security to get this part of Medicare. If you have not worked long enough, hospital insurance is still available by paying a monthly premium (currently $33). No work credits are needed for the medical insurance part of Medicare. However, there is a monthly premium to pay ($6.30 a month through June 30, 1974).

Types of Cash Benefits

This table shows the principal types of payments and the insured status needed for each.

Retirement	
Monthly payment to—	If you are—
*You as a retired worker (62 or over) and your wife and child	Fully insured
Your dependent husband 62 or over	Fully insured

Survivors	
Monthly payments to your—	If at death you are—
*Widow 60 or over or disabled widow 50–59	Fully insured
*Widow (regardless of age) if caring for your child who is under 18 or disabled and is entitled to benefits	Either fully or currently insured
Dependent child (under 18, student 18–22; over 18 and disabled before 22)	Either fully or currently insured
Dependent widower 60 or over and disabled dependent widower 50–59	Fully insured
Dependent parent at 62	Fully insured
Lump-sum death payment	Either fully or currently insured

Disability	
Monthly payments to—	If you are—
You and your dependents if you are disabled	Fully insured and if you meet special work requirements

*Under certain conditions, payments can also be made to your divorced wife or surviving divorced wife.

Reflecting on the relatively brief period of time necessary to attain Social Security insured status we might feel a person under certain circumstances can receive too much in benefits for the relatively small amount of premiums (FICA contributions). Recognizing this as insurance justifies the seeming inequity. For example, an individual getting an oral binder on a $100,000 apartment house fire policy could collect the full $100,000 if an unexpected fire started the next minute and destroyed the property, even though he had not paid anything at the time of loss.

Amount and Duration of Specific Benefits

Private insurance policies are typically based on a predetermined "face amount" ($100,000 fire insurance on a building, $100,000 life insurance on an individual); Social Security benefits are based on the *Primary Insurance*

Amount (PIA), which in turn is based on the *Average Monthly Earnings* (AME). The period for determining the average monthly earnings generally begins with 1951 or the year in which the insured became twenty-two, if later, and goes up to the year a person reaches retirement age, becomes disabled, or dies. The earnings *average* is computed from all earnings subject to social security contributions during the period divided by the total number of months in the period. Up to five years of low earnings (or no earnings) can be deleted in computing the average.

Within that period, if the insured does not work full-time in covered employment, the average monthly earnings (AME) would be significantly reduced. Another factor widening the gap between the AME and the actual earnings level is that only the amount of earnings subject to social security contributions for a particular year is counted. The maximum taxable earnings was much lower in earlier years, as shown in the following list.

Year	Maximum earnings taxed
1937–50	$ 3,000
1951–54	3,600
1955–58	4,200
1959–65	4,800
1966–67	6,600
1968–71	7,800
1972	9,000
1973	10,800
1974	12,000*

*The maximum amount of earnings that count for social security will rise automatically in the future as earnings levels rise, with the first increase possible no earlier than 1975.

Since up to five years of low or no earnings can be dropped, this helps the worker who either did not work in covered employment for a while or had below average earnings.

Figuring the Primary Insurance Amount. The present formula for figuring the primary insurance amount is as follows: 108.01 percent of the first $110 of average monthly earnings (AME); 39.29 percent of the next $290 AME; 36.71 percent of next $150; 43.15 percent of next $100; 24 percent of next $100; and 20 percent of balance of AME that can count for social security.

The above formula is generally used in figuring the primary insurance amount (PIA) for most workers. In some instances, however, a worker may be able to qualify for a PIA higher than he would normally be eligible for:

1. *Regular minimum benefit.* If a worker is insured but has a low AME (of $76 or less), he nevertheless is guaranteed a minimum benefit. In 1973 and 1974, this minimum was $84.50 a month.

2. *Special minimum benefit.* Under a 1972 change in the law, some people who work under Social Security many years, but at low pay, can receive a higher minimum benefit than would normally be paid. For example, a

Exhibit 16–1 Examples of Monthly Cash Benefits Under Old Age, Survivors and Disability Insurance

Benefit	% of PIA	Average monthly earnings									
		$76 or less	$150	$250	$350	$450	$550ᶜ	$650ᶜ	$750ᶜ	$850ᶜ	$1000ᶜ
		Primary insurance amount (PIA)									
		84ᵃ	134ᵃ	174	213	250	288	331	354	374	404
		Maximum family benefit									
		126	201	267	371	467	522	579	620	655	707
Retirement											
Insured, age 65	100 %	84	134	174	213	250	288	331	354	374	404
Insured, age 62	80 %	67	107	139	170	200	230	264	283	299	323
Wife, age 65	50 %	42	67	87	106	125	144	165	177	187	202
Wife, age 62	37.5%	31	50	65	80	94	108	124	133	140	152
Each child	50 %	42	67	87	106	125	144	165	177	187	202

328

Survivorship										
Widow, age 60	71.5%	73	96	125	152	179	206	236	253	267	289
Widow, age 65	100 %[b]	84	134	174	213	250	288	331	354	374	404
Widow any age with dependent child	75 %	84	100	131	160	188	216	248	265	280	303
Each child	75 %	84	100	131	160	188	216	248	265	280	303
Disability										
Insured, age 65	100 %	84	134	174	213	250	288	331	354	374	404
Wife with dependent child	50 %	42	67	87	106	125	144	165	177	187	202
Each child	50 %	42	67	87	106	125	144	165	177	187	202
Disabled widow at age 50	50 %	51	67	87	107	125	144	166	178	188	203
Lump sum death benefits		253	255	255	255	255	255	255	255	255	255

[a] A person who worked under social security more than 22 years, but at relatively low pay, may qualify for a special minimum benefit higher than the usual amount. With 30 or more years of coverage, the benefit would be $170 a month.

[b] If either the widow or her deceased spouse received reduced social security benefits before 65, then the widow will receive *less* than 100% at 65.

[c] Higher benefits shown in the columns on the right generally won't be payable until later. Top retirement benefit for a worker who was 65 in 1973 was $266.10 per month. Maximum family benefits in 1973: $490.10 for a retired worker and his family; $599.40 for a disabled worker and his family; and $620.40 for the family of a deceased worker.

worker retiring at sixty-five with twenty-five years of coverage could get
$127.50 a month, and one with thirty or more years coverage could get
$170 a month. Under the old law, he might have received only the min-
imum benefit of $84.50 if he had minimum wages.

3. *Delayed retirement credit.* A worker who does not start getting retirement checks until after sixty-five gets a special credit which can mean a
   benefit larger than his usual PIA. For each year between sixty-five and
   seventy-two that he delays retirement, his benefit amount is increased 1
   percent.

Range of Benefits. Maximum benefit for a man who retired at sixty-five in
1973 was $266.10 a month. Top family benefits in 1973 were $490.10 for a
retired worker and his family, $599.40 for a disabled worker and his family,
and $620.40 for the family of a young deceased worker. Exhibit 16–1 gives
examples of monthly cash benefits under OASDHI based on a wide range of
average monthly earnings.

It is possible for a younger worker to have a higher PIA because earnings
may be averaged over a shorter period of time (i.e., since age twenty-two) and
may include a larger percentage of years when the social security contribution
base was larger. For this reason, family benefits—in the case of disability or
death—can be higher.

Relation of Benefits to PIA. An insured worker's unreduced benefit is the primary insurance amount. All monthly social security benefits (including a worker's reduced benefit, if he starts drawing before sixty-five) are a certain percentage of the PIA:

1. *Worker.* His retirement benefit is reduced five-ninths of 1 percent for
   each month before sixty-five that he receives checks. If he retires at sixty-
   two, for example, this permanent reduction amounts to 20 percent, leaving him with 80 percent of the PIA.)

2. *Wife or dependent husband.* Either is potentially entitled to 50 percent
   of the worker's PIA. Benefits can start as early as sixty-two, but the
   amount is reduced $25/36$ of 1 percent for each month checks are taken
   early (25 percent reduction over three-year period).

3. *Aged widows and dependent widowers 60–65.* Both can get 100 percent
   of the PIA if they start getting benefits at sixty-five or later and the
   worker did not receive reduced benefits before his death. The reduction
   factor if a widow or widower becomes eligible between sixty and sixty-
   five is $19/40$ of 1 percent per month.

4. *Disabled Widows and Dependent Widowers 50–59.* In addition to a full
   reduction as shown in the category above, there would be an additional
   reduction of $43/240$ of 1 percent for each month benefits were taken early
   from age fifty through fifty-nine. A disabled widow's benefit at age fifty,
   then, would be 50 percent of the PIA, after all reductions are calculated.

5. *Child.* A child of a retired or disabled beneficiary is eligible for 50 percent of the PIA, and the child of a deceased worker can get up to 75 percent. There is no reduction factor involved, but the amount payable to each child (and other eligible beneficiaries) could be reduced so that total family benefits stay within the legal maximum payable for the particular PIA involved. Children eligible for benefits include natural children, adopted children, stepchildren, and (under certain conditions) grandchildren who are: under eighteen; full-time students eighteen to twenty-two; or over eighteen and become disabled before age twenty-two.

6. *Wife or widow with children.* A wife disabled or caring for eligible children under eighteen can get up to 50 percent of the PIA, and a widow with children 75 percent. There are no reduced benefits (except reduction because of maximum family benefits payable).

7. *Dependent parent (of deceased worker).* One parent is eligible for 82½ percent of the PIA at sixty-two or later (two dependent parents are eligible for 75 percent of the PIA each).

Benefits Are "Inflation Proof." Legislation in 1972 provided for automatic increases in Social Security benefits in future years to keep pace with increases in the cost of living. Whenever living costs rise 3 percent or more, benefits will be increased by the same amount the following January unless Congress has already acted to raise benefits. The first automatic increase cannot come before January 1, 1975.

Beneficiaries Who Work. It is not necessary to stop working completely to be eligible for social security benefits. A person can earn as much as $2,100 a year without having any benefits withheld. If annual earnings go above $2,100, $1 in benefits is withheld for each $2 in earnings above that amount.

No matter how much one earns in a year, however, he can still get full benefits for any month he does not earn more than $175 in wages or perform substantial services in self-employment. Both the annual and monthly limits will be raised automatically in future years as the level of average earnings rises.

Starting with the month a person is seventy-two, no benefits are withheld because of earnings.

Special rules apply to work performed by people getting benefits because of disability.

Earnings of a retired worker may affect his own and his dependents' checks, but earnings of a dependent or survivor affect only his own benefit.

Who Can Get Disability Checks?

Monthly disability benefits are payable to:

1. An insured disabled worker under sixty-five and his family.
2. A son or daughter who became severely disabled before twenty-two, when an insured parent receives retirement or disability benefits or when an insured parent dies.

3. A disabled widow (or dependent widower), fifty through fifty-nine, whose spouse was insured under social security.

Disability Defined. For social security purposes, "disability" means the inability to work because of (1) a severe physical or mental impairment that has lasted (or is expected to last) at least twelve months, or to result in death; or (2) "blindness," which is defined as either central visual acuity of 20/200 or less in the better eye with the use of corrective lenses, or visual field reduction to twenty degrees or less.

Payments to a disabled worker and his family or to a disabled widow or widower are generally payable for the sixth full month of disability. A son or daughter disabled in childhood is eligible as soon as a parent begins getting retirement or disability benefits or dies insured. Payments to a disabled worker are changed to retirement benefits, at the same rate, when he reaches sixty-five.

The test of inability to engage in *any* gainful activity is a stringent disability provision. Most commercial policies require only the inability to continue the type of employment engaged in at the time of the onset of disability for the first year or two; after that, they impose the inability to engage in *any* gainful occupation test.

The rules in the social security law for deciding whether a person is disabled also may be different from rules in some other government disability programs. A person may be eligible for disability benefits from another agency, for example, but be ineligible under social security.

Certain conditions which are ordinarily severe enough to be considered disabling under the law are described in the Social Security Regulations. Copies are available in any social security office.

If a person's social security disability claim is denied and he feels the decision is incorrect, he can ask the Social Security Administration to reconsider it. If the denial is upheld at this and two subsequent administrative levels, the individual can take his case to the federal courts.

Survivors Benefits

The value of survivorship protection under social security is significant. About 95 out of every 100 mothers and children in the country would be eligible for benefits in the event of death of the main breadwinner. The total of potential survivorship benefits is roughly equal to all life insurance in force in the private insurance industry.

Benefits are payable to: widowed mothers (with dependent children) at any age; dependent children who are under eighteen, or eighteen to twenty-two if in school full-time, or who have been seriously disabled since before age twenty-two; widows and dependent widowers at sixty or older (or at age fifty if disabled); and dependent parents sixty-two or older. Surviving divorced women also can qualify under certain conditions.

Survivor benefits for a widow with dependent children under age 18 are similar to decreasing term life insurance. In terms of what it does, it is like the family income life policy which will be described later in this chapter. A monthly income is paid from the time of the insured's death until the youngest dependent child reaches age 18, or 22 if in school full-time.

The survivorship monthly life income for a widow age sixty or over can be looked on as additional term life insurance on her husband. The amount of life insurance would be the cost of a life annuity for his widow starting at age sixty —or whatever later age she might be at his death prior to qualifying for retirement benefits.[3]

A lump-sum death payment can be made upon death of the insured, regardless of whether there are dependent survivors eligible for monthly benefits. The amount is usually $255 and generally is paid to the person who assumes responsibility for burial expenses, unless the surviving spouse is still living, in which case it usually is paid to her or him.

Qualifying for a surviving child's insurance benefit and a surviving widow's insurance benefit is not a problem in most cases, but more is involved than one might think. Because of the tremendous significance of survivorship benefits to every family and also to indicate the scope of technicalities involved in *any* of the OASDHI benefits, we are reproducing the following extracts from the *Social Security Handbook* as examples.[4]

419. A surviving child is entitled to child's insurance benefits if:

A. The worker-parent was either fully or currently insured at death (possible only if he died after 3/31/38); and

B. He (or she) is the child of the deceased; and

C. The child is:

1. Under age 18; or

2. Age 18 through 21 and a full-time student; or

3. Age 18 or over and under a disability as defined in § 507(A) (which began before age 18); and

D. The child was dependent upon the deceased parent (see §§ 342–345 for the dependency "tests"); and

E. The child is not married; and . . . .

420. The term "child" as used above, includes the insured worker's:

A. Legitimate child, or any other child who would have the right under applicable State law to inherit intestate personal property from the insured worker as his child. Applicable State law is that law which would be applied by the courts of the State in which the insured person was domiciled at his death, or if not then domiciled in any State, the courts of the District of Columbia.

B. Stepchild (under certain circumstances—see § 340).

---

[3]Actually, it is increasing term because every month the wife gets closer to age 60, the greater sum of money is required, with compound interest, to accumulate a fixed sum at her age 60—that sum being the amount of cash required to purchase a single premium life annuity of a stated amount.

[4]*The Social Security Handbook,* 4th ed. (U.S. Dept. of Health, Education, and Welfare, February, 1969), pp. 80–85.

C. Legally adopted child (see § 338).

D. Child of ceremonial marriage entered into under the conditions explained in § 337(A).

E. Illegitimate child (see § 334(E)) provided the insured worker:
   1. Had acknowledged in writing that the child is his son or daughter; or
   2. Had been decreed by a court, during his lifetime, to be the father of the child; or
   3. Had been ordered by a court, during his lifetime, to contribute to the support of the child because the child is his son or daughter; or
   4. Has been shown by satisfactory evidence to be the child's biological father, and was living with or contributing to the child's support at the time of his death. . . .

422. The child's insurance benefit may not be payable for some months if:

A. The child works and earns over $2,100 a year; or

B. The child is an alien living outside the U.S. for 6 months or more; or

C. The insured parent had been deported and the child is an alien living outside the U.S.; or

D. The disabled child, age 18 or over, refuses to accept vocational rehabilitation services without good cause. However, the child's insurance benefits are payable for all months in which the disabled child is still under age 22, if he is a full-time student, as defined in § 352; or . . . .

423. Surviving child's benefits end when:

A. The child dies; or

B. The child:
   1. Reaches age 18, unless it is established that the child is attending school full time or is under a disability that began before age 18; or
   2. Ceases, while age 18 through 21, to attend school full time *or* reaches age 22 while still attending school, unless it is established that the child is under a disability (which must have begun before age 18); or
   3. Ceases, while age 18 or over, to be under a disability, unless the child is still under age 22 and it is established that he is attending school full time; or

C. The child is adopted after the insured parent's death by someone other than a stepparent, grandparent, aunt, uncle, brother, or sister (or, in some cases, surviving natural parent); or

D. The child marries; however, if a disabled child age 18 or over marries another social security beneficiary, see § 1856. If the marriage is absolutely void or has been annulled *from the beginning,* see § 1857. . . .

424. A widow or "surviving divorced mother" is entitled to mother's insurance benefits (whether or not she has reached age 60) if:

A. The insured worker died either fully or currently insured (possible only if he died after 3/31/38); and

B. She has filed an application for mother's insurance benefits (see § 1511 for list of prescribed application forms; however, no application is required if she was entitled to wife's benefits for the month before the month in which the insured worker died); and

C. She is not entitled to a retirement benefit which is equal to or larger than the amount of the mother's insurance benefit, after any increase to the minimum (see § 720); and

D. She has in her care a child of the deceased worker under age 18 or disabled who is entitled to child's insurance benefits (see §§ 312–319 for definition of "in her care"); and

E. She is not married (see § 425); and

F. She meets one of the following conditions:

   1. She is the mother of the deceased worker's child (this requirement is met if she has borne her husband a live child, though the child need not still survive); or

   2. She legally adopted (as defined in § 338) his son or daughter before the child's eighteenth birthday and during her marriage to the worker; or . . . .

425. The remarriage of a widow or surviving divorced mother will prevent her from becoming entitled to mother's benefits on her prior deceased husband's social security record except where her subsequent marriage ends, whether by death, divorce, or annulment. If the subsequent marriage ends, she may become entitled or reentitled to mother's benefits on her prior deceased husband's (or former husband's) earnings record beginning with the month the subsequent marriage ends. If the remarriage was absolutely void or has been annulled *from the beginning,* see § 1857 . . . .

Even with the many qualifying requirements indicated by the preceding examples of specific provisions, most families with dependent children have this survivorship insurance protection. The likelihood of the deceased worker having a "currently insured" status (six quarters of coverage among the thirteen quarters preceding death) means this social insurance is in force in most instances by the time the insured has a dependent child.

A dependent *widower* (a husband who meets the requirements for qualifying as dependent on his wife's earnings) is entitled to similar survivorship benefits, but the wife must have been fully insured. In the typical family situation where both parents work, the husband is not eligible unless he was receiving at least one-half of his support from his wife.

We can see that social security protection against the loss of income due to disability or the insured's death or retirement provides a substantial base from which to build a family's financial security program in these areas. In Chapter 18, we will see that such is not the case with social insurance against the unemployment risk.

Life Insurance
Policies

In Chapter 14 we reasoned that there is one kind of life insurance, *term,* and that it is realistic to think of it as "one year" term. We further pointed out that the many differently named life insurance policies were *different* only in the number of years and amount of term life insurance which might be combined with a savings account in a contract.[5]

The contract may be made still more different by adding certain riders (separate contracts made a part of the basic contract). Two common examples are:

1. *Double indemnity,* which is a limited life policy paying additional amounts if death occurs by accident; and
2. *Premium waiver,* which is health insurance providing a disability income benefit equal to the annual premium on the policies. These riders will be further described shortly.

Description of Life Insurance Policies

Most descriptions of individual life insurance policies are organized under three headings: term, whole life, and endowment. *Term* policies are described as contracts which pay the face amount (or other stated benefit) *only* if death occurs during the stated term of the contract. *Whole life* policies are described as contracts paying the face amount at death or at age 100, whichever occurs earlier. *Endowment* policies are described as contracts paying the face amount at death or at the stated endowment date, whichever occurs earlier. The whole life, then, is an endowment at age 100. By this logic, our description of the different policies will be under two headings: term and endowment. This description will be presented in tabular form, in order to emphasize the basic similarity of the two groupings and to point out their differences.

No reference is made in the tabular presentation to *industrial* insurance. The key to understanding the term is to think of it as "the same basic plans but in smaller packages." One of the segments of the industry's marketing effort has been the industrial (also called "combination") sales force. This is a totally different branch organized originally to serve lower income groups. Since a laborer (and other large segments of the working population) cannot be interviewed on the job, the industrial sales force is primarily organized on a neighborhood basis, with only one agent of a company servicing any particular area. Policies with face amounts of $100 to $1,000 with the premiums payable weekly were offered as well as regular policies (unfortunately referred to as "ordinary" to distinguish them from industrial). Most of the larger life insurance companies no longer sell these small weekly premium policies, even though their industrial (combination) agencies remain a vigorous, important, and growing marketing force.

---

[5] A review of this part of Chapter 14 might be worthwhile at this point.

Exhibit 16–2   Classification of Individual Life Insurance Policies

Most usual name for policy	Premium paying period*	Basic benefits
Term policies		
One Year Term	One year	Pays face amount only if death occurs during the one-year term of the policy; usually provides for renewal for successive one-year periods to some stated age such as sixty, with premium increasing each year.
Five Year Term (also 10 year, 15 year, etc.)	Each year policy is in force	Pays face amount if death occurs during the stated number of years; usually provides for renewal until some stated age such as sixty, with premium increasing each renewal period.
Life Expectancy	Each year policy is in force	Pays face amount only if insured dies during a stated term period which represents the number of years "life expectancy at issue age" (even chance of living that many years).
Mortgage Cancellation (10 year, 15 year, 20 year, 25 year, 30 year) (also named the more generic "Reducing Term")	Usually several years less than the term of policy. Thus premiums payable first seven years on ten-year term period, twelve years on fifteen year period, sixteen years on twenty year period, etc.	Benefit period chosen to equal or exceed the number of years remaining on a mortgage. Amount of term insurance decreases each year roughly corresponding to reduced balance of mortgage that year. Face amount paid in the event of death during the stated term period. The beneficiary may be the mortgage company for the amount necessary to pay off mortgage at death with any remaining proceeds payable to insured's estate or named beneficiary.
Family Income (ten year, fifteen year, twenty year)	Premiums usually payable for fewer number of years than policy period, as in mortgage cancellation. Priced in units of $10 monthly income from date of death.	Pays monthly income to beneficiary from date of death to future date stated in policy, thus, twenty year family income issued in June, 1974, pays monthly income from date of death until June, 1994; no benefits unless insured dies prior to that date. By definition, this is reducing term, the amount in force at any one time being the sum necessary to provide the stated monthly income for the remainder of the income period.

Exhibit 16–2   (continued)

Most usual name for policy	Premium paying period*	Basic benefits
Endowment policies		

Whole Life (Endowment at age 100). Given different names depending on length of premium paying period:

Most usual name for policy	Premium paying period*	Basic benefits
1. Ordinary Life (also called Straight Life)	Continuous annual premiums while original policy in force	Face amount paid if death occurs prior to end of endowment period. Face amount paid to insured at end of endowment period if alive; thus, insured gets face amount of ten year endowment at the end of ten years. Stated *cash value* for each of the years policy in force equal to the total savings element less surrender charge during early years. Optional insurance benefits in the event original policy terminated prior to stated policy period (and if cash value is not withdrawn):
2. Twenty Pay Life (also fifteen pay, ten pay, etc.)	Premiums payable for the number of years stated; thus, twenty pay life calls for twenty annual premiums only, policy paid up for full face amount after twenty premium payments	
3. Life Paid Up at sixty-five, etc.	Premiums payable annually until insured's age 65, etc.	1. *Original endowment* policy continued for the *reduced face* amount that cash value would purchase on single premium basis at insured's attained age. 2. Continue *original face amount* for number of year's cash value will purchase *term insurance* at insured's attained age. This term option cannot run beyond the original insurance period. If cash value in excess of amount necessary to provide term insurance for remainder of original insurance period, such excess is paid to the insured only if alive at the end of the original insurance period.
10 Year Endowment (also fifteen year, twenty year, etc.) Endowment at age eighteen (also at age fifty, fifty-five, sixty, sixty-five, etc.)	Annual premiums payable for each year of policy period. The same plans may be purchased as "limited pay"; thus, twenty-pay endowment at age sixty-five requires annual payments first twenty years and none thereafter	
Retirement Income at sixty-five (also fifty-five, sixty, sixty-two)	Each year original policy in force until stated retirement age	As above with these differences: pays $10 a month for life at age sixty-five; savings account exceeds face amount in later years of policy in order to have enough cash to buy the single premium $10 a month life annuity for insured; death benefit is cash value any time it exceeds the face amount.

Most usual name for policy	*Premium paying period**	*Basic benefits*
	"Special package" policies	
"Jumping Juvenile" (each company has its own name such as Juvenile Increasing Estate, Estate Builder)	Same as basic policy, thus every year policy is in force (until age sixty-five if life paid up-at-sixty-five)	Basically a whole life policy issued on juveniles. Some companies issue it as a life paid-up at sixty-five. Different in that face amount is only $1,000 until age twenty-one and then automatically increases to $5,000. Same premium during entire policy period.
Double Insurance to sixty-five (combined package of Whole Life and Term to sixty-five)	If basically whole life, premiums payable annually while policy is in force. If life paid up at sixty-five, premiums payable to age sixty-five	Usually a whole life policy (with some companies a life paid-up at sixty-five) with an additional "term to sixty-five" built into the contract. Thus, if insured dies *prior* to age sixty-five he collects on the basic policy and that amount again on the term to sixty-five. Should be little difference from ordinary life in premium because term life cost at early ages is minimal.
Family Income (combined package of whole life and Family Income)	Premium reduces to that of base policy after stated family income period is past. Typically, twenty year family income provides for original premium for seventeen years; reduced premium continues while basic policy in force.	Usually combines in one policy form: ordinary life issued in minimum amounts of $5,000 to $10,000 with 5 to 10 units of family income (explained under term policies) built into it. If insured dies during family income period proceeds of whole life policy retained by insurance company with interest earnings from these proceeds made part of the monthly family income. At end of family income period, proceeds then paid to named beneficiary.
Family Plan (combined package insuring every member of family)	Varies greatly among the different companies, but premiums paid continuously while policy is in force on father's basic permanent insurance.	Usually a combination of basic whole life on father issued in minimum amount of $5,000 with $1,000 term to age twenty-one (some to twenty-five) on each child and term to sixty-five on the wife, face amount originally $3,000 to $5,000. Also children have right to convert at age twenty-one to larger policy without evidence of insurability. Great variations among companies.
College Senior Plan (relatively few companies	Continuously while original life policy in force unless issued	Varies with companies, but usually is an Ordinary Life or Life Paid-up at sixty-five. Modified so that it automa-

Exhibit 16–2   (continued)

Most usual name for policy	Premium paying period*	Basic benefits
offer this, sold on college campuses often by students). Usually whole life or life paid-up at sixty-five combined with personal note for first year premium. Sales approach: "Sold only to seniors; pay little or nothing first year; a fourth year endowment will pay off note for balance of first year premium plus interest."	on "Paid-up at sixty-five basis."	tically releases enough of savings account (cash value) at end of fourth year to pay off the note (plus interest) given by the senior for the first year premium. This note is "sold" to a bank or finance company by insurer; insured is liable on this note even if he discontinues policy. Annual premium normally higher than comparable whole life because of fourth year cash value release. Usually offered with several "extra benefit" riders. College senior normally can buy more suitable policy from same company.

*All can be purchased on a single premium basis, but most are purchased on an annual premium basis for a stated number of years with the privilege of paying these on a monthly, quarterly or semi-annual basis.

Annuities

Private life insurers also sell *life annuities*. Under a life annuity, the insurer agrees to pay the annuitant a regular income (usually monthly) as long as he lives ("a monthly income you cannot outlive" in the parlance of the insurance agent). An individual can purchase an annuity through regular deposits over a period of years (called *annual premium deferred life annuity*) or through the single payment of a sum necessary to purchase the desired immediate life income (*single premium life annuity*). If this single premium is paid before the life income is to start, it is called a single premium *deferred* life annuity.

What happens if this large sum is deposited and the annuitant draws only one monthly payment and dies? If the agreement calls for no further liability by the insurer, such an annuity is called a *straight* or *no-refund* life annuity. This arrangement allows the insurer to pay the maximum monthly life income for the money applied. If the annuitant requires that, in addition to the guarantee of an income for life to him, the insurer must agree to make a specified minimum number of payments in the event of the annuitant's early demise, the amount of life income payments must necessarily be reduced. The most usual *certain* periods chosen are five years, ten years, and twenty years. There is also a "full refund" (also called "installment refund") certain period which is the number of years and months necessary to guarantee payment of the full amount paid to purchase the life annuity. We cannot say one particular life annuity (no-refund, full refund, five year certain, etc.) is a "better deal" than the other. They are all mathematical equivalents involving ingredients which make up the life annuity: principal sum applied, interest on the principal, mortality factor (a pooling operation the same in principle to all insurance but different in operation), and expense factors.

Variable Annuities and Variable Life Insurance

Life insurance policies and life annuities described to this point are called "fixed dollar" contracts. The benefits to be paid (whether they be death benefits, cash values, or annuity payments) are fixed dollar amounts provided for in the contract. The insurer, in order to be able to meet these future commitments, has to invest mainly in bonds and mortgages (which pay fixed amounts of interest and principal).

Inflation decreases the purchasing power of dollars. Thus, a $10,000 life insurance policy purchased in 1950 is thought to have had in 1970 only $5,000 purchasing power (in 1950 dollars). On the theory that equities would keep pace in dollar value with inflation, the idea of tying life insurance and annuity benefits to common stocks developed. Under this system, the insurer invests reserves primarily in common stocks. The individual insured's share of these reserves is a stated number of *units*. A unit's value is determined by the market value of the total common stock reserve fund divided by the entire number of units. This amount is calculated daily, with the insured or annuitant's benefit share varying with the unit's value. Variable annuities have been marketed since the late 1960s. Approval for the sale of variable life insurance, was given by the Securities and Exchange Commission in early 1973. SEC guidelines require variable life insurance policies to have a minimum fixed dollar face amount with the provision for additional benefits through "unit" value increases. The relative merit of these *variable* plans depends basically on one's convictions concerning common stocks as an inflation hedge.

Contract Provisions Common to all Life Insurance Policies

Non-Forfeiture Benefits. The *death benefit* and *endowment benefit* (included in all policies except term) are the most important provisions in a life insurance policy. Closely following these in importance is that concerning the accumulation of the savings part of annual premiums. In Exhibit 16–2, this was called the "cash value" of the policy. This cash value, along with two paid-up insurance options (taken in lieu of the cash) make up what is called "non-forfeiture benefits." There is a value for each of these for each year the policy is in force. Usually, values for only the first twenty years, age sixty, sixty-two, and sixty-five are printed in the policy. Nevertheless, an insurance company cannot be arbitrary about the amounts for years not given in the policy form. This is regulated by state insurance laws and the value for each year is a precise mathematical function.

Understanding the cash value is not difficult. From the insured's point of view it is the same as the balance in his savings account at a bank. Understanding the two different *paid-up* insurance policies he can buy with that cash value (the non-forfeiture insurance options) is a little more difficult. They can best be explained by using an example. John Doe, at age thirty-five, buys a $10,000 ordinary life policy. Exactly ten years later, he gets the policy out of the vault to find out what his non-forfeiture values are. He finds the non-forfeiture table and looks at the "policy years elapsed" column down to the tenth year. He reads across and finds the following figures under three column headings:

1. "Cash or loan value: $1,715.30." He can either drop the policy and settle for $1,715.30, or he can "borrow" the amount and keep the policy in force.

2. "Paid-up Life Insurance: $2,950." This means his $1,715.30 will buy him $2,950 of paid-up whole life (no more premiums to be paid). This policy, then, will pay $2,950 at his death or to him at age 100. Incidentally, it immediately has a *cash* or *loan* value of about $1,700 which will continue to increase until it reaches $2,950 at his age 100.

3. Extended Insurance

   Years   Days
    16   87

   This means his $1,715.30 will buy him a paid-up $10,000 (the original face amount) *term* policy which will be in force 16 years and 87 days (through some day of his 62nd year of life). Ten thousand dollars will be paid if he dies during that period; nothing will be paid if he dies after that time.

Which non-forfeiture option he would choose would depend on his personal circumstance at the time. If he had a terminal illness—and did not have the premium waiver rider attached—he would no doubt choose the "Extended Insurance" option. If he needed the money and still needed the death benefit, he would "borrow" his cash value and continue the policy in force. If he did not particularly need the death benefit (having adequate other life insurance) and did not need the cash, he would possibly choose the "Paid-up Life Insurance" (an unfortunate label because the Extended Insurance is also paid-up for the period indicated). With this he would (1) continue to draw interest on his savings, (2) his funds would have some protection against future creditors that is unique to life insurance as opposed to other property, and (3) upon his death the funds would be paid directly to his named beneficiary without passing through the probating of his estate.

Settlement Options. Not to be confused with non-forfeiture options, the *settlement options* in a life insurance policy provide for other than immediate cash settlement of policy *proceeds*. These other ways all involve the insurance company *retaining* the proceeds and handling the funds under one of the following options.

1. *Interest only.* The full proceeds are kept intact and the interest is paid to the beneficiary. At some later date, either at the direction of the beneficiary or under provisions set out by the insured prior to his death, the

principal is paid out in cash or under one of the following other settlement options.

2. *Regular periodic payment* (usually monthly) *of principal and interest* until proceeds are fully disbursed. These payments may be for a *fixed amount* (e.g., $200 a month as long as it will last), or for a *fixed period* (e.g., pay whatever monthly amount is possible in order to make the payments last for forty-eight months).

3. *Life income.* This is an option to buy one of the immediate life annuities previously described (with a monthly income for life and choice of the *certain* period).

These settlement options are available for *any proceeds* of a life insurance policy. Thus, the surviving beneficiary spouse can apply the death benefit to any of the options; the insured can take the cash value or any endowment proceeds and apply the funds on any of the options. It is not unusual to apply the cash value of an ordinary life policy when the insured retires to a life income option, in order to augment the life income from social security and company retirement benefits.

Other Provisions. There are many other provisions in the basic life insurance policy form. Most important for the insured to understand are:

1. *Incontestable clause.* This is unique to life insurance not only in insurance, but in all contract law. The clause gives the insurer only a stated period (often one year, never more than two years—depending on state laws) to contest payment of a death claim or to seek to revoke the policy. This means that after the contestable period has passed, the insurer has *no* defense against the insured or his beneficiary in payment of claims (except non-payment of premiums).

2. *Reinstatement clause.* After a premium due date, a grace period of thirty-one days is allowed for payment, after which the policy lapses and goes out of benefit—except for the non-forfeiture benefits previously described. The reinstatement clause gives the insured the *right* to reinstate, subject to (1) being able to show evidence of insurability, (2) paying back premiums plus required interest, and (3) applying for reinstatement within a specified period (typically three to five years). An important aspect of lapsing and reinstating is that—depending on the state law and circumstances—the contestable period may start again.

3. *Suicide clause.* This clause also is unique in insurance and contract law. It provides that after a stated period (one–no more than two–years) depending on state law) the insurer cannot use suicide or attempt to commit suicide as a defense against paying the death benefit.

4. *Change of plan clause.* This clause gives the insured the right to change the policy plan to another plan (e.g. ordinary life to endowment at 65) without evidence of insurability as long as insurer's total mortality expo-

sure is not increased. The clause states the mathematical basis for making the change.

5. *Dividend options.* Life insurance sold on a participating (Par) basis provides payment of cash dividends (as explained in Chapter 15). They usually provide options to leave the dividend with the company to accumulate at compound interest, to purchase single premium paid-up additional insurance of the same kind, or to purchase one-year *term* at the price for the insured's current age in an amount that the dividend will purchase.

Riders to Life Insurance Policies

Contract law recognizes the existence of separate contracts made between two or more parties in connection with a basic contract. These contracts are known as "riders." The same terminology is used in insurance and there are a number of widely used policy riders issued in connection with basic life insurance policies. Exhibit 16–3 classifies and gives basic information concerning these.

Exhibit 16–3 Classification of Typical Life Policy Riders (premiums usually paid until insured's age when rider benefits cease or for length of premium paying period of basic policy, whichever is of shorter duration)

Most usual name	Basic benefits	Kind of insurance
Family Income	Same provisions as family income term policy (Exhibit 16–2) but issued as a rider to any number of different basic plans.	Term life insurance on the insured
Double Indemnity, Triple Indemnity, etc.	Double indemnity is $1,000 accidental death life insurance issued in connection with each $1,000 of the basic policy. Triple indemnity is the same except $2,000 accidental death life insurance for each $1,000 of the basic policy. Pays only if death is accidental according to conditions in policy.	Term life insurance limited to death by accident
Premium Waiver	Policy premium is "waived" for duration of total disability. Usually three to six months elimination period.	Health insurance; actually a disability income policy with benefit amount equal to policy premium
Disability Income	Priced in units of monthly income (usually $10) while totally disabled. Issued only in connection with a basic policy per $1,000 of face amount. Pays monthly income while insured totally disabled for illnesses lasting stated minimum period (varies from three to six months).	Health insurance Disability income

Most usual name	Basic benefits	Kind of insurance
Guaranteed insurability	Gives insured the right to purchase additional insurance even if uninsurable at certain stated option dates such as age twenty-five, thirty, thirty-five, forty. Face amount at each option date same as base policy amount, thus guaranteeing the right to purchase additional coverage at four times the face amount.	Health insurance (guarantees insurability)
Family Plan	Same as family benefits of the Family Plan described in Exhibit 16–2, but issued as a rider in connection with any number of different policy plans.	Term life insurance for the death benefit; health insurance for the guaranteed option to convert
Return Premium Benefit	If insured dies during "return premium benefit period" (usually fifteen or twenty years), additional amount is paid equal to total premiums paid prior to death.	Term life insurance on insured; increasing term, increasing yearly by amount of total premium for base policy and riders
Premium Payor Benefit	Issued in connection with juvenile policy. If premium payor (usually the father) dies before the juvenile attains age twenty-one all premiums from date of premium payor's death to juvenile's age twenty-one are waived. A few companies add premium waiver benefit on premium payor.	Term life insurance on premium payor; health insurance where waiver of premium in the event of disability

Which and how much of these many life insurance policies and riders to use in planning a family's financial security program will be considered in Chapter 17.

Health Insurance Policies

Health insurance, as was noted previously, is the one line that is sold by both life insurance companies and property insurance companies. In addition, Blue Cross and Blue Shield Associations exist solely for offering health insurance protection.[6]

Health insurance protection is available under group insurance policies—usually in connection with employment—and through the purchase of individ-

---

[6] A few of the Blue Cross Associations have wholly owned life insurance companies which exist primarily to offer group life insurance and group disability income as part of a personal insurance package for group insurance.

ual contracts from insurers. Where group protection is involved, the individual has little or no buying decision to make. The insurance is simply one part of the total employment contract where salary, working conditions, other fringe benefits and other considerations are involved. For this reason, we will not attempt to study group health insurance benefits and provisions in this chapter. Reference to these will be given in Chapter 18. Our concern here will be individual health insurance contracts.

Degree of Uniformity

A logical first question is, "to what extent are the various *individual* health insurance policies uniform in benefits and provisions?" The answer is made without hesitation and unequivocally: there is no uniformity in benefits and very little uniformity in provisions. Probably no field of insurance involves a greater heterogeneity among the thousands of individual policy forms available. The other extreme is illustrated by the uniform family automobile policy (essentially the same policy is issued by all companies in all states) and the homeowner's property insurance policy.

The one area of uniformity results from the *1950 Uniform Individual Accident and Sickness Policy Provisions Law* now in force in all but two states (the exceptions, Louisiana and Alaska, do have similar statutes). The law provides for twelve mandatory provisions in every policy issued and for eleven optional provisions. Even though entitled "uniform," some of the provisions allow optional wording with varying degrees of liberality to the insured. A summary of these provisions is given in the appendix.

Differences in Benefits: Medical Expense Policies

You may think these uniform provisions would result in a high degree of uniformity among various medical expense policies, but such is not the case. The extent of variance will be indicated in terms of benefits, renewal provisions, definitions, and exclusions and reductions.

In regard to the extent of benefits in individual medical expense policies there are three basic types:

> Basic hospital expense policies
> Major medical expense policies
> "Special Package" policies

Basic Hospital Policies. These policies typically provide a payment for room and board charges, miscellaneous hospital expenses, special maternity benefits, and emergency out-patient treatment for accidental injuries. The wording on each of these benefits varies greatly among different policies and insurers.

Room allowance. The room and board benefits may be expressed in terms of (1) a specified dollar amount for each day or (2) the payment of charges for a semi-private room in the hospital. The semi-private room allowance is more realistic during these times of constantly rising hospital costs.

Miscellaneous hospital expenses. The provision regarding miscellaneous expenses (laboratory fees, medicines and dressings, oxygen, x-ray services, etc.) is important.

There are two contrasting provisions in hospital policies for payment of these expenses:

1. A specified allocated payment for each type of expense, or
2. A specified blanket amount payable for all miscellaneous charges.

The blanket allowance is much more liberal. There is a big difference between a $500 miscellaneous *allocated* benefit and a $500 blanket benefit. In the latter, a particular illness might involve using the full $500 for x-ray; the same illness under an allocated provision might pay only the maximum $50 allowed for x-ray, reserving the balance of $450 for other specified miscellaneous expenses, many of which might not be incurred.

Out-patient benefit. The provisions for out-patient treatment for accidental injury varies from a very limited benefit paying only for setting of a broken bone in a hospital to a liberal allowance of payment for treatment of any injury administered by any doctor without restriction as to where the treatment was performed. This is one benefit where the buyer may want to consider less liberal coverage in order to keep the premium as low as possible.

Surgical expense benefit. This benefit is usually included (sometimes on an optional basis for an extra charge and, in other cases, as a part of the total package.) A surgical schedule in the policy lists the allowance for each type of surgery. It is desirable to look at the schedule of allowances to see how reasonable they are. There are instances of companies speaking in terms of a "$1,000 surgical schedule" allowing this $1,000 for some rare type of surgery and then scaling down the allowances on the more typical types to very meager amounts.

Other benefits. Other benefits usually included in the basic hospital expense policy are: (1) an allowance for doctors' visits while the patient is in the hospital, (2) a daily allowance for private nurses, and (3) a specified allowance for necessary ambulance service. With the emergence of intensive care service, it is desirable to have a specific daily intensive care benefit which can be used in lieu of hospital room and board and private nurses benefit.

Major Medical Expense Policies. The "major medical" expense coverage applies to all medical expenses without reference to whether they were incurred in a hospital. It is often referred to as "catastrophe" health insurance. Major medical coverage may be purchased in one of two ways: in connection with a basic hospital policy issued by the same insurer or as a separate policy without reference to any basic hospital coverage that may or may not exist. When offered in relation to a hospital policy, there usually is a provision for a stated "deductible," such as $100, beyond expenses covered by the basic policy. After this amount (technically called a *corridor*) of medical expenses has been incurred during a benefit period (calendar year or policy year depending on wording of the policy), the major medical then pays some stated percent of all *covered* medical expenses. When one benefit year ends, another deductible amount applies before the policy begins to pay 80 percent (usually, but some pay 75 percent, 85 percent and 90 percent) on covered expenses. The covered expenses are set out in the policy and generally include most medical expenses a person might incur, such as: hospital bills, professional services of physician and surgeon, drugs and medicine, medical appliances, x-ray, laboratory tests, private duty nursing, physiotherapy, ambulance service, and dental surgery made necessary as the result of an accident.

A major medical expense policy purchased without regard to a basic hospital policy is issued with a stated deductible chosen by the insured ($100 to $10,000, but more typically $500). After the stated deductible amount of medical expenses has been incurred, the insurer pays 80 percent of all covered expenses. In all major medical policies, there is a stated maximum amount of benefits. This maximum is set out in one of two ways: either with reference to any particular illness, or with reference to a lifetime of medical expenses with an annual "restoration" of benefit amount. For example, an insured has a $40,000 lifetime benefit maximum with $1,000 yearly restoration. He contracts tuberculosis and over a period of four years the insurer pays him $1,500 each year. He has used up $6,000 of his $40,000 benefit amount, but the four yearly $1,000 restorations of amount leaves him with a $38,000 lifetime benefit potential.

The typical exclusions in a major medical policy are: (1) expenses of an ordinary pregnancy and childbirth, (2) cosmetic surgery not resulting from an injury, (3) treatment of alcoholism and narcotics, (4) claims under workmen's compensation, (5) self-inflicted injuries, and (6) all coverage while in military service.

Another version of a combined basic hospital policy and major medical is called Comprehensive Medical Expense Insurance. It is basically major medical expense insurance modified to pay a stated amount of *hospital* expenses without applying the deductible. For example, a comprehensive policy might provide for paying the first $400, $500, or $600 of hospital expenses and 80 percent of all other medical expenses, whether in the hospital or not. There may or may not be a deductible on the hospital expenses and/or non-hospital medical expenses. The usual rate book permits you to name your own deductible with the premium adjusted accordingly.

The covered expenses and the exclusions are essentially the same in comprehensive and major medical policies.

"Special Package" Policies. As medical expense insurance progressed from non-existence to almost universal acceptance in three decades, many companies found it difficult to maintain their rate of growth in this field. Where previously the market consisted of selling to an entire population which had no protection, sales suddenly were limited to replacing existing policies of other companies or to providing new insurance for the relatively small group of new household units. The sales problem became increasingly acute as more and more people were offered health insurance in connection with their jobs. Another problem has been the matter of profitability on the conventional policies

in force resulting from the time lag between increasing hospital and other health insurance costs and raising premiums on policies. Added to this general situation has been the competition of the over 1,000 new life insurance companies alone which have appeared on the scene since 1950. A significant proportion of these new companies have tried to get premium volume generated through health insurance sales which are generally easier than life insurance sales. This would all seem to add up to an impossible growth situation for many health insurers, particularly the smaller and newer ones; but this has not been the case. An almost endless variety of *special, limited* health insurance packages have been devised, most of which have one or both of the following advantages to the insurance company.

1. A highly salable policy that appears to be a bargain and which many people will buy—motivated by their concern over ever increasing health costs.
2. A policy highly profitable to the company in terms of claims paid out and —for those which are sold by direct mail and through newspaper ads— in terms of reduced marketing costs.

Each company in this market (many have not entered it and others have become involved only to a limited degree) has its own unique package or packages and it is impossible to classify the many plans. However, the following groupings would include a significant percentage of the plans.

1. Policies which pay for accidents only.
2. Policies which pay for medical expenses incurred as a result of certain specified illnesses such as cancer, polio, spinal meningitis, encephalitis, diptheria, smallpox, leukemia, tetanus, rabies, Rocky Mountain fever, tularemia, etc.
3. Policies which pay a stated monthly amount of *extra* benefits while insured is in a hospital. This monthly benefit is usually paid on a per day basis; thus, a $1,000 monthly benefit policy would pay $33.33 for each day.
4. Policies which pay supplemental benefits to Medicare.

It is difficult to make a case for the first two categories. A sound medical expense insurance program for an individual or a family provides for payment of certain portions of total expenses. This needed protection is the same regardless of the cause of the medical expense—whether it be from an accident, cancer, polio, tularemia, appendicitis, heart conditions, or any other disease. The only possible justification would be that certain diseases—such as cancer and polio—often involve a catastrophe-type financial expense. With the advent of major medical and comprehensive plans, this justification no longer exists. These limited policies, in spite of a seemingly low premium, tend to be quite expensive in terms of percent of premiums paid out in claims by the insurer.

The cancer policy is an example of extremely high-cost protection. These special policies usually quote the same premium regardless of age of the insured. Even though there are instances of cancer at younger ages, it is basically a degenerative disease and therefore one that appears in late middle age and old age. If one-half of a company's insureds under cancer policies are under age thirty, there will be very little loss expense for that group for the first twenty years or more that they are insured. During those years, a significant percentage drop their coverage and are thus not a risk liability to the insurer at the age when most likely to have a claim.

In the marketing of these special package policies, great stress is put on the payment of benefits regardless of other insurance. Even so, a significant percentage of the insureds will collect little or no additional total benefits from their combined insurance coverages. Most group health policies and most individual basic policies have "other insurance" clauses which have the effect of reducing the amount the primary insurer pays by all or part of the amount he collects from other insurance.

The third described special package policy which involves payment of a (daily) fixed amount while the insured is in a hospital can be criticized principally on the basis that it is very expensive coverage for the benefits received. The various companies' plans differ greatly on policy provisions. With many, the benefits do not start until *after* the third day in the hospital—after the sixth day with some. Exclusions vary also; although most completely exclude emotional and nervous disorders, and others have two-year waiting periods on preexisting conditions.[7]

The authors analyzed the advertising (direct mail and newspaper) of seven companies' plans chosen at random. The accompanying table is an attempt to illustrate premium charges for approximately the same basic benefit and to indicate the percent of premium dollar paid out in benefits by each company on all their special package plans.

Company	Monthly premium for $1,000 monthly benefit while in hospital (male; age 30)	Percent of premium dollar paid out on individual guaranteed renewable health policies[8]
A	$7.58	47%
B	7.26	37
C	5.00	58
D	5.90	35
E	6.10	36
F	5.20	37
G	4.95	58

The fourth category of special package plans, medicare supplement policies, provide needed protection for those over sixty-five who feel their financial resources are not adequate to permit retention of risk on the hospital costs not covered by Medicare. Since policies of the various companies cover *specifically*

---

[7]One of the companies with the most restrictive provisions and highest premiums included in its ad a quote from the Congressional Record commending it—among other things—for bringing low-cost insurance to the general public.

[8]Data taken from 1971 *Argus Chart,* National Underwriter Company, Cincinnati.

the medicare gaps on hospitalization costs, there is a fairly high degree of uniformity in *benefits* among competing plans. The tendency to uniformity ceases, however, when we come to a consideration of various provisions in the policy (the optional uniform provisions noted previously and other provisions to be considered presently).

Differences in Benefits: Individual Disability Income Policies

A discussion of differences in benefits among individual disability income policies must center around the *duration* of the income payable. Among the many private plans sold, there are policies representing almost every possible duration—from as short a time as one month to payments for life. However, most plans would fall under two headings: short-term disability income and long-term disability income. Short-term plans, by arbitrary definition, include all those with a maximum duration for disability payments of up to two years; long-term plans include all those providing income payments for longer than two years.

The short-term plan *individual* policies in force would consist almost totally of those "loss of time" contracts sold by industrial insurance agents. These plans, as Exhibit 16–4 indicates, cover fewer than 14 million people, and seem to have reached a plateau in growth. The market for this type of plan primarily consists of laborers paid by the day or week who want insurance against "loss of time," even from illnesses or accidents of short duration. Payments start after three to seven days house confinement and continue for a maximum period—for example—of twenty-six weeks. Agents are often allowed to pay small claims on the spot. This insurance is necessarily quite expensive for benefits received and is not coverage most families would want to consider.

Important Other Provisions

We have seen how widely individual health insurance policies vary in *benefits* provided. In what other provisions are there significant differences? Many. So many, in fact, that the only feasible approach for the insurance buyer is to have a checklist from which he seeks specific answers to the more important ones. Such a list should include the following questions.

1. What rights do I have to renew this policy on exactly the same terms? What exceptions are there, if any? How many times can I renew it?
2. Are there any medical care facilities which are not covered under the hospitalization benefits?
3. Are there any physicians, either because of type of medical degree or by present employment, for whose services a benefit, otherwise payable, is not allowed?
4. Are there any periods of time when benefits, otherwise payable, are eliminated? (Such as first three days in hospital; two years after policy date on pre-existing conditions; treatment involving tonsils, appendix, cancer, pregnancy, or other disabilities.)
5. How is "pre-existing condition" defined?

6. Explain any situation under which part of a benefit payment is deducted?
7. How does the policy define an "accident"? What specific occurrences are excluded as accidents?
8. Are there any exclusions of any nature? What are they?

Exhibit 16–4   Number of Persons with Disability Income Protection by Type of Program—in the United States (000 omitted)

End of year	All programs*	Insurance companies			Formal paid sick leave plans	Other
		All insurance companies*	Group policies	Individual policies		
1946	26,229	14,369	7,135	8,684	8,400	3,460
1950	37,793	25,993	15,104	13,067	8,900	2,900
1955	39,513	29,813	19,171	13,642	8,500	1,200
1960	42,436	31,836	20,970	14,298	9,500	1,100
1961	43,055	32,055	21,186	14,301	9,900	1,100
1962	44,902	33,602	22,313	14,854	10,200	1,100
Short-term disability income protection						
1963	44,475	32,475	22,669	12,902	10,900	1,100
1964	45,270	33,270	23,177	13,280	10,900	1,100
1965	49,690	34,160	24,615	12,559	11,700	1,100
1966	50,003	36,403	26,322	13,264	12,500	1,100
1967	51,915	37,515	27,632	13,004	13,300	1,100
1968	55,677	40,777	30,229	13,879	13,800	1,100
1969	57,627	41,027	30,865	13,807	15,500	1,100
1970	57,833	40,833	31,498	12,683	15,900	1,100
1971	58,850	41,250	32,168	12,340	16,500	1,100
Long-term disability income protection						
1963	3,029	3,029	749	2,280	—	—
1964	3,420	3,420	1,257	2,163	—	—
1965	4,457	4,457	1,903	2,554	—	—
1966	5,002	5,002	2,376	2,626	—	—
1967	6,682	6,682	3,827	2,855	—	—
1968	7,718	7,718	4,710	3,008	—	—
1969	9,076	9,076	5,715	3,361	—	—
1970	10,740	10,740	7,176	3,564	—	—
1971	12,011	12,011	8,209	3,802	—	—

*Data for the years 1963–1970 have been revised for short-term disability income protection.

Note: Data in the category "insurance companies" refer to the net total of people protected, *i.e.,* duplication among persons with more than one insurance policy has been eliminated. However, for years prior to 1963, any duplication resulting from the combination of numbers covered for short-term and long-term protection has not been eliminated. The category "Formal paid sick leave plans" refers to people with formal paid sick leave plans but without insurance company coverage. The category "Other" includes Union-administered plans and the Federal Mutual Benefit Association.

Source: Health Insurance Council. 1972–1973 *Source Book of Health Insurance Data,* Health Insurance Institute, New York, p. 25.

The appendix to this chapter includes a discussion of the significance and justi-fication of provisions covering these and other pertinent questions.

A final note of caution is in order. All individual health policies of any sig-nificance attach your application to the policy, making it a part of the con-tract. An insured should carefully read this copy, looking for any important errors or omissions. If there are any, a certified letter should be written to the insurance company apprising it of factual discrepancies and requesting a letter stating your insurance is not affected by this.

Property Insurance Policies

An individual or family is in a far different position in planning a program of property insurance as opposed to personal (life and health) insurance. Fortu-nately, it is a much better position. The personal insurance needs of protecting earnings from loss of job, disability, premature death, and finally old age is very complex. In addition, there is a broad social insurance program providing a base for this protection; but, to supplement this with other insurance, the individual is faced with literally almost "a thousand ways to go." Not so with property insurance. For one thing, the problem is not as complex. For another, the private insurance industry has developed *two* policies which complement each other in providing a very adequate property insurance program for a family.

Because of this, we will describe the benefits and provisions of the property insurance policies in Chapter 18, which will be concerned with the specifics of reducing an individual's and family's potential property losses through insurance.

Discussion Questions

1. Name three tests for disability benefit entitlement.
2. What "kind" of insurance is involved in each of the following riders?
   a. double indemnity
   b. premium waiver
   c. return premium benefit
   d. guaranteed insurability
3. Individual life insurance policies are organized under three headings. Name and describe each.
4. Assuming identical earnings records, why will a person reaching age sixty-five in 1974 have a lower retirement benefit from social security than someone reaching age 65 in 1980 (disregard increases in basic benefit rates)?
5. What is meant by "settlement options"? Are they synonymous with "non-for-feiture options"? Why or why not?
6. Explain the incontestable clause.
7. Name and describe at least five typical life insurance policy riders.

8. Make a case for the "guaranteed renewable but with right to increase premiums by class" renewable clause as opposed to other such clauses.
9. Explain why the survivorship benefit of the OASDHI program is theoretically similar to the family income policy.
10. What is the "inflation proof" feature of OASDHI program as included in the 1972 amendments?
11. What do "fixed dollar" and "variable" mean with reference to life insurance policies and life annuities?

---

appendix

Summary of ''1950 Uniform Individual Accident and Sickness Policy Provisions''

Required Provisions

1. The policy with any endorsements and attached papers constitutes the entire contract.
2. After three years the policy is incontestable except for fraudulent misstatements made on the application.
3. A grace period of not less than seven days on weekly premium policies and thirty-one days on all others must be granted.
4. Where formal application for reinstatement of a lapsed policy is not required, the acceptance of a premium by the insurer or its agent immediately reinstates the policy. Where formal application is required, the reinstatement does not become effective until approved by the insurer (unless the insurer unduly delays approval beyond forty-five days).
5. Written notice of claim must be given to the insurer within twenty days after the occurrence or commencement of any loss or as soon thereafter as is reasonably possible under the circumstances.
6. If the insurer insists that claims be submitted on company forms, such forms must be furnished to the insured within fifteen days of receipt of notice of a claim. Otherwise, it must accept any reasonable written proof of loss submitted by the insured.
7. Written proof of loss must be furnished by the claimant within ninety days.
8. Claims for specific losses must be paid immediately upon proof of loss. Claims for periodic indemnities must be paid within the number of days specified in the contract, but in no case over a month.

9. Any benefits payable after the death of the insured will be paid to the named beneficiary or to the insured's estate if there is no living named beneficiary. All other benefits are paid to the insured.

10. Allows the insurer, at its own expense, to examine the insured when and as often as may be reasonably required; also gives the insurer the right to make an autopsy in case of death, unless forbidden by law. [Many individuals owning such policies are not aware of having contractually agreed to this.]

11. Relates to lawsuits under a policy. Insured may not institute a lawsuit prior to sixty days after furnishing proof of loss. No suit may be instituted at the end of three years from the time written proof of loss is required.

12. The insured is given the right to change the beneficiary, unless an irrevocable beneficiary has been designated.

Optional Provisions

The insurer may include any or none of the optional provisions in a particular policy. Where a provision is used, the wording must be the same or, if worded differently, must be as favorable to the insured. In the latter case, the state insurance department must approve. Where optional provisions are not included in the policy and the subject matter covered by such provision becomes an issue, existing laws, legal decisions, custom, and litigation determine the results.

Following is a brief summary of the more important optional provisions.

1. If the insured changes to a more hazardous occupation, the benefits payable will be reduced to whatever his premium would have purchased in the newer occupation. Conversely, if he changes to a less hazardous occupation, the insurer shall upon proof of such change, reduce the premium and refund on a pro rata basis the excess premium charged.

2. A provision similar in effect to the preceding one where there has been a misstatement of age and the difference in age would have caused a different premium.

3.–5. Duplicating coverages. If the insured has duplicating coverages with the *same company* exceeding a stated number of dollars, only the stated amount will be paid and the premium for the excess will be refunded upon request. If the insured has duplicating coverages with *other* insurers of which he has not given the insurer written notice, benefits will be reduced on a pro rata basis in relation to the actual expense incurred.

6. If the insured has two or more disability income plans whose aggregate income benefits exceed his average income for the preceding two years, the insurer is liable only for the proportionate amount the actual earnings bear to the total amount of benefits of all policies.

7. If the policy provides no non-cancellable or guaranteed renewable provisions, the insurer may cancel the contract at any time by giving five days written notice to the insured. Unearned premiums will be refunded. Conversely, the insured may cancel any time after the first contract period. Unearned premiums will be refunded, not on a pro rata basis, but on a short-rate table basis (returns substantially less than the pro rata amount).

8. The insurer shall not be liable for any loss where the insured's committing of a felony or attempting to do so is a contributing cause; also no liability where a contributing cause was the insured's being engaged in an illegal occupation. [Note the possible significance of the former provision where the insured was driving while intoxicated or under the influence of certain drugs. The next optional provision specifically excludes claims under these circumstances whether the insured's actions are judged felonious or not. This obviously is a very stringent provision.]

Other Important Provisions of Individual Health Insurance Policies

In the health insurance section, the differing provisions regarding specific benefits of individual health insurance policies are discussed. Following is a review of certain other important provisions.

Differing Renewal Provisions

In all voluntary private insurance, the insured has the right to drop the policy at any time. From the standpoint of the insurer's renewal rights and obligations, there are four basically different renewal provisions for health insurance policies:

1. Cancellable at any time upon due notice to insured
2. Renewable annually (sometime at any premium due date) at the option of the insurer
3. Guaranteed renewable to some specified date or age or for life, but with the right reserved to the insurer to increase premiums by *classes of insureds*
4. Non-cancellable and guaranteed renewable without the right to increase premiums at any time.

Cancellable. A cancellable policy is one that may be terminated by the insurer at any time. This is the typical provision in property insurance policies. Where there is not the problem of becoming uninsurable in the future, as is the general case in property insurance, a cancellable contract has some advantages to the insured. An insurance company can issue such a policy without having to do extensive underwriting. It can afford to actually charge a smaller premium at the inception of the policy because it has the right to insist on an increase and is protected by the right to cancel should the insured not agree to the increase. This also permits an insurance company to issue new types of coverages on which accurate cost data are not available. With health insurance, however, there is the problem of becoming uninsurable. For this reason, the cancellable provision is usually an undesirable provision in *individual* health insurance policies. In *group* health insurance, the insurer's right to cancel the group policy does not present a problem to the individual, because all employees would be covered under a new group plan with another insurer.

Renewable at the Option of the Company. This is essentially the same as the cancellable provision except that the insurer may not cancel (refuse to renew) until the end of the policy period. In some cases, the clause is worded to provide for this at any premium due date where premiums are payable more frequently than the typical annual term of the policy. Where the insurer exercises this right, it is technically not *cancelling* but is simply refusing to renew. Blue Cross and Blue Shield policies are issued on one of these two bases. Both renewable provisions have similar advantages and disadvantages to the insured. Because of public reaction to alleged abuse of the cancellation or non-renewing right, more and more states are setting out requirements limiting this right to reasons other than deterioration of health or frequency of claims. For example, they may allow such only (1) when a particular policy form is discontinued by a company, (2) where the insured is over-insured, (3) where there is a moral hazard, or (4) where there has been an indication of fraud. Where these limitations are imposed and where the insurer has a record of operations in good faith, this renewal provision is possibly the best for the insured. It makes possible the most policy benefits at the lowest premiums and more liberal underwriting procedures.

Guaranteed Renewable. The guaranteed renewable policy sets out a given number of years or a certain age of the insured to which the insurer *must* renew the policy. The right to increase the premium is retained, but it is limited only where premiums are increased by certain "classes" of insureds.

This is a relatively new contract provision and the full meaning of what constitutes classes of *insureds* has not been determined by litigation. Some states have cleared the matter by defining what may constitute *classes:* (1) sex (raising rates for female or male insureds only), (2) geographical (raising rates for all insureds in a certain state or region), (3) occupational (raising rates on those insureds in certain occupations), and (4) age (raising rates on insureds within stated age groupings).

This type of renewal provision was designed to permit guaranteed renewal and at the same time protect insurance companies from possible catastrophic losses from inadequate premiums. When practiced in good faith by the insurer, it is a very sensible and favorable renewal provision.

Non-Cancellable Policy. A non-cancellable policy is one which the insured may keep in force for some stated time or until some stated age set out in the policy and in which the insurer may not increase premiums or change other provisions of the contract. This provision is fraught with danger to the health insurer. Health costs, whether they be medical expenses or disability income, are difficult to determine even under assumptions of current conditions and almost impossible to determine for future conditions. A number of substantial companies in the past (principally in the 1920s and 1930s) have become insolvent or sustained substantial losses, maintaining solvency only because of sound financial resources and profits from other lines of insurance. For this reason, most states require very substantial reserves to be accumulated for such policies. This necessarily increases premiums from the start. For all these reasons—as liberal and protective as the provision may seem to the individual insured—it is probably the least desirable for the insurance buyer. Some companies, especially newer and smaller ones, may resort to such a policy provision in order to get new business even at the risk of their future solvency; or—as protection—they may put in an undue number of exclusions and conditions which have the effect of limiting the coverage.

As has been explained previously, the life risk is the most nearly perfect insurable risk and is therefore probably the only one where the non-cancellable provision as described here is suitable. Even then, a significant segment of the companies hedge by adopting the participating pricing method.

Differing Definitions

Hospital. In terms of the definition in some policies, some hospitals may not be classified as hospitals; this is true for a convalescent hospital. In policies issued years ago, there were many varying definitions, some very restrictive. There is a trend now toward more uniformity, but this is a definition a prospective buyer should check. The most usual current definition includes the requirement of a lawfully operated institution for care of sick or injured with twenty-four-hour nursing service. If there is the requirement of a physician on duty at all times, this would technically eliminate many small suburban and rural hospitals and clinics.

Physician. The definitions range in scope from "a legally qualified physician or surgeon" to the very restrictive: "a physician holding a degree of doctor of medicine or osteopathy." The broadest definition binds the insurer to the laws of each state and, in some cases, includes the services of naturopaths and chiropractors.

Elimination Period. Any period for which benefits are not paid on an otherwise covered sickness or accident may be called an elimination period; also referred to as "waiting period." Provision for an elimination period eliminates small disability income claims and thus permits lower rates and more liberal long-term benefits. They serve the same function as deductibles in medical expense insurance. Elimination periods are found, however, in some medical expense policies; for example, in supplemental hospital benefit policies where the first one, two, three, or even six days are eliminated. They are also found in some of the other special package plans previously mentioned. Specific elimination periods may apply to accidents occurring within a stated period after the policy date, to pre-existing conditions, to pregnancy, nervous disorders and to diseases involving tonsils, sex organs, genito-urinary tract, etc.

Preexisting Condition. This is an *all-important* definition where the policy has an elimination period or exclusion on preexisting conditions. Even if there is no "preexisting condition" exclusion, any wording that sicknesses covered include only those "first occurring," "first commencing," "beginning while this policy is in force" could give the insurer grounds to attempt to deny liability on illnesses where there is a question as to when it actually *began.* Any wording which would clearly include all illnesses first diagnosed as such after the effective policy date would protect the insured. Professor Mehr suggests the wording "first manifesting itself after the effective date" accomplishes this. He states:

> 'The first manifesting' provision . . . means in effect that if there was no diagnosis of a condition and no symptoms recognizable to a layman, the claim will be honored even though it can be proved beyond doubt by medical testimony that the disorder or disease had its actual origin prior to the effective date of the policy.*

---

*Robert I. Mehr, *Life Insurance Theory and Practice,* 4th ed. (Austin, Texas: Business Publications, 1970), pp. 315–16.

Deductible. Deductibles are used in hospital expense coverages usually for each hospital admittance and in connection with outpatient treatment of accidents. In major medical and comprehensive coverages, more significant deductible amounts are involved. There are many types of deductibles. As we know, deductibles permit the insured to retain small losses thus saving high costs that normally are involved in insuring against small losses. We should keep this in mind when comparing plans.

Accident. An often but now less frequently used definition of a "covered accident" requires that the injury be the result of "accidental means." The term has varying interpretations, but essentially it restricts benefits to injuries *caused* by unusual, unforeseen, and unexpected occurrences. This may preclude certain injuries that are the result of an intended act or non-accidental events (examples: a back injury from lifting weights; a broken arm resulting from a fainting spell; death under an anaesthetic; a broken nose from a friendly scuffle; a car accident resulting partly from a heart attack).

Many definitions (especially for life insurance double indemnity, but also for some health insurance) allow the accident benefit only when injuries are affected solely through external violent means and where there is a visible contusion or wound. Some definitions specifically exclude one or more of the following:

1. Taking drugs, medicine or anaesthetics
2. Inhaling gas or fumes
3. Sunstroke
4. Commission of or attempt to commit an assault or felony
5. Participation in a riot, civil commotion, or hostile action
6. Various types of flying

From all this, we can see the importance of determining the provisions of any policy regarding accidents, where the accident benefit is different from the sickness benefit (which we have maintained should not be the case).

Differing Exclusions and Reductions

Most health policies exclude suicide or attempts at suicide, anything covered by workmen's compensation, and contain some type of exclusion on injuries resulting from acts of war or while in the armed services. Usually excluded are costs of dental care and cosmetic and plastic surgery, except where these are made necessary by a covered accident; the same is true for eyeglasses and hearing aids.

Very few still have travel exclusions, but it is advisable to determine if there are any in a policy being considered. Most policies have exclusions or reductions for treatment of mental disorders. These vary from (1) complete exclusion, (2) one-half benefits, to (3) payment only while confined in a hospital *not* specializing primarily in such treatment. Regarding old-age, there is again a wide variety of exclusions or reductions. They include those just recited for mental disorders plus a complete change of policy benefits to insure medicare "gaps." It is *all-important* to know of any exclusions or restrictions regarding preexisting conditions (previously discussed under the "Definitions" section).

17

Reducing Earnings Losses Through Insurance

Most of us would still agree with Benjamin Franklin's adage "nothing is certain in life but death and taxes." The degree of uncertainty among the various facets of our future varies greatly. This is particularly true of uncertainty regarding the loss of future earnings. There are basically four possible exposures:

1. Loss of job (including reduction of pay)
2. Premature death
3. Disability
4. Old age

As we explore the means of reducing losses through insurance for each of these exposures, we will consider—

—the chance of loss

—means of loss reduction other than insurance

—the extent to which insurance can reduce the loss

—which individual insurance policy or policies to buy

Losses Resulting from Unemployment

Chance of Loss

No attempt will be made to explore statistically the matter of *chance of loss* of employment. Reliable measurement is impossible. Each person must make his own judgment of the personal situation. The causes of such loss are many: company failure, merger, and consolidation; departmental reorganization; personal relations with fellow workers and with management; industry obsolescence; technological displacement; economic fluctuations locally, regionally, nationally, and worldwide.

We should note the constant imbalance in the supply and demand for all categories of workers—unskilled and skilled, as well as the technically trained and those in professions. Examples of the latter are the oversupply of geologists in the 1950s following critical shortages two decades earlier; a similar glut of scientists in the 1970s following the sputnik-inspired near-panic in the 1950s; and the overabundance of Ph.D.'s for college teaching in the 1970s following a critical shortage when the post-World War II baby boom was felt by the colleges in the 1960s.

Further, who can measure the impact of the combined forces of technological displacement and lower birth rates on the one hand and a greatly increased labor force on the other? Still, there are other seemingly plausible factors adding up to a bullish prospect for general employment levels in the next half-century. From all of this, we can conclude that the *chance of loss* of earnings through unemployment (1) is unpredictable with any degree of accuracy and (2) the unpredictability applies to all categories of employment.

Reducing Losses by Means Other than Insurance

A few means of reducing the exposure to losses from unemployment would appear to be:

Developing individual attitudes, skills, and productivity in order to be among the most valued employees.

Learning other skills and trades as a hedge against reduced employment opportunities in one's present field of employment.

Becoming self-employed through ownership of a business. (This alternative introduces a whole new set of financial uncertainties.)

Other members of the family can seek employment, of course, to help off-set the loss of income. It may seem irrelevant—almost irreverent—to mention the financial opportunities attendant to choosing a marriage partner with substantial means. Even so, this is a means of reducing the financial consequences of loss of earnings.

How Much Can Insurance Reduce the Loss?

The only existing formal unemployment insurance program in this country was introduced by the Social Security Act of 1935. This act, with subsequent amendments, provides for individual state programs giving benefits to unemployed workers. The 1970 amendment extended coverage to include not only employees of private industry but also those of state hospitals, state colleges and universities, and certain non-profit institutions.

The program is financed basically by a 3.2 percent payroll tax on the first $4,200 of wages. An individual employer can get some reduction in this by maintaining a favorable record of employee terminations. The benefits, paid weekly, vary greatly in amounts among the fifty states. For example, maximum benefits for a worker without dependents range from $40 to $79 a week; with dependents, from $40 to $114. The *amount* and duration of the benefits are based on a formula each state has devised relating to average wage previous to loss of job. The most typical maximum duration is twenty-six weeks, with a few states allowing up to thirty-six weeks. There are also some states which automatically extend the duration when the general unemployment level of the state reaches a certain figure. The reader is urged to acquaint himself with information pertinent to his own state. Regardless of which state it is, he will find that this—the only form of unemployment insurance—leaves a wide gap between job earnings and insurance benefits.

What some consider an abuse of this particular social insurance program stems from the situation where both the father and mother work. The mother, feeling the need for occasional extended periods of being a full-time housewife, seeks employment of a nature where she is likely to be laid off at fairly regular intervals, thus collecting unemployment insurance benefits.

The "which policy to buy" question does not arise in the area of unemployment insurance. Voluntary individual unemployment insurance is not offered.

Losses Resulting
from Disability

Chance of Loss

In 1970, as Exhibit 17–1 shows, roughly one out of twenty persons age eighteen through sixty-four suffered "complete work disability"; one out of thirty-three suffered long term disability (two years or more). It is likely that the percent of workers disabled was even greater, since the data is based on

Exhibit 17–1   Persons Age 18 to 64 Years Old With Complete Work Disability, 1970

United States Urban and rural	Total	Complete work disability						
		Total	Less than 6 months	6 to 11 months	1 to 2 years	3 to 4 years	5 to 9 years	10 years or more
Total, 18 to 64 years old	112 289 642	4 930 709	405 265	318 372	796 342	803 310	974 449	1 632 971
18 to 24 years	23 210 261	328 939	57 080	34 545	40 638	37 529	28 534	130 613
25 to 34 years	24 661 442	421 968	57 092	34 399	64 886	57 268	53 770	154 553
35 to 44 years	22 960 719	670 114	64 358	47 280	107 776	103 435	119 830	227 435
45 to 49 years	11 977 878	557 435	44 755	34 354	87 357	91 954	114 304	184 711
50 to 54 years	10 986 401	710 202	49 900	43 148	114 287	120 559	150 788	231 520
55 to 59 years	9 936 662	968 339	61 261	55 988	160 679	164 594	216 761	309 056
60 to 64 years	8 556 279	1 273 712	70 819	68 658	220 719	227 971	290 462	395 083
60 and 61 years	3 639 421	478 204	27 734	26 679	82 687	82 129	108 758	150 217
62 to 64 years	4 916 858	795 508	43 085	41 979	138 032	145 842	181 704	244 866
Male, 18 to 64 years old	54 181 381	2 009 639	172 248	148 800	364 626	330 358	397 345	596 262
18 to 24 years	11 235 266	157 205	19 504	13 547	23 283	19 506	14 322	67 043
25 to 34 years	12 022 001	168 867	20 353	13 824	25 578	21 511	20 614	66 987
35 to 44 years	11 144 365	257 493	25 395	19 202	44 120	36 255	44 601	87 920
45 to 49 years	5 752 666	211 557	18 005	15 123	35 012	32 935	43 576	66 906
50 to 54 years	5 276 313	273 787	23 044	19 908	46 975	45 965	58 014	79 881
55 to 59 years	4 746 732	385 653	29 615	28 322	73 722	68 724	87 121	98 149
60 to 64 years	4 004 038	555 077	36 332	38 874	115 936	105 462	129 097	129 376
60 and 61 years	1 715 720	197 294	13 647	14 301	40 837	34 117	46 710	47 682
62 to 64 years	2 288 318	357 783	22 685	24 573	75 099	71 345	82 387	81 694

Exhibit 17–1 (continued)

United States Urban and rural	Total	Complete work disability						
		Total	Less than 6 months	6 to 11 months	1 to 2 years	3 to 4 years	5 to 9 years	10 years or more
Female, 18 to 64 years old	58 108 261	2 921 070	233 017	169 572	431 716	472 952	577 104	1 036 709
18 to 24 years	11 974 995	171 734	37 576	20 998	17 355	18 023	14 212	63 570
25 to 34 years	12 639 441	253 101	36 739	20 575	39 308	35 757	33 156	87 566
35 to 44 years	11 816 354	412 621	38 963	28 078	63 656	67 180	75 229	139 515
45 to 49 years	6 225 212	345 878	26 750	19 231	52 345	59 019	70 728	117 805
50 to 54 years	5 710 088	436 415	26 856	23 240	67 312	74 594	92 774	151 639
55 to 59 years	5 189 930	582 686	31 646	27 666	86 957	95 870	129 640	210 907
60 to 64 years	4 552 241	718 635	34 487	29 784	104 783	122 509	161 365	265 707
60 and 61 years	1 923 701	280 910	14 087	12 378	41 850	48 012	62 048	102 535
62 to 64 years	2 628 540	437 725	20 400	17 406	62 933	74 497	99 317	163 172

Source: "Persons With Work Disability," *1970 Census of Population,* U.S. Department of Commerce, Table 1, p. 1.

total population age eighteen to sixty-four, rather than the 80 million of that group on the labor market. It is also apparent the chance of becoming disabled increases significantly with advancing age.

It has been estimated that in 1971 about $16 billion of personal income loss was incurred from non-occupational, short-term sickness, and that about $2 billion was paid out during the same year in workmen's compensation disability income benefits.[1] The "odds" of income loss from disability, it seems, are great enough to warrant consideration of means of reducing the possible losses.

Reducing Losses from Disability through Means Other than Insurance

Prevention. Prevention of disabling illnesses and accidents and—where that is not possible—minimizing the incidence of such are means of reducing earnings losses from disability. This, of course, involves the fields of physical and mental health care and accident prevention.

Assistance from Employer. The scope of the ways the employer may help to prevent or reduce loss of pay in the event of disability extends from formal benefit programs to individual consideration of each case. The most typical formal benefit (other than group disability insurance, which will be discussed later) is an employee sick-leave program. In 1971, formal sick-leave plans covered some 16.5 million employees, approximately one out of five workers.[2] Another informal benefit might also be the employer's willingness to allow vacation time to extend the total period off the job with pay.

Spouse and Children Seek Employment. As in the case of unemployment, earnings losses resulting from disability can be partially offset by a non-employed spouse or child going to work. This often provides a disappointingly small net income due to relatively low pay, costs attendant to working, child care costs, and greater expenses in operating the home.

Spending accumulated capital or borrowing money are not ways of *reducing* losses from disability; rather, this is a reflection of absorbing the loss.

How Much Can Insurance Reduce Losses from Disability?

Insuring against loss of earnings resulting from disability confronts the family decision maker with perplexing questions. Protection is available from three areas: (1) compulsory insurance under federal social security and state workmen's compensation, (2) as part of the fringe benefit program in connection with employment, and (3) individual policies which one might decide to purchase from private insurers.

---

[1]Social Security Administration, *Social Security Bulletin*, January, 1973, p. 21, 62.
[2]*Source Book of Health Insurance*, 1972–73 (New York: Health Insurance Institute, 1973), p. 25.

Exhibit 17–2 Examples of Monthly Cash Benefits under Old Age, Survivors and Disability Insurance

					Average monthly earnings					
	$76 or less	$150	$250	$350	$450	$550c	$650c	$750c	$850c	$1000c
					Primary insurance amount (PIA)					
	84a	134a	174	213	250	288	331	354	374	404
					Maximum family benefit					
	126	201	267	371	467	522	579	620	655	707

Benefit	% of PIA										
Retirement											
Insured, age 65	100 %	84	134	174	213	250	288	331	354	374	404
Insured, age 62	80 %	67	107	139	170	200	230	264	283	299	323
Wife, age 65	50 %	42	67	87	106	125	144	165	177	187	202
Wife, age 62	37.5%	31	50	65	80	94	108	124	133	140	152
Each child	50 %	42	67	87	106	125	144	165	177	187	202

	%										
Survivorship											
Widow, age 60	71.5%	73	96	125	152	179	206	236	253	267	289
Widow, age 65	100 %[b]	84	134	174	213	250	288	331	354	374	404
Widow any age with dependent child	75 %	84	100	131	160	188	216	248	265	280	303
Each child	75 %	84	100	131	160	188	216	248	265	280	303
Disability											
Insured, age 65	100 %	84	134	174	213	250	288	331	354	374	404
Wife with dependent child	50 %	42	67	87	106	125	144	165	177	187	202
Each child	50 %	42	67	87	106	125	144	165	177	187	202
Disabled widow at age 50	50 %	51	67	87	107	125	144	166	178	188	203
Lump sum death benefits		253	255	255	255	255	255	255	255	255	255

[a]A person who worked under social security more than 22 years, but at relatively low pay, may qualify for a special minimum benefit higher than the usual amount. With 30 or more years of coverage, the benefit would be $170 a month.
[b]If either the widow or her deceased spouse received reduced social security benefits before 65, then the widow will receive *less* than 100% at 65.
[c]Higher benefits shown in the columns on the right generally won't be payable until later. Top retirement benefit for a worker who was 65 in 1973 is $266.10 per month. Maximum family benefits in 1973: $490.10 for a retired worker and his family; $599.40 for a disabled worker and his family; and $620.40 for the family of a deceased worker.

Social Security. Social security disability benefits provide a substantial base for developing a disability income insurance program. For example, as Exhibit 17–2 reflects, a worker with average monthly earnings of $850 who qualifies for the disability benefit would, starting six months after the onset of the disability, receive $375 per month. The payments would continue as long as the disability lasts, up to age sixty-five at which time he would start drawing the retirement benefit.[3] The wife of the same insured worker would receive $188 per month while there was a dependent child, and each child would receive $188 per month.[4] Thus, the total benefits for a family of four would be $939 which would be reduced to the maximum family benefit of $655.

Assuming the insured's current earnings were close to $850 at the onset of the disability and that there was adequate health insurance, the family would have near adequate recovery of earnings losses from the social security benefit alone. The waiting period could represent a substantial loss, but—as has been noted—many employers have sick-leave programs which would take care of part or all of this income period.

Recalling the discussion in Chapter 16 on determining average monthly earnings, we know that those who have been under Social Security for many years are more likely to have a significant gap between current earnings and social security benefits than a young person. The average monthly earnings for younger workers will be much closer to current wages because earnings levels of the past decade have been higher and a greater amount of annual earnings have been covered under Social Security.

From Exhibit 17–2 we note that the maximum average monthly earnings are $1,000. This produces a $405 monthly benefit to a worker and a $708 maximum family benefit. This means there will be significant income gaps for higher income families even where the maximum social security disability is received.

Disability Income from Job-Connected Accidents and Illnesses. All fifty states have special programs for partial replacement of income and for medical expenses for disabilities arising from employment. These limited benefits are based on *employer's liability* and *workmen's compensation* laws. Employer's liability is based on harm to employees arising from the *employer's negligence.* This concept proved to be unacceptable because of the difficulty of proving negligence in most job-connected accidents and illnesses. Accordingly, all states have supplemented employer's liability statutes with *workmen's compensation* laws. These eliminate the negligence factor and provide specific benefits for *any* job-connected disability.

The employer's negligence liability is still important to varying degrees among the states (1) as a possible action by the employee for benefits in addition to those of workmen's compensation where the employer has been grossly

---

[3]Exhibit 16–1 has been reproduced at this point as Exhibit 17–2 for reference convenience in this chapter.

[4]Qualifying conditions and definitions of terms such as "dependent child" were explained in Chapter 16.

negligent, (2) where state law permits an employee to "elect out" of the workmen's compensation coverage (thus relying on the possibly larger but less certain benefits from a negligence claim), (3) in the twelve states which apply workmen's compensation only to certain hazardous industries, (4) for certain diseases not on the list of "covered" diseases, and (5) where state law provides "small shop" workmen's compensation exemption. The latter applies to "small business," judged as such according to the number of employees.

Disability benefits under workmen's compensation are paid for *temporary total disability* and for *permanent total disability*. The amount is stated as a percent of wages at the time of disability with a stated (1) maximum weekly payment, (2) maximum time limit and, in some states, (3) a maximum total amount that will be paid. Except for a few states, disability income benefits fall significantly short of replacing earnings even in the limited area of job-connected disability.

Other Disability Benefits from Employment. More and more employers are providing, as part of the employment contract, provisions for continuation of income when an employee is unable to work because of sickness. Previous mention has been made of: a specified number of days off with pay due to illness, annual sick leave allowance, use of vacation time and other non-insurance benefits allowing pay for short-term illnesses.

Formal disability insurance programs are also provided by employers, primarily through group insurance contracts with commercial insurance companies.

Group Plans. The group plans are of two types:

1. Short-term disability income insurance
2. Long-term disability income insurance

In 1971 over 33.2 million workers had short-term disability income protection, in addition to the 16.5 million under formal paid sick-leave programs. Long-term disability income protection covered 8.2 million workers. Income benefits paid out under short-term and long-term protection amounted to $1,974,988,000.[5]

Short-term disability income insurance. As the name indicates, short-term disability group plans provide for relatively brief illnesses only. Usually there is a weekly benefit related to the employee's earning, but with a maximum benefit. Typical duration periods are thirteen weeks and twenty-six weeks—in fewer instances, one or two years.

The maximum amount varies greatly with the group policy purchased; most often it is one-half to two-thirds of current earnings with some stated maximum amount. The weekly benefit *is not in addition* to any workmen's compensation. Such payments are either deducted from or paid instead of the disability income benefit.

---

[5]Data in this paragraph obtained from *Source Book of Health Insurance,* 1972–73, p. 25.

There is usually a short period at the start of any disability for which no benefits are paid. This is typically one week and often coincides with pay continuation plans of the individual employer.

Long-term disability income insurance. The fact that fewer than 10 percent of all employees are provided long-term disability protection is an indication that insurance companies have been reluctant to offer this coverage. Basically this has been because, as was previously explained, the *permanent disability* risk is very weak on the important requirements of what constitutes an insurable risk. Many insurers had disastrous experience with permanent disability plans offered during the first three decades of this century. However, some companies are now venturing again into this field relying on the following underwriting safeguards to protect them from catastrophic claims experience.

1. Strict adherence to the indemnification principle. The amount of the benefit is stated as a percentage of earnings with a deduction from this amount for payments received from other sources as a result of this disability. This would include deducting benefits from social security, workmen's compensation, and any insurance other than individual disability income policies. Even the latter are deducted in some plans.

2. Elimination of benefit payments for short-term illnesses. There is a lengthy elimination period (no benefits payable for the number of days stated). The shortest such period is 30 days and more often is 60, 90, or 120 days.

3. Cooperation of employers and employees to prevent claims abuse. The permanent disability group policies are written on a yearly contract basis and are renewable at the option of the employer and the insurance company. The insurers are thus relying on the employer and the employees' eagerness to continue this protection and their recognition that it can be done so only if benefits are paid on valid claims.

The benefit amount is usually two-thirds to three-fourths of current earnings with some stated maximum amount such as $1,000 to $2,000 per month. Here again, we find the higher income groups faced with a serious income loss problem from disability.

There are disability benefits of lesser significance provided in group life insurance plans and pension plans. The typical benefit in the group life plan relates to waiving any future premiums for the life insurance when an employee is totally and permanently disabled. Pension plans frequently provide for early retirement in the event of total and permanent disability. Restraints on abuse of this provision are in the nature of rather restrictive definitions of *total and permanent disability* and also significant reductions in the amount of the benefit where early retirement is chosen.

Individual Disability Income Policies. From our study to this point of insurance as a means of reducing earnings losses resulting from disability, we can make some generalizations.

1. Workmen's compensation benefit levels are in most instances inadequate. In addition, protection is limited to job-connected disabilities.

2. Social Security disability income benefits are fairly adequate for families where earnings were less than $1,000 per month, *but only if the average monthly earnings closely approximate these earnings at the onset of disability.* Such would possibly be the case for only the younger worker whose higher earnings level has been fairly stable. Further, there is the matter of a five full month waiting period plus a highly restrictive definition of what constitutes total disability.

3. Disability income fringe benefits from employment vary widely among employers. Nearly 50 million workers enjoy short-term benefits or formal paid sick-leave benefits. These are of varying degrees of income adequacy. We can presume these plans are more and more being designed to coordinate with the waiting period of social security disability benefits.

4. Only about *10 percent of employed workers* are provided *long-term* disability income benefits by their employers. For those relatively few, the level of the benefit is adequate for those with lower and middle incomes, but inadequate for high-income employees.

5. Even if all workers had adequate short-term disability income coverage, there would remain the long-term disability problem. Acknowledgment of the *large loss principle* (which was explained in Chapter 14) would mean recognition that long-term disability poses a catastrophic threat to family finances.

With the just stated limitations of other protection (workmen's compensation, social security, employment benefits), there is an obvious high loss exposure for many. For these, the only remaining alternative is the purchase of individual long-term disability income policies. Yet, in 1971, only 4 million individuals owned such policies.[6] The reasons for this were related in Chapter

Exhibit 17–3   Examples of Annual Premiums for Individual Disability Income Policies Providing $500 Monthly Income to Age 65

| | Age at issue | | | | |
Company	25	30	35	40	45
A	$163	$189	$223	$269	$328
B	162	189	226	273	328
C	216	240	275	314	378
D	191	215	246	284	336
E	175	220	264	289	348

*Non-cancellable, premium guaranteed. Actual rates of five major companies. Policies vary markedly on individual provisions.

[6]*Source Book of Health Insurance*, p. 25.

16: few insurance companies and agents push the sale of this coverage and the premiums seem high for the benefits offered. It might be said that individual disability income policies are a product without an effective sales force. There are very few agents who specialize in or even push this coverage. This leaves the marketing to agents whose primary zeal is the sale of life or property insurance. Exhibit 17–3 gives an indication of the price range of long-term individual disability income policies.

Substantial as these rates are, many individuals should give serious consideration to purchasing long-term disability income protection. Unlikely as it is to happen, permanent disability probably poses the greatest threat of financial catastrophe of any of the insurable uncertainties facing a family.[7]

Losses Resulting from Premature Death

It is realistic to refer to modern man as a *money machine:* he works and he *makes* money. The logic of placing a present value on the future earnings potential of an individual was discussed in Chapter 14. Exhibit 17–4 illustrates the "human life value" of projected lifetime earnings potentials.[8]

Death of this "money machine" during its productive period is referred to as *premature death.* In terms of family finance, death poses its greatest threat from the chance that it will come to one of the parents while children are still dependent on them. [The word *parent* is used rather than *father* or *breadwinner,* because there are serious financial consequences attendant to the death of the mother whether she be a wage earner or housewife or both.]

Chance of Loss

The probability of the death of either parent prior to any given age can be determined with a high degree of accuracy. Exhibits 17–5, 17–6, and 17–7 show the probabilities for a range of typical family situations. The significance

---

[7]This is a most difficult personal insurance to obtain. One company's underwriting instructions to agents include limitations such as the following: maximum amount of all disability income benefits (excluding social security, but including group, other individual policies, and salary continuance plans) cannot exceed 50 percent of earned income; anyone earning under $7,500 annually is not eligible (except for college seniors, professionals, etc.); exclusion riders eliminate benefits from illnesses where there is a present medical history, such as kidney stones, hernia, poor hearing, etc.; unacceptable occupations include any hourly wage basis job, actors, aircraft pilots, appliance servicemen, armed forces, artists, professional athletes, authors, mechanics, bakers, bartenders, beauty parlor operators, all building trades, metal industry workers, miners, police, musicians, truck drivers.

[8]Amounts shown in this table, as noted, do not include a mortality factor for probability of death before age sixty-five as is customary in human life value projections. For reasoning relative to this, see J. B. Aponte and H. S. Denenberg "A New Concept of The Economics of Life Value and Human Life Values: A Rationale For Term Insurance As the Cornerstone of Insurance Marketing," *Journal of Risk and Insurance,* Vol. XXXV, Sept. 1968.

is obvious: *the likelihood of the father's death before his child reaches maturity is great enough to require adequate premature death insurance. This becomes even more urgent as older fathers have children.* Before reaching age twenty-five, one out of twenty to twenty-five children whose fathers were twenty-five at the time of their birth will lose his father. This will happen to one out of fourteen children where the fathers were age thirty, one out of eight where the fathers were age thirty-five, almost one out of five where the fathers were forty, and one out of four where the fathers were forty-five at the birth of the children. We should note also the much greater likelihood of a child losing his father than his mother.

Exhibit 17–4   Present Value of Future Earnings*

Number of years of earnings	Amount of monthly earnings				
	$750	*$1,000*	*$1,250*	*$1,500*	*$2,000*
10	$ 71,363	$ 95,151	$118,939	$142,726	$190,052
20	115,174	153,566	191,957	230,349	307,132
30	142,072	189,429	236,243	284,143	378,858
40	158,583	211,444	264,667	317,167	422,888

*No mortality factor included following the reasoning that earnings cut short by premature death should be insured. Earnings discounted at 5 percent.

Reducing Losses through Means Other than Insurance

Prevention. The scope and specifics of the many ways an individual can decrease the chance of his premature death are obvious, including diet, exercise, habits, attitudes, activities, and occupation. No attempt will be made to measure statistically the extent to which a person can lessen the chances of his premature death. It is generally recognized, however, that these premature death prevention measures are relatively insignificant compared to the forces beyond the control of an individual. Whatever the significance of prevention measures, most will agree this is not an acceptable single way of dealing with the financial consequences of the premature death of the parent.

Other Means. All other means of dealing with the premature death of a parent relate to the happening of such a tragic occurrence. Except for insurance to replace the earnings of the deceased, other means are normally considered undesirable. They include: spending accumulated or borrowed funds for current expenses; the taking of employment or additional employment by the surviving spouse and children; a hasty early remarriage; accepting a lower standard of living, moving in or sharing the home with others; breaking up the family unit.

At this point, the financial consequences to the family of the death of the mother should be reemphasized. The difficulty of finding and paying an accept-

Exhibit 17–5* *Number of Fathers Per 1,000, Who Will Die Within the Number of Years Stated Below*

Age at beginning	5 years	10 years	15 years	18 years	25 years
20	3	7	11	15	29
25	4	9	15	21	46
30	5	12	23	33	75
35	7	18	37	55	119
40	11	31	64	91	183
45	20	54	103	143	277
50	34	85	157	215	405

Exhibit 17–6* *Number of Newborn Children Per 1,000, Who, Before Age 18, Will Suffer the Death of Their Fathers or Mothers*

Age of parent at birth of child	Fathers	Mothers
20	15	12
25	21	15
30	33	21
35	55	33
40	91	55
45	143	91
50	215	143

Exhibit 17–7* *Number of Wives Per 1,000 (One Year Younger Than Husbands), Who Will Live at Least the Number of Years Stated Below and Will Become Widows Within That Period of Time*

Husband's age at beginning	10 years	15 years	20 years	40 years
20	7	11	18	120
25	8	15	26	172
30	12	22	41	240
35	18	37	68	312
40	30	62	106	360
45	52	97	156	340
50	81	142	220	235
55	117	202	291	112

*These three tables are based on a group mortality table and the assumption that the mortality of the adult males and females in a family is the same as that of the males and females in the group mortality table. The degree of error in this assumption is minor. It is further assumed that there is no mortality of the children. The group mortality table used is the Group Annuity Mortality Table for 1951 (male lives), projected to 1962 by Projection Scale C, set back five years for females. The three tables above were prepared by John J. Evans, Associate Actuary of Southwestern Life Insurance Company.

able housekeeper are convincing reasons for having adequate funds for this purpose.

How Much Can Insurance Reduce the Loss?

To the question "To what extent can insurance reduce financial loss resulting from the risk of premature death?" the answer is "almost completely." This affirmative answer must be qualified (1) to the extent it is not possible to accurately estimate future earnings and (2) by the relatively small "loss" incurred from life insurance premium payments. The next logical question is "Just how small *is* the certain loss (insurance premiums) that is being substituted for the large uncertain loss (from premature death)?" The answer again is favorable. This is especially so if we are thinking of insuring earnings against death during the *family period*. At the risk of undue repetition, it should be pointed out that this favorable situation exists because (1) the *chance of loss* is not great, and (2) the premature death *risk* rates most favorably on all the requirements of an insurable risk.

Which Policy or Policies to Buy

Insurance Available. Fortunately, there is no problem on the availability of life insurance, other than the insurability factor. Even this is not a problem in social insurance and group insurance. For most individuals the insurance available falls into three categories; social security survivorship benefits; group life insurance in connection with employment; and individual policies purchased from insurance companies.

Specific Needs. Why do we need income? This may seem a ridiculous question, but *specific* answers are necessary if we are to determine *how much* insurance and *which policy types* to buy as protection against loss of the income through premature death.

It is true, as an insurance company once advertised, "there's no one else exactly like *you*" in terms of specific income needs. It is possible, however, to categorize the most important needs. From the earnings of an individual's productive life, there are usually *these* minimum goals to achieve:

1. Have funds available for death expenses—usually referred to as a *clean-up fund*.
2. Provide the necessities and certain luxuries for the family unit for all dependents: *family period income* (until the children are grown), and *widow's income* (after the children are grown).
3. Pay for a home—often called the *mortgage redemption* need.
4. Provide for any special educational needs or desires of the children—thus, a *college education fund*.
5. Have a cash reserve for unforeseen and uninsured financial emergencies—thus, an *emergency fund*.
6. Assure a comfortable living following retirement from work—hence, a *retirement income*.

From this listing, it might appear a program of life insurance—especially the premature death aspect—is a very complicated matter. Actually, for most families, it should not be. Let's see why.

A starting point is to be aware of the two basic types of life insurance policies (as explained in Chapter 16):[9]

1. Term policies. These are contracts which provide insurance for a specified number of years. If the insured dies within that period, the policy pays the face amount; if not, there are no benefits. All other lines of insurance—health, fire, automobile, etc—are term policies.

2. "Permanent" policies. These are the "savings account plus insurance" contracts—endowment at age 100 (whole life) and shorter term endowments.

Next, three generalizations are in order.

1. Term policies are for *temporary* needs.

2. Permanent policies are for *continuing needs* and for those needs which might require cash before the death of the insured.

3. Of the many permanent policies, whole life (also called "ordinary" and "straight" life) usually should be purchased where "permanent" insurance is needed. This is valid only on the assumption that the same amount of premium dollars will be used to purchase whole life as an alternative permanent plan (i.e., endowment at sixty-five, twenty year endowment, endowment at eighteen, etc.). There are three reasons for this last generalization:

   a) The insurance cost of the policy is so minor compared to the savings account part that there is little difference in the savings account aspect, regardless of which "permanent" plan is purchased. Thus, we might as well have the extra insurance. Exhibit 17–8 illustrates this.

   b) Having a policy with a greater face amount and with no restrictions as to how long premium payments may be continued gives greater flexibility for the future.

   c) There is the possibility of getting a better buy in choosing a whole life policy as opposed to other plans—in terms of premiums, dividends, and non-forfeiture values. Whole life is the policy plan most widely purchased and on which there is likely to be the greatest competition among companies. In terms of face amount, during 1971, whole life purchases were three times greater than limited pay policies, and nine times greater than endowment policies.[10]

---

[9]A brief review of that section of Chapter 16 would be helpful at this point.

[10]*Life Insurance Fact Book* (New York: Institute of Life Insurance, 1972), p. 18. Probably included in the limited pay life total were such plans as Life Paid-Up at 85 and other old ages, which are basically whole life plans; thus the margin over limited pay life plans was probably much greater.

Professor Joseph M. Belth states the matter this way: "Most companies have dozens of basic policies and a number of riders that may be added to almost any one of the basic policies. The primary effect of this proliferation is to confuse and frustrate the buyer. Fortunately, there is a way out for the consumer. The life insurance needs of virtually any buyer can be met satisfactorily with just two policy forms—straight life and five-year renewable term—or some combination of the two."[11]

Exhibit 17–8   Examples of Death Benefit and Cash Values of Various Policies Purchased by $100 Annual Premium (age at issue 25)*

Death benefit	Ordinary life $7,160	20 pay life $3,930	Life paid-up at 65 $6,270	Endowment at 65 $5,340
Cash values at end of:				
10th year	963.31	1031.31	983.32	1,004.51
15th year	1508.11	1641.21	1543.72	1,580.69
20th year	2080.84	2302.15	2139.83	2,202.11

*Based on Commissioners Standard Ordinary Mortality Table, 3 percent interest reserve, net level premiums and reserves.

Choosing the Policy. A great deal of fanfare is often given to the matter of *programming* an individual or family's life insurance. Elaborate charts are prepared to show dollar amounts of year-by-year *income* needs and *special-purpose* (mortgage redemption, clean-up, college education, etc.) needs. Existing insurance is then applied to providing for these needs, and is shown on the graphs. The income and special-purpose needs *not covered* by existing protection (social security survivorship and old age income benefits, group life insurance, and individual life policies) are also shown graphically with recommendations given as to how much and what type *additional* protection to purchase.

This methodology of (1) determining amounts needed, (2) applying existing protection to these accounts and (3) determining the additional life insurance necessary to complete the protection is a rational approach. It has the weakness of being *static,* since all needs assumptions are based on present conditions. No allowance is made for likely changes such as greater earnings; inflation; family attitude, goals and size. It is also doubtful that the charts and graphs which accompany this procedure serve much purpose to the insured. Often the insured's efforts to understand and interpret the charts only add to

[11]Joseph M. Belth, *Life Insurance: A Consumer's Handbook* (Bloomington: Indiana University Press, 1973), p. 19.

the confusion. The same information can be presented in a more understandable narrative form. With this in mind, and following the

> *term* policies for *temporary* needs,
> *permanent* policies for *permanent* needs

concept, we are ready to start thinking about specific policies for specific needs.

Clean-up fund. This is a permanent need. Death is inevitable, and there will eventually be a need of funds for death expenses. This calls for permanent insurance, with the whole life policy ideal for this purpose. How much? This can vary from some amount such as $5,000 (to be sure to have ample funds for last expenses) to $1,000,000 or more (for the person whose estate will be subjected to that much or more federal estate taxes and state inheritance taxes).[12]

Family period income. This is a temporary need because (1) the amount required decreases each time a paycheck is brought home and the children are that many days closer to being self-sustaining financially (2) and the need disappears when the last child is no longer dependent.

This suggests that a term policy would be appropriate and that a decreasing term policy would be adequate. The social security survivorship benefit is, in essence, decreasing term life.

Happily, adequate life insurance for this, a most urgent protection need, can be afforded by most families. Let's consider two hypothetical cases, the Browns and the Greens.

The Jack Browns. Jack Brown is age twenty-five, has a wife and children ages one and three. His family budget is based on $800 a month "take-home pay," $120 of which are "his" expenses (food, clothing, transportation to work, recreation, insurance on his life, etc.). He has been working for three years since graduating from college and has gross social security average monthly earnings of $750. The family has just purchased a new home which has a $20,000, twenty-year mortgage on which the principal and interest payments are $160 monthly. If Jack Brown had died in 1973, for example, his family would have received monthly social security survivorship income of $620, the maximum family survivor benefit payable in 1973. With the mother's benefit of $265 monthly (three-fourths of Brown's $354 Primary Insurance Amount) and *each* child's benefit (until age eighteen or up to age twenty-two while a full-time student) the same $265, the total would be $795 were it not for the $620 maximum family benefit.[13] This $620 is only $60 less than the amount necessary to maintain the monthly budget ($800 less $120 of "his" expenses).

If the mortgage on the home were paid-off by other life insurance leaving only taxes and insurance to pay on the home, we can see that the social security survivorship benefit would provide more than the income necessary to maintain the present budget. Even had Jack's average monthly earnings been only $350 there would be little problem affording adequate life insurance to aug-

---

[12]The matter of estate conservation will be considered in Chapter 23.

[13]See Exhibit 17–2 for Social Security benefit amounts given in this discussion. Benefit amounts are those in effect in 1973.

ment the $371 maximum family benefit his survivors would receive. Exhibit 17–9 shows that Jack could provide the $60 a month income from the date of his death until his youngest child, now age one, reaches twenty-one for an annual premium of $31.30 ($3.55 for $10 monthly income × 6 + $10). A $310 a month twenty-year family income policy, combined with the $371 social security survivor's benefit, would give the family $681 monthly income. It would cost only $121.05 annual premium ($31 × $3.55 + $10 = $121.05).

*Exhibit 17–9 Annual Premiums for $10 per Month Family Income Policy**

	Family period			
Age at issue	15 years ($1481 initial insurance)	20 years ($1855 initial insurance)	To age 65	(initial ins.)
20	$2.56	$ 3.36	$ 9.03	($3,123)
25	2.63	3.55	9.23	($2,933)
30	2.99	4.22	9.80	($2,716)
35	4.02	5.87	10.97	($2,466)
40	5.51	8.31	11.80	($2,181)
45	7.93	12.21	12.21	($1,855)

*Premiums quoted by a major life insurance company. $10 annual charge is added for each policy issued.

The Tom Greens. Tom Green is thirty-five years old, has a wife and children ages ten and six. His family budget is based on $1,200 of monthly take-home pay of which $170 are "his" expenses. His $450 gross social security average monthly earnings is not as close to his current earnings because of lower earlier wages and a smaller part of his wages subjected to tax during the first decade of his business career. The family purchased a new home five years ago. Principal and interest payments on the $24,000 mortgage are $195 monthly. Tom Green would need to provide $563 monthly income from life insurance ($1,200 budget less $170 "his" expense equals $1,030 less $467 survivors maximum family benefit equals $563). At his age, we note from Exhibit 17–9 that $10 a month for a fifteen-year family period costs $4.02 annually; fifty-seven units of $10 income would provide $570 from the date of Tom's death until his youngest child is age 21. Thus, 57 × 4.02 + $10 = $239.14 annual premium. This premium of less than $20 a month is a remarkably low cost for Tom to guarantee a continuance through the family period of the current monthly income should he die during that time. For an approximate $10 additional monthly premium he could provide $280 additional income as a hedge against inflation and an increasing family budget.

From these two examples we can conclude that adequate *family period income* life insurance is within the means of any family.[14] A case could be made

---

[14] Many life insurance companies offer the family income plan only as a rider to a permanent policy. Usually this is no problem because most families need to purchase additional permanent insurance.

for providing the family period income protection with five-year renewable and convertible term. This allows more flexibility than the family income policy in which the insurance in force automatically decreases each month. From the initial insurance amounts given in Exhibit 17–9, the amount of five-year term to purchase in order to provide the equivalent amount of monthly income can be determined. Thus, $1,855 of five-year term will pay $10.00 per month for twenty years under a settlement option. Remember, the family income policy initial insurance amount *decreases* each month to the amount necessary to provide $10 per month for *the remainder of the initial period.* Thus, under a twenty-year family income policy, if the insured died at the end of the fourth policy year, $10 a month would be paid for sixteen years; if the five-year term policy had been chosen, the $10 per month would be paid for twenty years.

We will recall from Chapter 16, the renewable term policies renew at the rate for the attained age of the insured. An indication of the annual premiums involved should the insured choose the five-year term route can be seen from the following rates quoted for five-year term by a major insurer (Exhibit 17–10).

Exhibit 17–10   *Sample Rates for a Five-Year Term Policy*

Age at issue or renewal	Annual premium*	Age at issue or renewal	Annual premium*
20	$3.53	45	$ 8.27
25	3.57	50	12.02
30	3.73	55	17.07
35	4.36	60	26.17
40	5.77	64 (not issued after this age)	37.37

*$15 annual policy fee added to these rates.

A possible disadvantage of choosing the five-year term route over the family income policy would be the necessity of keeping the entire initial amount in force even if future events indicated the need for much less protection. However, if the insurer was unwilling to renew for a smaller face amount *and* if the insured was insurable, he could replace the policy with a new one with a smaller face amount. If he was not insurable, he probably would want to maintain the full amount in force.

Dependent spouse during social security "blackout" period. Social security survivorship benefits cease at the time there are no more "dependent children." This means the surviving spouse receives no more survivorship income until reaching age sixty (or age fifty if disabled). These years of no income have come to be called the *social security blackout period.* We must label this a "temporary" need in that it disappears with the passing of time and is not certain to occur. A parent with no dependent children and with a paid-for home could hope to find employment to meet current budget needs. In addition, there would be life insurance death benefits from policies intended for other purposes (retirement income, emergency funds, etc.) had premature death not occurred. These will be noted later in this discussion.

From Exhibit 17–9 we see that the cost of a family income policy which pays from the insured's death each month until what would have been his age sixty-five is substantially higher than the "family period" plans, but is still moderate in price. Considering the Tom Green example again, in order to provide his wife a monthly income during the social security "blackout" period, Tom may choose to provide $250 a month of the $570 on a "to age sixty-five" basis, with the remainder on the fifteen-year basis. This would make the total annual premium $375.89 ($284.25 for the "to age sixty-five policy; $91.64 for the fifteen-year policy). Even so, specific policies are not usually purchased for this "blackout" period, even though settlement provisions may be directed to this in other policies.

Mortgage redemption. This "temporary" need can be met adequately with a decreasing term life policy. In fact, most companies have just such a package policy. Many mortgage companies offer the policy and include the premiums in the mortgage payment. Since this is term insurance decreasing in face amount as the age of the insured increases, the premiums are nominal. This is not true where the age at issue plus the mortgage period carries the insurance into the insured's old age (his seventies and eighties). Exhibit 17–11 illustrates this.

Exhibit 17–11   *Examples of Premium Rates for $1,000 Mortgage Redemption Policy with Waiver of Premium Benefit Included**

Age at issue	Annual premium		
	20 year mortgage premiums payable for 16 years	25 year mortgage premiums payable for 19 years	30 year mortgage premium payable for 26 years
20	$2.37	$ 2.53	$ 2.75
25	2.63	2.94	3.27
30	3.18	3.72	4.36
35	4.21	5.11	6.14
40	5.97	7.42	9.02
45	8.94	11.18	13.52

*Premiums quoted by a major life insurance company. Add $12 annual policy fee for each policy: i.e., $20,000 twenty year mortgage redemption policy, issued at age thirty-five, costs 20 × $4.21 + $12 = $96.00 per year.

Jack Brown could purchase a mortgage policy which would leave his family a debt-free home for $64.60 annual premium (20M × $2.63 + $12 = $64.60). If Tom Green had bought the same protection when he purchased his home five years ago, the annual premium would have been $88.32 (24M × $3.18 + $12 = $88.32).

Another package Mortgage Redemption policy offered by many insurers involves a decreasing term rider combined with a whole-life policy (typically, $1,000 decreasing term with $1,000 whole life; or with a set amount of whole life, such as $5,000 or $10,000, plus the necessary additional decreasing term to total the amount of the mortgage). Such policies, of course, include the savings account element and are marketed with emphasis on the amount of the savings). There is nothing wrong with such a policy *per se,* but it should be noted that it introduces a savings element not related to this specific need. Since the agent makes a negligible commission on the simple term policy, the combined package helps give the agent enough commission to justify an aggressive sales effort.

College education. From the standpoint of considering life insurance for this need, two aspects of financing a child's education should be considered:

1. Making sure funds are available if the parent(s) are *alive* during the college years.
2. Making sure funds are available if the parent(s) are *deceased.*

Both can be handled through life insurance. A policy with a savings element in each premium puts the intention to save in the form of a semi-obligation (the premium) and thus increases the likelihood of completing the savings program. For many families, there are valid reasons for providing the premature death protection only. Again, the term insurance premium for this package is nominal—even less than for mortgage cancellation, since the "years to college degree" are usually fewer than those of a mortgage. Reasons for going the latter route include:

1. The parents' income during children's college years is likely to be higher than in the early family years.
2. The family budget during these earlier years may not permit a substantial college savings program for *each* child.
3. The proliferation of public junior and senior colleges has increased the opportunity of getting a college education with the general public paying much of the cost.
4. Veterans' benefits for those who choose a term in the armed forces subsidize a college education.
5. Substantial federal, state, and private loan programs permit a person to pay for much of his college education after graduation.

The premium rates for five-year term shown in Exhibit 17–10 show how little money is involved in providing specific funds for college education of each child, if the parent should die before the college years were completed. Provision could be made in a settlement option for the death proceeds to be paid to each child during college years, or the proceeds could be paid over to a life insurance trust (often the trustee would be a bank's trust department) to be disbursed for the stated purposes.

For most families, *college endowment* policies should not be used, for reasons just stated. Should a family have to use savings to send children to college, the cash values of permanent life insurance purchased for other purposes (clean-up funds, estate conservation funds, and retirement income) can be "borrowed" and put back in the policies after the children have graduated.

Emergency fund. Providing an emergency fund for survivors, over and above providing for other specific needs, is a "temporary" need and therefore can be handled with a term life insurance policy. The group life insurance employment benefit (which is usually a term "policy") is often considered for this need. Other life insurance intended for "permanent" needs (as in the case of provision for the "social security blackout period") is available. For this reason, specific policies are usually not purchased for this purpose even though certain permanent policies may have settlement provisions assuring funds in the event of premature death.

The retirement income need is being treated next as a separate "reducing losses through insurance" topic.

Reducing Losses in Earnings Resulting from Old Age

When an individual's employability is judged to be over because of old age, the question of premature death no longer exists.[15] The most general situation at that time is that the individual's spouse is the only likely dependent.

As recently as four or five decades ago, old age to most people meant there was no income of any consequence other than from assets accumulated from hard work and frugality. Personal finances of old age were a dreadful prospect. As social security retirement benefits have greatly increased and with the widespread development by employers of supplementary pension programs, the old age income prospects for most individuals has changed dramatically for the better. As previously noted, over 90 percent of all workers are now under social security. About one-half of all business employees and three-fourths of all civilian government employees are covered by pension programs other than social security.

Exhibit 17–12 reflects the growth and scope of old age pension programs in the United States.

Chance of Loss

The matter of chance of loss of earnings resulting from old age involves two aspects:

1. The chance of an individual surviving to old age, and
2. The chance of earnings losses as a consequence of old age.

---

[15]This "judgment" might be that of the individual. If it is the employer's, it could be the result of mandatory retirement rules or of a decision relating to the individual only.

Exhibit 17-12*   Number of Person's Covered by Major Pension and Retirement Programs in the United States (000 omitted)

| Year | Private plans | | Government-administered plans | | | | OASDI‡ |
	Insured	Noninsured	Railroad retirement	Federal civilian employees†	State and local employees	Total	
1930	100	2,700	1,445	432	800	5,477	—
1935	285	2,525	998	483	1,000	5,291	—
1940	695	3,565	1,346	745	1,527	7,878	30,512
1945	1,470	5,240	1,842	2,928	1,976	13,456	39,418
1950	2,755	7,500	1,745	1,856	2,854	16,710	42,171
1955	4,105	12,290	1,574	2,262	3,877	24,108	60,674
1960	5,475	17,540	1,246	2,557	5,090	31,908	67,517
1965	7,040	21,060	1,176	2,893	6,685	38,854	78,489
1966	7,835	21,640	1,168	3,086	7,112	40,841	81,756
1967	8,700	22,280	1,128	3,248	7,486	42,842	83,113
1958	9,155	22,860	1,104	3,297	7,880	44,296	85,017
1969	10,120	23,410	1,088	3,346	8,155	46,119	86,918
1970	10,980	24,100*	1,055*	3,327	8,450	47,912	87,545

Note: These data represent various dates during the year, since the fiscal years of the plans are not necessarily the same. Trends from year to year are not affected. The number of persons covered does not include survivors or dependents of deceased workers or beneficiaries, except in a few instances, and the total number included is estimated to be relatively small. Retirement arrangements for members of the armed forces, and provisions for veterans pensions, are not included in these data.

*Estimated.

†Includes members of the U.S. Civil Service Retirement System, the Tennessee Valley Retirement System, the Foreign Service Retirement System, and the Retirement System of the Federal Reserve Banks, which includes the Bank Plan and the Board of Governors' Plan.

‡Includes persons employed with coverage in effect at year-end (including the self-employed) and workers retired for age or disability.

Sources: Railroad Retirement Board, Social Security Administration, other administrative agencies, and the Institute of Life Insurance. Life Insurance Fact Book, (New York: Institute of life Insurance, 1972), p. 37.

Reasonably accurate data are available on each. The chance (probability) of living to age sixty-five at a given age of life is indicated in Exhibit 17–13.[16]

Exhibit 17–13   Age Probability Table (selected ages)

	Chance of living
Age	*to age 65*
15	.74%
20	.74
25	.74
30	.75
35	.76
40	.76
45	.78

Having attained age sixty-five, the average number of years of life remaining (the life expecancy) is 14.29, based on actual United States population data (1959–1961).

The chance of earnings losses because of old age varies with each individual's circumstance. We do not become superannuated overnight, but for most it becomes *official* at age sixty-five. For those working in industry, the chance of loss of *earnings* (from our current employment) at age sixty-five is almost a certainty. It seems that a substantial number do, however, continue a degree of gainful employment after sixty-five. A 1968 social security study indicates that almost half of the married couples age sixty-five (not living with others) had some earnings and that about 90 percent drew retirement benefits (principally social security).[17] The same study showed: 19 percent drew supplemental pensions from employers, 64 percent had income from assets; and 2 percent had individual life annuity income. Exhibit 17–14 reflects similar data for the entire sixty-five and over population.

Faced with the strong likelihood of living to age sixty-five and the even more likely retirement with the cessation or drastic reduction in earnings, most would agree to the wisdom of

1. Determining *now,* as closely as possible, what substitute income will be received, and
2. Providing for the *additional* minimum income thought necessary.

Reducing Losses through Means Other Than Insurance

Reducing the impact of old age earnings losses through means other than insurance would seem to include

---

[16]Public Health Service, *United States Life Tables: 1959–61* (U.S. Dept. of Health, Education and Welfare, Dec. 1964), pp. 8–9.

[17]Janet Murray, "Living Arrangements of People Age 65 and Older: Findings From A 1968 Survey," *Social Security Bulletin,* September, 1971.

—decreasing income needs

—spending accumulated capital

—acquiring income-producing capital and investments.

Exhibit 17–14*   Employment Status of Persons Age 65 and Older in U.S., 1970 (number in thousands)

Sex and age	Total population	Total in labor force	Percent in labor force
Male			
65–69 years	3,139	1,278	40.7
70 years and older	5,256	886	16.9
Female			
65–69 years	3,780	644	16.4
70 years and older	7,653	412	5.0

*Data taken from table E–2, page 220 of *The Manpower Report of the President* prepared by the U.S. Dept. of Labor, transmitted to the Congress, March 20, 1973. Labor force totals include those able and willing to work and, if unemployed, actively seeking employment.

Decreasing Income Needs. There are some automatic plus near-automatic budget items which disappear at or near retirement age. Automatic items would include (1) costs connected with working (clothes, transportation, meals, etc.), (2) reduction and elimination of certain insurance premiums (premature death policies no longer needed, medicare health cost advantages, disability income policies dropped), and (3) certain income and other tax advantages. Other items of the family period which might not be in the retirement budget are: dependent children, mortgage on home, large church and charitable contributions, and income allocated to providing for retirement needs. One other favorable budget factor might be reduction of the level of living. The degree to which this helps will obviously vary greatly among individuals. Still another mitigating factor is the production of goods and services which were previously purchased. The scope ranges from the vegetable garden with home canning to handling certain service items, such as maintenance on mechanical items and swimming pool care.

Spending Accumulated Capital. Many would argue that spending money saved through years of hard work is the least desirable means of handling the retirement earnings loss. It does have its possible traumatic "bottom of the barrel" psychology, but some would disagree. How fallacious is the philosophy "It's been a wonderful life so far; now I'll culminate it by indulging myself to age seventy, then retire to a peripatetic life and the rocking chair with T.V., good books and wonderful memories?" This reasoning is not as irresponsible as it might have seemed in other eras, what with the armor of social security, pensions, and medicare. Even so, most retirees would not like this alternative. As in the case of other causes of earnings losses, the spending of accumulated or borrowed funds is not a means of reducing losses; rather, it is reflection of having to incur the loss.

Acquiring Income From Capital and Investments. Except for those fortunate enough to receive a substantial inheritance, most of us must accumulate capital and investments from our personal earnings, either as an employee or from self-employment. Budgeting income to provide capital fund accumulation was discussed in Chapter 8. Part V which follows deals with investing these funds.

Our concern in this chapter is "how much" capital we should strive to accumulate to produce the desired monthly income. Exhibit 17–15 provides this information in terms of interest income.

Exhibit 17–15 Monthly Savings Necessary to Produce $100 per month Interest Income

Number of years of saving	at 5%	at 6%
10	$154.85	$122.50
20	58.88	43.89
30	29.31	20.42
40	16.12	10.40
Principal Sum at end of savings period*	$24,000	$20,000

*Only slight rounding off needed to produce even 000s.

The often-noted "magic of compound" interest is reflected in this table. Its significance to an individual considering interest income from savings as part of his retirement income is obvious: (1) the sooner one starts, the smaller the amount required in the monthly budget; (2) delaying the start of savings accumulations requires monthly deposits which many individuals or families could not make. Thus, a savings program to provide $400 a month interest income at age sixty-five, if started at age forty-five would require $175.56 a month, even if 6 percent compound interest were available.

Federal Incentives for Voluntary Commitment to Retirement Fund Accumulation. Employees working in industry have, as part of their fringe benefits, supplementary pension programs. The government has given tax incentives to their employers to provide such pensions. As Exhibit 17–12 reflects, in 1970 supplementary pension plans were in effect for some 35 million Americans.

But what about the self-employed, and their employees? And the employees of such non-profit institutions as charities, hospitals, public schools, colleges, and health foundations? There was a void for many years which was filled in the 1960s by

passage of the Keogh Act (HR10) for the self-employed and their employees, and

provision for individual tax-sheltered annuities under section 403(b) of
the Internal Revenue Code for employees of non-profit organizations.

Keogh Act (HR10). The Keogh Act, technically *The 1962 Self-Employed Individual Tax Retirement Act,* allows self-employed persons a deduction from
their earned income for payments into an approved investment plan. Up to 10
percent of earned income with a maximum of $2,500 in one year can be de-
ducted. If a self-employed person takes advantage of this, he must do the same
for any employee of three years service or more.

For the doctor, accountant, small businessman, plumber, and all other self-
employers, the Keogh plan provides a strong tax incentive to put aside funds
for old age. Not only is there the tax *deductible* feature, but there is a provision
that the *earnings* of the funds are not taxed during the accumulation period. At
retirement there are favorable tax provisions for the accumulated funds. An
individual in a 40 percent income tax bracket could save $1,000 in current year
income taxes. Considering the alternative of putting the $2,500 in an unap-
proved investment, the $1,000 tax saving can realistically be thought of as *an
additional 40 percent interest return.* A person in this higher income bracket
who invests $1,000 a year at 5 percent compound interest would accumulate
$13,206 in ten years, $34,719 in twenty years, and $69,760 in thirty years. *All
of this is money which would otherwise have been paid out as income tax.*

Insurance companies, mutual funds, banks, trade associations, and other institutions can submit plans to the IRS for approval, or can get automatic approval by complying with "master prototypes." It is easy to get assistance in
choosing a plan. Insurance agents, stock brokers, bankers, accountants and attorneys are all "in the business" of making recommendations. The merits of
anyone who is eligible seriously considering investing in this manner are
obvious.

Tax-Sheltered Annuities. An employee of a non-profit institution may participate in a "tax-sheltered" annuity plan. Existence of other fringe benefits, even
pension plans, does not prohibit such an employee from taking advantage of
this tax saving provision. An employee electing to do this requests a reduction
in salary (or that a salary increase not be given). The *employer* then *remits
direct to an insurer* the amount of the decreased salary as premiums on a non-
forfeitable retirement annuity. The full amount of the annuity premium is not
automatically freed from income tax. The amount varies depending on specific
formulas set out by IRS involving the amount of current earnings, the number
of years with current employer, how much the employer has contributed and
will contribute to a qualified pension plan, and how much the employer will
contribute each year to the "tax-sheltered" annuity. In many instances, tax-
sheltered annuities offer substantial *net additional* funds for providing retirement annuities. Anyone eligible should investigate this opportunity. The same

group of specialists just mentioned as capable of advising on Keogh plans, can be consulted about tax-sheltered annuities.

How Much Can Insurance Reduce Old Age Earnings Losses[18]

Insurance plans which can provide monthly income to replace earnings losses caused by old age are:

1. Social security old age benefit
2. Life insurance policies with cash values
3. Life insurance death benefits to a surviving beneficiary
4. Life annuities, both fixed dollar and variable. These can take the form of pensions from employers or unions and of individual annuities purchased by the annuitant.

To what extent *can* these various insurance plans replace *old age earnings losses?* A total replacement is possible—and feasible for lower and middle income workers—but is by no means certain. Among the variables are: how nearly the employment history produces *average monthly earnings* approaching actual earnings at time of retirement; amount of additional pensions from employment; amount of funds available from life insurance cash values and from possible beneficiary death benefits; and amount of total individual life annuities purchased.

Perhaps we can best illustrate the significance of these variables by relating the circumstances of four differing hypothetical cases. Bill, Tom, Dick, and Harry are all age sixty-five and are retiring. The specific assumptions for each are shown in Exhibit 17–16.

We might question how realistic the retirement income amounts are as a percent of take-home pay prior to retirement. Sixty percent or less is often suggested. There are several reasons for using the relatively high figures. Since the amounts are related to "take-home pay," not gross pay, such items as withholding taxes, social security taxes, and fringe benefit contributions which disappear at retirement have not been part of the family's cash flow budget. The mortgage on the home, the largest item in most family budgets, may or may not have been paid off by retirement time. In either case, the family's monthly income requirements on this item will likely continue unchanged at retirement. Further, it does not seem likely the retiree and dependent(s) will want to lower their level of living significantly.

Other *decreased income need factors* are: elimination of costs of going to work (which might be partially offset by leisure time activity costs), elimina-

---

[18]It is theoretically incorrect to think of insurance benefits as reducing old age earnings losses. When insurance funds owned by the insured are paid out as income, this represents liquidation of principal, and is thus better classified as *absorbing* the old age earnings loss. However, life annuities include both a capital liquidation factor and a mortality factor. Social security, under which the insurance premiums (FICA taxes) do not create cash values, more accurately reflects the concept of "insurance reducing old age earnings losses."

Exhibit 17–16

	1 Net monthly earnings at retire- ment*	2 Retirement income needed to maintain same level of living Percent　Amount		3 Social security average monthly earnings	4 Social security old age monthly benefit†	5 Income needed from other sources (3–4)	6 Funds necessary to produce required additional income (6% interest income)
Bill	$ 600	75%	$ 450	$450	$251	$ 199	$ 39,800
Tom	$ 900	75%	$ 675	$550	$288	$ 387	$ 77,400
Dick	$1,500	80%	$1,200	$650	$331	$ 869	$173,800
Harry	$2,500	80%	$2,000	$800	$375	$1,625	$325,000

*Used here as "take-home" pay: the earnings available for personal expenditures.
†If retiree's spouse is sixty-five, this would be increased 50 percent; if sixty-two, the in-crease would be 37½ percent.

tion of premature death insurance premiums (which probably were not great, as has been illustrated) and certain tax advantages (most of which, as payroll deductions, were not in the "cash budget" anyway). It is felt the net effect of this is that an income of less than 20 percent to 25 percent of the last paycheck would not be satisfactory for most household units.

Retirement Income from Life Insurance Policy Cash Values, Life Insurance Policy Death Benefits, and Life Annuities. In Chapter 16, it was explained that *any proceeds* from a life insurance policy can, instead of being paid immedi-ately in cash, be paid out under the "settlement options" agreement in the policy. Further, we explained that one of the settlement options was a life an-nuity with a choice of "certain" periods. It was also pointed out that life in-surance policy proceeds arise out of cash values and endowment values (which *are* cash values) and from death benefits to the deceased's beneficiary.

For retirement purposes, then, life annuities may be acquired by:

1. Applying cash and endowment values to a life annuity option
2. Applying death benefits (normally would come from life insurance on a deceased spouse) to a life annuity option
3. Taking cash from other sources (savings account, sale of bands, stock, real estate, etc.) to purchase life annuities

A person with proceeds from a life insurance policy has the choice of apply-ing these funds under a life annuity option in the policy or taking the cash and shopping on the open market for an immediate life annuity that would give more monthly income for the same money. Surprisingly, he might do better paying the latter "retail" price than choosing the former which includes no sales expense. There are many historical and current market factors involved, but we can keep it simple by generalizing: any one with funds to put in a life annuity, from whatever source the money originated, would do well to shop for the annuity providing the greatest monthly income for each $1,000 applied with due caution as to the stability of the insurer. In doing so, he should seek competent professional advice for any tax and legal factors that may be involved.

What magic does the life annuity offer in solving the income replacement problem of old age? Unfortunately, there is little *magic*. But it does represent a vehicle for converting cash into (1) a monthly income for life, (2) an amount of payments in excess of interest payments normally obtainable, and (3) income with maximum safety of principal. Exhibit 17–17 illustrates this.

Exhibit 17–17   *Cost of $10 a Month Immediate Life Annuity, Male, Age 65*[1]

Company	No refund annuity[2]	Installment refund annuity[3]
A	$ 1,250	$1,397
B	1,311	1,448
C	1,158	1,273
D	1,439	1,641
E	1,177	1,257
F	1,212	1,293
G	1,270	1,387

[1]Annuity rates of seven major companies taken from *1972 Life Rates and Data* (Cincinnati: National Underwriter Co.), pp. 613–627.

[2]$10 a month for life starting at age sixty-five, payments discontinued at death.

[3]$10 a month for life starting at age sixty-five, with guarantee that if annuitant dies before payments received equal purchase price, payments will be continued to designated beneficiary or to estate *until* full purchase price has been paid out.

From Exhibit 17–17 we note that the monthly life annuity payment amounts to about an 8.5 to 10 percent return on an annual basis, from a *no refund* annuity, 7½ to 9½ percent on an installment refund annuity.[19] Using $1,200 and $1,300 as the costs of $10 a month life annuities at age sixty-five on the two refund bases, we can see that each $100 a month life income requires $12,000 or $13,000 cash, depending on the choice of refund provisions.

If the retiree goes the variable annuity route, either partially or wholly, he is relating the amount of his monthly income to the securities market rather than to fixed dollar amounts. The factors involved in this decision are related to Chapters 20 and 21 in which stocks, bonds, and mutual funds are studied. A

---

[19]The reader is reminded the monthly annuity payment includes three elements: interest on principal, liquidation of principal, and mortality.

point which should be emphasized is that whatever dollar amount might be available at retirement date (either through fixed dollar or variable annuity unit accumulations), the retiree can decide *then* how much of this amount to apply on *variable life annuity income* and *fixed dollar life annuity income.*

With this discussion in mind, let us refer to Bill, Tom, Dick, and Harry.

Further Examination of Bill, Tom, Dick, and Harry. Bill has not worked for any firm long enough to qualify for additional pension or other retirement benefits of any kind.

Tom, in his last fifteen years of employment, worked for a national retail chain and has qualified for a company pension of $200 per month.

Dick completed a twenty-five year career as a district sales supervisor for a regional life insurance company. His company pension is $469 per month.

Harry is a dentist. For the past ten years he has been investing $1,000 per year in a Keogh investment plan. He has $13,000 net from this plan.

Relating the "Income Needed from Other Sources" amounts for each of these men with the assumptions on additional pension sources, we see the picture for each at retirement in Exhibit 17–18. This demonstrates how, by

Exhibit 17–18

	(5) Income needed from other sources (from p. 390)	7 Additional income from co. pensions	8 Remaining income needed	9 Funds necessary to provide remaining income from:	
				6% interest income	Installment refund annuity
Bill	$ 199	0.	$ 199	$ 39,800	$ 25,800
Tom	387	200.	187	37,400	24,310
Dick	869	469	400	80,000	52,000
Harry	1,625	—	1,625	325,000	211,000

requiring substantially less cash to provide the needed income, *insurance (life annuities) can significantly reduce old age earnings losses.*

Bill's retirement financial picture will vary greatly depending on other conditions existing. If he is still physically able to work, he can probably find part-time employment to provide the $199 monthly. With the first $2,100 of earning's exemption for social security, there is no great problem. If his wife is of a retirement age, her additional benefit would about fill the gap. If she is not old enough and if Bill is not able to work, he could face stringent retirement finances.

Tom's $37,400 or $24,310 cash need (depending on whether he chooses the interest income or the life annuity route) is a sizable sum. We can hope that he has had some kind of systematic personal investment plan. If, as is often the case, the only savings he has is the cash value of life insurance, he will have $450 to $550 cash values (depending on age at issue) for each $1,000 of whole life insurance he chooses to put on a life annuity option. Thus, the cash value of a $50,000 whole life policy would probably be enough to purchase a $187 life annuity ($500 cash value × 50 = $25M ÷ $1300 = $19.2 × 10 = $192 per month installment refund life annuity).

The extra funds needed by Dick could be a real problem. If the funds are not there at retirement, continuing to work is not an adequate solution because of the $2,100 earnings limit. Since he has enjoyed above average earnings through

Exhibit 17–19 *A Peek at the Future: Pensions of $33,000 a Year for a Retired Couple by the Year 2011?*

Assuming wage increases, subject to Social Security tax averaging 5 percent a year, and consumer price rises averaging 2.75 percent a year—

	Maximum wages subject to tax	Maximum monthly benefit for worker retiring at age 65 in the year		Maximum wages subject to tax	Maximum monthly benefit for worker retiring at age 65 in the year
1972	$9,000	$259	1992	$27,600	$681
1973	$10,800	$266	1993	$30,300	$730
1974	$12,000	$275	1994	$30,300	$742
1975	$12,600	$287	1995	$33,300	$803
1976	$12,600	$312	1996	$33,300	$824
1977	$13,800	$348	1997	$36,600	$892
1978	$13,800	$367	1998	$36,600	$915
1979	$15,300	$395	1999	$40,500	$989
1980	$15,300	$402	2000	$40,500	$1,015
1981	$16,800	$434	2001	$44,700	$1,098
1982	$16,800	$441	2002	$44,700	$1,124
1983	$18,600	$473	2003	$49,200	$1,215
1984	$18,600	$481	2004	$49,200	$1,245
1985	$20,400	$517	2005	$54,300	$1,346
1986	$20,400	$525	2006	$54,300	$1,378
1987	$22,500	$568	2007	$60,000	$1,440
1988	$22,500	$571	2008	$60,000	$1,525
1989	$24,900	$614	2009	$66,300	$1,648
1990	$24,900	$625	2010	$66,300	$1,685
1991	$27,600	$669	2011	$73,200	$1,819

Keep in mind: These figures show pensions for a retired worker alone. Add 50 percent for a wife, age 65, if she is not working. Thus, a worker and his wife by 2011 would collect a monthly pension of $2,729—or nearly $32,750 a year—if the assumptions about wages and prices hold true. Note, though, that inflation would wipe out much of the effect of the increase.

Source: U.S. Dept. of Health, Education and Welfare. Reprinted from *U.S. News & World Report,* Copyright 1972, U.S. News & World Report, Inc. December 18, 1972 issue.

the years, we can hope he has budgeted and invested successfully to produce the $52,000 to $80,000 (or the equivalent in income producing property) he must have.

Harry's picture reflects the reason for the preoccupation of most professional men with personal investments. His $13,000 net from the Keogh plan provides only a fraction of the over $200,000 he needs to purchase a $1,625 monthly life annuity.

Futility of Static *Assumptions of* Future *Income Needs.* The *magic* of compound interest works for us in accumulating funds. Working against us at the same time is the *deterioration* of dollar amounts from the compounding annually occurring inflation rates. Exhibit 17–19 (page 393) details a forty-year career of earnings beginning in 1972. Also, there will be an unpredictable amount of increase in *total* productivity. For the individual this will trigger a continually increasing *need* for additional income. Mirrored in these forces is the futility of *static assumptions* about *future income needs.*

In summary, we should emphasize again that no two persons' financial situations are alike and that no one person's remains the same. We must recognize the importance of careful financial planning and up-dating, using insurance where it is appropriate to reduce future earnings losses.

Discussion Questions

1. What suggested means, other than through insurance, are there to reduce the chance of loss of earnings through unemployment?

2. What factual evidence is there that "individual disability income insurance is a product without a sales force"?

3. John Bachelor graduated from college in 1974 at age twenty-four. He went to work immediately for $1,000 a month. Two years later he became *totally* and *permanently* disabled and qualified for the social security disability benefit. How much a month (using benefits rates of 1973) will he receive until age sixty-five?

4. What is the approximate probability that a daughter whose father was age forty-five at the time of her birth will lose him by death before she is age twenty-five?

5. Are the social security survivorship benefits and the cost of term insurance such that it is feasible for most families to protect themselves against all earnings losses caused by the premature death of the breadwinner? Illustrate with a hypothetical case.

6. Explain what is meant by "term life insurance for temporary needs, permanent life insurance for permanent or certain needs"?

7. With some family you know of in mind, estimate what percent of the husband's net earnings income at date of retirement they would need to continue their current standard of living after retirement. What pre-retirement family budget items would not be in the retirement budget?

8. Get the actual provisions of the pension program of some company. Make some logical assumptions as to savings and calculate the amount of the company and the social security retirement income.

*The years teach much which
the days never know.*

[*Emerson*]

18

Reducing Property Losses Through Insurance

Having completed our study of reducing *earnings losses* through insurance, we must feel a certain sense of frustration from an awareness of the complexity and pitfalls of the decisions facing us. Fortunately, the problem is much less involved regarding *property losses*.

A logical approach to the study of reducing property losses through insurance might be to raise the following questions, and to seek the best possible answers:

1. What property might we lose?
2. What can cause total or partial loss of these properties?
3. What are the causes of property losses which are not insurable?
4. What policies should we buy?

Potential
Property Loss

All individuals own at least some *personal* property. Most own substantial clothing and personal items, household furnishings, sport, recreational and other avocational equipment, and one or more autos. Middle income families are usually surprised at the total cost revealed by an inventory of these items; $8,000 to $30,000 is not unusual. Many other families have accumulated substantial intangible personal property, such as debts owed them, cash, savings accounts, stocks, bonds, mutual fund shares, and other securities. Earlier chapters have described the magnitude of the value of personal property in this country.

The principal *real* property owned by most families is their home. The home represents the largest single investment of the typical family. Other real property often owned by individuals and families are detached buildings and improvements on the homesite (greenhouses, workshops, swimming pools, cabanas, etc.); lake houses; and improvements on rural property and on rental property. It is not uncommon for the value of real property owned by middle income families to range from $20,000 to $75,000 and more.

Causes of Total or Partial
Loss of Property

The various causes of loss to property are classified as either *speculative* risks or *pure* risks. Speculative risks are those where there is the possibility of *loss* or *gain*. The operation of a business for profit is an example, as is gambling. Also, economic and political forces which can cause obsolescence or appreciation, inflation or deflation, prosperity or depression, as well as science and technology, which can cause windfall gains or unexpected losses may be called speculative risks. Insurance is not a device which can be used to reduce property losses caused by speculative risks.

Pure risks are those uncertainties which can result only in a loss. We have already commented on the personal *pure* risks of unemployment, disability, premature death, and retirement. The pure risks threatening loss of property are endless in number. Examples of risks threatening *direct* losses (physical damage) are fire, lightning, windstorm, tornadoes, explosion, earthquake, collision, riots, and theft. *Consequential* losses often result from *direct* losses. The inability to open up for business because of a fire loss is an example. For individuals, an auto accident creating the necessity of renting a car or making it impossible to get to work is an example. A fire loss to a home requiring a family to live in a motel temporarily and store furniture in a warehouse is another example of a consequential loss. Even though the usual textbook does not treat them as such, for the purpose of this text, we include medical expenses as a consequential *property* loss; property (money or the selling of property to get the money) is "lost" as a consequence of having to pay medical bills.[1]

Property losses can result from breaking the law (criminal and misdemeanor and other fines) and from civil liability. These are consequential losses (giving up of property as a consequence of legal liability to others).

Civil liability losses can result from: (1) *contract actions* (breach of contract, breach of warranty, recission, etc.), (2) *equitable actions* arising from fraud, errors, mistakes (restitution, injunctive relief and specific performance), (3) *tort actions* (intentional and unintentional). Intentional torts include trespass, false arrest, libel, slander, invasion of privacy, and assault and battery. Unintentional torts arise from negligent acts and omissions of someone (called the *tort-feasor*).

Among civil actions, the negligence tort poses the greatest property loss exposure to individual and families. Broadly speaking, a person is legally negligent when his carelessness causes harm to others. The laws of negligence are vast and complicated—changing and developing almost daily as new situations and court decisions develop. Being acquainted with negligence law can serve as an effective loss prevention factor.

Negligence is the failure to use the degree of care that a reasonably prudent man would have exercised in the same circumstances. This failure may arise from *acts* (driving a car carelessly) or from *not acting when one should* (not having the car's brakes relined when they obviously needed it). Since a number of factors may have contributed to the occurrence that caused the harm, the negligence of the individual must have been the *proximate cause* of the harm. Where a lack of prudence is exhibited by all parties involved, often it is held that the one with the *last clear* chance to avoid the occurrence is the tort-feasor. A person may be liable for the negligence of others: a car owner for the acts of someone driving his car with permission, a homeowner for the acts of household employees, a principal for the acts of his agent, and many other situations.

Of special significance is the fact that courts have extended the concept of negligence damages to include not only the actual monetary costs but allowance for pain, suffering, and mental anguish. Equally important is the fact that financial capacity of the tort-feasor to pay is not considered in determining the amount of damages. It is not unusual for an individual to find himself faced with a judgment on his future earnings and property accumulations amounting to several hundred thousand dollars.

---

[1] This is not to be taken as a suggestion that medical expense insurance be classified as property insurance rather than personal insurance. The posture is taken here only because medical expenses seem to fall more logically under the "loss of property" discussion than that of "loss of earnings" (through unemployment, disability, premature death and retirement).

Causes of Property Losses
Which Are Not Insurable

Reviewing our survey of "what can cause total or partial loss of property," we should note the type of risks which are not insurable:

All Speculative Risks

Certain Pure Risks[2]

  Direct loss from:
    flood, acts of war
  Consequential loss from civil liability incurred
  by your:
    fraud
    certain mistakes
    assault and battery
    divorce responsibility

Uninsurable risks which can cause property losses are extensive. An individual is left with two means of protecting himself from such losses: (1) gaining an understanding and awareness of the loss potential of these risks, and (2) conducting himself and his affairs in such a manner as to reduce the likelihood of their occurrence.

Which Policies
to Buy

HO + FAP = APIP. Now to the proposition that the family finance manager has fewer problems regarding property insurance buying decisions. Lest the mysterious equation, HO + FAP = APIP, worry us, we should hasten to explain its meaning. The *homeowner's policy* plus the *family automobile policy* equals an *adequate property insurance program* for most families. This must be qualified with the reminder that not all loss exposures can be insured.

---

[2]It is possible to get certain forms of insurance protection against some of the risks (perils) listed below. Flood insurance is available on automobiles and certain other personal property, probably on the theory that their portability decreases the likelihood of loss. Some insurance companies have long had flood insurance coverage, but it was rather meaningless in practice: underwriting procedures made it available to the house high on the hill, but not the one in the flood plain. A federal government program became effective in 1968 under which private insurers could offer flood insurance by reinsuring with a government agency against catastrophic losses. It is available only to property owners living in cities which have complied with certain government regulations intended to decrease flood losses. Other causes of damage suit losses for which insurance protection is difficult or impossible to get are breach of contract and trespassing.

Prior to the 1950s, an individual seeking to insure his property was faced with choosing from a morass of coverages involving several policies, often overlapping, often leaving important gaps in protection. Frequently, several different insurance companies and agents were involved in the many buying decisions made for one property. Insurance companies became increasingly aware of this unsatisfactory situation and, not wishing stronger government controls, worked together and through state regulatory agencies to correct the situation. The result was two policies: homeowner's (HO) and family automobile (FAP). Together, they do afford a fairly complete family property insurance program. True, the buyer is left with a number of decisions as to coverage within each policy, but the coverages in the two policies are designed to complement each other and greatly lessen the chance of serious omissions.

Homeowner's Policy

Prior to the appearance of the homeowner's policy, most people bought fire insurance on their homes; many added *extended coverage* (windstorm, hail, explosion, riot and civil commotion, aircraft and vehicle damage, and smoke damage). Many did not insure their personal property; some insured it against fire, but did not buy the extended coverage. More often than not, the amount on the personal property was inadequate. Personal liability was seldom purchased; the same was true of water damage, vandalism, malicious mischief, and theft. An element of adverse selection was present, making rates higher.

The answer was a single policy with mandatory broad coverages and with amounts rigidly controlled as fixed percentages of the amount on the dwelling. This is the homeowner's policy.

A Two-Section Policy. The homeowner's is more than just insurance on the home. Section I provides *insurance on the improvements* and *on personal property,* the latter being covered not only at home but anywhere in the world. Section II is a *comprehensive personal (family) liability* policy. There are five versions of the homeowner's (designated HO-1, HO-2, HO-3, HO-4, HO-5). Section II, the liability part, is *exactly the same for all five.* For a description of this policy, see the appendix to this chapter.

Buying the Homeowner's Policy. Other than the questions of which insurance company and which agent to choose, the two important decisions in purchasing the homeowner's are:

> Which of the five HO forms to choose. In some states this has been reduced to three dwelling forms and one renter's form.
>
> How much insurance to purchase.

Which HO Form? It is regrettable that the owner has to choose between several versions of the same policy, but we can presume there are situations justi-

Exhibit 18–1 Coverage Provided by Section I of Homeowner's Policies Example: $20,000 home (exclusive of lot)

	HO-1	HO-2	HO-3	HO-5	HO-4
Typical annual premium, $16,000 insurance on home	$105	$150	$165	$345	$100 (for $8,000 on personal property) No real property coverage
Perils covered	Personal Real	Personal Real	Personal Real	Personal Real	Renters form. Broad on personal, except broken window not covered
	Basic* Basic	Broad* Broad	Broad All risk*	All risk All risk	
Standard amount of insurance:		Based on value of property (80% coinsurance clause requires at least $16,000)			(not applicable)
Coverage A Home					
Coverage B Detached structures		10% of amount on home ($1,600)			

400

Coverage C Personal property on premises		50% of amount on home ($8,000)	Based on value of personal property $4,000 minimum, 80% co-insurance clause
Coverage C Personal property away from premises	10% of amount for personal property on premises (10% of $8,000 = $800)	50% of amount on home $8,000	10% of amount on personal property
Coverage D Additional living expenses	10% of amount on home ($1,600)	20% of amount on home ($3,200)	20% of insurance on personal property
Extension of A Trees, shrubs, plants, and lawns		5% of amount on home ($800)	10% of amount on personal property

*For an explanation of the terms "basic," "broad form," and "all risk," see the appendix to this chapter, pp. 417–18.

fying the choice of each of the four forms (HO-1, HO-2, HO-3, HO-5). For renters there is only one form, HO-4. The choice involves setting and balancing priorities on the matter of (1) cost, (2) scope of coverage (perils covered and exclusions), and (3) amounts of protection on each coverage. We can dispose of the latter as a really significant factor, since all the insurance amounts are stated as a percent of the insurance on the dwelling in Section I (Section II, the liability part, is exactly alike in all forms). Exhibit 18–1 reflects how little difference there is in these amounts.

Regarding the scope of coverage and perils, there is no question but that HO-1 is considerably less liberal than the others. The most liberal form, HO-5, has a correspondingly higher premium; many feel the extra premium outlay is not justified in view of the very adequate protection afforded by HO-2 and HO-3. In most states, one of these two is generally recognized as the "best buy." As Exhibit 18–1 reflects, the essential difference is that HO-2 has *broad-form* peril coverage for both real and personal property, where HO-3 has *broad-form* for *personal property* and *all-risk for real property*.[3] The decision between the two should be made on a judgment of the justification of the additional premium for the all-risk protection on the dwelling.

How Much Property Insurance?

Amount on Dwelling. There are some important and sometimes difficult considerations in determining the amount of insurance to purchase on a home. We cannot collect more than the actual cash value of the home no matter how much insurance we have in force.[4] What is the *actual cash value* of a home? The market value? The purchase price? The original cost less depreciation? The cost of replacement less depreciation? The cost of replacement without depreciation? Or should it be an average of two or more of these? Or should it be the higher (or lower) of some specified two or more of these?

A usual example to emphasize the significance of these differing value concepts is the necessity of repairing or replacing the roof of a home. Let's assume "twenty-year" shingles were used; the original cost was $1,000 but would be $1,600 now, and the roof is ten years old. If a hailstorm required the roof's replacement, what value should be refunded? Using the suggested valuation concepts, we could derive the following estimates: $1,000, $500, $800, $1,600. In any event, if the insured collects anything less than $1,600 he will be in the position of paying out the difference in cash. Since market value and replacement costs *tend* to equate, the problem is lessened somewhat, but there still is a depreciation and/or obsolescence factor for an older home.[5] The most usual definition of actual cash value is *replacement cost less depreciation.*

---

[3]See Appendix, Section I, for a description of the difference between the two.

[4]An exception to this would be the few states which have "valued policy" laws. These laws provide that in the event of a total loss, the insurer must pay the stated amount of insurance in the policy, regardless of how much that exceeds the value of the home.

[5]Often property values in older neighborhoods actually increase significantly over and above inflationary factors. In most large cities there are examples of almost identical homes on the same size lots but in different neighborhoods varying 500 percent and more in "value."

Related to this discussion is the "80 percent of replacement cost" requirement. The homeowner's policy states that, if the amount of insurance carried on the dwelling is 80 percent or more of replacement cost, the insurer will pay for *the total replacement* cost. Otherwise, it will pay the larger of:

1. Replacement cost less depreciation (actual cash value), or
2. The amount payable under an 80 percent coinsurance clause.

Our roof damage example will illustrate. Replacement cost less depreciation would be $1,600 less 50 percent (ten years on a twenty-year roof), or $800. To illustrate the workings of the coinsurance clause, we need to know the replacement cost of the home and the amount of insurance in force. We will assume $25,000 replacement cost for the home and $15,000 for the insurance amount. An 80 percent coinsurance clause of the type used in this instance says in effect: "If you don't carry insurance at least equal to 80 percent of the replacement cost, you will be a coinsurer." In determining the dollar amount of "coinsuring," the following formula is used:

$$\frac{\text{Amount of insurance carried}}{\text{Amount required to be carried (Replacement cost} \times 80\%)}$$
$$\times \text{ loss} = \text{amount insurer pays}$$

In the example, we substitute the actual figures:

$$\frac{\$15,000}{\$20,000(\$25,000 \times 80\%)} \times \$1,600 = \$1,200 \text{ paid by insurer}$$

In this case, the coinsurance basis provides more ($1,200) than the replacement cost less depreciation ($800), but the insured still has to pay out $400 cash to get a roof over his head.[6]

The homeowner's policy is often written for a three-year term. Because of inflation and appreciation factors, the amount of insurance on the home should be increased—or at least reconsidered—no less frequently than each renewal date. Both the insureds and some insurance agents overlook this and simply

---

[6]The reader may have noted that the "replacement cost" provision (without a depreciation deduction) violates the indemnification principle. In the example given, had the insured complied with the 80 percent requirement, he would have made an $800 "profit" on the loss by exchanging a $1,600 roof for an $800 roof. This violation of a basic insurance principle has produced its bad effects. An inordinate portion of homeowner's policy aggregate losses has come from this "replacement insurance" benefit. Insurance companies have tried to offset this by (1) getting higher premiums, (2) tightening up on underwriting, making older homes ineligible for the homeowner's, and (3) seeking higher deductibles. On the latter point, Texas and a few other states in recent years approved a deductible of 1 percent of the face amount without requiring corresponding rate reductions. In actual practice the $15,000 insurance is so close to the 80 percent requirement, it is likely the insurer could have been made to pay—and probably willingly would have paid—the full $1,600. The actual cash value concept is not so precise as to be tenable in close cases. We should note that the insurer has an effective bargaining tool when there is dispute over the actual cash value or the amount of the loss. The insurer can invoke the appraisal clause of the policy, under which each party has the right to demand the *actual cash value* and *loss* be determined by arbitration. The arbiters are a group of three, one appointed by each party and these two choosing a disinterested third arbiter. This option is rarely used.

renew the previous amounts. The family finance manager should avoid this pitfall.

Amount on Other Property Coverages. As previously noted and seen in Exhibit 18–1, the insurance amounts on the additional property coverages (detached structures, personal property, additional living expenses) are automatically set as a percent of the amount on the home. These standard amounts can be increased (and in some instances decreased) by adjusting the premium. It is desirable to check how well these standard amounts suit an individual family situation and to make appropriate changes.

The personal property coverage refers to "unscheduled personal property." Highly valuable individual pieces of property should be described separately on a schedule in the policy, with a previously agreed upon value. There is an additional premium charge for this. Frequently the insurer will require an appraisal before scheduling such property.

Deductibles on Property Coverages

Deductibles appropriately should be treated in the "amount of insurance" discussion, since they affect the amount of insurance we have. The purpose and the justification for deductible clauses were noted in Chapter 14. Deductibles of varying amounts and of two types are available for Section I coverages of the homeowners policy. Before deciding on the deductible type and amount, we should get the facts as to the effect of each deductible in determining the claim amount and make a judgment as to how much of the risk we should retain in order to get a premium reduction.

The homeowner's policy has a "disappearing deductible," the essence of which is "the larger the loss, the less the deductible." The purpose is to save premiums through elimination and reduction of small claims. It works this way. On claims of $500 or more, there is no deductible. On claims of less than $50, nothing is paid. On claims between these two amounts, 111 percent of loss less deductible is paid. For example, a $100 claim would pay $55.50 ($100 minus $50 deductible equals $50 times 111 percent equals $55.50). Where a $100 deductible is chosen, 125 percent is paid on the amount between $100 and $500. There is an industry trend for the disappearing deductible to "disappear." It is being replaced, state-by-state, by straight (also called "flat") deductibles which simply deduct the chosen deductible amount from each claim.

How Much Liability Insurance?

Previous discussions in this section have emphasized the importance of owning adequate liability protection. We recall the fallacy of reasoning that "little protection is needed because there is little property to lose." We also remember that the amount of negligence damage awards are set with reference to the damage done, not the ability of the defendant to pay. Accordingly we should stress again that judgments can be renewed and can threaten our future earnings and capital accumulations. Even bankruptcy is not a sure way out; other debts may be excused, but tort liability awards frequently are not.

Restating the matter, we should ask ourselves not only "How much can I lose through negligence liability?" but "How much damage might I and those for whom I am responsible do to other persons?"

Fortunately, there is little financial strain in conforming with this aspect of the large loss principle. The extra cost of increasing the liability limits varies among companies and states, but the $25,000 basic limit of the personal liability protection can be increased to $50,000 for about $2.00 more per year; to $100,000 for $3.00 more; to $300,000 for $5.00 more; to $500,000 for $7.00 more. If taking a larger deductible on property insurance than we feel we can handle is the only means of affording adequate personal liability protection, it is probably desirable to do so.

Endorsements to Extend Coverage on the Homeowner's

There are many endorsements which may be added to the homeowner's for an extra premium charge. Not knowing of these, we frequently do without protection which we particularly need. Following is a listing of a few of these.

HO-40	Appurtenant structures rented to others
HO-42	Office, Professional, Private School or Studio Occupancy; Described Premises Only
HO-44	Residence Premises: Three or Four-Family Dwelling
HO-46	Theft Coverage Extension
HO-47	Inflation Guard (automatic increase of amount by 1 percent each quarter)
HO-53	Credit Card Forgery and Depositors Forgery Coverage
HO-65	Increased limits on money and securities
HO-66	Additional amount on unscheduled personal property away from the premises
HO-67	Secondary Residence Premises
HO-69	Physicians, Surgeons, Dentists and Veterinarians Away-From-Premises Coverage (for medical supplies and equipment)
HO-192	Condominium Unit-Owner's Coverage

Property Not Eligible for Homeowner's

Some of us cannot qualify for the homeowner's policy. This may be because of the nature of the structure (homes of less than required minimum value, obsolescence with attendant valuation problems, etc.) or because of the insured himself (the liability, personal property floater and theft coverages raise certain underwriting problems). Where this is the case, a fire policy with extended coverage represents the minimum coverage to seek. Also, an attempt should be made to purchase an individual comprehensive personal liability policy. This approach would also apply to insuring other residential property we might own. Liability protection is afforded by the Owners, Landlord and Tenants policy.

Mobile homes have presented a special insuring problem to the owners, to the insurers, and to regulatory authorities. The start of the difficulties lies in how to classify them: vehicle or house? When first introduced on the market, there was no question they were vehicles; as the size has increased, the vehicle concept has become untenable. The underwriting situation has not been standardized, and the practice varies greatly among the states. In some few states, there are insurers offering protection under an automobile policy form, and others under a dwelling form. The former gives more liberal coverage, but the insurers tend not to be as well established.

Business property is an entirely different category and one which we will not attempt to explore. Liability on such property represents a great loss exposure and is not covered by the homeowner's policy. The Owners, Landlords and Tenants policy gives protection on business property leased to others. The Comprehensive General Liability Policy should be purchased by those operating a business.

The Family Automobile Policy

The other part of the family property insurance program is the *family automobile policy* (FAP). We have seen how the homeowner's policy affords protection from real property loss on the home premises and personal property loss anywhere in the world. It also provides all-risk loss protection from negligence liability. Exclusions are made in both the property and liability sections for losses arising from the ownership and use of an automobile. The family automobile policy can adequately fill this void.

Before studying the automobile policy, a brief look at pertinent data should help put the automobile loss exposure in proper perspective. In 1971, almost half the accidental deaths in the U.S. were caused by auto accidents (54,700). There were almost twice as many deaths from auto accidents as from home accidents.[7] Of about $36 billion property insurance premiums written by property and liability insurers in 1971, $15.45 billion was for automobile insurance, with the automobile liability premiums being almost twice the automobile physical damage premiums. The homeowner's policies accounted for $2.8 billion of the $36 billion total, with premiums for other fire and liability lines totaling $7.39 billion.[8]

The family automobile policy might best be presented, for our purposes, in outline form with brief explanations of the significant points.

Family Automobile Policy

Section 1. Liability Protection
           Liability limits
           Contract to defend
           Insured defined
           Owned and non-owned automobiles
           Definition of an "automobile"
           Exclusions

---

[7]*Insurance Facts, 1972* (New York: Insurance Information Institute, 1973), pp. 46, 56.
[8]*Insurance Facts,* p. 9.

Section 1. Liability Protection From Ownership and/or Use of An Automobile

Liability Limits. The limits the company will pay are stated in terms of the maximum per person per occurrence for bodily injury, and per occurrence for damage to property of others. $10,000/$20,000/$5,000 is a standard set of limits and provides for payments up to $10,000 to *each person* harmed, up to $20,000 total for all persons harmed *per occurrence,* and up to $5,000 for property damage liability per occurrence. As an example, Joyce negligently loses control of her car, crashing into the bedroom walls of a home, causing $5,000 injury to Joe, $3,000 injury to John, and $12,000 injury to Jim who owns the house. Damage to the house is $8,000. The $10,000 per person limit would take care of the liability to Joe and John, but would pay only $10,000 of the $12,000 bodily injury liability to Jim and only $5,000 of the $8,000 damage to Jim's house. Joyce, thus still personally owes Jim $5,000. These same "limits of liability" are available for any other separate occurrences.

This example illustrates the desirability of purchasing higher limits of liability. The following are illustrative of what higher limits cost:

If the premium for 10/20/5 is $100
    20/40/5 will cost $106
    50/100/5 will cost $112
    100/300/10 will cost $121
    300/500/10 will cost $126

A discussion in Chapter 14 suggested the desirability of taking a $50 or larger collision deductible than planned, using the savings to increase liability limits. The 100/300/10 limits probably should be a minimum for most families.

Contract to Defend. This clause closely parallels the "contract to defend" provision of the homeowner's policy. (See appendix, page 420.)

Insured Defined. Owned and Non-owned Automobiles. Persons insured (given the liability protection) in connection with "owned" automobiles are similar to those in the homeowner's. All members of the insured's household are insured, as well as anyone driving the car with the permission of the named insured or his spouse. If the borrower, in turn, lends it to another, the latter is not insured; the named insured, however, is protected in such a case. The named insured and members of his household have the same liability protection while driving any "non-owned" private passenger car which is not furnished regularly for their use. In the latter case, if the owner does not have adequate coverage, the insured should list the car on the policy and pay premiums on it.

Automobile Defined. For liability protection in the ownership and use of a vehicle, the FAP includes private passenger cars, jeep-type vehicles, station wagons, pickup and farm trucks with three-quarter ton or less load capacity, and trailers designed for use with private passenger automobiles. Motorcycles, motor scooters, and other vehicles with less than four wheels must be insured under a similar but more restrictive "special" auto policy form.

Exclusions. Other Insurance. The purpose of the exclusions is to avoid duplication of liability coverage. Thus, use of the car as a "livery" or taxi is excluded, as is liability caused by a service station attendant (the garage liability policy of the service station owner would cover). On liability arising out of use of non-owned cars, the insurance is *excess* coverage (pays only after other insurers have paid their full limit). In "non-owned" auto liability occurrences, both the owner and user usually have insurance; the rule in such cases is that "the insurance follows the car" and that the non-owner's insurance is excess coverage.

Cancellation. The liability coverage may be cancelled upon ten days' notice, with premiums refunded pro rata. Most states, however, limit the right to cancel to: nonpayment of premiums, fraud in securing the insurance, suspension of driver's license, certain physical disabilities, and criminal behavior.

Section 2. Medical Payments

To Whom Paid. Unlike the medical payments benefit under the homeowner's policy, the FAP provides that insureds, as well as others incurring medical expenses, are covered. Thus, *anyone* incurring medical expenses while "in or upon or entering into or alighting from" the automobile can collect up to the limits for medical expenses.

Limits of Liability: Other Insurance. The standard limit is $500 per person. This can be increased to $5,000 for about six dollars per year additional premium. This seeming bargain is available because (1) medical expense reimbursement is limited to occurrences involving an automobile; (2) many situations involve benefits from two or more automobile owners' insurance, which is handled on a pro rata basis; (3) insurers can reduce personal liability suits appreciably by paying for medical expenses regardless of any negligence "fault" being involved.

Exclusions. The exclusions are minor. They include occupying an automobile used as a "public or livery conveyance" or any vehicle as a residence. Also, the usual *automobile business* exclusion is included.

Section 3. Uninsured Motorists

This is a relatively new, unique coverage. The insurance company tells the insured: "If there is an occurrence causing bodily injury to you and involving a motorist who does not have bodily injury liability insurance, we will become his liability insurer for any possible damages to you." The insured is suddenly in the position of possibly having to sue his insurer. There is an obvious element of conflict of interest, but experience to date has not indicated any serious problems in this area.

It is important to remember that the uninsured motorist coverage applies to bodily injury claims only; property damage is excluded. There is still some question as to the feasibility of this coverage as a solution to the problem of the uncompensated motorist.

Section 4. Physical Damage

The collision peril is by far the greatest cause of physical damage to an automobile. Accordingly, the premium charge is much greater than for other perils. For this reason many insureds choose to reduce the premiums by having a greater deductible for collision than for other perils. Collision coverage, then, is logically separated from other peril coverage. For the other perils the insured can choose *comprehensive* coverage which is *all-risk* protection; or he can choose *fire, lightning and transportation* with or without *theft,* to which he can add *combined additional coverage,* a broad form listing additional physical damage perils covered. The exclusions in the physical damage section are much the same as those for liability protection.

Collision Coverage. Because of the differing deductibles between collision and other perils, this precise definition of collision in the FAP is important: "Collision of an automobile covered by this policy with another object or with a vehicle to which it is attached or by upset of such automobile." Then, for certain perils that might conceivably be judged collision, the FAP in the comprehensive coverage section specifically states the following are not collision: "breakage of glass, and loss caused by missiles, falling objects, fire, theft or larceny, explosion, earthquake, windstorm, hail, water, flood, malicious mischief or vandalism, riot or civil commotion, or colliding with a bird or animal."

How much deductible? The most usual deductible amount chosen for collision is $50. To illustrate the high cost of insuring relatively small losses: $100 deductible would cost 15 percent less; $150 deductible, 30 percent less; $250 deductible would cost 50 percent less. Thus, if the $50 deductible premium is $100 annually—

the $50 additional insurance over $100 deductible costs $15
the $100 additional insurance over $150 deductible costs $30
the $200 additional insurance over $250 deductible costs $50

Most would agree this is very expensive protection and that in the family insurance budget this $15 to $50 can be put to better use.

Comprehensive Coverage. Most insureds choose the all-risk comprehensive coverage to complete the physical damage protection of their automobile.[9] *Supplementary payments* are usually included. The *personal effects* benefit provides the insureds $100 protection for "robes, wearing apparel and other personal effects" against damage by fire or lightning while "in or upon" an owned automobile. A *loss of use* benefit provides for $10-a-day car rental for up to thirty days should the car be stolen, beginning forty-eight hours after the theft.

Comprehensive coverage with no deductible costs about one-half as much as $100 deductible collision insurance, and even less in some areas. A $100 deductible on comprehensive reduces the premium some 70 percent; a $50 deductible, 50 percent. Here again is an opportunity to reduce insurance costs substantially by retaining part of the risk.

The *towing and labor costs* provision allows up to $25 for towing and for labor costs incurred at the scene of the accident. The annual premium charge is $1 to $4.

Section 5. Conditions

The conditions in the FAP are similar to those of other property insurance coverages. The following are of special importance to the insured:

An automobile acquired during the policy year (as a replacement for one already insured) is automatically covered. *Additional cars* are automatically covered only if the insured has all his cars covered by the same insurer; in each case, the insurer should be notified within thirty days.

---

[9]In most cases it costs no more, or even less, than buying separately fire, lightning and transportation plus theft plus combined additional coverage.

Assistance and Cooperation. At the time of an accident it is common for one or more of those involved to express regret and admit fault. Often fault is not the case. Whether the insured seems at the time to be at fault or not, he should make no statement to that effect. The insured has agreed to abide by the FAP condition not to "voluntarily *make any payment, assume any obligation,* or *incur any expense* other than for such immediate medical and surgical relief to others as shall be imperative at the time of the accident." Should he breach this condition with such typical statements as "It was my fault; my insurance will take care of it," the insurer could deny liability.

Subrogation. Similar to the assistance and cooperation requirement is the condition that the insured "do nothing after (the) loss to prejudice" any rights he might have against other parties involved in the occurrence. The insurer is subrogated to such rights (has legal claim to your rights against others) to the extent of recovering any funds it has paid out.

Financial Responsibility Laws. As losses to persons and property from automobile accidents have increased, the issue of a person's *right* to drive unless he has financial resources to pay for damages he might do has become increasingly important. For most of us, auto liability insurance is our only source of adequate financial responsibility. The states are traditionally reluctant to make the purchase of any private insurance *compulsory.* As a result, there are fifty varying degrees of *compulsion,* with most state financial responsibility laws skirting the issue by providing penalties to those who are unable to pay for damages for which they are responsible. Loss of the driver's license until the damages are paid is the major penalty. This is of little satisfaction or help to the uncompensated person who was harmed. The uninsured motorists coverage is only a partial solution to the problem.

No-Fault Insurance. It would be difficult to find a public issue about which there is more confusion than the various no-fault auto insurance plans. Some of this confusion could have been avoided had there been a more appropriate —however lengthy—name, such as "Compulsory automobile medical and disability loss insurance; no *minor* pain and suffering claims." There are many "no-fault" plans with no two alike, but most involve:

1. Compulsory automobile medical and disability income insurance, thus making the insured's own company pay for such losses. Many of us already have a version of this in the FAP medical payments coverage. Further, there were fewer than 10 percent of the population in 1971 who did not have some type health insurance.
2. Compulsory liability insurance would presumably solve the problem of uncompensated claims within the range of minimum limits set out in the plan.
3. Negligence law would be modified in one area, automobile negligence, to provide that no *minor* pain and suffering damages would be paid. What is "minor pain and suffering"? Most plans measure it by the

amount of *medical expenses incurred,* with minimum limits such as $1,000, $2,000, $3,000 or more. The purpose of this provision would be to eliminate the many "nuisance" settlements made by insurers to avoid litigation. It is felt this would greatly reduce personal liability insurance premiums. Like all controversial changes, there will be beneficial and harmful results. The question is in which direction the net balance will lie.

Reducing Medical Expense Losses (Cost) through Insurance

The rationale for including *medical expense* costs in this chapter dealing with *property losses* was made earlier. Essentially, the rationale is that medical care involves giving up property (money, which is a claim on property) as a consequence of incurring the expense. The other aspect of sickness, *inability to work,* logically belongs in the *loss of earnings* discussion.

In the section of Chapter 16 on health insurance policies, we reviewed some of the important benefits and provisions present in the many policies on the market. *Individual* "basic hospital expense" and "major medical" expense policies were described in some detail, with the notation that group health coverage would be treated in this chapter.

There are two aspects of health care which relate to family finance. *First,* the frequency of loss is so high that we have to think of health insurance as partially a prepayment plan for almost certain, but sporadic, expenses. For some families a certain level of *average monthly health costs* could be most efficiently handled as a monthly budget item, setting up a reserve account from which the sporadic expenditures would be made. Over the many years of a family period and on through retirement, there is no way to "beat" (or decrease) these average monthly health costs by purchasing health insurance. The mere fact of administrative and acquisition expenses of voluntary insurance almost certainly will increase the average monthly health costs.

This reasoning is open to criticism in that all families do not have the same average monthly health costs over a period of years. Admittedly this is true, but the concept is presented to stress the prepaid medical expense aspect of insuring relatively small, frequently occurring medical expense. Each family should consider how much of this loss it can absorb by paying from current income and reserve funds. Having done so, consideration should be given to choosing a corresponding deductible amount for medical expense insurance.

Second, there is the *catastrophic illness* that occurs much less frequently, affecting relatively few families. In line with the large loss principle, this is the area where scarce insurance budget dollars should be allocated. Major medical insurance is the coverage which indeed does reduce losses from catastrophic illness. Adequate amounts of this protection should be a part of the insurance program of every family which is not depending on unlimited free medical care. This, unfortunately, is not the case. In 1971, of the 183,687,000[10] "under sixty-five" civilian population of the United States, only 78,218,000[11] had major medical expense coverage through group and individual insurance plans.

Sources of Health Insurance Protection

There are three major sources of health insurance protection: social insurance, group insurance, and individual policies.

Social Insurance. Individuals age sixty-five or over who are under social security may qualify for Medicare. The hospital insurance coverage under Medicare provides additionally *extended-care-facility* benefits and *home health-services* benefits. The hospital benefits include the costs of a semi-private room, general nursing service, operating rooms, and the usual miscellaneous charges. There is a $60 deductible for each "spell of illness" for which up to sixty days in the hospital are paid; thirty additional days are allowed with a $13 a day deductible.

Extended-care facilities are those institutions providing for individuals who do not need the care and facilities of a hospital. Medicare provides that after three days of hospital confinement, a patient can have up to 100 days in such a facility for each spell of illness. If the patient after the minimum three days in a hospital still needs home care services, there is a provision for visiting nurse care and medical appliances.

For a monthly premium of $6.30, a person under Medicare may purchase Supplementary Medical Insurance. The benefits include pay for doctors' services and certain medical services and supplies.

Group Insurance. Group health insurance is normally provided as one of the fringe benefits from the employer. In some instances, unions handle group insurance. A growing number of associations whose members are self-employed or whose business operations involve too few employees to qualify for a group policy of their own, provide group coverage to their members. Examples range from the American Medical Association on a national basis to local associations of independent service station operators.

There are many advantages to group insurance and a few disadvantages. There are five important advantages.

1. Lower cost. Usually the employer contributes part or even all of the premium cost for employees who choose to enroll. Even if we discount completely the employer's contribution, the benefits paid in relation to premiums charged are far greater than for individual policies. Exhibit 18–2 shows that in 1971 owners of *individual* health insurance policies

---

[10]Social Security Administration, *Social Security Bulletin,* Vol. 36, No. 1, January, 1973, p. 63.

[11]*Source Book of Health Insurance, 1972–73* (New York: Health Insurance Institute, 1973), p. 19.

received about $.50 for each dollar of earned premiums from life insurance companies and about $.57 for each dollar from fire and casualty companies; about $.53 of each dollar from the combined total. These figures do not compare favorably with the $.90 of each earned premium dollar paid out under group health insurance *by the same group of companies*.[12] It is interesting that the 90 percent of premiums paid out as benefits held true for the Blue Cross-Blue Shield organizations. More significant is the fact that their totals include both group and individual policy premiums and benefits. Judging from the *cost aspect alone,* it would seem that the *individual policies* of the Blue Cross-Blue Shield organizations have a decided advantage over the private insurers.

2. Usually broader coverage. The group health insurance benefits vary from employer to employer, but there is a growing tendency for uniformity and for increasing the benefit structure. This is one job benefit that is not taxed as income, and is an area where business management usually tries to be competitive with other employers.[13] Most plans provide a basic hospital coverage, plus a major medical benefit.

   The hospital coverage provides either a semi-private room or a stated amount for a room, plus a liberal allowance for other hospital expenses on an unallocated basis. There is usually a deductible (typically $25 to $50) for each hospital admission. Major medical limits, as explained in Chapter 16, have increased greatly and currently range from $20,000 to $50,000 or more per insured. The major medical benefit covers most medical expenses, with the insurer paying 80 percent and the insured 20 percent. There is usually an annual deductible of $100 incurred medical expenses before major medical benefits are payable.

3. Convenience of paying premiums. Group insurance premiums are usually handled as a payroll deduction. Not only is this a convenience, but there is less likelihood of inadvertent lapsing of the policy.

4. No insurability requirement. Pre-existing conditions covered. If the employee enrolls within a stated period after starting to work (thirty, sixty, or ninety days), there is automatic coverage regardless of whether the employee is insurable or not. In addition, pre-existing conditions are covered.

5. Effective claim service. The normal claim service with group policies can be described as very effective in terms of ease, speed, and likelihood of collecting where the claim or claim amount is in question. It is not a case of a single insured dealing with an insurer; rather, the entire group case is involved, with the obvious greater bargaining power. Most employers

---

[12]It should be noted that many insurance companies sell group coverage but do not offer individual policies.

[13]The irony of this trend to more liberal benefits is the greater utilization that results in higher costs for the insurance. These higher costs are the penalty for violating the insurance principle that calls for self-insurance (retention) of relatively small, relatively certain losses.

have an employee or staff unit which deals with the insurer for all employees.

There are disadvantages of group insurance as opposed to individual policies, but most knowledgeable persons would agree that the scales are tipped in favor of group coverage. Probably the greatest disadvantage is that an individual loses his coverage when he quits his job. A provision allowing conversion

Exhibit 18–2   Claims Experience for 1100 Insurers in 1971.* 913 Companies and 187 Hospitalization and Medical-surgical Organizations Figure in thousands (000 omitted)

	Premiums earned	Claims incurred	Ratio of premiums earned to claims incurred
Individual—			
Non-cancellable	538,330	234,038	43.47%
Guaranteed renewable	1,373,199	719,818	52.41%
Non-renew, for stated reasons	219,894	138,616	63.04%
Other	1,591,062	885,793	55.67%
Total individual—697 life companies	3,353,817	1,768,857	49.99%
216 fire & casualty	368,668	209,408	56.80%
Total group—697 life companies	8,259,854	7,460,048	90.41%
216 fire & casualty	1,531,436	1,373,665	89.69%
Grand total	13,513,775	10,819,978	79.48%
187 hospitalization and medical-surgical organizations			
91 hospitalization organizations (including Blue Cross)	6,793,530	6,145,179	90.46%
96 medical-surgical organizations (including Blue Shield)	3,023,732	2,714,344	89.76%

**Argus Chart, Health Insurance, 1972* (Cincinnati, Ohio: National Underwriter Company), p. 112.

to an individual policy even if uninsurable mitigates this possible problem. There often is little choice as to coverage under the individual conversion policy, and the premium is justifiably higher than similar contracts from the standpoint of an adverse selection factor. If an ex-employee is insurable, he will be able to shop for the best policy available. The appearance of Medicare in 1966 did away with a disadvantage of some group policies which had very restricted benefits at retirement.

Can this discussion which makes a strong case for choosing group coverage over individual policies gain any credence from what is happening in the marketplace? Exhibit 18–3 indicates definite trends. Between 1960 and 1971, group health insurance benefits increased 241 percent; individual policy benefits increased 106 percent. In the four years 1968 through 1971, group health benefits increased 50 percent; individual policy benefits, 9 percent. It seems likely this trend toward increased group coverage benefits as opposed to individual coverage benefits will continue.

Exhibit 18–3*   Health Insurance Benefit Payments of Insurance Companies, by Type of Policy, In the United States (000,000 omitted)

Year	Total	Group policies	Individual and family policies
1945	$ 278	$ 139	$ 139
1950	755	438	317
1955	1,785	1,252	533
1960	3,069	2,350	719
1961	3,395	2,616	779
1962	3,763	2,911	852
1963	4,152	3,203	949
1964	4,658	3,585	1,073
1965	5,160	4,000	1,160
1966	5,559	4,357	1,202
1967	6,029	4,790	1,239
1968	6,717	5,362	1,355
1969	7,575	6,202	1,373
1970	9,089	7,476	1,613
1971	9,497	8,017	1,480

Note: The data include loss of income benefits and exclude accidental death and dismemberment benefits.
Sources: *Health Insurance Review, Spectator Health Insurance Index,* Health Insurance Council and Health Insurance Association of America. *Source Book of Health Insurance, 1972–73* (New York: Health Insurance Institute), p. 34.

Individual Health Insurance. The various types and provisions of individual health insurance policies were presented in some detail in Chapter 16. The preceding discussion on group insurance was basically a comparison of group and individual coverage. If we accept the proposition that group coverage should be chosen where there is the opportunity, we are left with recommending individual policies for those who have no other choice—and there are many such persons.

In the individual policy field, an argument has continued for years over the relative merits of Blue Cross-Blue Shield and private insurer protection. As Exhibit 18–2 indicates (and as was previously noted), Blue Cross has a much more favorable record on the important statistic: *ratio of premiums to benefits paid.* An important aspect of that statistic favorable to Blue Cross-Blue Shield is the payment of practically all hospital expenses (other than the designated room benefit) on an unallocated basis. Private insurers have available similar provisions, although often at a higher price. A possible disadvantage of Blue Cross is that their policies do not have a guaranteed renewal right for the insured; however their record to date on granting renewals automatically has been most favorable. A prospective buyer of an individual health insurance policy should seek factual information relative to the factors raised in this and preceding discussions, keeping in mind the additional aspects of choosing an insurer and an agent.

Discussion Questions

1. Distinguish between "direct" losses and "consequential" losses.
2. Distinguish between "speculative" risks and "pure" risks. Give examples.
3. What does the formula $HO + FAP = APIP$ mean?
4. What insurance coverage other than for direct and consequential losses from damage to the house does the homeowner's policy provide?
5. What is the most usual definition of "actual cash value"?
6. The replacement cost of a building is $50,000. There is an 80 percent coinsurance clause in the insurance policy. $30,000 insurance is in force. There is a $10,000 fire loss? How much would the insurance company pay under the co-insurance provision?
7. What is the fallacy of the reasoning "I don't need much liability insurance protection because I don't own much property for them to attach"?
8. About what percent of all property insurance premiums are from automobile insurance coverage?
9. Why are there usually separate deductible amounts for collision and for comprehensive automobile insurance coverage?
10. In terms of the percent of premiums paid out as benefits, is individual or group health insurance more favorable to insured's? To what extent?

---

appendix

Coverage in the Homeowner's Policy

Section I. Direct and Consequential Loss
(Coverages A, B, C, and D)

Perils Covered

There are three groupings of perils: *basic, broad form,* and *all risk.* The *basic* perils give protection against losses caused by:

fire, including loss by removal from
  threat of fire
lightning
windstorm
explosion
riot and civil commotion

damage by aircraft
damage by vehicles (not owned or
  operated by insured)
smoke damage
vandalism and malicious mischief
theft
window breakage

The *broad form* perils include *all the basic perils* plus the following:

falling objects
weight of ice, snow, or sleet
collapse of all or part of building
sudden and accidental tearing asun-
  der, cracking, burning or bulging
  of a steam or hot water heating
  system or of a water heater

accidental discharge, leaking or
  overflow of water or steam from
  plumbing, heating or cooling systems
freezing of the same systems or appliances
sudden and accidental injury to
  electrical appliances, devices, fixtures and wiring (except TV and
  radio) from short circuits or other
  accidentally generated electrical
  currents

The *all-risk* coverage includes damage from *any cause except those specifically excluded*. Thus, damage done by a berserk elephant from the city zoo crashing into your home would be covered. There are exceptions and limitations on the coverage provided by many of the named perils; particularly this is true of the perils added to the basic to make up the broad form perils. All of these exceptions apply in the all-risk coverage.

Specific Benefits

Section I provides for losses sustained from covered perils to: the home; detached structures; trees, shrubs, and plants; personal property at home and away from home; and for additional living expenses caused by the loss. These coverages are detailed in the policy form as follows:

Coverage A. Protects the home, including:

awnings and blinds and wire screens
screen doors and storm doors
shades
storm sashes

permanently installed air cooling
  and heating equipment
permanently installed lighting and
  plumbing equipment

An extension of Coverage A allows 5 percent of the amount of insurance on the home to apply to damage to trees, shrubs, plants, and lawn caused by any of the *basic* perils.

Coverage B. The policy captions this as "appurtenant structures." It provides *additional* insurance, 10 percent of the amount in force on the home, for *separate* structures on the home premises. Examples would be detached garages, storage buildings, cabanas, guest houses, and playhouses. If the 10 percent on the dwelling is not enough, the amount can be increased by endorsement for an additional premium. Excluded are any structures used as rent property to someone other than a tenant in the dwelling. Thus, a person renting a room in the dwelling and paying an extra charge for use of a detached garage or even a detached building for storage or office purposes would *not* exclude such property from coverage.

Coverage C. Protects the personal property owned by the insured and members of his family who are still considered to be living at home. This includes college students while temporarily living away from home. Since the insurance on personal property located at home and away from home is of special interest to most families and is not generally understood, we will give more details on this coverage than on the others.

The exclusions are: animals, birds or fish, motorized vehicles (except unlicensed ones intended for use on the premises), property of non-related roomers or boarders, property held as samples or held for sale or actually sold but not delivered, rental property, business property *away from* premises, sound recording or playing devices installed in a motor vehicle, and property separately described and insured in the policy or in another policy.

Concerning these exclusions, we can be specific about the insured status of certain personal property about which we may be in doubt. The following is generally true, but may vary in individual states.

The "rented property" exclusion does not apply when the insured rents his home and furnishings to another temporarily while away from the vicinity. It also does not apply to furnishings of that part of the home rented to another.

The "property held for sale" exclusion is intended to apply to commercial property, not personal property which the insured has decided to sell.

The "business property away from premises" exclusion implies that any such property which is not intended for sale or rental is covered while on the premises. Thus, a carpenter's tools, a doctor's medical bag are insured when on the home premises.

Stereo tapes and tape players installed in a motor vehicle to be powered by the electrical system of vehicle are not covered. Battery operated portables would be insured (at this writing, Kansas, Louisiana, New Jersey, and Virginia do not have this exclusion).

Power mowers and other unlicensed motorized vehicles intended for use on the premise are covered.

Watercraft (including boats, trailers, furnishings, equipment) are insured on and off premises, but for losses only up to $500. Windstrom and hail perils are excluded when the watercraft is not in a fully enclosed building.

There is a $500 aggregate limit (per occurrence) on the theft of jewelry and furs. The limit does not apply on other covered perils.

Trailers are covered whether licensed or not, but there is a $500 loss limit per occurrence. Boat trailers are included in the watercraft limit and therefore do not get an extra $500 from this limitation. There is no theft protection while trailers are away from the premises.

Personal property taken from home to college by a student (if under 21) is insured.

Coverage D. "Additional Living Expenses" is the policy name for coverage D. HO-1 allows up to 10 percent of the insurance on the home for additional living expenses; HO-2, 3, and 5 allow 20 percent; HO-4 which, we recall, is the renter's version of the homeowner's, allows 20 percent of the amount of insurance on the personal property. All of this is *additional* insurance. The intent of this coverage is to reimburse the insured for additional expenses *actually incurred,* as a result of the home being untenable due to damage from a covered peril. Assume the family moves to a motel while repairs are being made. Not only is the daily room charge paid, but also the extra cost of eating out (including tips) over the cost of eating at home. This would apply also to home utility costs maintained during the repair period, storage costs, additional laundry, and transportation expenses.

Section II. Comprehensive Personal Liability Coverage (Coverage E), Medical Payments (Coverage F), and Property Damage Liability (Coverage G)

Comprehensive personal liability coverage is all-risk insurance protecting the insured from losses arising out of his negligence. There are relatively few exclusions. The section II coverages together make up the comprehensive personal liability policy which has been incorporated without change in the homeowner's. The provisions are the same in all five versions of the homeowner's.

Coverage E. Comprehensive Personal Liability. The insurer agrees under this coverage to pay the insured for all sums that he may become legally obligated to pay as damages because of bodily injury or property damage. In addition, the insurer agrees to defend any suit against the insured alleging such damages, even if the suit is groundless, false, or fraudulent. It is this benefit that has prompted the labeling of liability protection as "defense insurance" because most suits are settled out of court by negotiation between attorneys. The insured is thus spared the expense and much of the worry and emotional disturbance that goes with such negotiations. The insurer reserves the right to make settlement without the insured's permission. This is often a source of anger and chagrin to the defendant who feels he was "not guilty" and would like to "take it to the Supreme Court." Additionally, the insurer agrees to pay all expenses involved in the conduct of negotiations and in defense and appeal of the case in court. Emergency first-aid costs at the time of the occurrence are also paid by the insurer.

Since an individual needs protection from the negligent acts of others for whom he is liable, the policy defines the insured as (1) the named insured, and (2) (if residents of his household) his spouse, the relatives of either, and any other person under the age of twenty-one in the care of the insured.

The major exclusions are:

Business and professional activities.

Use of automobiles and aircraft away from the premises.

Use of large boats. Small boat use is covered. Actual dimensions and horsepower are stated to distinguish between large and small boats. Liability for the former can be insured by endorsement and extra premium.

Intentional acts of the insured. Biggest significance here lies in intentional acts of small children. Some states require protection for intentional acts of children up to some stated age, such as nine.

Liability arising for second residences (such as beach, lake and mountain cottages) *owned* by insured. If insured were renting the same properties, the policy would cover negligence in its use. Liability coverage for these secondary residences can be purchased for as little as $15 a year, depending on the state and the company.

Coverage F. Medical Payments. The medical payments benefit, $500 limit in most states, pays regardless of whether the insured is negligent. The insured, including all the persons defined as insured, *cannot* collect on this benefit. It is simply health insurance payable for medical expenses of *others* who might have incurred such expense because of an occurrence on the insured's premises or in connection with an act of the insured. This helps avoid some liability suits on minor injuries.

Coverage G. Physical Damage to Property. The physical damage to the property of others' benefit, $250 limit in most states, is like the medical payments benefit in that the question of negligence is not involved. The insurer pays for such damage as long as the damage was the result of an act of the insured, whether negligent or not.

References

Cohen, J., and M. Hansel, *Risk and Gambling* (New York: Philosophical Library, Inc., 1956).

Dublin, L. I., and A. J. Lotka, *The Money Value of Man,* rev. ed. (New York: Ronald Press, 1946).

Greene, Mark, *Risk and Insurance,* 2nd ed. (Cincinnati: South-Western Publishing Company, 1968).

Gregg, Davis W., ed., *Life and Health Insurance Handbook* (Homewood, Ill.: Richard D. Irwin, 1964).

Handbook of Health Insurance (Cincinnati: National Underwriter Co.), latest edition.

Huebner, S. S., *The Economics of Life Insurance,* 3rd ed. (New York: Appleton, 1959).

Insurance Facts (published annually by Insurance Information Institute, New York), latest edition.

Life Insurance Fact Book (published annually by The Institute of Life Insurance, New York), latest edition.

Mehr, Robert I., and Emerson Cammack, *Principles of Insurance,* 4th ed. (Homewood, Ill.: Richard D. Irwin, 1966).

O'Connell, Jeffrey, *The Injury Industry—and the Remedy of No-Fault Insurance* (Chicago: Commerce Clearing House, 1971).

Source Book of Health Insurance (published annually by Health Insurance Institute, New York), latest edition.

Volpe, John A., U.S. Department of Transportation, "Motor Vehicle Crash Losses and Their Compensation in the United States—A Report to the Congress and the President," March, 1971.

Williams, C. Arthur, Jr., and Richard M. Heins, *Risk Management and Insurance,* 2nd ed. (New York: McGraw-Hill, 1971).

part five

Investments

Annual income twenty pounds, annual expenditures
nineteen six, result happiness. Annual income
twenty pounds, annual expenditure twenty pounds,
aught and eight, result misery.

[*Dickens*]

19

Managing
to Save

Mr. Micawber was not accomplished in the art of managing money, but he learned from experience that when he spent less than his income, "result happiness," and when he spent more than his income, "result misery." Numerous changes have occurred since Dickens' time, but thrift still has its virtues, and learning to save is an essential key to getting the most out of the use of income.

In an economic sense, the word "save" has a broad meaning. We save by avoiding waste or loss. We save when we spend wisely. We save when we use properly the things we consume, such as clothing, furniture, appliances, automobiles, etc. We save by taking care of ourselves and thus avoiding the high costs of illness. Used in this broad sense, the verb "save" is synonymous with "economize."

In this chapter, however, we shall use "save" in a more restricted way to mean laying aside money (not spending all our income), although a moment's reflection tells us that we are better able to achieve this when we do economize or save in the broadest sense.

How to Save

The power to save wisely depends upon having an excess of income over necessary spending. It is bad management to force the family to save by stinting on necessities and running the risk of incurring major costs later or of impairing performance at work or in other activities. Thrift should never be confused with miserliness or stinginess.

The amount saved should come from "discretionary income," or that which is left after expenditures for food, clothing, and housing. People with very low incomes find it difficult to save despite the fact that they might be frugal, because they have little or no discretionary income. Obviously, then, the great bulk of savings comes from middle and upper income families, but even among them are some who are unable to save because they do not know how to manage and save.

Essentially, when a person saves, he is postponing consumption—withholding purchasing power for future use. The extent to which he does this often depends upon what he expects in the future. If he thinks he can obtain greater satisfaction out of the use of money later, he is likely to postpone consumption. If he expects to earn interest on his savings, he is more likely to save, although expectation of interest is no longer considered to be as much an inducement as it once was.

Studies show that the best way to save is to do so regularly, not haphazardly or sporadically. A good rule is to decide how much the family intends to save each week or month and resolve to set that amount aside. If a budget is prepared and kept, savings can be provided for in it as for any other planned item. It is also desirable to isolate savings from funds currently in use.

Regular savings accumulate surprisingly fast. For example, by setting aside only $25 a month, a family will save $1,500 in five years which will earn an additional $208.20 in interest at 5 percent compounded daily, making a total of $1,708.20. In ten years, this account will be $3,901.88, and in twenty years, $10,336.76 (see Exhibit 19–1).

Why Save

As a rule it is easier to save regularly if the savings program is for a specific purpose or purposes. Most of the things we do, we do better when we have a reason.

Exhibit 19–1   *Regular Monthly Savings Build Up Surprisingly with Earnings Compounded Daily at 5%*

How savings grow	$5 monthly	$10 monthly	$15 monthly	$20 monthly	$25 monthly	$50 monthly	$100 monthly
1 year	61.67	123.33	185.00	246.67	308.34	616.67	1233.35
2 years	126.50	252.99	379.49	505.99	632.50	1264.98	2529.97
3 years	194.66	389.30	583.96	778.62	973.28	1946.54	3893.11
4 years	266.32	532.60	798.92	1065.23	1331.55	2663.07	5326.17
5 years	341.65	683.25	1024.90	1366.55	1708.20	3416.35	6832.76
10 years	780.40	1560.68	2341.08	3121.48	3901.88	7803.64	15607.40
15 years	1343.84	2687.47	4031.32	5375.16	6719.01	13437.80	26875.81
20 years	2067.42	4134.50	6201.92	8269.34	10336.76	20673.19	41346.72

People save for a variety of reasons.

1. Perhaps the most common reason is to make money income last over a period of time. Suppose a worker receives a year's wages in one lump sum every December 31. Obviously, he will have to make it last until he is paid again a year hence. In other words, he will be foolish, indeed, if he spends the entire sum in one month, saving nothing for the other eleven months. Fortunately, however, those of us whose incomes are derived from employment are paid monthly, semimonthly, or weekly, and for us the problem of saving to spread income over time is less urgent than for those who receive income infrequently or irregularly.

2. A very sensible reason to save is to accumulate a fund for emergencies such as illnesses, accidents, and unemployment, or as the old expression goes: "saving for a rainy day." Most financial counselors agree that a family emergency fund should equal a third to a half of annual income, depending upon the family's insurance program and borrowing capacity.

3. Many persons prefer to save to make purchases which involve relatively large outlays to avoid using credit. Frequently, as in the case of buying a home, enough must be saved to make the down payment even when credit is involved. As we observed in Chapter 9, consumer credit is expensive, and should be avoided when possible. The actual cost of such things as furniture, home appliances, automobiles, etc. may be reduced considerably when bought for cash or when a large down payment can be made.

4. An important long-range goal, often reported by families when questioned about their reason or reasons for saving, is the accumulation of enough funds for a child's college education. In many instances, a savings program for this purpose is begun early in the child's life.

5. Some people save because "being ahead" gives them a sense of security. In most instances, there is a powerful psychological force behind the fel-

low who is ahead. It gives him confidence, frees him of constant worries that go with living from hand to mouth day after day, and gives him an air of independence . . . all of which could make him a better producer, eligible for promotion and more pay. Sociologists say that "being ahead" also strengthens family ties.[1]

6. In the days of Poor Richard's Almanack, people were urged to save because, as Poor Richard said, "A penny saved is a penny earned." Implied in the saying is a very important reason to save, namely, to improve one's income over time by putting savings to work in a self-owned business or in investments that yield a return. An individual may have one or more specific objectives in mind such as more income for current living purposes, for retirement to supplement social security and other benefits, and for building an estate for present dependents or future heirs.

After some reflection on the above reasons for saving, most will probably conclude that all are worthy and desirable, but it is not possible to save for all of them at the same time. This is certainly true for most families, especially young families. Each family should start with what it considers the most urgent or most important reason in relation to the family's particular conditions and circumstances.

Common Difficulties in Saving

Regardless of purpose, most people find it difficult to save consistently even when their income permits saving. Failure to control expenditures satisfactorily is the chief stumbling block in situations of this kind. Experienced counselors in the field of personal finance can cite many cases of families with identical incomes and with about the same responsibilities who get vastly different results from their incomes. Some families live quite well and at the same time save regularly, while others seem always to be in financial straits.

It is not easy to give helpful advice about family spending, because so many times the real trouble stems from something that is strictly personal in nature. Within broad limits, the way persons spend their own money is their own business—it's a matter of likes and dislikes, and of choices. Each person's sense of values is slightly different from any other's. Nevertheless, it is wise to remember an old adage: "To satisfy one's hunger is not so expensive as it is to gratify one's appetite." Status is very important to some persons. "Keeping up with the Joneses," as the saying goes, can be rather embarrassing, especially if one does not have the income and other circumstances comparable to those of the Joneses. Even then the Joneses themselves might do better.

How does one develop a good sense of values? He might grow up in a family

---

[1]Ray E. Baber, "Marriage and the Family," McGraw-Hill Book Company, Inc., New York, 1953, Chapter 12.

that has it and acquire it by association; or he may develop it from his schooling (as women learn to judge quality of materials, foods, etc. in home economics courses); or he can learn it by experience—the "hard way." Regardless of how one comes by a good sense of values, he must discipline himself to live by it, especially when the prevailing economic philosophy plays down the old virtues of frugality and thrift, and all the arts and skills of Madison Avenue lure us to spend for countless wonderful things.

As previously stated (Chapter 8), a family which keeps reasonably good records should be able to answer the question: Where has the money gone? Without that answer, it is almost futile to expect effective control of spending, yet control of spending is often the only way a family can improve its economic position enough to save.

We do not propose so much austerity in spending that the family's level of living is lowered, but rather we propose the kind of money management which provides as well and eliminates the leaks.

Young People Need to Save

Although it is highly desirable to start a savings program early, statistics indicate that young people save relatively little of the nation's total personal savings. Why is this true? Young persons, mostly because of inexperience, seem to respond more readily to aggressive salesmanship—sometimes unscrupulous salesmanship—and are inclined to spend too much for immediate consumption. In addition, some young married couples try to start out living on a scale that took twenty to twenty-five years for their parents to reach. Moreover, on the whole, young people do not have much discretionary income since their wages and salaries tend to be low in the early years. Yet, this is the very time when need for such items as furniture, appliances, and an automobile is relatively large. Finally, additional expenses are incurred when the family begins to grow.

What to Do with Savings

Next in difficulty to the problem of saving money is how to manage what is already saved. What a family should do with the funds it has accumulated varies with (a) the amount saved; (b) the purpose or purposes for saving; and (c) the extent to which a family is willing to assume risks with its funds.

It is desirable to arrange savings goals in order of their importance and to manage the savings program accordingly. Top priority must be given to making the income received periodically last from one payday to the next and having enough available to meet sizable recurring expense items, such as insurance premiums and taxes when they fall due.

Obviously there is an element of saving involved here in the effective management of current funds which can be helped by careful budgeting and by the use of a checking account at a commercial bank.

Most banks collect a service charge when the balance of a checking account falls below a set minimum and/or a certain number of checks are written. If a sufficient balance is carried to avoid this charge, the family has a savings start. Banks are legally prohibited from paying interest on checking account balances (defined as demand deposits), but there is an indirect benefit when an account is not assessed such a service charge.

Funds saved for emergencies and other specific purposes should be put where they will be safe, will earn a reasonable income, and will be readily available when needed. A savings account with a commercial bank, a mutual savings bank, a savings and loan association, or a credit union affords a convenient place to accumulate savings until the sum reaches an amount which can be put to work more advantageously elsewhere.

Segregating funds from a checking account not only places them where they will earn a return but removes them as a temptation to spend.

Savings Accounts

A savings account is a form of contract between a saver or savers and the institution which holds the savings. The parties agree to be bound by rules and regulations usually set forth in what is called a *passbook*. However, certain rights of the depositor and obligations of the institution are initially agreed to in the particular type of account selected and are evidenced by a signature card signed by the depositor when he opens the account.

There are different types of personal savings accounts. The most common is the individual account which is in one person's name only, and that person alone has control of it. The account balance becomes a part of the person's estate upon his death. A specimen of an *individual account* signature card is shown in Exhibit 19–2.

A *joint survivorship account* is held in the names of two or more persons who are called "joint tenants with right of survivorship." Most often this type is used by a husband and wife, and either may deposit or withdraw funds from the account. Legally, joint tenants are co-owners of the account and upon death of either tenant the account balance belongs to the surviving tenant. See Exhibit 19–3.

A third type of personal savings account is the *trustee account* which is opened by an individual acting for a beneficiary. This arrangement is called a *self-appointed trusteeship,* since no formal written trust agreement is necessary. The trustee has sole control of the account during his lifetime and upon his death the balance of the account goes to the designated beneficiary. The trustee has an unilateral right to withdraw funds at any time and use them as he wishes, or he can terminate the account without recourse by the beneficiary.

A trustee account is simple and easy to open. For example, John J. Brown wants to set up a trustee account indicating his son James Charles Brown as

Exhibit 19–2   Signature Card for Individual Account

THE SECURITY STATE BANK, Commerce, Texas

BELOW PLEASE FIND DULY AUTHORIZED SIGNATURE, WHICH YOU WILL RECOGNIZE IN PAYMENT
OF FUNDS OR THE TRANSACTION OF OTHER BUSINESS ON MY / OUR ACCOUNT.

SIGNATURE

SIGNATURE

BANK REFERENCE

PERSONAL REFERENCE   OCCUPATION

STECK-AUSTIN

Exhibit 19–3   Signature Card for Joint Account

Date _____ 19____

The undersigned, Joint Depositors, hereby agree, each with the other and with

THE SECURITY STATE BANK, COMMERCE, TEXAS

that all sums heretofore or hereafter deposited by said joint depositors or either of them, with said Bank, to their credit as such joint depositors, shall be owned by them jointly, with the right of survivorship, and be subject to the check, or order or receipt of either of them, or the SURVIVOR of them, and payment thereof shall discharge said Bank from liability to either, or the heirs, executors, administrators, or assigns of either. This agreement shall not be changed or terminated except by written notice to said Bank, and such notice shall not affect the right of the Bank or said depositors hereunder with relation to deposits theretofore made.

In case of the death of either, it is understood that no checks drawn on this account by the survivor, will be honored until evidence is furnished that the inheritance tax is paid in accordance with the requirements of law.

_____ }

_____ } Joint Depositors

THE SECURITY STATE BANK, COMMERCE, TEXAS

By _____

beneficiary. The account will be styled: John J. Brown, Trustee for James Charles Brown. The father will sign in that manner.

Why use a trustee account? Brown may be planning to set aside savings for his son's college education ten years hence, but wishes to maintain complete control over the funds at all times; yet in case of his death he wants the son to have the funds.

Safety. It is important to take time to check the safety of a savings account before selecting a depository. Are the savings protected against loss? All but a very few commercial banks are members of the Federal Deposit Insurance Corporation (FDIC) which insures both demand and savings deposits up to $20,000. Most mutual savings banks are similarly insured. Savings accounts in member savings and loan associations are insured to $20,000 by the Federal Savings and Loan Insurance Corporation (FSLIC).

Both the FDIC and the FSLIC collect regular premiums from insured institutions, and the premiums go into funds from which losses are paid, if and when losses occur to insured depositors. Since deposit insurance became effective in 1933, losses from bank and association failures have been so meager that both insurance corporations have accumulated large funds, and no insured depositor has ever lost.

In 1970, Congress passed and President Nixon signed the Federal Share Insurance Act creating an agency to insure savings placed in credit unions. The law requires all federally chartered credit unions to provide savings insurance, and state chartered credit unions may apply to the National Credit Union Administration for membership in the insurance program. In effect the Federal Share Insurance Act makes available to those who save with credit unions protection comparable to that offered by the FDIC to depositors in member commercial banks and by the FSLIC to savers in member savings and loan associations.

Families should be sure that all savings are insured, whether they are in a commercial bank, a mutual savings bank, a savings and loan association, or a credit union.

Yield. Next a depositor should ascertain what return he can expect on his savings: how often it is paid and how it is calculated. There is some variation in rates between commercial banks, mutual savings banks, savings and loan associations, and credit unions. If all else is equal, the best return is the logical choice.

A common practice among thrift institutions is to pay interest quarterly. Methods of calculation, however, vary considerably. Some calculate on a quarterly basis, some monthly, and an increasing number of institutions are doing so on a daily basis, thanks to modern electronic computers. Daily compounding of interest at a 5 percent annual rate results in a true return of about 5.13 percent.

Savings institutions also differ in their treatment of account balances in computing interest. For example, some may compute by applying a stated rate against the lowest balance in the account during the interest period while others may apply the rate to the average daily balance, even giving credit from the first of a month for deposits made any time within the first ten days.

Computation is also affected by the way withdrawals are handled. Under the FIFO, or first-in-first-out, method of interest computation, withdrawals are taken from the earliest deposits in a stated period. Since the oldest deposits in a period earn more interest at time of computation than later deposits, this reduction within a period obviously works against the depositor.

On the other hand, depositors get a better break with the LIFO, or last-in-first-out, method of computation under which withdrawals are subtracted from the last deposits made in a period.

As a generalization, mutual savings banks and savings and loan associations pay from ½ to 1 percent more in base rate than do commercial banks, attributable to differences in the nature of the institutions, to regulations under which they operate, and to services they render.[2]

In this connection, it should be pointed out that there is a legal difference in the positions of depositors in commercial banks and of savers in mutual savings banks, mutual savings and loan associations, and credit unions. As a commercial bank depositor, the depositor is a creditor of the bank. The latter owes the depositor what he has placed in an account. Where interest is involved, the bank is legally bound to pay, regardless of how much the bank earns. But, as a depositor in a mutual savings bank, in a mutual savings and loan association, or in a credit union, the depositor becomes a shareholder or owner of part of the business represented by the shares he has acquired with his deposits. The depositor will be paid dividends—not interest—because there technically is an owner-relationship involved, not a creditor relationship. Before dividends can be paid legally they must be voted or declared by the board of directors, as in the case of any business corporation, and when earnings are insufficient or low the board just might not declare dividends.

There was a time when the above difference was regarded as quite significant, and it will be again in the event of a serious recession or depression, but today little attention is paid to the point because mutual savings banks and savings and loan associations have a long record of uninterrupted dividend payments.

Here it should be mentioned that all savings institutions, including commercial banks, raise and lower the rate of return they pay on savings in relation to money market conditions and other circumstances, but the changes are infrequent.

Under what is known as Regulation Q, commercial banks are forbidden to pay more than maximum rates on respective kinds of savings and time deposits set by the Federal Reserve Board, but they can pay less.

Credit unions pay various rates of dividends on members' savings, depending primarily upon the amount of earnings left after meeting expenses and setting up reserves. After a credit union has been in existence several years, has stabilized its operations, and has proven its earning capacity, it is likely to adopt a set dividend rate policy. Most commonly the rate is from 5 percent to 6 percent inclusive (see Exhibit 19-4). Credit unions chartered by the Federal Government are not allowed to pay more than 6 percent.

Availability. After checking safety and yield, a depositor should investigate the extent to which his savings will be available in case he wants them. This is particularly important when an account is set aside for emergencies.

---

[2]An average annual rate of 5.13 percent was paid by mutual savings banks in 1971. The average of savings and loan associations was 5.33 percent. Commercial banks paid 4.5 percent.

Funds in a demand deposit account at a commercial bank are payable when they are requested or demanded. As a general rule, the same high degree of liquidity applies to savings accounts in a commercial bank, but legally the bank can require thirty days' notice before it has to honor a request for withdrawal from a savings account.

Mutual savings banks and savings and loan associations accept savings accounts, but not checking accounts. However, merely by presenting his passbook a depositor ordinarily can withdraw funds at any time from either type of savings institution, although either legally can require a period of notice which may be from sixty to ninety days.

Exhibit 19–4   Dividend Rates Reported by Credit Unions in 1970

Rates	Ratio of credit unions reporting
3.00% and below	4.08%
3.01–4.00	7.57
4.01–4.49	1.83
4.50	6.96
4.51–4.99	4.51
5.00	25.96
5.01–5.50	25.29
5.51–6.00	22.50
6.01 and over	1.30
	100.00%

Source: *The Credit Union Yearbook 1971,* Credit Union National Association Inc., Madison, Wisconsin.

Since only members may do business with credit unions, and savings deposits actually are credited in terms of shares to be owned, when a member wishes to withdraw some or all of his savings, he sells an equivalent number of shares back to the credit union. Although the latter may require a member to give written notice of intention to sell his shares and take his savings out, it seldom does.

Penalty. Regardless of which institution is chosen to hold a savings account, a depositor should inquire whether there is a penalty imposed when he withdraws savings on any date other than interest or dividend dates. This is no problem where an institution pays interest or dividends from date of deposit to date of withdrawal, but many institutions still follow the old practice of figuring and crediting earnings at quarterly intervals, and depositors who withdraw funds in between receive no earnings for the time since the last crediting date.

Example: Suppose interest or dividends are paid on January 1, April 1, July 1, and October 1. If a depositor withdraws all or part of the balance from his savings account on June 15, he will receive no earnings on the amount he withdrew for the time from April 1 to June 15.

Frequently the bank or savings and loan association will suggest that a depositor borrow the needed amount from it for fifteen days so he will not lose 2½ months' earnings, and repay the loan and interest from the account on July 1. This is obviously the thing to do, as long as the cost of the loan does not exceed earnings.

Certificates of Deposit

Another savings medium available at thrift institutions is a *savings certificate,* more commonly called a *certificate of deposit* or *CD.* Once almost solely used by businesses and local governments to put temporary surplus funds to work, certificates of deposit have become increasingly popular with individuals who agree to leave a definite sum of money with an institution for a specified period of time. Most institutions issuing these certificates require a minimum amount of money for a certificate, sometimes as low as $100, but generally $500 or more. Maturity period may vary from thirty days to as long as ten years.

Certificates of deposit have both advantages and disadvantages when compared with savings accounts. The advantages are:

1. The owner of a certificate of deposit is assured a certain rate of interest for a specific period, whereas the rate may change any time as it applies to savings accounts.
2. Interest computation is easier to understand.
3. Certificates of deposit generally pay higher rates of interest than passbook savings accounts because (a) CD money is usually sufficient in amount to be more competitively sought; (b) it is committed for a definite time and the institution can count on it; and (c) costs of handling certificates are less than costs of administering passbook savings accounts.
4. Certificates may be made payable on any date convenient for the depositor beyond thirty days.

The disadvantages of these certificates are:

1. A certificate of deposit is a definite contract for a stated sum payable with interest at maturity, whereas a savings account is an open-end instrument to which the owner may make additional deposits in any amounts at any time and from which he may make withdrawals at any time.
2. Generally it is more difficult to cash a certificate of deposit before maturity than it is to make a withdrawal from a savings account, and the penalty in form of lost interest is often greater.

As a rule, interest rates paid on certificates vary directly with amount of money involved and with length of maturity. For example, when it is paying 5 percent on passbook savings, a thrift institution might be paying 5¾ percent on CD's of $1,000 or more with maturities from one year to ten years and

6 percent on certificates of $5,000 or more with maturities from two years to ten years.

Certificates of deposit are insured up to $20,000 in the same manner as other kinds of deposits.

The Flow of Savings

The process of saving changes the direction and timing of income use. When people save, they abstain from spending currently all their income for consumption. What they do not spend now, they expect to have available for future use.

In the meantime, what becomes of what they save? As we have seen, much of it flows into thrift or savings institutions, commonly called financial intermediaries, to be loaned to businesses for use in production and to individuals to spend for consumption. In our type of industrial system, capital formation depends upon savings, or the return of money to production. People must abstain from consuming all their income so that some wealth may be used to produce more wealth.

Exhibit 19–5 shows the amount of savings in the four most common types of financial intermediaries.

Exhibit 19–5   Amount of Savings in Leading Thrift Institutions (in billions, year end)

Institution	1950	1955	1960	1965	1970	1971
Commercial banks	$34.9	$46.0	$66.8	$134.2	$208.2	$238.2
Savings and loan associations	14.0	32.1	62.1	110.4	146.4	174.5
Mutual savings banks	20.0	28.2	36.3	52.4	71.6	82.4
Credit unions	0.9	2.4	5.0	9.4	15.4	18.5

Source: Federal Home Loan Bank Board and Board of Governors of the Federal Reserve System

Since money is fungible, it is not possible to trace the flow of a particular savings deposit from a depositor through an intermediary to a borrower who actually uses it. Deposits are commingled, and their identity is lost on the books of the intermediary, a particular account showing only credits for deposits and debits for withdrawals. Similarly, loans are recorded, each borrower's account being debited with the amount borrowed plus interest charged and credited with each payment on the loan. The effect, in substance, is that an intermediary's liabilities are mostly deposits, and its assets largely are loans and investments made with the deposits; but no single deposit can be said to be the very funds that were loaned to a specific borrower. However, with their liquid reserves and two-way flow of funds, intermediaries stand ready and able to pay depositors who on any day might want their money.

For the great majority of savers, thrift institutions offer the best place for savings because deposits are:

1. Absolutely safe in the amount insured
2. Income-yielding
3. Readily available or "liquid"
4. Never less in dollar value than the amount on deposit.

In addition, thrift institutions are specialists in putting funds to work, whereas the average depositor may have neither time nor know-how to do so; and since intermediaries handle large volumes of funds, they are able to supply a wide range of loan amounts and spread losses thinly. Finally, deposits are acceptable in almost any sums—small or large—and at any time.

U.S. Savings Bonds

Millions of American families invest some or all their savings in U.S. savings bonds, of which there currently are two kinds popularly known as Series E bonds and Series H bonds. The U.S. Treasury has issued savings bonds since 1935, primarily to provide people with small or average income a place to invest savings safely at a reasonably good rate of return.[3] The bonds are direct obligations of the U.S. Government, and about $53 billion worth were outstanding at the end of 1972.

Series E Bonds. These bonds are issued in denominations ranging from $25 to $1,000 and are sold at a discount price of three-fourths of their face value. They increase in redemption value over time, reaching full face or denomination value when held five years and ten months.

For example, a person can now buy a $100 Series E Savings Bond for $75, hold it five years and ten months, and it then will be worth $100, having increased one-third over what was paid for it, or an average annual yield of 5½ percent.

The U.S. Treasury has modified the effective yield on Series E bonds several times by changing the length of maturity (but not the discount price of three-fourths). Earliest issues yielded an annual average rate of about 2.9 percent when held ten years to maturity.

Exhibit 19–6 shows denominations, issue prices, and maturity values of Series E bonds currently available.

It is important to remember that the owner of a Series E bond does not receive interest income as such. Instead he receives an increase or accrual in the worth of the bond depending upon the length of time the bond is held.

A Series E bond is redeemable on demand at the owner's option anytime after two months at the accrued value for the respective bracketed time held. Yield accrues through increases in redemption value at the beginning of each successive half-year period after issue date, with an additional increase for the final four-month period from 5½ years to maturity.

---

[3]Series E bonds were first issued in 1941, and Series H in 1952.

Exhibit 19–6   United States Savings Bonds (sold on and after June 1, 1970)

	Series E	*Series H*
Type:	Appreciation.	Current income.
Dated:	First day of month in which payment is received by an authorized issuing agent.	First day of month in which payment is received by a Federal Reserve Bank or the U.S. Treasury.
Maturity:	5 years and 10 months.	10 years from issue date.
Cost per $1,000:	$750.00.	$1,000.00
Maturity value per $1,000:	$1,000.00	$1,000.00
Yield to maturity:	5½% a year compounded semiannually.	5½% a year compounded semiannually for the first five years and 6% for the remaining five years to maturity.
Redemption:	By owner at any time not less than two months from issue date.	At par by owner on written notice after 6 months from issue date.
Denomination (maturity value):	$25, $50, $75, $100, $200, $500, $1,000.*	$500, $1,000, $5,000, $10,000.
Registration:	In the name of adults or minors, also coowners or beneficiaries; persons or organizations, public or private, as fiduciaries; public or private organizations, including corporations, partnerships, associations, public bodies, but not commercial banks.	Same as Series E.
Limitation on purchase per calendar year:	$5,000 (issue price).	$5,000 excluding bonds issued in exchange for Series E bonds or U.S. savings notes.
Exchange:	May be exchanged for Series H.	
Purchase place:	Commercial banks, Federal Reserve Banks, U.S. Treasury, other qualified agencies, and some post offices.	Federal Reserve Banks, Treasurer of the U.S.

*$10,000 and $100,000 for certain employee savings plans.

Source: Handbook of Securities of the United States Government and Federal Agencies, 25th ed. (First Boston Corporation, 1972) p. 57.

Current yield is 5½ percent, compounded semiannually, if held to maturity. The rate is 4.01 percent the first year; thereafter, it increases gradually, and at maturity a ½ percent bonus is added, raising the yield to 5½ percent over the full five years and ten months.

Obviously, then, yield is graduated with the length of time held, the intention of which is to encourage people to hold the bonds longer, preferably to maturity. By way of example, if an investor buys a $100 E bond, costing $75, and holds it less than two months and decides to turn it in, he cannot redeem it because he has not held it for at least two months. If he tries again after two months but less than six months, he will then get his $75 back; but no more, since yield accrual does not begin until he has owned the bond six months.

Suppose he holds the bond more than a half year, but less than one year. Then he will receive $76.20, or $1.20 more than he paid for it, which represents a 3.2 percent return. If he waits a full year (the 1 to 1½-year bracket), he will receive $78.04, or $3.04 more than he paid, which is a 4.01 percent return. Redemption values and yield graduate in this manner until maturity, when the overall yield amounts to 5½ percent compounded semiannually.

Series E bonds have proved attractive to investors, particularly small investors, for the following reasons:

1. The bonds are easy and convenient to buy because (a) commercial banks, savings and loan associations, and various other agencies sell them; (b) bonds can be bought for as little as $18.75 each; (c) many companies have Payroll Savings Plans which employees may join to make regular E bond purchases; and (d) many banks have Bond-a-Month plans under which you can buy automatically each month.

2. The bonds are safe because they are obligations of the U.S. Government.

3. Their yield compares favorably with yields on other investments of savings, considering all factors.

4. They are easily converted into cash anytime after two months.

5. They are in relatively small denominations so they can be redeemed in desired amounts without having to liquidate a large investment.

6. E bonds can be bought and redeemed without having to pay a broker's commission.

7. Owners have an option of reporting annually for federal income tax purposes the accrual on E bonds or waiting until redemption to report entire accrual.

8. E Bonds are exempt from state and local income taxes.

9. An owner of E bonds will never receive less than what the bonds cost him because their value is not subject to market fluctuations.

10. All E bonds may be registered either in single ownership form, co-ownership form, or beneficiary form, and if stolen, lost, or destroyed, they can be replaced.

11. E bonds cannot be called, and those now on sale may be retained at the option of the owner for a ten-year extended maturity period.

The following may be regarded as disadvantages of E bonds from an investment point of view:

1. Yield can be realized only by cashing or redeeming the bonds.
2. E bonds cannot be transferred, sold, or used as collateral for loans.
3. There is an annual limitation on an owner's holding of E bonds. The limit is $5,000 issue price each calendar year, a further indication that the government intended for ownership to be confined to small savers. (Incidentally, commercial banks are not allowed to own E bonds.)

Series H Savings Bonds. These bonds are available in denominations of $500, $1,000, and $5,000 and sell at par or face value. Yield is 5½ percent compounded semiannually if the bonds are held to maturity of ten years. If not held to maturity, H bonds, like E bonds, earn a rate graduated according to the length of time they are held. For example, the yield is 4.49 percent the first year, 5.30 percent the next four years, and 6.0 percent for the second five years, producing an average of 5½ percent for the ten-year period.

Semiannual interest checks are mailed to H bond holders, beginning six months from the issue date. This feature is attractive to savers and investors who want to use the interest as part of current income. Interest from H bonds, like the yield from E Bonds, is subject to the federal income tax, but exempt from state and local income taxes.

H bonds may be redeemed at par any time after six months from issue date.

These bonds are issued only by Federal Reserve Banks and their branches and the Office of the Treasurer of the United States, but commercial banks and other financial institutions will help buyers by accepting and forwarding applications for delivery of bonds by mail to the registered owner.

Life Insurance Saving

Cash or Loan Value. As we noted in Chapter 16, all life insurance policies, except individual term and group term policies, contain an element of savings which begins to accumulate after the first or second year and increases as long as the insurance is in force. It is identified in each policy as cash surrender value or loan value.

Because of the large amount of life insurance in force in the country, savings in this form ranks third in magnitude only to savings in commercial banks and savings in savings and loan associations. See Exhibit 19–7.

Some persons have no other savings except the cash value that has built up in their life insurance program. This form of savings is sometimes referred to as *forced saving* because it is derived from level premiums the insured is obliged to pay to obtain insurance.

Exhibit 19–7   Savings Held by Individuals in Selected Media, Selected Years, 1930–1971 (in millions of dollars)

| End of year | Total | Savings accounts | | | | | U.S. savings bonds | | Reserves of life insurance companies |
		Mutual savings banks	Commercial banks	Savings and loan associations	Credit unions	Postal savings	Series E and H	Other	
1930	48,304	9,384	18,647	6,296	37	250	—	—	13,690
1940	59,336	10,618	15,403	4,322	235	1,342	—	2,753	24,663
1945	136,483	15,332	29,929	7,365	400	3,013	30,727	12,208	37,509
1950	176,303	20,002	35,200	13,992	892	3,035	34,493	15,059	53,630
1955	234,979	28,113	46,331	32,142	2,446	1,985	40,063	10,166	73,733
1960	312,782	36,343	67,079	62,142	4,982	836	42,920	2,722	95,758
1965	479,108	52,443	134,247	110,385	9,224	309	48,800	900	122,800
1966	504,237	55,006	146,329	114,009	10,071	122	49,800	500	128,400
1967	549,689	60,121	167,634	124,531	11,103	—	50,900	300	135,100
1968	583,432	64,507	181,322	131,618	12,285	—	51,400	500	141,800
1969	592,693	67,086	177,029	135,538	13,740	—	51,100	700	147,500
1970	643,145	71,580	203,439	146,404	15,522	—	51,400	700	154,100
1971	732,979	81,440	239,548	174,472	18,319	—	53,800	600	164,800

Source: Federal Home Loan Bank Board and National Association of Mutual Savings Banks.

Interest earned on life insurance savings is generally below the rate of most other forms of saving, but the difference tends to be offset when other factors are considered, such as policy dividends and relatively low interest charged the policyholder if he borrows from the company against his policy's cash value.

Although life insurance savings are not insured, they are generally considered safe because of the exceptionally good record of the life insurance industry. They are not as readily available when needed as are savings in banks and other thrift institutions, but only a few days at most are required to obtain a policy's cash value.

With the exception of those of advanced age who feel they no longer need as much insurance, most policyholders do not care to reduce their insurance program by surrendering a policy for its cash value. Instead, they will borrow from the company, and the latter will readily make a loan up to full cash value of the policy, usually at a rate of interest considerably below the going rate at other financial institutions. Incidentally, the borrower is not obliged to repay the loan at any specified time, but may keep it as long as his policy is in force and he pays interest on the loan.

In 1971, life insurance companies in the United States paid $2,881,600,000 to policyholders who surrendered their policies for cash value. The companies had outstanding at the end of 1971 total policy loans amounting to $17,065,000,000, or 7.17 percent of assets.[4] Interest charged on policy loans was generally 5 or 6 percent. Quite often policyholders borrow from banks and other lenders on the cash value of their insurance.

Annuities. Another form of saving with life insurance companies is through an annuity contract. People whose saving objective is primarily to provide income to supplement social security and/or retirement plans sometimes find an annuity a suitable means of achieving their goal.

An *annuity* is an investment which pays a fixed income periodically for life or for a specified time, beginning at a definite date in return for one or more premiums paid by the buyer of the annuity.

The best type of annuity for purposes of retirement is known as a *deferred annuity* or one whose payments to the annuitant begin at some future date, say when the person reaches age 65, and continue periodically for the rest of his life.

As an example, let's say that Fred Green at age thirty-five decides to buy an annuity which will pay him a monthly sum for life beginning thirty years from now. He contacts an agent of a life insurance company and obtains a contract under whose terms Green obligates himself to pay thirty annual premiums of a fixed amount each, and the company in turn promises to pay Green a monthly amount beginning thirty years from the date of contract.

---

[4]"Life Insurance Fact Book 1972," Institute of Life Insurance, New York, N.Y., pp. 51 and 84. It should be noted that the discussion in this chapter on life insurance annuities and the Keogh plan is related to the matter of *managing to save.* In Chapter 16, the *theory of life insurance and annuities* was explained, and the varying *benefits and provisions* among the many different plans were noted. In Chapter 17, they were discussed in terms of *which plans* to use in *reducing earnings losses.*

This kind of arrangement is known as a *straight* or *pure annuity,* because installment payments cease when Green dies, even if he has received only one installment, and the contract terminates without any more money being paid by the company.[5] Incidentally, a straight annuity involving the life of one person is the least expensive kind. Green could have bought a straight annuity called a *joint and survivorship annuity* which would provide income for more than one person's lifetime. Under this type of annuity, income is paid as long as either of the persons, usually a husband and wife, remains alive. Obviously, the cost of a joint and survivorship annuity is more than the cost of a straight annuity involving only one life.

Straight annuities are not popular because many people do not care to take a chance on losing part of their investment on account of an early death, even though they would gain by outliving the actuarial prediction. Furthermore, they usually want to leave something to their heirs.

These objections can be met partially by a contract which guarantees a life annuity with a certain number of installments or a contract which assures that if the annuitant does not recoup all his investment, the remainder will go to his beneficiaries. These contracts are known as a *guaranteed annuity* and a *refund annuity* respectively.

What is called an *immediate annuity* may be bought with a single premium and after thirty days the insurance company will begin periodic payments to the annuitant. It can be a straight annuity or an annuity with guaranteed installments or guaranteed refund.

Most immediate annuities are bought by companies for retiring employees or by individuals who have a sizable sum of money available to pay as a single premium, having in mind freeing themselves of responsibility for investing it. Also, policyholders often instruct their life insurance companies to use insurance proceeds to set up an immediate annuity for designated beneficiaries upon death of the insured.

In recent years popular concern over the declining purchasing power of the dollar (inflation) has led some insurance companies to offer *variable annuity* contracts under which dollar payments to annuitants are not fixed but fluctuate with prices of common stocks into which the variable annuity premiums are invested.

Under one type of variable annuity, income payments to the annuitant vary with current value of investments which support the annuity. Another type pays a guaranteed fixed income whose initial size is based upon value of the investment fund when the contract matures. Still another type (mostly in group plans) has variable benefits based on a cost of living index.

Since managers of variable annuity funds put premium income into investments supposedly less vulnerable to inflation, such as common stocks, it is expected that funds will increase in dollar value along with inflation and therefore provide more income to annuitants to meet rising livings costs. In other

---

[5] If an annuity owner dies before the annuity matures, the contract's cash value is paid to his heirs or beneficiaries.

words, a variable annuity is intended to be a hedge against inflation, but much depends upon the success of the insurance company's investment policy.

Due to the fact that payments are not guaranteed in fixed dollar amounts, the risk of investment must be borne by the annuitant; whereas in the conventional type of annuity contract, the issuing company does guarantee a fixed payment.

So, the buyer of an annuity must decide whether he wants to buy a variable type and assume an investment risk in hopes of offsetting inflation in whole or part, or buy a conventional type in which the company assumes investment risk and promises to pay a certain regular dollar amount.

It is a little early to judge how well variable annuities fulfill their purpose. At the end of 1971, there were 171,600 individuals covered by variable annuity contracts with invested reserves of $296,392,000, but only 1,421 individuals were receiving benefits. At the same time there were 9,969 group plan variable annuities covering 746,400 persons and having $3,115,048,000 in invested reserves with 24,055 persons receiving benefits.[6]

Retirement Plans and Employee Savings Plans

Company Plans. Many companies and institutions have retirement plans for their personnel, the entire cost of which is borne by the employer. However, some plans permit employees to participate usually by matching the employer's contribution to the plan, thus providing a kind of forced savings program which will result in larger retirement benefits to supplement social security.

Employee savings programs, sometimes called thrift incentive plans, are being set up to an increasing extent by many companies. Annual contributions made by an employer as bonuses or deferred wages are credited to respective employee accounts. These contributions are deductible expenses of the employer, but are not taxable to the employee at the time they are credited to his savings account.

Employees are permitted to add a certain percentage of their monthly wages which is regularly deducted from the payroll. What an employee himself puts into the savings plan is from after-tax income.

Money accumulated in a thrift incentive plan is invested by managers of the fund, usually a trust company or the trust department of a bank, or the money can be deposited in trusteed savings accounts with any thrift institution or used to buy Series E Bonds.

Company savings plans may be set up for a specified number of years or be timed to coincide with an employee's retirement. In either case, the balance of his savings account, including both his and the employer's contributions plus account earnings, then becomes available to the employee.

Most plans allow a participant to borrow from his account from time to time, but as a rule only for emergency purposes and with approval of a committee.

---

[6]*Life Insurance Fact Book 1972,* p. 56.

Exhibit 19–8 Pension Coverage in Private Industry, June 1968 through January 1970

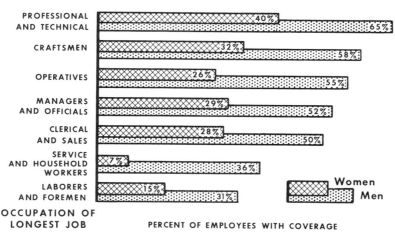

PROFESSIONAL AND TECHNICAL — 40%, 65%
CRAFTSMEN — 32%, 58%
OPERATIVES — 26%, 55%
MANAGERS AND OFFICIALS — 29%, 52%
CLERICAL AND SALES — 28%, 50%
SERVICE AND HOUSEHOLD WORKERS — 7%, 36%
LABORERS AND FOREMEN — 15%, 31%

Women / Men

OCCUPATION OF LONGEST JOB

PERCENT OF EMPLOYEES WITH COVERAGE

Source: *Social Security Administration* and U.S. Department of Agriculture.

We strongly recommend company savings plans because (1) the participant benefits from the company's contribution which is usually a substantial part of the account; (2) the participant commits himself to saving regularly through payroll deduction; and (3) there are worthwhile tax savings.

The Keogh Saving Plan. In 1962, Congress passed the Smathers-Keogh Act, also called the Self-Employed Individuals Tax Retirement Act, which provides a tax incentive to self-employed individuals to save for their retirement. Such self-employed persons as doctors, dentists, lawyers, architects, accountants, farmers, sole proprietors, and others who might be eligible and who receive approval from the Internal Revenue Service are permitted to save 10 percent of earned income, but not more than $2,500, each year and contribute this to an approved retirement fund, deducting the entire sum from taxable income in the year earned. Contributions are based only on earned income from personal services.

To qualify under the Keogh Plan an eligible self-employed individual must include in the retirement plan all of his full-time employees. Contributions he makes for them are tax deductible the same as wages.

Money set aside in a Keogh retirement fund may be used to buy annuities; be placed in a trust account at a bank, a savings and loan association, or some other qualifying thrift institution; be used to buy approved mutual fund shares; or be allocated to buy U.S. Government Retirement Plan Bonds.

Participants may set aside more than the statutory amount, but additional contributions are not tax deductible, although earnings therefrom are tax-free until distributed after retirement.

If a self-employed person contributes $2,500 each year to a Keogh Plan which invests the funds at 5 percent interest compounded daily, he will have credited to his retirement account $127,625 at the end of twenty-five years, consisting of $62,500 he himself contributed and $65,125 in accumulated interest.

When are benefits payable to a qualified self-employed individual and his employees? The answer is:

1. Upon retirement, but not before age 59½ or later than age 70½,
2. Upon permanent disability, or
3. Upon death, the benefits going to designated beneficiaries.

If an employee should terminate his employment for any reason prior to retirement, the balance in his account may be used to buy a nontransferable life annuity which will begin payments upon employee's normal retirement; or the balance may be transferred to another Keogh plan if his next employer has one.

Benefits are subject to income taxes in the years received to the extent that the benefits represent untaxed contributions and accumulations in the funds. If the individual beneficiary's income is lower, as it usually is after retirement, he will be in a lower tax bracket than he was when he contributed to the fund. Furthermore, he has tax-free contributions earning tax-free income for him until retirement. These tax concessions provide the incentive to save intended by the Smathers-Keogh Act.

The law does not discriminate in favor of self-employed persons, but simply allows them the same privileges previously available only to employees of corporations with retirement plans.

Discussion Questions

1. Name and describe three types of personal savings accounts.
2. What provisions are made under the Federal Share Insurance Act?
3. Explain how interest is computed under the FIFO and the LIFO methods.
4. Differentiate between a depositor in a commercial bank and a depositor in a mutual savings bank.
5. Explain the restriction that Regulation Q puts on commercial banks.
6. List four reasons why the majority of savers think thrift institutions offer the best place for savings.
7. List five reasons why series E bonds are attractive to investors.
8. From an investment point of view, list the disadvantages of Series E bonds.
9. Discuss the types of annuities listed below.
    a) pure annuity
    b) joint and survivorship annuity
    c) guaranteed annuity
    d) immediate annuity
10. What is the Keogh Saving Plan?

Money may not buy happiness but it certainly
helps you look for it in a lot more places.
[Anonymous]

20

Buying Securities

A sound investment program for most families consists of four parts: (1) an adequate amount of life insurance determined primarily by the number of dependents; (2) ownership of a home whose cost is not excessive in relation to family income; (3) a cash reserve, preferably in a bank or other type of thrift institution, sufficient to meet most contingencies that might arise; and (4) securities and/or real estate holdings.

Prudence dictates that the first three parts of this program be fulfilled before a family thinks about buying securities or real estate as investments. Home ownership and life insurance are the subjects of Chapters 10 and 16 respectively.

In the preceding chapter, we discussed the investment of savings in thrift institutions, in Series E and H Bonds, in insurance reserves, and in annuities

and retirement plans. For most people, especially small savers, these are recommended uses of savings because they rate high on the test of dollar safety.
With the exception of straight annuities and variable annuities, all may be regarded as fixed dollar commitments which assure the saver that he and/or his
beneficiaries will get back no less than the amount of dollars he put in plus the
rate of earnings agreed to.[1] In all of these, the saver has ready access to his
savings either by withdrawal, by redemption, or by borrowing against loan
value. Therefore, they tend to serve as a reserve to meet contingencies and to
fulfill other purposes.

In this chapter, we shall turn our attention to buying securities. Securities
are written evidences of either ownership or debt, issued by corporations, by
governments and their agencies, and—in some instances—by institutions.

A word of caution is in order for those who would invest their savings in
securities. The selection of securities requires more understanding, care, and
prudence than are required of a saver who, for example, keeps his money in
an insured savings account. In fact, not many individuals have sufficient knowledge of securities and of business conditions or are willing to devote enough
time to collect and study information upon which good investment judgment
is based. It is unfortunately true that some people depend almost entirely upon
luck as they would in a game of pure chance. Many securities of doubtful merit
have been sold because buyers have relied too much upon biased opinion and
too little upon personal investigation.

No one should put his savings in securities of any kind without first trying
to determine the degree of risk involved and then deciding for himself whether
his financial circumstances justify such a commitment.

Investing, Speculating and Gambling

This point leads us at once to differentiate between three commonly used terms:
investing, speculating, and *gambling. Investing* means using money under
conditions that are thought to provide reasonable assurance of safety for the
principal and a rate of return in keeping with the degree of safety. A true
investor is conservative and is motivated by a desire to find a long-term investment which is secure and yields a return he knows is satisfactory for the risk
involved.

Speculating may be defined as the use of money under conditions that are
thought to provide a capital gain through a change in market value. A speculator is motivated primarily by expectation of such a gain, usually in a short
time, and only secondarily by current yield on his commitment. Safety is not a
major consideration to a speculator. He is willing to assume a greater risk than

---

[1] Of course, that part of insurance premiums which goes for protection is not available to
the policyholder.

an investor. He is further encouraged by existing tax laws which give favorable treatment to a capital gain, if realized beyond six months.

Gambling per se is a nonproductive use of money under conditions whose outcome is dependent upon pure chance—that is, an outcome over which the gambler presumably has no control or influence.

Essentially, gambling differs from investing and speculating in the nature of risks involved. Gambling deals with artificially created risks not inherent in our industrial life. If four men sit down at a table to bet with cards, for example, they have created gambling risks that otherwise would not have existed and are not necessary to the economy. What one person wins another must lose.

Investing and speculating, on the other hand, involve risks of business which must be assumed by someone if we are to have goods and services to satisfy our wants. If no one had been willing to provide capital for an automobile factory, there would be few automobiles. Yet, many early automobile manufacturing companies failed, and millions of dollars were lost.

Occasionally we hear someone use the expression "stock market gambling," implying that buying stocks is like betting on horse races or on the roll of dice. Admittedly some people do buy securities, more especially stocks, so carelessly that their actions resemble gambling. A man is reported to have been watching the stock market tape in a brokerage office one day. He saw a three-letter stock symbol go through which happened to be the initials of an old sweetheart. Without any investigation whatsoever, he placed an order for 100 shares of the stock. This was indeed gambling.

But we must not conclude that the securities market is a casino. Ownership of business corporations in this country (some with billions of dollars in assets) is represented by millions of shares of stock owned by millions of widely scattered stockholders. Existence of a market or markets in which these shares can be bought and sold makes it easier for corporations to raise vast amounts of capital than would be the case if no such markets existed, simply because most people would hesitate to buy stocks if they knew they would have difficulty selling them.

Every commitment is a *risk,* and risk is defined as uncertainty with a chance of loss. The degree of risk that one thinks exists is a matter of judgment whose accuracy depends upon the care with which he investigates related facts and circumstances. A true investor, because of his objective, seeks to confine purchases to low-risk securities; while a speculator, whose objective is different, is willing to assume a large degree of risk, hoping to be rewarded by a high rate of return if he is successful.

Some individuals speculate deliberately and intelligently. They obtain and analyze as much pertinent information as they can about a company and its securities, arrive at a judgment about the degree of risk to be assumed, and then—in the light of their own circumstances—decide whether to buy. Still other individuals speculate so impulsively and unintelligently that they assume risks not unlike a gambler does.

A financial truism to be remembered is that if a person seeks a high rate of return, he must be willing to assume a high degree of risk. If he seeks safety of the principal, he must be satisfied with a more modest return. In other words, there is a direct relationship between risk and return. Beware of anyone who would sell "a safe investment which will pay you a big return." If the purchase is truly safe, the return will not be big.

Risk is a function of the quality of a security and the price at which it is selling. A good quality stock, for example, might be selling at a price so high that the risk of purchasing it at the time would actually be a speculative one. In other words, the price of a good quality stock can be so inflated at a given time as to increase risk of loss to a point where the security would not be an investment, despite its high quality.

A major factor affecting quality of a security is the strength and prospects of the issuing corporation. Quality is also affected by the kind of security being considered; and, for this reason, it is essential that we first know the inherent differences in various types of securities.

Corporate Securities

Corporate securities may be divided into three classes: (1) those that represent ownership, often referred to as "equities"; (2) those that represent debt solely; and (3) those that are issued basically as debt instruments but carry an equity option.

Stocks

Ownership securities are called stocks. They are issued in units or shares each representing a fractional equity in the issuing corporation. An owner's equity is evidenced (1) by a stock certificate or certificates in his name for the number of shares he owns and (2) by his name and shareholdings being recorded in a stockholder's ledger.[2]

Anyone who buys corporate securities should take care to know what rights and liabilities he has as owner. Stockholders have two kinds of rights: (1) *group rights,* which they exercise when they come together at regular and special stockholders' meetings; and (2) *individual rights,* which each stockholder has as an individual apart from other stockholders.

The following are group rights:

1. To elect directors of the company
2. To adopt and change company by-laws
3. To amend the company's charter, with the approval of the state where incorporated

---

[2]The record is kept in terms of shares, not in money.

4. To sell all the assets of the company
5. To dissolve the company
6. To exercise any other rights conferred by the charter

The following are individual stockholder rights:

1. To receive notices of stockholders' meetings and to vote at the meetings either in person or by proxy [A proxy is anyone who is authorized to vote in a stockholder's place. The term "proxy" also is used to mean the authorization itself. See Exhibit 20–1.]
2. To receive dividends if and when dividends are declared by the directors
3. To share in the assets of the corporation if it should be dissolved
4. To inspect certain records of the corporation
5. To participate in further issues of stock, called preemptive right[3]
6. To receive statements of the corporation's financial condition
7. To transfer stock to someone else

Exhibit 20–1   A Sample Proxy

Please Do Not Fold or Staple

THE DETROIT EDISON COMPANY

This proxy is solicited on behalf of the Management.

PROXY   The undersigned Common Shareholder of The Detroit Edison Company hereby appoints H. Glenn Bixby, E. Mandell de-Windt, and George M. Holley, Jr., and any of them, as proxies to vote the shares of the undersigned at the Annual Meeting of Shareholders to be held at the Henry and Edsel Ford Auditorium at 20 East Jefferson Avenue, Detroit, Michigan 48226, on Monday, April 16, 1973, at 10:00 a.m., Detroit Time, and at all adjournments thereof, upon the matters noted below, and upon such other matters as may come before the meeting, all as more fully set forth in the Proxy Statement received by the undersigned. Said proxies are instructed to vote:

1. The election of directors.   FOR ☐   WITHHELD ☐

2. The proposal to amend the Michigan Articles of Incorporation of the Company to remove a restriction on the use of sinking fund or redemption provisions in issuing series of Cumulative Preferred Stock.   FOR ☐   AGAINST ☐

3. The proposal to ratify the appointment of independent accountants.   FOR ☐   AGAINST ☐

(Please sign on reverse side)

---

[3]The right of each stockholder to purchase his proportion of any new stock sold by the corporation in order to maintain his relative interest in the business.

Although all stock represents ownership, corporation laws permit different classes of stock which have different rights of ownership. Many corporations issue more than one class. Stock which confers special privileges or preferences to owners is usually called *preferred stock,* while those issues that confer no such preferences are known as *common stock*.[4]

Corporations may issue preferred stock for a number of reasons, but for our purposes in personal finance preferred stock is generally issued to attract buyers who want less speculative equities than common stock. In certain respects, but not all, the position of preferred stockholders is stronger than that of common stockholders in the same corporation.[5] Perhaps the most important feature of preferred stock is that its owners have the right to receive a certain amount of dividends before dividends are distributed to holders of common stock. A preferred stock that carries a right to receive dividends beyond the fixed or stated rate is called a *participating preferred stock.*

Preferred stock may be either *cumulative* or *noncumulative.* When the specified rate of dividends is not paid in any year upon a cumulative preferred stock, the amount unpaid will accumulate as arrearage that must be paid at some time before the common stock can receive any dividends. Incidentally, arrearage on cumulative preferred stock is not a liability of the company and does not bear interest. Missed dividends on noncumulative preferred stock do not have to be made up.

Preferred stock almost always is preferred as to assets in the event of the company's liquidation, at which time preferred stockholders receive ahead of common stockholders a certain amount per share of what assets remain after all creditors are paid.

Some preferred stock carries a *conversion right* which is attractive to investors and speculators alike. This kind of stock is ordinarily *convertible* at the option of its owners into a stated number of shares of common stock.

Finally, it is important to know whether a preferred stock is *redeemable* or *callable.* If so, the issuing corporation has an option to redeem the stock in whole or in part by paying a stated or call price per share in cash for it. If there is arrearage on the stock, the company must pay that in addition to the redemption price. Almost always the call price of a preferred stock includes a premium above the issuing price.

Buyers of stocks, whether common or preferred, should not be confused or misled by the terms *par value* and *no par value.* Par value means that the stock was issued with a face or nominal value in dollars which may be any amount, but usually is $100, $50, $25, $10, $5, or $1. No par value means that the stock was issued without a face or nominal value being assigned to it.

Par value may cause an uninformed buyer to think that the nominal value of a stock is its real value; when, in fact, real value at any given time may be much less or much more than par value. An experienced investor pays little or

---

[4]Some companies have issued more than one class of common stock.
[5]Preferred stockholders ordinarily do not have voting rights unless the company fails to pay preferred dividends.

no attention to whether a stock is par or no par. True, from the issuing corporation's point of view there are some differences relating to taxes, etc.; but, as long as the stock is fully paid and nonassessable, the seasoned investor himself knows that the price he pays in the market reflects all conditions relating to the stock, and those arising from whether it is par or no par stock are of no consequence.

Another value term often applied to corporate stock is *book value per share* which is an accounting concept derived by taking a company's net worth or ownership equity and dividing by the number of common shares outstanding. Where a company has an issue of preferred stock, the book value per share of common is determined after deducting from net worth the liquidation value of the preferred.

As in the case of par value, it is generally not advisable to judge a stock's worth by book value despite the fact that many individuals persist in doing so. A company's earning power is a far more significant indication of a stock's value.

The characteristics of any particular stock are usually stated on the stock certificate itself.

Example: Union Oil of California has outstanding no par $2.50 cumulative convertible preferred stock. If you owned a 100-share certificate of this stock, you would see printed on the certificate's face the following wording:

> This certifies that (your name) is the record holder of 100 fully paid and nonassessable shares without par value of the $2.50 cumulative convertible shares of Union Oil of California transferable on the books of the corporation in person or by duly authorized attorney upon surrender of this certificate properly endorsed. This certificate is not valid unless countersigned by a transfer agent and registered by a registrar.

On the back of the certificate you would find other features of the stock stated in the following paragraph:

> Preferred shares are redeemable at the option of the corporation, at any time and from time to time, on or after July 1, 1970, at $67 per share if redeemed on or after July 1, 1970 and prior to July 1, 1971; at $66 per share if redeemed on or after July 1, 1971, and prior to July 1, 1972; and $65 per share if redeemed on or after July 1, 1972, together, in each case, with all accrued and unpaid dividends thereon to date of redemption. Preferred shares are convertible at the option of the record holder thereof into full common shares of the corporation at the rate of $1\frac{3}{10}$ (1.3) common shares for one preferred share subject to adjustment of the conversion rate in certain specified events.

Stockholder Liability. Since a corporation legally exists as an enterprise distinct and separate from persons who own it or control it, the liability of its stockholders is limited. If a person owns fully paid stock, he has no liability.

Limited liability of stockholders accounts, in part, for the popularity of the corporation as a form of business organization. Because of this feature, a corporation is in better position to raise large amounts of capital than a sole proprietorship, a partnership, or any other business form.

Stockholders, especially those of large companies, are far removed from any direct participation in management or control of the corporation. They elect directors who in turn employ operating officers, and in that way do exercise some indirect control.

In reality, the principal function of stockholders is to furnish risk capital of the business. As owners, they are in a residual position, standing to gain when the corporation prospers and to lose when the corporation does poorly. They stand at the end of the line.

When earnings are sufficient, dividends may be paid to stockholders, but the decision to pay dividends rests solely with the directors. Dividends are customarily paid quarterly.

Sometimes a company will pay a dividend in stock, in which case stockholders will receive additional shares. For example, if a 5 percent stock dividend is declared, an owner of 100 shares will receive five additional shares. Frequently, companies will declare both a cash and a stock dividend simultaneously.

In 1920, the U.S. Supreme Court ruled that stock dividends are not income subject to taxation, but merely the division of ownership into more shares.[6] The rule still stands.

Stock Rights. When a corporation increases its capital by issuing additional shares of common stock, it is obliged by law to offer existing stockholders an opportunity to buy, if they choose, enough new shares to maintain their relative ownership positions in the company. If a stockholder, for example, owns 5 percent of the company's common stock, he is entitled to buy 5 percent of the new issue. This stockholder privilege is known as a *preemptive right*.

Suppose X Company with 5 million listed shares of common stock outstanding decides to issue 1 million additional shares at a price of $82 a share when the market price of outstanding shares is $100. Each stockholder has a *preemptive right* to buy, within a stated time, one new share for each five outstanding shares he has. He will receive from the company a negotiable certificate indicating the number of rights he owns. If he does not care to exercise his rights, he may sell and transfer them to someone else. In our example, the rights would be worth approximately $3 each, calculated by subtracting from the market value per old share ($100) the subscription price of the new ($82) and dividing by the number of shares needed to buy one new share plus one (5 + 1).

In the case of fractional rights, the company usually will offer to buy or sell fractions. For example, a stockholder might own 43 shares which would entitle

---

[6]Eisner v. Macomber, 252 U.S. 189 (1920).

him to subscribe to 8.6 new shares, but since fractional shares of stock are not issued, he must either dispose of the .6 right or acquire .4 right.

Stock Split

Occasionally one hears that a corporation has declared a stock split. This simply means that the number of shares of common stock is being increased by giving stockholders a certain number of shares for each share they already own. For example, a two-for-one stock split results when one new share is issued for every share outstanding, so that each shareholder then has twice the number of shares he held before.

A 100 percent stock dividend also would result in doubling the number of shares; but, in case of a stock dividend, the surplus account is reduced in dollar value and the capital account is increased. In contrast, stock splits do not change these two accounts.

A corporation may split its stock for the purpose of lowering the price per share and attracting more stockholders and broadening the market for its stock.

Stock splits often stimulate public interest sufficiently to cause a greater total market value of the company's stock. As a consequence, investors generally like stock splits. For example, X Company's stock is selling at $150 per share, and the board of directors vote a three-for-one split. It might be expected that the price would go down to $50 a share when there are three times as many shares, but very likely the market price after the split will be higher than $50 since the shares are now in a more popular price range.

Straight Debt Securities

We turn now to that class of corporate securities which represent debt solely. These take two forms, notes and bonds. Both are promises to repay borrowed funds. Corporate notes need not concern us here because they are ordinarily issued to borrow money from institutional lenders such as banks, insurance companies, pension funds, etc. They are customarily used for short-term or intermediate term borrowing.[7]

Corporate bonds are very formal evidences of debt, issued under the respective corporation's seal, and generally for ten years or longer with a fixed interest rate, payable at specified dates, almost always semiannually. Corporate bond issues are ordinarily for very large sums, and each bond of an issue is one of many identical bonds in $1,000 denomination, as a rule.

Corporate bonds may be divided into two broad categories: (1) *secured bonds* and (2) *unsecured bonds*. Bonds called *mortgage bonds* are secured by a mortgage on fixed assets of the corporation. Those secured by a pledge of other securities or valuable papers are known as *collateral trust bonds;* while those secured by some kind of equipment, such as railroad locomotives, are

---

[7]Short-term notes sold in the open market by large companies are known as commercial paper.

known as *equipment trust bonds*. Those secured or backed by another corporation are referred to as *guaranteed bonds;* and, if responsibility for payment of an issue of bonds has been taken over by some other company, the bonds are identified as *assumed bonds*.

Unsecured bonds are called *debentures*. They are backed solely by the issuing company's promise to pay. In the past, only corporations of substantial economic strength and high credit rating could issue debentures successfully. Now many corporations, regardless of size or strength, use debentures. (Incidentally, all government bonds are debentures.)

Bonds, like preferred stock, may be subject to call by the issuer under certain specified terms. Usually the company's *call option* is not exercisable until after five years, sometimes ten. The call price almost always includes a premium above the bond's face value. Frequently, the first call-year's premium is equal to one year's interest, supposedly to compensate the owner for the inconvenience and trouble of reinvesting his money.[8]

The call option is valuable to the issuing corporation as a means of refinancing a debt that might have been contracted in a period of high interest rates.

For example, Corporation Y, a public utility, borrowed $10 million on December 1, 1969, when the supply of money was very tight in the money market. Despite its strong credit rating the company had to pay a 9¾ percent interest rate on its thirty-year bond issue. A five-year call option was specified in the bond indenture, enabling the company at its option to call the bonds at 109¾ percent of face value plus accrued interest any time after December 1, 1974, and until December 1, 1975, the call price declining annually thereafter down to par. On December 1, 1974, money market conditions were such that the company could issue new twenty-five year bonds at a 7 percent rate. Obviously the company's finance officers had good reason then to refinance the issue of December 1, 1969, namely to save $275,000 interest annually or $6,875,000 in twenty-five years, less the $975,000 premium paid on the call date.

Some corporate bonds have a *sinking fund* provision which means that the company is required to set aside funds regularly from earnings to retire all or part of the respective bonds. A fiscal agent or trustee is appointed to receive sinking funds which he uses to buy as many bonds as he can in the market or to pay for called bonds when bonds are not available in the market.

An alternative to sinking fund bonds for purposes of periodic retirement are *serial bonds* which are serially numbered units of a total issue, a part maturing each designated year until the entire issue has been paid off in the final year.

Convertible Bonds

A third class of corporate securities is *convertible bonds*. Basically these are debt instruments, but they can be exchanged or converted at some specific ratio into common stock if the owner wishes.

---

[8]The premium on most callable corporate bonds decreases each year of the call period.

In recent years, many debenture issues have carried conversion rights which add a speculative element and increase salability. By adding a conversion option, a corporation generally is able to sell its bonds at a lower rate of interest.

Companies sometimes will sell bonds with *stock purchase warrants* attached. Purchase warrants entitle their owner to buy the issuing company's common stock at a certain price any time within a specified period. In most instances, purchase warrants may be detached after a stated date and sold if the holder does not care to purchase the stock.

As in the case of convertible bonds, the purpose of attaching stock purchase warrants is to make the bonds more attractive to investors and speculators.

Bonds whose interest does not have to be paid unless the issuing company earns enough income to do so are known as *income bonds*. Uncertainty of yield accounts for the fact that income bonds are not popular and, therefore, are seldom issued.

All bonds are issued in either *registered* form or *coupon* form. In the case of registered bonds, names of bondholders are recorded or registered on the books of the issuing corporation; and when interest payments are due, the company mails interest checks to the bondholders.

On the other hand, coupon bonds are not registered and, hence, the issuing company does not have a record of ownership. Coupon bonds get their name from the dated interest coupons attached. When interest is due, bondholders simply clip the appropriate coupons and present them to a bank for collection.

Ownership of registered bonds can be transferred only by endorsement and issuance of new bonds to the new owners, but coupon bonds are bearer instruments, and title can be passed easily by delivering the bonds to anyone.

Almost all issues of corporate bonds now are registered. If lost, destroyed, or stolen, registered bonds are relatively easy to replace. Furthermore, the U.S. Internal Revenue Service urges corporations to use registered bonds so that taxpayers who receive taxable interest can be identified.

In relation to bonds, we distinguish between *nominal yield, current yield,* and *yield to maturity*.

Nominal yield is the amount of interest a bond pays as a percentage of the bond's par value. It is the rate which is stated in the bond itself.

Current yield is the amount of interest a bond pays related to the bond's cost. Suppose an investor buys a bond for $920 that pays 6 percent, or $60 interest annually. The current yield is $60 divided by $920, or 6.52 percent. In this case, current yield is greater than nominal yield because the bond is selling below par (at a discount). When a bond is selling above par (at a premium), its current yield will be less than its nominal yield.

Yield to maturity is a combination of current yield and the annual average gain of principal to maturity when the bond is bought at a discount or the average amortization to maturity of principal when the bond is bought at a premium.

Example: A 5 percent bond due May 1, 1979 was sold on May 1, 1973 at $880. Its current yield was 5.68 percent, but its yield to maturity was 7.41 percent because when the bond matures it will be worth par, thus gaining $120 in six years. (Note: A complicated formula is used to figure yields to maturity. However, most bondmen use a bond yield book to find the answer or use an electronic calculator programmed for bond calculations).

Corporate Bondholders vs. Stockholders

By now it should be evident that owners of corporate bonds are in a substantially different position from that of stockholders. Bondholders are creditors, having loaned the corporation a stated amount of money in exchange for the corporation's promise to repay principal plus a fixed rate of interest.

Failure to keep this promise constitutes a default which legally can lead to foreclosure steps by trustees acting for the bondholders. As a result, the company can be declared insolvent and its property be taken over by a receiver or trustee in bankruptcy for the benefit of all creditors, including bond owners.

If the respective bonds are secured by a mortgage on fixed assets, then the pledged assets may be taken and sold and proceeds used to pay the specific bonded debt plus accrued interest. On the other hand, if the bonds are unsecured (debentures), then the bondholders are considered general creditors and must share pro rata in proceeds of the assets with other general creditors. Some debentures, however, are subordinated to certain designated creditors, usually banks.[9]

When corporations are dissolved either voluntarily or involuntarily, bondholders, because of their creditor position, are paid before stockholders. In other words, in case of default bondholders are entitled to return of principal or face value of their bonds before stockholders receive anything. This is a very important difference between stocks and bonds.

As we learned earlier, common stockholders have an indirect voice in company management through voting rights; but holders of the company's bonds have no voting rights whatsoever and, hence, no role in managing the affairs of the business.

Finally, if a company fails to pay dividends on its stock, there is little or nothing stockholders can do; but if it fails to pay interest on bonded debt, bondholders can take the legal action described above. Remember that a corporation makes no promise or guarantee that it will pay a dividend, but it does promise to pay principal and interest on its bonds and is legally bound by that promise.

Securities Issued
by Governments

All securities issued by governments in the United States are debt instruments. Those issued by the U.S. Treasury are called "Governments" in financial circles, while securities issued by agencies of the Federal Government are called

---

[9]We call these "subordinated debentures."

"Agencies." State and local government securities are referred to as "Municipals."

Federal Government Securities

The U.S. Treasury uses four types of securities when borrowing from the public:

1. *Savings Bonds,* Series E and H, which are described in Chapter 19.
2. *Treasury Bills,* which are bearer obligations with maturities up to one year, sold at a discount and traded on a yield basis. Minimum denomination $10,000.
3. *Treasury Notes,* which are obligations with a stated rate of interest, issued for a term of not less than one year and no more than seven years in either bearer or registered form. Interest is paid semiannually. Minimum denomination $1,000.
4. *Treasury Bonds* which are long-term obligations, customarily for not less than five years and not more than forty years, bearing a stated interest rate payable semiannually. Minimum denomination is $1,000. Some Treasury bonds have the unique feature of being acceptable at par in payment of federal estate taxes when owned by a decedent at the time of death.

Federal government agencies and sponsored corporations are authorized to borrow funds from the public by issuing securities—mostly bonds, but sometimes certificates and notes. These "agencies," as they are called, are not direct obligations of the U.S. Treasury but are authorized by Congress and involve federal sponsorship. Some are actually guaranteed by the U.S. Government.

Exhibit 20–2 shows issuers of this category of securities and the distribution of ownership at the end of 1971.

State and Local Government Securities

Municipal bonds are almost always long-term obligations used to finance various state and local government projects. They are customarily bearer bonds with interest coupons attached.

Municipals may be divided into two broad categories: (1) *general obligation bonds,* sometimes referred to as *GOs,* and (2) *revenue bonds.* General obligation municipals are backed by the full faith and credit of the issuing government. This means that all the property of a community or district can be taxed to pay interest and principal of the debt.

Revenue bonds, as a class, include all municipal obligations whose interest and principal are not payable or guaranteed by the general taxing power of the issuing authority. Mostly these bonds represent debt incurred for the purpose of financing revenue-producing projects such as water systems, electric utilities, toll roads, airports, etc. Interest and principal are paid solely out of income or

Exhibit 20–2 Ownership of Securities Issued by Government Agencies and Sponsored Corporations, December 31, 1971 (in millions of dollars)

Issuer	Total amount outstanding	Com-mercial banks	Mutual savings banks	Insurance companies	Savings and loan associa-tions	Corpora-tions	State and local govern-ments	U.S. Gov-ernment investment accounts and Federal Reserve Banks	All other investors
Export-Import Bank	1,420	408	46	41	47	6	116	13	742
Federal Housing Administration	470	38	58	95	18	—	105	64	92
Government National Mortgage Association	5,915	757	353	284	137	22	697	1,977	1,687
Tennessee Valley Authority	1,595	39	63	24	54	6	163	190	1,056
Banks for Cooperatives	1,814	450	48	4	52	63	136	36	1,025
Farmers Home Administration	1,700	313	140	50	169	2	217	—	811
Federal Home Loan Banks	7,755	1,648	411	90	742	51	257	81	4,475
Federal Intermediate Credit Banks	5,531	1,306	178	32	254	90	283	123	3,265
Federal Land Banks	7,220	1,629	344	139	243	102	413	45	4,305
Federal National Mortgage Association	17,701	4,326	975	197	1,273	366	1,303	242	9,018
District of Columbia Armory Board	20	1	3	1	6	—	4	—	5

Source: Treasury Bulletin.

revenue from the respective projects. Sometimes revenue bonds will be secured by a particular tax, such as a tax on cigarettes.

A unique kind of municipals are *Public Housing Authority Bonds,* or *"PHA's."* These are issued by local housing agencies organized under state laws to develop and manage low-rent housing projects. The Federal Government is involved through the Public Housing Act of 1949, which provides that "the full faith and credit of the United States is pledged to the payment of all amounts agreed to be paid by the Authorities."

Almost all issues of municipals are in serial form, some bonds maturing each year until the entire issue is fully retired. This is a very practical arrangement for the issuing government, since the bonds are supported by taxes levied and collected annually or by steady revenues from some public service.

An important feature of municipal bonds is that interest received from them is fully exempt from federal incomes taxes.[10] The exemption results in a generally lower yield on municipal bonds because of two circumstances: (1) the progressive rate structure of the federal income tax and (2) differences in personal income. Example: Individual A has income sufficient to put him in the 50 percent income tax bracket, let us say. Individual B with much less income than A is in the 25 percent bracket. A municipal bond obviously is more attractive to A than to B as an investment, because every one dollar in interest from it is equivalent to $2.00 of taxable income to A, but to only $1.33 of taxable income to B. Or, to put it another way, a 4 percent yield to A from a municipal bond is equal to 8 percent to him from an investment (like a corporate bond, a stock, etc.) whose income is taxable, but to only 5.3 percent to B. If B can get more than 5.3 percent from some other equally safe source, he is better off buying it, even though he pays an income tax on it, rather than buying a municipal yielding 4 percent. On the other hand, A must find a taxable source yielding more than 8 percent to be better off than if he bought a 4 percent municipal.

Obviously the interest exemption feature of municipals means so much more to persons with high income than to persons with low income that the latter seldom find it advisable to invest in municipals.

The Mechanics of Buying and Selling Securities

There are two kinds of markets in which securities are bought and sold. One is called the *primary market* and the other the *secondary market*. The primary market is where entire new issues are bought from corporations by one or more investment banking firms and subsequently distributed at retail to the public.

---

[10]The celebrated Supreme Court decision in McCullough v. Maryland (1819) established the principle of reciprocal immunity of federal and state instrumentalities. Under this principle, the federal government cannot tax an instrumentality of a state and a state cannot tax an instrumentality of the federal government.

In the case of a large issue of securities, several investment banking companies usually form a purchasing group (often referred to as "the underwriting group") which functions under the direction of a manager. Each member of the underwriting group agrees to buy a stipulated amount of the new issue (shares of stock or number of bonds) at a price agreed to between the group and the issuing corporation.

The underwriters may, and often do, form a selling group to sell the securities to the public, hopefully at a price which will enable the participants to make a profit out of the *spread,* or difference between cost of the securities and the price paid for them. If all of the securities cannot be sold to the public, then members of the purchasing group are obliged to keep what are unsold or reduce the price enough to find buyers. Regardless of how the purchasing group fares, the issuing corporation is paid the total amount agreed to.

The secondary market is where stocks and bonds are bought and sold after they have left the primary market. In other words, securities traded in this market day by day are already owned by other investors and speculators.

It is in the secondary market that we are most interested as individuals, so let's look into it somewhat in detail.

It has been estimated that over 30 million persons in the United States directly own securities of some kind. Millions more can be said to own securities indirectly as policyholders of life insurance companies or as members of retirement plans whose funds are invested in stocks and bonds.

It is easy for anyone to buy securities if he has the means. Stocks and bonds are available through *brokers* and *dealers*. Brokers (usually part of a firm) execute customers' orders to buy or sell securities on organized exchanges, charging a commission for the service. In their role as brokers strictly, they do not own securities, but merely serve as members of exchanges through which buy and sell orders are brought together.

Dealers, on the other hand, own the securities they sell and derive their profits from the difference between cost and selling price. Most dealers operate in what are called "over-the-counter" (OTC) markets as distinguished from organized exchange markets, both of which are segments of the secondary market.

Prices are determined by an auction process when the securities are handled through brokerage firms with membership on organized exchanges; but, in over-the-counter markets, prices are determined by negotiation and trading among dealers who buy and sell for their own accounts.

By far the greatest volume of stock trading is handled through organized exchanges. These form continuous markets in which buying and selling of listed stocks takes place.

The two largest exchanges in the United States are the New York Stock Exchange (NYSE) and the American Stock Exchange (ASE), both centered in New York City; but brokerage firm members have offices scattered throughout the country.

The following are other exchanges:

Boston (Bo)	Midwest (MW)
Cincinnati (Ci)	National (NS)
Detroit (De)	Pacific Coast (PS)
Honolulu (Ho)	Richmond (Ri)
Intermountain (IS)	Spokane (Sp)

Only members may deal on an organized exchange. At the end of 1971, the New York Stock Exchange was composed of 1,366 members (seats). Members may act as brokers or dealers but never as both in the same transaction. The Exchange has strict control over its members through stiff membership qualifications and through rather rigid rules and regulations governing conduct.

Stocks of 1,426 companies represented by 1,927 different issues were listed on the New York Stock Exchange at the end of 1971. Total shares listed amounted to 17.5 billion. At the same time, 1,988 issues of bonds were listed having face value of over $145 billion.[11]

"To be listed on the New York Stock Exchange a company is expected to meet certain qualifications and be willing to keep the investing public informed on the progress of its affairs. The company must be a going concern, or be the successor to a going concern. In determining eligibility for listing, particular attention is given to such qualifications as (1) the degree of national interest in the company; (2) its relative position and stability in the industry; and (3) whether it is engaged in an expanding industry, with prospects of at least maintaining its relative position."[12]

In its listing agreement, the NYSE requires a company to release to the public all such information which "might reasonably be expected to materially affect the market for securities." This means that the company must disclose earnings statements, balance sheets, dividend notices, etc.

The following are minimum objective listing requirements which a company must meet:[13]

1. Have net tangible assets of $16 million.
2. Have pre-tax income of $2,500,000 in the latest year.
3. Have pre-tax income of $2 million in the preceding two years.
4. The aggregate market value of its publicly held shares must be at least $16 million.
5. It must have at least 1 million shares of stock publicly held.
6. It must have at least 2,000 shareholders of round lots (100 shares or more).

In early 1973, American Telephone & Telegraph Company had 3,010,000 shareholders and listed 553.7 million common shares with a market value of

---

[11]*New York Stock Exchange 1972 Fact Book* (New York: New York Stock Exchange, 1972), p. 79.

[12]*New York Stock Exchange Fact Book*, page 28.

[13]*New York Stock Exchange Fact Book*, page 29.

$27,690,000,000. General Motors ranked second in number of stockholders with 1,291,000, and listed 287.6 million shares whose market value was $20,420,000,000. Exhibit 20–3 shows fifty companies with the largest number of stockholders.

Although the largest proportion of stock trading is on organized exchanges, the volume of bond trading there is relatively small. Most bonds including all federal, state and local government issues, and a majority of public utility, railroad, and industrial bonds, are traded on over-the-counter markets.

Filling an Order for Stock

For our purposes, it is not essential to describe all technical details involved in executing a customer's order for a security, but we shall follow the major steps.

Suppose someone—say, John Doe—who has never bought stock before, wants to buy American Telephone & Telegraph Company common stock. He first talks with a broker who, after obtaining certain personal information, will open an account for him. The prospective customer asks about cost of the stock. The broker then obtains a current "quote" from a small terminal machine linked by wire to an electronics central in New York and does so by punching AT & T stock's symbol "T" on the terminal's keyboard. Immediately the quotation along with other information will be shown on a small screen in a form similar to the following:

T	↑				
LT	49⅞	B	49⅞	A	50⅛
O	49¾	H	49⅞	L	49¾
C	49⅞	N	10:00	V	14,700
D	2.80	Y	5.6%	T	:03
E	4.34	PE	11		

Here is what the above means:[14]

> T = Symbol for American Telephone and Telegraph Co.
>
> ↑ = Arrow pointing up means that last price change from previous sale was up.
>
> ↓ = Arrow pointing down means that last price change from previous sale was down.
>
> LT = Last trade or sale price, $49.875 per share
>
> B = Bid price at the time, $49.875
>
> A = Asked price, $50.125
>
> O = Opening price (first sale of the day), $49.75
>
> H = High price so far for the day, $49.875
>
> L = Low price so far for the day, $49.75

---

[14]Ultronic Videomaster Service.

C = Closing price of previous day, $49.875

N = Time of day when last news pertaining to this issue came across news wire, 10:00 a.m.

V = Volume of shares traded as of last transaction, 14,700

D = Dividend; latest indicated annual rate, $2.80

Y = Yield based on dividend and last price, 5.6%

T = Time since last sale, 3 minutes

E = Earnings, latest four quarters earnings per share, $4.34

PE = Price-earnings ratio, 11 (PE ratio means market price divided by earnings.)

Exhibit 20–3   50 NYSE Companies with the Largest Number of Common Stockholders of Record, Early 1972*

Company	Stock-holders	Company	Stock-holders
American Tel. & Tel.	3,010,000	Niagara Mohawk Power	167,000
General Motors	1,291,000	Phillips Petroleum	166,000
Standard Oil (New Jersey)	783,000	Greyhound Corp.	160,000
Int'l Business Machines	581,000	Transamerica Corp.	160,000
General Electric	514,000	Philadelphia Electric	157,000
General Tel. & Electronics	447,000	Public Service Elec. & Gas	157,000
U.S. Steel	342,000	Westinghouse Electric	156,000
Ford Motor	340,000	Detroit Edison	156,000
RCA Corp.	308,000	International Tel. & Tel.	154,000
Texaco Inc.	300,000	Pan Amer. World Airways	147,000
Standard Oil of California	280,000	Atlantic Richfield	145,000
Consolidated Edison	272,000	Xerox Corp.	144,000
Sears, Roebuck	254,000	Northeast Utilities	142,000
Gulf Oil	249,000	International Harvester	140,000
Tenneco Corp.	242,000	Penn Central	139,000
E. I. duPont de Nemours	229,000	American Brands	132,000
Eastman Kodak	223,000	American Motors	129,000
Mobil Oil	223,000	Sperry Rand	129,000
Bethlehem Steel	218,000	General Public Utilities	129,000
Union Carbide	207,000	Cities Service	128,000
Chrysler Corp.	202,000	Litton Industries	127,000
Columbia Gas System	175,000	El Paso Natural Gas	126,000
Standard Oil (Indiana)	173,000	Anaconda Company	123,000
Commonwealth Edison	170,000	American Can	122,000
Pacific Gas & Electric	169,000	R. J. Reynolds Industries	121,000

*A stockholder of record is the person whose name is recorded in the corporation's stock ledger.

Source: *New York Stock Exchange 1972 Fact Book,* p. 31.

The broker states that AT & T stock is "49⅞ bid, 50⅛ ask" and explains that the customer may place a *limit order* to buy at a set price, say at $50 per share or less, which is between the bid and ask price and hope that the order will be filled, or he may buy "at the market," known as a *market order,* in which case the order will be filled at once at some price, almost always at or very close to the ask price.

Since Doe has never bought stock before, the broker explains that stock prices are quoted in dollars and usually in fractions of eights minimum. For example, 50⅛ means $50.125 and 50¾ means $50.75.

The broker is also careful to point out that stocks are sold in *round lots* (usually 100 shares or multiples thereof) or in *odd lots* (less than 100 shares) and that prices of *odd lot transactions* are modified by what is called an *odd lot differential* which is added to round lot prices on purchases and subtracted on sales. For example, if you buy an odd lot of stock selling at $55 (or more) per share, the odd lot differential is ¼ or $.25 a share, making the odd lot price 55¼. In the case of a sale, the odd lot price becomes 54¾. The odd lot differential is only ⅛ when the round lot price of a stock is less than $55 a share. Odd lot differentials are part of the pricing process. They are not commissions.

Mr. Doe then asks what the commission will be if he buys 100 shares of A T & T common stock. From a seventy-nine-page booklet entitled "Commission Rates of the New York Stock Exchange, Inc. and the American Stock Exchange," the broker turns to a table of commissions on 100 shares and shows the customer that commissions vary with stock prices, but that on all selling prices of $50 or more the commission is $65 on a 100 share transaction.

Let's say the customer now places a market order for 100 shares of American Telephone & Telegraph Company common stock. The broker will fill out an order which will be sent at once by wire to New York and to the NYSE's trading floor for execution.

The order will be filled and quickly confirmed to the originating broker who probably will advise the buyer by telephone. But whether this is done or not, a written confirmation and statement will be mailed to the customer showing the following information:

Name of security—American Tel. and Tel. Common
Shares bought—100
Price—50⅛
Trade date—3–5–73
Settlement date—3–12–73
Account number—14 769 126 1
Gross amount—$5,012.50
Commission—$65.00
Amount due—$5,077.50
Name and address of customer— John Doe
         9209 Any Street
         Dallas, Texas 75230

The buyer has five business days in which to pay the amount due ($5,077.50). In about four weeks, perhaps sooner, he will receive a stock certificate showing that he is owner of 100 shares of A T & T common.

Suppose John Doe elects to place a limit order, good until cancelled (GTC), at $48 or less, about two points below the market, in hopes that he will be fortunate enough to buy at that figure. The broker will place the order as before; but, since it is a limit order, it will go to an Exchange floor broker registered as a *specialist*. The latter has the responsibility of maintaining an orderly market in the securities in which he specializes. Exchange rules permit a specialist to execute limit orders for other brokers. He may also act as a dealer for his own account.

When he receives a limit order, such as John Doe's order to buy A T & T at 48, the specialist records it in his "book" where he keeps a list of unfilled buy and sell orders. As soon as he receives a sell order at 48, he will match it with John Doe's buy order.

Doe might get the stock at less than 48 if there should be sufficient sell orders to drop the market price below 48. This sometimes happens. On the other hand, the market might go up and his order might never be filled at 48.

Margin Buying

Can a customer buy stock on credit? Yes, if he qualifies and if the price of the stock is $5 a share or more, he may buy "on margin," meaning that the brokerage firm will require him to put up a margin in cash and will lend him the balance, charging interest and holding the stock as security for the loan. The minimum margin on stocks is regulated by the Board of Governors of the Federal Reserve System. Currently it is 65 percent, which means that a customer can borrow no more than $35 on every $100 worth of stock purchased.

With a margin this large, the lending broker is well protected from even a substantial decline in stock prices. However, member brokerage firms are allowed to set even higher margins than the legal minimum, if they choose. Also, under NYSE regulations, brokers must require a margin customer to have an initial equity of not less than $2,000 in cash or its equivalent in securities. Currently brokerage firms have set $2,500 as initial equity.

When the price of a margined security drops and the margin becomes thin, the broker will call the customer for additional cash or securities to restore the margin. If the customer does not comply, the broker will sell the pledged security or securities to repay the loan plus interest. Whatever is left from the proceeds goes to the customer.

Trading on margin has the effect of increasing a customer's buying power in the securities market, and thus the amount he stands to gain or lose is greater than if he had used cash only.

The Short Sale

Reserved for speculators, mostly professionals, is an area of security trading known as *selling short*. Only the most sophisticated dare venture here. We certainly do not recommend it, but describe it solely for information.

When a person sells stock that he does not own but expects to buy later and deliver, he has *sold short*. Short sales are made in expectation of a decline in price of the stock. If a decline occurs, the trader then can buy and "cover" his short contract and make a profit out of the difference between the two transactions.

Example: Mr. Martin thinks that the price of X Company's common stock is going down in the near future. He sells 100 shares short at $75 a share. The buyer expects delivery of the stock within a specified time, but Martin has sold something he does not own so his broker will borrow 100 shares of X Company stock and make delivery to the buyer.

Let's say, as Martin expected, the stock he shorted drops in price to $60 a share. He now buys 100 shares and returns them through his broker to the person from whom they were borrowed. He has made $15 a share, less commissions, taxes, and any dividends paid in the meantime.

Suppose, however, Martin turns out to be wrong, and the stock goes up to $90 a share. If he buys and covers, he has lost $15 a share plus commissions, taxes, and dividends.

Short selling is strictly regulated and closely scrutinized by the Securities and Exchange Commission and by stock exchange authorities.

As a general principle, only experienced, knowledgeable speculators should engage in short trading. It is not for everybody.

Puts and Calls

Unfamiliar to most people are stock options, referred to as *puts* and *calls,* which until the organization of the Chicago Board Options Exchange (CBOE) in 1973, were traded solely in the over-the-counter market by *put* and *call brokers.* Customers are mostly sophisticated speculators, usually financially strong.

A *put* is an option contract under which the seller or maker for a consideration agrees to accept or buy a given number of shares (as a rule in lots of 100) of a designated stock at an agreed price during a stipulated option period, if the owner of the option calls upon him to do so.[15]

A *call* is an option contract under which the seller or maker for a consideration agrees to deliver a certain number of shares of a designated stock at an agreed price any time during the option period, if the owner of the option calls upon him to do so.

Here is an example of a put as handled over-the-counter: Mr. Wilson thinks that ABC common stock, currently selling at 80, is going to decline. He contacts a broker and asks the price of a sixty-day put of 100 shares of ABC common. The broker finds a speculator who is willing to sell for $400 a put contract under which the latter agrees to buy any time during the next sixty days 100 shares of ABC common at 80, if the option holder calls upon him to do so.

---

[15]A popular option period for tax reasons is six months and ten days, but other periods are used.

Wilson buys the contract. The stock declines to 72 about six weeks later and he "puts" 100 shares at 80. If the stock does not fall below 80 in sixty days, Wilson allows the option to expire. He will then lose what the option cost him ($400).

Suppose Mr. Wilson, instead of thinking ABC common is going down in price, believes it will go up. So he wants to buy a sixty-day call contract. The broker quotes him a price of $400 on a 100 share option at 80, which Wilson buys. Sometime during the option period, the price of ABC common goes to 90, and he "calls" on the maker of the contract to deliver to him 100 shares at 80. If the stock does not go above 80, Wilson will allow the option to expire.

How is the $400 consideration in the above examples determined? It is reached by negotiation. The put and call broker contacts "writers" of such contracts, and they make bids, the best of which is wired back to Wilson's broker who then advises Wilson. If the latter thinks the price is too high, he will reject it.

The broker's commission on puts and calls generally is 5 percent of the consideration, or $20 in our examples.

Most put and call contracts are "naked," that is, they do not involve actual delivery of stock. Rather they are settled by payment of cash equal to the difference between market price and option price when the option is exercised. For example, when Wilson bought the above put contract at 80 and the stock's price declined to 72, he could accept $800 without delivering 100 shares of ABC stock at 80. However, the contract cost him $400, so he would gain $400. (Commissions ignored.)

Wilson is sure of one thing; he cannot lose more than $400, but he can gain considerably more, if the stock falls.

Put and call trading has been assailed as gambling on the price behavior of stocks. It is said that the buyer of a put contract is betting that the price of a particular stock is going down, while the maker or seller is betting it will not by guaranteeing to accept at a fixed price a certain number of shares within an agreed period of time.

Those who defend put and call trading can and do cite situations where such a market renders a desirable service to institutions and investors, without involving a great deal of money. Many such situations are similar to those wherein individuals and businesses use commodity futures for hedging. In reality, hedging is a form of insurance to protect against price changes.

We do not propose to take one side or the other of this controversy. Suffice it to say that puts and calls, like short selling, are only for astute, well-informed speculators.

Stop Loss Orders

Employed by speculators more than by investors is a device called *stop order,* also known as *stop-loss order*. This order is used to limit a trader's losses. Here's how it is applied: Speculator Johnson buys 100 shares of common stock at 40 and immediately enters a stop order to sell at the market when and if the price drops to 36. The effect of the stop order is to assure Johnson that, if he made a mistake of selection, the most he will lose is approximately $4 a share.

Incidentally, a stop order also can be used to protect a gain already earned. Suppose Johnson owned stock selling at 52 which cost him 33, and he wanted to be assured of about $16 of the gain, he would place a stop order at 49.

Bond Trading

The mechanics of buying and selling listed bonds is quite similar to that of listed stocks. Brokers handle bond orders in the same general way as stock orders.

On the other hand, numerous issues of bonds are not listed on securities exchanges, but are traded in the over-the-counter market through dealers. This is true of governments, agencies, and municipals, as well as many corporate issues.

All bonds have a face or par value, generally $1,000. Listed bonds are quoted and sold at what actually amounts to percentages of par. For example, a bond quotation of 95 means 95 percent of $1,000 or $950. Fractions are usually in eights, as with stocks, but instead of an eighth meaning $.125, it means $1.25, or ⅛ of $10. Here are some additional examples:

Price quotation		*Dollar price*
97¾	=	$ 977.50
102⅞	=	1,028.75
100	=	1,000.00
100⅜	=	1,003.75
98½	=	985.00

Bonds pay interest semiannually from the date of issue. When bonds are traded, the buyer must pay to the seller not only the agreed price, but whatever interest has accrued since the last interest date. For example, a 6 percent bond issued April 1 pays $300 on each October 1 and each April 1, and if it is sold, say, on July 1 interest amounting to $150 will have accrued which the buyer must pay to the seller. On October 1 the buyer will get back the accrual he paid the seller plus three months interest he has earned on the bond.

The commission on corporate bond transactions is $5 per bond up to and including 100 bonds with a minimum of $25 on each order. On orders of more than 100 bonds there is a flat commission of $500 for all bonds up to 200, and $2.50 for each bond above 200.

Commission rates on bond transactions are less than they are on stock transactions relative to total value involved. Let's say an individual buys twenty General Telephone and Electronics 9¾ bonds of 1995 (meaning a 9¾ percent interest rate; bonds maturing 1995) at 114. He will pay a commission of $5 on each bond or $100 on the twenty-bond transaction, total value of which is 20 × $1,140, or $22,800. Suppose at the same time he bought 700 shares of

General Telephone and Electronics common stock at 30 amounting to $21,000. The commission on this transaction will be $250.

Bonds, like stocks, may be bought on margin. A 50 percent margin is required on convertible bonds selling above 50 percent of their face value regardless of quality and on those selling below 50 percent of face value if the bonds are rated high enough. All cash is required if convertible bonds are selling below 50 percent of face value and have a low rating. (See bond ratings in Chapter 21).

The margin on straight bonds is 35 percent under conditions identical to those applying to convertibles.

In the case of U.S. Government obligations, the margin is 10 percent of face amount or 10 percent of market value, whichever is greater.

Municipal bonds selling above 50 percent of face value can be bought on a margin of 20 percent of face value or 15 percent of market, whichever is greater. Municipal bonds selling for less than 50 percent of face value cannot be margined.

Institutional buyers are important in the bond market. For this reason orders tend to be quite large, especially for U.S. securities. Transactions in the latter take place in thirty-seconds, sometimes in sixty-fourths, rather than in eighths, as is true of listed corporate bonds. For example, a quotation on the $3\frac{1}{2}$ percent Treasury Bonds due February 1, 1990, might read as follows:

Bid   79.12   Ask   80.12   Yield   6.62%

This means that a $1,000 bond of this issue was bid $79\frac{12}{32}$ or $793.75 and was offered at $80\frac{12}{32}$, or $803.75.

In the above situation, dealers are saying that they will buy these bonds at the bid price and will sell at the ask price, making a profit margin of $10 per bond. But, if an institutional investor should be seeking to buy 1,500 bonds, there would be considerable negotiating with different dealers for the best price. Very likely the buyer would be able to improve somewhat on the ask price.

U.S. Treasury Bills, which also trade in very large amounts, are sold on a discount basis and, hence, are quoted in terms of percentage discount. For example, Treasury Bills maturing in twenty-nine days from date might be quoted as follows:

Bid   5.74   Ask   5.44

This indicates that the bid is 5.74 percent annual discount for 29 days, or $995.38 per $1,000 par value. At the same time, dealers are asking 5.44 percent discount, or $995.62. At maturity in twenty-nine days the bills are redeemed at par.

Only a relatively few individuals invest in Treasury Bills because the minimum denomination is $10,000 and maturities are short. Largest owners are Federal Reserve Banks, U.S. Government accounts, commercial banks, insurance companies, and state and local governments.

Discussion Questions

1. What are the three types of corporate securities?
2. List three group rights and three individual rights of stockholders.
3. Why is it important to know whether a preferred stock is redeemable or callable?
4. Differentiate between par value and no par value.
5. How do you calculate the book value per share?
6. What is meant by a "stock split"?
7. What is a sinking fund?
8. Discuss three securities issued by the Federal Government.

A rule to beat the stock market: Just find out what everybody else is doing, then do the opposite. But if too many follow the rule, it won't work.

[*Anonymous*]

21

Security Management

There is no simple rule or formula an investor can follow and be assured of success in buying and selling securities. If there were, all of us could get rich easily and no one would lose. However, there are some time-tested guidelines that, if observed, will be helpful.

1. Understand the various forms of securities and how they differ. A major part of the preceding chapter was devoted to this purpose.
2. Look upon the purchase of every security as a risk. In the vast array of securities available, the degree of risk ranges from small to quite large. Determine the risk of a specific security before buying it.
3. Decide whether personal financial and other circumstances justify assumption of the risk.

473

4. Ask yourself what you expect a security to do for you and seek the ones that will fulfill those objectives.

5. Understand the various factors which affect prices of securities, including overall movements of the market as a whole. Even the very strongest stocks and bonds fluctuate in price.

6. Avoid being swept away by mass psychology which occasionally causes stock prices in particular to swing to great extremes—sometimes up, sometimes down—without sound economic reasons.

7. As a rule, investors fare best financially when they select a security for its long-term prospects. If you do this, be sure you are in a position where you do not have to sell unexpectedly, possibly at the wrong time at a big loss.

8. Unless you have considerable resources, you should confine your holdings to securities that can be liquidated easily, if you need to sell. This means that your securities should have good marketability—that is, be actively traded.

9. Keep constant vigilance over securities you own because changes often can and do occur in the market. Risk, prices, and yields may vary from time to time, and your own financial situation may change also. Read annual and quarterly financial reports of companies whose securities you own and follow developments that may affect industries of which the companies are a part. For example, the emergence of the environmental protection movement in recent years has resulted in laws requiring major capital outlays in some industries resulting in adverse effects on earnings.

10. Do not hesitate to sell a security whose future begins to look unfavorable. Better to take a small loss than a large one.

11. Avoid "putting all your eggs in one basket." Diversify security holdings. As a general rule, over-all risk can be reduced by diversification—not only having securities of companies whose products and services are widely different, but having different forms of securities—common stocks, preferred stocks, and bonds.

12. Avoid acting on market "tips," rumors, and recommendations of biased persons. If you seek advice, go to someone qualified to advise you and in whom you have confidence.

13. Remember that there is no easy road to riches.

Finally, "Investigate before you invest" is a wise rule. Fortunately, an abundance of useful information about corporations and their securities is available to use. This information may be classified into two categories according to source: (1) that which comes directly from the respective companies themselves, and (2) that which comes from other sources.

As we shall see, corporations whose securities are publicly held are required by law to disclose all information which may relate to the value of their securities. Such information must be true and not misleading. Financial data in the form of operating statements and balance sheets, and other information are sent in quarterly and annual reports to stockholders, and at the same time are released to news media. Corporations also make public announcements of significant developments as the latter occur.

A vast amount of information about corporations and their securities is available through secondary sources such as financial journals, daily newspapers, radio and TV newscasts, financial services, and a wide range of investors' services. Brokerage offices generally maintain specialized libraries containing current information.

Two prominent financial services—Moody's and Standard & Poor's—publish what are generally regarded as the most comprehensive sources of information about corporations and their securities, including quarterly ratings of bonds and stocks.

Moody's publishes the following manuals annually and keeps them current with biweekly supplements:

> *Industrial Manual*
> *Public Utility Manual*
> *Transportation Manual*
> *Bank and Finance Manual*
> *OTC Industrial Manual*

Moody's also publishes weekly a stock survey and a bond survey.

The following are Standard & Poor's publications:

> *Corporation Records*
> *Stock Reports*
> *Stock Guide*
> *Bond Guide*

The contents of *Moody's Manuals* and *Standard & Poor's Corporation Records,* both published annually, are substantially similar. In fact, the two publications are competitive. Corporations are alphabetized by name and the following information is provided about each:

Capital structure
History of the company
Kind of business and products
Principal properties
Operating statistics
Income accounts
Record of earnings over a period of years
Balance sheets
Statistical record
  Per share earnings
  Dividends per share
  Range of prices
  Times charges earned
  Operating ratios
  Details about long-term debt
  Description of securities outstanding

Standard & Poor's Stock Reports supply condensed information about corporations that is more current than the longer treatment found in the annual publications. The *S & P Stock and Bond Guides* are issued monthly and are intended as quick references. Since only one line is devoted to each security, a great deal of abbreviating is used in the guides, but the information is quite meaningful.

Protecting the Buyer of Securities

Prior to 1911 there was little or no government regulation of the issuance and sale of securities. Many abuses arose whereby thousands of investors, particularly small investors, were victimized by fraudulent schemes of unscrupulous promoters and manipulators whose aim was to enrich themselves at the expense of the public.

Various devices were used to prey upon gullible individuals. Prices of stocks were manipulated through exaggerated publicity prepared by subsidized financial columnists, through such devices as *wash sales* and *matched orders,* and through insider schemes, and the use of buying or selling *pools.*

In a *wash sale,* one broker agreed to sell to another a certain security at a price higher than the market price at the time, neither broker having any intention whatsoever to deliver the stock or pay any money. The purpose of this fictitious transaction was to leave the impression that the price of the security was rising so as to lure the public into buying and give the scheme's operators a chance to sell at a profit.

The purpose of the *matched order* device was substantially the same as that of the wash sale, but the mechanics of the two were different. In the case of the matched order, an individual or a group of manipulators would hire two brokers, unknown to each other, one to sell a certain security and the other to buy the security at the same price, leaving the impression of great activity in the security in order to excite public interest, raise prices and enable the conspirators to unload.

Pools were formed to manipulate security prices through concentrated buying. After the operators of a pool had driven prices up, they would then sell before the public realized what had happened. Occasionally pools would be used to drive prices down so the operators could buy advantageously.

State Regulation

Forty-nine states, led by Kansas in 1911, now seek to protect the public from fraudulently offered securities through what are known as *blue sky laws.*[1] These laws are not strictly uniform among the states, but generally they provide for the filing of a registration statement with a designated state authority,

---

[1] Blue sky is a term coined from the sale of stocks in spurious business enterprises by unscrupulous promoters who were actually selling to gullible investors "nothing but the blue sky."

describing the securities to be issued and identifying the issuer. In some instances, this requirement takes the simple form of notification; while in other states, it is an application for permission to issue and offer for sale the described securities.

Securities issued by federal, state, and local governments and those listed on organized exchanges are exempt from blue sky laws because the public is presumed to be protected in other ways.

Blue sky laws also provide for registration and licensing of brokers and dealers, as well as the salesmen who work for them. Those who qualify for a license must establish evidence of good character and of financial responsibility.

Federal Regulation

The Federal Government seeks to protect the public from fraudulent securities offered through the mails or the channels of interstate commerce. The Securities Act of 1933, administered by the Securities and Exchange Commission,[2] requires companies to file a registration statement containing complete and accurate information about every new security offering and to make such information available to purchasers of the security in what is known as a *prospectus* (see Exhibit 21–1).

If the SEC, after investigation, finds that the information supplied in the registration statement is true and complies with the act, the Commission will approve the security—that is, register it. No new security can be sold interstate until it has been properly registered.

The principal function of the Securities Act of 1933 is to protect the public by requiring full disclosure of pertinent information. The Commission does not rate a security, express an opinion about its value, or advise its purchase.

In other words, an investor must not assume that because a security is registered with the SEC, that it is a good investment. However, he can assume that what he reads in a prospectus has been submitted to the SEC as factual and that it must be cleared by the Commission as a condition of registration.

Every prospectus contains at least the following information.

1. History and nature of the company's business.
2. Disclosure of risk factors pertaining to the security offered. Usually this section begins with a statement similar to the following: "The securities offered hereby involve certain risks and persons considering the purchase of such securities should carefully consider the matters disclosed in the prospectus, and in particular, the following risk factors concerning the offering."
3. How the proceeds from the sale of the security will be used.
4. Capitalization of the company.
5. Nature and extent of competition.
6. Names and experience of officers and directors of the company.

---

[2]At first the act was administered by the Federal Trade Commission.

Exhibit 21–1   A Sample Prospectus

PROSPECTUS

April 12, 1973

Decision Data Computer Corporation

510,000 Shares of Common Stock   ($.10 Par Value)

These securities involve a high degree of risk. See "Risk Factors," page 4.

Of these shares, 500,000 shares are being purchased by the Underwriters from the Company and 10,000 shares from the Selling Stockholders listed under "Principal and Selling Stockholders." The Company will receive no part of the proceeds from the sales of the shares by the Selling Stockholders.

On April 11, 1973, the representative closing bid quotation for the Common Stock in the over-the-counter market, as reported by the National Association of Securities Dealers Automated Quotation System (NASDAQ) was $16.50.

THESE SECURITIES HAVE NOT BEEN APPROVED OR DISAPPROVED BY THE SECURITIES AND EXCHANGE COMMISSION NOR HAS THE COMMISSION PASSED UPON THE ACCURACY OR ADEQUACY OF THIS PROSPECTUS. ANY REPRESENTATION TO THE CONTRARY IS A CRIMINAL OFFENSE.

	Price to Public	Underwriting Discount	Proceeds to Company(1)	Proceeds to Selling Stockholders
Per Share	$15.00	$1.20	$13.80	$13.80
Total	$7,650,000	$612,000	$6,900,000	$138,000

(1) Before deducting expenses estimated at $100,000, or $.20 per share, payable by the Company. See "Underwriting."

The 510,000 shares are offered subject to prior sales and when, as and if delivered to and accepted by the Underwriters. Delivery to the Underwriters is expected on or about April 23, 1973.

BACHE & CO.
Incorporated

---

7. Remuneration of officers and directors, including stock options.

8. Latest audited financial statements of the company.

9. Legal opinions.

10. The extent, if any, to which the company is involved in litigation.

11. Report of the certified public accounting firm which audited the company's financial statements.

In 1934, Congress enlarged the scope of federal regulation of securities marketing by passing the Securities and Exchange Act. Under this legislation each securities exchange is required to apply for registration with the SEC by submitting an application containing facts about its organization and its activities. Actually, the law brings every securities exchange and its members, unless exempt, under rules of the SEC.

The act also brings under regulation all securities listed on organized exchanges by requiring registration. Companies whose securities are listed must disclose publicly all information which might have a bearing upon market value of the respective securities.

Regulation reaches over-the-counter securities through the National Association of Securities Dealers, Inc., which was created and registered under the law.

The act contains certain provisions designed to control the use of credit (margin trading) in security transactions. The Board of Governors of the Federal Reserve System is given power to fix margin requirements.

Use of false and misleading information to induce anyone to buy or sell a security is forbidden, as are wash sales, matched orders, pools, and other devices which have the effect of raising or depressing prices or creating false appearances of active trading in a security.

Corporate officers must reveal the amount of securities they own in their own companies and must report to the SEC any changes in their holdings as the changes occur. This regulation is for the purpose of discouraging the use of information by insiders for their own selfish benefit.

In 1970, Congress created the Securities Investor Protection Corporation (SIPC) to protect investors from loss of securities resulting from failure of a broker or dealer. Maximum protection is $50,000 per account. Enactment of the law followed the failure of a number of brokers and dealers with whom customers left securities or maintained credit balances. All security dealers and brokers operating an interstate security business must join the SIPC and pay annual assessments into an insurance fund from which losses are met.

The purpose of government regulation of the issuance and sale of stocks and bonds is to protect the public from fraud, conspiracy, and misleading information. No agency, state or federal, attempts to determine whether a security is a good or bad investment. The law offers no guarantee that a registered security is going to make or lose money for its owner. Each individual must assume whatever risks are inherent in the securities he buys.

Factors Affecting Bond Prices

Changes in Interest Rates

As we learned in Chapter 20, bonds are formal long-term debt instruments which promise to pay a fixed rate of interest during the life of the bonds and to return the principal at maturity. When bonds are issued, their rate of interest at the time reflects what the issuer has to pay in the money market for borrowed funds for a given period.

An interest rate is composed of two elements, (1) pure cost of borrowed money, and (2) a premium relating to the degree of risk associated with the loan. Let's consider, for example, the case of Corporation K, a very strong company with an excellent credit record. If it had issued twenty-five year first mortgage bonds with a five-year call option on January 15, 1970, it probably would have had to pay 8.5 percent interest because, at that time, the supply of money was quite scarce in relation to demand; but, if the company had issued the bonds on, say, January 15, 1972, the rate probably would have been 7.25 percent since money market conditions had eased considerably and the cost of borrowed funds of the type in our example was much less.

Now suppose that Corporation J, a company not as strong credit-wise as Corporation K, also had sought to issue first mortgage bonds for twenty-five years with a five-year call, and to do this at the same time as Corporation K. It might have had to pay 9.0 percent on January 15, 1970, and 7.75 percent on January 15, 1972. The difference of 0.5 percent between the rate which Corporation K had to pay and the rate Corporation J had to pay is a risk differential by which the market says that Corporation K is a better risk than Corporation J.

On the other hand, the difference of 1.25 percent between the rates both companies paid in January, 1970, and what they paid in January, 1972, reflects changes in money market conditions from one time to the other—that is, a change in the cost of money.

Continuing with our example, let's suppose that Corporation K did issue its bonds on January 15, 1970, at 8.5 percent and that at the time of issue an investor bought ten bonds for $10,000. In substance, what he bought was a contract under which Corporation K obligates itself to pay $425 interest, no more no less, every January 15 and July 15 as long as the bonds are outstanding, and pay $10,000 on January 15, 1995, regardless of changes in the money market. The company has no obligation to redeem the bonds before January 15, 1995, although it can call them after January 14, 1975, if it wants to.

Let's say that this investor decided to sell his bonds after owning them exactly two years. Interest rates in the money market had gone down in the meantime, and companies like Corporation K could borrow long-term money at 7.25 percent on January 15, 1972. His bonds, which yield 8.5 percent on their par value, then would sell above par.

It was no surprise to the investor when his bonds sold at 112 on January 15, 1972, because he had followed price quotations on them from time to time in financial journals, and he had observed that as interest rates moved down the price of his bonds went up. Also he observed that the reverse was true—namely, as interest rates rose, the price of his bonds declined.

The principle demonstrated here is that market prices of bonds move inversely with interest rate changes. Therefore, interest rates are a basic factor in bond valuation.

Credit Risk

A corollary of the above principle is that the higher the quality of bond (that is, the safer it is), the more its price will respond to the interest rate factor.

For example, U.S. Government Bonds are regarded as riskless; and, as a consequence, their market valuation is responsive to interest rate changes almost solely. In other words, the interest yield on a riskless obligation includes no premium for risk. It is pure interest, or the true cost of money.

There actually is no such thing as a riskless obligation, not even United States Government bonds; but just as the physicist may assume the existence of a perfect vacuum for purposes of demonstrating a scientific principle, so we may assume the existence of a riskless obligation to emphasize the relation of yield to risk.

How is the lay investor going to determine the degree of credit risk associated with bonds that he might consider buying? He cannot do so himself unless he is willing to acquire as much expertise as a security analyst; but he can use the widely accepted bond ratings prepared by either Moody's Investment Services or Standard and Poor's Corporation, or both.

The following are Standard & Poor's corporate bond ratings as described in the S & P Bond Guide.

> AAA = Highest grade, with ultimate degree of protection of principal and interest. Prices move with interest rates.
>
> AA = High grade. Differ from AAA issues only in small degree. Prices move with interest rates.
>
> A = Upper medium grade. Principal and interest regarded as safe, but market prices tend to reflect economic and trade conditions more than is true of AAA and AA issues. Prices influenced by interest rates.
>
> BBB = Medium grade. Have adequate asset coverage and normally are protected by satisfactory earnings. Market prices are more affected by general economic, business, and trade conditions than by interest rates.
>
> BB = Lower medium grade. Have only minor investment characteristics. Very susceptible to changing economic conditions.
>
> B = In speculative realm. Interest cannot be assured under difficult economic conditions.
>
> CCC-CC = Outright speculative. May be paying interest, but continuation very questionable in periods of poor conditions.
>
> C = Income bonds on which no interest is being paid.
>
> DDD-DD-D = All in default, with the rating indicating relative salvage value.

Moody's corporate bond ratings are divided into nine graduations to which have been assigned the following symbols from highest to the poorest:

Aaa	B
Aa	Caa
A	Ca
Baa	C
Ba	

Moody's Investment Service carefully points out in the following statement that there are limitations in the uses of bond ratings: "As ratings are designed exclusively for the purpose of grading bonds according to their investment qualities, they should not be used alone as a basis for investment operations. For example, they have no value in forecasting the direction of future movements of market prices. Market price movements in bonds are influenced not only by the quality of individual issues but also by changes in money rates and in general economic trends, as well as by the length of maturity, etc. During its life even the best quality bond may have wide price movements, although its high investment status remains unchanged."[3]

In essence what investors buy in bonds is a contract under which the issuer promises to do two things: (1) pay bondholders a limited return periodically; and (2) at the end of the bond's term, pay back the principal of the debt. No bondholder has a right to expect more because that is all that is promised. Therefore, what basically concerns investors is the question of whether the company will be able to fulfill its contract.

Analysts in measuring the quality of corporate bonds apply several financial ratios. Among the most common are:

1. Earnings coverage, or times charges earned, which is the relationship between fixed charges (interest on bonded debt) and earnings. This is sometimes called the margin of safety test. A company that is barely earning enough to meet fixed charges would be considered weak, and its bonds be rated low, perhaps regarded as being in danger of default; whereas, a company whose earnings are many times fixed charges likely would be able to continue paying interest on its bonds even if the company suffered a decline in profits from a recession or depression. General Motors Corporation, for example, whose bonds are rated AAA, earned 64.18 times its fixed charges in 1971 on a bonded debt of almost $700 million.[4]

2. Another objective test is the *tangible assets ratio*. At the close of 1971, General Motors had $18,469 worth of tangible assets for each $1,000 of long-term debt.

3. Similar to the above ratio is the relationship between *net current assets* and *funded debt*. In GM's case the amount was $39,670 for each $1,000 of long-term debt, a strong position, indeed.

4. Since bonds, as credit obligations, are in a senior position to stocks, a significant financial ratio is that of *equity value to bonded debt*. This tells us how much capital value there is which is subordinate to bonded debt. The greater the ratio of equity to bonded debt, the greater the margin of safety of the latter. By using market value of outstanding preferred and common stocks, we find the ratio of equity capital to bonded debt of

---

[3]Moody's Investors Service, Inc., *Moody's Industrial Manual, 1972* (New York, 1972), Vol. 1, pp. v-vi.

[4]*Moody's Industrial Manual 1972*, Vol. 1, p. 1367.

General Motors to be about 30, meaning the company's bonded debt is ahead of equity capital valued thirty times as much.

5. Security analysts also carefully examine a company's working capital position. *Working capital* may be defined as assets available for use in everyday operations of a business, and more specifically it is the excess of current assets over current liabilities. The presumption underlying this test is that a company strong in working capital is in a good situation to earn and also to meet unforeseen contingencies, all of which affords added assurance that debt service requirements will be met.

The above actually are tests of strength and soundness of a corporation as a business unit and, therefore, indicate ability to meet debt requirements. Competent security analysts always stress the point that safety of bonds is not increased by any specific lien on property but by the capacity of the issuer to carry out contractual obligations. There have been numerous instances of values of property pledged to secure bonds declining sharply when a company has failed.

Bonds in the top four ratings of both S & P and Moody's are considered to be investment securities, and regulations permit commercial banks to own them. Bonds rated below BBB and Baa fall in purely speculative categories.

Since ratings are essentially measures of credit risk, an investor would expect bond yields to reflect ratings. Exhibit 21–2 shows this to be true. AAA bonds consistently sell at the lowest yields; AA bonds next lowest, then A bonds, with BBB the lowest of the four investment grades. There is not, however, a precise mathematical relationship. This indicates that there must be other factors than interest which affect bond prices.

Effect of Length of Maturity

As bonds approach maturity when the principal will be repaid, their price, as a rule, will move toward par regardless of their nominal interest rate. Prices of bonds that are selling at a discount (below par) will tend to rise and prices of bonds that are selling at a premium (above par) will tend to decline as maturity nears.

This is shown clearly by two issues of American Telephone & Telegraph Company's Debentures, each with 2¾ percent nominal interest rate, because they were sold originally in 1945 when interest rates were quite low. One issue is due October 1, 1975 and the other August 1, 1980. On March 1, 1973 the market price of the bonds maturing October 1, 1975 was 91¼, yielding 3.01 percent currently and 6.48 percent to maturity and the market price of those maturing August 1, 1980 was 76, yielding 3.62 percent currently and 6.94 percent to maturity.

The only difference between the above two issues is in maturity, one maturing four years and ten months earlier than the other. Yet, the market prices of the two issues on the same day differed by 15¼ or $152.50 per bond in favor of the shorter maturity.

Exhibit 21–2   Average Yields for Corporate Bonds by Ratings, 1972*

	AAA	AA	A	BBB
January	7.11%	7.42%	7.66%	8.16%
February	7.16	7.44	7.62	8.16
March	7.22	7.45	7.64	8.16
April	7.36	7.58	7.74	8.32
May	7.34	7.54	7.67	8.28
June	7.30	7.57	7.70	8.31
July	7.30	7.60	7.74	8.35
August	7.27	7.53	7.64	8.29
September	7.30	7.56	7.68	8.29
October	7.31	7.58	7.66	8.28
November	7.26	7.51	7.59	8.22
December	7.24	7.41	7.57	8.09

*Composite group, non-convertibles
Source: Standard and Poor's Bond Guide

Another way to state the rule is that interest rate changes affect market prices of bonds more when the maturity is long than when the maturity is short. When the market rate of interest rises above a bond's nominal rate, the bond will sell at a discount; and, if all else remains the same, the longer the maturity the greater the discount. If, however, the market rate of interest falls below a bond's nominal rate, the bond will sell at a premium; and, if all else remains the same, the longer the maturity the greater the premium. This is shown in Exhibit 21–3.

Exhibit 21–3   The Effect of Maturity on the Value of a 5% Bond

	When market rate of interest is:	
Years to maturity	6%	4%
1	99.04	100.97
2	98.14	101.90
3	97.29	102.80
4	96.49	103.66
5	95.73	104.49
6	95.02	105.29
7	94.37	106.05
8	93.72	106.79
9	93.12	107.50
10	92.56	108.18
11	92.03	108.83
12	91.53	109.46
20	88.44	113.68
25	87.14	115.71
30	86.16	117.38
35	85.44	118.75

Effect of a Call Option

Most corporate bonds have a call option which permits the issuing company to redeem them after a stated number of years. A call option tends to modify the price effect of a change in the market rate of interest sufficiently that an investor always should know the details of a call provision before he buys bonds.

Look again at our hypothetical case of Corporation K, whose twenty-five-year 8.5 percent bonds are rated AAA. Let's assume that there is no call provision whatsoever in these bonds and that they sold at par when issued January 15, 1970. By January 15, 1972, AAA bonds were selling in the market to yield 7.25 percent for twenty-three years. The price of AAA bonds with an 8.5 percent interest rate would rise to 113⅞ or $1,138.75 in order to bring their yield down to 7.25 percent for the remaining life of the bonds.

On the other hand, if the bonds have a five-year call at 108½ or $1,085 (par plus one year's interest), the investor must reckon with the possibility that the company will call the bonds in three years (January 15, 1975). If he is sure the bonds will be called then, and everybody else is equally certain, the bonds will sell at the market rate for three-year AAA obligations. If that rate happens to be 6.75 percent, then the price of the bonds will be 111⅝ or $1,116.25, because the buyers not only will receive $85 interest per bond for each of the three years, but an additional $85 premium when the call option is exercised.

But we cannot be certain that the company will call the bonds at the end of three years or any time thereafter. All we know for sure is that the company has that option beginning January 15, 1975. Obviously, the bonds will not be called unless it is economically feasible for the company to do so. Feasibility, in turn, depends upon what money is worth at the time a call is being considered.

So, actually, investors about to buy the bonds would have to exercise judgment as to the future of interest rates, realizing the risk involved in such judgment. In most situations like the above, sophisticated buyers will add perhaps another ⅛ to the base rate, making it 6⅞ percent, to cover the possibility that the bonds will not be called three years hence. At a base rate of 6⅞ percent, the price of the bonds would be 111¼ or $1,112.50 per bond.

Effect of the Conversion Option

As we noted in the previous chapter, companies sometimes issue bonds which give holders the right, if the latter choose, to convert the bonds into common stock at a stated ratio. The conversion right is considered a kind of "sweetener" to attract investors and speculators, and generally it adds to market value which enables the issuing company to sell the bonds in the primary market at a lower nominal rate and which similarly affects prices of the bonds in the secondary market.

Here is an example: On a certain date, the 5½ percent convertible bonds of Houston Lighting & Power Company, due in 1985 and rated AA by Standard

& Poor's, were selling at a price of 124 to yield currently 4.44 percent. At the same time, the company's 5¼ percent first mortgage bonds due in 1996 and rated AAA by Standard & Poor's were selling at 78 to yield 6.73 percent currently.

In this example, price and yield differentials between the two kinds of bonds of the same company are due almost entirely to the value of the conversion option in one of the issues. Each of the company's convertible bonds can be exchanged at the owner's option into 22.73 shares of common stock which at the time of the above prices was selling at 54⅜ per share, giving each bond a stock value of 123⅝ (22.73 × 54.375).

Obviously investors were willing to pay about $460 per bond (the difference between $1,240 and $780) more for the conversion privilege at a time when the price of the common stock was 54⅜. Had the price of the common stock been $64, the conversion option would have been worth about $675, putting the bonds nearer 145 or $1,450 and reducing the current yield to 3.79 percent at that price.

Let's suppose, however, that the market price of the company's common stock is only $34 a share, making the stock value of each bond 22.73 × $34, or $772.82. What effect would this have? The market price per bond would now be determined more by yield than by the conversion privilege. If yield ruled completely, an investor would expect the bonds to sell at about the same yield as the company's long-term nonconvertible bonds, namely 6.73 percent, or at a price of $817.25. But, since the conversion option almost certainly would have some value in the market, perhaps enough to reduce the yield to 6.5 percent causing the price per bond to be about $846.

Some of the above figures are only hypothetical, but we have made them plausible in light of the principle we are demonstrating. The principle may be stated as follows: a convertible bond's market price will follow very closely the bond's stock value when the latter moves above the bond's yield value, but when the bond's stock value falls below yield value, the yield value will tend to keep the bond's market price from falling. The principle is illustrated in Exhibit 21–4.

Exhibit 21–4   Effect of Conversion Option

Company	S-P rating	Convertible bond	Market price	Stock value	Current yield
Baxter Laboratories	BBB	4%, 1987	307	307½	1.30%
Black and Decker	BBB	4%, 1992	335⅞	335⅞	1.19%
McCall Corp.	BB	4¾%, 1992	495	495¾	0.96%
National Can	BB	5%, 1993	78	57	6.41%
Revere Copper and Brass	BB	5½%, 1992	68¼	27⅝	8.06%
Stauffer Chemical	BBB	4½%, 1991	90½	82	4.97%

Source: *S & P Bond Guide*, December, 1972.

Effect of Inflation

The United States and most countries of the world have experienced serious monetary inflation in the past third of a century. As explained in Chapter 7, monetary inflation simply means a condition of rising prices—not just a rise in the prices of a few things, but a rise in the general level of prices. Since the purchasing power of money is reciprocally related to the level of prices, inflation lowers the real value of money (the amount of things money will buy).

For example, consumer prices increased 125 percent between 1940 and 1965 in the United States and, as a result, buying power of the dollar declined about 56 percent.

Because bonds are fixed dollar obligations they pay a fixed amount of interest in dollars and a fixed principal sum in dollars at maturity, regardless of what those dollars will buy at various times. Anyone who bought at par twenty-five-year, 5 percent bonds in 1940 and held them to maturity received dollars whose real worth was 56 percent less in 1965 than that of the dollars used to buy the bonds. And because the increase in the price level averaged about 5 percent a year during the twenty-five year period, the interest rate on the bonds was virtually eaten up by inflation.

An investor might ask at this point: why does anyone buy bonds at all? Certainly the fellow in our example who bought in 1940 had no way of knowing what would happen inflation-wise in the years ahead. The future is not easy to read. Not even the best qualified economists and the most expert market analysts foresaw in 1940 what would happen to the dollar in twenty-five years. Even if someone had made a correct forecast, not enough people would have believed him to make any difference in the bond market.

Despite the worst inflation in our history to date and no assurance that it will be checked, bonds continue to be issued and sold. Why? One reason is that current inflated or cheap dollars are available to buy them. Secondly, interest rates are relatively high for long-term bonds, as if to say that the money market has added three to four percentage points to compensate for the purchasing power risk (for expected inflation). Third, financial institutions such as commercial banks, mutual savings banks, savings and loan associations, and insurance companies take in and pay out current dollars and, therefore, are not functionally concerned with the purchasing power of money. They continue to invest in bonds both as secondary reserves and for income. In fact, many financial institutions and fiduciaries are limited by law to investments from a list of "legal investments" made up of bond issues approved by government authorities.

Effect of Changes in the Economy

Bond prices like stock prices are influenced by changes in the level of the economy, but not in the same way and not as violently. In periods of recession, high-grade bond prices tend to hold up well and often advance because interest rates are lower, bonds are in a superior position to stocks, and demand for bonds is strengthened, since investment money is inclined to favor bonds over stocks in recession periods.

In periods of prosperity, when the economy is booming, stocks generally rise and high-grade bonds decline. When business is quite active and expanding, demand for money is strong, causing interest rates to go up, thus lowering bond prices. When times are good, corporations generally earn greater profits and pay larger dividends, which stimulate investor and speculator interest in stocks and away from bonds.

Low-grade bonds, on the other hand, tend to behave price-wise more like common stocks, whatever the level of the economy. Their prices are likely to fall rather deeply in recessions when business is bad because of the greater possibility of default. The opposite holds true in prosperous times.

Effect of Market Swings

On the whole, prices of securities whether bonds or stocks are susceptible to psychological and other forces which crop up in the market from time to time and are very difficult to explain. Again, however, high-grade bonds are not likely to fluctuate very much as a result of these factors, certainly not as much as common stocks are. Since the chief reason for buying such bonds is income, prices are not as subject to emotional expectations as are stock prices. Furthermore, institutional buyers and sellers usually dominate the high-grade bond market and they are far more objective and "hardnosed" in their decision making than the public.

Factors Affecting
Preferred Stock Prices

Although a preferred stock represents a part of the equity of the issuing corporation and, therefore, is basically different from a bond, there is a contractual aspect which makes it similar to a bond, subject to some of the same price determinants. This is particularly true of high grade *straight preferreds*.

For example, General Motors has two preferreds outstanding. One is a $5 cumulative preferred which was issued in 1930. The other is a $3.75 cumulative preferred which was issued in 1947. Both are non-callable. Both are rated AAA by Standard and Poor's.[5]

Because of the great strength of the company, few persons would argue that there is much difference between GM's preferred stocks and its bonds as investments, even though the preferreds are in a legal position inferior to the bonds.

---

[5]Standard & Poor's quality ratings on preferred stocks are as follows:

AAA or Prime grade	BB or Lower grade
AA or High grade	B or Speculative
A or Sound	C or Submarginal
BBB or Medium grade	

Both securities are of the fixed-income type; but, due to his creditor position, a bondholder has an enforceable claim for the amount of interest as it is due and for the principal sum at maturity; whereas, a preferred stockholder has no such enforceable claim. Rather, the stockholder has merely a claim to be paid dividends before common stockholders are paid. Yet, this legal difference melts into insignificance when the issuing company is as strong as GM.

The situation is different, however, when the issuing company is not strong. Then the market price of a straight preferred tends to reflect a contractual weakness of the stock which is the possibility that dividends may be interrupted. If this happens, there is nothing a preferred stockholder can do.

There are not many new issues of straight preferred stock anymore, because high corporation income tax rates make it more economical to issue bonds. Interest a company pays on its outstanding bond indebtedness is a deductible item for income tax purposes, but dividends it pays are not. Therefore, rather than issue straight preferred stocks, most strong companies now use subordinated debentures and take advantage of the tax saving.

There is another tax factor which affects the position of straight preferred stock in a way that discriminates against an individual investor. A corporation can own straight preferred stock of another corporation and exclude from taxable income 85 percent of the dividends received on the preferred, but an individual has no such tax advantage. This means that corporations tend to bid up the market price of the relatively few high-grade straight preferreds outstanding, bringing the yield about equal to the yield on high-grade bonds. Consequently, straight preferreds as a rule are fundamentally unsatisfactory investments for individuals.

On the other hand, *convertible preferreds* often have considerable attraction for individuals because of the chance to gain from appreciation in the price of the company's common stock. Market price behavior of convertible preferreds is similar on the whole to that of convertible bonds.

One problem with convertible preferreds, however, is finding issues of high quality. This is understandable when the conditions that usually are responsible for the use of this type of security by a company are considered. Remember we said that the conversion privilege is a "sweetener" to make the security more attractive than it otherwise would be. In the case of a convertible preferred stock, the company feels that convertibility is necessary to raise additional equity capital. Very strong companies would not have to do this.

Another problem is the difficulty of valuing properly the conversion privilege.

In selecting a preferred stock, whether convertible or not, a security analyst would consider, among other things, certain financial ratios similar to those used for selecting bonds. It is not necessary to repeat these, but we should point out that some of them are applied differently. For example, margin of safety ratios would relate the position of the preferred to that of the common stock. Since preferred dividends must be paid before common dividends, it is significant to know "times preferred dividends earned" which is calculated simply by dividing total earnings by the number of preferred shares outstanding to get per share earnings, then dividing that figure by the annual preferred dividend.

Let's look at an actual situation. Armstrong Cork has outstanding 218,000 shares of $3.75 cumulative preferred and 25,694,000 shares of common stock. The company's total earnings in 1971 when divided by the preferred shares amounted to $300.20 per share, or eighty times the annual dividend of $3.75. In 1968, times preferred dividends earned was 77; it was 70 in 1969; and 40 in 1970: all indicating very strong earnings coverage of preferred dividend requirements.

Factors Affecting
Common Stock Prices

Unlike bonds, common stocks are not contractual instruments. In fact, a common stock certificate simply states that the named owner owns a specified number of shares of the company's capital stock. There is no promise to pay dividends; there is no promise to redeem the shares. In other words, there is no contract similar to what exists in the debtor-creditor relationship represented by a bond.

Anyone who buys common stock does so because he expects the business to do well—that is, to earn profits and pay dividends—or he simply expects the market price of the stock for one reason or another to rise so that he can make a capital gain.

Unlike a corporate bondholder, a stockholder is not so much concerned about whether his company will live up to a definite contract as he is about whether the company will fulfill his expectations.

In the preceding chapter, we used the example of a fictional John Doe buying 100 shares of A T & T common stock. Let's pursue the example further.

Why did Doe decide to buy this particular security out of thousands of others available in the market? Only he himself can answer accurately, but we can presume that he did so because he expected good results from his investment. Like all who buy securities, he was optimistic about the future of the stock or he would not have bought it.

He may have been advised by a friend, a relative, a banker, or a financial counselor. Or it is possible that he was influenced by something he read or something he overheard. He may have examined various sources of information and made a thorough investigation of many securities. Perhaps he followed a recommendation of some investment service to which he subscribes.

These are only a few of countless possible determinants which could explain why a person decides to buy a certain security rather than some other, or why he buys a security at all.

We once knew a woman who was a successful buyer of securities. Asked how she knew what to buy, she replied that when she used a product she liked very much, she looked for the maker's name on the label and bought the company's stock.

The important ingredient is *expectation* which at any given time can be either positive (optimistic) or negative (pessimistic). It's not necessary for expectations to be soundly conceived. Often they are not. Furthermore, it's not

"*I recommend a planned program, Mrs. Sneedby, designed to reach
specific investment goals in a few years . . . like breaking even!*"

Reprinted by permission: Publishers-Hall Syndicate.

necessary for them to be fulfilled. There are some disappointments, of course.

Keep in mind that for every buyer there is a seller, and it is obvious that both are not motivated by the same expectation. Why? Each might have identical information about a company and its stock, but interpret the information differently. Or they might have different information at the outset. It is also possible that their personal circumstances are very different.

Regardless of the reason, one has decided to buy and the other to sell. When there are more buy decisions than sell decisions in the market at a given time, stock prices will rise, and vice versa.

It is not possible for us to examine, even very briefly, the multitude of determinants which can shape expectations about stocks and in turn affect stock prices. They range all the way from unfounded rumors to carefully reasoned conclusions derived from painstaking analysis.

Let's consider some of the ones which are examined by security analysts and rating agencies.

Standard & Poor's common stock ratings, for example, are derived from a scoring system based upon earnings and dividend records. Emphasis is placed upon *stability* and *growth*. Out of the formula all common stocks are graded and grouped into seven classes:

A+	Highest	B	Below average
A	High	B−	Low
A−	Above average	C	Lowest
B+	Average		

Standard & Poor's Corporation warns that the ratings are not to be regarded as recommendations to buy or sell a security. "They must not be used as a substitute for market recommendations; a high graded stock may at times be so over priced as to justify its sale, while a low score stock may be attractively priced for purchase. Rankings based upon earnings and dividend record are no substitute for analysis. Nor are they quality ratings in the complete sense of the term. They cannot take into account potential effects of management changes, internal company policies not yet fully reflected in the earnings and dividends record, public relations standing, recent competitive shifts, and a host of other factors that may be relevant to investment status."

Despite the warning, most people who buy common stocks are influenced by ratings; and, like bonds, high-rated stocks generally sell at prices above those of lower ratings.

Investors also tend to look with favor upon the common stock of a company which:

1. Has a history of good performance: has grown steadily, has earned well, and has a long unbroken dividend record.
2. Is in a strong financial position.
3. Is known to have capable management.
4. Is research and development oriented.
5. Can boast that its common stock is held by a large number of institutional investors.

Speculators, on the other hand, because of their primary objective of capital gains, tend to look favorably upon stocks of a company which:

1. Is relatively new, perhaps even its industry is new.
2. Has a certain amount of glamour about it, such as was true of uranium companies in the mid-1950s.
3. Has imaginative and venturesome management.
4. Has patents on promising products.

However, more is involved in the selection of common stocks than the identification of suitable companies, as essential as that is. An investor must decide whether the stocks are worth the prices at which they are selling.

Suppose Corporation M is recognized as well-managed, financially strong, a leader in its industry, and otherwise an outstanding company. It has consistently earned on its capital considerably more than the industry average. It has paid dividends every year of its existence, and in the past ten years dividends have averaged 65 percent of earnings. The company's public image is good. Many financial counselors have the company's common stock on their recommended buy lists.

Company M's common stock is selling at 78. Earnings for the last twelve months were $3 a share. The dividend is $2, or $.50 quarterly.

Should an investor buy at 78? At that price the stock is selling at 26 times earnings, or a price-earnings (PE) ratio of 26. The dividend yield is only 2.56 percent.

Clearly "the market" thinks highly of this stock for the price to be 78. In fact, the stock is regarded as a growth stock, or one likely to experience exceptional price appreciation over a period of years because much is expected of the company's future performance. But, there is no assurance or guarantee that this will happen. Therefore, those who pay 78 for this stock are actually speculating on what will occur. Yet, the stock is investment quality.

If we assume that the long-run yield on an investment quality stock should be 6 percent, then the dividend on this stock will have to reach $4.68 a year to justify a price of 78. If the company adheres to the policy of paying dividends equal to 65 percent of earnings, then earnings will have to be $7.20, or a PE ratio of about 11.

So many factors are involved in whether to buy at 78 that we cannot discuss them all. Suffice it to say that an investor should not buy:

1. If yield is of prime and immediate importance; because an investor can do better elsewhere, even with a commercial bank savings account.
2. If he has a policy of never buying a stock whose PE ratio is more than, say, 12. Some investors do set a certain PE ratio beyond which they will not buy.
3. If he is convinced that the market is paying too much for the growth feature.

Essentially both investors and speculators try to anticipate price changes in the market, but the former do so more for good yields on safe investments and the latter more for capital gain with less emphasis on safety.

Both realize that stock price changes may be the result of factors relating to respective companies and/or the result of conditions that exist in the stock market as a whole. Obviously the advantage belongs to the one who can forecast these factors and the magnitude of their market effect. Few individuals are qualified to do this. Even the most expert professional forecasters are not always correct, most particularly in their predictions of market movements, because market swings are more difficult of all to predict.

Stock Market Behavior

We return to the role of expectation. Expectation is often arrived at by purely subjective means, and at times it is stimulated by a good dose of imagination. When expectation is combined with a booster shot of imagination, there is no telling what price a speculator would be willing to pay; and, if enough people do likewise, the price of a stock might go into the stratosphere—say, to as much as 100 times earnings or more, as some electronics stocks did a few years ago. The so-called glamour stocks (those that cast a spell over people) fall in this category. There is a tendency to overprice not only these, but all stocks at times; because people are inclined to swing to extremes in expectation. Part of the explanation of every major drop in the stock market is that prices have been carried too high and ultimately are bound to react downward because expectation is not a constant thing; rather it is a changeable thing conceived by people whose patience is not durable.

The stock market is an imponderable phenomenon. What it does is a composite of the expectations of millions of people (the crowd). Its movements are fickle, indeed; fickle because moods of the crowd are fickle. On occasions the market seems to defy flauntingly all the time-tested basic principles of economics and to say: "There are no rules. I am a game of pure chance."

Sometimes during prolonged periods it swings to great extremes, severs itself from the world of economic reality, and appears to go into an orbit all of its own. It is then generally that speculative forces are dominant, speculative forces propelled by widespread optimistic expectations—not always related to anticipated earnings and dividends but often to the notion that stock prices will keep on going up willy-nilly, compulsorily! The crowd is then looking through rose-colored glasses happily. At that moment, the market is booming; it is a major bull market.[6] In essence, it resembles the Florida land boom of the 1920s or the speculative "tulip mania" in Holland several centuries ago when speculators paid thousands of guilders for a single bulb, nobody buying to keep at these prices, but to sell to someone else for still more.

But prices do not continue to go up and up forever. Something happens. Maybe reason finally subdues emotion, or maybe emotion itself swings 180 degrees around, and optimistic expectations give way to pessimistic expectations. The future that looked bright yesterday looks not so bright today and darker tomorrow. The crowd begins to peer through smoky glasses sadly. And, just as the market on occasions swings to extremes on the up side, so it can swing to extremes on the down side (a bear market), without any more rhyme or reason in the latter direction than in the former. Certainly there can be a basic reason or reasons for a rise or a decline, but the great heights or the great depths seem irrational for sure.

Sometimes erroneous generalizations express themselves forcefully in the stock market. One of these, for example, is the idea that common stocks are a good hedge against inflation at almost any prices. It is true that common stocks are considered, as a class, to be better protection against inflation in the long run than are creditors' claims such as bonds, notes, and similar obligations payable in a fixed amount of dollars. However, it is not correct to deduce from this that common stocks are perfect inflation hedges or that every common stock is as good an inflation hedge as every other common stock.

Some common stocks are much better hedges than others; and there are some that might turn out to be no better inflation protection than some bonds,

---

[6]In stock market parlance a *bull* is an individual who believes that prices of stocks are going up. His attitude toward the market is that of an optimist. When stock prices have gone up rather impressively over a prolonged period of time, we say that we are in a *bull market.*

The opposite of a bull is called a *bear* who thinks stock prices are going down. His attitude is pessimistic. A *bear market* refers to a prolonged decline in stock prices.

The terms "bull" and "bear" supposedly came from the different ways the two animals handle their adversaries. A bull uses his horns to toss his adversary up, whereas a bear throws his adversary down.

if as good. This latter point is based on the fact that stocks are in a residual position as sharer of corporate results; whereas bonds are in a preferred, although fixed, position, and if the corporation fares badly even in a period of inflation (and some always do), stockholders likely would lose.

In other words, an investor cannot close his eyes and take any stock and regard it as protection against inflation, any more than he can expect any and every stock to increase in value, inflation or no inflation.

For centuries people who distrust the future value of money (paper money) have, as a rule, sought to hedge. When and where the laws permit, precious metals (gold, silver, platinum) have been the most popular things to own. They have universal value, have large value in small bulk (hence, are easily moved and easily hidden), and hold their real value relatively well. Diamonds and other precious stones likewise have served as stores of value against depreciating currency, especially for those who can judge quality of such stones. Rare works of art afford excellent inflation hedges because of their scarcity; but a collector must know what he is doing. Real estate (land improved and unimproved), is perhaps the most popular inflation hedge in this country, but like common stocks, it cannot be bought blindly, and a buyer has to pay taxes on it, taxes that tend to rise with inflation.

Some astute investors and speculators buy stocks in companies that have large holdings of gas, oil, minerals, and timber lands, and these do tend to be good protection against long-run inflation as do several chemical companies. But if an investor looks carefully, he will find that the best inflation hedges among these stocks already sell at relatively high current price earnings ratios with low yields, indicating the willingness of buyers to pay something for what seems good inflation protection. Others aware of the age-old fact that there are very few things in life that are absolutely certain—even about the future course of inflation—watch convertibles. These hybrids have considerable attraction to the more cautious investor, and they may afford some protection against inflation in the long run.

Using Professional Assistance

There is so much to know and so much information to collect, assimilate, and analyze in order to get the best results from an investment program that some people prefer to seek professional help rather than spend the time and effort necessary to select and supervise a securities portfolio themselves.

Investors with above-average means often use *investment counselors*. The latter will recommend securities they think are best suited to the investment objectives and circumstances of their respective clients, will maintain constant watch over market behavior of those securities, and will advise changes when they think changes will strengthen a client's portfolio.

Investment counselors range from individuals to large firms with extensive libraries and research departments well staffed with capable security analysts.

Services of investment counselors are generally not available to small investors because fees charged are based upon asset holdings managed for each client, and counselors, as a rule, will not accept a client with less than $50,000 in assets to be managed.

Commercial banks with trust departments are another source of professional securities management. This service is available either under a *living trust agreement* or a *simple management agreement*.

In the case of a living trust, the trustor or creator of the trust transfers funds and/or securities to a bank which, acting as trustee, manages the account for the benefit of the trustor himself or some other designated beneficiary.

Under a simple management agreement, the customer authorizes the bank to act as agent to handle his securities. This service includes physical custody of the securities, collecting dividends and interest, and keeping records. Periodically, the bank will submit an investment review and a statement of income to the customer. The bank supervises the portfolio and, depending upon terms of the agreement, may have complete management authority—that is, power to buy and sell securities. Usually, however, the bank will make recommendations and will not act without the customer's approval.

In recent years, banks have set up *common* or *commingled trust funds* which permit common investment of funds of a number of small trusts, allowing greater asset diversification as well as certain economies of handling.

As a rule, bank trust departments employ highly trained, capable personnel, including security analysts, investment officers, tax experts, accountants, and lawyers—all of which means that a customer may expect a high standard of performance from a bank. Furthermore, trust activities are strictly regulated by law, and a bank can be held legally liable for any violation of its fiduciary powers.

Investment Companies

Many people have been attracted to *investment companies* in recent years, more especially to *mutual funds* whose popularity has grown substantially since World War II.

An investment company, sometimes referred to as an investment trust, is a corporation that sells its shares and invests the proceeds in securities of various other corporations not only for income but for capital gains from the underlying securities.

There are two types of investment companies: *closed-end* and *open-end*. The closed-end type is very similar to ordinary corporations. It has a fixed amount of capital derived from a limited authorized stock issue which it sells to the public. It also may sell its bonds and otherwise borrow, if it chooses. Its stock and bonds are traded on the market like the securities of other companies.

Open-end investment companies are generally identified as *mutual funds*. The number of shares they can sell is not limited, since their capitalization is not legally fixed. They can sell whatever number of shares investors are willing to buy.

Perhaps the most significant difference from an investor's point of view is in the manner in which shares in the two types are bought and sold. If a person invests in a closed-end company, he must buy its stock on the market from someone who wants to sell, just as he would if he were buying shares in General Motors, paying the market price plus brokerage commissions. He must sell closed-end shares in the same manner. Closed-end investment companies do not redeem their shares. On the other hand, when an investor buys shares in a mutual fund, he must buy them from the company itself at a price determined by the per share market value of the underlying securities owned by the fund. When a person sells shares in a mutual fund, he must sell them to the fund itself at a price determined in the same manner.

Some mutual funds have sales organizations of their own and also will pay commissions to brokerage firms, when orders come through the latter. Selling costs which are added to the asset value of a mutual fund share are called *loading costs*. Mutual funds which operate this way are known as *load funds*.

Fewer in number, but increasing, are *no-load mutual funds* which sell their shares directly to the public at asset value solely and will redeem at the same price. They do not have sales organizations and do not pay commissions to brokers, hence there is no loading.

Because they avoid having to pay loading costs, many investors prefer to buy shares in no-load mutual funds. However, since the latter do not sell their shares aggressively, an investor must seek them out and make direct contact in order to buy. Similarly, when he sells, he must go directly to the issuing company.

Prices of shares of mutual funds (both load and no-load) are quoted daily in the Wall Street Journal and in some metropolitan newspapers. For example, on a given day the shares of Dreyfus Fund, a load fund, were quoted at 11.36 bid, 12.45 ask, meaning that to buy into the fund an investor would have to pay $12.45 a share, and anyone redeeming his shares would receive $11.36. The difference between bid and ask prices (the load) is $1.09 in this instance, or 8.75 percent of ask price.[7]

On the same day, shares of The Johnston Mutual Fund, Inc., a no-load fund, were quoted at 25.58 bid, 25.58 ask, representing net asset value only. It can be determined from price quotations which funds are no-load, because bid and ask prices are always the same.

There are over 800 investment companies in the United States, all but about fifty of which are open-end or mutual funds. The latter offer a wide range of objectives and risks tailored to the economic circumstances and personalities

---

[7] A few mutual funds charge a small redemption fee which is subtracted from per share asset value to give the bid price.

of different investors and speculators. In fact, an individual has such a large choice among investment companies that the task of selection requires almost as much diligence and care as he would need to build his own portfolio.

Anyone who contemplates buying investment company shares must find a fund (1) whose objective is to his liking, (2) which will fit his needs, and (3) which has demonstrated by past results that it is well-managed.

Types of Mutual Funds

Based upon their respective objectives or purposes, mutual funds may be classified as follows:

1. *Balanced funds,* those generally regarded as the most conservative type, since their objective is to minimize investment risk and at the same time provide a reasonable income and an opportunity for capital gain. The term "balanced" comes from their policy of industrial diversification and of holding bonds and preferred stocks as well as common stocks.
2. *Capital gain funds,* those generally regarded as the most speculative because their policy is to buy securities primarily for capital gain, or increase in market value, and only incidentally for income.
3. *Growth funds,* those that may be regarded as less speculative than capital gains funds and yet less conservative than balanced funds. They seek to acquire securities of companies whose long-term growth is promising and who at the same time pay dividends.
4. *Income funds,* those whose objective is to acquire securities with liberal current yield, whether stocks or bonds.
5. *Specialized stock funds,* those which confine their portfolio holdings to a particular industrial category—for example, public utility stocks or insurance company stocks.

An excellent source of information about various mutual funds is *Investment Companies,* a large compendium published annually by Wiesenberger Services, Inc.

The Mutual Fund Concept

Mutual funds operate on the premise that professional money managers handling a large sum of funds can do better with a diversified group of securities than most individuals can do with a much smaller amount of money. This idea has had great appeal to small investors who have little or no skill with which to build a securities investment program, and often do not have the inclination to do so.

Most mutual funds also have catered to the small investor by offering him different kinds of accounts and savings plans to fit his convenience. Not only may an investor buy shares at any time by paying in a lump sum of money;

but, if he chooses, he may open an *accumulation account* by signing a contract to make regular periodic (usually monthly) investments for a certain number of years. He may also request the fund to use his dividends and other distributions to buy additional shares.

For investors who have accumulated $10,000 or more, most mutual funds have what is known as a *withdrawal account* under which periodic withdrawals are made. The withdrawal account usually appeals to investors who have reached retirement and want to start using savings they have accumulated during their working years.

Some mutual funds provide declining balance term life insurance with investment plans. Should an investor die before his entire plan is paid up, the insurance will complete his program. Let's say an investor contracts with a mutual fund for a fifteen-year, $50.00 a month investment program along with a declining balance form of life insurance. His investment objective is 180 monthly payments of $50.00 each which he plans to make if he lives. Suppose he dies after he has made four payments totaling $200. The remaining 176 payments or $8,800 will be paid immediately from the insurance. If he should die after making, say, 179 monthly payments, the insurance will make the remaining payment of $50. But, if he completes the 180 monthly investment contract, the insurance expires.

Some eager mutual fund salesmen have been known to advise prospects to cancel lifetime insurance and use the cash surrender value along with future premiums to buy an investment contract with a declining balance term insurance policy. Although the use of insurance along with an investment contract is sensible, no one should disturb his permanent life insurance program, as we have made clear in Chapter 16.

Most mutual funds employ under contract an investment management company on a fee basis, usually one-half of one percent of assets up to a certain sum, with a reduced rate thereafter. Often there is an interlocking of directors and officers of the fund and of the management company.

A fund's securities and cash are placed with a bank or trust company which acts as custodian. It is the custodian's responsibility to receive dividends, interest, and all other income of the fund and make all disbursements, all of which requires considerable record keeping.

Investment companies are relieved of federal income taxes under Sub-Chapter M of the Internal Revenue Code, provided they file an income tax return as a regulated investment company showing that they have distributed as taxable dividends to shareholders not less than 90 percent of net income for the taxable year.

Investment companies are subject to both state and federal regulation, but the most comprehensive regulation is under the Federal Investment Company Act of 1940 (administered by the Securities and Exchange Commission). All investment companies subject to the act must register with SEC. The act's primary objective is to protect investors, not against the results of poor management, but against possible abuses of management.

Here are some of the safeguards:

1. Sound and uniform accounting records must be kept.
2. Investors must be provided with complete and accurate information about the company's policies, operations and management.
3. No major changes in organization can be made without the consent of shareholders.
4. Adequate reserves must be maintained for the conduct of business.
5. A limit is set on the amount of money a mutual fund can borrow.
6. There must be a certain number of outsiders on the board of directors who are not connected with management.

Mutual funds of the load type have been criticized for their relatively high acquisition costs or loading fees. Whereas closed-end investment company shares are bought and sold in the open market with buyer and seller paying standard brokerage commissions, the shares of mutual funds are bought at asset value plus loading that typically ranges from 7 to 9 percent. However, when it is observed that most mutual funds redeem their shares without charging a fee, the cost of getting in and out of mutual funds does not seem to be unreasonable after all, unless the investor happens to contract for what is known as a front end load plan. The latter is sold somewhat like a life insurance contract where a large percentage of early premiums goes to the salesman.

Suppose Miss Evans, a schoolteacher, contracts for a ten-year investment plan, agreeing to buy $50 worth of shares each month. If she fulfills her contract, the loading fees may average not over 8.5 percent of the $6,000 she has paid in, or $510; but a large part of this, perhaps as much as a half, may have been charged against or loaded on to the first twelve payments. If Miss Evans, for some reason, should be obliged to give up her investment plan after two years, she would discover that the loading cost of the shares credited to her may have amounted to as much as 30, 40, or even 50 percent of what she paid in.

The whole matter of acquisition costs is under the scrutiny of the Securities and Exchange Commission. The outcome very probably will be changes favorable to the mutual fund buyer.

People who contemplate purchase of mutual funds should realize that the relatively high fees charged make such an investment questionable unless the buyer is reasonably sure he can stay over a long period. In other words, we do not recommend mutual funds as short-term investments.

Discussion Questions

1. Prior to 1911, there were no laws protecting the public from fraudulently offered securities. In 1911, forty-nine states sought to regulate this market by introducing the *blue sky laws*. Briefly describe these laws.
2. Discuss the scope of federal regulation brought about with the passing of the Securities Act of 1933.

3. What is the relationship between bond prices and the rate of interest of money? Why does this relationship occur?

4. Monetary inflation has been common in the United States for a third of a century. How does inflation affect stock and bond holders? Describe some of the "inflation hedge" investments.

5. Differentiate between common stock and preferred stocks.

6. "Stock market behavior is a highly complex game, but with enough research, experience, and analysis, it can be predicted accurately." Discuss the merit of the above statement.

We all live under the same sky, but we
don't all have the same horizon.

[*Konrad Adenauer*]

22

Investing in
Real Estate

Unique Nature
of Land

From our study of principles of economics, we have observed that production of goods and services comes from combining scarce resources, referred to as the *factors of production*. They are land, labor, capital, and management. The price of any one unit of these resources at any one time is based on its scarcity relative to the current demand. Among the four categories, land is unique in that the supply cannot be increased, regardless of the demand. This is not true

502

of labor, capital, or management.[1] Other unique characteristics of land include its heterogeneity (no two pieces are exactly alike), fixity of location (as compared to the mobility of the other factors), and (3) indestructibility.

Individual land sites vary greatly in value. A dramatic illustration of this comes from headlines of two separate stories from the same issue of a recent newspaper:[2]

BRAZILIAN LAND: 32¢ PER ACRE

DOWNTOWN TOKYO SITE SELLS
FOR $1090 A SQUARE FOOT

The contrast is more obvious when we realize that at the quoted Tokyo rate, an acre of land would cost $47,480,000 (43,560 square feet per acre).

In addition to the factors just noted there are others which, interacting, impose a value on each parcel of land at any one time. Among them are productivity, location, technology, laws, lack of an organized market, individual and group psychology, desires and leadership of influential individuals, and the state of local, national, and world political economies. Ghost towns which dot every section of our country are evidence of varying influences. Similarly, the changing values of certain urban properties as their classifications moved from raw land to speculative residential development, to blighted areas, to commercial sites, to freeway right-of-way, etc., illustrate the dynamic nature of real estate values.

Growth of
Land Values

However much individual land sites have varied in value, there has been a constant long-range growth of total land values. Exhibit 22–1 illustrates this. These values, of necessity, have to be rough estimates because of the inherent problems of real estate valuation, including separating land values from structures built on land. The same sources estimated the value of structures in 1968 to be over one and a half trillion dollars, almost three times the 1952 total.

As we know, land prices increase from inflation and from a rising demand. It is interesting to note the results of the competition for land use in the various sectors of our economy. Exhibit 22–2 shows that households commanded the greatest share, 34.6 percent; agriculture the next largest, 22.5 percent; with federal, state, and local governments owning 19.8 percent, about the same as industry. Land investors and speculators are involved in all the sectors except public lands.

---

[1] The *productivity* of land can be increased by such acts as: improving its location through transportation facilities, fertilizing farm land; and reclaiming land areas from inundation through levees, drainage and the like; however, the same can be said of the other factors.
[2] *Dallas Times Herald,* December 17, 1972.

Exhibit 22–1* Value of Land in U.S., 1900 to 1968 (in billions of dollars; excludes Alaska and Hawaii; data are approximate only.)

	Private				
Year	Farm	Nonfarm	Total private	Public	Total
1900	$ 16.0	$ 10.9	$ 26.9	$ 4.0	$ 30.9
1910	31.4	16.3	47.7	6.8	54.5
1920	54.0	36.9	90.9	12.5	103.9
1930	34.6	54.2	88.8	15.2	104.0
1940	26.9	47.3	74.2	18.0	92.2
1950	70.3	83.9	154.2	35.5	189.7
1960	92.9	239.8	322.7	79.0	411.7
1968	152.6	418.6	571.2	144.2	715.4

*Compiled from national wealth tables, *United States Statistical Abstracts*. Structures not included. Excludes subsoil assets. This includes data from: U.S. Congress, *Institutional Investor Study Report of the Securities and Exchange Commission, Supplementary Volume I*, House Documents 92–64, Part 6, March 10, 1971.

Exhibit 22–2* Percentage Distribution of Land Value Among Sectors, United States, 1952, 1960 and 1968

Sector	1952	1960	1968
All sectors	100.0	100.0	100.0
Nonfarm households	29.2	35.4	34.6
Institutions	3.1	3.5	3.9
Unincorporated business	5.4	4.3	4.0
Agriculture	34.3	24.2	22.5
Nonfarm corporations	10.8	13.8	15.1
State and local governments	11.8	14.4	15.2
Federal government	5.4	4.4	4.6

*U.S. Congress: *Institutional Investor Study Report of the Securities and Exchange Commission, Supplementary, Volume I*, House Documents 92–64, March 10, 1971, Table II–2, p. 321.

Reasons for Growth in Land Values

Reasons for this growth in land values are many. With the supply of land a fixed quantity, any factor having the effect of increasing the demand will increase land prices. The most significant such factors can be categorized under eight headings:

1. Personal satisfaction from land ownership.
2. Population growth.

3. Increased income and wealth of the nation, accompanied by a broader distribution among household units.

4. Development of a political economy embracing inflation as necessary and even desirable within limits.

5. An accompanying heightened demand for inflationary hedge type investments.

6. Relatively high income potential.

7. Ideal for leverage operations.

8. A federal tax system which is advantageous to real estate investments.

Personal Satisfaction from Land Ownership

There are very real ego and self-fulfillment aspects to the ownership of land. We can wonder how deep-rooted in our ancestral past is the desire—even the need—to be able to say, "This land is mine." Where we might hesitate to display our stocks, bonds, and savings account passbooks, our land is there for all to see. Other basic human need satisfactions resulting from land ownership are the needs for economic security, for play and recreation, for controlling material objects, and for providing pleasure for others.

An aspect of all these personal factors is that the investor can do things himself in a direct way that can improve and increase the value of his property. This is not so much the case with alternative investments. Such activities range from personal labor on improvements to working to influence actions of others (on zoning matters, rural water systems, farm-to-market roads, etc.). These personal physical activities can be thought of as providing additional employment to the investor and his family. In comparing real estate investment to alternatives, even if all other factors were equal, these personal aspects would make the difference in the choice of many investors.

Population Growth

From the first census in 1790, it took until 1915, 125 years later, to reach the first 100 million of population. The second 100 million was reached in 1967, only fifty-two years later. Demographers have less confidence in their projections now, but some feel the third 100 million will be reached soon after the turn of the century.

Increased and Broader Based Wealth

Reference to the data in Chapter 7 on the growth of our gross national product and the relative affluence of most of our population further explains the tremendous growth in land values. This affluence plus the urbanization of the population not only has increased urban land values but has created an unprecedented demand by city dwellers for rural properties for recreation and investment purposes. New freeways have brought rural sites "closer" to the cities. The result of all this has been to raise prices on land within a hundred miles or so of urban areas to a level several times greater than its productivity. Ironically, the poorer farmland often brings the higher price, because it is scenic, with its wooded areas, creeks, and pastures.

Continued Inflation as a Fact of Life

In Chapter 2, we noted the effect of inflation on the family unit. Not only is the present purchasing power of income reduced, but savings in the form of monetary units are eroded. In two decades, 1950 to 1970, a savings account of $100 was reduced to approximately $50 in terms of its 1950 purchasing power.[3] Exhibit 22–3 reflects the inflationary character of our economy thus far in this century, especially since the advent of the "new economics" in mid-century. Of special note is that not since 1955 has the cost-of-living decreased in any *one* year.

Demand for "Inflation-Hedge" Investments

What do we mean by "inflation-hedge" investments? Let's start by saying what they are not. Any contract calling for repayment at a later date in a *stated amount of fixed dollars* would be classified as a "deflation hedge." This is so because, as the purchasing power of the dollar becomes *greater* as a result of deflation, more valuable dollars would be paid back. Examples of such contracts are savings accounts, bonds, life insurance, and "fixed dollar" annuities.[4] Property, or claims on property, *the value of which will be determined by market forces at the time of disposition,* can properly be called inflation hedges. Three major categories of inflation hedges are (1) common stocks (and certain other securities), (2) real estate, and (3) art objects (including paintings, pictures, sculpture, china and glass, antiques, rare books, coins and stamps).

How have these three categories "fared" as inflation hedges? It is a little unrealistic to compare purchasing power of a unit of anything over any ex-

---

[3]We should keep in mind, however, the savings account produced $100 in income, assuming 5 percent annual interest. Also, if that income had been left at compound interest, its balance in 1970 would have been $265.33, roughly $130 in 1950 dollars. In this vein, the following quote from Forbes magazine is appropriate: "One last myth about Manhattan real estate deserves to be exploded. Every school kid knows that crafty Peter Minuit put one over on the Manhattoes Indians in 1626 by buying their island for $24 worth of doodads. But, Salomon Bros.' Sidney Homer, author of *The History of Interest Rates,* provides figures that show that the Indians got the best of the deal. Had they taken a boat to Holland, invested the $24 in Dutch securities returning 6% per year and kept the money invested at 6%, they would now have $13 billion. With that sum, they could buy back all the land on the island, and still have $4 billion left for trinkets. Or the Indians could keep the money invested at 6%, so it could continue yielding $780 million a year —without the risk of doing business amid urban decay." (From "Who Owns New York," *Forbes Magazine,* June 1, 1971, p. 32.) One wonders how many billions there would be had all the profits and rents resulting from Manhattan Island operations during that period been accumulated at 6% compound interest. Reprinted by permission of *Forbes* Magazine.

[4]Anyone selling life insurance and bonds during the 1930s used the "deflation-hedge" characteristic as a prime selling point. Since then, the phrase has gradually been dropped from our vocabulary. For instance, in how many finance textbooks—and how often—do we encounter the phrase?

Exhibit 22–3   Seven Decades of Inflation

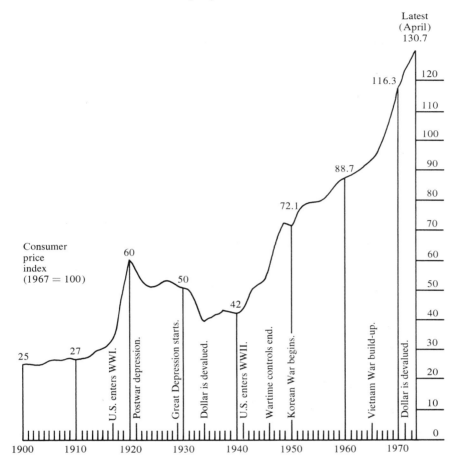

In the last 73 years: Consumer prices—the cost of living—more than quintupled, going higher in 54 of those years, or about 3 of every 4. Prices, on the average, stayed the same in only 6 years, and went down in only 13. Not since 1955—nearly two decades ago—has the cost of living declined.

Source: U.S. Dept. of Labor. Reprinted from 'U.S. News & World Report.' Copyright 1973. U.S. News & World Report, Inc. June 4, 1973.

tended period in this century. We need think only of how different were the "things" purchased by individuals in 1900, 1925, and 1950 from today's purchases. Any statistical attempt to do so is a valiant effort, at best, but can still serve some purpose. A "Dow-Jones" dollar (a theoretical unit of purchase of Dow-Jones stocks, adjusted for inflation) in 1971 is thought to be worth over three times such a 1900 dollar. It would be unrealistic to try to compute a weighted "land dollar" for such a period of time, but it is obvious the general level of land values has more than kept pace with inflation. Exhibit 22–1 relates to that conclusion.

A comparison of the performance of inflation-hedge investments since World War II might be significant as an indication of how they will fare in the so-called "new era" political economy. Between 1950 and 1969, land values in the United States are estimated to have increased about four times (400 percent). Exhibit 22–4 and 22–5 give special situation data which indicate both land and art objects have fared better than stocks in recent decades.

Exhibit 22–4   How Art and Rare Objects Have Outpaced Stocks

	Number of times that the price Index multiplied 1950 through 1969	*Percentage increase 1970 to present*
D. J. Industrial Index	3	*18%*
Old master prints	37	40% to 60%
Modern pictures	29	50% to 70%
Chinese porcelain	24½	30% to 50%
Old books	13	20% to 40%
Modern books	9	30% to 50%
Old master drawings	22	40% to 60%
Impressionist pictures	18	40% to 60%
Old master pictures	7	30% to 50%
English glass	9	25% to 35%
French furniture	5	20% to 40%
English porcelain	4	20% to 30%
English pictures	8½	50% to 70%
English silver	10½	(down 30% to 50%)

Average price increases for art, porcelain, books, glass, furniture and silver obtained from The London Times-Sotheby Index, which was discontinued after 1969.

Estimates for 1970 to the present for art and rare objects were obtained from a study of Parke Bernel auction records.

Source: Lee Berton, "Arts As An Investment Outpaces Stocks," *Financial World,* May 23, 1973, p. 22.

A strong case can be made for art objects as inflation hedges. Indeed, art has value characteristics similar to land in terms of heterogeneity and limited supply. We should be mindful, however, that art purchases by the individual investor are fraught with the perils of fraud, unscrupulous sales efforts and ignorance. We should be armed with a high degree of expertise, both personally and from competent advisors, before venturing into this area of investments.

Regarding real estate and securities, we can conclude their performance as inflation-hedge investments has been satisfactory for many investors—especially in the past quarter-century. An attempt to rate one over the other is unwarranted. It is much like comparing apples and oranges. Even the experts disagree as to how they will fare in the political and economic climates of the future.

Exhibit 22–5   Real Estate vs. the Dow

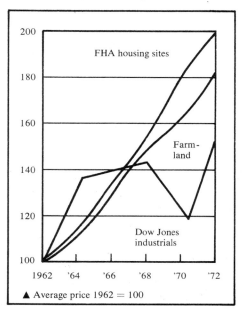

Data: Dow Jones, U.S. Dept. of Agriculture, Federal Housing Admin.
Source: *Business Week:* June 9, 1973, p. 96.

Relatively High Income Potential

It is not reasonable to hope for very high interest rates on savings accounts or bonds. The same tends to be true of dividends from investment-type stocks and from investment companies. Real estate, on the other hand, has the potential for relatively high rental income. There is no assurance of this on any particular piece of property, but it is not unusual to hear of properties netting 8 percent to 12 percent and even more. When we consider "leverage," the income potential gets really exciting.

Ideal For Leverage Operations

Obtaining title to an investment by borrowing part of the purchase price is known as *leverage.* Real estate is especially adaptable for leverage operations. Compare it with stocks. The great depression of the 1930s was heralded by the crash of the stock market in 1929, when thousands who had purchased stocks on the *margin* (a type of leverage) were wiped out. An inopportune call from a banker for more collateral for a loan secured by stocks or from a brokerage firm for more margin can cause a total loss of funds invested. The banker cannot do that on a real estate loan. The mortgagor need only meet the principal and interest payments to retain title to the property.

Let us study an example. Investor Dr. P. Rowe Fessor purchases a $100,000 apartment house by putting up $20,000 cash, and getting a twenty-year mortgage for $80,000 at 7 percent interest. The net annual rental income, after depreciation and paying all bills, insurance, taxes, and maintenance costs, is $10,000. The mortgage payments are $620.40 monthly, amounting to $7,442.88 each year.

Percent Return on Cost of Apartment House
$$\frac{\text{Net rent of } \$10,000}{\text{Cost of } \$100,000} = 10\% \text{ annual return on } Cost$$

Percent Return on Actual Investment:
$$\frac{\text{Net rent of } \$10,000}{\text{Investment of } \$20,000} = 50\% \text{ gross annual return on } Cash \ invested$$

But Dr. Fessor had to make $7,442.88 mortgage payments. $10,000 net rent less $7,442.88 leaves $2,557.12 cash return for the year.

Percent Net Cash Return on Investment
$$\frac{\text{Net cash received of } \$2,557.12}{\text{Investment of } \$20,000} = 12.77 + \% \text{ net annual return on } Cash \ invested$$

This calculation is appropriate in comparing likely annual return on this investment as opposed to alternatives.

Dr. Fessor's investment becomes even more attractive when we consider certain tax advantages. These tax advantages, while largely available on other types of investments, are particularly adaptable and advantageous on real estate investments.

Tax Advantages

There are certain federal income tax advantages which accrue to real estate because it meets the test of being classified as a "capital asset." There are several requirements but, essentially, to qualify as a capital asset a piece of property must not be an item to be consumed or property held for resale in pursuit of the regular operation of one's business.

Deductible Interest Payments. Interest payments are deductible from gross income. Thus, if Dr. Fessor is in a 25 percent income tax bracket and if $4,800 of the $7,442.88 mortgage payment is interest, there could be a $1,200 income tax saving. If thought of as an interest return on the $20,000 investment, it would be an additional 6 percent. Obviously, the higher the tax bracket, the greater is the tax saving potential.

Deductible Depreciation. Depreciation of improvements (all the property value except the land itself) is a deductible expense. If Dr. Fessor's apartments were depreciated over thirty years on a *straight line* basis[5] and if the apartments were

---

[5]See Chapter 5.

valued at $90,000 (making the land value $10,000), he would have a $3,000 ($90,000 cost/30) years depreciation deduction each year. Again, this could plausibly be considered an additional 3.75 percent interest return ($3,000 × 25%/$20,000). For most properties, income tax laws permit depreciation schedules which allow greater depreciation amounts in early years, with resulting lesser amounts as the property gets older.[6] Totaling the 12.77 percent net cash return plus the return in the form of income tax savings from interest payments (6 percent) and depreciation (3.75 percent), we get a 22.52 percent "cash flow" return on the $20,000 investment.

Deductible Property Taxes and Maintenance Expenses. Property taxes and maintenance expense including labor and materials are deductible. As is the case with interest payments and depreciation, these costs are deducted by the investor in determining his net earnings on his investment but actually are sources of additional returns in the form of income tax savings. The amount of these savings would be added to the "cash flow" total.

Receiving Cash from Appreciation in Value without Paying Tax on the Gain. Let's suppose the market value of Dr. Fessor's apartments later increased to $150,000. His original $80,000 loan has been reduced by that time to $60,000. He negotiates a new 80 percent mortgage of $120,000 which gives him net cash of $60,000. This represents a $20,000 return of investment (payments on principal from mortgage payments) and $40,000 income from appreciation in value. No income tax is paid at the time or will be paid until the property is no longer owned by Dr. Fessor. Thus, the gain is "tax sheltered." Through estate conservation measures (see Chapter 23), the tax might be lessened or even avoided in later years.

Substantial Long-term Capital Gains Savings. It takes only a quick glance at the federal income tax schedule to recognize the importance of the long-term capital gains tax provision. This provision applies to gains (and losses) on the sale of any capital assets. It is especially advantageous on real estate transactions. A distinction is made between "short-term" and "long-term" capital gains. Gains made by an individual investor who sells property *within* six months after acquiring it are taxed as ordinary income. If sold after six months, only one-half the gain is reported.

Thus, if Dr. Fessor had a taxable income from his teaching of $20,000 and sold his apartments for a $30,000 net gain two months after buying them, the gain would have been taxed as ordinary income (a short-term capital gain). Had he waited until after six months to sell, *only one-half* of the $30,000 net gain would be reported as income (a long-term capital gain). Following is a calculation of Dr. Fessor's income tax on the $30,000 gain both as short-term and long-term capital gains.

---

[6]See Chapter 5.

		Amount of tax	
		As a short-term	As a long-term
	Tax rate	capital gain	capital gain (one-half
Tax bracket	for each bracket	(full $30,000 taxed)	$30,000 taxed)
$20,000 to 24,000	32%	$ 1,280	$ 1280
24,000 to 28,000	36%	1440	1440
28,000 to 32,000	39%	1560	1560
32,000 to 36,000	42%	1680	1260 (3,000 @ 42%)
36,000 to 40,000	45%	1800	—
40,000 to 44,000	48%	1920	—
44,000 to 52,000	50%	3000 (6,000 @ 50%)	—
Total tax paid on $30,000 gain		$12,680	$5,540

This concession allowing the reporting of only one-half of long-term gains is the heart of the capital gains tax.[7] There are many other regulations and provisions, but reference to only two of them will serve our purposes as regards individual investors.

1. For the individual investor, there is an alternative tax rate of 25 percent on the first $50,000 of net long-term capital gains. In Dr. Fessor's case, he would not have chosen this because his tax was considerably less than $12,500 (25 percent of $50,000).
2. Net losses up to $1,000 on capital asset transactions can be deducted from taxable income. If the net loss is in excess of $1,000 for the tax year, the excess can be carried over as future deductions up to $1,000 a year. One dollar of long-term losses may be used to offset $.50 of ordinary income; thus, a $2,000 long-term capital loss in a year can offset $1,000 of ordinary income that year.

Trading Real Estate for other Real Estate and Postponing Tax on any Gain. Suppose Dr. Fessor trades his apartments, now worth $150,000, for other real estate of the same type which he feels is worth more and will increase in value in the near future. Even though he has received possibly a $200,000 property for his original $100,000 property, he may pay no tax on the gain at the time.[8] When the property eventually is transferred to others, there will be a tax. Again, this eventual tax can be minimized through estate conservation methods. This is another example of a "tax-sheltered" gain from real estate.

---

[7] It is incorrect to think of there being a "capital gains" tax applying to *each* gain or loss. Each tax year, the individual separates all his sales of capital items into either short-term or long-term gains. He may have had gains on some and losses on others. The net gain or loss in each category is reported.

[8] Not all real estate can be exchanged on a "non-taxable" basis. There is a "like-kind" requirement, which means the properties must be of the same character or nature but not necessarily of the same grade or quality.

Postponing or Decreasing Taxes on Real Estate Investment Gains through Installment Sales. If payments to the seller during the year of the sale do not exceed 30 percent of the "selling price," the seller can report the profit from the sale of realty over the period of time it takes to receive full payment of the sale price. The part of the profit reported any year is determined by applying the gross profit *percentage* on the sale to the payments received in that year. In addition to spreading the amount of the profit over a period of years, it—in some instances—can actually reduce the total tax on the total gain. This can result from the seller being in lower tax brackets in subsequent years or from tax schedules being reduced. In the latter case, of course, the reverse could also happen, to the detriment of the seller.

Problems and Disadvantages of Real Estate as an Investment

There are some very distinct disadvantages and problems related to the purchase, ownership, and disposition of real estate. The very same negative factors might be looked on by some as advantages in that their presence creates opportunities for discerning investors.

Heterogeneity

As previously noted, no two pieces of real estate are exactly alike. This means no one can become an expert on the value of any one parcel of land without specifically researching the parcel. It is not the case to the same degree with common stocks, coins, stamps and the like. If an investor becomes convinced XYZ company's common stock is underpriced, he can—within limits—proceed to buy as many identical shares as he likes.

Lack of an Organized Market

The fact of the heterogeneity of land precludes the existence of organized markets such as we have in securities, in commodities and—to a lesser extent—with certain art objects. This creates some problems in real estate investing activities. For one thing, there is the question of determining the value of a parcel. Real estate valuation is a very inexact science. It has been said that qualified appraisers admit they decide on a property's value by inspecting it, and then set about to "prove" this value by one or more of the accepted methodologies (replacement cost, capitalization of income, and/or market comparisons). The lack of a marketplace can cause real estate values to react slower to market forces than other types of investments. Depending on the circumstances, this could be an advantage or a disadvantage to an individual investor.

Another resulting disadvantage is the relatively *low liquidity* of real estate investments. Where a share of stock or a certain coin can be sold in a very short time at a known price, it might take months or years to dispose of a piece of real estate, and the seller might still not be sure that the sale price was right.

Relatively Large Purchase Units

Real estate is not the type of investment a buyer can make anytime he has $200 or so on hand. This one factor keeps many investors out of the land market. This condition has opened the door to questionable land sales promotions. They typically involve high pressure sales efforts pushing barren plots in far-away places by offering terms of a few hundred dollars down and small monthly payments. The development of *real estate investment trusts* (REITs) has opened the door to unit purchases of smaller amounts. The same is true of shares of real estate corporations. These will be discussed later in this chapter.

Vulnerability to Acts of Others

The value of a parcel of real estate can be greatly lessened by acts of others. This possibility ranges from such things as the city opening a trash dump on property next to investment acreage, to successful petitions for unfavorable re-zoning, to by-passing of property by new freeways.

Management Problems

We could put a stock certificate for 500 shares at A T & T in a safe deposit box, then sit back and worry only about future dividends and the value of the stock. With real estate, particularly with improved property, there are management problems. In fact, part of the rent received should be recognized to include a return for management activities performed by the investor. Even where property management specialists are hired to perform most of this function, the owner still has to make decisions regarding their activities and protecting the property value from outside forces. Among the decisions and activities involved in property management are: planning, utilization of space, type and duration of leases, establishing rent levels, attracting and selecting tenants, operations and maintenance, collecting rents, keeping records, conforming to regulatory codes and restrictions, handling taxes, and maintaining proper insurance.

Lest this listing of problems and disadvantages of investing in real estate seem too imposing, we should keep in mind they are merely counterbalances to factors which tend to make realty a good investment, recognizing that other types of investments have their own special problems.

Acquiring and Financing Various Real Estate Ownership Interests

Individual Ownership

Under individual ownership, title and control of the property rests solely with one individual, be it a person or other legal entity. An individual can acquire a piece of land by direct approach to the owner or through a real estate broker.

There are situations where each method is preferable. Ownership of real property is a public record, and it is possible to determine the owner of any particular property at the appropriate local agency, usually the city or county tax collector.

Financing the purchase involves either (1) the seller taking a mortgage for the unpaid balance or (2) the purchaser arranging a mortgage loan from individuals or institutions with funds to lend for such purposes. The former method is easier because the time, effort and expense of obtaining a third-party mortgage are avoided. Whatever method is used (and this would apply to all forms of direct ownership), it is desirable to have a minimum or no *prepayment penalty*. Many mortgages provide for a substantial cash penalty if the mortgage is paid off prior to the end of the mortgage period. Also, if there is the possibility that the buyer will sell off part of the original tract, it is important to have a *release clause*. A release clause in the mortgage provides for releasing parts of the property from the mortgage upon payment of an agreed amount per acre, lot, or other unit. For example, suppose an investor buys a forty-acre tract for $500 an acre, expecting to sell it off later in ten-acre tracts for $1,000 an acre. The mortgage is $15,000. If he immediately sells a ten-acre tract for $10,000, the investor—in the absence of a release clause—would have to pay off the $15,000 mortgage in order to convey title to the purchaser. In this example, a $700 per acre release clause would be reasonable. It would permit the investor to pay a $7,000 lump sum on the mortgage, transfer the ten-acre tract to the buyer unemcumbered by the mortgage, and still have roughly $3,000 cash from the transaction.

Tenants in Common

Tenants in common ownership involves two or more persons owning undivided, but not necessarily equal, interests in the land. A part-owner may transfer his interests at his own will. This interest at death will pass on to his heirs. This form is often used where a small group of investors wants to purchase a certain tract. The purchase and financing of joint tenancy and tenancy in common forms of ownership are accomplished in the same way as in individual ownership.

Joint Tenancy[9]

In joint tenancy two or more persons own undivided interests in the land. There are two significant aspects to this form of ownership:

1. If a joint tenant dies, his interest goes to the remaining owners on a proportionate basis.
2. If a joint tenant transfers his interest to a third party, the joint-tenancy is destroyed, creating a *tenancy in common*.

---

[9] In some states, where a husband and wife acquire real estate, a "tenancy by the entireties" exists. Under this form of tenancy, neither tenant can sell his share or force partition. The survivor gets the deceased's share. Upon divorce, they become tenants in common.

These characteristics make this form of ownership appropriate only for special situations where this is desirable.

Ownership Groups

Beyond investing in real estate as an individual or with a few associates, investors may want to join with relatively large groups. The array of such groups varies greatly in the individual organization. The labels for each type of organization are not always precise and mutually exclusive. One way to categorize them is as:

1. Non-corporate groups organized to accomplish a specified purpose.
2. Corporate groups organized as a continuing operation.

The non-corporate groups organized to accomplish a specific purpose are usually referred to as "joint-ventures"[10] or "syndicates." Examples of "specific purposes" would be:

1. Organizing a group of investors to purchase a relatively large tract of raw land to hold for appreciation in value.
2. Grouping an investor or investors, with a developer, loan specialist, possibly several would-be merchant tenants, and even a contractor to develop and promote a shopping center. The joint-venturers would construct and develop the project, then sell to an investing and operating company.

Investments in such groups may be made by being one of the original syndicators or by buying someone's share in an existing one. Syndicates of this type by their non-corporate nature are not "visible," and would-be investors have to seek them out through contacts with developers, bankers, accountants, realtors, and attorneys who have a large practice in this type activity. These same people should be sought out for information they can give on the desirability of a particular group. As for financing a participating share, an investor usually has his own funds available or the collateral for borrowing the cash required. He would normally be hard-put to find someone to finance him in the venture.

Real estate corporations and real estate investment trusts (REIT) are examples of corporate groups organized for continuing investment in real estate.

Real Estate Corporations.[11] There are many companies whose operations largely involve real estate as a base. The variety is almost endless. Some are truly real estate corporations in that their operations are totally committed to real estate. There are others: cemeteries, warehouses, automobile service stations, shopping centers, parking facilities, office buildings, hotels and motels,

---

[10]The joint-venture agreement is also widely used by as few as two persons working together on a project. Further, the terms "corporate" and "non-corporate" are used here in the sense of whether or not the grouping of individuals creates an entity in itself separate from the individual investors.

[11]This discussion of real estate corporations relates to public corporations of relatively large size.

mobile home parks, recreational facilities, mortgage loan companies, and savings and loan associations. Such corporations afford varying degrees of investment in real estate.

There are advantages and disadvantages to the corporation form of investing in real estate, most of which are characteristic of the corporate vehicle for operating a business. Among the advantages are:

1. Liability of the investor is limited.
2. Acquiring and selling ownership is easy and inexpensive; thus, there is *high liquidity.*
3. Small units of purchases are available.
4. Scope of operations can be increased more readily through borrowing and sale of additional shares.
5. Centralized and specialized management are more likely than in group ownership involving fewer investors.

Disadvantages include:

1. Double taxation resulting from taxing the corporation on earnings and the investor for dividends received.
2. Depreciation, while advantageous to the corporation, is not allowed the investor and he therefore loses this cash flow tax advantage.
3. Operating losses cannot be deducted by the investor.
4. Influence on management decisions by the individual investor is very limited.

Suggested procedures for researching, financing and acquiring shares in real estate corporations would be the same as for the purchase of other securities. This was discussed in Chapters 20 and 21.

Real Estate Investment Trusts. Just as a mutual fund is a vehicle by which individual investors can pool their funds for joint investment in common stocks, a *real estate investment trust* (REIT) offers the same opportunity for those interested in investing in real estate. The types of investments of the various REIT's fall under one of three headings: (1) equity (actual ownership of realty), (2) intermediate and long-term mortgage-type loans, and (3) short-term construction and development (C and D) loans. Most of the original REIT's were equity trusts. However, the great surge in growth beginning in the late 1960s came from trusts specializing in loans, with the greatest growth from those handling construction and development financing. Exhibit 22–6 reflects this trend from 1968 to 1972. From this table and from Exhibit 22–7, which gives the size distribution of the 185 REITs at the end of 1972, we see a phenomenal growth pattern during the short five-year period. We should note that even though most of these trusts are either equity or loan trusts, some engage in both types of investments.

Exhibit 22–6*   Aggregate Balance Sheet Data for REIT's, Final Quarter, 1968–71, and Second Quarter, 1972 (in millions of dollars)

Assets, liabilities, and net worth	Final quarter[1]				Second quarter
	1968	1969	1970	1971	1972
Assets:					
C & D loans[2]	260	848	2,576	4,254	5,480
Real property investments	553	702	949	1,353	1,898
Long-term conventional first mortgages	26	26	97	569	1,041
Second, short- and intermediate-term mortgages[3]	3	85	404	765	865
FHA & VA mortgages	94	148	142	175	206
Other assets	98	222	558	607	854
Total	1,034	2,031	4,726	7,723	10,344
Liabilities & net worth:					
Short-term debt[4]	90	231	797	2,238	3,395
Mortgage liabilities[5]	357	430	546	680	935
Other liabilities	122	133	197	373	714
Net worth	465	1,237	3,186	4,432	5,300
Total	1,034	2,031	4,726	7,723	10,344

[1]Data for first quarter 1969 substituted for last quarter 1968 data, which were not available. The quarters are not strictly comparable by component, as not all REIT's reported on a March, June, September, December schedule. In a limited number of instances full balance sheet data were available in the annual reports and quarterly information was estimated.

[2]This category includes land loans.

[3]"Second, short- and intermediate-term mortgages" is composed principally of second mortgage loans including "wrap-around" mortgages, and short- and intermediate-term mortgages on completed properties.

[4]"Short-term debt" includes both bank loans and commercial paper. It is estimated that at least three-quarters of the total is in commercial paper. Since only a handful of REIT's had issued nonconvertible long-term debt, long-term debt was not included in any category.

[5]"Mortgage liabilities" refers to the mortgage on real property owned by REIT's.

Source: Data for this table were obtained from REIT quarterly and annual financial statements. Data for the fourth quarter of 1971 represent 127 REIT's. Several small REIT's with total assets of less than $3 million were excluded because adequate data could not be obtained. This study did confirm the existence of 145 REIT's at yearend 1971, but it is likely that a few very small local REIT's were not identified.

*From an Article "Recent Developments In The REIT Industry" by Peter A. Schulkin, Director of Research, National Association of Real Estate Trusts, which originally appeared in the *New England Economic Review*, published by the Federal Reserve Bank of Boston. Reprinted in the *Federal Home Loan Bank Board Journal*, February, 1973.

Advantages of the REIT. From the standpoint of the investor of relatively limited means, the primary contribution of the REIT is this: he is given a choice between investing in common stocks (by purchasing mutual fund shares) or in

Exhibit 22–7* REIT Assets by Asset Size Categories

Asset category	Number of REIT's	Total assets (millions)	Percentage of REIT assets
Over $500 million	2	$ 1,083.7	8.5
$200–$500 million	10	2,582.4	20.2
$100–$199 million	31	4,298.7	33.7
$50–$99 million	40	2,832.8	22.2
$10–$49 million	67	1,835.8	14.4
Less than $10 million	35	133.5	1.0
Total	185	$12,766.9	100.0

Source: Most recent financial report available of each REIT as of December 31, 1972. A number of small organizations which were being operated in the REIT format but which were not filling their tax returns as REIT's were not included. It is possible that several small intra-state REIT's have been excluded from this table because they have not yet been identified by NAREIT.

*From an Article "Recent Developments In The REIT Industry" by Peter A. Schulkin, Director of Research, National Association of Real Estate Trusts, which originally appeared in the *New England Economic Review*, published by the Federal Reserve Bank of Boston. Reprinted in the *Federal Home Loan Bank Board Journal*, February, 1973.

real estate (by purchasing REIT shares). In developing his investment program, he may well decide to invest in both. In early 1973, more than fifty REIT's were listed on either the New York or American Stock Exchange, with many applications pending. Information concerning any specific trust is available from the same sources as for securities and bonds, as described in Chapter 21. Exhibit 22–8 indicates the type of data reported. The trusts shown are all listed on the NYSE.

1. If affairs of the trust are conducted in compliance with Real Estate Investment Trust Act of 1960, earnings of the trust, including capital gains, are not subject to the corporate income tax. This makes it possible for the investor to avoid the double taxation of corporation earnings and dividends to shareholders. Hence, the REIT has the same advantage afforded mutual funds.

2. The small investor is able to participate in major real estate operations not otherwise available to him. This participation offers the possibility of both high yields and asset appreciation. Exhibit 22–8 gives a sampling of the yields. Exhibit 22–9 illustrates a range of gains in share prices from original issue prices.

3. It has created an organized market for real estate investment in this particular area. Accordingly, high liquidity at a price reasonably close to value is available, as well as reduction of purchase and resale costs.

4. Important facts are available to the investor for making his own judgments regarding specific investment decisions. Daily quotations are available for those REIT's traded on the organized exchanges and the over-

Exhibit 22–8 Statistical Position of Certain Leading Real Estate Investment Trusts, June 14, 1973

Real estate investment trusts	Year ended	Total assets[2]	Long term debt[2]	Short term debt[2]	Book value[2]	Primary earns 1972	Primary earns E1973	Dividends[1]	Price range 1973	6-14-73 price	% yield
C.I. Mortgage Group*	Oct.	238	29	117	18.92	2.29	2.25	2.52	25 -17⅝	19	13.2
Chase Manh. Mtge. & Rlty.*	May	717	139	439	27.41	4.19	4.75	4.95	70 -50¼	50	9.9
Citizens & Southern Rlty.*	Sept.	329	27	223	20.32	2.60	3.05	2.76	39¾-32⅜	34	8.1
Continental Mtge. Investors*	Mar.	588	138	324	6.65	1.09[3]	1.20[3]	1.09	14 - 9⅝	10	10.9
Cousins Mortgage & Equity*	Aug.	183	67	34	21.85	1.95	2.35	2.22	30⅞-24⅛	27	8.2
Diversified Mtge. Investors*	Dec.	330	40	136	20.02	2.71	3.05	2.77	29⅜-22⅛	22	12.6
Equitable Life Mtge. & Rlty.*	Oct.	218	9	71	24.19	2.26	2.30	2.23	31¼-24	24	9.3
Fidelity Mtge. Investors*	Oct.	235	29	145	21.04	3.12	3.65	3.32	38 -25¾	29	11.4
First Mortgage Investors*	Jan.	463	114	204	15.15	2.27[3]	1.95	2.18	27⅞-18¼	17	12.8
Great American Mtge.*	July	361	40	249	15.07	2.52	3.20	2.98	40⅜-29½	31	9.6
Guardian Mtge. Inv.*	Feb.	319	55	198	28.89	4.20[3]	4.40[3]	4.11	46⅞-37	38	10.8
Lomas & Nettleton Mtge.*	June	349	32	187	33.21	3.34	3.75	3.63	52¾-40	43	8.4
North American Mtge.*	Dec.	200	27	104	15.49	2.41	2.40	2.50	35 -24¼	25	10.0
N'western Mutual Life Mtge. & Rlty.*	Mar.	175	5	59	19.29	1.80[3]	2.05[3]	1.86	27¼-22⅜	24	7.8
Tri-South Mtge. Inv.*	Dec.	143	40	58	20.30	2.78	3.00	2.69	37 -28½	30	7.3
Wells Fargo Mortgage*	June	206	Nil	129	18.28	1.75	2.20	2.06	25⅞-20½	22	9.4

*N.Y.S.E.

E—Estimated.

[1] Paid in last 12 months.

[2] Latest available.

[3] Of following year.

Source: *Standard and Poor's Industry Surveys*, p. I 38.

Exhibit 22–9   A Sampling of REITs

	Assets millions of dollars	Date of initial offering	Issue share price	1972 range	Recent price
Short-term trusts					
First Mortgage Investors	$380	9/61	$9⅜ †	$27¼–22¼	$23⅞
First Wisconsin Mortgage Investors	60	12/71	25	34¼–24½	34¼
Fidelity Mortgage Investors	198	10/71	20	32⅜–23½	32⅜
Larwin Mortgage Investors	97	7/69	20	32½–25⅞	28¼
Lomas & Nettleton Mortgage Investors	249	10/69	25	47¾–36½	44¼
Mortgage Trust of America	159	11/69	20*	25⅛–21⅝	23¼
Long-term trusts					
BankAmerica Reality Investors	170	7/70	20	28⅞–22½	28⅞
BT Mortgage Investors	106	9/71	12.50‡	31⅞–23½	31⅞
Equitable Life Mortgage & Realty Investors	187	11/70	25	31¾–26¾	28¾
Fidelco Growth Investors	52	9/70	25*	37⅝–31⅝	37½
PNB Mortgage & Realty Investors	98	12/70	20*	27¾–22½	24⅞
Equity trusts					
Cabot, Cabot & Forbes Land Trust	100	4/71	20	30⅜–23⅜	26½
C. I. Realty Investors	146	4/72	25*	23–18¼	21¼
General Grown Properties	109	9/70	6⅜ ‡	28–23¾	23¾

*Included warrants
†Adjusted for 8-for-5 stock split
‡Adjusted for 2-for-1 stock split
Source: *Business Week,* October 28, 1972, p. 82

the-counter markets. Such investment services as *Moody's* and *Standard and Poor's* (which are available at most libraries) give extensive information on each trust.

5. Federal regulations require that 90 percent of earnings be distributed each year, thus eliminating the chance of earnings not being disbursed regularly.

6. Investment expertise in managing the trusts is afforded from their managers and advisors.

Disadvantages of the REIT.

1. Management and operating expenses of the trust reduce the net earnings available to investors.

2. Tax benefits available under other forms of real estate investments are not available directly to the individual investor. Even though depreciation, interest, and maintenance expenses on a particular property owned by the trust are absorbed by it in the form of decreased earnings, the same items—if the property were owned directly by individual investors —would be deductible from their other income.

3. Regulatory restrictions imposed on it limit the trust's earnings potential somewhat. These same restrictions, however, do provide some protection to the investor.

Real estate investment trusts, contrary to mutual funds, should be considered as an investment primarily for its relatively high annual earnings potential, even though there is the hope of capital gains. The family decision maker(s) on investment policy should in most instances purchase REIT shares with money on hand.

Discussion Questions

1. Land values have skyrocketed in recent years. List and briefly discuss reasons for this rapid growth.
2. What do we mean by "inflation-hedge" investments? Is land such an investment? If so, why?
3. Is land a suitable investment for leverage operations? Why or why not?
4. List and briefly describe the tax advantages of investing in land.
5. What are some of the unfavorable aspects of real estate as an investment?
6. Distinguish between non-corporate and corporate groups that are both involved in land investment.
7. What is the essential difference between mutual funds and real estate investment trusts as inflation-hedge investments?
8. In financing land purchases, why is it important to have a "release" clause in the mortgage?
9. Relate briefly the growth of real estate investment trusts from 1968 to 1972.
10. With reference to real estate investment trusts, distinguish between "equity" trusts and "mortgage" trusts.

We live in a risky world. Few of
us will get out of it alive.

[*Anonymous*]

23

Estate
Planning

All of us at sometime have heard the quip, "You can't take it with you," and occasionally a sharp rejoinder, "Yes, but it is nice to have it while you are around."

Do most people know what would happen to their possessions if they were to die suddenly? Are people afraid to make plans for the distribution of their property after death? While there may be a growing public awareness of the need to consider this in personal business planning, too many persons still fail to make the best possible arrangements for their heirs. Estate planning is simply a matter of making preparations so that property will be distributed as the owner wishes it to be after his death.

Our laws confer upon us the right of property ownership. The laws give us broad—but not unlimited—powers respecting the use of what we own during our lifetime, including the power to say who shall have our property after death.

The property or assets owned at any time constitute a person's estate. Because of the uncertain time of death, a very important part of estate management is to determine how that estate is to be distributed in the event of death. Failure to do this could result in (a) property not being distributed as the owner would have liked, (b) unnecessary administrative costs, and (c) greater estate tax liabilities. Even worse, it could cause worry and trouble to the surviving family.

Making
a Will

The preparation of a written will is the only way to be reasonably certain that what wealth is left behind will go to those the owner wants to have it and under those conditions under which they should receive it. These instructions will be carried out by an *executor* designated by the person writing the will (one in whom he places his confidence). Furthermore, a properly prepared will should assure that the estate will be settled in the most efficient manner and with the least possible tax liabilities.

A will also provides the means of designating a guardian for minor children in the event of the parents' death. In the absence of such designation, a court will appoint a guardian.

The person who makes a will is known as a *testator,* if a man, or a *testatrix,* if a woman. One who dies leaving a valid will is said to have died *testate;* if no will is left, the person has died *intestate.*

Personal property transmitted by will is called a *bequest* or *legacy.* The beneficiary is a *legatee.* Real property transmitted by will is a *devise,* and the beneficiary is a *devisee.* It is legally correct in a will to say that one *bequeaths* personal property and *devises* real property. When a person leaves a legatee a stated amount of money, it is known as a *general legacy.* But if the deceased leaves him a certain item of personal property—such as an automobile—he has made a *specific legacy.*

There are three distinct types of wills based on the method of preparation.

1. The most common of these is the *witnessed will* either handwritten or typewritten. It is recognized in every state of the union. It is usually prepared by an attorney, is always signed by the testator, and is witnessed by two or more witnesses who saw the testator sign and heard him state that the document was his will.[1]

2. A *holographic* will is one written entirely in his own handwriting by the testator and signed by him. It does not require the signature of witnesses.

---

[1]Witnesses to a will should be persons of legal age who have no interest in the will's contents.

Difficulty of proving the validity of this type of will has caused some states not to recognize it at all. Other states whose laws permit such a will specify that certain requirements must be followed for it to be valid. Unless the testator knows exactly what the law requires in this respect, it is unfair to his family to make a handwritten, unwitnessed will.

3. A *nuncupative* will, sometimes called a "death-bed will," is an oral declaration made before witnesses when the person is not able to sign a written document. About one-fourth of the states do not permit this type of will, chiefly because it is generally made under critical circumstances and great emotional stress. Most of the states that do recognize it limit it to personal property.

The advantages of a witnessed will are obvious, and careful estate planning makes its use mandatory.

A witnessed will commonly begins with what is known as an *exordium* in which the testator identifies himself, states where he lives, declares the instrument to be his last will, and revokes all prior wills that he may have made. Here is an example: "I, John M. Doe, Sr., now domiciled in Any Town, Kansas, do make, publish and declare this to be my last will and testament, hereby revoking all wills and codicils heretofore made by me."

There then generally follow articles which:

1. Direct the payment of funeral expenses and all debts.
2. Direct payment of all taxes, federal, and state.
3. Dispose of property, both personal and real.
4. Name a guardian for minor children, if any.
5. Name an executor (called executrix, if a woman).

The next to last part of the will is known as a *testimonium* in which the testator establishes the fact that the will is his. Words similar to these may be used: "In testimony whereof, I hereunto sign my name to this last will and testament, consisting of this and five preceding pages, each of which I am initialing or signing for the purpose of identification, all in the presence of the undersigned who witnessed the same at my request, on this twelfth day of June, 1973, at Any Town, Kansas." And then the testator signs his name on a line below.

The final part of a will is the *attestation*. It may be worded as follows: "The foregoing instrument, consisting of this and five preceding pages, was signed, published and declared by John M. Doe, Sr., to be his last will and testament, in our presence, and we, at his request, and in his presence, and in the presence of each other, have hereunto subscribed our names as witnesses, this twelfth day of June, 1973." The witnesses, two or three, then sign their names and give their addresses.[2]

Some states have a provision which authorizes a "self-proved will." The procedure simply requires the testator and witnesses to appear before a notary

---

[2] Seven states require three witnesses, the other states two.

public or any official authorized to administer oaths and declare under oath that the will is the testator's last will and that it was executed "as his free act and deed for the purpose therein expressed." (See Exhibit 23–1.)

The self-proving provision makes it unnecessary for witnesses to testify when the will is probated.

After a will is made, it should be kept in a safe place. When an attorney prepares a will, he usually retains a copy in his files. A bank safe deposit box is a good place to keep the original.

It is helpful in the settlement of an estate for the testator to prepare a last letter of instructions to be kept in a readily accessible place. The letter should reveal the location of valuable papers, identify safe deposit box or boxes, and tell where keys are kept.

The court before which a will is probated is almost certain to uphold the will if it has been properly prepared by a person of legal age, sound of mind, and

Exhibit 23–1   A Form of Self-Proving Affidavit

The State of Texas
County of Dallas

Before me, the undersigned authority, on this day personally appeared Richard R. Roe, Elton P. Green, Charles M. Brown, and Frank D. Black, known to me to be the testator and the witnesses, respectively, whose names are subscribed to the attached instrument in their respective capacities, and, all of said persons being by me duly sworn, the said Richard R. Roe, the testator, declared to me and to the said witnesses in my presence that said instrument is his last will and testament, and that he had willingly made and executed it as his free act and deed for the purposes therein expressed; and the said witnesses, each on his oath, stated to me, in the presence and hearing of said testator, that the said testator had declared to them that said instrument is his last will and testament, and that he executed same as such and wanted each of them to sign as a witness; and upon their oaths each witness stated that they did sign their names as witnesses in the presence of the said testator and at his request; that he was at the time eighteen years of age or over and was of sound mind, and that each of said witnesses was then at least fourteen years of age.

_____Testator
_____Witness
_____Witness
_____Witness

Subscribed and acknowledged before me by the said Richard R. Roe, the testator, and subscribed and sworn to before me by the said Elton P. Green, Charles M. Brown, and Frank D. Black, witnesses, this 23rd day of June, 1973.

(Signed)_____
                                    Notary Public

(Seal)

free from undue influence at the time the will was signed. Occasionally, wills are contested on the grounds of mental incompetency; but when a will is prepared under the guidance of an attorney and duly witnessed, such contest is rarely upheld. Charges of undue influence are equally difficult to prove.

Role of the Executor or Administrator

A will is nothing more than a set of instructions as to what a person wants done with the property he possesses at the time of his death. Since someone has to carry out these instructions, the testator should designate an executor or executors to be responsible for this. If no executor is named in the will or if a named executor dies or is unable to serve, the court will appoint an administrator.

Executors and administrators must be of legal age, mentally competent, and without a criminal record.

A testator with an above average estate may designate a bank with trust powers as executor along with one or more co-executors. This arrangement is particularly desirable because trust departments of banks are experienced and responsible.

It is customary for a testator to name as executor or co-executor someone with whom he is acquainted (often a good friend) and in whom he has confidence, and to ask that person or persons beforehand to agree to serve. Frequently, a spouse or other relative is designated. Before a bank is named, it is well to consult with an officer of the bank regarding fees and other matters that may be important to the testator.

Upon the death of a testator, an executor must locate and read the will, secure a death certificate to present to the probate court along with the will, and petition the court for a document known as *letters testamentary* which give him authority to act. With this authority he will take immediate steps to safeguard the assets of the estate, will assemble the property in the form of an inventory, get appraisals, manage the assets during the settlement, investigate and pay all valid claims and debts, see that federal estate and state inheritance tax returns are properly prepared, pay taxes and help negotiate the settlement, and distribute the property according to the testator's instructions. Finally, the executor will make a complete report on his stewardship to the court which will then discharge him.

In a few states, a testator may provide for independent administration of his estate and thereby withdraw the estate from the general jurisdiction of the courts. To do this, a testator must designate the executor as "independent executor." Although not absolutely necessary, it is well for the testator to include an article worded somewhat like the following: "It is my will that no other action shall be had in the County Court in the administration of my estate than to prove and record this will and to return an inventory and appraisement of my estate and list of claims as required by law." (See Exhibit 23–2.)

The effect of this is to give the independent executor full power to perform without court order any act necessary for the complete settlement of the estate. It is particularly useful when a bank is designated as independent executor.

Exhibit 23–2   A Simple Will in Which a Husband Leaves All his Property to his Wife

---

STATE OF TEXAS   )
)
COUNTY OF DALLAS)

    I, *Richard R. Roe,* of the State and County aforesaid, being of sound and disposing mind and memory, do hereby make and publish this my last will and testament, hereby revoking all other wills heretofore made by me.

    1. I direct that all my just debts, taxes, and funeral expenses shall be paid out of my estate.

    2. After the payment of all debts, I give and bequeath to my beloved wife, *Nancy W. Roe,* all real and personal property and all rights and interests of whatsoever kind and character and wherever situated of which I may be possessed, or upon which I may have any claim at the time of my death.

    3. I hereby constitute and appoint my said wife, *Nancy W. Roe,* independent executrix of this my last will and testament, and I direct that no bond or security shall be required of her as such executrix.

    4. It is my will that no other action shall be had in the County Court in the administration of my estate than to prove and record this will and to return an inventory and appraisement of my estate and list of claims as required by law.

    In testimony whereof I have set my hand this the *23rd* day of *June,* 1973 A.D.

_____

We, the attesting witnesses, hereby declare that we sign our names to the foregoing will in the presence of *Richard R. Roe,* testator, who is, in our opinion of sound and disposing mind and memory, and in the presence of each other, at the request of the said *Richard R. Roe,* and that we have each witnessed him attach his signature hereto, this the *23rd* day of *June,* 1973 A.D.

_____	_____
(Witness)	(Address)
_____	_____
(Witness)	(Address)
_____	_____
(Witness)	(Address)

    When a husband has complete confidence in his wife's ability to manage matters, he may appoint his spouse as "independent executrix."

When Someone is Disinherited

Great care should be taken when a person disinherits a member of his family. But if that is what a testator wants to do, then he should be reasonably certain that his objective will be carried out. He should mention the disinherited person by name and give a reason or reasons for disinheriting him. Language similar to the following should suffice: "I have deliberately made no provision herein for the benefit of my son, John M. Doe, Jr., not because of any lack of love or affection, but because he has ample property of his own."

Sometimes a testator will simply leave the person "the sum of one dollar." This clearly indicates that the person was not forgotten.

In many states, it is difficult for a wife to be cut off. She is entitled, as a rule, to one-third of the deceased husband's estate. But states vary on this matter, and again we emphasize the importance of using a lawyer's services in preparing a will.

Changing a Will

Family circumstances change to such an extent that most wills should be reviewed about every five years to see if they need to be altered. When a will needs changing, the testator should not take a pen and mark out the part he wants eliminated and write in something new or different. The process is somewhat more complicated than that. To modify a will, a testator must prepare a *codicil*. This is a separate instrument in which changes to be made in the original will are expressed. A reference is made to the will which actually makes the codicil a part of the will. A codicil must be prepared with the same care as the original will and witnesses are necessary.

Codicils should be used only to make minor changes in a will. If extensive changes are necessary, it is wise to prepare a completely new will. Anyone can revoke a will as long as he is alive and of sound mind, since wills do not take effect until death. When a new will is written, the testator includes a statement expressing his intent to revoke all prior wills. Another method is simply to destroy the old will when a new one is made.

Since a will should be prepared according to the laws of the state in which the testator has his legal residence, a person should make a new will if he moves to another state.

Why People
Die Intestate

Young persons often postpone making a will, perhaps thinking there is plenty of time. This is a mistake, because an accident could result in instantaneous death.

Some persons do not prepare a will because they say they do not have enough property to worry about. Only a few persons do not have enough property to be concerned with estate planning, especially if they are married. Until we actually make an inventory of our assets and liabilities, we do not realize the amount of our estate. Most people now accumulate assets of various kinds faster than in previous years.

Occasionally someone says that he has not made a will because "lawyers charge too much." This is a flimsy excuse. The guidance of a lawyer is not only essential but valuable in the preparation of a will. A competent legal advisor is well worth the fee he charges, because he can help to avoid certain pitfalls, can suggest ways of saving taxes, and can assist in estate planning for the greatest benefit to the family.

For some inexplicable reason, many wives do not think about a will, when, in fact, it is as important for the wife to make a will as it is for the husband. Often, a desirable arrangement is for husband and wife to prepare what are known as *reciprocal* or *interlocking wills,* which are separate instruments, each inter-relating with the other. In this way, the mutual objectives of both persons can be set forth.

Husband and wife may make a *joint will* which is simply one instrument signed by both parties. However, this kind of will is not used very much because it is less flexible and, for most couples, is less desirable than reciprocal wills.

Intestate
Distribution

When a person dies without leaving a will, the state where he had his legal residence will distribute his estate according to the state's laws of inheritance (sometimes referred to as descent or intestate distribution laws). These laws determine how all personal property and all real estate within the state will be distributed. If real estate is owned in another state, the inheritance laws of that state will prevail.

The word "heirs" is used to refer to persons who would receive property according to state laws when there is no will. Blood relatives of the intestate may be lineal heirs (by direct line) and be either descending (the intestate's children) or ascending (the intestate's parents); or the blood relatives of the intestate may be collateral, meaning they are of a common ancestor (first, brothers and sisters of the intestate and their descendants; second, uncles and aunts of the intestate and their descendents; and so on).[3] All children have equal inheritance rights regardless of their order of birth.

Laws of descent and distribution vary from state to state but they do have a tendency to adhere to a pattern. In general, the following are in line to receive property of those who die without leaving a will.

1. Surviving spouse. A surviving spouse receives a specified share, usually one-third or one-half, if there are children. When no blood relatives survive, the spouse receives the entire estate.
2. Children. When a spouse survives, the percentage amount left after his or her share is divided equally among the children. If no spouse survives, all property is divided equally among the children. When one of the children who is to receive property is deceased and has offspring, the latter will share equally in their parent's part.

---

[3]Joseph L. Frascona, *C.P.A. Law Review,* 4th ed. (Homewood, Illinois: Richard D. Irwin, 1972), p. 935.

3. Surviving parents. A certain percentage goes to the surviving spouse and the remainder is divided equally between the parents when there are no children. When the spouse is not living and there are no children, the entire estate is divided between the parents.

4. Brothers and sisters. When no spouse, children, or parents survive, the brothers and sisters are next in line. They share equally in the estate and if one brother or sister is deceased, his or her children will receive the parent's share.

A similar pattern would be followed to distribute the property of a deceased single person who never married. Parents would be first in line of succession and brothers and sisters next if the parents are deceased.

What happens to property when there is no will and no blood relatives can be found? Most states have what are called laws of *escheat,* which require the state to assume ownership of property when no legal heirs exist.

Intestate Administration

When a person dies intestate, the court must appoint someone to administer his estate. The administrator may or may not be a relative of the deceased, but usually the court will appoint the surviving spouse if that person is capable and wants to serve.

In the absence of a suitable relative, a public administrator will be appointed. Once an administrator is appointed, the process of settling the estate is similar to that which we have discussed concerning the executor of a will. He will have to locate and make an *inventory* of the property and pay all claims of creditors against the estate. After all claims and taxes have been paid, the property is distributed to heirs according to state laws.

There is one important thing to remember about the laws of intestate succession and that is that the testator and his family will lose control of what happens to the property. The laws must be followed explicitly when there is no will.

Trusts

The subject of estate planning would not be complete without a discussion of trusts. Trusts appear to be growing in popularity as estates get larger and owners seek new ways to transfer their wealth to others.

As we shall use the term here, a trust is a legal arrangement whereby a person may transfer any or all of his property to another person or an institution to be managed by the latter for the benefit of whomever he designates. The document transferring the property and setting forth terms and powers under the trust is called a *trust agreement.* The one who creates the trust and furnishes the property to be put in trust is called the *trustor,* sometimes *settlor* or *grantor.* The trust property is known as the *trust principal* or *corpus.* The person or institution who holds the property and administers the trust is known as *trustee*. Those for whose benefit trusts are created are known as *trust beneficiaries*.

Types of Trusts

Trusts for purposes of estate planning are principally of two types: *living trust* or *inter vivos trust,* and *testamentary trust.* A living trust is established and is in effect during the life of the trustor who may designate himself as beneficiary to receive income from the trust property; or he may designate his wife, his children, his parents, or anyone else as beneficiaries. A living trust may be used when a person wishes to relieve himself of the management of his property in whole or part and provide income for his retirement. Or, a trustor may wish to set up a living trust to provide continuous income to a favorite charity or educational institution.

Perhaps the most important reason for creating such a living trust is to remove property from a person's estate and thus reduce the amount that will be probated at death. In the case of large estates, this will eliminate a portion of settlement costs and very likely will produce estate tax savings. But to accomplish this, the trustor must not retain any rights over the trust property or the trust income. In other words, the living trust must be *irrevocable*.

An irrevocable trust legally separates the trust property completely from the trustor's estate which means that the creation of this kind of a trust amounts to a gift, and it may be subject to gift taxes. If a gift tax is incurred when the trust is created, it can mean a savings, because gift tax rates are usually 25 percent lower than federal estate tax rates.

Suppose a person's taxable estate is $400,000. The top $150,000 of the estate assets will be subject to a 32 percent federal estate tax, or $48,000. But, if the owner placed the same $150,000 in an irrevocable living trust for the benefit of others, the gift tax rate could range from 2¼ percent to 22½ percent. Even if he did not apply his lifetime exemption and annual exclusion to the gift, the gift tax could be about $21,000 less than the estate tax would be if he transferred the property to his beneficiary or beneficiaries under his will.

If a trustor creates a living trust over which he retains the right to change or cancel the trust agreement whenever he wishes, he has created a *revocable* trust. The trust property, however, will be counted in his estate and be subject to estate taxes at death.

A trustor can provide that a revocable living trust be continued beyond his lifetime. In such a situation, the trust automatically becomes irrevocable at his death and the income from the trust will go to the beneficiary or beneficiaries without interruption. Although the trust property will be subject to estate taxes, it will not be administered as a part of the estate, and this will reduce probate costs.

Mention should be made of what is called a *short-term irrevocable living trust* which can be used to reduce income taxes. Here is an example: Mr. M, who is in a relatively high income tax bracket, wishes to make regular contributions to the support of a less fortunate relative or friend. He can set up a short-term irrevocable living trust and place in it enough property to produce the desired income for the beneficiary. The effect of this arrangement is to reduce the trustor's income tax by removing the income from his own taxable income and taxing it to the beneficiary who, presumably, will be in a much lower income tax bracket. This kind of trust must continue for a specified period of time, at least ten years in most states, or for the life of the beneficiary should the latter die during the period. When the trust terminates, the property may revert to the trustor. It should be noted here that the trustor may be subject to paying a gift tax if the value of the income from a short-term irrevocable trust exceeds the gift tax exemptions of the trustor ($30,000 lifetime exemption and $3,000 annual exclusion).

A *testamentary trust* is one which is created by will and becomes effective upon the testator's death. In other words, a testamentary trust is simply a provision in a person's will whereby he delegates to his chosen trustee the responsibility of holding, managing, and distributing part or all of his property and the income therefrom in accordance with the conditions and objectives set forth in his will.

There are two good reasons for the use of a testamentary trust. (1) The testator may hesitate to give full control of his property at death to his wife or to a child, either not caring to burden the beneficiary with the responsibility of managing the property or not having confidence in the beneficiary's ability to do so. (2) The testator may want to save estate taxes by skipping one or two generations.

Very often a widow is shielded by a testamentary trust. She may be a person who finds it difficult to resist pressures and temptations put on her by friends or relatives. Or she may need protection from swindlers who might find her easy prey for their schemes. If she can say that a trustee must be consulted, she often can be saved both money and embarrassment. Occasionally, a husband may use this option to protect his widow from the possibility that a second husband will marry her for the estate money.

Our federal estate tax laws permit generation skipping, and this is one of the greatest motivators in the creation of testamentary trusts.

Each time an estate transfers by death of the owner it is subject to the estate tax. By skipping a generation or two a considerable amount of taxes can be saved. This can be done by use of a testamentary trust. Example: A husband wants his estate to go to his wife and then upon her death to the children. If he leaves his property directly to his wife and then upon her death she leaves the remainder of the estate to the children, taxes are paid two times. One tax can be avoided by the husband providing in his will that the property be put in trust for the benefit of the wife as long as she lives, then be distributed to the children upon the widow's death.

Even more taxes can be saved if the trust continues for the life of the children and the property is then distributed to grandchildren. The amount saved in this way depends upon the amount of the estate. Not only are federal estate taxes saved, but state inheritance taxes also, as well as costs of successive probates.[4]

Purpose and Duties
of a Trustee

For a trust to be functional, there must be a manager or trustee. Any person who is considered legally capable to transact business affairs is eligible to serve as a trustee. No special training is required. A corporation, such as a bank with trust powers, may serve as a trustee. In fact, there is an advantage to selecting a bank instead of an individual. Although a trustor has provided for a trust to begin at his death and has named a person in the will to serve as trustee, the latter may still decide not to serve. The court would then have to name a trustee for the estate.

A court-appointed trustee must agree to serve in the position and, after the trust begins, he cannot resign except by agreement of the beneficiaries, or by permission of a court. Usually, court-appointed trustees must post a bond to protect beneficiaries of the trust.

It is desirable to use the trust department of a bank as trustee because the successful administration of a trust calls for the trustee to have training and experience in many fields, such as accounting, investments, finance, taxation, and wide areas of business. Furthermore, trust departments of banks are carefully examined periodically by government authorities. Finally, a bank trustee is permanently available, whereas the services of a person acting as trustee may be interrupted by accident, illness, or death.

Duties of a trustee are primarily to (1) administer the trust according to its purpose, (2) administer the trust in a reasonable manner, and (3) be loyal and honest with the beneficiaries. Of course, the first duty of a trustee is to follow the wishes of the trustor to accomplish the purpose of the trust. If it was established to benefit named persons, it is called a "private trust." Most trusts are created to benefit family members and/or other relatives. Some trusts are established to benefit society and are known as "charitable trusts."

Administering a trust in a reasonable manner simply means that the trustee should give it the same care as he would use in managing his own property. He should follow a reasonably safe course in making investments to obtain a moderate return while preserving capital. Many states restrict trustees from making investments in corporation stocks. Sometimes investments are limited to bonds of governments, first mortgages on real estate, and some types of corporation bonds. Prudent investments are not always easy to judge.

---

[4]It is your legal right to reduce your taxes by lawful means. The courts have ruled: "Anyone may so arrange his affairs that taxes shall be as low as possible; he is not bound to choose that pattern which will best pay the Treasury: it is not even a patriotic duty to increase one's taxes."

A trustee is employed to work for the beneficiaries. Loyalty of employee to employer should be no different here than in any other working relationship. There is more reason than just wanting to do a good job; the trustee is liable for his work. When beneficiaries become dissatisfied with the work of a trustee, they can petition a court to remove him from the trust. In the court's investigation, if it is found that the trust has not been properly managed, the trustee can be assessed damages to restore any loss. A trustee must be especially careful to keep his private business affairs separated from the trust to show that he is not benefiting from its management. A trustee is paid a fee for his services.

Powers of a Trustee

Limits are placed on a trustee by provisions written in the trust by the trustor and by state laws. State laws are more concerned with how trust funds are invested. Forbidden types of investment under state laws may be made if specifically provided for in the trust by the trustor. For example, the trust may include a family corporation in which the trustor wants the stock to be held. Where no instructions are given, investments must be sold to satisfy state laws.

A trustee has considerable power over an estate, and he needs this authority to obtain a reasonable return on the property. He has power to lease property and in some instances to sell it. Usually property that is considered unproductive can be sold. His powers are restricted in borrowing money and pledging property as security. He has authority to vote shares of stock held by the trust. A most important part of a trustee's work is to keep good records of all transactions relating to the trust and make regular reports to the beneficiaries.

Laws governing trust agreements, like those relating to wills, vary among the several states. True, the variations are more in detail than in principle. We have made no attempt to present here more than a general description of trusts and the reasons for their use. Anyone who contemplates the setting up of a trust must realize that the services of an attorney are absolutely essential.

Since a trust can be adapted to almost any legal purpose, and every trust involves factors peculiar to the circumstances and desires of the trustor, each trust agreement must be carefully drawn so as to avoid later entanglements.

Taxes

Estate planning must take account of certain types of taxes. Passing property to others and receiving property from someone through inheritance are rights granted by law, but governments have reserved the power to take a share of the property in the form of taxes. These are called death taxes and are of two types: (1) estate taxes and (2) inheritance taxes.

An estate tax is an excise tax on the right of transferring property from the dead to the living. On the other hand, inheritance taxes are excise taxes on the right of the living to receive property from the dead. The federal government does not have an inheritance tax, but all states except Nevada do.

The Federal Estate Tax

The federal estate tax is on the gross value of the estate of the deceased, less debts, administration expenses, and charitable bequests.

All types of property, both real and personal, tangible and intangible, are valued in an estate for tax purposes. In most instances, life insurance on the deceased is also a part of the estate. As we have already learned, revocable type trusts which have been set up by the deceased are a part of the estate.

In order to prevent them from being used as tax dodges, gifts made within three years of death must be reported as part of the gross estate. Such gifts are by law deemed to have been made "in contemplation of death."

Under the current federal estate tax law, a basic exemption of $60,000 is allowed. In other words, if the remaining value of an estate for tax purposes is not over $60,000, it is not necessary to file a tax return.

A very significant provision of the current law relates to what is called the marital deduction. A husband may leave up to 50 percent of his gross estate minus deductions to his wife tax free, provided she survives him and also that by terms of his will she is allowed to dispose of the property as she chooses when she dies. A wife may do the same thing for her husband. To obtain full advantage of the marital deduction, a will must be prepared.

In states having the community property law, the marital deduction applies to one-half of the testator's separate property and not at all to his part of the community property.

Federal estate tax rates are graduated to a maximum of 77 percent on estates above $10,000,000. Exhibit 23–3 shows how the rates increase as the estate gets larger.

Let's take the case of a husband and wife who live in Ohio where there is no community property law. The husband dies leaving a will in which he takes full advantage of the marital deduction. If the value of the estate after allowable deductions is $180,000, the estate tax will apply only to $30,000 ($180,000 less the basic exemption of $60,000 and the marital exemption of $90,000). The amount of the estate tax is $3,000.

Now suppose this couple lived in Texas, one of the states having a community property law. One-half of the estate is presumed to belong to the surviving spouse, leaving $90,000 as the value of the deceased spouse's estate. After the $60,000 basic exemption is subtracted the new taxable estate is $30,000, and the tax is $3,000.

You will observe that the amount of the tax works out the same in both instances. Congress provided for the marital deduction in order to give married couples in states not have the community property law an equal break with couples in community property states.

Inheritance Taxes

Since an inheritance tax is levied on the privilege of inheriting property, the tax is paid by the individual beneficiary, and not by the estate, as is true of the estate tax.

Exhibit 23–3 *Estate Tax Rates*

I. Estates of U.S. Citizens and Residents

The federal estate tax on estates of U.S. citizens and residents is computed on a "taxable estate," after deduction of a $60,000 exemption, at the rates below. This amount is further reduced by a state death tax credit computed under Table IV, below, or by the actual amount of state death taxes, whichever is less. (Credits are also available for foreign death taxes, certain gift taxes, and federal estate taxes on prior transfers.)

Taxable estate (after deducting the $60,000 exemption) From	To	Tax =	+ %	Of excess over
0 $	5,000	0	3	0
$ 5,000	10,000	$ 150	7	$ 5,000
10,000	20,000	500	11	10,000
20,000	30,000	1,600	14	20,000
30,000	40,000	3,000	18	30,000
40,000	50,000	4,800	22	40,000
50,000	60,000	7,000	25	50,000
60,000	100,000	9,500	28	60,000
100,000	250,000	20,700	30	100,000
250,000	500,000	65,700	32	250,000
500,000	750,000	145,700	35	500,000
750,000	1,000,000	233,200	37	750,000
1,000,000	1,250,000	325,700	39	1,000,000
1,250,000	1,500,000	423,200	42	1,250,000
1,500,000	2,000,000	528,200	45	1,500,000
2,000,000	2,500,000	753,200	49	2,000,000
2,500,000	3,000,000	998,200	53	2,500,000
3,000,000	3,500,000	1,263,200	56	3,000,000
3,500,000	4,000,000	1,543,200	59	3,500,000
4,000,000	5,000,000	1,838,200	63	4,000,000
5,000,000	6,000,000	2,468,200	67	5,000,000
6,000,000	7,000,000	3,138,200	70	6,000,000
7,000,000	8,000,000	3,838,200	73	7,000,000
8,000,000	10,000,000	4,568,200	76	8,000,000
10,000,000	. . . .	6,088,200	77	10,000,000

Source: Reproduced by permission from Federal Estate and Gift Taxes—Code and Regulations—April 1, 1973, published and copyrighted 1973 by Commerce Clearing House, Inc., Chicago, Ill. 60646.

Most states exempt a certain amount of wealth from the inheritance tax. Exemptions vary in magnitude with the relationship of beneficiaries to the deceased, the highest exemption being allowed to those beneficiaries most closely related. A spouse has the greatest exemption, with children a lesser amount, and collateral heirs still less.

Exhibit 23–4   Gift Tax Rates and Computation

From	To	Tax =	+ %	Of excess over
. . . .	$ 5,000	0	2¼ %	. . . .
$ 5,000	10,000	$ 112.50	5¼ %	$ 5,000
10,000	20,000	375	8¼ %	10,000
20,000	30,000	1,200	10½ %	20,000
30,000	40,000	2,250	13½ %	30,000
40,000	50,000	3,600	16½ %	40,000
50,000	60,000	5,250	18¾ %	50,000
60,000	100,000	7,125	21 %	60,000
100,000	250,000	15,525	22½ %	100,000
250,000	500,000	49,275	24 %	250,000
500,000	750,000	109,275	26¼ %	500,000
750,000	1,000,000	174,900	27¾ %	750,000
1,000,000	1,250,000	244,275	29¼ %	1,000,000
1,250,000	1,500,000	317,400	31½ %	1,250,000
1,500,000	2,000,000	396,150	33¾ %	1,500,000
2,000,000	2,500,000	564,900	36¾ %	2,000,000
2,500,000	3,000,000	748,650	39¾ %	2,500,000
3,000,000	3,500,000	947,400	42 %	3,000,000
3,500,000	4,000,000	1,157,400	44¼ %	3,500,000
4,000,000	5,000,000	1,378,650	47¼ %	4,000,000
5,000,000	6,000,000	1,851,150	50¼ %	5,000,000
6,000,000	7,000,000	2,353,650	52½ %	6,000,000
7,000,000	8,000,000	2,878,650	54¾ %	7,000,000
8,000,000	10,000,000	3,426,150	57 %	8,000,000
10,000,000	. . . .	4,566,150	57¾ %	10,000,000

Taxable gifts* (From/To columns)

*After deducting exemption of $30,000, and after taking annual exclusions for individual donees ($5,000 through 1938; $4,000 after 1938 and through 1942; and $3,000 after 1942). The annual exclusions do not apply to gifts of future interests. Neither do they apply to gifts in trust made after 1938 but before 1943.

Source: Reproduced by permission from Federal Estate and Gift Taxes—Code and Regulations, April 1, 1973, Copyrighted 1973 by Commerce Clearing House, Chicago.

Inheritance tax rates are usually graduated with progressively higher rates as the net value of the inheritance increases. Rates, however, are lower than for the federal estate tax.

Inheritance taxes paid to any state are deductible up to a certain amount from the estate tax payable to the federal government. Most states try to take full advantage of the credit allowed on the estate tax, although the maximum credit is not large.

Gift Taxes

In the early days of death taxes, a person could avoid paying such taxes in whole or part simply by giving his property away in contemplation of death. This loophole was soon closed by the enactment of gift tax laws—federal and state—upon the privilege of making gifts. We shall discuss briefly the federal gift tax.

So as to afford some encouragement to people to make gifts of their property while living, Congress set gift tax rates lower than the estate tax rates (see Exhibit 23–4). The two taxes are intended to compliment each other and provide some assurance that taxes will be collected as property passes from one generation to the next.

How Gifts Save Money. All gifts of money and property to any person are taxable, but the law provides liberal exemptions and deductions. Good estate planning requires that wealthy families make gifts while living to reduce estate taxes at death. It is important for the gifts to begin early for large estates, since gifts made "in contemplation of death" are taxed at estate tax rates. Gifts made three years or longer prior to death are considered not to be in contemplation of death, unless it is proven that the giver had a known terminal illness when the gift was made.

Although gift taxes are lower than estate taxes, it is possible to plan gift-giving in ways that allow large gifts without paying any tax. Most family members make regular, small gifts to each other. Since it would be difficult to keep records of these gifts, each person has a $3,000 annual exemption for making gifts to one person before the tax begins. This amount can be given to any number of individuals in one year and the gifts can be repeated each year.

Suppose John Green wants to give each of his twin daughters a new car as a college graduation present. He can do so without paying a gift tax if the cars cost $3,000 or less each. Actually, he can make any number of gifts tax-free as long as not more than $3,000 goes to any one person. But most givers limit their gifts to members of the family, which tends to keep total giving to relatively small amounts.

Gift taxes, like estate taxes, have exemptions and progressive rates. When persons take advantage of both methods of passing property to their heirs, they get to use a combination of exemptions and avoid the highest tax rates. By making a gift and paying a gift tax, a family reduces the estate by that amount and, on large estates, the rate would have been high. In effect, the gifts are taken from the top of the estate.

Charitable Deductions. Some types of gifts are not taxable. You can give an unlimited amount to recognized charitable and non-profit type organizations without paying a gift tax. If the gift is above $3,000, it must be reported, but no tax will be due. Organizations qualified to provide this exemption are religious groups, fraternal orders, foundations, war veterans groups, colleges, and others. It is possible to give property to a charitable organization and reserve the income from the property for your lifetime. For example, John Green can make an irrevocable gift of certain property to his favorite university, while reserving income from it as long as he lives. He gets a double benefit. He can deduct part of the gift from his income tax as a donation to charity and the gift pays no gift tax. Income from the property continues, yet he gets the benefit from making a donation.

The Marital Deduction. A marital deduction is allowed for one-half the value of gifts made by husband to wife or by wife to husband. This deduction is in addition to the $3,000 annual exemption. For example, a husband can make a gift to his wife valued at $6,000 and not owe any tax; the marital deduction reduces it to $3,000 and the annual exemption removes the balance. He could continue to give her $6,000 each year as long as he lives. Filing a return will be necessary, since the amount is over $3,000, but no tax will be owed. This is a very important deduction because it allows large amounts to be transferred between husband and wife tax-free. Suppose Mr. Green decides to give his wife $50,000. The marital deduction reduces it to $25,000 and the $3,000 annual exemption reduces the taxable gift to $22,000. Marital deductions are allowed on the assumption that property of married persons belongs equally to both of them, therefore a gift from one to the other is equal to only half its value.

Husband and Wife Splitting Gifts. Another important exemption is the right of a married couple to split gifts. When a husband and wife make a joint gift, each one gets to claim a $3,000 annual exemption. Suppose Mr. and Mrs. Green decide to give their son $5,000 for a birthday present. Each can file a gift tax return showing a gift of $2,500 and by claiming their exemption, no tax is due.

Lifetime Exemption. In addition to the annual $3,000 exemption allowed in making gifts, each person has a tax-free lifetime exemption of $30,000. This amount can be taken in one year or spread over many years. Now we can examine how large gifts are made by a married couple by taking advantage of all exemptions and gift-splitting. A gift of $66,000 can be made to one person in one year without paying a tax. How is this done? Husband and wife both use their total lifetime exemption of $30,000 each plus the $3,000 annual exemption.

Mr. Green decides to give his son $5,000—will there be a gift tax? He can take his $3,000 annual exemption and apply $2,000 to his lifetime exemption if it has not been used. Mr. and Mrs. Green decide to give their daughter $10,000. Each one takes the annual $3,000 exemption and applies $2,000 to the lifetime exemption. After the full lifetime exemption is used, a family can continue to split the gifts and give $6,000 each year to one person tax-free.

Special provisions are made for gifts to minors. There are times when parents want to make gifts to minor children to reduce the size of an estate. Minor children cannot legally manage property and there is considerable trouble and expense involved with court-supervised guardianship which is necessary to manage property for minors.

Most states have passed laws which permit parents to make gifts of securities to their children and manage the ownership for the benefit of the child. This is known as "The Uniform Gift of Securities to Minors Act." Stocks, bonds, and shares in a mutual fund can be bought and sold in the child's name and not be a part of the estate of the parents unless the latter die before the child reaches legal age. The custodianship ends and the child begins to manage his business affairs when he attains legal age.

Points to Remember
About Estate Planning

Since estate planning and the preparation of legal documents can be complicated and confusing to persons who have little knowledge about such matters, we are listing a few important points as a summary of this topic.

1. A will is a legal instrument by which the maker provides for the passing of his property to others after his death.
2. For a will to be valid, it must be (a) made by a person of sound mind, (b) signed by the maker, and (c) signed by witnesses.
3. A will may be revoked at any time before the maker's death.
4. When a person dies without a valid will, his property is disposed of according to the laws of descent (real property) and distribution (personal property) of the state where he had legal residence.
5. When a person dies with a valid will, his property is disposed of according to provisions of the will.
6. A trust may be established in which legal title to property is given to the trustee to be managed for the benefit of another person.
7. A trustee is a person or institution holding property in trust.
8. The federal government levies an estate tax on the net value of all estates before they are distributed to heirs after allowing certain exemptions and deductions.
9. Most state governments levy an inheritance tax on persons who inherit property, after allowing certain exemptions and deductions.
10. A gift tax is levied by the federal government on gifts made by one person to another when the value exceeds $3,000 in one year. Other exemptions and deductions are available.
11. Good estate planning is best accomplished by seeking the aid of a competent attorney.

Discussion Questions

1. Differentiate between "intestate" and "testate."
2. Explain why you should make a new will when you move to a different state.
3. Discuss four reasons for making a will.
4. List and explain three special types of wills.
5. Name six of the items normally included in a will.
6. What is a codicil?
7. What are "laws of escheat"?
8. Who are the three persons included in a trust?
9. Differentiate between the living trust and the testamentary trust.

10. What is the rule against perpetuities?

11. If Mr. Dodd gave his wife $40,000, how much of it would be taxable?

References

Babcock, Henry A., *Appraisal Principles and Procedures,* Homewood, Ill., Richard D. Irwin, 1968.

Baber, Ray E., *Marriage and the Family,* New York, McGraw-Hill, 1953, Ch. 12. Some Economic Aspects of Family Life.

Ball, Richard E., *Readings In Investments,* Boston, Allyn & Bacon, 1965.

Bellemore, Douglas, H., *Investments: Principles, Practices, Analysis,* Cincinnati, South-Western Publishing, 1966.

Bockl, George, *How Real Estate Fortunes Are Made,* Englewood Cliffs, N.J., Prentice-Hall, 1972.

Bogen, Jules I., *Financial Handbook.,* 4th ed., New York, Ronald Press, 1964.

Casey, William J., *Real Estate Desk Book,* New York, Institute for Business Planning, 1971.

Claycamp, John, *The Composition of Consumer Savings Portfolios,* Urbana, Bureau of Economic and Business Research, University of Illinois, 1963.

Cohen, Jerome B. and Arthur W. Hanson, *Personal Finance,* 4th ed., Homewood, Ill., Richard D. Irwin, 1972.

Crane, Burton, *The Sophisticated Investor,* New York, Simon & Schuster, 1964.

Donaldson, Elvin F. and Pfahl, John K., *Personal Finance,* New York, Ronald Press, 1964.

Engel, Louis, *How To Buy Stocks,* 5th ed., Boston, Little Brown, 1971.

Fisher, Philip, *Paths To Wealth Through Common Stocks,* New York, Harper & Brothers, 1960.

Frascona, Joseph L., *C. P. A. Law Review,* 4th ed., Homewood, Ill., Richard D. Irwin, 1972.

Graham, Benjamin; Dodd, David L.; and Cottle, Sidney, *Security Analysis,* 4th ed., New York, McGraw-Hill, 1962.

Graham, Benjamin, *The Intelligent Investor,* New York, Harper & Brothers, 1959.

Handbook of Savings and Loan, 3rd ed., Chicago, American Savings and Loan Institute, 1972.

Hastings, Paul and Norbert Mietus, *Personal Finance,* New York, McGraw-Hill, 1972.

Hayes, Douglas A., *Investments: Analysis and Management,* New York, Macmillan, 1966.

Internal Revenue Service, *Retirement Plans for the Self-Employed,* Washington, D.C., U.S. Government Printing Office, 1962.

Investment Companies, 1972 ed., New York, Weisenberger Services, Inc.

Lasser, J. K., *What You Should Know About Estate and Gift Taxes,* New York, Henry Holt, 1951.

Leffler, George L. and Farwell, Loring C., *The Stock Market,* 3rd ed., New York, Ronald Press, 1963.

Lerner, Eugene M., *Readings In Financial Analysis and Investment Management,* Homewood, Ill., Richard D. Irwin, 1963.

Life Insurance Fact Book 1972, New York, Institute of Life Insurance, 1972.

Main, Roger, *Guide To Successful Real Estate Investing, Buying, Financing and Leasing,* Englewood Cliffs, N.J., Prentice-Hall, 1971.

Markowitz, Harry M., *Portfolio Selection,* New York, John Wiley & Sons, 1959.

Mayer, Martin, *Wall Street: Men and Money,* New York, Collier, 1966.

National Fact Book: Mutual Savings Banking 1972, New York, National Association of Mutual Savings Banks, 1972.

New York Stock Exchange Fact Book, published annually by the New York Stock Exchange.

Personal Money Management, New York, Savings Division, The American Bankers Association, 1967.

Rabinowitz, Martin J., and Morris L. Kramer, *Real Estate Investment Trusts,* New York, Practicing Law Institute, 1972.

Sauvain, Harry, *Investment Management,* Englewood Cliffs, N.J., Prentice-Hall, 1967.

The Savings and Loan Association: An American Financial Institution, Chicago, U.S. Savings and Loan League, 1972.

Savings and Loan Fact Book 1972, Chicago, U.S. Savings and Loan League, 1972. 1972.

Schaefer, George E., *How I Helped More Than 10,000 Investors To Profit In Stocks,* Englewood Cliffs, N.J., Prentice-Hall, 1960.

Seldin, Murry, and Richard Swesnik, *Real Estate Investment Strategy,* New York, Wiley-Interscience, 1970.

Shultz, Birl E. and Squier, Albert P., *The Securities Market and How It Works,* rev. ed., New York, Harper and Row, 1963.

Smith, Len Young and G. Gale Roberson, *Business Law,* 3rd ed., St. Paul, Minn., West Publishing Co., 1971.

Standard and Poor's Stock Guide, New York, Standard and Poor's Corporation.

Sterns, Linhart, *How To Live With Your Investments,* New York, Simon and Schuster, 1955.

Unger, Maurice A. and Wolf, Harold A., *Personal Finance,* 3rd ed., Boston, Allyn and Bacon, 1972, Ch. 14.

West, David A. and Wood, Glenn L., *Personal Financial Management,* New York, Houghton Mifflin, 1972, Ch. 13.

Willett, Edward R., *Personal Finance,* Columbus, Ohio, Charles E. Merrill, 1964.

Wyatt, John W. and Madie B. Wyatt, *Business Law,* 4th ed., New York, McGraw-Hill, 1971.

index